MW01599828

100 Magic Miles
of the Great Barrier Reef

the Whitsunday Islands

by David Colfelt

with

Illustrations by Carolyn Colfelt

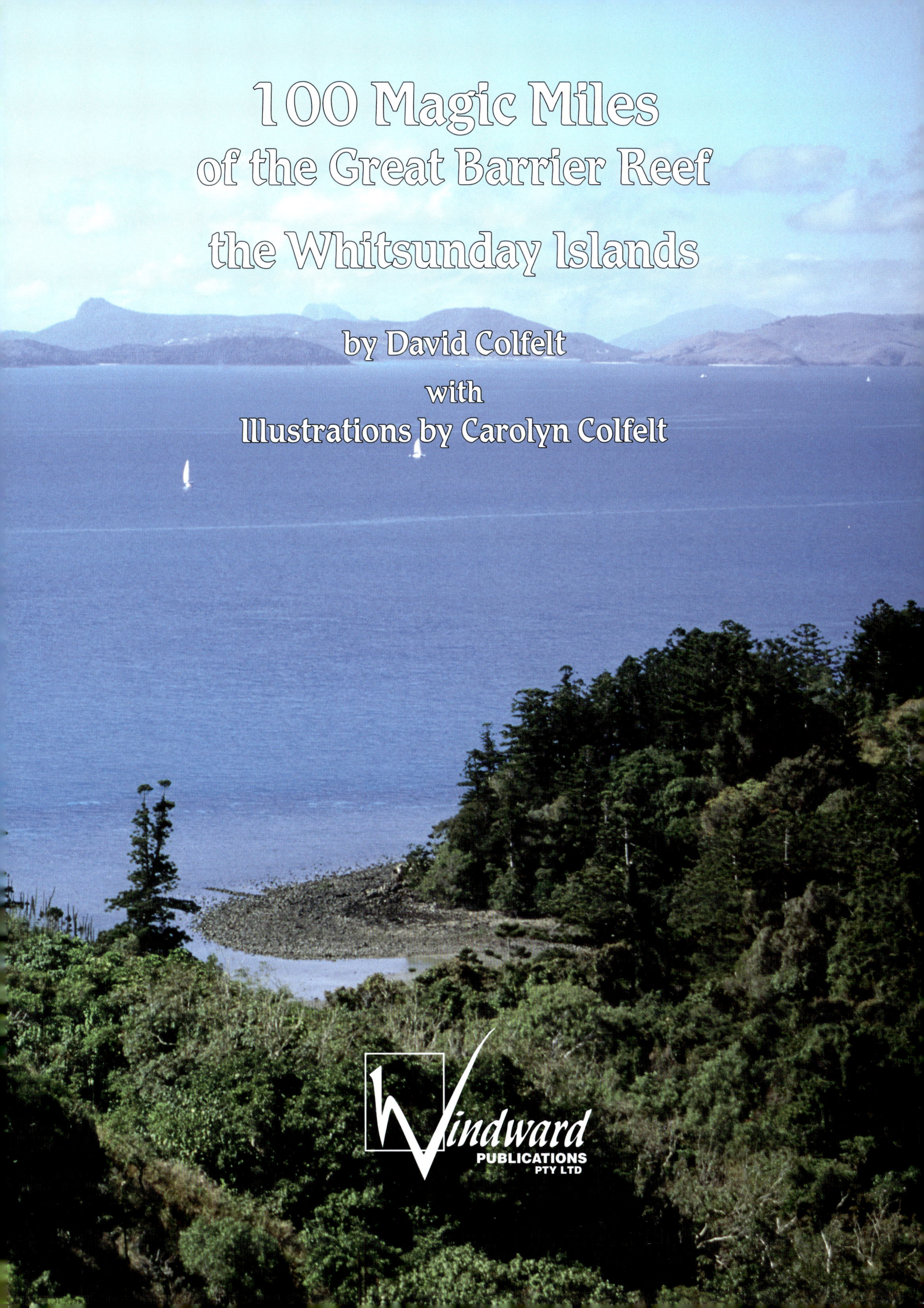

Windward
PUBLICATIONS
PTY LTD

Published by:
Windward Publications Pty Ltd
PO Box 361
464 Woodhill Mountain Road
Berry NSW 2535
Tel. 61 2 4464 1977 Fax 61 2 4464 1906

National Library of Australia
    Cataloguing-in-Publication entry

Colfelt, David, 1939–.
    100 Magic Miles of the Great Barrier Reef: the Whitsunday Islands.
    9th edn (revised)
    Includes index.
    ISBN 978-0-9586989-6-2.
    1. Pilot guides – Queensland – Whitsunday Group.
    2. Whitsunday Group (Qld.) – Description and travel.
    I. Colfelt, Carolyn, 1941–. II. Title. III. Title: One hundred magic miles of the
    Great Barrier Reef.
623.89299436

© David and Carolyn Colfelt 2010

This publication is copyright. Other than for the purposes and subject to the
conditions prescribed under the *Copyright Act 1968*, no part of it may in any form
or by any means (electronic, mechanical, microcopying, photo-indexing, recording or otherwise), be reproduced, stored in a retrieval system or transmitted
without prior written permission. Inquiries should be addressed to the publisher.

Printed and bound by Tien Wah Press (Pte.) Ltd., Singapore

First Published 1985   *Sixth Edition 2000*   *Ninth Edition (Revised) 2012*
Second Edition 1987   *Seventh Edition 2003*
Third Edition 1990   *Seventh Edition (Revised) 2004*
Fourth Edition 1993   *Eight Edition 2007–2008*
Fifth Edition 1997   *Ninth Edition 2010*

Acknowledgements

The Revised Ninth Edition of *100 Magic Miles* represents an accumulation of knowledge about
the Whitsunday Islands gathered with a very long, wide net over three decades. The contributors are too numerous to mention individually, but all may take satisfaction from the fact that
they are in some measure responsible for this book, which makes it easier to get around the
Whitsundays with some confidence that there are probably no unpleasant surprises in store.

Thanks are due to the following, whose contributions have been especially valuable at
one time or another: Tony and Denise Allsop; Greg Andrews; Briony Barnett; Kevin Bowe;
Nigel and Lisa Brown; Mel Day; Corrie de Waard; Terry Done; Cmdr Joe Doyle, RAN; Tony
Fontes and the members of OUCH; Meredith Hall; Hamilton Island Enterprises; Hayman
Island; Martin Hindle; Peter Holland; Rob Hughes; David Hutchen; Artie and Sandy
Jacobson; Yvonne and Bernie Katchor; Tony Kelly; Donald Kinsey; John Latchford; Dr Peter
Lavarack; Phil and Rhada Luks; Kurt Maring, Kim McClymont; Leon O'Donahue; Peter
Phillips; Bob Porter; Maureen Prior; Des Ward; Doug White; Leon Zann; Len Zell.

A few people deserve extra-special thanks: Andrew Colfelt; Anthony Colfelt; Harry
Smith; Anne Smith; Ray Blackwood; Wendy Craik; Carlo Grossman; Margie and David
Allsopp; David Bradley; the Great Barrier Reef Marine Park Authority; the Queensland Parks
and Wildlife Service; Ella Martin.

David and Carolyn Colfelt, 2012

FRONT COVER PHOTO: DAVID COLFELT

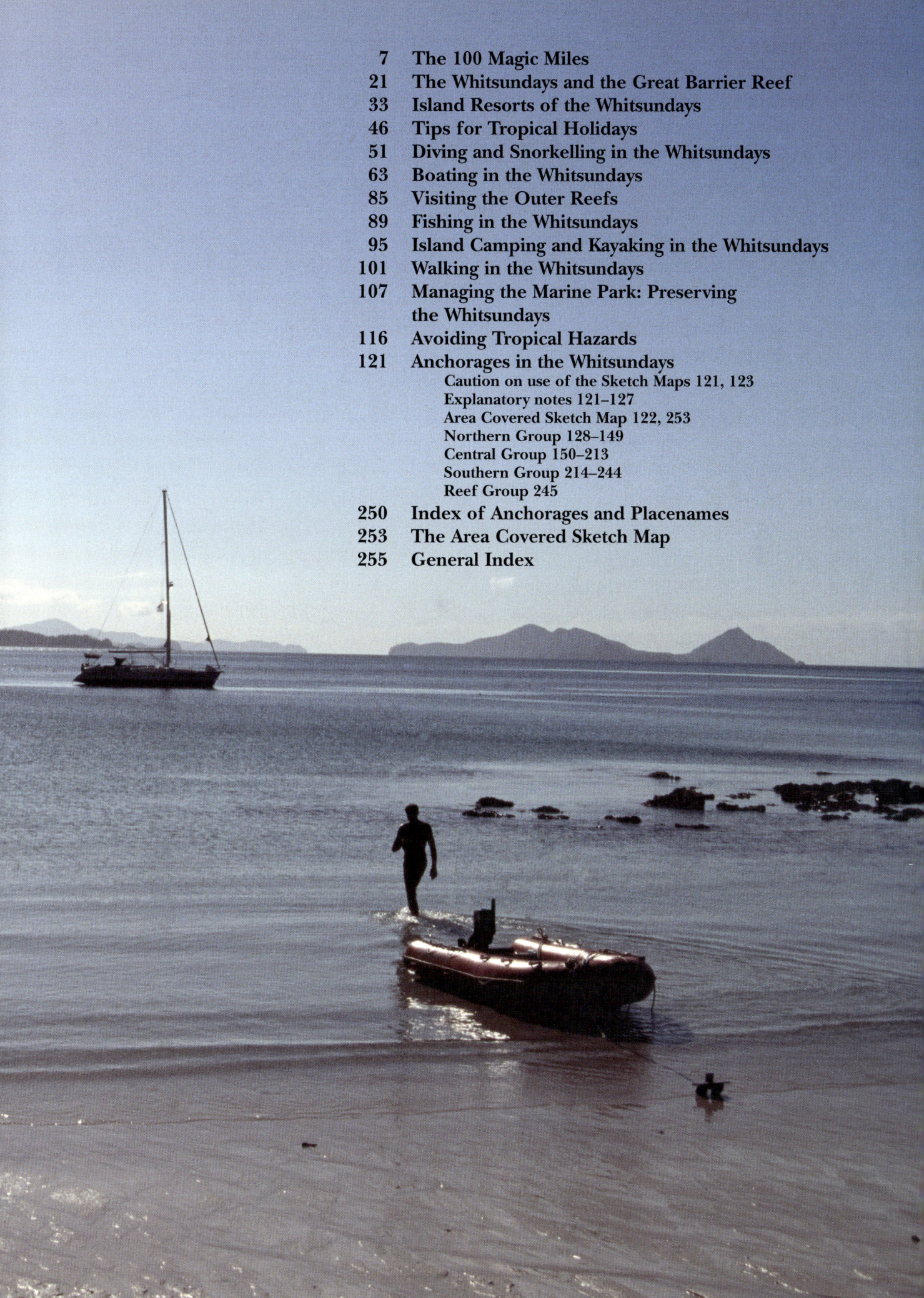

David Colfelt

Above:
The continental islands of the Whitsundays have fringing coral reefs
that give them a 'reef island' character, but they are made of the same stuff as
the mainland, being a coastal mountain range that was inundated
when the sea level rose at the end of the last ice age.
Opposite:
View north from Airlie Beach

THE 100 MAGIC MILES

In the distance the islands rise majestically, their dark silhouettes like pyramids on the shimmering horizon. Along their rocky shores, patches of brilliant white sand merge with the sea turning at first aquamarine, then emerald, their fringing coral reefs iridescent beneath the surface, their voluptuous hills becoming yellow-green in tropical sunlight. The Cumberland Islands span almost one degree of latitude on the eastern coast of Australia. They lie close to Queensland and the heart of that State's 'sugar belt', their limits marked on the mainland by the coastal towns of Mackay in the south (about latitude 21° south) and Bowen in the north (latitude 20° south).

The route north takes one from Scawfell Island, the southern gateway, along a vibrant blue passage through some one hundred islands and islets on the way to Bowen. Brisk trade winds fan a passing landscape which was, until geologically recent times, the preserve of eagles – yesterday's mountain tops, which rise steeply out of coral waters that are now about one hundred metres deeper than when the Aboriginal people probably first came here. It is about one hundred nautical miles by the shortest course from Mackay to the quiet little town of Bowen through a tropical island paradise in the heart of Australia's Great Barrier Reef Marine Park. The magic of these islands has been appreciated since they were first recorded in the history books of the 18th century, by Lieutenant James Cook – during his first voyage of discovery – on Whit Sunday, in the year 1770.

Drowned mountain ranges

The Cumberlands, or Whitsundays as they are more often referred to these days, are actually two drowned mountain ranges cut off from the mainland by past geologic events.

Since Cook, the islands have been divided, for the convenience of the map makers, into smaller groups – the Whitsunday Group, the Lindeman Group, the Anchor Islands, and the Sir James Smith Group. The Whitsunday Group first drew the attention of the pioneers who came to this part of the mainland coast in the mid-1800s, and this group's name is now generalised to refer to any of the Cumberlands.

Opposite above:
A view from Hamilton Island looking west towards Dent Island (left) and Henning Island (right) with little Plum Pudding Island in the centre foreground and the Whitsunday mainland in the background.
Opposite below:
Shades of fading day in the Whitsunday Passage.

The Whitsundays are called 'continental islands' because they are composed of the same rock and have generally the same flora and fauna as the adjacent mainland. Their colourful fringing coral reefs pulsating with marine life are generally absent on the mainland. Some twenty-five nautical miles further north-east is the nearest of the platform reefs that are usually associated with the Great Barrier Reef, and these are referred to locally as the 'outer reefs'.

Since the earliest days of this maritime nation when it was discovered that there was a route up the Australian east coast inside the Great Barrier Reef, vessels have been using the Whitsunday Passage as part of the shortest route north. At one time the government planted coconut palms on some of the islands to provide an energy-rich food for the shipwrecked, and the passing sailors went one better and turned pigs and goats loose to run wild. The more than one hundred islands and islets offer scores of sheltered anchorages, and it isn't surprising that they became the favourite of yachtsmen because of these hundreds of hideaways all within easy sailing distance of each other. Later exploration proved that the mainland coast, too, between Bowen and Airlie Beach, is studded with anchorages, almost all protected from the prevailing south-east trade winds. In these sheltered bays mangrove communities are often found, the primeval aquatic nurseries, so typical of the northern Queensland coast, which make for fascinating exploring and good fishing.

Pioneer settlers on the adjacent mainland in the mid-19th century needed timber to build their houses, and their land was both difficult to fence and subject to visitation by large salt-water crocodiles. The islands were sought out for the tall pines and for safe paddocks on which to graze sheep and cattle. By the 1920s, half a dozen or so of the islands had full-time residents, some of whom started up small resorts, with huts made out of corrugated iron, floors of coral fragments. The Whitsundays were to become popular island retreats after World War II. The resorts were generally homely and very much a product of post-war Queensland. Seasoned sailors with time on their hands knew that the islands offered excellent cruising. Even so, the Whitsundays remained a relatively well-kept secret.

The 1970s brought great change. Cyclone Ada, in 1970, devastated the area, levelling trees and extensively damaging several of the resorts. This was the beginning of a period of historic development. The creation of the Hamilton Island in the 1980s as a major tourist destination started a chain reaction that saw redevelopment of every island resort, four of them razed and begun again from scratch. Hayman, always a magic name in Australia, closed its doors for more than two years to undergo a complete metamorphosis, emerging a 'brilliantly coloured butterfly', stunning in form and style. Lindeman was rebuilt virtually from the bottom up, as were the resorts at Happy Bay, Long Island and Daydream Island. Brampton was extensively refurbished; Palm Bay was completely rebuilt. The ownership and financial base of the resorts is no longer just a family matter but is, in many cases, the business of major corporations, and this has brought in capital to bring facilities in line with 'contemporary standards'.

Airlie Beach is the adjacent mainland holiday centre, and it has expanded west towards Cannonvale. There are a number of mainland resorts now, from smart hotels to backpackers accommodation, as well as motels and holiday flats. The marina at Abell Point has become a major point of embarkation for the islands; other marinas are planned.

The Whitsundays have the largest bareboat charter fleet in the South Pacific. The islands offer all manner of adventure holidays – diving, camping, cruising among unspoilt national park islands. Every day hundreds of day-trippers get a taste of the islands or catch a first glimpse of the Great Barrier Reef from the deck of one of many vessels that ply the Whitsunday Passage and beyond. For those who want resort comfort combined with a holiday afloat, there are skippered charter yachts taking cruises among the islands and to the Barrier Reef.

David Colfelt

David Colfelt

David Colfelt

Above:
Stopping off at Whitehaven Beach,
Whitsunday Island.

Right:
The most spectacular beach in all the
Whitsundays, Whitehaven stretches for some
three nautical miles up the eastern side of the
largest island, of the group. The Aboriginal
name for it meant 'whispering sands'. The beach
is composed of virtually pure, white silica, a
bountiful gift from the geologic past.

Sandy Peacock

David Colfelt

David Colfelt

Above:
A mother humpback whale beats the water with her tail, her calf (to her right) like a 'ditto' mark beside her. Humpbacks migrate from their Antarctic feeding grounds to breed and give birth in tropical and subtropical waters, favouring the continental shores as they travel. They are a common sight in the Whitsundays from July through September. Those pictured were photographed just south of Whitsunday Island early on a September morning; the mother put on a spectacular five-minute display of 'breaching' – leaping completely out of the water – before she and her calf went on their way.

Left:
The Whitsundays are among the finest cruising grounds in the world and the home of the largest fleet of bareboat charter yachts in the South Pacific. The area is visited by many of itinerant yachts each winter.

Andrew B W Colfelt

Above:
Day-sailing in the Whitsunday Passage

Right:
View north-west from Daydream Island

Below:
Lazy days, Gloucester Passage

David Colfelt

David Colfelt

David Colfelt

Above and right:
Airlie Beach surveys a brilliant blue expanse of
water, and the islands to the north sit up majestically,
breaking the line of the horizon. Airlie's large
man-made lagoon provides a year-round swimming
and wading facility for young and old and a place for
sunbakers to relax and enjoy the magnificent scenery.

Below:
Shute Harbour is the the finest mainland harbour
for many miles along this part of the coast and is a
centre for island transport and charter operators.

David Colfelt

David Collett

Before the Dawn of Man

How the islands arose

Looking at a globe you can't help but notice a remarkable, if rough, 'fit' between the west coast of Africa and the east coast of South America. Analysis of offshore depths allows Africa and South America to be fitted together, very snugly, at the 100-metre contour. The same is true of North America and Europe, and of Africa, Australia, South America and Antarctica.

Scientists believe that all of the earth's present land masses were, about two hundred million years ago, part of a supercontinent, 'Pangaea' ('all earth'), named by Alfred Wegener, the German inventor of the theory of continental drift. Nobody believed him at first, because existing knowledge made drifting continents unlikely. But in the 1960s the theory of plate tectonics provided an explanation which gave Wegener's theory more or less the same degree of scientific acceptability as Darwin's theory of evolution by natural selection.

The theory of plate tectonics holds that the continents 'float', like logs on water, on denser but plastic basaltic crustal rock 'plates'. The plates fit together around the globe like pieces in a giant jigsaw puzzle. Throughout the history of the earth great blocks of continental crust have been moved by expanding suboceanic plates. These plates are being enlarged by a spreading process that takes place in a direction away from great mid-ocean rift areas. In parts of the world some of the plates are tearing apart, or sliding past each other. When plates collide, one slides beneath the other (is subducted). Fractured blocks of continental rock accumulate and others are folded in these areas of contact. Mountains are formed. The movement of the plates against each other causes them to heat and become viscous. This hot, viscous material begins to rise towards the surface. If it cools and crystallises below the surface it is granite. If it breaks through while still hot, volcanoes form, and lava flows. People have noticed for ages that earthquakes recur at the same places around the globe. Definite earthquake belts have been identified and lie mainly where the crustal plates are colliding.

About sixty-five million years ago Australia began to detach itself from Antarctica. At that time the whole of the continent was south of latitude 40° south. India was advancing on the Asian continent (the ultimate catastrophic collision would form the Himalayas). The advancing 'active' edges of moving continents are where mountain ranges are thrown up. The Rocky Mountain chain in western USA is at the 'leading' edge of the North American continent. Queensland's volcanic eastern coastal ranges are near its leading edge, but some also occur where the drifting Australia has passed over a deep 'hot spot'.

You can safely assume that the continents will continue to move in geologic time; Australia is heading north-east, at about five centimetres a year, into the Pacific which is itself shrinking. The Mediterranean Sea will, one day, close up completely as Africa completes its collision with southern Europe.

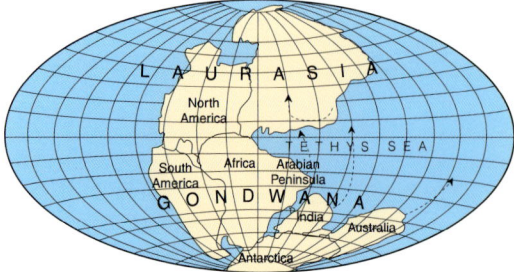

Two hundred million years ago all of the earth's continents were united in a single land mass dubbed Pangaea ('all earth') by a German meteorologist, Alfred Wegener. Gondwana began to break up about a hundred and eighty million years ago. Australia started to separate from Antarctica some sixty-five million years ago and became an island continent about forty-five million years ago, moving north-eastwards into the Pacific.

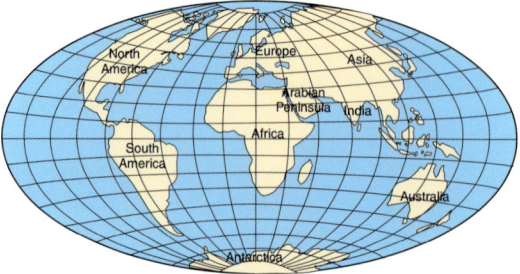

The position of the continents is explained today in terms of the theory of plate tectonics, which suggests that the continents are carried on rigid plates that 'float' around the globe driven by the thermal dynamics of the planet's interior. Today Australia continues its north-easterly movement into the Pacific, moving about five centimetres a year.

How the mountains were drowned

Throughout most of the earth's four and a half thousand million year history there was little or no ice, and the climate was warmer than during the last one million years. The breaking up of the land mass, and the movement of continents across the earth's surface, caused new heat transfer patterns to be established, and cooling probably began when North America and Europe reached their present positions several tens of millions of years ago.

Glacial ice began to form on Antarctica about thirty million years ago, after it had separated from South America and was cut off from the circulation of warm equatorial waters, and colder southern ocean waters were able to circle the earth, especially after Australia moved clear of the Antarctic.

Present knowledge suggests that the build-up of ice on earth has to do with the amount of solar radiation that reaches the large land masses that now lie in the northern latitudes. This, in turn, is controlled by periodic variations in the earth's tilt on its axis and the shape of its orbit around the sun. The cycle takes about one hundred thousand years.

Eighteen thousand years ago ice was several kilometres thick over most of Canada and much of northern USA. Two-thirds of the earth's land was covered with it. So much water was locked up in the ice that sea level was about one hundred metres lower than it is today. This glaciation was the most recent of ten ice ages during the past million years.

About eighteen thousand years ago the earth entered a new orbital cycle that caused the northern latitude land masses to receive a net increase in heat from the sun. Ice began to melt. During the next twelve thousand or so years the sea rose some one hundred metres, isolating two mountain ridges from the Queensland central coast, cutting off Tasmania from the mainland and flooding all of the current natural harbours around the Australian coast. During this period the corals of today's Great Barrier Reef grew upwards, on top of the ancient remains of earlier reefs, matching the advance of the sea. Today, if all global ice melted, the sea level would rise by eighty-five metres; in recent times it has been rising about one millimetre a year, but this rate is accelerating due to the 'greenhouse effect' caused by man-made gases in the atmosphere.

The Whitsunday coast 10,000 years ago was further east than it is today; the sea level at the time was about 35 metres lower. The islands were lofty hills on a coastal plain, cut off from the Queensland mainland when the last great thaw began to flood the continental shelf.

David Colfelt

The Discovery of the Whitsundays

Dreams of South Pacific isles have infected the minds of European men since the day in September 1513 that Vasco de Balboa scrambled up a hill on the isthmus of Panama and saw that there was water beyond. The fever really took hold in the 17th and 18th centuries as the Spanish, French, Dutch and English successively rediscovered the many islands, flung across the vast Pacific Ocean, that the Melanesians and Polynesians had made their homes some four and a half thousand years earlier – when sailors in Europe and Asia barely dared to go out of sight of land.

The first remarks by a white man about the great quality of the Cumberland Islands were made by James Cook and, like many of his observations, they have stood up to modern critical appraisal. He was not the first to appreciate the islands, however; Aboriginal people have been in Australia for at least forty thousand years, and they were in the Whitsundays for thousands of years before Cook sailed up the Passage.

Cook was a lieutenant in His Majesty George III's Navy, promoted from the rank of master in May 1768. He was nearly forty years old, and his rise from the lower deck since joining the Navy as a seaman in 1755 was an indication of the talent that was ultimately to bring him world recognition.

The 18th century was an age of science and reason – and one of aggressive economic imperialism. While Great Britain's North American empire was cracking, she was thinking about laying the first bricks of another. Cook had attracted the favourable attention of his superiors for his meticulous charting of Newfoundland, and he had been noted in scientific circles for his observations on the eclipse of the sun in 1766.

An event of immense scientific importance was to take place in June 1769 – the phenomenon of the transit of Venus with the Sun. The British nation was not to be left behind in the quest for scientific discovery and the Crown agreed, at the behest of the Royal Society, to pay the expenses of an exhibition to observe this once-in-a-lifetime astronomic occurrence from Tahiti, where southern hemisphere observations could be related to those made at various positions on the northern half of the globe to help determine the distance of the earth from the sun. The Admiralty was to provide a ship, and James Cook got the job.

Some five years before the Americans dumped tea into Boston Harbour, Cook was given the 368-tonne *Endeavour Bark* (the 'Bark' in the name was included because there was already another *Endeavour* in the Royal Navy). The ship was cat-rigged, roomy and seaworthy. After making his observations of Venus, Cook was to proceed to latitude 40° south to try to find the supposed great southern continent. He left Plymouth in August 1768.

Early mainland settlers sought out tall pines from the islands for timber to build their houses. A mill was operated on Whitsunday Island, at Cid Harbour, from 1888 to 1904.

David Colfelt

Whit Sunday, 1770

Almost two event-filled years and many discoveries later, on Whit Sunday June 3, 1770 (as the time was reckoned then – it was actually Monday, June 4 in Australia), he was sailing up the central coast of what is today Queensland, and at noon on that day he was in the entrance of a passage between the mainland and a group of lofty islands to the east, with 'Everywhere good anchorages ... Indeed the whole passage is one continued safe harbour'. He named the passage 'Whitsundays Passage' after the day of its discovery, and the islands the Cumberlands, after Henry Frederick, Duke of Cumberland, the younger brother of King George III, the reigning monarch. Cook put a number of names on the map as he made his way through the Passage, and some of these that remain today are Cape Hillsborough[1], at the southern extremity of Repulse Bay[2], Cape Conway[3], Cape Gloucester[4], Holbourne Island[5] and Edgecumbe Bay[6].

Australian Aboriginal people in strength roamed all of the coast between Mackay and Bowen long before pioneer explorer George Dalrymple founded the settlement at Bowen in 1861. Evidence suggests that Aboriginal people from the mainland visited the islands seasonally in search of available foods rather than establishing permanent settlements on the islands.

European man's early encounters with natives of the South Pacific were frequently troubled, and there is little doubt that the coming of the white man was extremely unsettling. In many encounters it is difficult to decide who did what to whom first. Some white historians have noted that the 'natives' of the Whitsunday area were unpredictable and belligerent. No doubt if there were any recorded notes of the Aboriginal people's thoughts on the coming of the white man, these would also reflect considerable misgivings.

After Cook, the next white visitor to the area was Lieutenant Phillip Parker King, in 1819, on the *Mermaid*. His party found Aboriginal huts and the remains of a canoe on the northern side of Conway Peninsula. Throughout the 19th century a series of British naval surveys were undertaken among the islands during which the presence of Aboriginal people was noted on some islands.

In 1878 *Louisa Maria* called in at Whitsunday Island for water; it is not clear what provocation was or was not given, but the ship was scuttled and burned by the tribesmen there; three of her four crew were picked up later by a schooner and taken to Bowen, but the cook was never found. Aboriginal people, according to some reports, were still on the island when, in 1888, James Withnall set up his sawmill there. Withnall employed some of them in building a dam for the mill and in gathering timber.

The lure of the islands

There is no doubt that James Cook's favourable impressions of the Whitsunday area were echoed by many who followed him. The botanist Jukes, aboard *Fly* when Captain Blackwood surveyed the area, noted: 'Shores rise in a very steep slope, with occasional precipices to a height of several hundred feet and are completely covered by a magnificent forest, the greater part of which is pine tree ... if it should be desirable to push settlements of N.S.W. further to the north, I think this part of the coast has greater natural advantage than any other we have seen'.

After the settlement of Bowen and Proserpine, the islands were sought out. Timber from Whitsunday and Hook islands was used extensively in early buildings at Bowen. Some of the islands were leased for grazing cattle and sheep or for breeding goats.

By the end of the 1920s there were fledgling resorts on a number of the islands, although the ensuing world depression, and then the war, held back any extensive development for another fifteen years.

A number of the islands, such as South Molle, had grasslands that attracted the eye of early graziers.

1. Hillsborough was named after Wills Hill, the first Viscount Hillsborough, who was Secretary of State for the Colonies.
2. Cook, at first, thought that Repulse Bay might be the way north along the coast. He anchored in the mouth of the bay until sunrise, but then he noted that the flood of the tide came in from seawards, and his first assumption was wrong. His intended route thus 'repulsed', he so named the bay.
3. Henry Seymour Conway, Secretary of State from 1765 to 1768.
4. William Henry, Duke of Gloucester, second younger brother of George III.
5. Francis Holbourne, Commander of the North American fleet in which Cook served in 1757, and Lord of the Admiralty, 1770–71.
6. George Edgecumbe, Naval Commander-in-Chief at Plymouth, 1766–70.

Tony Fontes

Above:
This 'flowering coral' is actually a coral head with many colourful Christmas tree worms *Spirobranchus giganteus* that live in calcium tubes embedded in the surface. The worms withdraw quickly into their tubes when alarmed.

Opposite:
Bait Reef is the nearest platform reef (of the Great Barrier Reef system) to the Whitsunday Group, and it is very popular with scuba divers

Tony Fontes

THE WHITSUNDAYS AND THE GREAT BARRIER REEF

The Great Barrier Reef is said to be the largest structure on earth ever created by living creatures. It is a submarine chain of small limestone hills that stretches some two thousand kilometres along the eastern coast of Australia from above Cape York (latitude 10º 41' south) to Fraser Island (24º south) and covers some three hundred and fifty thousand square kilometres on the Australian continental shelf. The limestone has been created in part by tiny colonising animals which absorb calcium and oxygen dissolved in sea water and, with some help from tiny plants that live in their tissues, secrete calcium carbonate (limestone) skeletons which become massive reefs.

In spite of its name, the Great Barrier Reef is not a single reef, nor is it a 'barrier reef' in the sense that Charles Darwin used the term. 'Barrier reef' was first used by Darwin in his attempts to classify coral reefs seen at mid-ocean islands around which they formed a close offshore barrier. This type of reef began life as a fringing reef, skirting the shores of an island that was slowly sinking into the ocean as a result of the tectonic movements of the earth's crust. Eventually, when the island submerged, only a ring of coral with a central lagoon was left at the surface – an atoll. There are no atolls in Australia's reef system, which sits on our relatively stable continental shelf, although the term is used by some tourist promoters who are ignorant of its true meaning but knowledgeable about the promotional magic of the word!

'Barrier' was probably first used in describing Australia's system of reefs by Matthew Flinders when he explored the coast in the early 1800s. The term had a certain logic, especially in the northern sections of the Reef Region, where the reefs form almost a continuous rampart, and in other parts, such as the Hard Line Reefs east of Mackay, are an almost impenetrable maze perforated by intricate channels. Throughout the Region the reef structures bar the incursion of huge oceanic swells from the east, rendering the waters behind them smooth in comparison with the ocean. And they certainly constitute a barrier to easy navigation even today.

David Colfelt

Continental islands are structurally similar to the continental mainland, which is why they are so named. In tropical waters these islands may grow fringing coral reefs that have many similarities to reefs found further offshore. The quality of fringing reefs can be adversely affected by freshwater runoff from the island to which they are attached or from the nearby mainland. Pictured is Neck Bay, Shaw Island.

The Great Barrier Reef Region

After years of growing concern about how oil and mineral exploration might affect this magnificent living structure and marine habitat, the *Great Barrier Reef Marine Park Act 1975* was passed by Federal Parliament. The Act defined a Region which incorporates roughly all of the Queensland coast from the shoreline to the edge of the continental shelf, from the tip of Cape York to just north of Bundaberg. Within it are approximately three thousand individual coral reefs (including some three hundred cays, about seventy of which are vegetated) as well as a host of other islands which lie closer to the mainland and which are referred to as 'continental islands' because they are geologically similar to the continental mainland. Many of these have their own fringing coral reefs with associated reef life similar to that of the offshore reefs.

All places where reefs form in the Pacific are located on major oceanic rises or on the continental shelf. Greatest development is near the shelf edges next to deep water. Reef development declines as the distance from deep water increases, because water pooled in lagoonal or shelf environments does not favour good reef growth. Corals, moreover, do not like fresh water or sediment found close to larger mainland rivers. Reefs tend to reflect the range of physical and biological possibilities; the direction and extent of their growth closely reflects the bottom that they grow on and the influences of currents and the contents of the water around them.

In the northern section of the Great Barrier Reef Region, where the continental shelf is narrow, the 'typical' reef is a long, linear 'ribbon' close to the shelf edge and running parallel to it. These are separated by narrow passes. The shelf slopes off steeply east of the reefs to depths of about two thousand metres. Inshore are oval platform reefs and low wooded coral islands.

In the central Region the continental shelf is wider. Opposite the Whitsundays it is about seventy-two nautical miles wide, and it expands rapidly to reach maximum width just south of Mackay (21° south), where its edge is almost two hundred nautical miles from the mainland. Continental islands with fringing reefs lie close to the mainland – Hinchinbrook, Orpheus, the Palm Islands, Magnetic Island, the Whitsundays. Beyond them out towards the shelf edge are platform reefs.

The southern Region is a vast wilderness of patch reefs separated by open water or narrow winding channels. Further south the continental shelf narrows again, and east of Gladstone close to the shelf edge there is a series of well-developed lagoonal platform reefs and vegetated cays, the best known of which is probably Heron Island.

A modern veneer over ancient animal ruins

The individual reefs of the Region are composed of a cemented base of accumulated plant and animal calcium carbonate skeletons upon which grows a veneer of living coral animals and plants. In the Region there are some three hundred cays, islands which have in a sense lifted themselves out of the ocean, when enough reef debris – broken bits of corals, shells and the skeletal remains of other marine life – has been piled up by currents and storms to remain above water even at high tide. Sea birds then provide the organic matter to form a soil base.

The Great Barrier Reef is the world's largest and most complex expanse of living coral reefs, supporting many unique forms of marine life. There are over fifteen hundred species of fish, about four hundred species of coral animals – and a host of sponges, anemones, worms, crustaceans, shells, sea stars, urchins. The cays are nesting places for around two hundred and forty-two species of birds, and six species of turtle (it is one of the world's significant turtle-breeding areas). Whales, dolphins and dugong are found in the area.

The great diversity of life forms makes the Great Barrier Reef an area of immense scientific importance. It was declared a World Heritage Area in 1981, internationally recognised for its outstanding natural values and only one of a few ever nominated for all four natural criteria. It was also the first time a listing went beyond the bounds of individual sites

and embraced a whole region. Whilst coral reef, mangrove and seagrass habitats occur elsewhere on the planet, no other World Heritage Area contains such biological diversity.

'The Reef'

Today anything that lies within the Region is often referred to by the all-encompassing term, 'the Reef', which is confusing as it can refer to an outlying shelf-edge reef, a near-shore platform reef, a coral cay or (sometimes) a continental island with its fringing reef. However, 'the Reef' seems to communicate an idea of the locality with a certain economy of words, and although less than precise, it satisfies the desire to express a sense of magic that most visitors feel about the area.

What are corals?

Corals baffled men for ages. The ancient poet Ovid referred to them as organisms that were soft underwater but hardened on contact with air (the soft living animal dies out of water, leaving behind the calcium carbonate skeleton). Because they were attached and didn't move about, it's perhaps easy to understand how even scientists of old declared these underwater 'shrubs' to be plants, although credulity must have waned after they'd picked one and taken it home to Mum. Even today, no one has figured out a way to prevent dead corals from losing colour or, more significantly, smelling like last month's prawns.

Back in 1723 a French scientist dared to challenge this herbal notion of coral. Jean Peysonnel put it to the French Académie des Sciences that corals were, in fact, animals! Many colleagues thought Peysonnel had momentarily taken leave of his senses, and they tried to persuade him not to publish his findings lest he ruin his reputation.

Today with hindsight and more study we know that the truth lies in both camps. Coral polyps are carnivorous; they are relatives of jellyfish, the link being that they are armed with stinging cells – nematocysts – which are a devastating weapon for immobilising their animal prey. But living within their tissues they have microscopic algae called zooxanthellae which provide a substantial proportion of their total food energy. Reef-building corals with their resident algae can lay down hard skeleton far more quickly that they could by themselves.

How a coral reef is formed

The reef begins when, after drifting in the plankton community for several weeks, a coral planula (the larval stage which results when a coral egg and sperm get together) settles, attaches itself to a clean piece of shallow ocean floor and secretes a cup-like calcium carbonate skeleton, thus insuring its survival. Now a 'polyp', the individual coral animal proceeds to reproduce itself simply by growing another. When this process

Above:
Continental island fringing reefs can produce beaches of a very similar nature to the beaches of true coral islands (cays). Langford Island, for example, has an expansive reef on which a small sand cay has formed, giving the island a somewhat 'dual' character – part continental island, part cay.

Above left:
True coral islands, such as North West Island in the Capricorn Group off Gladstone, have grown up on top of coral reefs and are composed entirely of calcareous sands. Their beach vegetation is distinctive and is made up of plants that can tolerate a salty environment.

Tony Fontes

Tony Fontes

has occurred enough times to produce a structure, other organisms join the project for protection.

Corals are the initiators and the visually dominant organisms, but algae and all of the animal life associated with the fledgling reef contribute to its success. As already noted, corals have living in their tissues single-celled plants, algae, called zooxanthellae, which, like all plants, have the ability to create food by a process called photosynthesis. Given the energy of sunlight to drive their factory, the algae turn basic nutrients (nitrogen, phosphorus, carbon dioxide) into chemical energy in the form of carbohydrates and amino acids (the building blocks of protein and fats). Like all plants, they also produce oxygen, helping to keep the reef water well oxygenated. These resident algae get their own needs – nitrogen and CO_2 – from the by-products that corals create in digesting their tiny animal food and by their respiration. It has been estimated that somewhere between 30 and 90% of the corals' food requirements are provided by these symbiotic algae, and the corals are thus free to concentrate on building skeleton and dividing into more polyps.

The reef has begun, and little fishes and other creatures have sought protection among the corals' branches and intricate folds. Algae have grown here and there, various planktonic animals have sought protection, and soon bigger fishes have come around looking for algae to graze on or for little creatures to eat. Some of the zooplankton have grown up into shells and crabs and fishes. And so on and on.

The reef grows upwards seeking maximum light for the benefit of the corals' resident algae. It continues until it reaches the surface, where it can grow up no more, so it continues outwards. The best growth is on the seaward/windward side of the reef, subjected to the clean ocean water and high turbulence. However, most of this growth is not realised.

Having reached the surface the reef begins to reflect the physical factors that now impinge upon it. The pounding of the waves soon breaks bits of coral away from the exposed surface and tosses the debris back away from the weather side. When coral dies, algae grows on the dead reef, and in the very punishing surf zone a species of tough, calcareous algae thrives. It cements-over the abraded surface forming a durable pavement called the 'algal rim', or reef crest, behind which, the wave energy having been dissipated, corals can again survive and grow. Debris consisting of dead coral skeletons, pulverised calcareous algae, shells and the skeletal remains of other animals eventually accumulates behind the crest and the living coral zone, creating another kind of physical zone – a sand flat – which in turn provides another biological environment. Nothing succeeds like success, and the mature reef becomes a marine habitat.

The Great Barrier Reef Region has been described as a watery desert,

Top left:
Corals' colourful polyps are extended at night for feeding. In the daytime they typically exhibit more muted tones (like those on the opposite page). The species pictured (*Tubastrea* Sp.), is often found in dimly-lit caves.

Top right:
The underwater reef displays a rich variety of co-habiting species. The purple sea anemone in the centre (it is an animal in spite of its plantlike appearance), is surrounded by corals of widely differing forms.

Bottom right:
The feather star is another colourful reef inhabitant (it, too, is an animal).

Opposite:
Corals adopt a number of forms appropriate to their habitat, such as the platelike species (*top*), whose shape maximises its exposure to sunlight for the benefit of its resident algae.

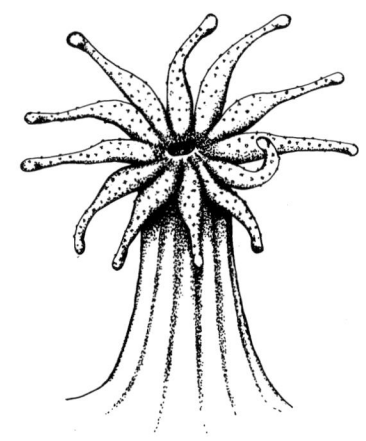

A single coral polyp.

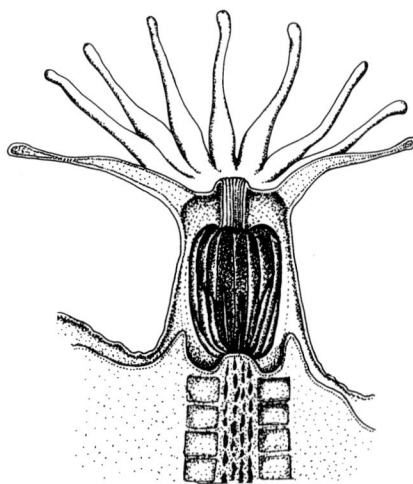

Polyp in cross-section.

The individual coral polyp is a sac with a hole surrounded by multiples of six waving tentacles, each armed with batteries of stinging cells which immobilise planktonic prey. From the mouth a muscular gullet descends into the central digestive cavity which is connected to the body by vertical partitions. The cells lining the digestive cavity have symbiotic algae which live and divide in them and which contribute greatly to the efficiency of the coral as a reef builder. The polyps secrete a protective limestone cup, consisting of radiating vertical plates, which interleaf with the partitions.

a vast expanse of clear, warm tropical waters that are low in nutrients, its reefs oases, marvels of evolution. It is now considered questionable whether the tropical ocean is necessarily a watery desert, and in fact reefs occur in waters with quite a wide range of nutrient levels. Nevertheless the reef is certainly a finely tuned complex, creating and consuming much of its own food supply, and it maintains the delicate balance of production and consumption. Every member of the community has some part in the equation. This critical balance of species is important for human reef visitors to remember; spear fishing, excessive line fishing, shell collecting or even just inconsiderate viewing can, theoretically, upset normal predation patterns and thereby the balance of the reef, which would threaten its survival.

There are many ways to enjoy coral reefs – diving over the unearthly landscape of a reef slope, or snorkelling in the coral pools of a lagoon while a fantasia is acted out for you by the local inhabitants, or walking on the reef rubble at low tide watching crabs skitter and shells going about their business.

There are many different types of reef to enjoy, from oceanic platforms to continental island fringing reefs. Although there are differences between them, certain fundamental characteristics are always present. As reefs expand, they have an influence on the water circulation around them. Different sorts of conditions are created which suit different sorts of marine life and, with this in mind, some sort of order emerges from the chaos that confronts the novice reef explorer. Pages 30–31 provide a brief glimpse of the life that is associated with the coral reef. In 'Tips for tropical holidays', some words of advice are offered on how to get the best out of your day on a reef.

The Great Barrier Reef Marine Park Authority (GBRMPA)

GBRMPA is the Federal authority charged with overall responsibility for planning and management of the Great Barrier Reef Marine Park. The main object of the 1975 Act that gave birth to this organisation was to provide for the long-term protection and conservation of the environment, biodiversity and heritage values of the Great Barrier Reef Region. Unlike other Marine Parks around the world, the Marine Park is a multiple-use marine protected area meaning that people can undertake a wide range of activities from commercial fishing to tourism and recreation. This is achieved through the introduction of specific zones within the park. Zoning has often been a balancing act and has been accomplished with imagination and a remarkable lack of conflict, considering the widely varying interest groups that use Queensland's coastal waters. GBRMPA works closely with all community and stakeholder groups to ensure that their interests are considered when management decisions are made in a consistent and transparent process.

The Marine Park

The Great Barrier Reef Marine Park covers most of Australia's north-eastern continental shelf, and it is quite different from a 'park' as in 'national park', where everything is totally protected. The Marine Park incorporates a vast area of water and islands, with a 'town plan' superimposed; it has various zones that cater for the equivalent of a town's residential, commercial, light-industrial, and recreational areas, along with areas that are off limits (which are usually for wildlife preservation). The Marine Park provides the framework for managing and preserving the Reef.

Within the boundaries, everything from low water mark to the edge of the continental shelf is under Commonwealth Marine Park jurisdiction; it is complemented and overlapped by a system of Queensland State Marine Parks which protect from high water out to 3 miles offshore. Above high water mark the islands are either Queensland national parks or are covered by State or Federal Government lease or, in a few cases, by freehold title.

In zoning the Marine Park, GBRMPA had to consider pre-existing activities on the continental shelf; for example, commercial fishing, amateur

David Colfelt

fishing, tourist resorts, shipping. It was apparent that a model much more flexible than a national park was needed. A zoning scheme was devised allowing different uses of the park to coexist without undue interference between them. It took about ten years to zone the entire Reef, section by section, a process completed not long ago. Under its legislation, the GBRMPA may not amend the Zoning Plan unless the zoning has been in operation for at least seven years.

The Marine Park is managed on a day-to-day basis jointly by GBRMPA and the Queensland Parks and Wildlife Service (QPWS), a division of Queensland's Department of Environment and Resource Management (DERM). Queensland's Boating and Fisheries Patrol also has a role. Whitsunday visitors can obtain extensive information about the Reef, the Marine Park and the Whitsunday area (including some excellent publications which outline the various zones and explain the types of activities permitted) seven days a week from the Whitsunday Information Centre located on the Bruce Highway at Proserpine (next to the museum, on the left just before the turnoff to Airlie Beach), or during the week from QPWS headquarters at the corner of Mandalay Road and Shute Harbour roads (about one and a half kilometres from the centre of town), Airlie Beach, Qld 4802. QPWS's telephone number is (07) 4967 7355.

In conjunction with zoning, GBRMPA has devised a permit system controlling collecting, research, and tourist activities in zoned sections of the Park. Permits are a simple way to keep a reasonable check without the need for total prohibition. Unlike national parks, where nothing may be taken, in certain Marine Park areas you may fish, and in some areas you may collect a small number of shells without a permit. In still others you may be granted a permit to collect, if you have formally requested and received permission to do so. The desirability of permits is easier to understand when one reflects on the delicately balanced ecology of coral reefs.

The Great Barrier Reef is made up of thousands of individual reefs.

The Marine Park has been divided into sections with separate management plans and zones worked out according to the desires of users and the dictates of conservation. The Whitsunday islands fall in the Central Section (yellow infill). The other sections are (north to south): Far Northern; Cairns (including Cormorant Passage); Mackay–Capricorn.

The crown-of-thorns starfish (*Acanthaster planci*) is a predator of corals and has caused extensive damage to some reefs. There is a question whether the starfish represents a real threat to the future wellbeing of the Reef or whether it is just an occasional phenomenon. Another question is whether the activities of man have started to alter the pattern of nature to the detriment of the Reef.

Crown-of-thorns starfish

The crown-of-thorns starfish (*Acanthaster planci*) (COT) has become a major worry for the Reef because in the past three decades it has swarmed over reefs (primarily from Lizard Island to Bowen) in plague proportions causing a significant amount of damage to corals. Minor (controllable) outbreaks have occurred in the Whitsunday area in recent years, principally at Butterfly Bay, northern Hook Island, and at Blue Pearl Bay, north-western Hayman Island. The crown-of-thorns is a normal part of the Reef community and is but one of a number of coral predators and parasites, which include a variety of fishes, crabs, nudibranch and gastropod molluscs, worms, an encrusting sponge and one other starfish. However, it is the only one that is known to cause physical damage on such a large scale.

Population explosions of the crown-of-thorns may have occurred periodically throughout history and in recent times throughout the Indo-Pacific region. The first of recent outbreaks on the Barrier Reef was noticed in the 1960s. It began at Green Island, off Cairns, where there is a tourist resort and where thousands of people get their first look at a coral reef. Green Island's reef was devastated. *Acanthaster* attacks particularly staghorn corals, the fastest growing and most plentiful species. These starfishes have no table manners; they lie on top of the corals, turn their stomach out through their mouth, release digestive juices all over the corals, and then slurp up the 'polyp soup'. One starfish can wipe out an area the size of a dinner plate a day, leaving nothing but a bleached white skeleton. In aggregations of millions, they can devastate an entire reef in a matter of months.

By 1976 the COT started to disappear as suddenly as they came, and an advisory committee concluded that there wasn't sufficient evidence to suggest that the starfish posed a real threat to the Reef. In 1979 the crown-of-thorns returned with a vengeance, and some people began predicting the end for the Reef, that it would crumble and be destroyed by the sea (which wouldn't happen, as the living corals of any reef form only a thin veneer, the rest being limestone). The media created an atmosphere of panic, there were loud calls of 'somebody do something' – although, without understanding the cause of the phenomenon, it is difficult to see just what anyone could do. Practical field work suggested that the cost of killing the starfish wholesale would soon bankrupt the country. One reef may have starfish in the millions, and estimates put the cost (at the time) at about ten dollars per starfish killed. Small-scale eradication on parts of reefs used for coral viewing – done by injecting starfish with small amounts of copper sulphate, a poison – have proved more feasible but still expensive and time-consuming. Other methods of control suggested

Peter Moran

so far, such as dusting reefs with lime, are neither ecologically sound nor feasible.

The reasons for population explosions are not yet known. The starfish is extremely fecund, one female producing up to one hundred million eggs per year. That sort of population economy is known in other animals, such as giant clams, and it is one characterised by the survival of only a few offspring. Anything that tips the balance in favour of survival of the larvae, which are produced in such great numbers, even if the survival rate is increased only by a minute percentage, can result in a plague.

Several theories have been advanced. One is that human beings are responsible, because they have removed in great numbers one or more natural enemies of the COT, particularly the triton shell and some species of fishes. Man has also been implicated by his activities on the land – clearing and agriculture – which have increased runoff of nutrients which have, in turn, fertilised the phytoplankton upon which the COT larvae survive. There is evidence that there have been fewer outbreaks in 'no-take' areas of the Reef, suggesting that, although exploited fishes are unlikely to prey on COT directly, indirectly they may affect populations of invertebrates that prey on juvenile starfish. Another argument holds that starfish plagues are a natural phenomenon that recurs from time to time, a caprice of nature.

Researchers now mostly agree that the crown-of-thorns phenomenon is not a simple cause-and-effect relationship. There may be many reasons for the outbreaks, perhaps even a combination of natural and man-induced factors. The managers of the Marine Park feel that, until most crown-of-thorns experts can agree that the infestations are unnatural, measures to control them should be limited to areas of scientific importance or importance to tourists. As noted above, there's not much that can be done anyway.

Skeletal remains of the crown-of-thorns have been found in core samples taken from reefs, yielding sediments dating back thousands of years and suggesting that outbreaks may not be just a recent phenomenon. This evidence may indicate that nature is taking its course, but it is also subject to a number of doubts.

Since the effect of humans on nature is now being felt more regularly, what used to be an infrequent natural disaster may have become a more frequent unnatural one. The earth and oceans are becoming warmer. Science is, by definition, conservative, so the final proof may not be available until after the truth is apparent to all.

The Reef Authority continues to follow the situation closely. Significant new sightings of crown-of-thorns should be reported to GBRMPA, PO Box 1379, Townsville Qld 4810 (telephone 07 4750 0700). The Authority is also interested in *negative* reports from reefs off the beaten track, where it is difficult to maintain up-to-date data.

The deep channel between Hook and Hardy reefs.

Green turtles are often seen around the Whitsundays. .

A jungle in the sea

A coral reef could be said to be a 'jungle in the sea' with an amazing quantity and diversity of life, so diverse that a whole book scarcely provides an introduction. Detailed discussion is beyond the scope of this author, and those interested should obtain one of several good general books about the Reef, such as Isobel Bennett's The Great Barrier Reef *or the* Reader's Digest Book of the Great Barrier Reef, *and read more about it. The following is a superficial smattering of facts about some of the more obvious forms of life encountered on a coral reef.*

Corals

For simplification, reef-building corals can be grouped into categories based upon their general appearance: branching; digitate; massive; tabulate (table-like); encrusting; foliaceous (leaf-like); free-living. Simplifying further, these are often described using words such as staghorn, brain, plate, mushroom, slipper, microatoll, 'bommie'. The most prolific coral growth usually takes place at the windward edge on the slope of the reef, and this is where to look for the greatest variety of, and the most colourful, coral, although it is also possible to find excellent coral on protected leeward sides of islands in the Whitsundays. Staghorn and plate forms are the most abundant; staghorns are the fastest growing and they are great contributors to the debris of the reef. On continental islands the sand beaches usually begin as piles of coral fingers, the broken tips of staghorns.

In the coral zone you will see beautiful blue-tipped antlers; massive rounded corals with intricate patterns on their surface that resemble brains; 'microatolls', circular formations of smoother massive corals so called because they have a depression in the top that holds water like the lagoon of an atoll (typically these have purple coral around the sides and are found in the coral and sand flats); encrusting corals; corals that have soft leathery bodies and look as if they have been 'plopped' on the reef; mushrooms, or slipper corals, which have slits like mushroom gills and resemble a fluffy slipper (these corals are not colonies but individual polyps).

Coral reproduction

The economy of life in the sea is as flamboyant as the handling of money in a Monte Carlo casino; heaps of it is thrown around, most of it disappears.

Corals reproduce by budding (like having your own do-it-yourself clone kit), or when individual polyps 'bail out' of the colony and re-establish themselves. Corals also reproduce sexually. Reef-building corals usually contain both male and female sex cells. The cells mature rapidly in spring; eggs coloured pink, red, orange, blue, green, or purple will attract sperm with long wiggly tails.

When the corals of the Barrier Reef mate, they do it in one great orgy a few nights after the full moon in late spring. Marine biologists have wondered at this mass spawning of corals which has been described as an 'upside-down snow storm' that goes on for perhaps a week, reaching a peak just after 'mid-week'. Mass spawning – which other forms of reef life, such as clams, do also – increases the chances of survival of these immobile animals which cannot move into sexual contact and which live in an environment of continuous water movement. The behaviour may also serve to 'overwhelm' predators by giving them a plethora of targets, a strategy employed by schools of fish which distract predators by presenting a blur of prospective meals, rendering a decision about 'which one' very difficult and reducing the chance that any one will be caught.

The food of the reef

Plankton on which many of the reef community feed is of two basic types: animal (zooplankton) and vegetable (phytoplankton).

The zooplankton has representatives from all the major divisions of the marine community. They consist of small animal organisms, some which always remain plankton, and some which are temporary, larval stages of animals that will grow up to be fishes, lobsters, crabs, snails, and corals. Phytoplankton is a principal food source for all sea life, especially small larval life forms. Because plants actually create food by photosynthesis, they are the fundamental element of the reef food web. Filamentous algae are the most significant source of plant food on the reef.

All plankton generally live in the upper, sunlit part of the oceans, although upwards and downwards migration of zooplankton takes place. In daylight zooplankton go well below the surface, some burrowing (in shallow water) in the sand. After dark they rise. This behaviour helps them to avoid being eaten. It is the reason that corals have learned that night-time is the best time to feed (night-time, of course, also renders the corals less subject to being eaten). It is also why many visitors to a reef never see coral at its most beautiful, in 'full bloom'.

The reef economy thus goes around and around. All other members of the reef contribute to the zooplankton – the fish, snails, slugs, bivalves, and corals themselves. The waste products of consumption and digestion of zooplankton create a source of nitrogen for the algae to assimilate and convert back to food.

The role of algae as food of the reef should not be underestimated. The corals' resident algae (zooxanthellae) produce a significant proportion of their total food requirements, and many reef dwellers are vegetarian and depend upon algae for their food. Many others are detritus feeders and consume the animal and plant debris that abounds in the reef environment.

Molluscs

One of the most populous divisions of the animal kingdom, molluscs include all shells, plus a few shell-less types, squids and octopuses. Molluscs are important in the reef ecology as food (zooplankton) producers and algae mowers. The dead skeletons are also converted into actual reef structure by cementing algae.

These animals have a soft body with a flap of skin called a mantle which secretes the shell. All (except bivalves, e.g. clams) have a 'tongue' coated with teeth (called a radula) with which they rasp algae from the reef or with which they bore through other shells. They have eyes sensitive to light but which don't form images; some eyes are on stalks, some are on the surface of the shell, and some are deep in the skin.

The vast majority of molluscs live in the intertidal zone.

High water

Low water

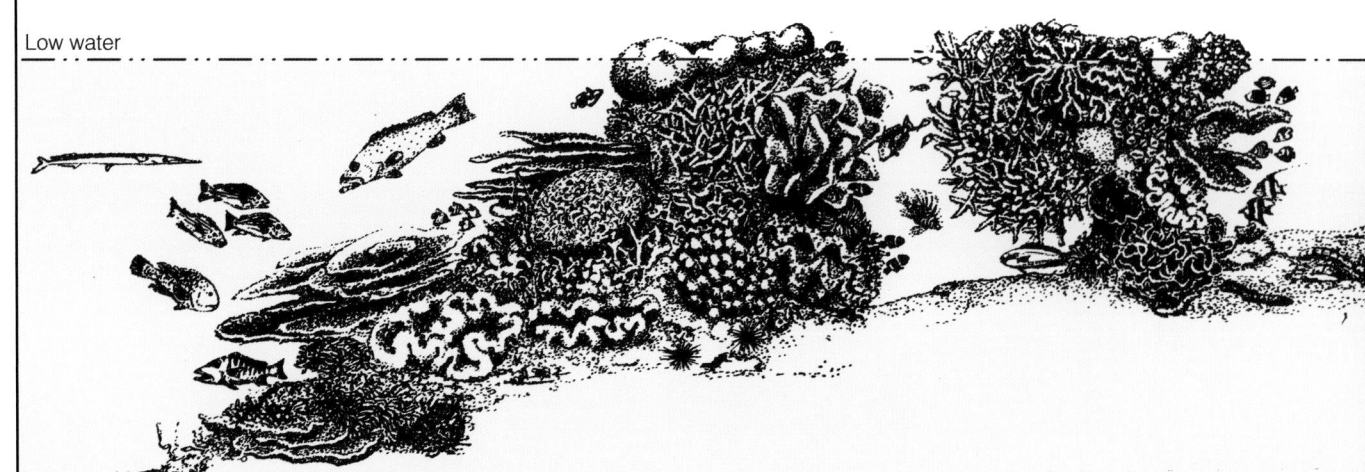

Bivalves

Clams. Large clams lie on the top of the reef, with brilliant, fleshy lips (the colour is caused by microscopic layers of crystalline, colourless pigments – the purpose of which is unknown). They filter water for phytoplankton. Clams are primarily photosynthetic and have in their mantle tissues zooxanthellae similar to those in corals. Clams close their shells when a reefwalker's shadow falls on them, and they occasionally squirt reefwalkers up the pants leg. They are quite harmless, even the giants, in spite of B-grade movie images of giant clams entrapping divers who were silly enough to insert a foot in them. Some burrowing clams actually dig their way into coral boulders, so that all you can see is their 'smile'.

Snails

There is a large variety of snails, all with an acute sense of smell. They have a specialised organ in their mantle cavity which senses chemicals in the water. Many carnivorous snails have a long siphon which they wave around, sensing the direction of smells.

Cowries. These beautiful, smooth shiny shells have always been attractive to man and used to be employed as money in some of the Pacific islands. They are active at night, when they crawl out from under their boulders with their mantle completely covering their shell.

Spider shells are among the most graceful, with long curved projections on one side. They are grazers and have a long green 'foot' with an eyeball on the end. Usually difficult to see because of brown slime which covers the top, their undershells are shiny and delicate reddish-pink. They often hang around in pairs.

Helmet shells. Helmets, or Cassids, are found on reefs in intertidal sand flats. They are beautiful shells whose name comes from their similarity to the headgear worn by early Roman soldiers. Helmets eat sea urchins, including (believe it or not) those with the long poisonous black spines.

Tritons are among the most spectacular (if not common) shells which grow to almost sixty centimetres; they are totally protected and are an enemy of the crown-of-thorns which somehow they manage to eat.

Cone shells are plentiful, each with a distinctive colour pattern which is usually obscured by a horny browny-green slime, or periostracum. Their radular teeth have become tubes through which they can eject poisonous harpoons. These species can be venomous and therefore dangerous to your health; don't pick them up in your bare hands.

Sea slugs

These shell-less animals, called nudibranchs, come in a variety of vivid colours and shapes. Many have bad-tasting poisonous skins, their bright colour being a warning to predators. They eat coelenterates (corals, jellyfish, anemones); some have projections on their backs in which they can store the stinging cells of the animals they've eaten and re-use them for their own defence.

Echinoderms

This ancient group includes stars, cucumbers, sea urchins. They have been around for some five hundred million years and are a mixture of the primitive and of ultra-sophisticated engineering. Their space-age skeleton is light, strong and self-repairing and replacing. They have a water vascular system with a diversity of form and function, including 'tube feet' which serve as legs, suckers, chemical sensors, breathers and execretors. Some are carnivorous but most are algae eaters.

Stars come in a variety of colours and forms, including the blue linckia commonly seen on reef flats and the brittle stars – (they look like a cross between a tarantula and a starfish and are able to shed a limb if molested (hence 'brittle'). Starfish limbs can regrow a body, and vice versa. The crown-of-thorns, currently notorious because it eats corals and causes extensive reef damage, has spines covered with toxin which inflict a painful wound. (Triton shells eat them, and trigger fish flip them upside down and attack them from underneath.)

Sea urchins are common on the reef. They are algae grazers. Watch out for their long black spines which cause a painful wound if trodden on.

Sea cucumbers are sedentary detritus feeders. The Chinese, in the past, for some reason decided that they could make one virile if taken in soup. A burgeoning industry existed for 'bêche-de-mer', so-called by the French, who misunderstood the Portuguese fishermen's name for them – 'bicho da mar' or sea worm/slug. Sea slugs are also called 'trepang' which is an English corruption of the Malay teripang, a term used by the hoards of Macassan fishermen who used to descend on northern Australian shores for the cucumbers; at one time this was Australia's largest export industry. They come in all sizes and colours and when spawning assume a posture that resembles a rampant penis in the act of ejaculating, which may have been what gave the Chinese the idea of eating them in soup. When frightened, sea slugs can 'ejaculate' sticky, milky threads that entrap their antagonists.

Fishes

More species of fishes may be found on coral reefs than anywhere else. Every conceivable size and shape and lifestyle is represented. They have specific feeding habits and locations. There are algae grazers and carnivores.

Fishes have evolved from sea squirts and have made a number of changes, including the development of jaws and paired fins. Some left the bottom to become mid-water predators.

Bony fishes are the most successful of water animals, with more than twenty thousand known species. Their success lies in their bony structure and their 'buoyancy tank' which enables them to control their ascent and descent without having to swim forward, a big evolutionary step ahead of the cartilaginous fishes such as sharks and rays. They have achieved vertical flattening which facilitates lateral movement, and they are capable of very subtle movements and apparently effortless swimming.

It is common among reef fishes to be sexually ambidextrous; some start life as male, some as female, and change over as they grow older. They are territorial; a dominant male patrols his area, which contains a number of females; if he gets killed, the dominant female in the group changes sex in a few days and takes over the male role.

Reef fishes have adopted some fascinating habits. The clown fish, or anemone fish, for example, lives with impunity among the poisonous tentacles of the anemone. Another, the little cleaner fish, swims boldly inside the mouths of larger fishes which permit him to do so because he rids them of parasites. As always, life throws up its opportunists, and there is also a false cleaner fish; you can imagine the mischief he gets up to. (As the clown fish says, with friends like that, who needs anemone?)

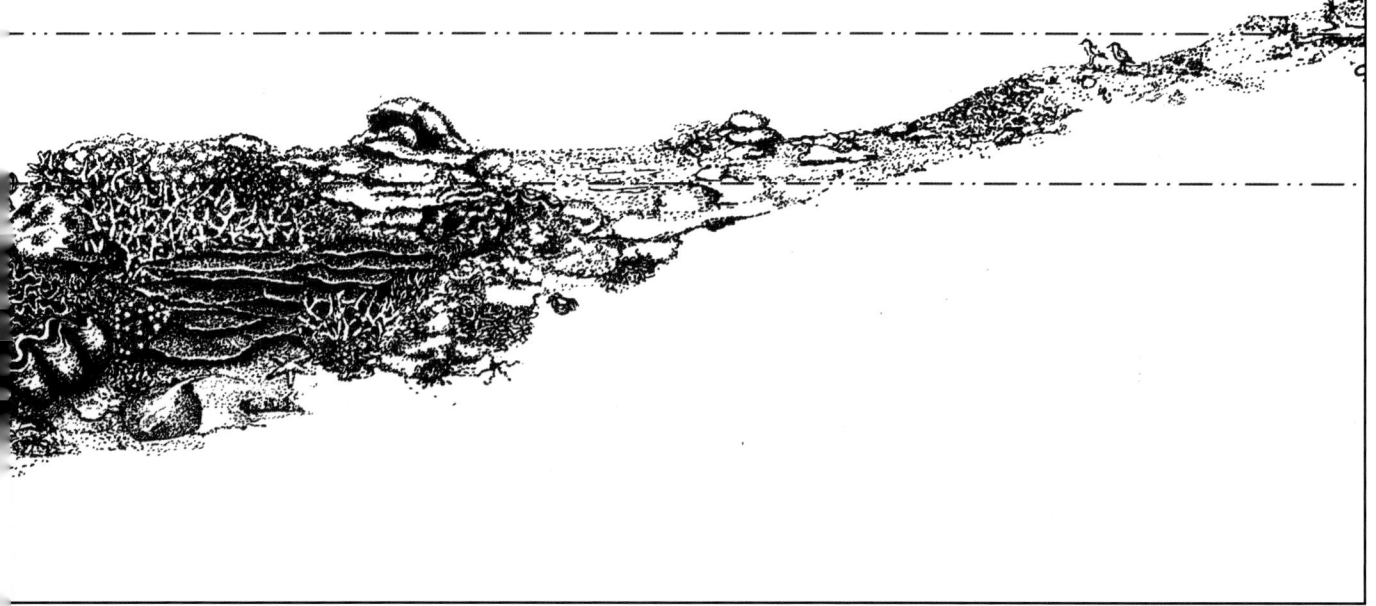

David Colfelt

Above:
Looking north from the Long Pavilion of Hamilton Island's luxury 'qualia' resort

Opposite:
Sunlight on the water through the palms at Palm Bay, Long Island

David Colfelt

ISLAND RESORTS
OF THE WHITSUNDAYS

The islands of the Whitsundays were first sought out by early settlers around the turn of the century for timber to build houses for the mainland settlements and for grazing land. By the 1920s a number of leases were held, and the first families began to establish permanent residence. In 1923 the Nicolson family was living on Lindeman Island, and the first manifestations of tourism began when they dabbled at having the occasional paying guests.

By the late 1920s groups of enchanted holidaymakers were beginning to carry tales of adventures on 'Robinson Crusoe' islands back to their home States throughout Australia. The resort accommodation was pretty primitive; in some cases it was tents, and guests were expected to supply their own plate, cutlery, linen and lamp. But in surroundings like the Whitsundays this just added to the magic.

By the mid-1930s accommodation for holidaymakers was being provided on Lindeman, South Molle, Long, Daydream and Hayman islands. Guests arrived by coastal passenger vessels which plied between Melbourne, Sydney, Brisbane, Townsville and Cairns. It was then that the concept of 'package' tours, so widely employed today, was first established. They were, with one or two exceptions, very much family affairs, homely and informal, a pleasant quality they shared with many Queensland resorts but which, in later years, became a fault; 'informality' became an excuse for not keeping up with the times.

During the war the resorts were, for the most part, closed; they re-opened in 1946. Flying boats later replaced the coastal passenger vessels, and what a romantic way to arrive that was! Today the islands and the adjacent mainland have some of the most up-to-date resort accommodation found anywhere. They are served by two jet airports, one at Hamilton Island and one at Proserpine on the adjacent mainland.

David Colfelt

Emma Reeves

Hayman

Hayman has been an exciting name in Australian tourism ever since the first tourists arrived in about 1931, when school teacher Monty Embury used it as a base for 'scientific expeditions' during school holidays. Zane Grey made the island his headquarters while filming *White Death* in 1936. Today's resort can trace its origins back to July 1950, when Sir Reginald Ansett opened 'Royal Hayman' which was fashioned after the Royal Hawaiian Hotel. At the time, Hayman was Australia's most fashionable island retreat. A complete reconstruction of the resort was finished in 1987; the island had undergone a total metamorphosis.

Hayman has a range of luxurious accommodation, a total 212 rooms, suites and penthouses in: the Pool Wing (*pictured at right*) overlooking the gigantic saltwater pool (*above*) with a magnificent vista of the islands to the south (*opposite top*); the Lagoon Wing, overlooking the lily lagoon with its white swans (above); Beachfront Villas and Beachfront Rooms; peaceful Retreat Rooms with private rockery gardens.

Emma Reeves

David Colfelt

No expense was spared in creating a grand hotel and spa which borrowed architectural and decorative themes from around the world. Landscaping was given equal, meticulous attention, with literally millions of trees and plants brought to the resort area to create magnificent lush tropical gardens. These, in their own right, might justify a visit to the island.

Today the resort has a range of restaurants offering a variety of cuisine – from exotic Asian to formal modern European. It has six day/night tennis courts, a sports centre with two squash courts, ping pong tables, a golf target range, nine-hole putting green, a health club, and three swimming pools. Dinghies and outboards are available for hire. Water-skiing and parasailing are available. It also has a chapel with a spectacular view down the Passage. The island has some good walking tracks with lookouts onto some impressive scenery.

Scuba diving is catered for with a diver training facility and water sports area; the island also operates a purpose-built dive boat, *Reef Goddess,* which does day trips for divers and snorkellers to the islands and out to the Barrier Reef.

Hayman has its own game-fishing boat and experienced local skippers. Other yachts based at Hayman's marina run casual day and sunset cruises.

Visitors to Hayman are checked into the resort while travelling to the island on a luxury cruiser that meets flights arriving at Hamilton airport. The island has a helipad, and amphibious aircraft regularly taxi through the boat harbour and up the ramp to pick up passengers for trips to the outer reefs. The marina has floating berths for about twenty-five yachts; casual visitors are welcome provided they make arrangements well in advance. Hamilton Island Aviation based at the airport offers a range of sightseeing and reef flights.

Carolyn Colfelt

As much attention has been devoted to Hayman's gardens as to its accommodation and decoration. Literally millions of plants and trees brought from the mainland create a very special garden environment. Pictured above is the richly planted entrance to the Pool Wing.

Top:
Three mermaids stand vigil on the north-east tip of Daydream Island.
Middle:
Along the western shore is a lovely, white sand beach.
Bottom:
Daydream's Rejuvenation Spa offers the latest in body-treatment equipment, massage and other therapies.
Right:
One of three 'lagoon' pools on the island (right) is set among accommodation units at the northern end of the island.

Daydream Island Resort and Spa

Daydream Island is located just across the Molle Channel, about two and a half nautical miles north-east from Shute Harbour. The story is told that in 1930 Major Lee 'Paddy' Murray, with his wife Connie, a deckhand and an Airedale dog called Toby, left Sydney in the yacht *Day Dream* on a cruise to Cape York. They got as far as the Whitsundays, where the Murrays fell in love with the islands and particularly with what was then called West Molle Island. They went over to South Molle to meet the owner (well-known author Henry Lamond) and persuaded him to sell them West Molle. Murray renamed it Day Dream after his yacht (it later became Daydream), and he and his wife set about establishing tourist accommodation.

The island's resort of today has received accolades from tourism authorities. Daydream Island Resort and Spa has 296 rooms in a range of styles, most with balconies and ocean or garden views (it's difficult to find anywhere on tiny Daydream Island that doesn't offer a spectacular view in one direction or another). A pleasant, short walking track runs north–south along the ridge of the island through native bush.

At the northern extreme of the resort area is Daydream's modern Rejuvenation Spa, with 14 treatment rooms and the latest in hydro-therapy equipment, thermal tables, steam effusion showers and solarium rooms. Naturopathy, iridology, aroma therapy, body maintenance and massage are available.

At the southern end of the island there is a 19-hole putt-your-way-around-Australia putt-putt course. The island has three restaurants, four tropical bars, three 'lagoon' swimming pools and outdoor spas, gymnasium, sauna, tennis courts and outdoor cinema. A chapel caters for the now-familiar Whitsunday island wedding. Daydream's 'Living Reef' located at the entrance to the resort is one of the world's largest man-made living coral reef lagoons and features more than 80 species of marine fish and 50 species of coral.

As with all of the island resorts, island-hopping and reef cruises are available with vessels that collect passengers daily from the resort. Daydream welcomes visitors by sea and has six moorings outside the man-made harbour along the eastern side of the island (see page 168 for specific information for yachts visiting Daydream).

South Molle – Koala Adventure Resort

South Molle Island is relatively close to the mainland, and because of its protected anchorage, its beach and its bountiful grasslands, it was one of the first to attract the attention of graziers and, later, settlers in search of an idyllic island life. Long before that time Aboriginal people in the area discovered that the island had a natural wealth of basaltic stones that made good cutting tools, and they called the island 'Whyrriba' for that reason (the remains of their stone quarry may be seen today on the track to Spion Kop).

The Lamond family lived on South Molle from 1927 to 1937 during which time Henry Lamond, a grazier-turned-author who escaped the searing heat of western Queensland to come to this paradise island, had articles published around the world about the idyllic Whitsundays. These, along with stories such as Banfield's tales of paradise on Dunk Island – *Confessions of a Beachcomber* – undoubtedly were a major factor in development of tourism in this part of Queensland.

Ernest Bauer, farmer-turned-adventurer, acquired the lease in 1937 and it was he and his family who established tourist accommodation on the island with a relaxed informality that has always been a hallmark of South Molle's resorts. The lease has changed hands a number of times since then and has been extensively renovated over the years.

South Molle is now known as Koala Adventure Resort and is aimed at the youth market (exclusively for 18+), where one can be as active at night as through the day. Accommodation is relatively inexpensive (based on multiple occupancy) in Rainforest, Reef, Ocean View rooms and Beachfront Bungalows. As well as a nine-hole golf course, there is a gym, two floodlit tennis courts and a swimming pool. Scuba diving instruction is available. The beach is crowded with catamarans, water bikes, and other water sports equipment. Trips to the Barrier Reef operate several days a week.

Most of South Molle is national park, and the walking tracks are public; the island has some excellent tracks to promontories, offering spectacular views; some lead to secluded beaches around the shorelines – pleasant places for a picnic lunch. The tracks are reached by following the signs that guide you along the pavement leading back from the jetty and across the golf course. Visitors by sea are welcome (see page 170 for details).

Top:
The Molle Islands National Park has a number of excellent graded walking tracks with spectacular views over the Whitsunday Passage to the surrounding islands and mainland. A lookout (top) at the end of the Spion Kop track surveys the view to the east and south towards Whitsunday and Hamilton islands.

A second lookout (left) near Spion Kop looks down over the resort and Bauer Bay.
Middle:
The summit of the Mt Jeffreys track rewards walkers with the best views in the Whitsundays.

Bottom:
South Molle's nine-hole golf course

A. Francolini

Hamilton Island's man-made harbour is a principal yachting centre in the Whitsunday region with a full range of marine facilities. The harbour precinct is a small township in its own right, with restaurants and shops, charter operators and comprehensive marine infrastructure.
The marina offers a complete range of services – slipways with on-site lifts, power, water and storage facilities, equipment servicing, repairs, refits, provisioning and refuelling. Diesel, leaded, unleaded and outboard fuels are available.

Hamilton Island

Hamilton is not just an island with two resorts but a complete holiday destination with a wide range of accommodation, restaurants and activities. It is also a site of considerable real estate development, with holiday apartments, condominiums and private mansions all over the northern half of the island. Its jet airport, with daily flights from major capital cities, has made Hamilton a major trans-shipment centre for all the islands.

Founded by the free-wheeling, unstoppable Keith Williams in 1982, the island lease was acquired in 2003 by Robert Oatley, perhaps best known as founder of the fabulously successful Rosemount Estate winery in the NSW Hunter Valley. He and his son, Sandy, who is now executive director, have determined to make Hamilton a world-class destination. The completion in 2007 of a major new five-star resort, 'qualia', at the northern end of the island, was their opening salvo, followed in 2009 by the completion of an 18-hole golf course on neighbouring Dent Island and a magnificent new yacht club christened in August 2009 during what has become Australia's most popular yacht racing regatta, Hamilton Island Race Week.

Hamilton has a bustling marina village built around a man-made harbour on the western side; it is a tiny town with facilities that include the most comprehensive marine services in the Whitsunday area, a bank, post office, newsagency, laundromat, general store, bottle shop, chemist, boutiques, yacht club, buggy hire and bakery. A number of restaurants, a nightclub and tavern, keep this part of the island buzzing at night. A major bareboat charter company operates from an office on one of the six marina arms. The harbour is the debarkation point for a ferry service to the mainland, day cruises to the Barrier Reef and a number of island cruise and fishing charter operations.

The original resort complex is on the opposite side of the island overlooking Catseye Bay, along with high-rise accommodation, individual stand-alone units and holiday flats. At the top of the beach a deluxe boutique hotel, the Beach Club, provides luxury beachfront rooms with

David Collett

an elegantly furnished Club Lounge incorporating meeting facilities, buffet, music and reading library as well as a private pool and bar. The multi-storey Reef View Hotel has large suites with balconies and panoramic views over Catseye Bay. The Whitsunday Holiday Apartments are fully equipped high-rise units that sleep up to five people; they all have views over Catseye Bay. The buré-style Coconut Palm Bungalows are set on green lawns under palms and gum trees. Self-catering apartments and villas nestle throughout the north-western side of the island with water and bushland views. The resort has a licensed child day-care centre which provides organised activities for children 4–14 years.

Other facilities include a golf driving range, mini golf, go-karts, target sports range, tennis and squash courts, gymnasium, and a wide choice of water sports. Bushwalking tracks offer excellent views over the surrounding islands. Golf-cart style buggies are available for hire – a great way to explore.

At the northern tip of the island is Hamilton's signature resort, 'qualia', designed by local architect Chris Beckingham, consisting of 60 stand-alone units fanning out from the central pavilion. The unique structures, which make rich use of local hardwoods and hoop pine, sit beautifully within an Australian landscape. The Long Pavilion is the central resort complex with its luxurious lounge and restaurant affording serene views of the Whitsunday Passage to the north, a sumptuous library with internet terminals and comfortable chairs for relaxing and reading. Spa qualia offers a unique range of body-pampering treatments in elegant peaceful surroundings, with ajacent yoga hall for contemplation. The resort has its own Pebble Beach sports complex consisting of swimming pool, luncheon restaurant, gymnasium; beach sports are available.

Guests at Hamilton Island have a variety of choice in tours of the Whitsundays and the Great Barrier Reef, by sea or by air. Fantasea Cruises operates daily trips to Reefworld at Hardy Reef as well as half-day excursions to Whitehaven Beach on Whitsunday Island.

High-rise accommodation in the Reef View Hotel and in fully-equipped Whitsunday Holiday Apartments provides spectacular views over Catseye Bay.

Emma Reeves

Carolyn Colfelt

David Colfelt

Emma Reeves

Andrea Francolini

Andrea Francolini

Right top:
Yachts participating in Hamilton Island Race Week, racing in Dent Passage

Right middle:
The Beach Club provides top-of-the-range accommodation immediately adjacent to the beach.

Right bottom:
The 18-hole golf course on neighbouring Dent Island offers players a challenge as well as stunning views of the surrounding islands

Left top:
One of the island's resident koalas

Left middle:
Catseye Bay is Hamilton's playground in front of the main activities centre.

Left bottom:
The yacht club, designed by Walter Barda, with its soaring copper roof, has facilities for both recreation and business as well as a restaurant and bar overlooking the marina and Dent Passage. Members have access to a gymnasium and heated indoor lap pool.

David Colfelt

David Colfelt

David Colfelt

Carolyn Colfelt

David Colfelt

Left top:
View from One Tree Hill over the Whitsunday Passage

Left centre:
Entrance to the yoga hall, Spa qualia

Left bottom:
Buré-style Coconut Palm Bungalows

Right top:
Tranquil view of a yacht emerging from Fitzalan Passage

Right above:
One of the meandering pools surrounded by lawns and palms

Right top:
Palm Bay viewed from The Narrows
Left top:
The units sit just behind the beach
amongst the palms
Left centre:
View from the lagoon
towards the mainland
Left bottom:
Freshwater pool and spa
Right:
Yachts moored in the quiet lagoon and
tie stern-to to a palm tree on the shore.

Palm Bay

Palm Bay was traditionally the home of a quiet, low-key resort set on the shores of a reef lagoon about half a mile south of Happy Bay, Long Island. It became a popular overnight spot for bareboat charterers looking for a safe anchorage immediately adjacent to the mainland on their first or last night out. The resort was subsequently completely rebuilt as a boutique retreat, with attractive bungalows, burés, and cabins, a swimming pool, dining room, deck area. For several years it was operated on behalf of the resort owners by the well-known Peppers hotel group. Peppers is no longer involved, and the property, as we go to print, is not operating as a resort. Some of the units are privately owned and some are owned by the resort owners. There is no food and drink available, so visitors need to be self-sufficient; they may use the communal barbecue area for cooking. There is a swimming pool.

Visiting yachts may avail themselves of a mooring outside the lagoon (there are two) or occupy one of five moorings inside, where the vessels are tied stern-to to a palm tree on the shore. (See page 162 for more information about bookings and visiting the resort.)

David Colfelt

Long Island Resort

Happy Bay was the original name of the resort situated on Long Island's northern beach facing Port Molle. It opened in the 1930s and it operated in a homely style for many years. Happy Bay has a sense of history about it, cannonballs and old wrecks having been found on the beach, testimony that the island and Port Molle used to be a favoured stopover for early ships – including bêche-de-mer fishermen and survey ships, some of the latter probably having had some gunnery practice while at anchor.

Today's Long Island resort caters for all types, from backpackers to honeymooners, from families to lone adventure-seekers. Accommodation is in Beachfront or Garden Rooms with private facilities and basic Lodge Rooms with shared facilities. The island offers a choice of activie pastimes, such as tennis, parasailing, waterskiing, snorkelling and diving. Entertainment is organised on most nights – karaoke, cabaret, casino night, beach parties. Moorings are available for visiting yachts (see Happy Bay, page 162 for specifics for visiting yachts).

Long Island is a national park and has several good walking tracks through vine forests with tantalising glimpses of The Narrows (between the island and the mainland) and of the Passage to seaward.

Hook Island Wilderness Resort

The Hook Island underwater observatory, located in the narrow passage between Hook Island and Whitsunday Island, first opened in 1969, before it was possible to take day-trips to the Barrier Reef. Today it still stands as part of the history of Whitsundays and provides an opportunity to view fish and a few corals at close quarters, without getting wet. For legal reasons there are signs inside the observatory warning that the building contains asbestos and that visitors may possibly come in contact with asbestos dust.

Immediately north of the observatory is a small eco-resort with 'low-key' facilities and a 'retreat' atmosphere. There is a range of accommodation including campsites, small dormitory units, standard cabins and ensuite cabins (the cabins are air-conditioned). An amenities block provides showers, basins and toilets. The resort has a small camp kitchen with gas cooking rings and barbecue, and meals are served day and night in the Island Cafe. Guests gather in the Barefoot Bar for drinks.

A range of beach activities is on offer, and snorkelling and kayaking are available just off the beach. The resort also operates snorkelling trips across to the Coral Gardens on Whitsunday Island. Scuba diving can be arranged by appointment. Milk, ice and bread may be purchased at the small kiosk. Visitors by sea are welcome; two moorings are currently available (see page 187 for specifics about visiting the resort by boat).

David Colfelt

David Colfelt

Left top:
Relaxing by one of Long Island Resort's swimming pools
Top:
Units under the palms
Middle:
Happy Bay's beach looks north onto Port Molle.
Right below:
Hook Island underwater observatory
Right bottom:
Hook Island Wilderness Resort

David Colfelt

David Colfelt

Lindeman Island

Located in the centre of the Cumberlands, Lindeman is a little off the beaten track, between the gateways of Shute Harbour to the north and Mackay to the south. It is a Club Med village, the central complex of which is a series of open pavilions by the sea which take full advantage of the setting; its buildings, in natural timbers with pyramid-shaped shingled roofs, impart a village atmosphere. Accommodation on the side of a steep hill has views out over Seaforth and Shaw islands.

Club Med's philosophy is to offer activities and entertainment day and night, but it's up to guests whether they want to join the sports, pool games, concerts and late-night disco or be left alone to idle away the hours, enjoying the view and the carefree atmosphere. The talented staff organise nightly shows that involve resort guests, much to everyone's enjoyment.

Lindeman's grasslands made it an obvious place for a golf course, and the island has a true links, a full-length nine-hole course with some spectacular vistas out to the Passage (and some severe penalties for golfers who slice). There are five day/night tennis courts (one covered). The Club Med circus school gives guests a chance to learn the thrill of a flying trapeze. Other activities include archery, sailing, windsurfing, basketball, volleyball, aerobics, squash and scuba diving. A number of attractive beaches may be found on Lindeman, as well as on the adjacent Seaforth and Shaw Islands, where it is possible to escape with a picnic lunch.

Club Med Lindeman's meals are massive smorgasbords presenting an amazing variety of food from many cultures; free beer and wine are included. The more intimate Nicolson Restaurant offers table service and a wine list.

Being a national park, Lindeman has several excellent graded bush tracks, one which meanders through forest and a valley of butterflies until it makes the ascent up a grassy slope to the summit of Mt Oldfield, a spectacular place from which to watch the sunset. The island has three moorings for use by visiting yachts (see page 216 for specific information for visitors by sea).

Top right:
Lindeman's Club Med Resort pool with an aquarobics class in session
Top:
The nine-hole golf course is a true links with panoramic views out over the surrounding Whitsunday waters.
Middle:
Lindeman Island is a national park with some excellent graded walks that offer spectacular views, this one overlooking Plantation Bay with Neck Bay, Shaw Island, in the background
Bottom:
Sunset from the top of Mt Oldfield.

Brampton Island

It is said that the scenery in the southern Cumberland Islands resembles the Lake District of north-western England, which inspired a 19th century marine surveyor to bestow place names of the Lake District onto the chart of this part of the Whitsundays – St Bees, Keswick, Cockermouth, Wigton, Calder, Skiddaw, Maryport, Helvellyn, Scawfell, Carlisle, Brampton. In the early 1930s, the Busuttin family set up a fledgling resort on Brampton, the island having a good anchorage, beautiful beaches, water, and abundant wildlife.

Brampton Island is for the most part a national park and has a system of graded walking tracks, which are regarded by many as among the most scenic in the Cumberland Group, with many spectacular views, particularly over the southern bays of the island. The track system commences not far from the jetty and is signposted. Queensland Parks and Wildlife Service has constructed a lookout above the resort on Brampton Peak, well worth the small effort to get there. The island has a number of secluded sand beaches accessible from the walking tracks.

The resort was closed in 2010 and at the time of printing its future is not known.

Visiting the resorts in a yacht

Calling in at one of the resort islands can provide a welcome change of pace during a week of cruising, an opportunity to 'make port', to go ashore and enjoy a walk, a meal in a restaurant and perhaps some evening entertainment. Visitors in yachts are welcome at most resorts, with a few provisos. Arrangements usually must be made before landing, and once ashore, it is necessary to register with the reception desk or the harbourmaster. Resorts expect visitors to conform to the usual standards of dress 'good Queensland casual' (see 'What to wear', page 46) in the evening and in the more formal areas. Visitors are also expected to behave appropriately (the fact that this bears mentioning at all indicates simply that, in the past, some yachties have behaved like pirates).

Resorts generally charge for use of mooring facilities, and in most cases this entitles you to a free run, enjoying the same privileges as the in-house guests. Specific information about visiting the resorts in a yacht (radio contact channels and other information) is provided in the relevant anchorage details later in the book.

Top centre and right:
Brampton's beach and pool look northwards towards the Sir James Smith Group of islands which sit on the horizon like volcanic cones.
Middle:
National parks walking tracks on the island afford beautiful views over all sides of the island.
Bottom:
Native wildlife abounds and is frequently encountered on the tracks.

David Colfelt

TIPS FOR TROPICAL HOLIDAYS

Whitsunday weather

The Whitsundays are located a little over one hundred nautical miles north of the Tropic of Capricorn. From March/April through September the islands and most of the coast of Queensland are fanned by trade winds. During these months the temperature is always equable. In the dead of winter one may be wearing a bathing suit by day and will probably want to put on a jumper when the sun goes down. If you are on the water and the trade winds are piping fresh, warm gear may be the order of the day. For sailors, the winds blow stronger from May through August, tending lighter from then on, although seasons are not clearly defined. The summer months are warm and sultry. July is the coldest month, January the warmest.

Whitsunday weather	Jan.	Apr.	July	Oct.
Av. daily high temp.	31°C	28°C	23°C	28°C
Av. daily low temp.	25°C	23°C	17°C	21°C
Days rain (over 0.2 mm)	13	14	5	5
Normal rainfall	203 mm	115 mm	36 mm	16 mm
Mean sea temp.	27°C	26°C	22°C	24°C

Normal annual rainfall: 1445 mm

The wet season is January to March. The peak of tourist activity falls between May and October, although holiday times are very busy. Cyclones, if they happen at all, are most likely from February to March, although very occasionally one has come as early as November and as late as May.

What to wear

At night, if out in company, one is expected to conform to a standard of dress known as 'good Queensland casual' – neat, and comfortable for the tropics. For men, this means sports shirt, trousers and shoes. Women are expected to wear a dress or long pants, not shorts. Two items not considered good casual, particularly for evening wear, are T-shirts and thongs.

Four simple tips

Sunscreen cream, polarised sunglasses, good solid footwear and a broad-brimmed hat: these are the essentials – not necessarily in that order – for the Whitsundays. A lightweight, long-sleeved shirt may also come in handy.

Polarised sunglasses. Imagine skippering your drive-it-yourself yacht, approaching the night's peaceful anchorage, your heart warming at the sound of your beloved one mixing Mai Tai cocktails in the galley. Because of the reflections on the surface of the water you fail to see the edge of the island's fringing reef. Without as much as a last-minute croak acknowledging imminent doom, you drive-it-yourself right up on the reef. You are now sitting on the floor in the main saloon, next to your love, having catapulted over the wheel and straight down through the companionway. The Mai Tais are dripping from the ceiling onto both of you, and the foredeck hand is flat on his back halfway up the beach.

Polaroids (or any sunglasses with polarised lenses) are invaluable in coral waters because they reduce reflections; you can see into the water rather than just the reflections of the sky on it. Reefs become much more visible. Even if you're not a yachtie, polarised glasses make the sky a deeper blue, the clouds stand out like balls of fluff, and colours become more vivid. (A polarising filter on your camera can yield dramatic results, too.)

Sunscreens. The sun in Queensland is very strong. Even those who can tolerate a lot of sun down south get burned in the Whitsundays. If you arrive looking like you just crawled out from under a rock and try to convert your Melbourne alabaster to Bo Derek brown on the first day, you will give your skin an insult it will never forget. Take along plenty of sunscreen, consider upping your normal grade to one that is waterproof and gives greater protection.

Footwear. Good solid footwear can get you off the number one casualty list – those with oyster cuts on their feet – and may also protect you in the unlikely event that 'Thomas the Terrible' toadfish happens to be around when you're wading in Shute Harbour or Pioneer Bay (see Avoiding Tropical Hazards). Be sure to take along an old pair of sand shoes that you don't mind getting wet.

Hat. A broad-brimmed hat will provide extra protection from the very strong Queensland sun when your layer of sunscreen cream has been thinned by salt spray, perspiration or wiping your face. It will also protect the shoulders and tops of the ears, which don't always get their full measure of protection. Experienced snorkellers frequently wear a long-sleeved lightweight shirt in the water to provide some protection to those parts of the body which remain exposed when the sunscreen gets washed off. Such a shirt is often welcome when reef walking on a hot afternoon, too.

Tips for enjoying a coral reef

The best way to really appreciate a reef is while in the water yourself, where you have intimate contact with the corals and other living inhabitants. Reefs can also provide hours of entertainment from on top – just exploring.

First and foremost, wear that pair of old sneakers or running shoes. Decent footwear (the thicker the soles, the better) is essential for reef walking, not only because of all the bits of coral and shells that are there but also because if you tread barefoot on a stonefish lying concealed in the rubble at low tide, you can get a very painful foot. Socks are also a good idea, to protect your ankles and calves from inevitable coral scratches. Thongs are useless on a reef.

Many tourists who have heard all about wondrous colourful corals are dumbfounded when they have their first look at a continental island reef

Polarised   Un-polarised

Polaroid sunglasses can be a great help to sailors because they allow underwater reefs to be seen much more readily. The lens on the left is polarised; the right one isn't. The difference can be even more obvious than shown here.

All reefs have distinctive physical and biological zones, moulded by the physical factors that impinge upon them. The offshore platform reefs of the Great Barrier system have grown up on top of ancient sedimentary structures, away from mainland influences such as sediments and freshwater runoff. Depending upon their particular circumstances and their age, some have lagoons, while in others the lagoon has, over time, become filled with sand.

Fringing reefs formed on the rocky shores of the continental islands when the sea level rose after the last ice age. They have parallels with offshore reefs, but being adjacent to land masses, are vulnerable to freshwater runoff, which can kill the coral animals. These reefs usually have wide mud/sand flats and expanses of algae-covered coral rubble between the beach and the edge of the reef. They also lack the deep pools or lagoons found in the leeward areas of some platform reefs on the continental shelf. The best coral growth on island fringing reefs is at the edge and on the reef slope.

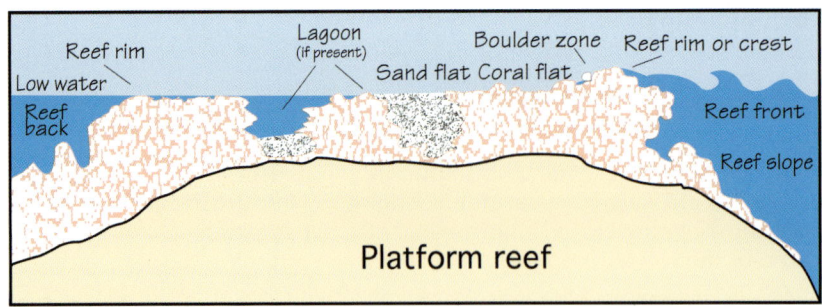

Platform reef

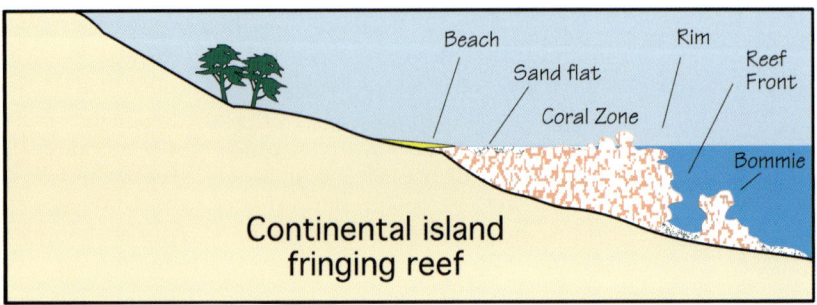

Continental island fringing reef

as it is drying at low tide; from all appearances, it is a vast expanse of dead, slimy, brown rubble. The part of a fringing reef that you first reach from the beach is 'dead' on the surface (although many animals live there). Reefs grow upwards until the top remains exposed at low tide, whereupon the corals on the surface die and are covered over by the characteristic yellow-brown coat of algae. The reef continues to grow outwards, and it's at the edges that you find the most living coral growth.

Physical factors impinging upon a reef create zones with various physical characteristics, which are preferred by different kinds of marine life. The intertidal reef flat (the part that exposes between high and low tide) is the habitat of the shells, crabs, sea cucumbers, starfish, and tiny fishes. Generally, as you get further out towards the growing edge, the reef life becomes more prolific. It is amazing how much there is to see, besides coral, if you are patient and use your eyes.

Naturally, better coral is usually found on the offshore reefs where, away from adverse mainland influences such as silting and freshwater runoff, coral achieves its true potential. Walking and snorkelling in the lagoon of one of these 'mid-ocean' reefs is a magical experience.

Walking on the surface of reefs is to be discouraged if we wish to preserve them for future generations. If you do find yourself on one, watch where you put your feet. If you step on live coral and break it, it will almost certainly die. Walk on the sandy spots in between the patches of coral or on those places that appear 'cemented over'. A walking stick may be useful, especially if you're not good at balancing on one foot while deciding where to put the other.

If you want to pick up anything to have a closer look, wear gloves, and replace it just where you found it.

Watch the state of the tide. Reefs are mostly flat with a slightly raised crest out towards the edge. They are often very wide, and you may have wandered a considerable distance from your boat or from the beach. When the tide comes over the crest, the water comes in with a rush, along with the marine traffic jam of hungry creatures that have been stuck at a red light for the past six or so hours. You simply cannot walk fast over a reef, and in water that's up to your calves, walking gets even harder.

Geography cone
Conus geographus

Textile cone
Conus textile

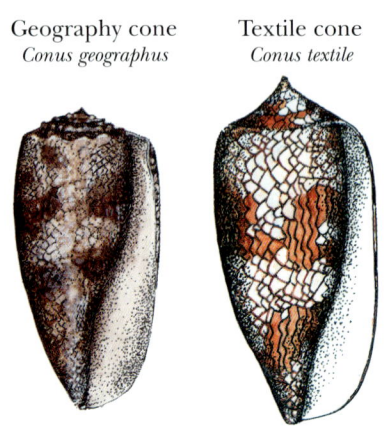

Cone shells are among the more beautifully patterned shells, although they are often covered with a thick greeny-brown slime which hides their beauty. They are more or less straight-sided, with a low pointed spire and straight narrow aperture. A few species are highly venomous and potentially very dangerous to man (both of those pictured). Don't pick up any cone shell with your bare hands.

Keeping Safe and Well

The following tips are based on the observations of a general practitioner with considerable experience in the Whitsunday area. More information is found in 'Avoiding Tropical Hazards'

Oyster cuts and coral grazes are Problem Number One (statistically). To begin with, in the tropics any cut that results from contact with something that lies beneath the level of high tide is guaranteed to be infected within seconds. If not treated properly, it can develop into a major infection. A twofold reaction is caused, first, by marine bacteria, some of which multiply with blinding speed, and second, by the physical presence of slimy gunk which produces an allergic response in some people.

Cleaning oyster wounds in particular is most important; if an injury is more than a graze, and if it's early in the holidays, go to a doctor, have a local anaesthetic, and get the wound cleaned properly. Oyster shells disintegrate as they cut; they're like shale, in layers, and they shatter, leaving mica-like slivers in the wound. The incidence of complications is virtually 100 per cent.

If it's the last two days of the holiday and you're catching lots of fish, you can probably sweat it out and see the doctor when you get back to the mainland.

Always clean wounds thoroughly and apply a disinfectant (any lingering moisture in the tropics is 'bad', so use a disinfectant with an alcohol or aqueous base (such as 'Betadine') or one in powder form rather than a cream.

'Tropical ear' (inflammation of the external ear, which doctors call *otitis externa*) spoils more holidays than just about anything on the list. It is caused by too much water in the ears too frequently; the ear gets waterlogged, never dries out, infection (bacterial or fungal) sets in. It occurs most frequently in people who have a tendency to 'waxy ears'.

Before going to the tropics and doing a lot of swimming, those with a tendency to get ear trouble should see a doctor and make sure that their ears are clean. Chemists have ear drops, and mouldable ear plugs that fit comfortably, and one or both of these may help.

Minor barotrauma in divers, a pressure-induced ear problem, is very common in tropical travellers. If in the plane on the way to the Whitsundays you had difficulty with your ears (equalising the pressure), you will probably have a problem if you go diving. Don't dive if you are having any difficulty equalising pressure.

Sea creatures. Everyone has read about tropical horrors – sharks, stingrays, man-eating clams, giant squid that wrap their arms around you and love you to death. Evil-doing by creatures of the sea is vastly exaggerated and always gets very extensive press. It is unlikely that you will ever have a run-in with any of the following, but some discussion is necessary (for more details, see the section 'Avoiding tropical hazards' (pages 116–120).

Sharks are a natural feature of all tropical waters. The species most commonly seen in the Whitsundays are timid blacktips, which are reef fossickers, and unaggressive whitetips. Divers sometimes encounter tiger sharks and hammerheads. The Whitsundays are on a broad part of the continental shelf, where everyone in the sea gets plenty to eat. Whenever one is in the water in the tropics, however, it is prudent to avoid attracting unwanted attention, such as by making a huge splash diving into the water from the deck of a yacht, or by doing 'wounded fish' impressions while swimming or snorkelling. Slip quietly into the water. Swimming and fishing are incompatible activities, for obvious reasons. Don't fish near swimmers or swim near anglers. Sharks have excellent vision, but they need light in order to see; to avoid being mistaken for a fish, don't swim at night, and if the sky is heavily overcast and visibility in the water is not good, consider postponing your swim until conditions are better. Sharks are scavengers; don't throw food scraps into the water. If on a reef, don't pick up a reef shark by the tail (yes, that did happen, and the person, understandably, got a good bite on the hand).

Stingrays are, biologically, flattened sharks that have taken to the bottom to feed on shellfish. Their teeth are flattened too, for crushing instead of cutting. Most species are very timid and will run away if they have the choice. Stingrays lie on the bottom and flick up sand on their back, rendering them better able to surprise the unsuspecting mollusc on its way to grandmother's house. Stingrays frighten the pants off you when they 'erupt' from the sand half a metre in front of you and skitter away. Problems can occur when a stingray is inadvertently pinned to the sand by a foot, for example, and cannot skitter away..

Always shuffle the feet when wading in shallow sandy areas. If you encounter one stingray, there are probably more of them about. The wound they inflict with a venomous barb in their tail is painful and will require the attention of a doctor, but unless you get stung on the torso, the wound is seldom serious. If scuba diving or snorkelling and cruising close along a sandy bottom, keep enough distance between yourself and the bottom to avoid getting lanced if you surprise a ray and it lashes upwards with its tail.

Pressure-immobilisation of stingray wounds is not recommended. Use warm to hot water to relieve pain. Medical attention should be sought as wounds invariably require expert attention. (See 'Avoiding tropical hazards'.)

Stonefish are diabolically ugly creatures that look akin to a warthog that ran into a brick wall at a hundred and sixty kilometres an hour, resulting in (1) much of its bulk being permanently shifted forward on its frame, (2) the pugging of its face, and (3) the accordion-plaiting of its brow. Cover that lot with brown slime and carbuncles, and you have a stonefish, more or less.

At the outset let it be said that you are highly unlikely ever to see one, because they are so perfectly disguised, where they lie on algae-encrusted coral rubble, that they virtually defy detection.

Stonefish have thirteen dorsal spines (this may appeal to the superstitious) each attached to a poisonous venom sack, and if you tread on one it can give you an agonisingly painful wound. About one-half of the people treated for stonefish wounds have been wearing nothing on their feet. The moral is, always wear a solid pair of sneakers when reefwalking. Never run on a reef top; walk very gingerly.

Stonefish stings shouldn't be treated by pressure-immobilisation (see 'Avoiding Tropical Hazards'). Pain is severe and may be alleviated by immersing the wound in warm to hot water (but not scalding). Antivenom is available; always consult a doctor.

Keeping Safe and Well

Jellyfishes. There are a couple of jellyfishes about which visitors to the Whitsundays need to be aware, particularly in the warm months (November–May). The box jellyfish *Chironex fleckeri* is a well-known and potentially lethal species that inhabits coastal estuaries and mainland near-shore areas and is the reason why most Queensland beaches have netted swimming enclosures. In recent years another species of box (cuboid) jellyfish has been associated with several deaths, and it is potentially a worry to those on the water in the Whitsundays because it is not confined to the coast – it inhabits offshore reefs. Called the irukandji (after the Aboriginal tribe in north Queensland who live where one of this species (*Carukia barnesi*) was first discovered), it is now believed that there may be as many as six species of these much smaller cuboids. Whereas the box jellyfish *Chironex* inflicts an immediately excruciatingly painful sting, the irukandji sting is often barely noticed, and it is only 30 or so minutes afterwards that a typical syndrome sets in – severe low back pain, cramping that comes in waves in all four limbs, the abdomen and chest, goose pimples, sweating, a feeling of impending doom and, in some cases, spiking blood pressure.

There is more discussion of these jellyfishes and first-aid treatment in the section entitled 'Avoiding Tropical Hazards'. Suffice it to say here that one can greatly reduce the chances of a sting by wearing a stinger suit when snorkelling or diving, as much of the body's surface area will be protected. Until more is known of the phenomenon, stingers suits are highly recommended particularly after there have been several days of northerly winds (which can carry the irukandji in from offshore reefs). These jellyfishes are also attracted to light, so one should avoid diving at night under floodlights.

Observe warning signs posted on mainland beaches and be aware if a 'jellyfish alert' has been announced on the radio. Beach stinger nets are too coarse to screen out irukandji. In cases of stings, the adhering tentacles and sting area should be doused liberally with household vinegar for at least 30 seconds before attempting to remove them (vinegar inactivates the stinger cells preventing further injection of venom). Antivenom is available for *Chironex* stings and should be administered; medical assistance should be sought in all cases.

Cone shells are among the most strikingly beautiful shells (although they are frequently covered with a tenacious green slime that hides their beauty). They are common on reefs and are found all along the coastline. A number of species are poisonous and can give a potentially lethal sting.

Don't pick up cone shells, as the animal is capable of harpooning you from anywhere along the cleft entrance to its shell. In the event of a sting, treat with pressure-immobilisation, and seek medical advice.

Tony Fontes

Tony Fortes

DIVING AND SNORKELLING IN THE WHITSUNDAYS

The Whitsundays and the surrounding hundred or so miles of Great Barrier Reef Marine Park offer a wide variety of diving and snorkelling opportunities. The islands are ringed by fringing coral reefs with a high diversity of coral and fish species; the mid-shelf reef complexes of the Great Barrier system some twenty to thirty nautical miles further to the north-east offer the visitor a real taste of what the Barrier Reef is about.

Diving is well catered for in the area. Opportunities range from feet-wetting courses for beginners, in mainland and island resort swimming pools, to full certificate courses, to extended excursions to the outer reefs aboard purpose-oriented dive vessels. Because of the number of dive operators on the mainland and islands, diving can play some part in holidays of various kinds – a diversion from lazy resort life, an interlude in a bareboat charter, an event on an extended island cruise, or just part of a day-trip out of Shute Harbour or Abel Point Marina. If you are bare-boating, for example, you might even arrange to have an instructor run a private course for you and your friends right on your yacht. Or you can join up with a dive boat at various locations throughout the islands.

Snorkelling

Snorkelling is one of the most popular pastimes on the Great Barrier Reef and one of the best ways to appreciate it – in shallow water, where the light and colours are brightest. Snorkelling involves a minimum of fuss with equipment and it gives complete freedom to explore and to observe the creatures of a reef in their own environment. If you are venturing for the first time into tropical waters, or if it's been a few years since you donned your face mask and flippers, a few hours practice before you leave for your holiday will be very well spent. You will miss many of the delights of the Great Barrier Reef Marine Park if you can't get into the water and be relaxed and confident while you're there.

All of your attention when snorkelling ought to be directed at what you're looking at rather than at keeping yourself watertight, and this is where practice comes in. You should be able to lie face down in the water and breathe through the snorkel in a relaxed, easy way. When floating in a world full of strange creatures and your mask starts to leak, or you inhale a little water through the snorkel, you may find that anxiety will cause your breathing to become erratic and you will tend to gulp water. Just when you have cleared your mask and wiped the salt water from your eyes is the moment you fancy that 'Jaws' is coming at you around a bend in the reef. Normally a cool, rational person, in these circumstances you may do a massive twitch, spit out your snorkel, and inhale enough water to make the water level at the reef fall several centimetres. Adrenalin pumping and all senses now ready for a life-and-death struggle, you will notice for

Reef fishes commonly seen in the Whitsundays

Many-lined sweetlip (60 cm)
Plectorhynchus goldmanni (Bleeker)

Six-banded angelfish (46 cm)
Promacanthus sexstriatus (Cuvier)

Yellow-tailed fusilier (45 cm)
Caesio cuning (Bloch)

Six-banded parrotfish (40 cm)
Scarus sexvittatus (Ruppell)

Blue angelfish (38 cm)
Pomacanthus semicirculatus (Cuvier)

Harlequin tuskfish (30 cm)
Choerodon fasciatus (Gunther)

Scarlet-breasted maori wrasse (36 cm)
Cheilinus fasciatus (Bloch)

the first time that the current has carried you a hundred and fifty metres from the boat, a distance you couldn't swim in your peak of fitness at high school even with a shove off the diving board from your swimming instructor. Your cry for help is a mere gargle that attracts only the attention of a nearby seagull. A number of points are illustrated here.

How to get the most out of snorkelling

First and foremost, have a mask that fits. Even if the holiday brochure said that you would be supplied a face mask and snorkel at no charge, consider buying your own face mask. If you think about what you are paying for your holiday, the cost of a mask is peanuts, but not having one that works properly for you can assume unpeanutlike proportions. Go to a good dive shop and make sure that the mask you buy makes a good seal around your face. To check that a mask fits properly, put the strap in front of the faceplate, out of the way, and with one hand hold your hair back away from your face and put the mask into place with your other hand. Holding it lightly against your face with your index finger, breathe in gently through your nose. When you take your finger away, the mask should stay in place by suction, and no air should get in around the seal. Shake your head gently from side to side; the mask should still stay in place. If it does, you've got a good fit.

Children who are going with you will also need masks that fit. Small masks can be obtained relatively inexpensively. You will be lucky, indeed, if your charter yacht has masks that will fit children's small faces properly. An ill-fitting mask is worse for children because their irritation threshold is usually lower, and if they're unhappy, you probably will be, too! Make sure that all hair is away from the face when putting the mask in place.

Mastering the basic technique

The secret of snorkelling is learning how to relax with your face in the water. Breathing easily and normally is the key; it may take a few moments to overcome the natural anxiety that most people have when their mouth and nose are underwater. Spend a little time in a pool (with the kids, too), or in shallow water by the beach, where you can stand up immediately if you feel the need to. Legs and feet should float out straight behind you. Once you can control your breathing you will feel confident to deal with the odd bit of water that gets into your snorkel; for example, when a wave slops over the top or you put your head in too deep. Small amounts of water in the snorkel will be trapped in the U-bend under the mouthpiece and will gurgle as you breathe in. To clear this, inhale slowly and gently (so as not to draw in this water with the air) until you have a deep breath, then exhale sharply into the mouthpiece. Remember, never inhale sharply through your snorkel – always slowly and gently.

Finning is almost a straight-legged action, with the knees slightly bent. Some people say it helps to imagine having splints on your legs; it may be easier to get the hang of it on your back.

More-advanced technique

When you're happy about snorkelling on the surface, you may wish to try some shallow diving. The first thing to remember about diving is that you will need to equalise the pressure in your ears from the very moment you start to go down. Pressure increases rapidly as you descend. Everyone is familiar with equalising – 'popping' their ears – when landing in a plane; the principal in diving is the same. Divers start equalising from the moment they are beneath the surface, and they keep equalising all the way down. Pinch your nose and exhale gently with your mouth blocked. You shouldn't wait to actually feel the pressure coming onto the eardrums; if you wait until you feel it, you may not be able equalise. If you feel pain, go back up.

'Duck diving', as it is sometimes called, is done from a position flat on the surface with arms by your sides. Take a deep breath and swing your arms straight down and forward, which will force your head and trunk down. As you go head down, point your legs straight up in the air. The

David Collett

Pink anenome-fish (9 cm)
Amphiprion perideraion (Bleeker)

Yellow damselfish (7.5 cm)
Pomacentrus pomei (Jordon & Seale)

Banded humbug (8.5 cm)
Dascyllus aruanus (Linnaeus)

Blue Puller (9 cm)
Chromis viridis (Cuvier)

Five-banded damselfish (15 cm)
Abudefduf saxatilis (Linnaeus)

Beaked coralfish (20 cm)
Chelmon rostratus (Linnaeus)

Threadfin butterflyfish (20 cm)
Chaetodon auriga (Forskal)

Moon wrasse (18 cm)
Thalassoma lunare (Linnaeus)

weight of your legs above water will force your body down, and then you can begin finning downwards.

Watch the boat and the time

In spite of the relatively warm water you will experience in the Whitsundays all year round, most people cannot tolerate more than 20–30 minutes without getting chilled (unless they wear a wet suit). The more vigorous your activity the quicker you become chilled. Watch the boat to see that you are not getting too far away. By the time you realise that you are too far away, you may already be cold and tired.

Another hazard of prolonged snorkelling is sunburn. Lying face down on the surface you will not have your usual cue – heat – to tell you that you may be getting burned. A small portion of your back or shoulders usually floats just above the surface. This exposed part may get seriously sunburned.

Many snorkellers actually wear clothes in the water – shirt and trousers. This helps to protect you from the sun, it provides some small degree of 'wet suit' effect, and it also protects you from coral grazes if you get too close to the reef (it's amazing how often people get scratched on reefs through failure to appreciate their own draught).

Underwater visibility in the Whitsundays

Contrast is the principal visual cue by which objects may be distinguished from their background, and the water medium is a greater reducer of contrast. Light is scattered by particles suspended in the water, and it is absorbed by water itself. As a result, even in water of exceptional clarity the greatest distance at which an object of any size may be seen is about two hundred metres. In practice, it is usually much less; scuba divers the world over consider visibility of 30–50 metres to be exceptionally good. This sort of visibility is usually available only in waters far away from land masses where freshwater runoff laden with sediments greatly reduces clarity.

Hump-headed maori wrasse (229 cm)
Cheilinus undulatus Ruppell

Pinnate batfish (30 cm)
Platax pinnatus (Linnaeus 1758)

Tony Fontes

Above:
Little wonder corals were for so long considered plants. These are tube corals, with polyps extended.

The islands of the Whitsundays are high continental islands which create their own freshwater runoff, and they are adjacent to the mainland river systems. Moreover, they are swept by very strong tidal currents, particularly at times of spring tides, that race to and from Broad Sound just south of Mackay, which has the greatest tidal range of anywhere on the Australian east coast. The result is that Whitsunday waters carry, from time to time, a heavy load of suspended sediment particles; these scatter the light and give the water a brilliant turquoise colour, enhancing the view above water but diminishing it underwater.

Visibility among the islands ranges from 15 metres down to as low as 1.5 metres depending upon the winds and the range of the tide; average visibility is perhaps 6 metres. Corals, with their resident algae, are sensitive to (dependent upon) light penetration of the water, and they find the depth that suits them best. This fact gives another side to the coin; there is a greater diversity of corals within a shorter vertical distance in Whitsunday waters than in clearer waters out on the Reef itself – a real bonus for snorkellers and in some ways for divers, too, who have less tendency to rush here and there to the detriment of really seeing what is in any one place.

Beware currents

Reefs require clean new water for optimum growth. The best coral development is found at the outer edges of a reef. The windward slope is where the most virulent growth is taking place. Reef development is also strongly moulded by the flow of currents, and for this reason some of the best reef development in the Whitsundays is adjacent to areas of swift currents. The tide when flooding (southswards) is first obstructed by the northern side of Hook Island (sketch map C14/15), and here some of the best diving and snorkelling in the Whitsundays is found. Cateran Bay, on the northern side of Border Island (C29), sports a rich growth of fringing reef.

Tony Fontes

Currents sweeping south around Langford Island (C12) have fostered a substantial kidney-shaped reef there.

The corollary of all this is important to divers and snorkellers alike: beware strong currents. In certain locations you have no choice but to drift dive (for example, at Bird Island (C12), and in others great care must be exercised to avoid being swept too far from your boat.

'Never dive by yourself' is especially true in the Whitsundays, and if at all possible, always leave someone tending the dive boat so that you can be assisted if you get into difficulty with currents.

What about sharks?

The species of sharks most commonly seen in the Whitsundays are the timid blacktip, a reef fossicker, and the whitetip, which is not aggressive. Divers have reported encounters with hammerheads and tiger sharks. As is true of all tropical waters, sharks are a natural part of the scene. You probably have a better chance of losing a toe to a giant toadfish in Shute Harbour than you have of being bitten by a shark (see 'Avoiding Tropical Hazards' for diabolical tales of terrible toadfish). However, it is prudent when in the water to behave in a manner that will not attract undue attention (see the following discussion). Swimming and fishing are not compatible activities, for obvious reasons. Don't fish near swimmers, and don't swim near anglers. Sharks have excellent vision, but they need light in order to see. Don't swim at night, as this obviously increases your chances of being mistaken for a fish. Sharks are scavengers; don't throw food scraps into the water.

When in the water

When in the water, assume the attitude that you are a 'visitor' in a foreign environment. Behave the same way that you would expect a visitor to behave in your home – not to damage your furniture or insult your

Tony Fontes

Top:
Among the most spectacular of the corals are the gorgonians (fan corals).
Above:
The nudibranch, or sea slug, is a shell-less mollusc whose bright colour warns predators that it is unpleasant to the taste.

Diving and Snorkelling

- Check you are weighted correctly before diving and practise buoyancy control away from coral or reef animals
- Secure diving equipment such as spare regulators and gauges to your body
- Move slowly and deliberately in the water, relax and take your time
- Avoid leaning on, standing on, holding onto or touching any part of the reef and take extra care when taking photographs underwater
- Avoid touching anything with your fins and try not to disturb the sand
- Observe animals and do not touch, poke, handle, prod or chase them
- Do not disturb the environment as all creatures play an important role in the Marine Park.

family and friends. Sea creatures can be as curious about you as you are about them. They will often show little fear, especially if they haven't been mistreated by man before. Don't be deceived by all appearances. A moray eel, for example, peering at you from under a reef ledge, opening and closing its mouth as though practising how it is going to chew you up, is actually gulping water and forcing it over its gills, that is, it is breathing. These reef eels are not aggressive. In the water, do unto others as you would have them do unto you – not before they do it unto you. If you provoke anything enough, it will have a go at you.

Slip quietly into the water rather than jump or dive. Don't thrash around on the surface making a lot of noise or doing an impersonation of a wounded fish. Marine creatures depend upon a spectrum of low-frequency sounds that might almost be called 'vibrations'. They use these for communication as well as for navigation. For example, some fish attract mates by vibrating certain muscles in their air sacs. The spiny lobster, by vibrating an apparatus at the base of its antennae, makes a sound that you can feel as well as hear if you pick it up.

The lateral line of fishes and sharks is exquisitely sensitive to low frequency sounds. This is one way that fish maintain their perfect formations when schooling and escaping predators. The lateral line is made up of gelatinous canals along their sides which communicate with the external environment through pores in the skin. These canals have millions of tiny hair cells which act like the cells in the ears of land animals; displacement of the hairs by pressure gives the fish information about the direction and speed of an approaching object. Sharks are particularly sensitive to such vibrations. They have additional pores scattered about their head which are connected via jelly-filled tubes to sensory cells called Lorenzini's ampullae.

Sharks are attracted to wounded-fish-like vibrations. This fact has led to incidents on the Great Barrier Reef where sharks have been attracted to divers who have stayed underwater with a fish wiggling on the end of a spear for too long.

Sound travels much further in water than light does, so this sense assumes greater importance in water. Whales, for example, communicate with each other near the surface for distances of over forty nautical miles, and further down they use temperature barriers (thermoclines) to make their voices travel even further. Swim smoothly and quietly. You will see very much more if you do. If you spear a fish while snorkelling, take it to the surface and hold it out of the water until you can put it into the boat (there are limits on spearfishing in the marine park; see 'Fishing in the Whitsundays' and 'Managing the Marine Park').

Nasty jellyfishes

The box jellyfish (*Chironex fleckeri*) and irukandji (*Carukia* sp.) are potential hazards for snorkellers and divers, mostly during the hot summer months. You can protect a large portion of your body by wearing a stinger suit (a light-weight, body-stocking sort of wet suit)) which are available including a head mask, gloves and booties, and they are not expensive. They will give you added protection from sunburn and coral grazes and will keep you warmer in the water, too.

Diver training in the Whitsundays

The Whitsundays are now the second largest diver training centre in Australia (Cairns is the largest), and some of Australia's most qualified sports diving professionals work in the area. The Whitsundays are ideal for diver training because it is possible to dive there virtually every day of the year at a choice of Great Barrier Reef or island sites. The Barrier Reef lies 32 nautical miles north-east of the Whitsunday mainland, about one and a half to two hours by motorised catamaran or fast launch. If it's too windy to go out to the Reef, there will be somewhere amongst the many island fringing reefs that will be sheltered enough to dive in comfort.

BEST DIVING IN THE WHITSUNDAYS

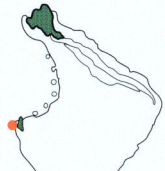

Bird Island (C12)

Visibility: 2–12 metres
Diving depth: 2–15 metres
Bottom: Rock in the shallows down to 6–8 metres, then dropping off to coral rubble and silty sand.

This site very open to currents; best to plan a drift dive or stay close to the island. Interesting rock formations down to 8 metres; shallow caves, ledges and gullies. Not a lot of coral, but the fish life can be quite good with large cod, sweetlip and trevally.

Snorkelling: Only mediocre.

Black Island (West Reef) (C12)

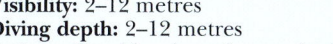

Visibility: 2–10 metres
Diving depth: 3–12 metres
Bottom: Small, scattered coral heads on a silty sand bottom gently sloping from the beach to 15 metres.

An easy shore dive (as the majority of interesting corals are very near the shore) from the north-western corner of Black Island. Fish life rather small, but colourful. Current can be strong offshore, particularly near the northern end of the beach.

Snorkelling: Yes, but a bit deep at high tide.

Border Island (Cataran Bay) (C29)

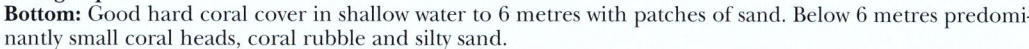

Visibility: 2–12 metres
Diving depth: 2–12 metres
Bottom: Good hard coral cover in shallow water to 6 metres with patches of sand. Below 6 metres predominantly small coral heads, coral rubble and silty sand.

Best diving on either side of entrance into bay. Coral reefs are relatively shallow, dominated by large beautiful plate coral. From the top of reef a small wall drops down to 6 metres. Scattered coral bommies continue down to 12 metres. Plenty of gullies and ledges to explore. Fish life average, though some larger sweetlip and cod can be found under the ledges. Inside the bay, current is minimal; however, beware strong currents at the entrance, particularly off the northwest tip.

Snorkelling: Coral very shallow, making for easy snorkelling.

Haslewood Island (Waite Bay) (C31)

Visibility: 3–15 metres
Diving depth: 3–18 metres
Bottom: Very good coral cover with scattered small bommies and sand patches in shallow water gradually sloping from 3 metres to 6 metres. Good wall down to 12–18 metres then coral rubble and silty sand.

Very diverse dive site. A maze of interesting coral bommies in shallow water from 6 metres. Good quality coral. A descent wall dive from 6 metres to as deep as 18 metres on reef edge. Again, good coral cover, plenty of gullies and ledges to explore. Good fish life of all sizes. Watch for manta rays in the winter months, May to September. Current is not normally a problem except during spring tides. Bay is open to south-easterlies. Can only be dived during light winds or northerlies.

Snorkelling: Best in shallows near beach, though is also very good for the interepid snorkeller who prefers something a bit deeper on the reef edge.

Hayman Island (Blue Pearl Bay) (C13a/b)

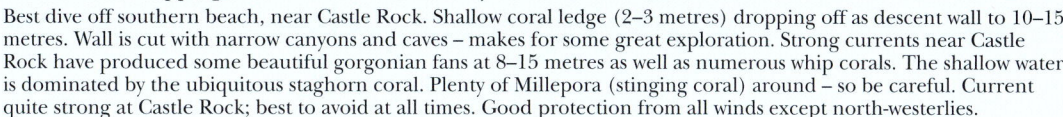

Visibility: 3–15 metres
Diving depth: 3–18 metres
Bottom: Best coral cover in shallow water off southern beach. Scattered bommies with silty sand bottom at 5–18 metres, dropping off to coral rubble and silty sand below 18 metres.

Best dive off southern beach, near Castle Rock. Shallow coral ledge (2–3 metres) dropping off as descent wall to 10–15 metres. Wall is cut with narrow canyons and caves – makes for some great exploration. Strong currents near Castle Rock have produced some beautiful gorgonian fans at 8–15 metres as well as numerous whip corals. The shallow water is dominated by the ubiquitous staghorn coral. Plenty of Millepora (stinging coral) around – so be careful. Current quite strong at Castle Rock; best to avoid at all times. Good protection from all winds except north-westerlies.

Snorkelling: Very good off southern beach, near Castle Rock.

Hayman Island (Dolphin Point) (C13a/b)

Visibility: 3–15 metres
Diving depth: 5–18 metres
Bottom: Rugged terrain of coral outcrops and huge boulders set on coral rubble and sand.

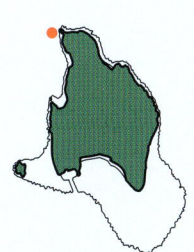

An unusual dive amongst house-sized rock slabs making for great exploration. Large coral bommies at 5–15 metres add to the diversity of the dive. Excellent large fish life for island diving, including trevally, mackerel, barracuda and the odd shark. This is a relatively deep dive with potential currents near the point. Good anchorage in all but northerly winds.

Snorkelling: Not really. Too deep.

 Dive sites with a mixture of black and grey symbols rate differently depending upon conditions

BEST DIVING IN THE WHITSUNDAYS

Hayman Island (East Reef) (C13a)

Visibility: 5–15 metres
Diving depth: 2–12 metres
Bottom: Very good coral cover in shallow water (6–8 metres) cut with numerous small canyons. Small bommies and sand–coral rubble from 8 to 15 metres.

A very pretty shallow dive and snorkel site. The shallow coral cover is dominated by large plates, creating numerous small canyons and ledges which make for interesting exploration. Plenty of small, friendly reef fish. Access to this site is difficult due to its exposure to wind from every direction and to currents. A site for very calm days at slack tide.

Snorkelling: Excellent shallow coral.

Hook Island (Alcyonaria Point) (C14/15)

Visibility: 3–15 metres
Diving depth: 3–18 metres
Bottom: Good coral cover with patches of coral rubble and silty sand.

Excellent coral and fish life, particularly along the shallow ledge that runs along the point to Flat Rock. Plate corals dominate the shallow water. Ledge drops vertically with wall penetrated by numerous gullies and small caves. Many colourful soft corals at 10 metres, hence the site name. Large wrasse, cod and sweetlip found at depth. Current can be a problem, particularly at midtide. Anchorage is difficult due to drop-off. Exposed to northerlies and strong south-easterlies.

Snorkelling: Excellent shallow corals but prone to strong current.

Hook Island (Butterfly Bay) (C14/15)

Visibility: 2–10 metres
Diving depth: 5–12 metres
Bottom: Coral cover with large patches of coral rubble and silty sand.

This popular bareboat anchorage offers coral outcrops with shallow walls. Many small, colourful fish. Best of the bommies is found in the centre of the bay, though difficult to locate at high tide. Tidal currents can be a problem as one moves away from the bay edge towards the centre.

Snorkelling: Only along the bay edge or just off the beach

Hook Island (Luncheon Bay) (C14/15)

Visibility: 3–15 metres
Diving depth: 3–15 metres
Bottom: Good shallow coral cover to 8–10 metres, coral rubble and silty sand at depth. Large bommie on eastern point.

Interesting terrain along foreshore down to 10 metres, best along eastern side of bay with coral gullies and ledges. Best part of dive is the bommie on the eastern point. Large fish life including wrasse, sweetlip and red emperor. Tidal current on point can be quite strong, particularly at midtide. Open to northerly winds.

Snorkelling: Good coral cover in shallow water all along the the bay.

Hook Island (Mackerel Bay) (C14/15)

Visibility: 2–10 metres
Diving depth: 2–12 metres
Bottom: Good coral cover in shallow water, dropping off to scattered bommies at 7–12 metres.

A dive better at some times than others depending upon visibility. This is a popular dive site during northerlies when most of the more popular sites are untenable. A relatively shallow dive through a maze of coral bommies, which form shallow canyons, ledges and swim-throughs. Fish life is medium in size and quite good. Exposed to southerly winds.

Snorkelling: Visibility adversely affected by the tide. Best during neap tides.

Hook Island (Manta Ray Bay) (C14/15)

Visibility: 3–15 metres
Diving depth: 3–15 metres
Bottom: Scattered coral bommies with sandy bottom. Below 15 metres mainly silty sand and coral rubble.

Hundreds of small damselfishes make this a top island dive. The fish of Manta Ray Bay include some not-so-small Maori wrasses. The terrain is diverse with scattered bommies starting at 10–12 metres and reaching up to within 2 metres of the surface. Acropora corals dominate, with large plates on the top of the bommies and fields of staghorns in the shallow waters near the beach. A small but spectacular coral canyon (10 metres) can be found about 50 metres off the western end of the beach. Manta rays are common in the winter months, May to September. Excellent protection from all winds except the northerlies.

Snorkelling: Very good throughout the bay.

Hook Island (Maureen's Cove) (C14/15)

Visibility. 3–15 metres
Diving depth: 3–15 metres
Bottom: Large coral bommies and sandy bottom at back of cove. Good shallow coral cover with coral rubble and silty sand on eastern side of cove.

There are two dive sites here. At the back of the cove off the western side of the beach is a series of bommies starting at 12–15 metres and rising to within 3 metres of the surface parallel to the shoreline. Gullies and shallow caves make for an interesting dive. Good medium-sized fish life. Along the eastern edge of Maureen's Cove is another good dive site locally known as the Boulders. Plate corals and other acropora dominate the shallow ledge which drops off as a small wall to 10–12 metres. Best corals, including large gorgonian fans, are near the point, but beware of strong currents. Open to northerly winds.

Snorkelling: Best on the east side of the cove (otherwise, becomes too deep).

BEST DIVING IN THE WHITSUNDAYS

Hook Island (The Pinnacles)(C14/15)

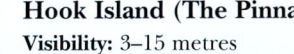

Visibility: 3–15 metres
Diving depth: 3–18 metres
Bottom: Near solid coral cover in shallow water, breaking up into scattered but dense bommies from 5 to 18 metres. Below 18 metres only coral rubble and sand with the odd small coral head.

Arguably the best dive site in the Whitsunday islands – certainly the best hard corals which compare favourably to the Great Barrier Reef. The best dive is off the western beach, adjacent to the Woodpile and swim east at a depth of 7–15 metres. Large coral bommies dominate the terrain, reaching nearly to the surface. As usual, acropora corals are everywhere, but huge porites corals in the shape of boulders and massive towers can also be seen. The fish life is medium in size and average in quality. Manta rays are very common in the cooler months, May to September. In the shallow water, particularly off the western beach, the coral cover is nearly solid, mostly staghorn, with only a few sandy patches. The quality of the corals diminishes the further east one goes (towards the rock pinnacles). This site is open to northerly winds and swell from strong south-easterlies.

Snorkelling: Some of the best in the Whitsundays just off the western beach.

Hook Island (Saba Bay)(C14/15)

Visibility: 2–12 metres
Diving depth: 2–15 metres
Bottom: Good coral cover in shallow water, dropping of to scattered bommies at 7–12 metres

As with Mackerel Bay, this is another popular dive site during northerly winds which can be better at some times than others depending upon visibility. The northern end of the bay is studded with numerous small bommies in relatively shallow water, dropping down to 10–15 metres with scattered bommies among coral rubble and sand. Plenty of shallow canyons, ledges and swimthroughs. The fish are small- to medium-sized and in good numbers. Visibility is adversely affected by tide. Best dives during neap tides. Exposed to southerly winds.

Snorkelling: Interesting bommies on both sides of bay.

Hook Island (The Woodpile) (C14/15)

Visibility: 4–15 metres
Diving depth: 5–30 metres
Bottom: Rock wall drop-off with scattered deep coral and sandy bottom.

The unusual rock formation known as the Woodpile has created the best wall dive in the Whitsunday islands. The wall drops down to nearly 30 metres on the point. Best to start the dive about halfway between the beach and the point. Here the wall is covered in soft corals down to 5–7 metres. Below 7 metres, the wall is somewhat devoid of corals but provides some excellent exploring, with large overhanging ledges and shallow caves. Some fairly large black coral trees can be found between 10 and 15 metres. Back away from the wall is a maze of coral bommies, including some large porite corals. Approaching the point the landscape becomes rather barren due to strong currents – an area to be avoided. This site is exposed to northerlies, and swell from strong south-easterlies can make anchoring quite uncomfortable.

Snorkelling: No.

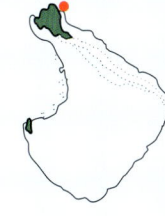

Langford Island (Langford Reef North)(C12)

Visibility: 2–10 metres
Diving depth: 3–15 metres
Bottom: Scattered small coral bommies on sandy bottom, gradually sloping from shore to 15 metres. Below 15 metres mostly coral rubble and silty sand.

A very popular day-trip destination for sailors, snorkellers and divers. Best diving is found on north-western end of beach, where current is strongest at mid-tide. Scattered bommies offer an interesting maze to explore. Some shallow walls at the eastern end of the island. The majority of fish life is small but abundant. Expec t to encounter tidal currents at all times except slack water. Reasonable protection from all but the strongest wind condition.

Snorkelling: Just offshore along the beach; best towards the island.

Whitsunday Island (The Gardens)(C18)

Visibility: 4–15 metres
Diving depth: 5–15 metres
Bottom: Reasonable coral cover on a gently descending slope with silty sand patches.

Easy, shallow dive just off Hook Island, very near the Underwater Observatory. Coral cover dominated by large plate corals. Plenty of small friendly reef fish looking for a handout. Occasionally, large pelagic fishes will cruise through. Excellent protection in all wind conditions. Current can be a problem during spring tides.

Snorkelling: Watch current during big tides.

BEST DIVING AT THE REEF

Bait Reef (Gary's Inlet) (R1/1b)

Visibility: 10–20 metres
Diving depth: 4–18 metres
Bottom: Walls forming inlets are solid coral, bottom is sand with scattered, low coral bommies.

An easy site offering two very different dives. The outside edge and entrance into the inlet is a relatively deep dive, 10–18 metres among the low coral bommies and along the wall that forms the edge of Bait Reef. The coral is excellent including soft corals and gorgonian fans. Fish life can be reasonably large with cod, mackerel, barracuda and trout. Once outside the inlet, current can be a problem. Diving within the inlet is easy and relaxing with minimal to no current and 4–12 metres of water. The walls are cut with canyons and deep ledges. Numerous giant anemones at the back of the inlet. Look for wobbegong sharks under the ledges. Good protection in all winds but north-westerlies.

Snorkelling: Very good shallow coral along the edge of the inlet. A 100-metre swim to the east at high tide is a beautiful shallow, unnamed lagoon with a couple of resident reef sharks. Worth the effort.

Bait Reef (Manta Ray Drop-off) (R1)

Visibility: 12–30 metres
Diving depth: 3–36 metres
Bottom: Total coral cover in shallow water to 5 metres, wall dropping to 30 metres cut with crevices. From 30 metres down, bottom is made up of coral rubble, sand and scattered coral heads.

Great Barrier Reef diving at its best. A spectacular wall dive from 5 to 30 metres vertical. At the top of the wall is a gorgeous coral garden with a diverse array of hard corals. The wall itself is covered in small colourful soft corals, gorgonian fans, whips and feather stars. The most interesting aspect of the dive is exploring the deep fissures that cut deep into the wall, including a vertical tunnel or chimney. At the base of the wall the bottom continues down and is covered with numerous small coral heads. At 30–35 metres are tall, corkscrew sea whips that reach upwards 3–4 metres towards the surface. The fish life is never-ending, with an array of big and small forms. Schools of fusiliers cruise the drop-off, large wrasse and bumpheaded parrotfish are often seen along the wall, trevally, mackerel, barracuda and sharks come up from the deep and, of course, manta rays. This site is exposed to southerly winds and is very prone to strong currents. Best to dive during slack water, neap tides.

Snorkelling: Excellent coral garden in shallow water but very prone to current.

Bait Reef (Stepping Stones) (R1/1b)

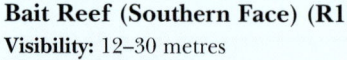

Visibility: 10–20 metres
Diving depth: 3–30 metres
Bottom: Very large coral bommies on sand. Behind the Stepping Stones sand often covered by huge thickets of staghorn coral.

The Stepping Stones are a unique feature of Bait Reef. They are made up of 18 or more flat-topped coral pinnacles lined up in a row along the south-west side of the reef. Each pinnacle rises from a depth of 15–25 metres and stops within 1 metre of the surface. The pinnacles are circular in shape and have absolutely vertical sides. Each of the stepping stones is completely covered with coral of all varieties – huge plates on top, soft corals and gorgonian fans on the sides. The stones vary in size from small (15 metres in diameter) to large (50 metres in diameter). Clouds of small colourful tropical fishes swarm around the tops of the stones, while large wrasse, sweetlip, cod, trevally, trout and others cruise the numerous canyons, ledges and caves at depth. Large rays are common, especially manta rays from May to September. Watch the tidal movement as currents are fairly consistent. There are numerous dive sites within the Stepping Stones complex. Some of the highlights are:

- The Maze: located at the southern end of the Stepping Stones, this dive site is literally a maze of canyons, caves and crevices and relatively shallow (5–15 metres). Large fish are often found in the caves and under ledges. Angelfish are also common. Minimum current within the maze.
- Hawaii: this large solitary Stepping Stone is located near the northern end of the chain. It drops to nearly 20 metres on the seaward side. Plenty of big fish life but also plenty of current at mid-tide.
- Cluster of Four: as the name implies, four medium-sized stones in close proximity have created some excellent terrain for exploring – deep canyons and narrow crevices full of whip corals and large fish life. Some current on outside.
- The Lost Stone: at the northern end of the chain, the stones seem to disappear but are actually just deeper, rising to within 5 metres of the surface. Very good fish life, medium- to large-sized. Fairly deep dive, 8–30 metres. Current at mid-tide.

Snorkelling: Excellent shallow coral on top of the Stepping Stones.

Bait Reef (Southern Face) (R1)

Visibility: 12–30 metres
Diving depth: 5–30 metres
Bottom: Shallow water dominated by flat terrain completely covered by hard corals with the odd sand patch. Drops away quickly from 5 metres down to 20–30 metres. The slope is cut with numerous gullies with coral rubble and sand bottoms.

This dive is very similar to Gorgonia Hill without as many fans at depth. The numerous deep gullies make for very interesting diving, often filled with a variety of fish life including angelfish, sweetlip, cod and soldier fish. Large turtles, manta rays and some pelagic fishes such as mackerel and barracuda are often seen cruising along the drop-off. Open to southerly winds and current. Best to dive at slack water.

Snorkelling: Excellent.

BEST DIVING AT THE REEF

Fairey Reef (Henry's Bommie)

Visibility: 10–20 metres
Diving depth: 5–15 metres
Bottom: Relatively flat, sandy bottom studded with small coral outcrops. Largest bommie cut with ledges and a large cave.

An interesting dive in the lagoon at Fairey Reef, Henry's Bommie is considered to be a premier attraction. The bommie reaches from 12 metres to near the surface. A narrow gap opens into a cave which is worth exploring but beware the small opening. Inside you may find a huge clam, 1 metre across. In years past there has also a resident turtle that is often spotted at night. Circumnavigation of Henry's Bommie is the usual dive plan. Good coral cover and clouds of small tropical fish.

Snorkelling: Excellent with minimal current.

Fairey Reef (Little Fairey Inlet)

Visibillty: 10–20 metres
Diving Depth: 10–18 metres
Bottom: Shallow wall at back of inlet dropping to 10 metres, sandy bottom sloping down to 16 metres, studded with small coral outcrops.

Classic dive starting at wall along entrance to inlet, depth 16 metres. Excellent coral cover which tends to degenerate below about 18 metres. Possible to miss inlet if deeper than 16 metres. Swimming along wall and into inlet brings you in contact with very good fish life including brightly coloured angelfish, cod, trout and sweetlip. Plenty of nooks and crannies to explore when going into the inlet, and shallower water (10 metres). Small current should be expected outside the inlet but good protection once inside.

Snorkelling: Excellent along the wall of the inlet. Some current at opening of inlet.

Fairey Reef (The Shoals)

Visibility: 10–20 metres
Diving depth: 5–25 metres
Bottom: Relatively flat, sandy bottom at 6–8 metres backed by a shallow coral wail cut with shallow canyons opening into small lagoons. Eventually drops to 25 metres with small coral bommies on sandy bottom, some coral rubble.

A very 'easy diving site with negligible current at almost all tidal conditions. Swim-throughs into small lagoons make for good exploration. Heaps of giant clams, sea cucumbers and all the small tropical fish. Blue spotted rays. Maori wrasse and the odd reef shark are also common. Average depth is only 8 metres but does drop away to 24 metres. Current can be a problem at depth.

Snorkelling: Quite good, with little current.

Fairey Reef (Tina's Arm)

Visibility: 15–30 metres
Diving depth: 5–30 metres
Bottom: Small bommies extending from coral wall. Bommies and wall bottom out at 20–30 metres, then relatively flat, sandy bottom with coral rubble.

This is one of the prettiest sites on Fairey Reef. Very good coral cover including large porites coral and gorgonian fan, the largest found at 25 metres. Plenty of fish life of all sizes and colours, regular encounters with reef sharks, barracuda and turtles. As with most of the better dive sites, currents can be a problem, best to dive at slack water. However there are plenty of swim-throughs to explore if current poses a problem.

Snorkelling: Excellent, but prone to currents.

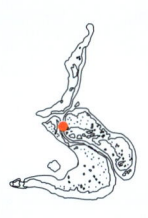

Hardy Reef (Fantasea Reef World pontoon) (R1)

Visibility: 8–18 metres
Diving depth: 5–18 metres
Bottom: Wall with good coral cover down to 10 metres, cut with numerous shallow curves, canyons and ledges. Below 10 metres, there are steep slopes of coral rubble and sand, with low coral outcrops.

An easy dive, good for exploring the undersides of numerous ledges and caves covered with small, colourful gorgonian fans and soft corals, down to 10 metres. Best hard coral cover found in the shallow water of the reef face down to 5 metres. However, the fish life is where it's at. For years the pontoon has been feeding the locals who are now big and quite friendly. Largest among the residents is a groper coming in at 2 metres in length and nearly 200 kilograms! Large Maori wrasse, trevally, trout and cod are always there to greet the diver. Plenty of small colourful reef fish as well. Good protection in most wind conditions except northerlies. Consistent currents particularly away from the wall. Possibly opt for a drift. Extremely deep water (60 metres) in the channel away from the wall.

Snorkelling: Excellent fish life; some current.

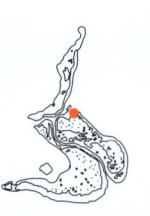

Hardy Reef (The Canyons) (R1)

Visibility: 10–20 metres
Diving depth: 3–18 metres
Bottom: Wall cut with caves, tunnels and canyons down to 15 metres, then steep slope of coral rubble and sand.

This dive offers great opportunity to explore an endless maze of tunnels, canyons and shallow caves which start as deep as 15 metres and take the diver right up to the surface. Gorgonian fans often shroud the tunnel entrances and crayfish are common in dark recesses. Large and small reef fish in abundance. One cave is always jammed with 100 or more morwong. Good protection from all but strong northerly winds. Outside of the canyons, current can be quite strong. Very deep water off wall (60 metres) in the channel.

Snorkelling: Current often strong over the reef flat.

BEST DIVING AT THE REEF

Hardy Reef (Shark Alley) (R1)

Visibility: 6–15 metres (varies tremendously with tides)
Diving depth: 4–20 metres
Bottom: Wall drops quite steeply; below 20 metres mostly coral rubble.

Plenty of action here, particularly at the bottom of the tide when the waterfalls are running. Sharks are known to cruise this area looking for a feed. White tips and black tips with the odd whaler, hammerhead and even tiger shark. Visibility is often low due to strong currents and outflow from Hardy Lagoon. Generally protected from strong winds of all directions.

Snorkelling: Not recommended.

Hardy Reef (Hardy Reef South) (R1)

Visibility: 12–30 metres
Diving depth: 5–30 metres
Bottom: Shallow water dominated by flat terrain completely covered by hard corals and cut by numerous shallow gullies. Some shallow pools with sandy bottom.

The southern face of Hardy Reef, when accessible, offers really spectacular diving, both shallow and deep. The steep slope drops from 3 to 30 metres very quickly and is covered in a variety of hard and soft corals. The numerous deep gullies are often full of fish life, including angelfish, sweetlip, cod and wrasse. Pelagic fishes can be seen off the reef face, including mackerel, trevally and barracuda. Open to southerly winds and current.

Snorkelling: not recommended.

Line Reef (R1)

Visibility: 8–18 metres
Diving depth: 3–25 metres
Bottom: Basically a coral wall with small gullies and deep ledges. Wall drops to 10–15 metres then steep slope of coral rubble and sand.

A good drift dive along a wall full of nooks and crannies. Small, brightly-coloured soft corals, fans and feather stars are common under the ledges. Fish life is medium in size with cod, sweetlip, wrasse, trout and angelfish. Good protection from wind but no protection from current.

Snorkelling: Prone to current; best to drift with current.

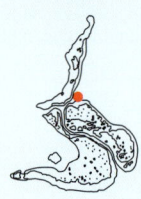

Sinker Reef (R1/1b)

Visibility: 8–18 metres
Diving depth: 5–30 metres
Bottom: Top of reef covered with staghorn coral (although some fairly extensive anchor damage). Steep walls dominate the sides, with lots of ledges and short caves to explore.

This is a relatively small reef located in the middle of the channel between two very large reefs. Line and Hardy. Watch the current. The dive is similar in character to Line Reef; a good wall dive with nooks and crannies full of small, brightly coloured soft corals, fans and feather stars. Fish life includes cod, sweetlip, wrasse, trout and angelfish.

Snorkelling: Not recommended due to current.

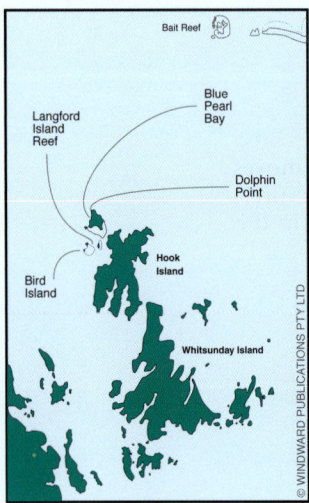

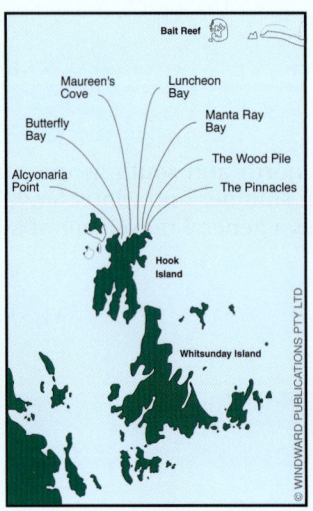

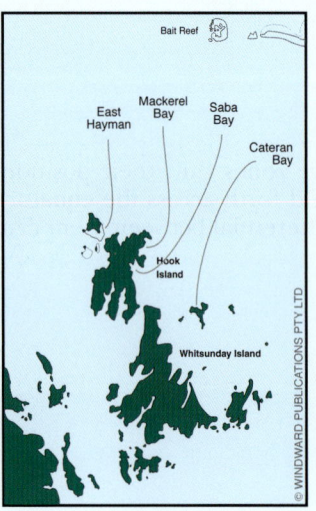

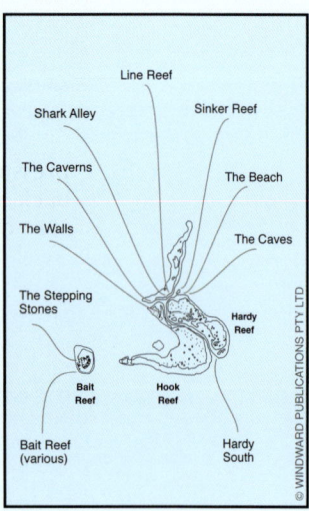

David Collett

BOATING IN THE WHITSUNDAYS

The Cumberland Islands*, now more often referred to as the Whitsundays, are arguably the best cruising grounds found anywhere in Australia, and they rival the best in the world. These wrinkled and indented mountain tops of a bygone era today provide a wide variety of anchorages, one seldom more than ten miles from the next. At least fifty of the more than one hundred islands and islets in the group afford comfortable anchorage, many of them several anchorages. Almost all of the islands are national parks, covered with trees and bush, creating the impression that they have yet to be discovered and offering visitors the faint smell of adventure.

In the past, by the time sailors made their way to the Whitsundays they knew all about trade winds, and coral, and how the big tides of this part of the coast play merry hell with contrary winds. With the advent of the sail-it-yourself yacht, this assumption of experience is no longer always true. This chapter provides an introduction to the winds and tides of the area, a few tips on cruising in coral, and some suggestions for getting around happily. The sketch maps and sailing directions later in the book take up the finer points of finding anchorage in the Whitsundays.

The weather and the winds

The Whitsunday islands, at about latitude 20° south, lie between a band of subtropical high pressure and the equatorial low pressure belt. These pressure zones shift their positions north and south as the sun moves back and forth across the equator in summer and winter, and the pressure differential between them causes a general movement of air (in the southern hemisphere) from south to north. In 1835, a French physicist, Gaspard de Coriolis, pointed out that any particle moving relative to the earth's surface is deflected to the right (in the northern hemisphere) or left (in the southern hemisphere) when viewed from the respective poles. Although the force of this deflection is only one millionth the magnitude of the gravitational force of the earth, it nevertheless has a significant effect on the horizontal movements of the atmosphere and the oceans, even on water swirling down the plughole.

---

*Cumberland was the name that Lieutenant James Cook gave to the islands he discovered on the Whitsunday coast in 1770. Other surveyors and the navy hydrographers later sub-grouped the Cumberlands into the Whitsunday Group, Lindeman Group, Sir James Smith Group, the Anchor Islands and the Repulse Islands. The name 'Whitsundays' today is generalised to refer to all of them.

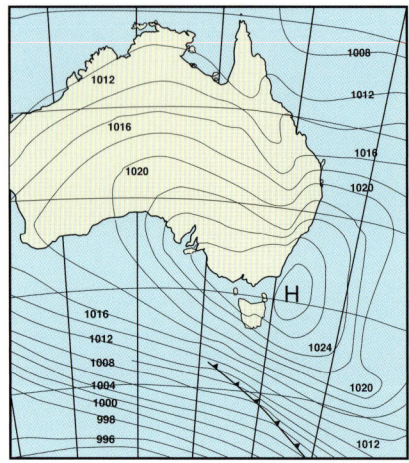

Typical April weather map showing high pressure, well south, ridging up the Queensland coast.

The engine of Australia's weather

Our weather in Australia is marked by a series of 'highs' which march across the continent from west to east, centred over the mainland at about 30° in winter and at about 35° in summer. They are set spinning in an anti-clockwise direction by the rotational force described by Coriolis and, from autumn to spring, these highs tend to produce ridges of high pressure all up the east coast of Queensland. The winds course around the ridges, producing persistent fresh south-east-to-east trades, their strength varying according to the central pressure of the highs.

It is important for sailors in the Queensland central coast to watch the high pressure systems which are way down south, as remote as they are from the tropics; strong wind warnings for St Lawrence to Double Island Point often have to do with a strong high in Bass Strait, producing on the weather map a spate of isobars across the coast between New South Wales and Queensland. The ridge of the high, where the isobars undergo maximum local curvature, produces acceleration of winds. Keep in mind, too, especially if your eye is trained to anticipate the strength of winds based on the relative spacing of isobars on a weather map, that in the lower latitudes of central Queensland, air is more easily moved than it is at, say, latitude 40° south, and what looks like 10–20 knots to the southerner may in fact produce 20–30 knots in the Whitsundays. The strongest highs usually occur during March–April, and Whitsunday winds tend to follow suit.

Weather is always capricious, and generalisations frequently leave egg on the face of the generaliser. Seasons have blurry edges, but the 'wet' season in the Whitsundays is January–March, the windiest months are March–May, the driest months are August–September. From late September onwards the trade winds abate, and some say late September to early November is the best cruising weather in the Whitsundays. At any time of year you can almost always be assured of having enough wind for a pleasant sail, with flat calm days occurring less than 5% of the time.

Whitsunday Wind Strength (knots)
Incidence of winds in given range, 1500 hours, Hayman Island (observations over 15-year period)

Month	0–11	11–16	17–22	22+
Jan.	55%	29%	9%	6%
Feb.	42%	34%	19%	6%
Mar.	47%	29%	16%	8%
Apr.	44%	28%	20%	8%
May	47%	33%	15%	5%
June	64%	25%	9%	1%
July	65%	27%	6%	1%
Aug.	61%	26%	10%	2%
Sept.	63%	22%	12%	3%
Oct.	54%	33%	11%	3%
Nov.	56%	28%	12%	4%
Dec.	54%	30%	12%	5%

This wind strength table shows the per cent incidence of winds of various strengths (knots). Figures add across to 100% (more or less). They confirm T.S. Eliot's observation that 'April is the cruellest month' when, in the Whitsundays, on almost one in three days, the mean wind strength at 1500 hours is over 16 knots (stronger gusts will, of course, be common). Weather is confounding. All these figures are based on 15 years' statistics, but quite exceptional weather is always on the cards.

Whitsunday Wind Direction
Incidence of winds from given direction, 1500 hours, Hayman Island (observations over 15-year period)

Month	Calm	N	NE	E	SE	S	SW	W	NW
Jan.	2%	7%	22%	31%	21%	2%	1%	4%	10%
Feb.	2%	5%	11%	32%	33%	6%	1%	2%	8%
Mar.	1%	2%	13%	35%	37%	6%	1%	*	5%
Apr.	3%	1%	6%	30%	46%	7%	*	3%	4%
May	4%	*	4%	24%	46%	18%	1%	2%	1%
June	3%	1%	3%	14%	41%	25%	4%	5%	4%
July	3%	1%	6%	23%	40%	16%	5%	3%	3%
Aug.	3%	4%	13%	26%	35%	5%	1%	4%	9%
Sept.	2%	5%	19%	33%	25%	2%	2%	5%	7%
Oct.	*	6%	20%	32%	21%	2%	*	4%	14%
Nov.	1%	10%	22%	27%	16%	1%	*	5%	18%
Dec.	*	10%	21%	29%	17%	1%	*	5%	16%

*Occurs, but incidence is less than 0.5%   = predominant wind direction

The predominant winds in the Whitsundays are south-east and east; north-east winds occur with increasing frequency from September onwards through January, giving sailors an opportunity to visit some of the south-exposed anchorages.

Buys Ballot's law says that, if you stand (in the southern hemisphere) facing the true wind, the centre of the low pressure will be 8 to 12 points of the compass to your left (one point of the compass is 11.25°, so 8 to 12 points is 90 to 135°). Facing the predominant south-east-to-east winds in the Whitsundays, your left arm, when extended 90 to 135°, will point to low pressure somewhere north of the islands. The almost total absence of afternoon south-west and west winds confirms the point – that the tropical lows are to the north. South-west winds do occur with thunder squalls and, sometimes, overnight.

The march of the weather systems over Australia results in periodic bursts of trade wind activity throughout the season, which lasts from March or April through September. Winds can spring up from a southerly direction on the spur of the moment, even in the middle of the night. For this reason, local skippers strongly advise against the overnight use of south-exposed anchorages from March through September. Exceptions are Nara and Macona inlets (sketch map C11), which are deeply embayed and are not as exposed, for example, as are the anchorages on the southern side of Whitsunday and Haslewood islands – Turtle Bay, Chance Bay, Waite Bay (White Bay).

Bullets

Gusty winds that joust with the lofty Whitsunday Island profiles increase in velocity as they whistle over the peaks and funnel down into the anchorages, producing what are locally referred to as 'bullets'. Bullets can be almost twice the strength of the ambient wind. Anchorages on the north side of Hook Island – Stonehaven and Butterfly Bay – are particularly bullet-prone, as are some others. Bullets needn't worry you unnecessarily, but it is good practice to get your sails down before you enter the confines of an anchorage, where all your attention should be directed towards locating the fringing reef and any scattered coral heads, not towards retrieving sails or articles of clothing blown overboard by a sudden unexpected gust.

Cyclones

Cyclones, or tropical revolving storms, when they do occur on the Queensland coast, come most often between December and April. It is unfortunate that 'cyclone' is such an innocuous name; it is correct in describing the clockwise circulation of an air mass around a low pressure system but deceptively meek-sounding compared with the hurricanes and typhoons of the Caribbean and South China Sea. A cyclone heads the list of sea experiences to be avoided.

Fortunately Queensland has a very good cyclone warning system, and yachtsmen, particularly those on bareboat charter, are most unlikely ever to have to cope with one. Cyclones breed in low tropical latitudes, and at latitudes 10° to 20° move at an average speed of only 6—12 knots. You will almost always hear of one days before it might pose any threat. Whenever a cyclone is within 434 nautical miles, the Bureau of Meteorology initiates a programme of regular warnings which are broadcast through the media with increasing frequency as danger becomes more imminent. Yacht charterers will be advised by their bases what action to take and when.

Riding out a cyclone

In the unlikely event that you are caught out and need to take shelter from a cyclone, the most ready shelter is one of the man-made harbours in the area – Meridien Abel Point Marina at Airlie Beach, Hamilton Harbour at Hamilton Island, or the Mackay marina. There are some other traditional refuges – sheltered creeks, where the yacht can be tied or anchored amongst mangroves. Some of the best 'anchorages' in this respect are Trammel Bay (sketch map C5), Funnel Bay (C2), the creek at the head of Airlie Bay (past Edge's Boat Yard) (C2), Woodcutter Bay (C6), and Upper Gulnare Inlet (C21).

Anchorages in creeks are obviously shallow and must be entered with a tide that gives you a little more water than your draught. Among mangroves, there are probably not too many rocks around, and the yacht will settle comfortably in soft mud as the tide goes out. Don't get too close to the shoreline; stay amongst the mangroves and allow enough room for the boat to lay over however much it will. A powerful motor left ticking over slowly in reverse will wash out mud from under the boat and may prevent the angle of heel from becoming uncomfortable. If you find a natural 'hole' the boat will hardly lean over at all.

Heavy rains accompany cyclones, and creeks when flooded will be

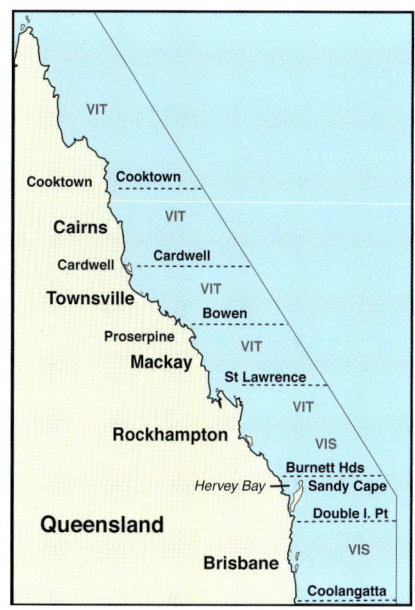

Weather forecasts for the Queensland coast are issued covering eight sections: Torres Strait to Cooktown, Cooktown to Cardwell, Cardwell to Bowen, Bowen to St Lawrence, St Lawrence to Burnett Heads, Hervey Bay, Sandy Cape to Double Island Point, and Double Island Point to Coolangatta (NSW border). The forecast of prime interest for yachting in the Whitsundays is

Weather information

Bareboat charter companies conduct their schedules morning and afternoon chiefly on VHF channels 81 & 82 and the latest weather report is always read at these times.

Whitsunday Volunteer Marine Rescue (VMR 442) also broadcasts the latest forecast three times a day seven days a week. VMR can be contacted on VHF channels 16, 22, 80 & 81 and on HF 2524 kHz and marine CB channel 27.88 MHz

For vessels with HF radios, the **Bureau of Meteorology** broadcasts weather from Charleville (call sign VMC) at 0330, 0730, 1130, 1530, 1930, & 2330 EST.
The frequencies are:
(0700–1800 hrs)
4426, 8176, 12365 & 16546 kHz
(1800–0700 hrs)
2201, 6507, 8176 & 12365 kHz

Weather information may also be heard on commercial and ABC radio stations, from Townsville to Mackay, at various times throughout the day:

4QN ABC Townsville (630 kHz AM)
4RR Townsville (891 kHz AM)
4ABCRR ABC Airlie Beach (89.9 MHz FM)
4QA ABC Mackay (756 kHz AM; 101.1 MHz FM)
4MK Mackay (1026 kHz AM ; 91.5 MHz FM)

Sandy Peacock

Wind against tide produces lumpy sailing in the Passage.

awash with logs and debris coming down from the land, especially if the particular creek has not flooded for a while. Keep your lines high and tied onto solid mangrove trees. If necessary, run anchors out around trees before dropping them into the mud. Secure several bow lines to keep you headed upstream.

Batten down all hatches, close all ports and deadlights, close skin-fitting valves (except those needed for the engine), board up large windows (if this is not possible, run vertical and horizontal strips of tape across them to prevent flying glass if they fracture), pump the bilges, clear the decks, stow all gear, turn on the radio so that you can hear all about the fun you're about to have, break out the OP rum, and pray!

Tides

Tides in the Whitsundays rise and fall more than those experienced by many yachtsmen, and they are the single most important consideration in cruising the area. Their effect on sea conditions, particularly when they oppose fresh south-east trade winds causing the sea to 'stand up' a bit, can be important to trip planning as is the swift ebb and flow of the tide through the narrow passages between islands. Spring tides may influence a decision on the use of a few shallow anchorages, for as well as providing more water at high tide, they give less water than normal under the keel at low tide.

The direction of tidal flood (rising tide) is southwards through the Passage, and the ebb (falling tide) sets to the north. This is worth making a note of and remembering; it is the single most important factor in trip planning.

Broad Sound, south of Mackay, has the highest tides of any place on the east coast of Australia, with a maximum in some estuaries of 10 metres. The magnitude of tides decreases to the north and south of Broad Sound. Mackay Outer Harbour, which is the Standard Port for tidal predictions for some of the islands, has a maximum astronomical tide of about 6.95 metres. As you move north through the islands, the tides decrease until, at Butterfly Bay on the northern side of Hook Island, the range is just half that of Mackay. As a rule of thumb, tide range in the Whitsunday Group is about 60% of that at Mackay; further south, in the Lindeman Group for example, the range is about 75%; and still further south, at Brampton Island, the figure is about 90%. Keep this in mind if you sail from Shute Harbour to southern anchorages.

Tidal waves (i.e. standing waves of tide as opposed to tsunamis, the latter being monstrous, so-called 'tidal' waves created by undersea earthquakes) approach the Queensland coast in a general easterly direction and converge around the broad eastern expanse of continental shelf east of Mackay. The shape of the shelf accentuates the effects of convergence, and shoaling produces bottom interference, resulting in a tremendous build-up of water, some hundred cubic nautical miles of it. The tide floods south through the Whitsundays on the way to Broad Sound, and these islands form an obstruction to the flow of water. In the restricted passages, currents can be very swift.

The Official Tide Tables & Boating Safety Guide, published by the Queensland Government (Maritime Safety Queensland), a copy of which should be aboard every yacht, is a very useful book with lots of valuable information. Among other things, it provides the means for calculating tides at points throughout the islands, and there are interpolation diagrams for calculating the height of tide at any time (see also the note 'Estimating tide' later in this chapter for the 'rule of twelfths' method).

The *Tide Tables* gives data for the Standard Ports of which there are four that are used to calculate tides for various parts of the Cumberlands – Hay Point, Mackay Outer Harbour, Shute Harbour and Townsville. Under the Standard Ports are listed various Secondary Places; for example, under Shute Harbour are listed Airlie Beach, Cid Harbour, Double Bay, East Repulse Island, Hamilton Island, Hayman Island, Hook Island, Lindeman Island, Nara Inlet (southern Hook Island). Because, as already mentioned, the tidal range varies tremendously throughout the islands, one needs to consult the data on the appropriate Standard Port to calculate the tide for a particular anchorage – for example, to determine how much scope to let out on the anchor at Butterfly Bay, or how much water there may be at a given time at the entrance to Gulnare Inlet.

Calculating Whitsunday tidal range and times

The *Tide Tables* gives a series of figures for the various Secondary Places – time difference, ratio, and a constant – which enable exact tide heights to be calculated. The following gives an example of some of the data for Secondary Places listed under the Standard Port, Shute Harbour.

Sailing with the tides

Secondary Place	Relative time high (mins)	Relative time low (mins)	Ratio	Constant
Hamilton Island	+2	+2	1.13	+0.07
Hayman Island	-25	-25	–	–
Lindeman Island	+6	+8	1.13	+0.05
Nara Inlet	-12	-12	0.97	+0.06

Explanation: At Nara Inlet the time of the high and low tides is 12 minutes earlier than at Shute Harbour (-12 means subtract 12 minutes from the times at Shute Harbour). The ratio 0.97 means the height is about 97% that of Shute Harbour with a constant of +0.06 metres to be applied afterwards, which raises the previously calculated height somewhat. The height of high or low water above the depths shown on the chart at Nara Inlet is calculated by extracting from the *Tide Tables* the figure for high (or low) tide at Shute Harbour, multiplying that figure by 0.97, then applying the constant (in this case, adding 0.06 to the result. (See the marginal note 'Calculating scope and tide'.)

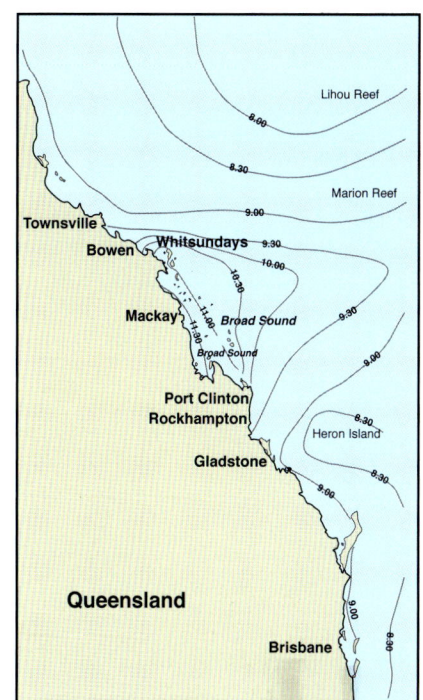

In this illustration, lines depict equal points in time, and they trace the advance of the tide on the Queensland central coast. Note the convergence around the broad expanse of continental shelf, which reaches its widest point off Broad Sound south of Mackay. Tide range decreases north and south from Broad Sound; at the top of the Whitsundays, the range is about one half that at Mackay.

(*After Maxwell, W.G.H., Atlas of the Great Barrier Reef, Elsevier, 1968.*)

Calculating scope and tide

Calculating the amount of scope to put out involves determining the tidal range (the difference between high and low tide) and then using the tide tables to determine the maximum height of water that will be expected in your anchorage (which determines your need for scope). The large range of tides in the Whitsundays and their variabilty at different time of the month (due to phases of the moon) makes this a necessary exercise.

'Standard Ports' are used by the people who make the tables, and then figures ('ratios' and 'constants') are supplied for other locations to bring those localities into line with the standard port – thus greatly reducing the number of pages in the tables but leaving some of the work to be done by you! (As you move north and south up the coast, the tidal range varies from place to place.)

The following shows the steps to go through.

Example

Lindeman Island, June 8–9

(Figures are from a past tide table and are for example only.)

The *Tide Tables* shows the following details for the Standard Port, Shute Harbour.

8	0413	3.34
SA	1057	0.55
◑	1709	2.81
	2259	1.00
9	0522	3.24
SU	1158	0.46
	1819	3.03

The highest tides in the winter are at night, and the difference between the low at 2259 on the 8th and the high at 0522 on the 9th is the greatest, so this one is used to calculate the scope required.

The high on the 9th is 3.24 metres. The range between this and the previous low is 3.24–1.00 = 2.24.

The tables show that Lindeman Island has a ratio of 1.13 (meaning the height of water will be 13% greater than the standard port) and a constant to be applied of +0.05. Applying the ratio and the correction factor:

Tide range 2.24 x 1.13 = 2.53 m

plus constant + 0.05 m

2.58 m

Chart depth at anchorage ③ = 2.40 m

Add high tide = 2.58 m

Total depth = 4.98 m

Scope factor (because depth < 7 m) = x 4

Total scope at least 19.92 or 20 m

The use of the 'constant' gives a degree of precision that, in practice, you probably wont be bothered with. To simplify it all, determine the tidal range for your location during your period at anchor and then add to that the chart depth in your anchorage and then multiply that by 5x to achieve a good safe amount of scope with a margin of safety.

When a spring tide is flooding south through the Whitsunday Passage against a fresh south-east trade wind, the tidal current opposes surface drift set up by the wind and the waves stack up into short, steep lumps. Yachts sailing against the wind will take plenty of spray and occasionally a bit of green water over the bow. Some sailors revel in these conditions; some prefer to avoid them.

The first note in the daily log should be the time of high and low tides for the day, and plan all trips accordingly. Spring tides can cause currents to run at several knots in the Passage, and currents in Fitzalan and Solway Passages may attain 4–5 knots. Even in calm conditions this can have a significant effect on your travel time, and at times of fresh winds against the tide it may be foolish to even attempt passage.

Navigation

There are so many readily identifiable landmarks throughout the Whitsundays that 'navigating' almost seems unnecessary. There is a temptation not to be formal about it, nor to be scrupulous in recording one's position; after all, it may be obtained at a moment's notice by glancing at the chart plotter (or GPS).

To revert to the old truths about the necessity of fixing one's position at every opportunity may sound schoolmarmish in Whitsunday conditions. There may be something to be gained, therefore, from relating a true story of the chap who was crossing the Passage in fresh breezes and spring tides. He disappeared into one of those 'occasional' Whitsunday showers, only to find that, on this occasion, the shower didn't clear immediately – in fact, not for 45 minutes. He hadn't a clue what he was closing in on, at a rate of 7.5 knots, nor did he really know the precise direction in which he was travelling, as there was 2 knots of tide setting up the Passage and it was on his beam. Under such circumstances the book says you should immediately go into a defensive posture; however, feeling certain that the shower was only momentary, he continued on at speed for an imprudently long time. The story ended happily, the only permanent casualty being the captain's image in the eyes of his crew as, in spite of the jaunty angle of his sun visor and the presence of his mirror sunglasses, there was no mistaking that on this occasion he was not in control of their destinies. He has since gone back to more formal navigating and log-keeping in accordance with the ancient prophets of seamanship.

Currents accelerate around points of land and edges of reefs, and if the skipper is not alert he may find himself careering towards a hazard faster than the yacht's sails are carrying him away from it. It is, of course, just at this moment, his having called for full steam ahead, that the key breaks off in the ignition and the engine can't be started. Or ,perhaps, the 'engineer' is otherwise occupied and can't respond immediately to his request to start the engine and so avoid the 'pickle you shouldn't have got yourself into, stupid' (these words were flung back in his face on the rescue craft as they went back to port to explain to the charter company that the security deposit is all that remains of their ship). Be particularly watchful when negotiating the reef off the southern end of Daydream Island (sketch map C9); 'The Beak' on the northern entrance to Shute Harbour (C3); Roma Point at the south-west end of South Molle Island (C9); Reef Point at the southern entrance of Cid Harbour; and the channel between Cid and Whitsunday islands (C19) – to mention a few potential trouble spots.

Preparing to anchor

The moment of achieving anchorage is a very special one in cruising, signalling the beginning of a whole series of pleasures. Refuge attained, the crew can peel off gear after an exhilarating sail, the galley slave breaks out the drinks and lunch, and everyone languishes in the sun. The joy of this can occasionally be dampened, however, by the few moments that preceded anchoring.

The anchorages of the Whitsundays are almost invariably surrounded by majestic hills and, along the shorelines, fringing coral reefs. The hills behave like funnels and air foils; they create very disturbed air which makes sailing difficult, with wind coming from all directions, causing the occasional surprise jibe and sometimes even a knockdown. It is advisable to get your sails down and start your motor before you enter an anchorage in order to allow you and your crew to concentrate fully on picking out the fringing reef and sighting scattered coral heads rather than retrieving hats or sunglasses lost in a last-minute battle with flogging sails.

The best way to detect a reef is to wear polarised sunglasses. Then, with the sun behind you, use an oblique angle when approaching the reef rather than a straight course; you will see the reef merging from the right or left, and you can gently manoeuvre yourself at a respectable distance without violent turns that tend to make the crew depart the deck and the sauce invert over the cabin sole (cabin sole is not, in this case, a Queensland fish dish).

It is very important both to have a lookout on the foredeck and to be able to communicate effectively with this person. Establish a set of signals and agree upon their meaning. If you haven't done this you may repeat the drama so frequently re-enacted: the lookout points to one or other side of the bow while yelling a startled instruction which, because the lookout is facing forward, carries away over the bow and the helmsman doesn't hear it. The helmsman responds by turning the yacht in the direction the lookout pointed, thinking this was the meaning, only to run square onto the coral head that was the original cause of the lookout's alarm. 'You idiot!' screams the lookout, saved only by a few fingernails clinging to the headstay.

'You blind idiot!' the helmsman retorts. He is momentarily at a loss for words, still trying to comprehend why his skippership has suddenly come unstuck.

His wife, who is lying on the galley floor, wearing the drinks and savouries she was preparing in anticipation of at last having attained the evening's peaceful anchorage, screams, 'You idiot, George, why don't you watch out where you're going?'

This is all easily avoided. The lookout, when communicating with the person on the helm, should always turn his or her head full around so that the helmsman can see his or her face. This way, even if the sound is dissipated by the wind or noise of the motor, the person at the helm has some chance of reading the lips or of getting some message from the expression. Agree on signals for steering right or left, for reversing, and for cutting the engine.

Anchoring

Many yachtsmen these days who sail off marinas or moorings gain their anchoring experience largely in rafting up on a mate's anchor for Sunday lunch or, perhaps on Easter weekend, dropping a lunch hook in a sheltered estuary where the maximum wind encountered may be 10 knots, the maximum seas four centimetres, and the bottom of muddy clay that would hold the anchor by suction even if it were upside down and the anchor chain straight up and down.

The Whitsundays demand good anchoring technique. Many of the most beautiful anchorages are subject to sharp gusts which may be twice the average velocity of the wind, which places extra demands on the ground tackle. There is also a large rise and fall in tide which makes extra demands on scope. The anchorages are surrounded by coral reefs, too.

The recommended ground tackle for most Whitsunday anchoring has traditionally been all-chain cable with a CQR (plough) anchor. The debate between Danforth and CQR devotees about which of the two is best may never be laid to rest, and the introduction of new anchor designs, such as the Delta, with enthusiastic claims about their supposed advantages, hasn't settled the matter. Locals have favoured the CQR because it cannot be jammed by coral, as sometimes happens when a piece of staghorn lodges in the flukes of a Danforth, preventing it from resetting if the yacht has ridden over and dislodged it because of a change in wind or tide. Delta anchors, the design of which also precludes jamming, are appearing on some newer bareboats; however, until

Use the largest-scale Hydrographic Office chart available when navigating.

The charts for the Whitsunday area are:

AUS 250
Plans for Hay Point and Mackay Harbour
Scale: 1:10 000

AUS 251
Bailey Islet to Repulse Islands,
including The Sir James Smith Group,
Brampton & Carlisle islands,
Keswick and St Bees islands
Scale: 1:75 000

AUS 252
Whitsunday Group & Laguna Quays
Scale: 1:75 000; 1:12 500

AUS 253
Whitsunday Passage & Shute Harbour
Scale: 1:37 500; 1:15 000

AUS 254
Plans in the Whitsundays: Lindeman I.,
Fitzalan Passage, Hayman I., Stonehaven,
Hamilton I., Dent I., Hook Reef
Scale: 1:75 000; 1:12 500

AUS 268
Plans of Airlie Beach & Bowen,
Gloucester Passage, Approaches to Bowen
Scale: 1:25 000; 1:10 000

AUS 825
Whitsunday Islands to Bowen
Scale: 1:150 000

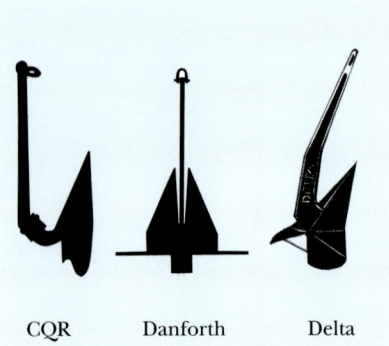

CQR   Danforth   Delta

Estimating the state of the tide

Tidal ebb and flow is not a linear function, i.e. is not equal over time but is a wave that may be described as a cosine curve (bell curve). The rise and fall of water is much greater in the middle of the cycle (as the wave builds up) than it is in the first or last hours, for example.

There is a simple, easy-to-remember 'rule of twelfths' for interpolating the state of the tide at various intervals between low and high tide.

Rise/fall during	Rise/fall by rule of twelfths	% of total rise/fall
1st hour	1/12	8%
2nd hour	2/12	17%
3rd hour	3/12	25%
4th hour	3/12	25%
5th hour	2/12	17%
6th hour	1/12	8%
6 hours	12/12	100%

Only a small proportion of tidal movement occurs during the first hour before or after the change of the tide. Twice as much movement occurs in the second hour, and the middle two hours account for fully one-half of the total rise or fall.

Tidal stream, or lateral movement of water, is not the same thing as 'tide' (tidal amplitude), which is the rise and fall in water level. Stream, or tidal current, reflects the constrictions of land and of the bottom. Tidal currents may run swiftly right up until the time of high or low water (and sometimes afterwards), and the rule of twelfths is therefore not necessarily useful in predicting the best time to negotiate a passage, which will, as often as not, be at the turn of the tide. Sea conditions are a more important consideration in the Whitsundays than the direction of set, and state of sea has to do with the net effects of wind and tide.

In the Whitsundays:

● with winds from the south, the water is smoother on a falling tide;

● with winds from the north, the sea is smoother on a rising tide.

David Colfelt

more exhaustive testing under all conditions has proven the superiority of newer designs, mariners, always conservative, will probably continue to favour the conventional plough.

Chain anchor cable has several advantages. Corals can quickly sever fibre ropes, and there are patches of coral everywhere. Chain ensures that the pull on the anchor remains horizontal, or nearly so, as long as sufficient scope has been put out; this guarantees that, once set, the anchor stays set. Chain puts extra catenary (sag) in the line, which acts as a shock absorber and prevents tugs and jerks from being transmitted directly to the anchor. Sag also considerably shortens the swinging distance at anchor, a great advantage in deep anchorages where lots of scope is required, or in crowded anchorages. Any yacht in the Whitsundays should carry at least 30 metres of chain.

Holding in the Whitsundays is generally good, the commonest type of ground in these continental island anchorages being a combination of mud and sand or coral and sand. Some anchorages have patches of live coral and coral bommies, which appear as dark patches. Try to drop your anchor over a light, sandy patch and keep your chain away from coral.

Setting the anchor

First, select a spot which is (1) a sufficient distance from any other yacht not to create a swinging problem or a social problem (see 'Anchoring etiquette') and (2) not directly over a dark patch on the bottom (coral). Then, with the yacht moving slowly backwards, pay out your cable in a straight line to avoid the anchor being fouled by its own chain. With all-chain cable, three times the maximum expected depth should be enough scope if the water at high tide will be seven metres deep or more; in blustery conditions four times the depth is a good idea. In shallow anchorages (where depth will be less than seven metres) pay out at least four times the depth (no matter what the wind) to be sure that the angle of pull remains horizontal. Yachts with rope anchor cables should pay out at least six times the depth.

Having let out the required scope, reverse slowly, watching a stationary landmark until the yacht ceases to go backwards, then slowly increase power (to about half cruising revs) until it is clear that the anchor isn't going to budge. When the engine is turned off the yacht will move forward as the chain settles; make a note of your position by taking transits or bearings on stationary landmarks so that if the wind comes up in the night you will know that you're not dragging (and will spare yourself a lot of needless uneasiness). If you follow this routine religiously, you will seldom get into trouble.

There are a couple of anchoring styles that you will see employed which will serve as an example of what not to do: the first is that of the skipper who enters the anchorage, circles around and, with obvious care, picks a spot – not too close to anyone else and with apparent calculation as to how much the yacht will drop back on its line – and then, as the yacht continues moving just perceptibly forward, the loud clatter of the entire predetermined length of chain can be heard exiting the bow, in one fell swoop. It's all over in six seconds. One can imagine either a tidy pile of anchor and chain on the bottom, like a galvanised wedding cake, or equally risky, noodles of chain lying immediately to windward of the anchor waiting to be dragged right over the top of the anchor, fouling the flukes as the yacht settles back.

The other example which works for some but which is not recommended in Whitsunday anchorages is called 'the cruising drop', a technique employed by the salty, round-the-world single-hander type. He steams through the anchorage at a relatively brisk two knots, weaving and winding nonchalantly until he has surreptitiously identified his spot, whereupon he wheels around, and steaming downwind, still at two knots, drops the anchor and cuts the engine. The momentum of the yacht carries it on until all the chain has been laid down and the yacht snubs up against the end of the scope. The skipper has a drink in his hand and is settled in the cockpit almost before the last ripples cease to radiate from the stationary hull.

This dashing technique has more to recommend it than the previous one, although it leaves a bit to chance – the anchor could initially become fouled with weed or something else that prevents its penetrating the bottom. It at least gets all of the chain laid down in a straight line and in such a way that it doesn't itself foul the anchor. Of course, if the anchor does become fouled and doesn't set, this technique will give everybody else in the anchorage something to laugh about for months to come.

The more conventional technique of anchoring is recommended. Before you start, **shorten up on the dinghy painter so that this doesn't get wrapped around the propeller when you are reversing to set the anchor.**

Calculating scope

Vertical pull on an anchor stock at an angle of more than about $8°$ starts to dislodge rather than bury it, even with chain cable, and to maintain an $8°$ angle you must put down enough scope. Allow for the maximum depth that will occur at high tide, which is simply the depth shown on the chart added to the height of tide you've calculated according to the formula already discussed.

Anchoring etiquette

The Whitsundays are being discovered by more and more sailors, and good anchoring etiquette is important. Enter anchorages quietly (i.e. slowly and being careful not to create more than a few centimetres of wake). If you are dragging half the Pacific Ocean behind you in your large, square-sterned motor vessel, remember that those sailboats with masts sticking up have, in effect, a pendulum above deck, and once set in motion by large waves side-on, they unfailingly set up an action that throws all drinks, plates of nibbles and perhaps even the baby and its bowl of mashed dinner onto the floor in the cockpit. It is akin to walking up to a stranger's table in a restaurant and raising one side of it off the ground.

Observe the basic laws of not violating others' 'space' – by not dropping anchor right next to someone else when it is possible to get further away. In some crowded anchorages even the most seamanlike efforts will sometimes result in one yacht ending up too close to another. If good seamanship doesn't make it immediately clear just how close 'too close' is, then anxious looks from the yacht already anchored should. In such instances the yacht which was anchored first has the right of prior occupancy, and any moving should be done by the latest to arrive and before it has become necessary to physically intervene to separate the yachts.

The importance of swinging circle

The swinging circle of a yacht describes its potential at anchor for interaction with other yachts, fringing reefs, or nearby coral heads. It is a function of the amount of scope paid out on the anchor and is the radius of a circle which the yacht can scribe around the point where the anchor is fixed to the bottom. Theoretically this is the hypotenuse of a right-angled triangle (see diagram), but because of sag in the anchor line it is, in fact, somewhat less. Without going into all the many imponderables, suffice it to say that one should assume that the yacht will swing around the anchor on a radius that is about 80% of the amount of scope paid out.

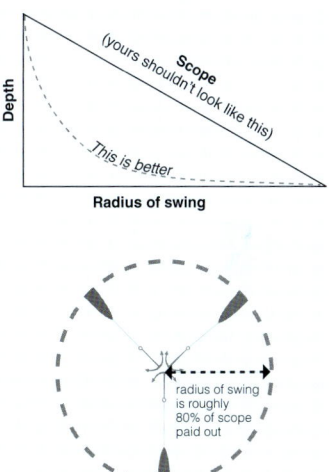

If all boats in an anchorage swing the same way, as usually happens if a steady breeze is blowing and there is no tidal influence, life at anchor remains uncomplicated. When the wind drops and the tide starts to do its capricious tricks, swirling around the anchorage, and where there are yachts with different underwater profiles using different types of anchor cables, that's when the fun begins. As a general rule, try to anchor next to yachts similar to your own and next to those using similar ground tackle – big keel yachts next to big keel yachts, motor vessels with flat bottoms next to motor vessels. If you see rope hanging off the bow of the yacht next to which you are about to anchor, ask how much scope is down. This personal 'intrusion' will not be objected to by a good seaman, rather it will be appreciated for the forethought it demonstrates.

Obviously if the gods have decided to play havoc, and they suck the breath from an anchorage while sending in the tidal clowns, yachts will need more than just one swinging distance between them to avoid collision. In uncrowded anchorages the ideal of maintaining a distance of two swinging radii can be achieved, but it is often impracticable where there is congestion.

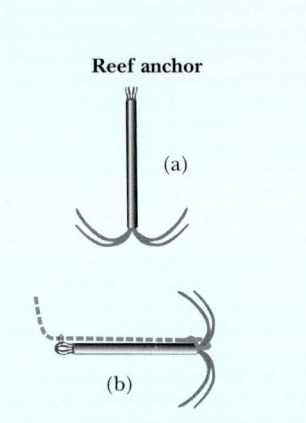

Reef anchor

(a)

(b)

The reef anchor ('reef pick') is a kind of grapnel with multiple flukes (not flattened at the ends) designed for temporary daytime use and intended to hook into coral and to be retrieved doing less damage than is done by a sand anchor. If you must anchor over coral, always use a reef pick. (For the future good of the Marine Park, and to keep you out of trouble with park managers, anchoring over coral should be avoided, if at all possible.) Attach the anchor line to the crown and lead it back alongside the ring at the end of the shank, as in (b), tying it loosely to the ring with twine. This method ensures that, if the anchor gets stuck, a strong vertical pull will break the twine and the anchor will come up crown-first (that's the theory, anyway).

Never leave a yacht hanging from a reef pick unattended.

Best environmental practices for anchoring

Increasing pressure on corals in the Whitsundays places an onus on all Park users to avoid anchor damage to corals. It is an offence to damage coral except when anchoring with a reef pick and taking due care to avoid the coral. More important than penalties for offences is the future health of the Marine Park, and the following practices should always be followed.

- Pay out enough chain (or chain and line) for the depth.
- Check out the area before anchoring.
- Anchor in sand or mud away from corals.
- Motor towards the anchor when hauling in.
- Use approved public moorings in preference to anchoring.

Don't wait until a collision has occurred; the worry about whether one is going to will spoil everyone's relaxation.

And for those who may love having the comforts of home wherever they are, including microwave ovens, TVs, dishwashers, etc. – all of which require that the yacht's engine be run constantly to keep the batteries from being sucked inside out – spare a thought for those who have come to the Whitsundays to enjoy a bit of wilderness, away from the constant reminders of urban civilisation. Use of generators should be restricted to times when they will not interfere unduly with the serenity of the anchorage and the peace of others.

Sailors should remove all halyards and tie them away from the mast to prevent these keeping themselves and everyone else in the anchorage awake all night. In light and variable winds the dinghy may bump the hull annoyingly at just the moment you have fallen asleep. Either strap it alongside with fenders to cushion it or hold it off by rigging a spinnaker pole.

Anchor light
Vessels at anchor are required to display a white light at the masthead between the hours of sunset and sunrise.

Anchor noise
Chain dragging over the bottom in some Whitsunday anchorages makes a noise which resonates through a fibreglass hull like a troll rolling boulders around in the cellar. The racket is transmitted right up the chain making sleep impossible for all but the comatose. The noise may be dampened by using a rope 'snubber'. To make a snubber, attach a piece of line to a link in the anchor chain and lead this through the fairlead or over the bow roller and secure it to the sampson post, bollard or cleat, letting it take the strain. Keep the chain secured to the yacht as well (but let it hang loose over the bow) so that if the snubber should part the yacht will not go exploring the anchorage while you sleep.

Stern anchors
There are times, particularly in anchorages open to the sea, when swell may be refracted around points and headlands into the anchorage. Just as a slice of buttered bread falls butter-side down, yachts turn side-on to the swell and roll uncomfortably. Butterfly Bay, Cateran Bay and Whitehaven Beach are notorious for this, and it can happen elsewhere.

A stern anchor may make life more pleasant by keeping the yacht headed into whatever is making it roll. It's sometimes a good idea to buoy a stern anchor with a trip line attached to the crown to make it easier to retrieve, especially if this is done from a dinghy where, if the anchor is set well, you may well pull yourself down to Davy Jones's locker before the anchor starts to dislodge. Keep the buoy line as short as possible or you may find another yacht winding up your stern anchor with its propeller. If a stern anchor has been taken ashore (for example, at Whitehaven) tie a float to the line so that others will know it is there.

Getting the anchor up
Getting the anchor up is the time when you are likely to see more of the colour puce than at a flower show – on the straining face of the foredeck hand (if the yacht doesn't have an electric winch; fortunately, most do these days). There is undoubtedly a certain amount of hard physical labour involved in raising the anchor and chain by hand, and considerable strain is put on the system regardless of how the power is supplied – manual or power-assisted. Many foredeck hands abandon their cool and become embroiled in a battle with the anchor, chain, wind and the full inertia of the boat. **Whether or not the boat has a windlass, the skipper should use the engine to move the boat up to a position where the chain becomes vertical**. This relieves strain on the windlass and is environmentally much friendlier to coral. Hand signals to keep the person at the helm steering straight to the anchor are useful here.

Normally, with a vertical pull the anchor will break out without incident, but if it starts to pull the foredeck hand overboard, he or she should take a few quick turns of the chain around the bollard and then call for the person at the helm to give a short burst ahead with the engine. If the yacht's nose dips violently and it spins around, the anchor is snagged, and further direct confrontation is likely to be of no avail.

An anchor snagged in coral will not let go as long as there is pressure on it. Release the strain: let out plenty of slack. Ideally, if the yacht is in shallow water and there is a capable hand aboard, to avoid doing further damage to the coral, someone should dive down and free it manually. Otherwise, motor slowly to the right or left and upwind. If the anchor snags again, stop, retrieve the slack, then let it all out again and try going to the left. By slacking off and pulling in a different direction you may free it. If the chain has wrapped itself around a bommie, ascertain the direction in which it is wrapped and then circle slowly, keeping a little tension on the cable. If all this fails, there may be no choice but to abandon the anchor and cable, but buoy it so that it can be retrieved later.

No-anchoring areas in the Whitsundays

There are a number of areas in the Whitsundays where anchoring is not permitted. These are chiefly anchorages where reef protection markers have been installed (white, pyramid-shaped buoys) to protect the fringing reefs. Other no-anchoring areas include those where there are power or sewage lines (for example, no anchoring is permitted anywhere between the southern end of Henning Island down to Dent island and all of the area between the top of Dent Island and Hamilton Island as far down as Cowrie Island (see sketch map C22)). Anchoring is also not recommended where there are 'mooring grids' (high-density mooring areas) such as: in Shute Harbour; part of Bauer Bay, South Molle Island; Muddy Bay (Port of Airlie) from Mantaray Point to Airlie Beach; and off Abel Point Marina (see sketch map C01) because (a) of the likelihood of swinging room problems and (b) one can easily foul one's anchor on a mooring.

Discharge of marine toilets in Queensland waters

It is illegal in Queensland to discharge sewage in a boat harbour, a canal, a marina or a 'designated area'. The 'designated areas' for the Whitsundays are noted in the anchorage diagrams (a brown line inside the box describing the wind conditions and depths). Designated areas of principal interest in the central Whitsundays are the northern side of Hook Island (sketch map C14/15 and the enlarged sketch maps of the bays between Alcyonaria Point and The Woodpile), all around Border Island (sketch map C29) and the eastern and southern sides of Hazlewood Island (sketch map C31).

It is also a requirement that, in waters where discharge is permitted, sewage must be passed through a mascerator to assist dispersion. In other words, vessels with a fixed marine toilet that discharges through the hull must have a mascerator fitted. (See page 126 for more details on discharge of sewage.)

Protecting reefs from anchor damage

It is a serious offence to damage coral in the marine park.

Reef protection markers

To prevent further damage to corals in the Whitsundays caused by yachts anchoring, a number of reef protection markers have been installed. These buoys measure about 0.75 metres on the base and sides and are fixed to the bottom along the edge of the fringing reefs. Anchoring inshore of an imaginary straight line between the marker buoys is prohibited. There is always more than one of these in an anchorage (to establish the 'imaginary line').

Since the first marker buoys were installed the incidence of damage to the fringing reefs has declined dramatically. **The marker buoys are not moorings, and tying up to them is both unsafe and prohibited.**

Reef protection marker buoys are installed at a number of anchorages to reduce anchor damage. They are white, triangular buoys, measuring about 75-cm across the base; they show anchoring limits. Anchoring inshore of an imaginary straight line between buoys is prohibited.

These are never found alone (i.e. only one in an anchorage), so look for others to establish the imaginary line between them.

They are not moorings and may not be used as such, even for dinghies.

Public moorings

To reduce coral damage and to maintain access for reef appreciation activities, public moorings have been installed at a number of sites around the islands. Public moorings have blue, beehive-shaped floats with a colour-coded band indicating the size of vessel that may occupy the mooring (see table below), and an engraved tag attached to the mooring pennant explains other conditions of use (e.g. wind conditions and other instructions, such as 'vessel masters are responsible for safety of their vessel while on the mooring; vessels not to be left unattended; shortening of the rope is not permitted'). Mooring sites have been carefully placed, in some cases in close proximity to reefs. It is therefore imperative that the mooring pennant **not be lengthened in any way**, for example, by reeving another line through the loop (other than the shortest-possible length if the bulky mooring line won't fit under the bow cleat). Moorings may be occupied for a maximum two (and in some cases four) hours during the day (between 0700 and 1700 hours) in order to ensure fair and equitable use. A vessel legally occupying a mooring at 1700 hours may remain overnight until 0900 hours the next morning. Using a mooring if one is available is much easier than anchoring, and it is better for the Marine Park.

Band Colour		Class	Vessel length limit		Wind Speed Limit
			monohull	multihull	
	brown	T	6m (tender only)		24 knots
	yellow	A	10m	9m	24 knots
	green	B	20m	18m	34 knots
	blue	C	25m	22m	34 knots
	orange	D	35m	30m	34 knots

In consideration of others, as a general rule, try to occupy a mooring of appropriate rating for your vessel if one is available (e.g. if you have a 20-metre monohull, pick up a 'B' class-mooring (green band) rather than occupying a 'C' class mooring (blue band, suitable for vessels up to 25 metres) because to do the latter may deprive a larger boat of a mooring. It is an offence to occupy a mooring contrary to the condistions displayed on the tag (for example, if your vessel's length exceeds that shown on the tag), and fines may apply.

Other moorings

There are other moorings, sometimes referred to as 'Service moorings', throughout the area, usually associated with resorts or other privately owned facilities. These have varying types of floats. Use of these moorings is the same in the Whitsundays as anywhere in Australia (i.e. they are private property and the owner has a right to object to unauthorised use). On the other hand, if the rightful occupant isn't on the mooring, there may be no problem using it. Never leave a yacht unattended on such a mooring.

General note about moorings

A table showing the placement of public moorings is found on page 125, and the sketch maps also show individual mooring locations. Moorings can be subject to misadventures, from propellors to storms, and are subject to periodic maintence; thus, from time to time they may not be in place as shown in this book.

IALA Maritime Buoyage System 'A'

Queensland employs the IALA (International Association of Lighthouse Authorities) 'A' buoyage system – navigation buoys, beacons and marks

Public moorings have a blue beehive-shaped float with pennant and tag that gives information on conditions of use.

A 2-hour time limit applies to their use between 0700 and 1700 hours.

designed to safely guide the mariner. The types of these beacons and marks most frequently encountered in the Whitsundays include lateral marks, cardinal marks, isolated danger marks, and special marks (see marginal notes).

Lateral marks are usually positioned to show well-established channels and they indicate the constraints of the safe navigation route into a port. They are red or green floating buoys (anchored to the bottom) or beacons or marks fixed to the substrate. Ports in the Whitsunday area include the Port of Mackay to the south or the Port of Bowen to the north. Thus, marks south from Pioneer Point (sketch map C2) are laid towards Mackay, and marks along the coast northwards from Pioneer Point are laid towards Bowen. In some instances marks are laid towards the obvious destination; for example, going into Nara Inlet (sketch map C10b), where the mark on the entrance shoal is a port mark identifying the left side of the navigation route into Nara Inlet.

Cardinal marks indicate the direction in which the safest course lies; for example, a north cardinal mark indicates that the 'best water' lies northwards from the mark, an east cardinal mark 'best water east', etc. Two examples of cardinal marks are those surrounding Low Rocks at the north-east entrance to Shute Harbour (sketch map C3) and the south cardinal mark on the southern extremity of Langford Reef (sketch map C12).

Isolated danger marks indicate a hazard to navigation of limited extent (i.e. with safe water around them). Don't pass too closely. A good example of this type of mark is on Pioneer Rocks (sketch map C2).

Special marks indicate a special area (in major ports, things like spoil grounds, cables and pipelines, or perhaps a channel within a channel). In the Whitsundays these marks are employed, for example, on the northern and southern extremities of Black Island's reef (sketch map C12), or on the south-east tip of the deceptive reef off the northern side of Refuge Bay, Nara Inlet (sketch map C10b).

'Red tide'

Visitors to the Whitsundays will sometimes see masses of 'red tide' – rust-coloured or yellow-green streaks of algae – floating in long slicks through the islands. Red tide is a misnomer in that, in other parts of the world, it is a term associated with a dinoflagellate algae that renders fish and some shellfishes temporarily poisonous. The Whitsunday 'red tide' is produced by the phytoplankton *Trichodesmium erythraeum*, a little hairy red bundle which periodically blooms (usually August–October) and blows in wind rows along the surface giving off a slightly rank smell. It is also called 'red sawdust', because that's what it looks like, or sometimes 'coral spawn', which is a misnomer (see below). *Trichodesmium* is a cyanophyte, a close relative of bacteria. Another type of slick is sometimes caused by coral spawn (late October to early December), which is coral sperm and eggs released in a mass reproduction orgy. Slicks can also be caused by oil. The three types are sometimes confused. *Trichodesmium*, examined closely, always reveals bundles of tiny threads.

Going ashore

Remember, the large tidal range in the Whitsundays may mean that there will be much more beach or reef flat to get across when you're ready to return to the boat. Always be aware of the state of the tide to avoid getting stranded. For example, leave the dinghy well out if the tide is falling; a good example of an expansive reef flat that can cause stranding is at Neck Bay (sketch map S2).

Mosquitoes, sandflies and various types of biting insects are abundant on some of the islands, including Whitsunday Island, home of the fabulous Whitehaven Beach which looks just too nice to have sandflies but which, nevertheless, does. Take plenty of insect repellent whenever you venture ashore.

The islands have the same wildlife as the mainland, including lizards, goannas, and snakes (some poisonous). Carry a torch with you at night. Queensland has a stinging tree which Aboriginal people named the

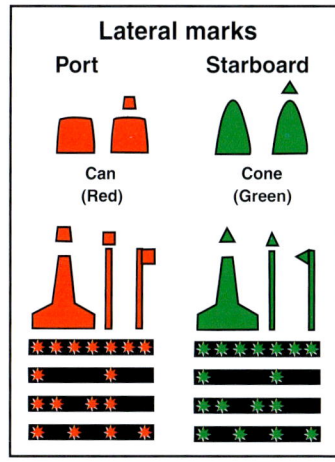

Lateral marks

Port lateral marks are coloured red, have a basic can shape, the topmark is square, and if they have a light, it is red. Starboard lateral marks are green, the basic shape is conical, the topmark is triangular or cone-shaped, and if they have a light, it is green. Port marks are kept on the port side of the yacht, starboard marks on the starboard side, when proceeding into port.

There are a number of mnemonics to help keep this straight. One simple one is 'port to port to port', meaning that one should keep the port-coloured (red) mark on the port (left) side when going into port (PPP). Another is 'green gauche going' (keep the green (starboard) mark on one's left side (gauche is French for 'left') when going out of port) (GGG).

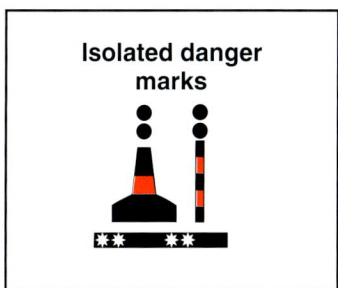

The topmark of isolated danger marks is two black spheres, one on top of the other, clearly separated. At night they exhibit a white flashing light in a group of two flashes (two balls, two flashes).

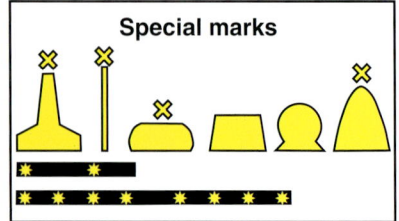

Special marks

Special marks have a yellow 'x' topmark; at night they exhibit a yellow light with any rhythm other than that used for the white lights on cardinal or isolated danger marks.

Cardinal marks

Cardinal marks have distinctive triangular or conical topmarks, which are relatively easy to remember (see below), and a code of coloured stripes, which are not so easy to remember.

North (cones/triangles pointing upwards, following the convention that north on a map is upwards)

South (cones/triangles pointing downwards following the convention that south on a map is downwards)

East (cones/triangles with apexes apart/bases together)

West (cones/triangles with apexes together/bases apart)

The east and west marks are perhaps easier to confuse than the north and south. The following may help: 'E' comes before 'W'. And, the west cardinal topmark, if turned on its side, is somewhat reminiscent of a 'w' (with a bit of imagination).

At night, cardinal marks exhibit a white flashing) light with easily identified patterns (3, 6, 9 and continuous flashing). These can be related to the positions of 3, 6, and 9 on a clock face, which also represent east, south and west on a compass rose.

'gympie' bush; it has heart-shaped green leaves covered with minute pale green hairs. If you brush the leaves with your bare skin you can get an intensely uncomfortable burning itch which is made worse by rubbing it and which does not respond particularly well to any treatment. The effects may last several days. Gympie bush is best avoided.

Making your way around the Whitsundays

Polarised sunglasses are essential in coral waters for the person at the helm and for the lookout. They cut reflections on the surface, making it possible to distinguish reefs that are otherwise almost invisible. Reefs are difficult to see when the sun is low in the sky and on overcast days. They are impossible to see at night. It pays to move around when the sun is high and be in an anchorage not later than 1600 hours or so. While there are no real coral surprises in store among the islands, some of the island fringing reefs are extensive and deceptive.

Coral which is an immediate hazard to navigation has a brownish appearance in the water; shoaling coral and/or sand appears light green (beware); deep coral patches appear black or deep blue and are usually out of harm's way.

Planning the day's travel

The first consideration of getting around in the Whitsundays is the tide – making an assessment of what effect it will have in the prevailing winds and how this may affect the sea and your yacht. Wind against tide can create rough conditions, especially fresh winds against spring tides. Remember, the tide in the Whitsundays floods to the south and ebbs to the north. If the wind is fresh south-east and the tide is flooding, the Passage itself can be very lumpy, Solway Passage (sketch map C26) can be hair-raising and Fitzalan Passage (C22) can be breathtaking. You may well be advised to postpone a trip until the wind and tide are together.

The 'Index to anchorages and placenames' lists all the anchorages that have a name and also the most prominent placenames found on the sketch maps. Their approximate geographic centre, in latitude and longitude, is given along with a map reference. At the beginning of each section (Northern, Central, Southern, Reef) is a map showing the area covered in that section and the area covered by individual sketch maps, as well as an index of sketch maps and anchorages. Armed with these and the official Hydrographic Office charts, you should be able to locate, and get yourself into, any anchorage. It must be stressed that the official charts are the final authority for navigators. The sketch maps are indicative only and are not intended for navigation. In some instances, they have 'displacement errors' as they are based on uncorrected aerial photographs and other sources, and they have not been created with sophisticated map-making equipment nor by a professional cartographer. They are intended to assist with orientation, to help you better read the charts and to provide some additional details, but you should use the official charts for navigation.

So, always have the chart of the largest scale available and use it as your primary navigation aid (the sketch maps indicate, in the upper right-hand corner of the page, the largest-scale chart that covers the particular area).

Use of the time available to you

There is a temptation to try to see too much of the Whitsundays in a short time, particularly for those with only a week on their hands. A leisurely look at four anchorages is about as much as you can really digest in one week; doing more will tend to make you feel rushed.

The most popular anchorages are Cid Harbour and Nara Inlet because they are all-weather anchorages and are close to Shute Harbour. The further south you go the more alone you will be. Some south-exposed anchorages, such as Chance Bay (sketch map C25)) or Saba Bay (C14/15), should not be used overnight during the trade winds season (May through September) because of the possibility of a strong southerly change in the middle of the night.

Principal causes of accidents

Analysis of marine incidents in the Whitsundays shows that poor anchoring technique is the principal cause of grief – dragging anchors and resulting groundings due to improperly setting the anchor or failure to calculate the necessary scope; anchoring too close to reefs resulting in contact with the reef (failure to correctly assess swinging circle); collisions with other yachts at anchor (failure to correctly assess swinging circle). Be sure that you understand good anchoring technique (see anchoring notes on pages 69–73).

Another common cause of mishap is failure to observe navigation marks (either through ignorance of their meaning or simply inattention). The previous two pages deal with navigation marks in the Whitsundays and how to negotiate them (also see the *Tide Tables*).

Areas requiring special caution

A number of areas require particular attention, some having been dubbed 'black spots' because of the high number of incidents that have occurred there. Areas requiring particular caution when you're out and about are:

- the Stonehaven/Hayman area (sketch map C12), particularly the passage between Hook and Hayman islands; the extensive and deceptive reef off the south side of Hayman; the reef off the south side of Black Island; the bulging reef projecting south and east from Langford Island;
- the entrances to Nara and Macona Inlets and reefs in these anchorages (C10a and C10b);
- French Shoal, Whitehaven Bay (C26–C27);
- the reef off Chalkie's Beach (C26).

Other areas requiring particular caution are:

- the patch of reef just south-west of the entrance to Gulnare Inlet (sketch map C20);
- the area south-east of the southern tip of Haslewood Island, between Haslewood and Nicolson islands (sketch map C31);
- Solway Passage, because of currents and sometimes rough conditions (sketch map C26);
- Fitzalan Passage, because of currents and disturbed water (sketch maps C21 and C22);
- Long Island Sound, between Long Island and the mainland, because of strong currents and rough seas;
- Cape Conway, because of potentially wild water in wind-against-tide conditions, and a number of underwater hazards;
- the shoal area to the south-east of the passage between Hook and Whitsunday islands (C17), where there are isolated bommies.

Radio communications in the Whitsundays

VHF is the prime means of communicating on the water within the Whitsundays. It is now used by virtually all the marinas, island resorts, cruise vessels, and bareboat charter companies and by Volunteer Marine Rescue Whitsunday (VMR442) whose base is located at Altman Avenue, Cannonvale.

The lofty hills of the Whitsunday mainland and islands create difficulties for line-of-sight communications, such as VHF and 27 MHz. The problems have been partially overcome in the case of VHF through the use of repeaters: channel 22 (located behind Woodwark Bay); channel 81 (located on Mt Robinson, above Cid Harbour); and channel 82 (located on 'Cook's Look', Hayman Island). Channel 82 is especially useful along the northern side of Hook Island where the lofty Hook Peak and other hills create a radio 'shadow'.

Some basic rules of the road

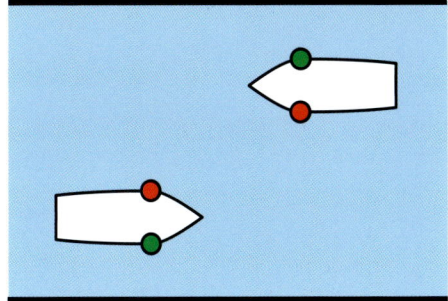

Navigating in restricted passages
In restricted passages and channels, vessels must always be navigated on the starboard side of the waterway.

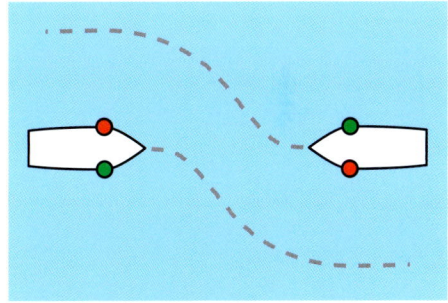

Vessels approaching head-on
Both vessels alter course to starboard.

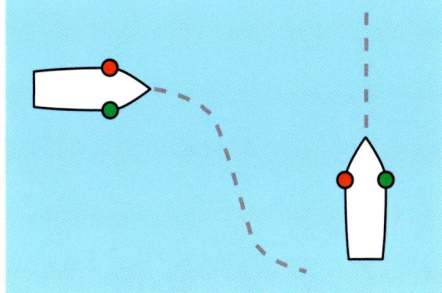

Vessels approaching at right angles
The vessel approaching from the starboard side has the right of way and the other vessel must alter course. However, the necessity to avoid a collision takes precedence over any right of way, if it comes down to that.

Vessels at anchor
Vessels at anchor must display a white light at the masthead from sun-down to sun-up.

Relaxing in a peaceful anchorage after the day's cruising.

David Colfelt

VHF channels 16 and 67 are available 24/7 for emergency calls, providing coverage from 54 nautical miles north of Hayman Island and 27 nautical miles south of Mackay. These channels may also be used to establish contact but are not 'chat' channels.

There is a lot of 'traffic' on the repeater channels, especially on channel 81, which is used by bareboat charter companies for their twice-daily 'skeds'. To relieve congestion on the air, the VHF repeaters should not be used for inter-yacht communication by vessels that can 'see' each other, when channels 72, 73 or 77 will suffice. Commercial vessels may use channels 6, 8 or 72. The repeaters have a 'cut-out' to discourage lengthy communications (timed at about 20–25 seconds).

Mobile telephones will work in some locations around the islands, generally on the western side of Whitsunday Island, but these are not to be relied upon and are not a substitute for VHF.

Most resorts, islands and marinas use VHF channel 16 for calling. Marinas generally use channel 68 for working (except Meridien Abel Point Marina and Laguna Marinas, which use channel 09 for working, Daydream Island, which uses channel 17 exclusively, and the jettymaster at Shute Harbour, who uses channel 10 for working).

Trailer sailing in the Whitsundays

Are trailer sailers safe in the Whitsundays? This question is often asked, and the answer is a qualified 'yes'. A trailer sailer is safe in competent hands – if the skipper knows the limitations of the yacht, of the crew, and can handle the boat within these limitations. If no one else in the crew is capable of taking the helm and reefing the mainsail, then the skipper will sooner or later be in an awkward situation. Whitsunday weather can be blustery, seas can be short and steep, and currents can be strong. These test a trailer sailer just that much more than a fixed-keel yacht. Trailer sailers are overpowered more easily and demand more expertise from the crew when the going gets stiff.

Launching

Launching ramps are located at: Abell Point (just west of the marina); at the Whitsunday Sailing Club, Airlie Beach; at Shute Harbour (a ramp and pontoon next to the public jetty); next to the Whitsunday Air Sea Rescue, Shingley Drive. Shute Harbour can be busy on weekends and is relatively exposed in south-east weather. The Whitsunday Sailing Club has an excellent ramp and dinghy harbour, but it is a private club. Reciprocal rights are in place with a number of yacht clubs, and visitors are welcomed at the clubhouse, but permission should be obtained from the secretary before using the launching ramp.

There is a lock-up garage next to the service station at Shute Harbour, and trailer parking is available at Shute Harbour (along the road between the service station and the harbour). Trailers may also be parked next to the sailing club at Airlie Beach and in the public parking area at Abell Point.

Be sure to wear sand shoes when launching, as the ramps are located in areas where giant toadfish have been known to attack the feet of fishermen wading in the water.

Trailer sailer gear

Trailer sailers can get up to some of their usual anchoring tricks in the Whitsundays (i.e. stern-to and close in on a sandy beach), but if you wish to explore an island where you must anchor offshore, your ground tackle and anchoring technique will need to be different. The importance of having anchor line of sufficient circumference to be easy on the hands cannot be stressed too much. If you've been trailer sailing on the Gippsland or Myall Lakes and are using clothesline for anchor cable, get rid of it before you go to the Whitsundays.

Trailer sailers should carry a 15 or 20 pound CQR anchor, must have at least 10 metres of 6 millimetre or 8 millimetre chain (depending upon the yacht) and 40 metres of rope cable of a good-sized diameter (breaking strain has nothing to do with it; line should be sufficiently thick to be comfortable to pull on). CQR anchors are preferred to Danforths (see notes on anchoring earlier in this chapter). A small reef anchor is a useful addition.

Check that your reefing system is working, and have a No. 3 or storm jib aboard. Other useful items of equipment are a boom tent (for protection from sun, dew and rain); containers for transporting water to the yacht; a portable transistor radio for receiving weather reports; a VHF radio.

It is necessary to carry certain items of safety equipment – the usual gear, including a proper liquid-damped compass, flares, oars, life jackets, buckets with lanyards, bilge pump, waterproof torch, etc. A complete list is contained in *The Official Tide Tables & Boating Safety Guide*, which itself is essential and which contains a wealth of other useful information about weather, fishing, navigation, buoyage, etc. You will need a copy of the appropriate charts (see page 69).

An outboard motor in good working order is an absolute necessity in the Whitsundays. Take a spare 20-litre fuel container if you can. Outboard fuel is available in reasonable proximity to the water at Abel Point Marina, the service station at Shute Harbour, at Mandalay Point jetty and at Hamilton Harbour.

A dinghy is also a necessity. The island fringing reefs are extensive and anchorage is sometimes a long way from shore; a small outboard motor for the dinghy may be a desirable 'luxury' as well.

On the water

The best time in the Whitsundays for trailer sailers is after the trade winds season, generally from September onwards, when the winds are usually lighter.

Pay particular attention to the little wavy lines and curlicues on the chart, which indicate that disturbed water or eddies occur in some conditions. Remember that the tide floods south and ebbs north through the Passage and that it gets rough when fresh winds oppose spring tides. Plan your trip accordingly. Avoid Long Island Sound – the narrow strait between Long Island and the mainland – which can be dangerous for trailer sailers in all sorts of conditions – wind against tide, wind with tide, fresh winds. Be sure not to attempt Fitzalan Passage (sketch maps C20 and C22) and Solway Passage (sketch map C26) in fresh winds with contrary tides.

The most popular trailer sailer anchorages are Cid Harbour (sketch map C19), which has a large all-tide sand beach and national park campsites; water is available here for much of the year. Nara and Macona inlets have a number of good little beaches, the best trailer sailer spot being

David Colfelt

anchorage No. 5 (sketch map C10b). Water is available during much of the year from a waterfall at the head of Nara Inlet. Hill Inlet (sketch map C27) was made for trailer sailers (take plenty of insect repellent). Camping is permitted on some islands provided you have a permit. Airlie Beach and Shute Harbour have public facilities for emptying the toilet.

Bareboat chartering in the Whitsundays

Crewed yacht charter began in the Whitsundays in the early 1970s when a Sydney couple, Yvonne and Bernie Katchor, sailed into Shute Harbour, fell in love with the Whitsundays and stayed. They used to take day-trippers around the islands in their auxiliary ketch *Nari*, and in those days *Nari* used to be the only way that visitors could savour a tantalising bit of these islands in a way that took full advantage of the remoteness and beauty of the setting.

It wasn't until about 1978 that the first drive-it-yourself yachts were licensed by the Queensland Department of Harbours and Marine, years after 'bareboat' was part of the international yachting vocabulary and only after a certain amount of official red tape had been unwound by two enterprising Sydneysiders, David Bradley and John Landau. They succeeded in overcoming a bureaucratic scepticism about the ability of unlicensed sailors to survive the rigours of the Queensland coast, and they were able to negotiate a compromise on the exacting survey regulations that were written for commercial passenger and fishing vessels. In 1978 they opened for business as Whitsunday Yachting World, a company that is no longer operating but which set a new a standard for the charter industry in Australia. From that time on the bareboat industry really began to grow, and more and more sailors from the south were able to live out fantasies of tropical sailing that were previously only to be hankered after. The size of the bareboat fleet grew and charter companies have proliferated.

Bareboating is the ideal way to get the most out of the Whitsundays. It offers virtually complete freedom to go anywhere you want, at your own pace. Bareboating means you are the skipper, your friends the crew. In spite of the name, most bareboats these days are rather luxuriously appointed. Those over ten metres in length will usually be equipped with freezer and fridge, stereo radio, elaborate galley, hot and cold running water, shower, roller-furling headsail, electric anchor windlass, and so on. In order to become licensed the boats have to be solidly constructed, with safety features that most sailors wouldn't put on their own yachts. Charter yachts are available ranging in size from about seven metres up to about fifteen metres, with four berths up to ten berths. For comfort, as a rule of thumb subtract two from the number of berths available, and limit your crew to that number. There are monohull sailing vessels, catamarans (both sail and motorised) and power yachts.

How to go about it

Bookings may be made either directly with the charter company or through travel agents. At the time of booking, a deposit must be lodged, and the balance of the charter fee is payable 30–60 days before the charter commences. A security bond on the vessel and equipment must also be paid before heading off on the holiday; this acts as collateral against any damage or loss during the charter, and it represents the limit of the charterer's liability for the yacht (except in cases of wilful negligence). The bond is refunded immediately after (or within a short time of) completing the charter, less any deductibles (lost winch handles, etc.). Some companies offer insurance on a daily basis which further reduces any liability for damage sustained to the yacht or equipment.

Cancellations received more than 60 days before the charter attract only an administration fee; notice given in less than 60 days renders the charterer liable for the full fee unless an alternative charterer is found by the company (one frequently is). Cancellation insurance is available, although there are some limitations on what constitutes a legitimate excuse for cancelling.

David Cofelt

Above:
Afternoon shower in Shute Harbour
Right:
The Whitsunday Fun Race is an annual
event and features the
'Miss Figurehead' contest which is
always keenly contested

Bob Porter

How much experience is needed?

Charterers don't need any formal qualifications or licence, but someone in the crew should have a few clues about handling a boat and how to set an anchor properly. Anchoring is the most demanding task undertaken, and prospective charterers should be familiar with good technique (described earlier). Navigation is quite simple among the islands because land is always in sight, so one really only needs to be able to interpret a nautical chart. If there isn't someone in the crew who is capable of both of the above, then someone needs to take a course to bring them up to scratch. You will be in charge of a very expensive piece of equipment (perhaps in excess of $500,000), and that fact in itself should make it obvious that a certain degree of proficiency is necessary.

Charterers are given a briefing and check-out aboard the yacht before being permitted to sail away. If the charter company is uncertain about your ability to handle the yacht, you may be required to take an experienced sailing guide along for a couple of days until you are ready to go it alone. Or, you may prefer to have someone with you for the duration. You will pay extra for the sailing guide.

A charter in the Whitsundays is not the ideal time and place for beginners to cut their baby teeth or to learn for the first time how to drop an anchor, but anyone with some experience and a crew capable of helping them should not be frightened off by tall tales. History has shown that it is often the most experienced sailors who come unstuck; perhaps less confident skippers are more vigilant.

How long to charter?

Charters are measured in 'nights' and begin at midday on day one. Most of the first afternoon is spent being briefed and checked out on the boat, and thus charterers need to anchor nearby on the first night because there won't be time to sail very far. A sketch map showing anchorages nearby to the charter centres is found on pages 154–155. Most companies insist that charterers be anchored by 1600 hours due to the difficulty of seeing coral when the sun is low. Charters end, depending upon the company, from 0900 to 1100 hours on the last day, so one needs to anchor nearby on the last night. That leaves five nights of real freedom of choice of anchorages (on a one-week charter). Unless you are a roadrunner, it's much better to allow at least ten days to experience a number of different anchorages at leisure. Seven days just isn't enough; you may be just getting into the pleasant rhythm of life aboard a yacht in the Whitsundays when it's time to come home.

One imponderable as to how long is long enough is the compatibility of the crew. This wild card can make a few days seem like a lifetime, or time may fly. Living at very close quarters as one does aboard a yacht, hidden dimensions even in old mates may be uncovered. The charter boat log books tell all manner of tales, mostly of laughter, love and good times. There are a few tales of mutiny and abandonment, crew being put ashore on a deserted isle with a message sent to the charter base to have the water taxi go pick up the marooned member who will have to pay for the taxi – himself. It goes without saying that one should choose companions carefully.

What costs are involved?

Costs of a bareboat holiday include the hire of the vessel and food and may also include fuel used while motoring, plus perhaps a few extras such as mooring fees when visiting an island resort and a nominal Marine Parks user fee. The size of the vessel and how new it is are the principal factors governing rental charges. Rates are higher during holiday seasons. Shared amongst a group, the costs of a bareboat holiday are not inordinately high.

Provisioning the yacht with food can be done for you, and most companies offer several different standards, from survival rations to gourmet

David Collett

dining. This saves you the bother of planning meals and is a decided plus for whoever has the job of chief-of-galley. The most frequently selected regime, for a seven-night charter, caters for seven breakfasts and lunches and five dinners, the assumption being that the other two dinners will be eaten at an island resort (this is referred to as 'partial provisioning'). You can opt to have your own list of food put aboard by the charter company, for which a handling fee is charged. The same applies for liquor. If you're on a tight budget and don't mind the inconvenience, you can provision the yacht yourself.

All companies charge for fuel used by power vessels; some charge fuel used on sailboats, others don't. Mooring and marina fees vary from resort to resort, but having paid the fee, you usually have complete freedom to use all resort facilities; shared amongst all those on the yacht, it is a small expense.

The charter area

There are well over one hundred rocky islands, islets, rocks and shoals in the Cumberland Islands which are spread out over one degree of latitude (20° to 21° south). The charter area varies from company to company but generally extends from George Point (sketch map N9) to Hayman Island (C13) to Thomas Island (S6). (Some companies permit yachts to travel as far north as Bowen and as far south as Mackay.) Not many first-time charterers find time to get all the way to either the western mainland anchorages or the southern anchorages. Some restrictions apply when strong wind warnings are current, some companies insisting that in these circumstance, yachts should be in an anchorage between Hayman and Hamilton islands and on the western side of Whitsunday Island.

There are more than enough good anchorages within a twenty-mile radius of Shute Harbour to make it unnecessary to travel further. Seven of the islands in this area have resorts, and most will accommodate visiting sailors provided that certain procedures are followed (specific information about visiting resorts by sea is found in the sailing directions later in this book). Many charterers at some time during their charter go ashore at a resort, providing that unique sensation in cruising of 'making port', to have a shower and a meal and enjoy the entertainment.

When is the best time to come?

For most people, the time of their holidays is the determining factor, but if you have some flexibility, here are a few considerations. The weather is pleasant almost any time in the Whitsundays, with temperatures not often above 30°C in summer nor below 20°C in winter. You can swim year-round. The trade winds are re-established after the summer monsoon in April–May, providing brisk sailing for the most part throughout the winter; the weather is generally more settled after June, and the winds get progressively lighter after mid-September. Charter rates are lower in non-holiday seasons. When the trade winds have abated (late September to mid October), balmy conditions make it possible to get into some south-exposed anchorages that cannot be used overnight during the trade winds season. Christmas holiday season is always a very busy time.

Crewed charter

A number of companies offer crewed charters; you charter the yacht and the company supplies a skipper and mate who do all the worrying and work for you. There are also a number of luxurious charter vessels ranging in size from about fourteen to twenty-one metres, with full-time crew, completely equipped with everything that might be wished for.

David Coffelt

Snorkellers at Fantasea Reefworld meet some of the local inhabitants.

David Colfelt

VISITING THE OUTER REEFS

The individual coral reefs of the Great Barrier system lie on Australia's eastern continental shelf, generally towards its outer margin. Along the northern Queensland coastline the shelf is narrower than it is in the south, and the reefs are closer to the mainland. In the Whitsunday region (south-central Queensland) the continental shelf is about 75 nautical miles wide (measured from the mainland out to the 200-metre depth contour in a north-easterly direction). The first reef to be reached from the mainland is Bait Reef, about 34 nautical miles away. It is one of a group of reefs associated by name; their particular shapes and proximity to each other suggested, to early chart-makers, the angler's basic equipment – hook, line, sinker and bait. Immediately east is a large lagoonal platform reef, Hardy Reef, separated from the rest by a very long, deep channel through which tidal currents flow swiftly. About nine miles to the north lies Knuckle Reef. These reefs are the focal point of Reef daytrip activity in this part of the Barrier Reef Marine Park.

Bareboats are not permitted to venture as far out as the Barrier Reef, but high-speed, motorised catamarans capable of carrying several hundred passengers depart from the mainland most days of the week. The trip is about two and a half to three hours each way, and guests have 3–4 hours out there to snorkel or dive or just enjoy the amazing feeling of being anchored in smooth, crystal-clear water 'in the middle of the ocean'. Interpretive videos of the Reef are shown on the way out, the bar is open, tips on snorkelling are given by the crew and arrangements can be made to take a guided snorkel tour conducted by a marine biologist, a good way to enhance one's appreciation of reef life.

Pontoons moored out at the reefs provide platforms from which snorkellers and scuba divers enjoy themselves in the water right next to the Reef, with its incredible abundance of sea life. For those who don't want to get into the water, specially designed craft are available, some with glassed-in compartments below the level of the water (semi-submersed 'submarines'), which allow lateral views along the edges and underneath ledges of the reef, and glass-bottom boats, which give a bird's-eye view of the reef below. Some pontoons have an underwater viewing chamber from which spectators can watch the fish, plus snorkellers and scuba divers exploring the local geography. A freshwater shower followed by a smorgasbord lunch and perhaps a lie in the sun afterwards – all out in the middle of the ocean – caps off an unforgettable experience.

Fantasea Adventure Cruising

Shimpei Ito

David Colfelt

Top:
Reefworld pontoon moored in the
channel between Hook and Hardy reefs
Middle
Fantasy 'Reef Sleep' diners get a close-
up look at a resident giant Maori wrasse
Above:
Warming up on the sun deck
after snorkelling

Fantasy Adventure Cruising's operations at the Reefworld pontoon offer the unique 'Reef Sleep' experience, which includes overnight accommodation, alfresco dinner including wine, full breakfast, buffet lunches, sunset drinks, one scuba dive or guided snorkelling safari, and use of Reefworld facilities including the underwater viewing chamber, semi-submersible, waterslide as well as optional extras such as heli-scenics and massage.

The lagoon at Hardy Reef serves as the landing strip for amphibious aircraft, which bring sightseers out from the mainland and island resorts, sometimes picking up passengers from island anchorages.

Cruise Whitsundays operates an outer Reef cruise to Knuckle Reef departing from Abel Point Marina, calling in at Hayman Island if required.

Bait Reef, about eight nautical miles west of Hardy Reef, is a beautiful, pristine, kidney-shaped reef that is one of the favoured sites for scuba diving in this area, particularly its 'Stepping Stones', a series of large coral bommies on its western side. A number of vessels take divers to this reef, on day trips and overnight cruises.

Another way of getting out to the Reef is with the area's air taxi service whose mainland operations are based at Whitsunday Airstrip and Hamilton Island. This is a most exciting means of travel, offering, as a bonus, magnificent aerial views of the islands and reefs (and, in late winter, frequent sightings of whales). Pick-ups can also be arranged for bareboat charterers from some locations, such as at resorts or at certain anchorages. The flight to the Reef takes about twenty-five minutes, and visitors then spend two hours exploring Hardy Reef in glass-bottom boats, sub, or snorkelling.

A number of vessels do Reef trips for special interest groups, such as divers or those who are on an extended cruise throughout the islands.

What to take with you
Remember to take plenty of sunscreen, wear a broad-brimmed hat, and a lightweight cotton long-sleeved shirt is also a bonus on hot afternoons. Take along a windcheater for the trip out and back.

Cruise Whitsundays

Cruise Whitsundays

David Colfelt

Top left:
Cruise Whitsundays catamaran and pontoon at Knuckle Reef

Middle left:
Snorkellers at Hardy Reef

Bottom left:
Fantasea Adventure Cruising's Incat Crowther 24-metre, fully air-conditioned catamaran can carry 170 passengers to Hardy Reef.

Above:
Mutual admiration, Knuckle Reef.

Below:
Underwater viewing chamber, Reefworld

Fantasea Adventure Cruising

David Colfelt

Above:
Some fishes of the coral reef (top to bottom):
surf parrotfish (*Saurus rivulatus*),
blue tuskfish (*Choerodon albigena*),
coral trout (*Plectropomus leopardus*)

Opposite:
A prized eating fish, the coral trout brings joy to the angler's face.

David Collelt

FISHING IN THE WHITSUNDAYS

Fishing in the Whitsundays can mean drifting along island reefs waiting to hook a coral trout or sweetlip; or it may mean trolling the deeper waters of the Molle Channel for big mackerel, queenfish and trevally, or rod fishing from rocks along the mainland shore. The many estuaries and mangrove inlets of the Whitsunday coast are virtual fish nurseries.

Tips for coral fishing
If it's your first experience of coral fishing, there are a few tips that will be helpful. It's always desirable to fish as 'light' as possible, using minimum weight and hardware. Having said that, coral fishing requires a line of *at least* 25 kilograms breaking strain, not so much because of the monstrous fish waiting to pull you from the dinghy but because coral is hell on fishing gear. Take plenty of spares. Thin line will be chewed to pieces by coral in no time, and coral-dwelling fish tend to take the bait and run for cover under the nearest bommie. This line attached to a fleeting fish can be quickly severed and it can also cut your fingers (many anglers tape their finger joints). Keep enough tension on the line to register bites and to avoid snagging. The weight of sinker can be adjusted to suit the current.

Fish over the edge of the reef one hour before or after high tide for best results (neap tides are better); early morning and evening are better than when the sun is high. Night-time on a rising tide can be excellent.

Trolling along the edge of a reef may also produce dividends; the Nils Master lure is effective for coral trout (and may also yield cod or mangrove jack in estuaries).

Cutting the fish's throat immediately and bleeding it will usually improve the eating quality.

Baits readily available in the Whitsundays are prawns, squid, a small fish known locally as 'herring', and garfish. If you have a throw net, small fresh fish from the shallows make excellent bait.

Gear
Whether to use a rod or handline is your own choice; rods may have advantages when fishing from rocks, and hand lines may be easier to manage on a yacht, and a handline with a large-diameter casting reel will facilitate line management. The basic recommended configurations of hooks and sinkers are shown on the following page.

Identifying your fish

The best way to identify fish caught in the Whitsundays is to ask a local. Otherwise, have a look at a book called *Fishes of the Great Barrier Reef and Coral Sea* by J. Randall, G. Allen and R. Steene, or the *Guide to Fishes* by E.M. Grant.

Miscellaneous general prohibitions

- Jagging or foul-hooking fish
- Use of explosives, poisons or electrical devices to take fish
- Possession or carriage of prohibited apparatus in closed water unless the apparatus is dismantled, secured or stowed
- Collection of coral without lawful authority
- Selling fish without a licence or permit

Important note

Before dropping a line in Whitsunday waters, anglers should be aware of marine park zones and the limits on fishing in some of these (see zoning maps on pages 110–113).

Moreover, the information in this chapter is subject to change from time to time (e.g. changes in fish sizes and bag limits), and the onus is on the angler to be aware of current regulations to avoid violating the law.

Check for latest information with the Department of Primary Industries and Fisheries (DPI&F):

freecall in Queensland 13 25 23

out of State (07) 3404 6999

or visit the department's web site

http://www.dpi.qld.gov.au/fishweb/

Qld Boating and Fisheries Patrol Whitsunday office: (07) 4946 7003

Fishing gear for the Whitsundays

For sand and mud

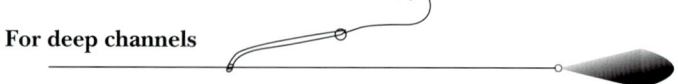

Line, running ball sinker (threaded but not attached), swivel, wire trace and hook. Good over sand and mud, where some movement helps to attract fish such as flathead. Bean-shaped sinkers are sometimes preferred when line must be kept in place.

For reef fishing

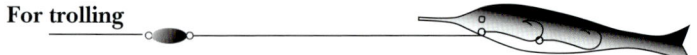

Recommended by pros for working reef areas. A line threaded through a ball sinker and attached to the hook runs freely and maximises sensitivity to bites, minimises snagging, and does not deter timid fish that might baulk at the sinker's dead weight.

For deep channels

The snapper rig is useful for deep channels where currents may be swift. Pass a loop through the eye of the hook and back over the shank (or use a three-way swivel). Attach a heavy sinker (perhaps as much as 225 grams).

For trolling

The 'floater' is for trolling and is simply a gang of hooks at the end of a long wire trace which in turn is attached to the line with a swivel. The hooks are embedded in a garfish (or other bait) and made to look as natural as possible. A single live fish may also be used, hooked through the back above the spine. Size, number of hooks and bait depend upon the quarry sought. Use shock cord or rubber tube as a shock absorber where the line is fixed to the boat.

Where to fish and not to fish

Fishing is permitted in most areas of the Whitsundays, but some areas are totally protected (e.g. green zones – see pages 108–111), and there are some other restrictions (see notes in the left margin of page 114.) When fishing, always wear footwear, especially around the mainland harbours and estuaries, where giant toadfish have been known to nibble toes (see 'Avoiding Tropical Hazards' for lurid details). Fishing of any kind is prohibited with 100-metre radius of the Hook Island observatory. When navigating a vessel in no-fishing zones, all fishing gear must be stowed or secured (meaning it is inboard and completely out of the water).

Spearfishing

Limited spearfishing – which means fishing with a spear gun without a powerhead, a firearm, a light or underwater breathing apparatus other than a snorkel – is allowed only in these zones: General Use (light blue), Habit Protection (dark blue), and Conservation Park (yellow). However, spearfishing is prohibited in yellow zones that lie within the Public Appreciation Area (see dotted pink line on the map on page 111).

Spearfishing is also prohibited in the following areas:

- Brampton and Carlisle Islands: waters between the islands.
- Seaforth Island.
- Lindeman Island: the western and southern sides.
- Long Island: the western side.
- South Molle Island: the northern side.
- West Molle Island (Daydream Island): surrounding waters.
- Hook Island: the eastern, south-eastern and southern sides.
- Hayman Island: the southern and western sides.

Spearfishing with scuba gear is prohibited throughout Queensland (see also Fishing Activities on pages 114–115). The use of underwater breathing apparatus other than a snorkel is not permitted when taking any fish, whether by spear, spear gun, hand or any other means.

Closed seasons

Closed seasons exist for several species; check with the Department of Primary Industries and Fisheries (see contact details at left).

No-take fish; size and bag limits

The taking of some species is totally prohibited; others are subject to size and bag limits (see the chart on pages 92–93 which summarises information on some reef and pelagic species commonly seen in the Whitsundays). For more assistance with fish identification, visit

http://www.dpi.qld.gov.au/cps/rde/dpi/hs.xsl/28_2981_ENA_HTML.htm.

Fish are under general heavy pressure from commercial and recreational fishing; take only what you need for the next meal, and observe the size limits.

Oysters

Oysters may be taken only for immediate consumption *on the spot* in most of the Whitsundays, except in the totally protected Marine National Park Zone where they may not be taken at all. Under Queensland fisheries legislation you **may not collect oysters in a container to eat later.**

Fish poisoning

There are a few fishes in Queensland which are known to cause tropical fish poisoning (ciguatera) and which should not be eaten: Chinaman fish (juvenile and adult); paddle tail; red bass (it is illegal to take any of these, but why would you want to?); barracuda; moray eel. It's a good idea to check with locals to see that others have not temporarily been added to the 'don't eat' list, as the toxin is sometimes a transitory phenomenon. Generally, larger fishes are more likely to be ciguatoxic; avoid eating any fish larger than four-kilograms and don't eat repeated meals from the same fish. There are illustrations of the main ciguatoxic species and more details about ciguatera in 'Avoiding Tropical Hazards'. Puffer fishes are inherently poisonous and should never be eaten.

Game fishing

The Whitsundays are renowned for billfish and the area holds a number of world light tackle records. The outer islands from the Edward Group to 'The Paddock' north of Hayman is generally best for pelagic fishing, and excellent catches of mackerel and tuna may be had during the season when these fishes are running. The outer islands and near offshore reefs yield black marlin, sailfish, turum, barracuda, Spanish mackerel, cobia, yellowfin and bluefin tuna, kawa kawa and various species of shark. Game-fishing charters are available ex Hamilton Island, Abel Point Marina, Shute Harbour, and Hayman Island (for guests only).

Crab measurement and identification

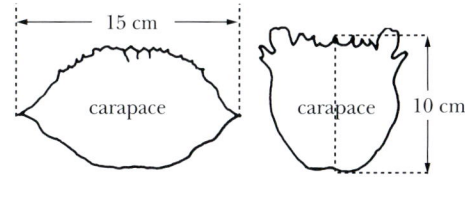

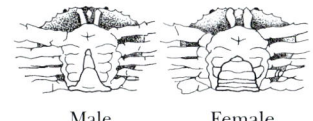

Male   Female

Fish measurement

TOTAL LENGTH

Fishing Tips
- Study zoning maps for the area you are visiting to ensure fishing is allowed
- Take only what you need and abide by possession and size limits
- Return all undersized or unwanted fish to the water carefully and quickly
- If intending to keep a fish, remove it from the hook or net quickly and kill it humanely
- Never feed bread, cooked seafood or processed food to fish
- Take all rubbish home including line, tackle and bait bags.

Some common Whitsunday reef fin fish species with size and/or bag limits

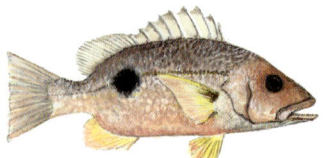

Fingermark
Lutjanus johnii
35 cm/5 fish

Hussar
Lutjanus adetii
25 cm/10 fish

Large mouth nannygai
Lutjanus malabaricus
40 cm/9 in species

Small mouth nannygai
Lutjanus erythropterus
40 cm/9 in species

Moses perch
Lutjanus russeli
25 cm/5 in species

Red emperor
Lutjanus sebae
55 cm/5 fish

Mangrove jack
Lutjanus argentimaculatus
35 cm/5 fish

Stripey
Lutjanus carponotatus
25 cm/5 fish

Estuary cod
Epinephelus tauvina (= coioides)
38–100 cm/5 combined limit all cods & groupers

Grass sweetlip
Lethrinus laticaudis
30 cm/10 fish

Red throat emperor
Lethrinus miniatus
38 cm/8 fish

Long-nosed sweetlip
Lethrinus olivaceus
38 cm/5 fish

Coral trout
Plectropomus species
38 cm/combined 7 all trout species

Snapper
Pagrus auratus
35 cm/5 fish

Spangled emperor
Lethrinus nebulosus
45 cm/5 fish

Venus tusk fish
Choerodon venustus
30 cm/combined 6 all tuskfish

Purple tusk fish
Choerodon cephalotes
30 cm/combined 6 all tuskfish

Black spot tusk fish
Choerodon schoenleinii
30 cm/combined 6 all tuskfish

Surf parrotfish
Saurus rivulatus
All parrotfishes 25 cm/5 per species

Rosy job fish
Pristipomoides species
38 cm/8 fish

Pearl perch
Glaucosoma scapulare
35 cm/5 fish

Information current as at March 2009. Size and bag limits are subject to change, and anglers should seek the latest information from the Qld. Dept. of Primary Industries (free call 13 25 23; web site: www.dpi.qld.gov.au/fishweb) or Queensland Boating and Fisheries Patrol, Combined Marine Operations Base, Shingley Drive, Airlie Beach (07 4946 7003)

Some Whitsunday reef fin and pelagic fish species with size and/or bag limits

Spotted (black) jew
Protonibea diacanthus
75 cm/2 fish

Teraglin jew
Atractoscion aequidens
38 cm/5 fish

Mulloway
Argyrosomus hololepidotus
75 cm/2 fish

School mackerel
Scomberomorus queenslandicus
50 cm/10 fish

Broad barred (grey) mackerel
Scomberomorus semifasciatus
60 cm/5 fish

Sharkey mackerel
Grammatorcynus bicarinatus
50 cm/ 10 fish

Spanish mackerel
Scomberomorus commerson
75 cm/3 fish

Wahoo
Acanthocybium solandri
75 cm/2 fish

Spotted mackerel
Scomberomorus munroi
60 cm/5 fish

Yellowtail kingfish
Seriola lalandi
60 cm/2 fish

Black kingfish
Rachycentron canadus
75 cm/2 fish

Dolphin fish (Mahi Mahi)
Coryphaena hippurus
60 cm/5 fish

Coral reef fin fish

Coral reef fin fish species incorporate all coral trout, emperors, cods and groupers, parrot fishes, surgeon fishes and sweetlips, tropical snappers, sea perches, fusiliers, banana fishes and wrasses.

In addition to individual take and possession limits for each species above, all coral reef fin fish species have a combined take and possession limit of 20.

Example

45 cm–120 cm/10 fish
The smallest size of this species that may be kept is 45 centimetres; fish over 120 centimetres may not be kept. The maximum number in one's possession at any one time is 10. If no figure given, no limit.

No Take
Potato cod
Epinephelus tukula

No Take
Queensland grouper
Epinephelus lanceolatus

No Take
Maori wrasse
Chelinus undulatus

No Take
Red Bass
(Lutjanus bohar)
(poisonous)

No Take
Paddletail
(Lutjanus gibbus)
(poisonous)

No Take
Juvenile Chinaman fish
(Symphorus nematophorus)
(poisonous)

No Take
Adult Chinaman fish
(Symphorus nematophorus)
(poisonous)

David Colfelt

Above:
Camping on an island in the Whitsundays can provide what some regard as the 'ultimate' camping experience.
Opposite:
A million miles from care

David Coffelt

ISLAND CAMPING AND KAYAKING IN THE WHITSUNDAYS

Almost all of the Whitsunday Islands are national parks, and they provide a chance to indulge in what many believe to be the ultimate camping experience, sleeping out under the stars on a 'south sea isle'. The Queensland Parks and Wildlife Service (QPWS) permits eco-friendly use of its campsites by both independent and commercial campers. The national park campsites are used by people seeking a range of different adventures, including camping in small groups, sea kayaking tours, large sailing vessel safaris or individuals looking for a remote wilderness experience. The number of people and the size and number of tent sites vary with each location and the time of year.

There are a couple of options for camping on the islands. You can join a camping or kayaking tour organised by a commercial operator, or you can book your own site and make your own arrangements for getting there, either in your own boat or with a ferry service for campers and kayakers. It is possible to hire all the necessary gear from camping and kayaking operators, and a delivery service can take care of your water requirements if, for example, you cannot carry enough in a kayak for the duration of your adventure.

Permits

Once you have selected a suitable campsite and arranged transport, a camping permit can be purchased several ways: (1) by visiting the Queensland Government's internet website (www.qld.gov.au/camping); (2) by ringing the QPWS camping permits information line on 13 74 68; (3) call in at the QPWS headquarters (during normal office hours), corner Mandalay and Shute Harbour roads, Airlie Beach (about three kilometres out of Airlie Beach towards Shute Harbour). Once you have booked and paid for your permit, you will be given a booking number and issued a camping tent tag.

Getting to an island site

Ferry services that specialise in camper and kayaker drop-offs are the easiest option. They are used to dealing with the needs of campers and kayakers, and they usually have all the necessary equipment available for hire. There are a couple of experienced camping and kayaking companies operating from Shute Harbour. A specialised boat, such as a mini-barge with a drop-down bow platform, makes unloading at an island beach much easier. If your interest is in kayaking rather than just camping, one company specialises in supplying all the needs of both individual kayakers, or it can organise guided kayaking tours. Not all island sites can be reached at all tides (some access information is given in the following list of campsites), and this is an important consideration in planning your adventure.

Some of the information in this chapter is based on materials supplied by courtesy of the Queensland Parks and Wildlife Service, Whitsunday District Office.

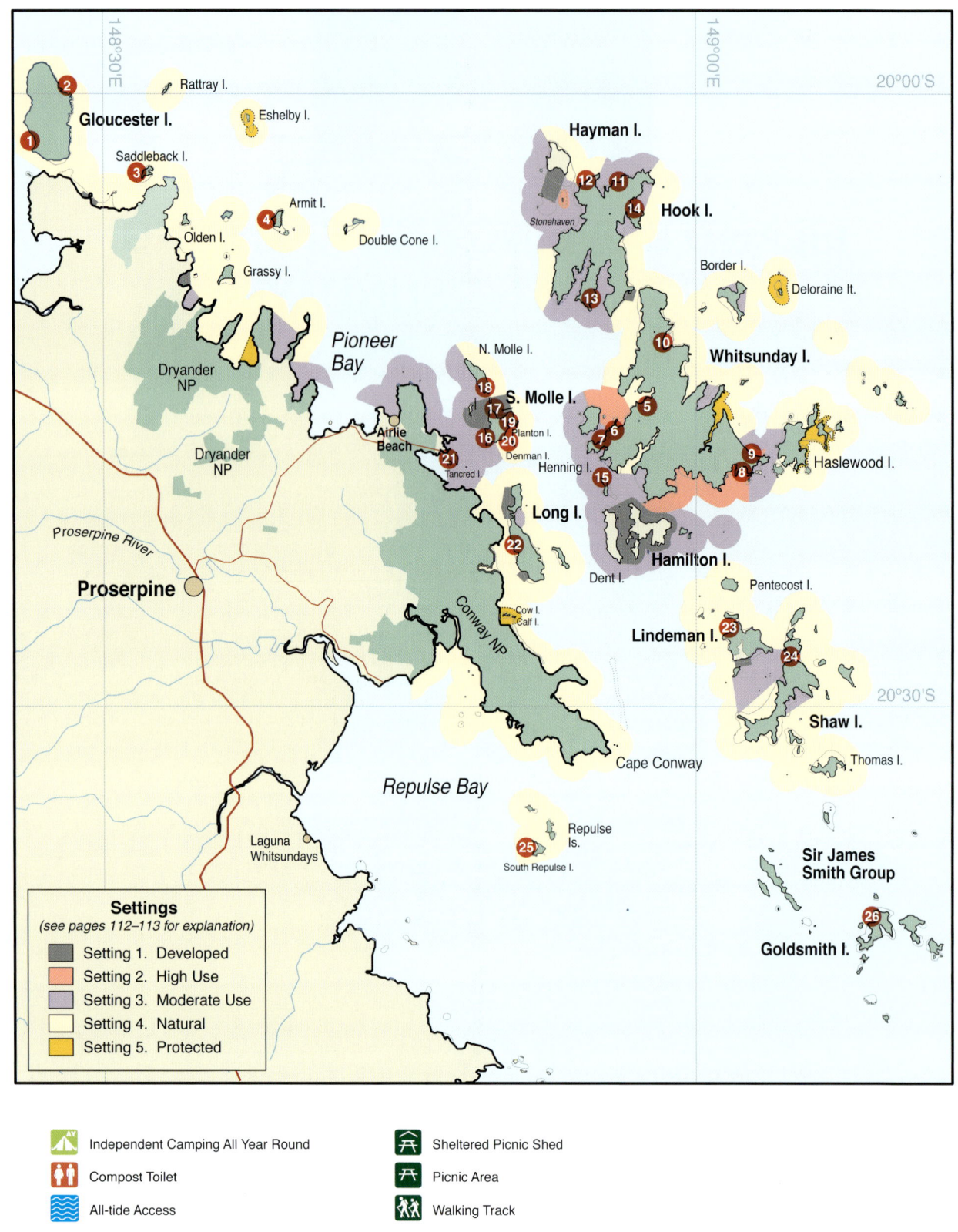

Setting 1. Developed
Setting 2. High Use
Setting 3. Moderate Use
Setting 4. Natural
Setting 5. Protected

Settings
(see pages 112–113 for explanation)

Independent Camping All Year Round

Compost Toilet

All-tide Access

Sheltered Picnic Shed

Picnic Area

Walking Track

A camping tag is issued when a permit is purchased. Your booking number
is to be written on the front of the tag and the tag attached to your tent.

Island Campsites

Gloucester Island

1. Bona Bay 36 people

Access: Sheltered from SE winds but exposed to northerlies (rough in north winds). Reached by boat from Dingo Beach or Bowen.

Pleasant outook and a good sandy beach and anchorage.

2. East Side Bay 6 people

Access: By boat. Exposed to all winds and can be rough.

East Side Bay is set between two rocky headlands. The east-facing beach is steep, and the anchorage is unreliable. The campsite is set in the vegetation behind the beach adjacent to a seasonal freshwater lagoon.

Saddleback Island

3. 12 people

Access: By boat at mid to high tide. Sheltered from SE winds but exposed to northerlies.

Can be reached by boat from either Earlando or Dingo Beach. This small site offers a wilderness camping experience on the island's western side. The anchorage is reasonable for small boats; be aware of the current. Watch out for death adders.

Armit Island

4. 12 people

Access: Sheltered from SE winds but exposed to northerlies.

This camping site is situated on the south-western side of an attractive island among casuarina trees; suitable for small groups. The beach is sandy and the boat anchorage is good. A seasonal bird closure (October–April) is in effect around the southern beach (see sketch map N10b).

Whitsunday Island

5. Dugong Beach 36 people

    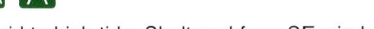

Access: By boat at mid to high tide. Sheltered from SE winds.

This is a suitable campsite for larger groups, with a good sandy beach backed by rainforest. A 1 km walking track connects this beach with Sawmill Beach. Access to track to Whitsunday Peak.

6. Nari's Beach 6 people

Access: Boat only at mid to high tide (reef flat). Sheltered from SE winds.

This site has excellent views of Cid Island. The campsite is set under the rainforest canopy, tucked against a steep hill. A reef line is close to shore with good access at mid-tide and plenty of anchorage.

7. Joe's Beach 12 people

Access: Mid to high tide only (reef flat). Sheltered from SE winds.

Joe's Beach provides a secluded campsite and beach area with excellent views of Cid Island and the Molle islands. The fringing reef provides good snorkelling, and is exposed during low tide.

8. Chance Bay 12 people

Access: By boat at mid to high tide. Good anchorage in northerly winds; access can be difficult in S-SE winds.

Elevated campsite with great views across the sandy beach to the islands to the south. Walking track to Whitehaven Beach.

9. South Whitehaven Beach 36 people

Access: Rough in northerlies, partially sheltered from SE winds.

The dazzling white, pure silica sands of Whitehaven Beach are one of the best known sites within the Whitsundays. This spectacular beach is backed by lowland vine forest and eucalyptus woodland which provides good shade. Walking track to Solway Circuit and Chance Bay.

10. Peter Bay 12 people

Access: Mid to high tide only (sand bars, fringing reef and sand flat). Sheltered from all but easterlies.

This site has outstanding physical beauty with excellent views across the bay to Border and Dumbell islands. A large intertidal sand and rock flat is fed by a winding creek behind the beach.

Hook Island

11. Maureen's Cove 24 people

Access: All tides except low-low tides. Steep coral beach. Sheltered from SE winds but exposed to northerlies (OK in light winds).

The bays of Hook Island offer some of the most beautiful fringing reefs, providing good diving and snorkelling. Maureen's Cove has a coral rubble beach popular with snorkellers and divers. This is a frequently visited anchorage with public moorings. Anchoring is not permitted in some areas of the bay. As there is no fishing allowed, please ensure that you are familiar with Marine Park Regulations before visiting this site.

12. Steen's Beach 12 people

Access: High tide only. Sheltered from SE but exposed to northerlies.

This campsite is set in the rainforest behind a sandy beach and overlooking Hayman Island. A small reef flat provides good snorkelling.

13. Curlew Beach 12 people

Access: Mid to high tide only (sand bars, fringing reef and sand flat). Sheltered from northerlies and light SE winds.

A sandy beach backed with rainforest. Accessible at mid to high tide by shallow craft only.

14. Crayfish Beach 12 people

Access: Mid to high tide only (reef flat), shallow craft. Sheltered from SE winds, but exposed to northerlies (OK if light).

Beach of great physical beauty with an extensive reef flat area.

Henning Island

15. Northern Spit 18 people

Access: All tides, but can be rough. Exposed to all prevailing winds.

Located on the northern side of the island, this pleasant sandy beach is backed by closed forest canopy. While it is accessible at all tides, it is not a suitable overnight anchorage.

Molle Group (South Molle, North Molle, Planton & Denman islands)

16. Sandy Bay, South Molle Island 36 people

Access: Mid to high tide. Generally well sheltered.

A good campsite for bush walkers, with 15 km of graded walking tracks passing through grasslands, open forests and rainforests to lookouts with spectacular views. Has a pleasant beach fringed with casuarinas and can be readily accessed at mid-high tides. This site also provides good snorkelling.

17. Paddle Bay, South Molle Island 12 people

Access: Mid to high tide only in most winds, for small boats, but is an exposed anchorage.

This rainforest site backs onto a sandy beach and overlooks Daydream Island. South Molle Island is a favourite with bushwalkers with more than 15 km of walking tracks. Access to the track system from Paddle Bay is possible only at low tide.

18. Cockatoo Beach, North Molle Island 24 people

Access: Mid to high tide. Sheltered from northerlies, partially exposed to SE winds.

A number of large campsites around the forest edge are a feature of the camping area at the southern end of North Molle Island. Access is limited by tide. Anchorage off the beach is not recommended as it is exposed to currents and weather. Smaller boats may be left on the beach.

19. Planton Island 6 people

Access: Mid to high tide. Sheltered from SE winds, but exposed to northerlies.

An island that offers a pleasant experience with that 'deserted island' feel. The campsite is set in dry rainforest behind the beach.

20. Denman Island 6 people

Access: Mid to high tide. Sheltered from SE winds, but exposed to northerlies.

A small island offering pleasant bush camping with a remote feel. The campsite is set in dry rainforest behind the beach.

Shute Harbour

21. Tancred Island 6 people

Access: Mid to high tide (fringing reef and mud flat). Generally well sheltered.

While close to mainland facilities, it is still a very private campsite, with Shute Harbour being hidden from view by Repair Island. This island can be easily accessed by small boat, though care should be taken on the fringing reefs at mid to low tide.

Long Island

22. Sandy Bay 12 people

Access: Mid to high tide, shallow-draft vessel.

This site features a small, secluded beach lined with mangroves and backed by rainforest. A walking track from the campsite allows exploration of more of Long island

Lindeman Island

23. Boat Port 12 people

Access: Mid to high tide.

A quiet campsite with sandy beaches backed by rainforest. Lindeman has more than 20 km of walking tracks, some of which afford some spectacular views of the surrounding islands.

Shaw Island

24. Neck Bay 12 people

Access: Mid to high tide. Sheltered from SE winds, but exposed to northerlies.

This small, quiet campsite has a beautiful sandy beach. The reef flat dries a long way out. A short track leads across to the eastern side of the island. A good anchorage frequented by cruising yachts.

South Repulse Island

25. South Repulse Island 12 people

Access: Mid to high tide. Sheltered from SE winds.

A sheltered bay and campsite with views of the Conway Range. The anchorage is good and access to the beach is good during mid to high tide. A seasonal bird closure (October–March) is in place south-west of the camping area (see sketch map S18).

Goldsmith Island

26. Roylen Bay 12 People

Access: Mid to high tide; the fringing reef and mud flat are exposed at low tide.

This is a quiet campsite with a long, sandy beach and seasonal creek. It affords good views to the other islands of the Smith Group.

Carlisle Island (see sketch map S11)

Neils Beach – 12 people

    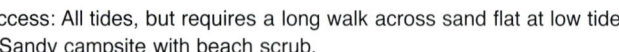

Access: All tides, but requires a long walk across sand flat at low tide.
Sandy campsite with beach scrub.

Rabbit Island (see sketch map S20)

Tugs Point – 12 people

Access: All tides, but there is a mud flat and rocks at low tide.
Grassy campsite with shading trees

Newry Island

Newry Island campground

Access: All tides, but soft mud flat at spring low tide.

The largest camping area in the Newry Group, this island has a walking track through rainforest and open forest offering excellent views of nearby islands and the mainland.

Outer Newry Island (see sketch map S20)

Hut Site – 6 people in single group

Access: All tides, but very soft mud flat at spring low tide.

Hut at site is suitable for camping in. Walking track access to weather side of island. Dirt campsite with little shading

Scawfell Island (see sketch map S16)

Refuge Bay – 12 people

Access: all tides (via channel through coral to beach at low tide).

Campsite is beside the day-use area; also visited by cruising vessels and tourist operators. A grassy site under casuarina forest.

Keswick Island (see sketch map S15)

Singapore Bay – 12 people

Access: mid to high tide. There is a large tidal reef flat with restricted access at low tide.

Camping available in the small margin between high tide and beach dunes.

Victor Bay – 6 people

Access: All tides, but a long walk across sand flat at low tide.

Camping in the small margin between high tide and beach dunes.

Some basic camping considerations

- Campers should be completely self-sufficient regardless of the facilities present at each campsite.
- Fresh water is an essential item. Do not risk running short. The recommended amount is at least 5 litres per person per day.
- Take enough food for your intended stay plus meals for three extra days in case you are stranded in adverse weather.
- No fires are permitted in island national parks or on beaches.
- To reduce the risk of native animals raiding your food, securely store or seal all foods in plastic or similar containers (bags of any description do not afford security!). Do not hang food in plastic bags from tree limbs. Do not leave food unattended.
- A basic first aid kit which includes vinegar to treat marine stingers and insect repellent for protection against sandflies and mosquitoes is essential.
- Sunscreen, a hat and sturdy footwear are very important.

Continued next page

Minimal impact camping

Help protect the camping areas of the Whitsunday Islands by following the Minimal Impact Camping Code:

- The surrounding landscape, plants and animals should be left undisturbed. Remember the islands are national parks.
- Use beach access walkways and camp only at designated campsites.
- Keep to the walking tracks. Do not create new trails by taking shortcuts.
- Do not light fires on island national parks or beaches. Use gas or fuel stoves and lanterns.
- Soaps and detergents harm marine life. Wash away from waterways and the foreshore area and scatter wash water when finished.
- Domestic animals are not permitted on national park islands nor on beaches of islands in the State Marine Park (which includes most of them). Check locally.
- Do not feed native animals. Human food will harm them and feeding can lead to aggression.
- Firearms must not be taken onto national park islands.
- Generators and diving compressors are not permitted in national parks.
- 'Ship it in – ship it out': take all rubbish with you when you leave.
- Fishing is prohibited at campsites located in Marine National Park (green) zones: Whitehaven Beach (No.9), Denman Island (No.20), Armit Island(No.4) and Maureen's Cove (No.11).

- Strong garbage bags are needed for removal of rubbish. Do not bury or leave any rubbish. What you carried in must be carried back to the mainland.
- Where toilet facilities are not provided, a hand trowel is useful for digging toilet holes. Please bury human waste at least 100 metres from a watercourse or campsite and all faecal waste at least 15 cm deep.
- Warm clothes should be taken as winter nights can be cool.
- An insectproof and waterproof tent, sleeping mat and sleeping bag will make your stay more comfortable. Always keep your tent zipped up, whether you are in it or not.
- The camping situation is subject to change; check with QPWS Whitsunday headquarters, cnr. Shute Harbour and Mandalay roads, Airlie Beach, or go to the Queensland Government website to get the latest information about site availability. Also note marine park regulations about fishing, spearfishing, and collecting as these are restricted in some areas.

Kayaking

Kayaking in the Whitsundays is becoming increasingly popular and can provide an exhilarating experience with potentially a variety of encounters with nature including sea turtles and, in season, whales. The Whitsunday area, with its big tides that can generate swift currents and fresh SE trade winds, can be demanding on kayakers, but with a little planning, weather and sea conditions can be taken in one's stride. Many kayakers, for example, going on a guided six-day tour are having their first experience in a sea kayak; all that is required is a reasonable level of physical fitness. If winds are forecast to be in excess of 15–20 knots, then it is a place only for the well-experienced. The guides are good at assessing competence, and the wide-bodied kayaks used are extremely stable, safer and more comfortable than, say, a 4-metre tinny would be in similar conditions. Moreover, starting the paddle one hour before high tide usually ensures at least a couple of hours of reasonable conditions, and trips can be broken up to accommodate challenging weather.

Courtesy Salty Dog Kayaking

Kayakers are given a thorough briefing; depending upon level of competence and previous experience in the area, briefings may last from 30 minutes to two and a half hours. All necessary gear can be supplied; those with their own kayak and gear may need only hire perhaps a camp stove (as these, with their gas bottles, are usually not acceptable to airlines). Participants in guided trips are supplied maps, flares, V-sheets, tide tables, a hand-held VHF for emergency use and a list of emergency contacts. Mobile phone coverage with 3G is good on the western sides of the islands; some coverage is possible on the northern sides. Fishing gear is not supplied; kayakers are usually given the following advice about fishing: "If you've got lots of food, you'll probably catch a fish; if you're relying on fish, you'll probably go hungry"!

A major consideration, again, is tides; not all convenient stopping places can be accessed at any stage of the tide. Your itinerary may have to be juggled accordingly.

A typical kayak itinerary

A popular itinerary for kayakers starts with ferrying the kayaks and gear to Whitehaven (sketch map C26; No.9 on campsite chart page 96) aboard the specialist craft, where kayakers pitch their tents at this spectacular silica sand beach campsite. From there they proceed northwards via campsites at Peter Bay, Whitsunday Island (C28; No.10); to Crayfish Beach, Mackerel Bay, Hook Island (C14/15; No.14); then up around the north-east tip of Hook (Pallion Point – watch weather conditions carefully when planning to negotiate this point, which can be extremely turbulent), around the top of Hook Island and down to Curlew Beach, Macona Inlet (C10a; No.9), then back to a pick-up spot at Cid Harbour (C19) or Bauer Bay, South Molle Island (C9).

J. Heitman (QPWS)

WALKING IN THE WHITSUNDAYS

The national park islands of the Whitsundays have significant tracks that reward walkers with spectacular views of this magic island group. The tracks range from gently graded climbs through diverse bushland and across grasslands to scrambles up some of the highest promontories in the Whitsundays.

In the busy central section of the Whitsundays, Queensland Parks and Wildlife Service (QPWS) has created the Whitsunday Ngaro Sea Trail, which integrates some exciting new tracks on Whitsunday Island with the established, beautiful walks on South Molle Island and an upgrade to the Ngaro Cultural Site at Nara Inlet. The Trail provides opportunities for yachtsmen, kayakers, campers and trekkers of all persuasions to stretch their legs and appreciate some of the finest seascapes in the world and to visit some of the oldest sites of human habitation on earth. Other islands in the Whitsundays also have some wonderful walking tracks, such as Lindeman Island and Brampton Island, for those who venture further south.

The Ngaro

The Ngaro people after whom the Trail is named are the original inhabitants of the Whitsundays; they frequented the area more than 8000 years ago, according to carbon dating of shell fragments found at the Ngaro Cultural Site. There evidently were no permanent large settlements on the islands, but the Ngaro used to move seasonally through the islands in search of food.

Early reports of the Aborigines invariably describe them as a fine race of people, well built and well fed, the young men in particular carrying themselves confidently and proudly. The Whitsundays must have been a reasonably benign habitat, with fish and other marine creatures abounding.

Their watercraft were simple bark canoes 2.4–3.0 metres long, made either from a single sheet of bark or, for larger craft, from three sheets, one for the bottom and one for each side, sewn together with a cane-like creeper. The larger canoes could carry up to five persons. The expertise with which the Ngaro handled their frail boats and the speed they could attain earned comment in early writings about the Whitsundays. In waters that can be treacherous to small craft, the extent of their travel among the islands was remarkable. They were highly skilled in the use of their spears, some of which were long with a detachable head that parted company with the shaft when the target was struck.

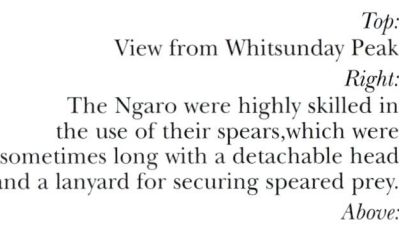

Top:
View from Whitsunday Peak
Right:
The Ngaro were highly skilled in
the use of their spears,which were
sometimes long with a detachable head
and a lanyard for securing speared prey.
Above:
Aborigine with spear, Lindeman Island,
in the 1930s.

Highlights of the Whitsunday Ngaro Sea Trail
(Descriptions courtesy QPWS)
Ngaro Cultural Site, Hook Island – 170 m one way (30 mins return)
Short and initially moderately steep, the track climbs the banks of Nara Inlet to
a rock shelter containing Ngaro art motifs and extensive cultural deposits. The
site includes a boardwalk, viewing area and interpretive displays.

Sandy Bay to Spion Kop and the Mt Jeffreys loop – 5.6 km one way (4 hrs return)
Winding its way through open forest, grasslands, dry rainforest and stands of hoop pine, the track starts at Sandy Bay and traverses the length of South Molle Island. Culturally significant sites can be visited en route to Spion Kop, and spectacular views are a highlight from the higher elevations of the track.

Whitsunday Peak, Whitsunday I. – 2.5 km one way (4 hrs return)
The Whitsunday Peak track is one of the most challenging of the Whitsunday Ngaro Sea Trail. Reaching an elevation of 437 m, the summit offers spectacular views over the Whitsunday islands and the mainland. Accessed from the Sawmill Beach picnic area at Cid Harbour, the track climbs steeply through rocky dry rainforest. A reasonable level of fitness is required to walk this track.

Whitehaven Beach to Chance Bay, Whitsunday I. – 3.6 km one way (2.5 hrs return)
The track extends between Chance Bay, a secluded bay on the southern side of Whitsunday Island, and the iconic Whitehaven Beach. It branches off the Solway Circuit and winds through some of the Whitsundays' finest forest and woodland.

Solway Circuit – 1.2 km round trip (40 minutes total)
The circuit departs from Whitehaven Beach and climbs through impressive grass trees and pandanus with sensational views over Solway Passage, Pentecost and Haslewood islands before returning to Whitehaven.

Tongue Point, Whitsunday I. – 1.5 km one way (1 hr return)
This moderate, winding track travels through woodland and dry rainforest communities to lookouts and beaches. Visitors can walk uphill to take in the vistas over: Hill Inlet – a highly significant area for the Ngaro people; the islands emerging from surrounding turquoise waters; and, the sweeping sands of Whitehaven Beach. An alternative is to walk over the ridge and along the cycad-lined boardwalk to the extensive white sands of Lookout Beach.

Whitsunday Cairn, Whitsunday I. — 2 km one way (4 hrs return)
Steep and challenging, this marker-guided track route leads to a rocky summit with breathtaking views of Hook Island and beyond to Border Island. A reasonable level of fitness is required to walk this track. The track is steep and challenging in places, but walkers are rewarded with a sense of isolation and numerous vantage points to take in the views on their climb to this unusual monolith.

Camping areas are provided at South Whitehaven Beach, Chance Bay, Dugong Beach (Whitsunday Island) and Sandy Bay (South Molle Island). These camping areas are immediately adjacent to the various walking tracks. All have toilet facilities and tables. There are other QPWS camping areas in the vicinity of the walking tracks, e.g. Peter Bay on Whitsunday Island, Curlew Beach and Crayfish Beach on Hook Island, Northern Spit on Henning Island, Paddle Bay on South Molle Island and Cockatoo

Top left:
Ngaro Cultural Site reflection area
Top right:
Platform leading to the Ngaro Cultural Site, Nara Inlet, Hook Island.
Above:
Whitsunday Cairn

Top::
One of the walks in of the Ngaro Sea Trail leads from Whitehaven Beach to a secluded beach on the southern side of Whitsunday Island, Chance Bay.
Above:
Art motif of the Ngaro Cultural Site

- Wear sensible footwear and carry plenty of water.
- Stay on the track.
- Always tell someone responsible where you are going and when you expect to return.

Beach on North Molle Island. Drinking water is not provided at any of the camping areas.

There are day use areas with toilets and tables at South Whitehaven Beach Sawmill Beach, Whitsunday Island, and Sandy Bay, South Molle Island. Throughout the trail, interpretative signs inform visitors of the unique natural values and the culture significance of this area to the traditional owners - the Ngaro people.

Other walks in the Whitsundays

Long Island (sketch map C4)

Circuit Track – 3 km

From the resort north along the eastern shore, giving views across to Dent and Hamilton islands, circling back to the northern end of the beach at Happy Bay.

Palm Bay Track – 2.2 km

An easy walk with possible detour along the way to Humpy Point, where elevated views of Palm Bay are available. Goes through dense vine forest before descending into the saddle where Peppers Palm Bay is nestled.

Sandy Bay Track – 5 km

There is a turnoff about 500 m from Peppers Palm Bay that takes a circuit to the east, giving views of the passage, then continues through vine forest to Sandy Bay.

Brampton Island (sketch map S11)

Circuit Track – 8.4 km

A scenic walk right around the island passing secluded bays with glorious views seaward. A track to Brampton Peak (3.6 km return to circuit track) affords panoramic views across the islands. At Western Bay there is a day-use facility with toilet and picnic shelter.

Lindeman Island (sketch map S1)

Mt Oldfield – 3.6 km one way

A steady climb features some of the most diverse vegetation on the island – eucalypt forest, thick vine forest and grassland dotted with grass trees. The peak rewards trekkers with magnificent 360° views of the surrounding islands.

Plantation Beach – 2.1 km one way
The walk is mainly over grasslands broken by the scattered pointed outlines of pandanus palms, and it offers excellent views of neighbouring Shaw Island. The track winds down into rainforest and emerges on a rocky foreshore. Following the track to the other side of the valley brings one to a sandy beach with mangrove forest and beach shrubs. At high tide one will need to ford a small creek.

Coconut Beach to Boat Port circuit – 6.5 km
This walk can be done as a circuit or separate sections either to Coconut Beach or Boat Port.

Coconut Beach – 2.7 km one way
This track takes one through eucalypt forest past the resort dam (good place for spotting birds), then descends to a sandy beach through light scrub which gives Coconut Beach a secluded feel.

Boat Port – 2.7 km one way
The track goes through open eucalypt forest into a closed woodland community and rainforest. Stonework stairs descend to a sheltered beach lined with sheoaks (*Casuarina equisetifolia*). Hermit crabs are active at low tide. Boat Port was used by the Nicolson family because it provided protection from the southeast trade winds.

Gap Beach – 2.7 km one way
Winding through eucalypt forest and a dry rainforest valley the track emerges at a small pebble beach and rocky foreshore with mangroves. Beautiful views north to Pentecost Island.

Left top:
Glimpses of native wildlife are commonplace along the Brampton circuit track.

Left middle:
View of Dinghy Bay from the Brampton circuit track

Top right:
The track to Spion Kop leads past the site where natives of the Whitsundays got their 'whyribba' stones for making axe heads.

Above:
Grass tree (*Xanthorrhoea sp.*) – a common sight along Whitsunday tracks

Andrew BW Colfelt

Above:
Sunset in the Sir James Smith Group
Opposite:
Hill Inlet, Whitsunday Island

David Colfelt

MANAGING THE MARINE PARK: PRESERVING THE WHITSUNDAYS

The Great Barrier Reef Marine Park

The Great Barrier Reef Marine Park was created to protect, preserve and manage the largest and richest system of coral reefs in the world. The Park, for all intents, includes everything below the low tide limit, from the tip of Cape York right down to Bundaberg, including the waters surrounding the Whitsundays and their beautiful fringing coral reefs and fascinating marine life.

The Marine Park is a multi-use park that provides for all reasonable uses. A spectrum of zone types specifies which activities (including extraction activities such as fishing and collecting) are allowed in which zones while ensuring the overriding objective of conservation. Just what constitutes 'reasonable use' is set out in the Marine Park zoning plans and the Whitsundays Plan of Management, both of which are explained below.

State Marine Parks and Island National Parks

Most of the Whitsunday islands are national parks under the laws of the State of Queensland and, as such, all flora and fauna above high water mark on these islands are totally protected – one reason for their great appeal to tourists. Between high and low water – the intertidal zone – the islands are protected by a system of Queensland State Marine Parks that mirror the federal Marine Park. Thus the whole continuum, from sea bed to island peak, is provided for.

Marine Park plans of management

The Great Barrier Reef Marine Park Authority (GBRMPA), which has overall responsibility for the Park, uses a number of management tools, including zoning plans, to preserve and conserve the Great Barrier Reef. These define the activities that are permitted in various zones to ensure a balance between short-term human needs to use the Park and the long-term dictates of conservation. Zoning plans allow multiple use of the Reef and its resources and they separate conflicting uses. Levels of protection vary from general use (all reasonable activities allowed) to Preservation Zones (no access without a permit). The Whitsundays are in the Townsville/Whitsunday Management Area of the Great Barrier Reef Marine Park which extends from Dunk Island in the north to just below Thomas Island in the south.

To allow an additional measure of fine tuning in management of the Whitsunday area, the Whitsundays Plan of Management includes a series of 'Settings' and is an 'overlay' to Marine Park zones. The Whitsunday

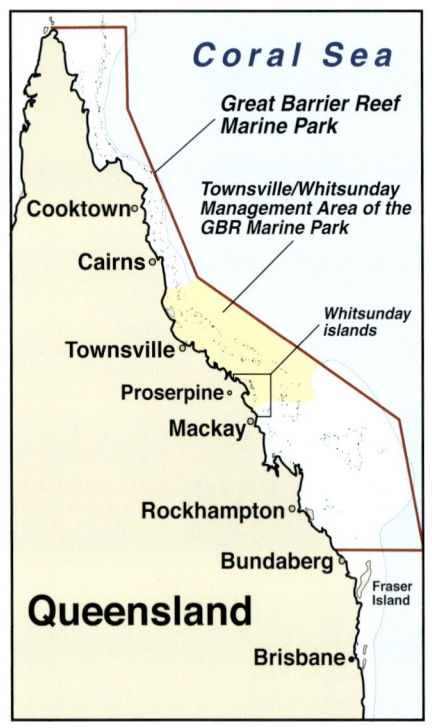

Planning Area covers the area from Middle Island (sketch map N2, page 131) in the north-west along a parallel that extends east of the islands down to and including Thomas Island (sketch map S6) and the Repulse Group (sketch map S18). It also includes the Hook/Hardy/Line/Bait reef complex (sketch map R1).

Marine Park zones

The map on pages 110–111 shows the colour-coded zones that apply in the Whitsundays and the activities that are permitted within these zones.

General Use (light blue) Zone
The objective of the General Use Zone is to provide opportunities for reasonable use of the Great Barrier Reef Marine Park, while still allowing for the conservation of these areas. Activities such as shipping and trawling are allowed in the General Use Zone without written permission.

Habitat Protection (dark blue) Zone
The Habitat Protection Zone provides for the conservation of areas of the Great Barrier Reef Marine Park by protecting and managing sensitive habitats and ensuring they are generally free from potentially damaging activities. Trawling is not permitted in the Habitat Protection Zone.

Conservation Park (yellow) Zone
The Conservation Park Zone (yellow zone) allows for increased protection and conservation of areas of the Great Barrier Reef Marine Park while providing opportunities for reasonable use and enjoyment including limited line fishing. Limited spearfishing is also allowed except within the Public Appreciation Area (shown as broken pink lines on the zoning map). However, there are additional restrictions for most fishing activities. For more information about fishing and spearfishing restrictions, see 'Fishing Activities' on pages 114–115.

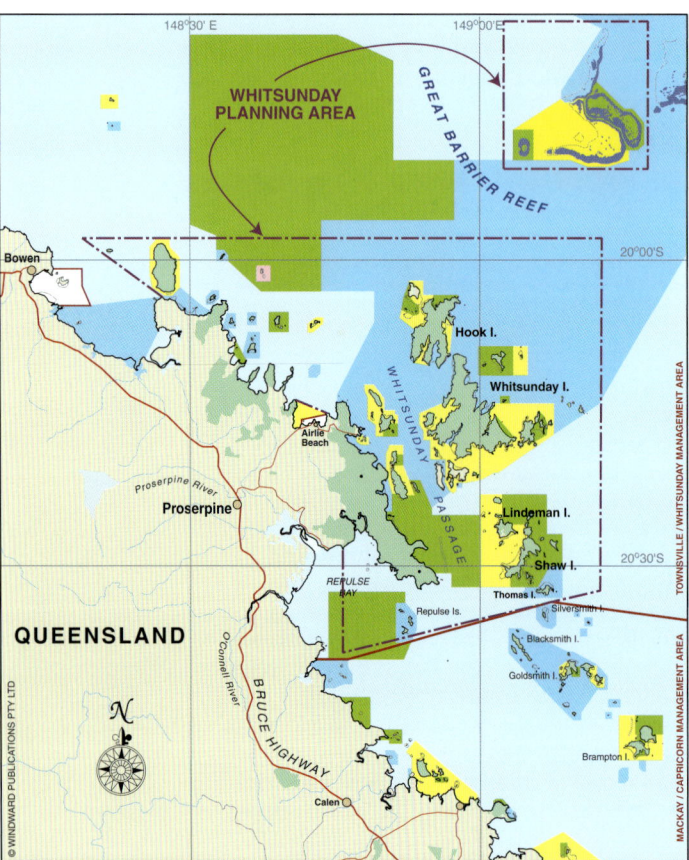

Marine National Park (green) Zone
The Marine National Park Zone (green zone) is a 'no-take' area, and extractive activities like fishing or collecting are not allowed without written permission. Anyone can enter a green zone and participate in activities such as boating, swimming, snorkelling and sailing. Travelling through a green zone with fish on board is also allowed (it is only an offence to fish in a green zone). Fishing gear, such as rods with hooks attached, must be stowed on board or in a rod holder while in a green zone. Anchoring is also allowed in a green zone; however, in high use and sensitive areas, use of a mooring may be necessary.

Preservation (pink) Zone
The Preservation Zone (pink zone) is a 'no go' area for the general public. A person should not enter a Pink Zone (except in an emergency) unless they have special permission, and extractive activities are strictly prohibited. Research may occur in a pink zone, but only if the research is relevant to, and a priority for, management and cannot be conducted elsewhere. A permit for such research is required

Marine Park zones south of the Whitsunday Planning Area
The Marine Park zones shown on the map on pages 110–111 include the mainland and islands of the Whitsunday Planning Area. Those visiting the Whitsundays on a yacht may travel south of this area. The maps opposite show zoning for the islands south of Thomas Island.

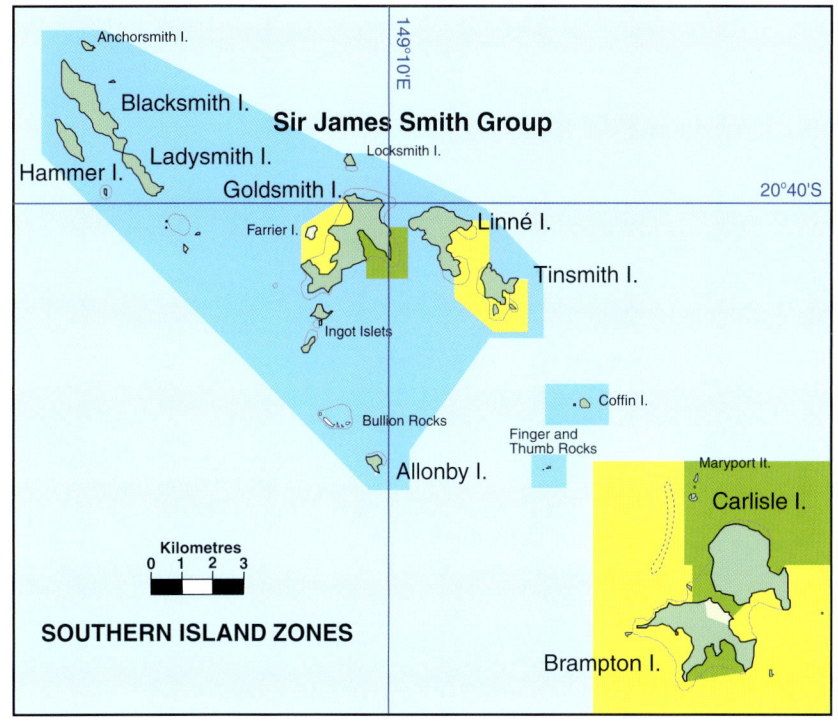

SOUTHERN ISLAND ZONES

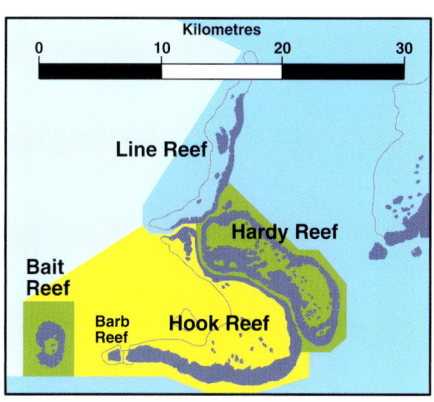

Above:
The group of reefs, including Hook, Line, Bait and Hardy, is the centre of outer reef activities for the Whitsundays. These are the reefs of the Barrier system nearest to the Whitsundays. They lie on the continental shelf about seventeen nautical miles from the nearest of the islands. Hardy Reef, with its magnificent lagoon, is the destination of amphibious aircraft, helicopters and high-speed catamarans which bring tourists out for a day on the Reef. Hardy is a Marine National Park Zone. Bait Reef is a pristine oceanic platform south-east of Hardy and is popular with scuba divers.

The Whitsundays Plan of Management

The Whitsundays Plan of Management was gazetted in 1998 and has been updated several times to continue to address a range of management issues in the area. In conjunction with the existing Zoning Plan, it is designed to ensure continued use of the area without compromising the special values that users come to enjoy.

Settings

Under the plan, settings (numbered 1 to 5 – see map on pages 112–113) have been assigned to reefs and coastal waters of the Whitsundays to provide for a range of recreational activities. Settings describe the type of activities to expect when visiting particular parts of the Whitsundays. For example, Setting 1 allows for activities such as water-skiing, parasailing, and the landing of float planes, whereas these activities are not permitted in other areas. Settings may put limits on the length of vessel and size of group that may use an area. These limits apply to everyone, from tourism operators to private individuals.

Setting	Colour Code	Max. Vessel Length	Group Size
1 – Developed		70 metres	No limit
2 – High Use		35 metres	No limit
3 – Moderate Use		35 metres	40 people
4 – Natural		35 metres	15 people
5 – Protected		20 metres	15 people

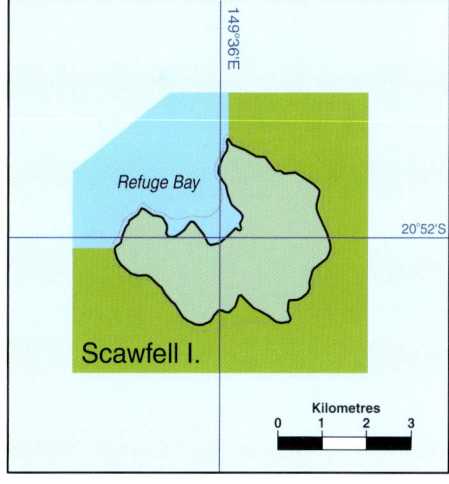

Above:
Scawfell Island, at the southern end of the Whitsundays, a popular stopover for itinerants and professional trawlers.

Site plans

Detailed site plans have been developed for sensitive sites, including Setting 5 areas (the latter can be viewed at *gbrmpa.gov.au/corp_site/management/pom/whitsundays/draft_setting_5_plans*). The Protected setting is used to manage, for example, areas such as the nesting beaches of threatened species, e.g. the beach stone-curlew (*Esacus neglectus*), or where unique

(Continued on page 114)

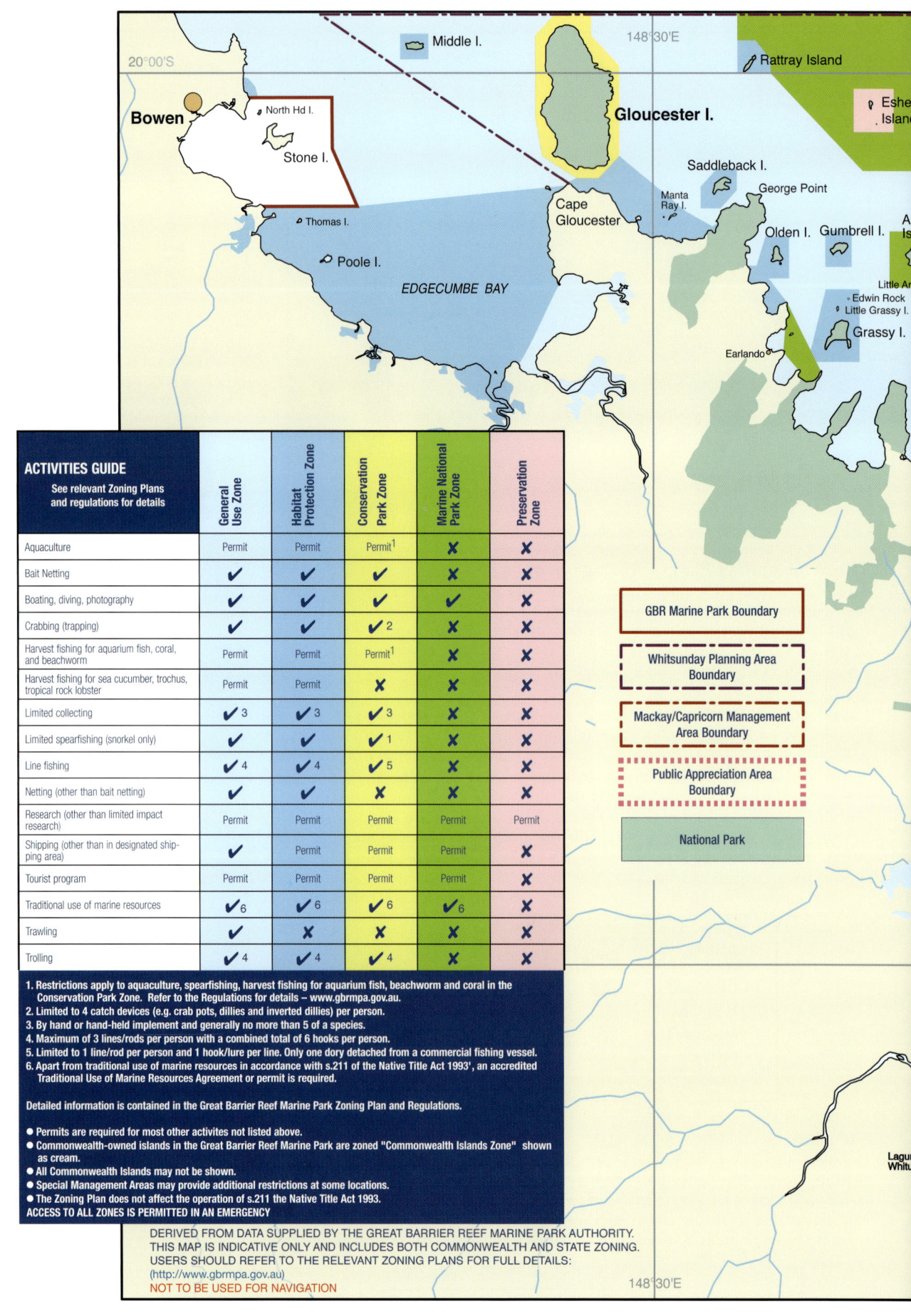

Map labels: Middle I., Rattray Island, 20°00'S, 148°30'E, Bowen, North Hd I., Stone I., Gloucester I., Eshell Island, Saddleback I., George Point, Cape Gloucester, Manta Ray I., Olden I., Gumbrell I., Thomas I., Little Arr Is, Poole I., Edwin Rock, Little Grassy I., EDGECUMBE BAY, Grassy I., Earlando, Lagur Whitu

ACTIVITIES GUIDE — See relevant Zoning Plans and regulations for details	General Use Zone	Habitat Protection Zone	Conservation Park Zone	Marine National Park Zone	Preservation Zone
Aquaculture	Permit	Permit	Permit[1]	✘	✘
Bait Netting	✔	✔	✔	✘	✘
Boating, diving, photography	✔	✔	✔	✔	✘
Crabbing (trapping)	✔	✔	✔[2]	✘	✘
Harvest fishing for aquarium fish, coral, and beachworm	Permit	Permit	Permit[1]	✘	✘
Harvest fishing for sea cucumber, trochus, tropical rock lobster	Permit	Permit	✘	✘	✘
Limited collecting	✔[3]	✔[3]	✔[3]	✘	✘
Limited spearfishing (snorkel only)	✔	✔	✔[1]	✘	✘
Line fishing	✔[4]	✔[4]	✔[5]	✘	✘
Netting (other than bait netting)	✔	✔	✘	✘	✘
Research (other than limited impact research)	Permit	Permit	Permit	Permit	Permit
Shipping (other than in designated shipping area)	✔	Permit	Permit	Permit	✘
Tourist program	Permit	Permit	Permit	Permit	✘
Traditional use of marine resources	✔[6]	✔[6]	✔[6]	✔[6]	✘
Trawling	✔	✘	✘	✘	✘
Trolling	✔[4]	✔[4]	✔[4]	✘	✘

1. Restrictions apply to aquaculture, spearfishing, harvest fishing for aquarium fish, beachworm and coral in the Conservation Park Zone. Refer to the Regulations for details – www.gbrmpa.gov.au.
2. Limited to 4 catch devices (e.g. crab pots, dillies and inverted dillies) per person.
3. By hand or hand-held implement and generally no more than 5 of a species.
4. Maximum of 3 lines/rods per person with a combined total of 6 hooks per person.
5. Limited to 1 line/rod per person and 1 hook/lure per line. Only one dory detached from a commercial fishing vessel.
6. Apart from traditional use of marine resources in accordance with s.211 of the Native Title Act 1993', an accredited Traditional Use of Marine Resources Agreement or permit is required.

Detailed information is contained in the Great Barrier Reef Marine Park Zoning Plan and Regulations.

- Permits are required for most other activites not listed above.
- Commonwealth-owned islands in the Great Barrier Reef Marine Park are zoned "Commonwealth Islands Zone" shown as cream.
- All Commonwealth Islands may not be shown.
- Special Management Areas may provide additional restrictions at some locations.
- The Zoning Plan does not affect the operation of s.211 the Native Title Act 1993.

ACCESS TO ALL ZONES IS PERMITTED IN AN EMERGENCY

Legend:
- GBR Marine Park Boundary
- Whitsunday Planning Area Boundary
- Mackay/Capricorn Management Area Boundary
- Public Appreciation Area Boundary
- National Park

DERIVED FROM DATA SUPPLIED BY THE GREAT BARRIER REEF MARINE PARK AUTHORITY. THIS MAP IS INDICATIVE ONLY AND INCLUDES BOTH COMMONWEALTH AND STATE ZONING. USERS SHOULD REFER TO THE RELEVANT ZONING PLANS FOR FULL DETAILS: (http://www.gbrmpa.gov.au)
NOT TO BE USED FOR NAVIGATION

148°30'E

TOWNSVILLE / WHITSUNDAY MANAGEMENT AREA

149°00'E

20°00'S

Approximate Scale 1:300 000

0   10
Nautical Miles

0   5   10   15   20
Kilometres

N

Hayman I.

Blue Pearl Bay

Butterfly Bay

Mackerel Bay

Bird I.   Black I.

Stonehaven Anchorage

Saba Bay

Hook I.

Nara Inlet

Macona Inlet

Double Cone I.

Grimston Point

Roseric Shoal

Border I.

Deloraine It

Dumbell I.

Petrel It

Peter Bay

Whitsunday I.

North Molle I.

WHITSUNDAY

Pioneer Rocks

Almora It

Aposte Bay

Tongue Bay

Esk I.

Harold I.

Edward I.

South Molle I.

Daydream I.

Cid Harbour

Hill Inlet

Whitehaven Beach

Waite Bay

Pioneer Bay

Cid I.

Haslewood I.

Nicolson I.

Airlie Beach   Shutehaven

Shute I.

Tancred I.

Henning I.

Turtle Bay

Chance Bay

Teague I.

East Rock

Long I.

Perseverance I.

Public Appreciation Area Boundary

Dent I.

Surprise Rk

Pine I.

Hamilton I.

Pentecost I.

Anne I.

Little Lindeman I.

Maher I.

Cow I.

Cole I.

Baynham I.

Calf I.

Lindeman I.

Comston I.

Sidney It

Mansell I.

CONWAY NATIONAL PARK

Seaforth I.

Volskow I.

20°30'S

Genesta Bay

Shaw Island

Keyser I.

Cape Conway

Thomas I.

REPULSE BAY

Repulse Islands

Silversmith I.

MACKAY / CAPRICORN MANAGEMENT AREA

THE ANCHOR ISLANDS

Blacksmith I.

Midge Point

Hammer I.   Ladysmith I.

Linné I.

Goldsmith I.

Farrier I.

149°00'E

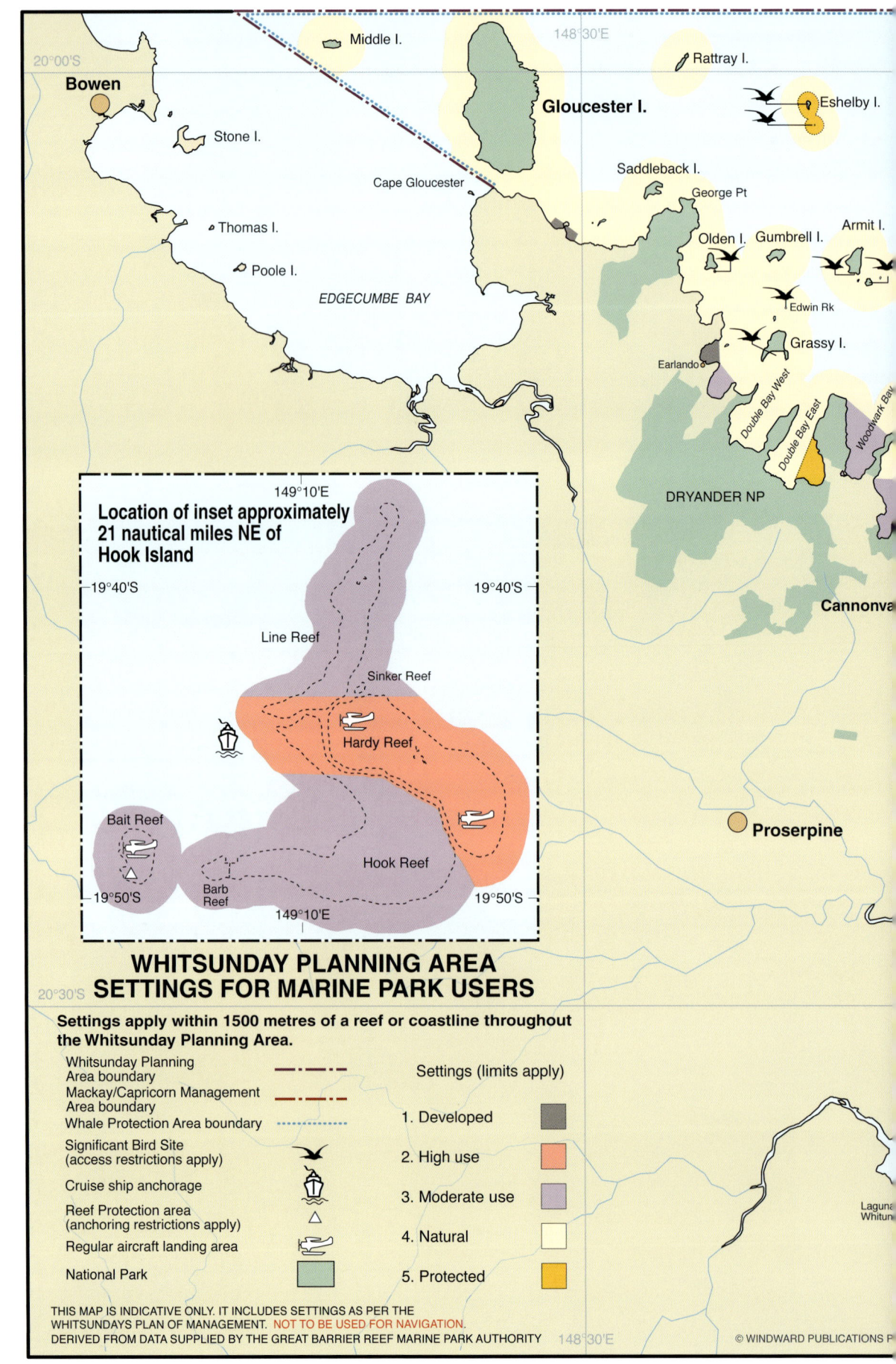

20°00'S

Middle I.

148°30'E

Rattray I.

Bowen

Eshelby I.

Stone I.

Gloucester I.

Saddleback I.

Cape Gloucester

George Pt

Thomas I.

Olden I. Gumbrell I. Armit I.

Poole I.

Edwin Rk

EDGECUMBE BAY

Grassy I.

Earlando

Double Bay West Double Bay East Woodwark Bay

DRYANDER NP

149°10'E

Location of inset approximately 21 nautical miles NE of Hook Island

19°40'S   19°40'S

Cannonva

Line Reef

Sinker Reef

Hardy Reef

Bait Reef

Proserpine

Hook Reef

Barb Reef

19°50'S   19°50'S

149°10'E

WHITSUNDAY PLANNING AREA
SETTINGS FOR MARINE PARK USERS

20°30'S

Settings apply within 1500 metres of a reef or coastline throughout the Whitsunday Planning Area.

Whitsunday Planning Area boundary — · — · —
Mackay/Capricorn Management Area boundary — · — · —
Whale Protection Area boundary ············

Settings (limits apply)

Significant Bird Site (access restrictions apply)

1. Developed

Cruise ship anchorage

2. High use

Reef Protection area (anchoring restrictions apply) △

3. Moderate use

Regular aircraft landing area

4. Natural

National Park

5. Protected

Laguna Whitun

THIS MAP IS INDICATIVE ONLY. IT INCLUDES SETTINGS AS PER THE WHITSUNDAYS PLAN OF MANAGEMENT. NOT TO BE USED FOR NAVIGATION. DERIVED FROM DATA SUPPLIED BY THE GREAT BARRIER REEF MARINE PARK AUTHORITY

148°30'E

© WINDWARD PUBLICATIONS P

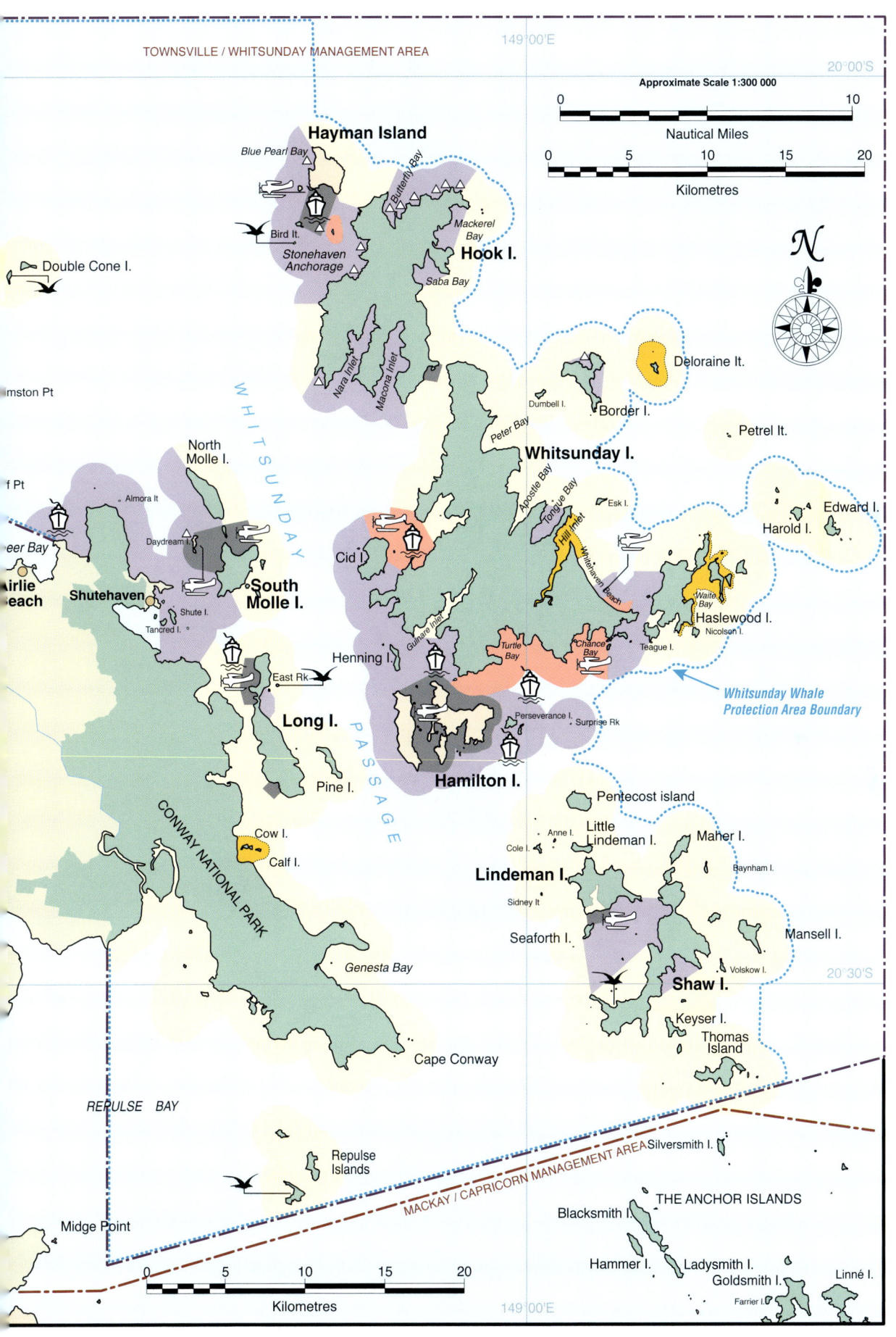

149°00'E

20°00'S

Approximate Scale 1:300 000

0   10

Nautical Miles

0   5   10   15   20

Kilometres

Hayman Island

Blue Pearl Bay

Butterfly Bay

Bird It.

Stonehaven
Anchorage

Mackerel
Bay

Hook I.

Saba Bay

Double Cone I.

Nara Inlet

Macona Inlet

rmston Pt

Peter Bay

Dumbell I.

Border I.

Deloraine It.

Petrel It.

Whitsunday I.

North
Molle I.

Almora It

f Pt

Apostle Bay

Tongue Bay

Esk I.

Edward I.

Harold I.

eer Bay

Daydream I.

Hill Inlet

Whitehaven Beach

**South
Molle I.**

Cid I.

Waite
Bay

Haslewood I.

irlie
each

Shutehaven

Shute I.

Nicolson I.

Tancred I.

Henning I.

East Rk.

Turtle
Bay

Chance
Bay

Teague I.

Long I.

*Whitsunday Whale
Protection Area Boundary*

Hamilton I.

Perseverance I.

Surprise Rk

Pine I.

Pentecost island

Anne I.

Little
Lindeman I.

Maher I.

Cow I.

Cole I.

Baynham I.

Calf I.

CONWAY NATIONAL PARK

Lindeman I.

Sidney It

Seaforth I.

Mansell I.

Volskow I.

20°30'S

Shaw I.

Keyser I.

Genesta Bay

Cape Conway

Thomas
Island

REPULSE BAY

Silversmith I.

Repulse
Islands

THE ANCHOR ISLANDS

Blacksmith I.

Midge Point

Hammer I.

Ladysmith I.

Linné I.

Goldsmith I.

Farrier I.

0   5   10   15   20

Kilometres

149°00'E

WHITSUNDAY PASSAGE

Fishing activities

Line fishing is allowed in the General Use (light blue) and Habitat Protection (dark blue) Zones. Line fishing is fishing using not more than three hand-held rods or handlines per person with a combined number of not more than six hooks attached to the line(s).

Limited line fishing is allowed in the Conservation Park (yellow) Zone. Limited line fishing is fishing using not more than one hand-held rod or one hand-line per person, with no more than one hook attached to that line. See below for the definition of a hook.

Definition of a hook

In addition to the ordinary meaning, **a hook** means:
- a single-shanked double or treble hook; or
- an artificial fly; or
- a lure (an artificial bait with not more than three hooks attached to it); or
- a jig (for taking squid); or
- a bait jig (a hook or group of hooks consisting of no more than six hooks, each hook being of a size from number 1 though number 12 or their equivalent); or
- a ganged-hook set (consisting of no more than six hooks, each of which is in contact with at least one of the other hooks in the set).

Trolling is allowed in the General Use (light blue), Habitat Protection (dark blue) and Conservation Park (yellow) Zones. Trolling is fishing by means of a line or lines trailed behind a vessel that is underway using not more than three lines per person and up to six hooks combined total per person.

Bait netting is allowed in the General Use (light blue), Habitat Protection (dark blue) and Conservation Park (yellow) Zones. Bait netting means the use of a net of dimension and mesh size as prescribed in relevant Queensland fisheries legislation. For more detail of bait netting and the relevant Queensland fisheries legislation, see the Great Barrier Reef Marine Park Regulations 1983.

Crabbing (trapping) may be undertaken by recreational fishers using no more than four apparatus per person in the General Use (blue), Habitat Protection (dark blue) and Conservation (yellow) Zones. Crabbing (trapping) is using apparatus such as crab pots, collapsible traps, dillies of the number and dimensions described in Queensland fisheries legislation. Crabbing (trapping) undertaken by commercial fishers is also limited to no more than four apparatus in the Conservation Park (yellow) Zone.

Limited spearfishing is allowed in the General Use (light blue), Habitat Protection (dark blue) and Conservation Park (yellow) Zones. **Spearfishing in yellow zones that lie within Public Appreciation Areas is not permitted.** Public Appreciation Areas are shown as broken pink lines on the zoning map. Limited spearfishing means fishing with a spear or speargun not using a powerhead, a firearm, a light or underwater breathing apparatus other than a snorkel. A person must not have a loaded speargun in his or her possession out of the water.

(continued next page)

(Continued from page 109)

coral communities may exist, or where an area may have cultural significance. Limits on access to protected settings may be applied from time to time in accordance with the dictates of good environmental management. Some examples of Setting 5 (Protected) are Double Bay (eastern) (sketch map N13) (significant mangrove community and sclerophyll forest), Hill Inlet (sketch map C27) (significant sea bird site and stopover for itinerant wading birds, significant mangroves, unique silica sand inlet and delta), Waite Bay (sketch map C31) (source reef for coral recruitment in the area, significant vegetation communities, turtle feeding and nesting area).

Coral protection

The Whitsunday reefs, particularly around the northern islands, are outstanding in the coral cover and diversity. The increasing use of the fringing reefs makes them vulnerable to damage by careless anchoring and vessel groundings. Coral collecting (either live, dead or beach-washed) without a permit is illegal. It is generally an offence to damage coral. But prevention is far preferable to cure, and to this end reef protection markers and public moorings have been installed in a number of bays to protect coral (see 'Boating in the Whitsundays', pages 73–74, for more about moorings and reef protection buoys).

Wildlife protection

The Whitsundays have a wide diversity of marine wildlife including sea birds (which are increasingly threatened by loss of nesting habitats along our coastlines), sea turtles and marine mammals, such as dugongs and whales. A number of species of sea birds are very sensitive to interference by humans during their nesting season.

Birds

Throughout the islands a number of sites have exclusion zones at certain times of year and there are a number where beach access is prohibited all year round (see list opposite top). These sites are all identified on the sketch maps by a broken red circle and a seabird symbol.

Dugongs and turtles

Dugong populations in the southern Great Barrier Reef Marine Park are severely depleted and under pressure from habitat loss, gill netting, illegal hunting and boat strikes. Marine turtles, which pass through the Whitsundays on their way to nesting sites, or which are full-time residents foraging in the waters, are listed as protected species. The taking of dugongs and marine turtles in the Whitsundays is prohibited. Dugong sanctuaries or dugong protection areas have been established in Edgecumbe Bay and Repulse Bay and restrictions apply on the use of mesh nets in these areas.

Whales

The Whitsunday islands are an important calving ground for humpback whales between May and September each year. Most of the waters around the islands are part of a 'whale protection area' (see map on pages 112–113) to minimise disturbance to whales. Inside the whale protection area boats must not approach within 300 metres of a whale. Outside the whale protection area boats must not approach within 100 metres of a whale.

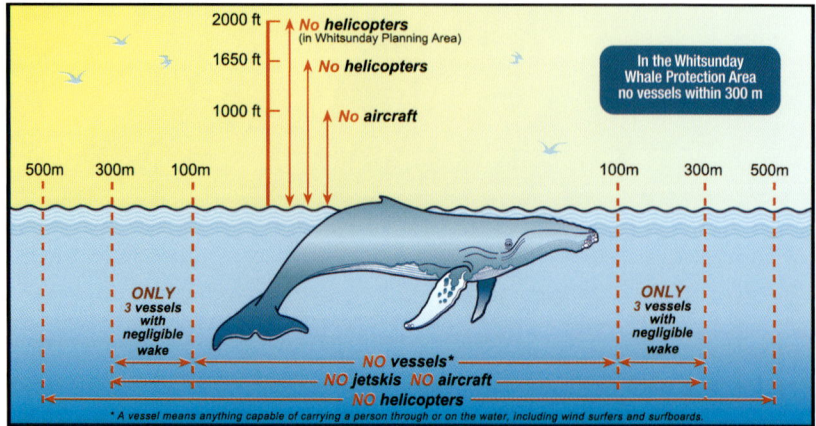

Significant bird sites with restriction periods

A number of sites throughout the islands have significant bird populations and certain restrictions apply, some seasonal and some year-round. The sites in question (with sketch map numbers) are:

Armit Island and Little Armit Island (N10b)
Bird Island (C12)
Double Cone Island (western island) N10c
East Rock (C4)
Edwin Rock (N11)
Eshelby Island and Little Eshelby Island (N8b)
Grassy Island (N11)
Olden Rock (N9)
Shaw Island (Burning Point) S3
South Repulse Island (S18)

Symbol for
restricted bird sites

Details of the restrictions that apply are given on the sketch maps and in accompanying text.

Best environmental practice

Best environmental practice is a way of describing the best way for park users to protect the environment. Throughout this book are notes on best environmental practice, and if everyone who visits the islands behaves according to these, there will be less need to rely on additional legal requirements to manage the park. In the end, the wellbeing of the area will really depend upon people doing the 'right thing' because they understand the need for it rather than because they are forced to do it.

Best environmental practices for all activities:

- Respect other people using the World Heritage Area.
- Avoid conflicting activities in the same area.
- Learn about the World Heritage Area and how to minimise your impact.

Reporting procedures

You can help manage the Great Barrier Reef World Heritage Area by reporting any of the following activities or incidents:

- suspected breaches in law (QPWS Whitsunday (07 4967 7355), GBRMPA (07 4750 0700/*www.gbrmpa.gov.au*) or DDM Compliance Unit (07 4726 0510))
- vessel collisions, groundings or oil spills (AMSA 1800 624 792)
- marine mammal sightings or strandings (strandings hotline 1300 130 372)
- crown-of-thorns starfish sightings (GBRMPA (07 4750 0700/*www.gbrmpa.gov.au*)
- natural history observations such as fish spawning, coral bleaching or algal blooms (GBRMPA (07 4750 0700)/*www.gbrmpa.gov.au*)

Reports should be directed as above or to QPWS Whitsunday (07 4967 7355).

The beach stone-curlew (*Esacus neglectus*) may be found on lonely beaches during the day, foraging with a mate in the intertidal zone. At night its haunted, mournful wail may be heard around island beaches. This species is easily disturbed by humans during the nesting season, which is one of the reasons for restricted access to some beaches. Increased human activity threatens the survival of these birds.

Fishing activities *(continued from previous page)*
Limited collecting is the taking of shells (except helmuts, tritons and giant clams, which may not be taken), fish, crustaceans or other invertebrates, other than corals of Classes *Anthozoa* and *Hydrozoa*, by hand or hand-held implement and subject to any limitations prescribed in the Great Barrier Reef Marine Park Regulations 1983. Generally not more than five of any one species can be taken except when collecting bait or oysters for immediate consumption.

AVOIDING TROPICAL HAZARDS

These notes are provided for curiosity seekers as much as for any real hazards posed by tropical marine creatures. One has to marvel at the ingenious behaviours and weaponry that have evolved, and no matter how remote the danger posed by any of the animals discussed below, it's useful to be aware of them. Unlike man, the creatures described here almost always inflict their damage in self-defence only, or after extreme provocation.

Poisonous fishes

Of the many and varied fishes that may be found in the waters of the Whitsundays, there are a few which can be 'poisonous'. Some are rendered so by their behaviour (such as Thomas the Terrible Toadfish), some can cause poisoning if eaten (such as Thomas the Terrible Toadfish, Chinaman fish, paddletail, etc.), and some cause 'poisoning' if stepped on, such as the stonefish – this is, actually, 'envenomation'.

Toadfish

The toadfish belongs to the order of tetraodontiformes, a mouthful that describes these fishes' four (tetra) large, fused teeth (odontiformes). Toadfish lurk around shallow coastal estuaries and inlets; they lie waiting for passing crabs which they crunch up with their beaklike teeth. They are normally only about 13 centimetres long, but certain species grow as big as 96 centimetres, with teeth to match and capable of shearing through a number 4/0 hook.

Giant toadfish have from time to time conducted campaigns of terror in the Whitsundays. For example, during the Easter weekend of 1979, six-year-old Margaret Lewis had two toes bitten off at the first joint while wading barefoot in Shute Harbour. Some time later that year a toadfish removed a walnut-sized chunk from the leg of a boy wading in Cid Harbour, and Richard Timperley was fishing in water about 35 centimetres deep over gravel near the Shute Harbour ramp when a 65 centimetre toadfish came like a torpedo for his sneakered feet. Undeterred by jabs from a fishing rod, the toadfish pursued the rapidly retreating fisherman until it had

Thomas the Terrible Toadfish had this portrait taken in 1979 after he unsuccessfully attempted to eat the sneaker-clad toes of a fisherman in Shute Harbour. This giant toadfish was 65 centimetres in length, but they can grow as large as 96 centimetres.

almost beached itself. Timperley later made up a 'wanted' poster to warn local residents about a vile fish which he dubbed 'Thomas the Terrible Toadfish'.

In early March 1984 61-year-old Robert Crompton was prawning at Earlando (sketch map N11) in waist-deep water when a giant toadfish tore away the top of the middle toe on his left foot. In spite of Robert's kicking, the fish circled back in a second attack and took yet a little more of the toe, which later had to be amputated completely. (As fate would have it, this was the first time Crompton had ever gone into the water barefoot.)

Toadfish are sometimes referred to in the area as 'toefish', and the lessons of the past should be heeded. Never wade in coastal inlets in bare feet.

Toadfish are members of the family of puffers which are capable of inflating themselves like basketballs, a practice which evidently intimidates would-be predators, or at least it makes the puffers jolly difficult to swallow. Puffers were known to be poisonous well before the advent of Christ. Hieroglyphics of 2700 BC mention the toxicity of Red Sea puffer fish, and there are biblical warnings against eating fish with no scales (puffer fish have no scales). The Greeks and Chinese knew of the danger, and it is surprising that neither Captain James Cook nor his cook were aware of it, for the great explorer was poisoned by a puffer in New Caledonia on his second voyage of discovery in 1774.

Puffer fishes can inflate themselves to relatively enormous proportions, making them difficult to swallow and, perhaps, formidable to predators.

The Japanese play a form of culinary Russian roulette with puffer fish and, like so much of what they do in Japan, the game is taken to the extremes of art. Fugu, as it is called, is a prized delicacy which may be prepared only by licensed fugu chefs who have gone to school and taken exams on the subject of its preparation. These chefs create *tours de forces* in their restaurants, laying out the thin slices of the fish in delicate floral patterns. Traces of tetrodotoxin (TTX) produce a pleasant tingling sensation which has been likened by enthusiasts to that produced by a white Burgundy of a good year. The sense of danger obviously heightens the experience, and it is said that to eat fugu liver, in which the concentration of toxin may be very great indeed, is the ultimate in fugu culture; even trained chefs are prohibited from serving it; but what can they do when a dejected haiku poet comes in and says:

I cannot see her tonight,
I have to give her up,
So I will eat fugu.

TTX is one of the most toxic poisons known. James Bond, at the end of *From Russia with Love*, was left for dead on the floor after being kicked in the leg by a poison-tipped boot which, 'M' explains in the sequel, *Dr No*, was tainted with fugu poison, from the sex organs of the Japanese globe fish (the sex organs, roe, viscera and skin also have very high concentrations of toxin). Nine millionths of one gram (0.000009 gram) per kilogram of TTX administered intravenously will kill 50% of mice injected with the poison.

Symptoms of puffer poisoning

The onset of symptoms is relatively rapid (10–45 minutes); the speed of onset and severity is relative to the amount of toxin ingested. Symptoms begin with a tingling sensation and numbness about the mouth and lips; sometimes there is nausea but seldom vomiting. Symptoms progress to numbness of the tongue and face, followed by slurred speech and progressive muscle paralysis, with ultimate respiratory paralysis and death, which evidently occurs in about 60% of cases. TTX is said to be used by voodoo specialists in Haiti to create their 'zombies' – the walking dead who survive being 'buried alive'. Conventional medicine reports that, in some serious cases where the patients have apparently been unconscious, they have recovered and reported being mentally alert right throughout the ordeal. (Don't say anything that you wouldn't say in front of the hapless patient or he may remember you for it later.)

First aid

If the victim is conscious, induce vomiting; stick fingers down the throat or administer an emetic (syrup of ipecac).

Avoidance

Don't eat puffer fishes or, as the Bible says, any scaleless fishes.

Ciguatera (tropical fish poisoning)

The word ciguatera comes from a Spanish word, 'cigua', and was coined by a Cuban ichthyologist, F. Poey, in 1866. Cigua is the name for a small mollusc which causes digestive and nervous disorders when eaten. Ciguatera is usually acquired by eating predatory tropical reef fishes or reef-feeding pelagic fishes that have accumulated a toxin through eating smaller fishes which contain the toxin. Ciguatoxin is believed to originate from a dinoflagellate (plankton), *Gambierdiscus toxicus*, which is passed along the food web via small herbivorous fishes; the toxin is firmly tissue-bound, very little being excreted, and it thus can reach high concentrations in larger carnivorous fishes.

Gambierdiscus toxicus proliferates around coral reefs where the corals have been killed either by storms or by the intervention of man, or by silting after heavy rainfall. Thus, from time to time, many different species of fish may be affected by ciguatoxin, and the list of fishes that have been implicated at one time or another reads like a peerage, everything from coral trout to scallops having been named. The list is of little practical value as a guide to which fish to avoid if you want to eat any fish at all. It is a good idea to check with local fishermen as to which fish to avoid.

Certain species of fish in Queensland are known to be toxic, and these should always be avoided: Chinaman fish (*Symphorus nematophorus*), paddletail or red snapper (*Lutjanus gibbus*), red bass (*Lutjanus bohar*), and moray eel (*Gymnothorax* sp.).

Because of the cumulative nature of the poison, it is possible that one may on one occasion ingest a dose which is not sufficient to produce symptoms, and then on a subsequent occasion develop a fullblown case after eating what would normally be a subclinical dose of toxin.

Several members of Cook's crew got ciguatera in the New Hebrides (now Vanuatu), and a pig on board which was fed some of the suspect fish died the next day, in spite of the fish having been cooked together with a silver spoon. Other folklore heard even today says that ciguatera may be avoided by boiling the fish together with a coin, and perhaps both of these fables have a common origin. There is no fact known to support either notion. Ciguatoxin is heat stable and is not destroyed by cooking. While the water soluble fraction may be reduced by repeatedly soaking fillets and discarding the water (incidentally, the broth of boiled ciguatoxic fish is very poisonous), this will not prevent poisoning by the insoluble fraction.

Symptoms of ciguatera – abdominal pain, nausea, vomiting and diarrhoea – develop between two and twelve hours after ingestion (usually in about five hours). There is a developing numbness or tingling about the mouth and in the extremities, and victims experience a characteristic inversion of hot and cold perception (ice cream and cold drinks burn the mouth and throat, a cold can of beer feels hot). Muscle aches and pains are common. Sometimes victims say their teeth feel like they're falling out of their sockets, and that

they have a metallic taste in the mouth. Rash is common. Recovery usually occurs in forty-eight hours to one week. Tingling and disturbance of temperature perception may last much longer. A good dose of poison may produce subsequent allergic reactions, particularly to fish.

First aid
If the victim is conscious, induce vomiting; stick fingers down the throat or administer an emetic (syrup of ipecac). If a large amount of toxin has been ingested symptoms can be life-threatening, and medical attention should therefore always be sought.

Avoidance
- Never eat Chinaman fish, red bass or red snapper, paddletail or moray eel. And always ask the locals which other fish to avoid.
- Avoid eating any fish larger than four kilograms; bigger fish are likely to have larger accumulations of toxin.
- Don't eat repeated meals from the same fish.
- If there are more than the usual number of dead sea birds around, don't eat any fish for several weeks.

Envenomation
The kind of serious envenomations that visitors to the Queensland coast are at all likely to have to deal with are stonefish stings, box jellyfish and irukandji stings, snake bite, stingray wounds, cone shell stings, blue-ringed octopus bites, and sea snake bites. As unlikely as it is that any of these will occur, they are all discussed, along with tips for avoiding trouble and measures to be taken should they happen.

Fortunately our scientists have developed specific antivenoms for some of the worst offenders, but prevention is better than treatment, which may be many hours away.

Venoms have a number of ways of working their mischief – by such means as destroying blood cells, by inactivating nerves that control vital muscles, by poisoning muscle tissues

themselves. Some venoms do most damage at the site of injection; others, usually with more significant results, travel via the circulatory or lymphatic systems to places where they can disrupt the functioning of the body. It is important to prevent the systemic spread of venom by keeping the victim as still as possible; for example, walking should not be attempted in cases of snake bite on the leg. In other cases, venoms do local damage at the site of injection but do not produce serious systemic effects; in these cases it is best not to restrict the movement of venom from the wound.

Pressure-immobilisation
A procedure known as 'pressure-immobilisation' is now widely accepted in first aid for venomous bites and stings. It simply involves applying pressure generally to the bite and surrounding tissues which restricts the flow of venom through the lymphatic system; immobilising the affected limb prevents spread of the poison. Pressure-immobilisation is indicated in all cases of bites and stings which are not immediately painful (pain signifies that local tissue damage is taking place, and in these cases the procedure is sometimes not recommended). Pressure-immobilisation is recommended in all cases of snake bite, cone shell stings, blue-ringed octopus bite; it is not recommended for fish envenomations.

- Apply a broad crepe bandage (or any flexible material) over the site of the bite as soon as possible. Don't struggle with removal of pants or shirt if this requires a lot of movement of the affected limb. In cases of bites to the trunk, administration of pressure-immobilisation is more difficult but may be used if it doesn't impair breathing. In bites to the groin and neck, it is probably not feasible.
- Bandage over the wound and upwards (away from the toes or fingers) as tightly as you would bind a sprained ankle, extending

Poisonous Fishes

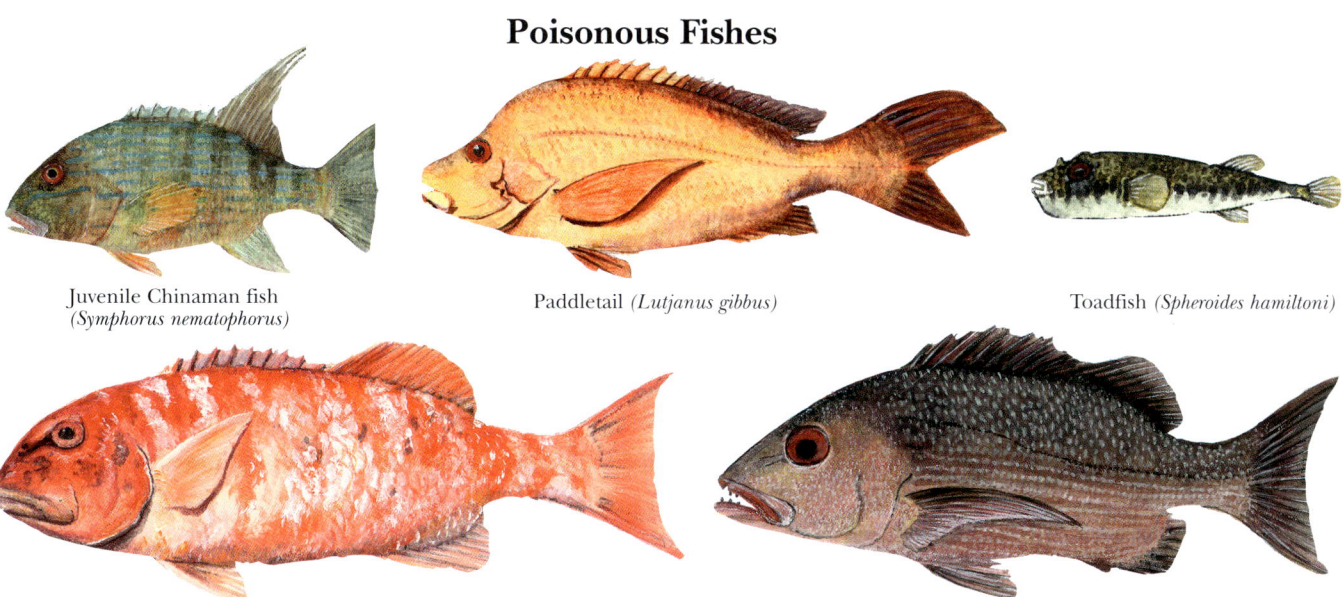

Juvenile Chinaman fish
(*Symphorus nematophorus*)

Paddletail (*Lutjanus gibbus*)

Toadfish (*Spheroides hamiltoni*)

Adult Chinaman fish (*Symphorus nematophorus*)
(note pit in front of eye)

Red Bass (*Lutjanus bohar*)

the bandage as high as possible. If the victim complains of discomfort it probably means that the bandage is too tight and it should be readjusted.

- Bind a splint firmly to as much of the limb as possible (up to the elbow in the case of an arm).
- Reassure the victim. Seek medical assistance.
- Bandages should be left in place until the victim is in capable hands and emergency resuscitation measures have been prepared.

Stonefish

There are two principal species of stone fish in Queensland – the estuarine stonefish (*Synanceia trachynis*) and the reef stonefish (*S. verrucosa*). The estuarine stonefish is much more common than the reef stonefish, but they are both equally ugly and equally poisonous.

Estuarine stonefish *(Synanceia trachynis)*

Stonefish are usually about 20 centimetres long, are scaleless, and their skin is covered with 'warts' and a slime which is toxic to small marine animals and which evidently tastes bitter (the mind boggles at the desperate hunger of the man who established this fact, his bravery far exceeding that even of the man who ate the first oyster). Stonefish have spines along their back which become erect when the fish is disturbed; these thirteen spines (which will appeal to the superstitious) are fitted with venom sacs. Normally, stonefish lie in rubble, defying detection. They scoop out a little nesting place with their large pectoral fins and wait for an unsuspecting fish to come by, whereupon the prey is 'inhaled as if by a rock with a hideous upturned frog mouth'. Man describes stonefish as 'lethargic' because they make little attempt to move even when discovered. Discovery must be a rarity; having managed to find one, if you take your eyes off it for one second it will be gone when you look back (actually, it won't have moved, but such is the quality of their deception). Stonefish can remain exposed at low tide apparently without ill effect – to themselves.

The skin on the spines, when these are trodden on, presses down over the venom sacks causing venom to explode upwards along the sheath. The spines are capable of penetrating the sole of a sneaker, and the experience of a local general practitioner over a number of years showed that about one-half of treated cases were wearing something on their feet. About three-quarters of stonefish wounds are to feet, one-quarter to hands.

Stonefish stings are agonisingly painful. No deaths have been reported in Australia (although some have been reported in the Indo-Pacific). There is laboratory evidence that the venom can produce loss of function in all types of muscle. The wound is usually accompanied by acute swelling, spreading up the limb from the wound, which may persist for many weeks.

First aid

- Control of pain is most important. Do not apply pressure-immobilisation. The venom is protein; soaking in hot water has been found useful in relieving pain (it should not be so hot as to scald).
- Antivenom is available and probably should be administered in all but mild cases.

Avoidance

- Always wear substantial footwear when reef fossicking or when walking on rubble around mainland beaches. Don't run in these areas.

Stingray

Stingrays are flattened sharks that lie on the sea bottom looking for shells to crunch up with their pavement of flat teeth. They flick sand onto their backs, and very often the first hint of their presence is when one 'explodes' from the sand immediately in front of or just between your feet! Rays are timid, and given the chance they will move away rather than do battle. For this reason it is always a good idea to shuffle one's feet or to carry a stick with which to 'test' the sand in front.

A foot planted on the back of a stingray makes it very difficult for the ray to fly away; its response is a forwards/upwards flick of the tail, which is armed with venomous, serrated spines. A similar response may be evoked by divers or snorkellers cruising close over the bottom, in which case the whole torso is offered as a target instead of just a foot or leg. Wounds to the trunk are possibly worse than those to the limbs.

As much damage, if not more, is done by the physical trauma caused by the barbed spines as is done by the stingray venom itself, which, like that of the stonefish, is protein. The wounds may be ugly, painful, and they are invariably contaminated with animal tissue and foreign matter that needs to be cleaned out. It is likely that proper treatment will be beyond the capability and the resources of the average holidaymaker, and medical attention for these wounds is a good idea. Considering the great number of rays that are about, it is surprising that there are so few wounds inflicted by them.

As is true with a number of venomous fishes, the sting apparatus can be dangerous long after the animal is dead, so treat dead rays with some respect.

First aid

- Pressure-immobilisation is not recommended.
- Wash the wound and clean it out thoroughly to remove venom and foreign tissue that may be in it.
- Hot water may be useful in controlling pain. Because of the nature of these wounds and possible loss of sensitivity in the affected limb, it is recommended that the unaffected foot or leg also be soaked in hot water of the same temperature to provide some gauge as to how much heat is 'too much'; overcooking the wounded limb may lead to serious complications.

Avoidance

- Shuffle your feet or prod the sand in front of you with a stick when walking in stingray country, i.e. shallow sand and mud flats.
- Don't cruise close along sandy bottom when diving or snorkelling.

Zebrafish, fire cod
Pterois volitans – butterfly cod, lionfish

Butterfly cod *(Pterois volitans)*

Butterfly cod are found around coral reefs. Curious creatures, they will sometimes approach divers in the water, pointing their dorsal spines in front of them as they get near. These spines have glands that produce venom akin to that of one species of stonefish. It produces a severely distressing sting, which usually subsides within a couple of hours (although it can last for several days). Local effects of the sting are usually the most significant (vomiting and fever are sometimes reported).

First aid

- Immerse the wound in hot (but not scalding) water. Do not use pressure- immobilisation.

Conus sp. – cone shells

Cone shells are numerous (some seventy species) in Australian waters, some seven species being potentially dangerous to man. They have beautifully patterned and coloured shells, although their beauty is not always obvious due to a thick green covering of slime.

Cones are carnivorous gastropods that inhabit shallow intertidal waters of coral reefs, where they remain buried or under a rock by day and come out at night to do their marauding. They eat worms, fish, other gastropods and octopuses, all of which they immobilise with a poisoned 'harpoon'. This barbed tooth, of up to a centimetre in length, is firmly held in the end of the proboscis and is jammed into their prey while venom is squeezed through the tooth cavity. Each barbed tooth is used only once, which is usually enough, although cones have a quiverful of them held in reserve. Cones can distend their proboscis to envelope an object about their own size. They have an acute sense of smell which they localise by sampling the water with their waving tube-like siphon.

The species that eat fish are potentially most dangerous to man, but since you cannot ask them what they eat, it is best to assume that, whatever that cone is that you shouldn't have in your hand, it is potentially lethal. A myth has been perpetuated that cones can safely be held by the thick end; alas, they can reach either end from the cleft in their shell, so don't pick them up and don't slip them into your pocket.

The sting is sometimes very painful, and it may be followed by incoordination and muscular weakness, blurred vision, difficulty in swallowing, slurred speech; the ultimate symptom is respiratory paralysis. There have been some sixteen reported fatalities.

First aid
● Immediately apply pressure-immobilisation and be ready to give resuscitation. Keep the bandages in place until medical assistance and resuscitation equipment are available. Prolonged resuscitation may be required.

Avoidance
● Don't pick up cone shells.

Sea snakes
Virtually unknown in the Atlantic Ocean, there are some thirty-two species of sea snakes recorded in northern Australian waters. Lucky us! Sea snakes look like their land brethren but have flaps over their nostrils and a paddle-like tail which aids their swimming. Their nostrils, flattened tail and scaly appearance helps to differentiate them from eels. They can absorb about one-fifth of their oxygen requirements directly from the water and are capable of extended (two-hour), deep (100 metre) dives. They shed their skin frequently, perhaps every two weeks, which solves their antifouling problems. Most are born alive at sea.

One hears some conflicting opinion about the danger of sea snakes, and caution is prudent. Their venom is very toxic, but they do not put out a great deal; pain is notably absent and this may be a distinguishing feature in the case of bites of unknown origin received at night. Clinical illness following bites is evidently uncommon.

Some say sea snakes are curious, some say they can be downright aggressive (at mating time), and both of these observations may be valid. Divers say that their 'curiosity' can be a damned nuisance. When they bite a flipper, they continue to hang on, probably behaviour required in the marine environment to avoid losing prey. Sea snakes are not all that frequently seen in the Whitsundays.

Where first-aid measures are not taken, symptoms of bites occur within half an hour and include visual disturbance, muscular weakness, pain, progressing in severe cases to paralysis and respiratory failure. Antivenom is available for treatment of bites.

First aid
● Pressure-immobilisation and resuscitation.

Hapalochlaena maculosa – blue-ringed octopus
The blue-ringed octopus is found all around Australia and is the only octopus with a potentially lethal bite. It is very small (only about twenty centimetres from the tip of one arm/leg to another) and has a characteristic dark brown to ochre coloured body with blue rings which 'glow' brightly when it is disturbed, making it 'irresistible' to people who happen upon it in shallow rock pools where it fossicks for crabs, its favourite food. The octopus has a small beak at the junction of its eight arms and, unlike many other octopuses, it manufactures a toxic saliva rather than ink. The toxin closely resembles tetrodotoxin, and its bite can produce flabby paralysis very much more rapidly than after puffer fish is consumed because the poison is injected rather than absorbed from the victim's gut. The bite may be almost imperceptible, many victims having been unaware that they were bitten except for a tiny drop of blood at the site. Bites have always occurred when the creature is being handled out of water, for example picked up and draped over an arm, hand or shoulder.

First aid
● Speed of action is important. Apply pressure-immobilisation immediately.
● Give resuscitation if necessary. Get the victim to medical help as soon as possible.

Avoidance
● These octopuses never bother any human unless picked up out of water. Tell children to leave them alone, irresistible though they may be with their glowing blue circles.

Box jellyfish
The box jellyfish (*Chironex fleckeri*) is a potential hazard to swimmers along the Queensland coast north from Gladstone from November through May. The peak season along the Whitsunday mainland seems to be March–April.

Chironex belongs to a class of cuboid jellyfishes so-called because of their box-like shape. They are agile swimmers and are capable of maintaining a pace of three to four knots all day; they can swim at a rate of five knots in a sprint. They have four sensory organs that register posture and attitude, change of direction, change of light intensity, and one of their 'eyes' has a convex lens capable of forming crude images. When approached slowly at an oblique angle (not directly ahead or behind) they will move away, and they tend to avoid dark objects in the water. Stings often occur when swimmers rush headlong into the water, not giving it a chance to get away.

The extended threads of the nematocysts are 0.2 millimetres long – long enough to penetrate the skin of most adults (except that on the palms of the hands and undersides of the fingers, where the skin is thicker). An encounter with the tentacles can produce a very high number of individual envenomations over a broad area. Only those nematocysts in contact with the skin discharge.

Box jellyfish (Chironex fleckeri)

Robert Hartwick

The venom is an extremely toxic protein that affects the skin, blood and the heart muscle. When the bell of a box jellyfish is more than eleven centimetres in diameter, stings are extremely severe, with death a probability if the total length of weals is greater than six to seven metres. The stings produce a characteristic frosted crosshatching on the skin. Children are very susceptible because their skin is thin and because, relative to their body weight, they receive a high dose of venom.

Box jellyfish are creatures of the mainland coast rather than outer Whitsunday islands. The adults breed in coastal rivers and estuaries, and in summer they come out of the rivers and cruise along the coastal shores, patrolling for little prawns which they find in dense accumulations just outside the 'chop zone' where detritus is stirred up from the bottom by the waves. They tend to stay offshore from beaches in rough weather. They are seldom found far from the mainland. The classic weather to watch out for is glassy calm or light northerly winds.

Household vinegar is the most effective readily available commodity to inactivate the nematocysts, and this is the recommended first step before attempting to remove any adhering tentacles. Vinegar is recommended for all cuboid jellyfish stings e.g. *Chironex, Tamoya sp.*, irukandji, jimble). Vinegar has no effect on the venom nor the damage it has caused, but it does prevent any unfired nematocysts from going off and causing a more serious envenomation.

'Stinger suits' are sold throughout Queensland and are worn by many locals during the stinger season, November–May.

First aid – *Chironex*
● Remove the victim from the water. Douse the area of the sting and any adhering tentacles with household vinegar for at least thirty seconds before attempting to remove them. Do not rub with sand.
● Be prepared to give resuscitation. Seek medical help.
● Pain is usually only temporarily relieved by topical applications.
● Antivenom is available; early administration will help reduce the incidence of scarring.

Avoidance
● Listen for jellyfish alerts and observe signs on beaches during the November–May season.
● During the season when swimming on

mainland beaches (if not in a stinger-free enclosure) wear protective clothing or a 'stinger suit'.
- Don't rush headlong down the beach into the water.

Carukia barnesi – irukandji

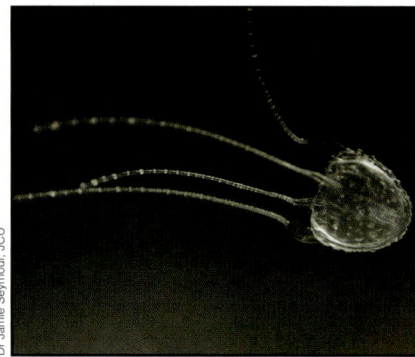

*Irukandji (*Carukia barnesi*) has a single tentacle emanating from each corner of the bell. Venom is delivered by nematocysts (stinging cells) on both the bell and the tentacles. Nematocysts may be evenly distributed along the tentacle or aggregated creating a 'string-of-pearls' appearance. This is a relatively small jellyfish (about 25 mm across) and is almost transparent in the water, making it difficult to spot. Most victims never see the animal that stung them.*

Irukandji is a very small, cuboid jellyfish (10–25 mm) that has been associated with deaths in recent years. There may actually be as many as six species of irukandji, most of which are as yet undescribed by science. Irukandji have four tentacles only, one emanating from each corner of the bell; they also have stinging cells on the bell itself as well as the tentacles. They are nearly transparent, which makes them very difficult to spot in the water. Their small size means they can pass through the stinger enclosures on mainland beaches that protect swimmers from the larger box jellyfish.

Whereas the box jellyfish inflicts an immediately excruciatingly painful sting, the irukandji sting is often barely noticed, perhaps only mildly painful with a goose-pimple effect and redness around the sting site. Most victims have not seen what stung them. Then, 20–30 minutes later, in some cases a symptom complex emerges – severe lower back pain; excruciating muscle cramps in all four limbs, the abdomen and chest; sweating; anxiety (a sense of 'impending doom' is often reported); restlessness, nausea, vomiting, headache; palpitations; spiking blood pressure. Medical help should be sought immediately if this symptom complex is present. It is encouraging to note that some success in reversing the syndrome has been achieved in hospitals by the intravenous administration of magnesium.

Unlike *Chironex*, which inhabits mainland estuaries and patrols coastal beaches, irukandji make their home at coral reefs. Spawning aggregations may occur on offshore reefs 8–10 days after a full moon. Their presence closer to the mainland may be higher after two days of north to north-east winds together with an afternoon high tide. The incidence of stings has varied greatly, the greatest number having occurred when there were loſng periods of onshore northerly winds.

Irukandji are attſracted to lights at night, and for this reason night-divers should not enter the water under lights (dive boats often play lights into the water at the other end of the vessel in order to draw them away).

Stings usually occur in water deeper than one metre and just below the surface – usually on the trunk or upper arms of swimmers or on the back or back of the neck when divers surface. Only 24% of reported stings have been on the face, hands and feet, so wearing a 'Lycra' stinger suit may help to avert as much as 75% of potential stings, and if a face mask, gloves and booties are also worn, a high degree of prevention may be achieved. (A stinger suit will also help to protect against sunburn and minor scratches which become infected quickly in tropical waters.)

First aid – irukandji
- Douse with vinegar (to inactivate undischarged nematocysts) and apply a vinegar-soaked pad.
- Restrain the victim (or others) from rubbing the site of the sting.
- Reassure victim and seek medical aid immediately.

Avoidance
- Wear a stinger suit when in the water, particularly during the summer months.

Carybdea rastoni – jimble
The jimble is another small (1–3 centimetres) cuboid jellyfish, transparent, with four tentacles, one at each corner, measuring 5–30 centimetres depending upon whether or not they are retracted. Jimbles rise to the surface in the morning and evening, are active swimmers, and can deliver an immediately painful sting (characterised frequently by four weals, sometimes with a sharp bend producing a box-like shape on the skin) which may last for several hours.

First aid – jimble
- Douse adhering tentacles with household vinegar.
- Apply cold packs for ten minutes. Reapply cold packs if skin pain persists.
- Send for medical aid if symptoms persist.

Cyanea capillata, C. sp. – sea blubber, hairy stinger, sea nettle, hairy jelly, lion's mane
The sea blubber has been described as a repulsive big slimy jellyfish that resembles a mop hiding under a dinner plate (Barnes). It has a large, flattened bell (25–30 centimetres across) and is found all around Australia. The sting is characterised by white weals which rapidly change to bright red zigzags with surrounding red flare. Sometimes nausea and abdominal pains develop after stings.

First aid – Cyanea
- Wash sting area with water.
- Apply cold packs for ten minutes; reapply if skin pain persists.
- Send for medical aid if symptoms persist.

Pelagia noctiluca – little mauve stinger
'Little mauve stinger' pronounced rapidly and indistinctly sounds like what a resident of Harlem might say after being stung by one. They are found all around Australia, have a rounded, mushroom-shaped body (4–12 centimetres in diameter) with wartlike nematocysts on their mauve to pink-coloured bodies. The brownish-yellow tentacles vary in length from ten to thirty centimetres. The sting can be painful, but is seldom serious, producing irregularly shaped weals that look like insect stings or hives.

First aid – Pelagia
- Wash sting area with water.
- Apply cold packs for ten minutes; reapply if skin pain persists.
- Send for medical aid if symptoms persist.

Physalia physalis – bluebottle, Portuguese man-of-war
Bluebottles occur right around Australia. This jellyfish with its inflated pale translucent blue bag for a sail is actually a colony of specialised animals, some of which are the sail trimmers and some the executioners (the latter being the mass of deep blue stingers, some quite long). The sting is painful and produces a characteristic line of separate oval weals, white in the centre with red edges.

First aid – Physalia
- Wash sting area with water.
- Apply cold packs for ten minutes; reapply if skin pain persists.
- Send for medical aid if symptoms persist.

Catostylus sp. – blubber jellyfish
The blubber jellyfish has been called a giant mushroom wearing frilly pants. It is milky-white to brown with a large bell (up to thirty centimetres). Easily seen and avoided, the sting is usually mild.

First aid – Catostylus
- Wash sting area with water.
- Apply cold packs for ten minutes; reapply if skin pain persists.
- Send for medical aid if symptoms persist.

Lytocarpus phillipinus – stinging hydroid
These beautiful white fern-like 'plants' pack a sting which belies their appearance. They have a penchant for finding the gaps in divers' wet suits, and any contact can produce an extremely uncomfortable sting with rash and, in more severe cases, gastro-intestinal symptoms.

First aid – stinging hydroid
- Apply cold packs for ten minutes. Reapply if skin pain persists.

Millepora sp. – fire coral, stinging coral
Millepora looks like greenish-brown staghorn coral with white–yellow tips. It has thousands of minute 'pores' (hence the name) through which it can poke its nematocysts. If it touches bare skin, millepora can produce an uncomfortable burning itchy sting with swelling and, in severe cases, associated nausea and vomiting.

First aid – stinging coral
- Apply cold packs for ten minutes. Reapply if skin pain persists.

David Collett

ANCHORAGES
IN THE WHITSUNDAYS

The following pages contain sketch maps and sailing directions covering the principal anchorages of the Whitsundays and some of the adjacent mainland from Bowen in the north to Mackay in the south. They will be immensely helpful to anyone making their way around the area, and they may provide an interesting souvenir record for others. Also included are some aerial photographs to provide another view of some of the anchorages.

The maps (and photographs, where present) are in four groups:

Group	Sketch Map	Location covered
Northern	N1–N15	Bowen to Airlie Beach
Central	C1–C33	Airlie Beach to Lindeman I
Southern	S1–S21	Lindeman I. to Mackay
Reef	R1–R1b	Hook/Hardy/Line/Bait Reefs

Photographs communicate a wealth of information at a single glance and may be helpful when used in conjunction with the sketch maps.

A word of caution

The sketch maps have been prepared from vertical aerial photographs. The authors have endeavoured to make them reliable by using maps and charts as cross-references. However, the sketch maps were not prepared for navigation and they should not under any circumstances be used as a substitute for the official Hydrographic Office charts. For navigation you should always refer to the largest-scale official Hydrographic Office chart. The publishers and authors expressly disclaim responsibility and liability for any error or omission in any sketch map arising out of reliance upon any sketch map for navigation.

The Hydrograhic Office Charts

The Hydrographic Office now issues metric charts of the Whitsunday area. The most important charts for the Whitsundays are:

AUS 250

Plans for Hay Point and Mackay Harbour
Scale: 1:10 000

AUS 251

Bailey Islet to Repulse Islands, including the Sir James Smith Group, Brampton & Carlisle islands, Goldsmith & Linne islands, Keswick & St Bees islands
Scale: 1:75 000

AUS 252

Whitsunday Group & Laguna Quays
Scale: 1:75 000; 1:12 500

AUS 253

Whitsunday Passage & Shute Harbour
Scale: 1:37 500; 1:15 000

AUS 254

Plans in the Whitsundays: Lindeman I., Fitzalan Passage, Hayman I., Stonehaven, Hamilton I., Dent I., Hook Reef
Scale: 1:75 000; 1:12 500

AUS 268

Plans of Airlie Beach & Bowen,
Gloucester Passage, Approaches to Bowen
Scale: 1:25 000; 1:10 000

AUS 825

Whitsunday Islands to Bowen
Scale: 1:150 000

Top: Bauer Bay, South Molle Island, looking north to Mid Molle and North Molle islands.

THE AREA COVERED

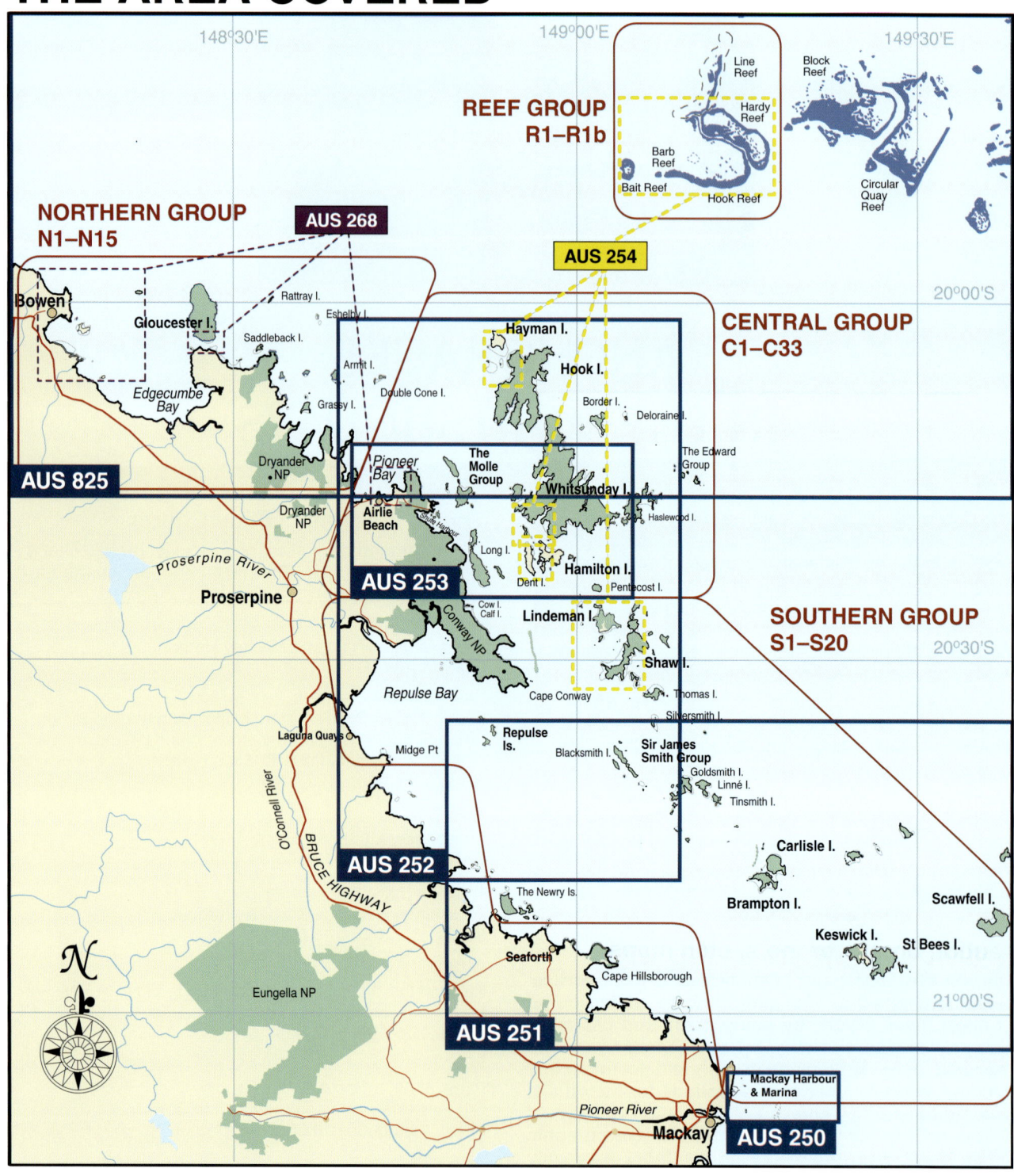

About the sketch maps

Sketch map sequence

The cruising area has been divided into northern, central southern and reef sections, and the sketch maps each have a corresponding letter prefix 'N', 'C', 'S' and 'R'. The order of the maps is generally from north to south, as illustrated below, according to the way yachts often circulate among the islands. A few maps that were added at a later date, e.g. Laguna Whitsundays, Cape Conway, the Repulse Islands and Newry Island, have been placed at the end of the southern ('S') group.

At the top, bottom and sides of most sketch maps is found an adjoining map reference, e.g. 'joins sketch map N15' (where maps are contiguous) or 'next sketch map N15' (where sketch maps do not butt up against each other). The sides of contiguous maps may not necessarily butt squarely.

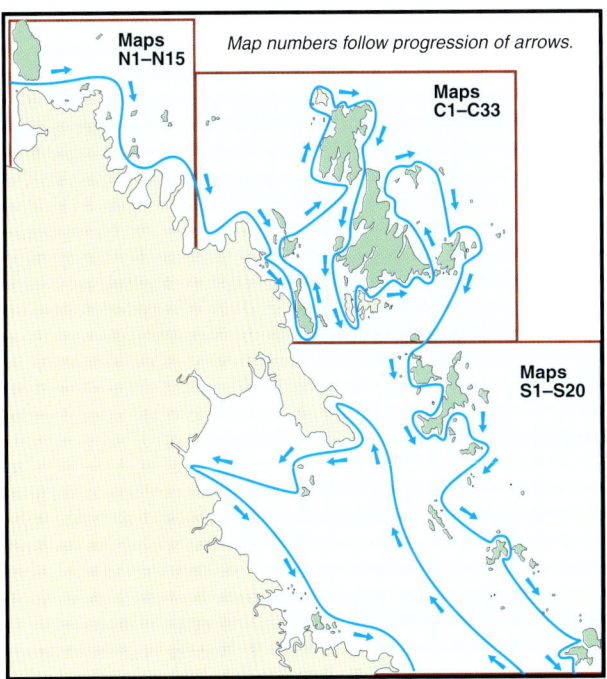

Caution on use of the sketch maps

Although every effort has been made to make the maps and descriptions in this book as accurate as possible, there may be errors, including some displacement errors in the maps (caused by using uncorrected aerial photographs). **The maps cannot be used for position fixing.** They are intended to assist with orientation, to help you read the charts more easily and to provide some additional details, but you should always use the official Hydrographic Office charts for navigation. The publisher and the authors expressly disclaim responsibility and liability for any error or omission in any sketch map or arising out of reliance on any sketch map for navigation.

Scale

The scale of the sketch maps varies from approximately 1:14 000 to 1:32 000. It may be useful to note that on a 1:30 000 chart a 1-millimetre line represents a distance of 30 metres. Every attempt has been made to maintain the appropriate scale of charted objects, but this is sometimes not practicable (as in the case of buoys, etc.).

Soundings, elevations, distances

Depths on the sketch maps are in metres and tenths of metres (e.g. 3_4 is 3.4 metres). Elevations of principal landmarks (in metres) are shown in parentheses. Distances over water continue the world over to be measured in 'nautical miles' (referred to simply as 'miles' in this book) rather than kilometres. A nautical mile is about 1852 metres. Its origin is fundamental to our whole system of navigation, which measures in degrees of longitude and latitude and which is based upon a notion of angles measured from the centre of the earth to the earth's surface. One minute of latitude at the earth's surface ($1/60$ of a degree) is one 'nautical mile', and it is that distance described by one minute of angle measured from the earth's centre. (Other nautical measurements, such as the fathom, are also based upon the nautical mile – the fathom is about $1/100$ of a nautical mile, the cable $1/10$ of a nautical mile.) That the nautical mile refused to fit into a neat metric package incensed the Metric Conversion Board when Australia underwent metrication in the late 1960s (they at first insisted that we use metres, but the issue was too big for them). Metres *are* used on the sketch maps for measuring *small* distances, such as a rock or shoal a short distance away; this is because a small figure, such as 100 metres, is easier to comprehend than, say, '0.054 mile' would be.

Anchorage symbols

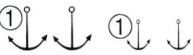

Numbers are used to differentiate anchorages where there are several in close proximity. In some cases anchor symbols are not numbered (where there is no ambiguity, or where maps overlap and the unnumbered anchorage is discussed on a different page). A small anchor denotes a temporary anchorage provided the weather is suitable; these are rarely suitable overnight anchorages.

Anchorage diagrams

CATERAN BAY (C29)

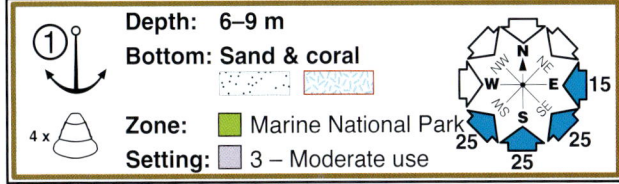

At the beginning of the descriptions of anchorages throughout the remainder of this book there is a graphic giving information about the depth, type of bottom, wind conditions in which the anchorage is 'comfortable', as well as marine park zoning information (in the square labelled 'Zone'), usage settings under the Whitsunday Management Plan (in the square labelled 'Setting'), and an indication of whether there are moorings in the anchorage. Be aware of the marine park zoning information (see pages 110–111 for a zoning map) as it has a direct impact on some activities (for example, fishing is not permitted in a green zone). A brown border within the black border of the graphic indicates a 'nil discharge area' (no flushing of marine toilets – see more about discharge of sewage later in this section).

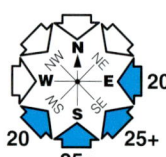

The wind directions and strengths (in knots) in which an anchorage is considered habitable (with some degree of comfort when on an anchor) are shown with arrows around an 8-point compass rose.

An infilled blue arrow indicates that the anchorage offers protection in winds from that direction; the number next to the arrow indicates in how much wind it will be 'comfortable'. White arrows without numbers indicate that not a lot of protection is available, i.e. if it's blowing more than 10 knots from that direction, the anchorage may not be comfortable.

Reef protection markers

Reef protection markers (white, pyramid-shaped buoys) have been installed in a number of bays where coral damage has been a problem. They delineate no-anchor areas, i.e. anchoring inshore of an imaginary straight line between the buoys is prohibited. They are not suitable to use as a mooring, and using them as such is not allowed.

Moorings

There are presently two different types of moorings in the Whitsundays: public moorings, available to all vessels including recreational and commercial users, and private, or 'service', moorings usually owned by resorts or commercial operators or located in marinas. Public moorings (blue, beehive-shaped moorings) have been installed to protect coral from anchor damage, to enhance public access to popular bays and to facilitate reef appreciation. Private moorings (in various colours) are privately owned and can be used with the permission of the owner (a list of private mooring permits is available at *www.gbrmpa.gov.au* (search for 'mooring register')).

A list of public mooring locations may be found on the opposite page.

Reef appreciation/protection moorings

There are public moorings in a number of anchorages as well. Public moorings have a blue beehive-shaped float with colour-coded band indicating the size of vessel that may occupy the mooring.

They have an engraved tag on the pennant that describes conditions of use (see page 74 for more about moorings).

Public moorings may be occupied for a maximum of 2 hours during the day (between 0700 and 1700 hours), or they may be occupied overnight provided they are picked up after 1500 hours (in other words, the vessel legally occupying the mooring at 1700 hours may stay there overnight).

Public moorings have been placed carefully, sometimes in fairly close proximity to reefs. Follow the use instructions for your own safety, and **never lengthen the pennant by any means**, as this may allow you to swing too close to an obstruction.

On the sketch maps the colour-coded public mooring symbols are used. Private moorings are shown thus ⬣.

A generic mooring symbol is used in the anchorage description summary boxes already referred to. The generic symbol is: ⬣.

Moorings locations

Moorings have been installed in the areas of highest use in the central islands (see oppsite). Moorings can be subject to misadventures from propellors and storms and are periodically removed for maintenance, so from time to time they may not be in place as shown in this book.

Anchoring in some areas not advisable

In a number of locations, for example, Pioneer Bay and Airlie Beach (sketch map C1), Shute Harbour (C3), South Molle Island (C9) and in the Dent Passage opposite Hamilton Harbor (C22), there are what are known as designated 'Small Craft Mooring Areas'. These are bounded on the sketch maps by a broken orange line like the one around this text. Anchoring within the area should be avoided. The moorings have allotted positions in a grid with adequate minimum swing room. Anchoring within a designated grid style mooring area could compromise the swing room and may lead to vessels coming into contact, possibly damaging each other. Legally this would constitute 'a marine incident' and a penalty could be incurred.

The Great Barrier Reef Marine Park

The waters around the islands are part of the Great Barrier Reef Marine Park, and visitors should be aware of the various park zones that exist and how these may impinge on certain activities (see zoning map and other information on pages 107–115).

Whitsunday management settings

The day-to-day management of the Marine Park is carried out by Queensland Parks and Wildlife Service (QPWS) in conjunction with the Great Barrier Reef Marine Park Authority (GBRMPA), which has overall responsibility for this World Heritage Area. The Authority's zoning plan provides the basis for overall management of the Marine Park, which stretches from Bundaberg in the south to Cape York in the north. Fine adjustments in managing the local Whitsunday area are made by the Whitsundays

LOCATION OF MOORINGS IN THE CENTRAL WHITSUNDAY AREA

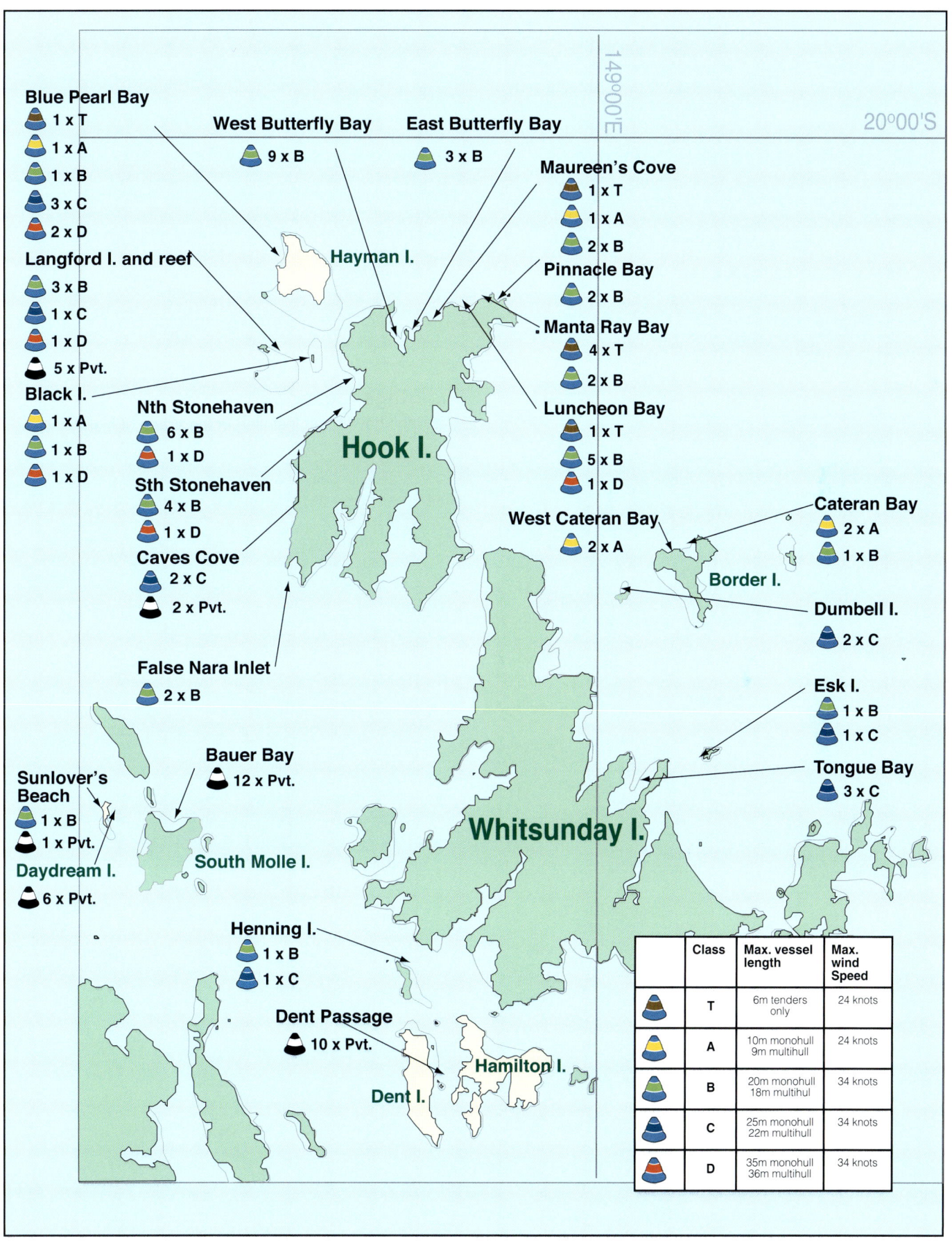

Blue Pearl Bay
- 1 x T
- 1 x A
- 1 x B
- 3 x C
- 2 x D

Langford I. and reef
- 3 x B
- 1 x C
- 1 x D
- 5 x Pvt.

Black I.
- 1 x A
- 1 x B
- 1 x D

West Butterfly Bay
- 9 x B

East Butterfly Bay
- 3 x B

Hayman I.

Maureen's Cove
- 1 x T
- 1 x A
- 2 x B

Pinnacle Bay
- 2 x B

Manta Ray Bay
- 4 x T
- 2 x B

Luncheon Bay
- 1 x T
- 5 x B
- 1 x D

Nth Stonehaven
- 6 x B
- 1 x D

Sth Stonehaven
- 4 x B
- 1 x D

Caves Cove
- 2 x C
- 2 x Pvt.

False Nara Inlet
- 2 x B

Hook I.

West Cateran Bay
- 2 x A

Cateran Bay
- 2 x A
- 1 x B

Border I.

Dumbell I.
- 2 x C

Esk I.
- 1 x B
- 1 x C

Tongue Bay
- 3 x C

Sunlover's Beach
- 1 x B
- 1 x Pvt.

Daydream I.
- 6 x Pvt.

Bauer Bay
- 12 x Pvt.

South Molle I.

Whitsunday I.

Henning I.
- 1 x B
- 1 x C

Dent Passage
- 10 x Pvt.

Hamilton I.

Dent I.

	Class	Max. vessel length	Max. wind Speed
	T	6m tenders only	24 knots
	A	10m monohull 9m multihull	24 knots
	B	20m monohull 18m multihul	34 knots
	C	25m monohull 22m multihull	34 knots
	D	35m monohull 36m multihull	34 knots

149°00'E

20°00'S

Plan of Management, which provides an overlay of five settings, ranging from Setting 1 (Developed) to Setting 5 (Protected). As these names suggest, different types of activities are permitted in the different setting areas. See pages 108–113 for more explanation of marine park zones and settings.

GPS positions in the Whitsundays

Satellite derived positions can be transcribed directly onto the Hydrographic Office metric charts for the Whitsundays. No reference to GPS positions is madeon sketch maps in this book as they are not designed for navigation.

Environmental notes

Throughout the Anchorages section (as space permits) we have placed some reminders that should be borne in mind for the benefit of the environment and the enjoyment of the Whitsunday experience.

Anchor over sand or mud and avoid coral to prevent further damage to the reefs.

Feeding sea gulls turns them into pests. Thereafter, they badger humans for food, and they can also become a positive threat to other seabirds.

Try to avoid disturbing seabirds (you can tell when they're upset by their agitated behaviour – circling, squawking, divebombing). Observe access restrictions and speed limits around significant bird sites, which are marked with red broken circles on the sketch maps.
(See also pages 114–115.)

Don't fish in a green zone (Marine National Park Zone), and observe the fishing restrictions within a yellow zone (Conservation Park Zone). Be mindful of size and bag limits and seasonal closures when these apply (see pages 88–93).

Discharge of sewage in Whitsunday waters

It is a requirement in Queensland waters that any vessel with a fixed toilet must also have a macerator installed (that cannot be bypassed) to facilitate the dispersal of waste and reduce visual pollution. Moreover, it is illegal in Queensland to discharge treated or untreated sewage in a boat harbour, a canal, a marina or a designated 'Prohibited Discharge Area' (see below for what this means in practice for Whitsunday cruising). The rules vary depending upon the type of ship and number of persons on board. In summary, in the Whitsunday area, the discharge of untreated sewage is prohibited in:

For vessels carrying 6 or fewer persons:

(1) boat harbours, marinas, canals, designated smooth waters, rivers and creeks

(2) designated Prohibited Discharge Areas*

(3) within 1/2 nautical mile of a wharf or jetty (that is not a marina)

(4) within 1 nautical mile of an aquaculture fisheries resource (e.g. oyster lease, prawn farm, etc.)

For vessels carrying 7–15 persons, the above rules (1)–(4) apply and in addition, discharge of untreated sewage is prohibited:

(5) within 1 nautical mile of a reef, or the mean low water mark of an island or the mainland

For vessels carrying 16 or more persons, discharge is prohibited:

(6) anywhere in Queensland waters

*Prohibited Discharge Areas which are relevant to anchorages in the Whitsunday area:

(a) along the northern side of Hook Island from the Woodpile to Alcyonaria Point (sketch map C14/15);

(b) within 100m of Border Island (C29);

(c) around the western and southern sides of Haslewood Island (C31);

(d) the southern anchorage (No. 4) at Carlisle Island and anchorage (No. 1) at Brampton island (off the jetty) (S11);

(e) the southern anchorage (No. 4) at Scawfell Island (S16).

For full details and the most up-to-date requirements, always refer to the Maritime Safety Queensland website http://www.msq.qld.gov.au.

General Legend

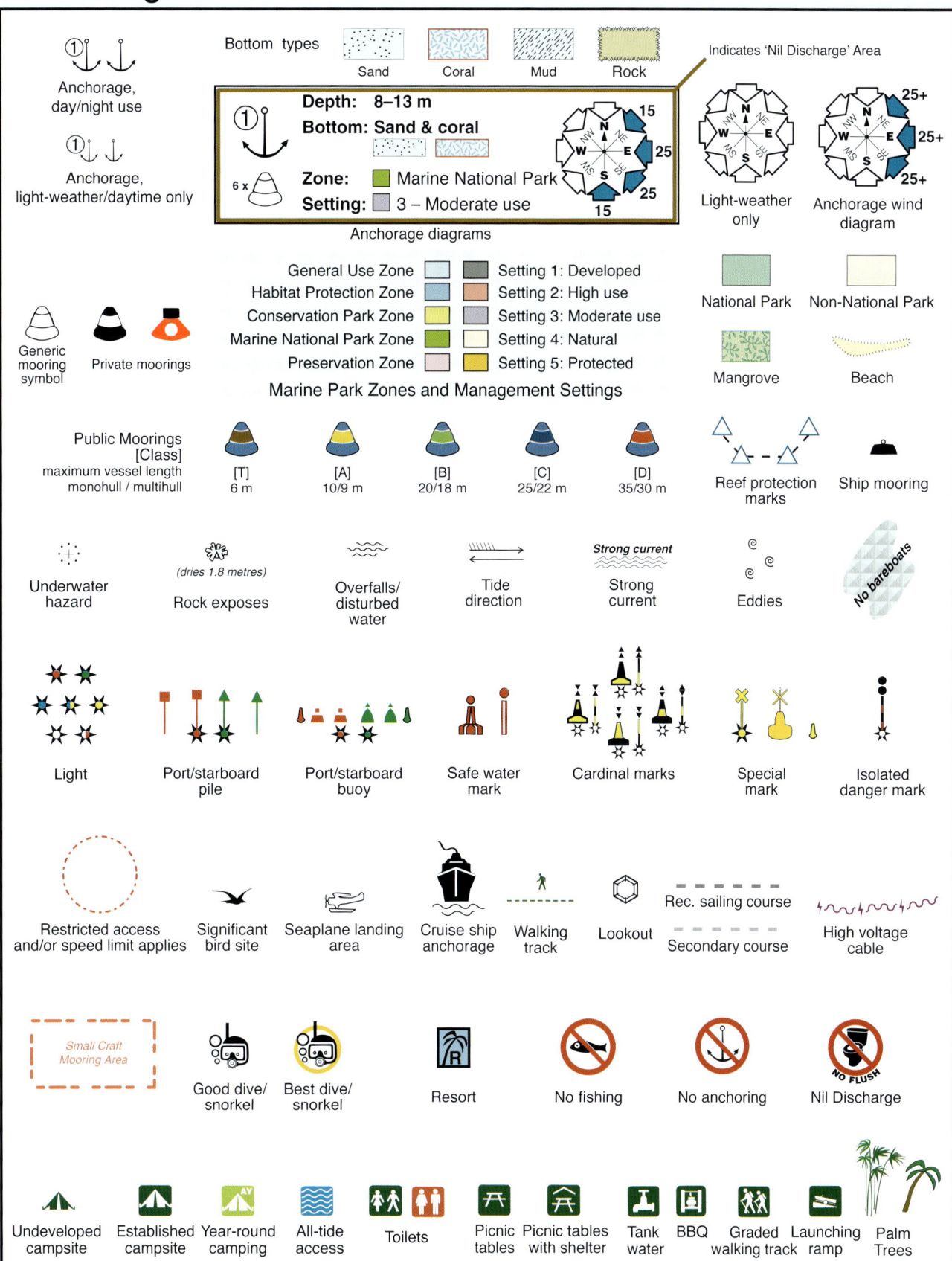

Anchorage, day/night use

Anchorage, light-weather/daytime only

Bottom types — Sand, Coral, Mud, Rock

Indicates 'Nil Discharge' Area

Depth: 8–13 m
Bottom: Sand & coral
Zone: Marine National Park
Setting: 3 – Moderate use
6 x
Anchorage diagrams

Light-weather only

Anchorage wind diagram

Generic mooring symbol — **Private moorings**

General Use Zone · Setting 1: Developed
Habitat Protection Zone · Setting 2: High use
Conservation Park Zone · Setting 3: Moderate use
Marine National Park Zone · Setting 4: Natural
Preservation Zone · Setting 5: Protected
Marine Park Zones and Management Settings

National Park · Non-National Park

Mangrove · Beach

Public Moorings [Class]
maximum vessel length
monohull / multihull

[T] 6 m · [A] 10/9 m · [B] 20/18 m · [C] 25/22 m · [D] 35/30 m

Reef protection marks · **Ship mooring**

Underwater hazard · **Rock exposes** *(dries 1.8 metres)* · **Overfalls/ disturbed water** · **Tide direction** · ***Strong current*** · **Eddies** · **No bareboats**

Light · **Port/starboard pile** · **Port/starboard buoy** · **Safe water mark** · **Cardinal marks** · **Special mark** · **Isolated danger mark**

Restricted access and/or speed limit applies · **Significant bird site** · **Seaplane landing area** · **Cruise ship anchorage** · **Walking track** · **Lookout** · **Rec. sailing course** / **Secondary course** · **High voltage cable**

Small Craft Mooring Area · **Good dive/ snorkel** · **Best dive/ snorkel** · **Resort** · **No fishing** · **No anchoring** · **Nil Discharge**

Undeveloped campsite · **Established campsite** · **Year-round camping** · **All-tide access** · **Toilets** · **Picnic tables** · **Picnic tables with shelter** · **Tank water** · **BBQ** · **Graded walking track** · **Launching ramp** · **Palm Trees**

THE NORTHERN GROUP N1–N15

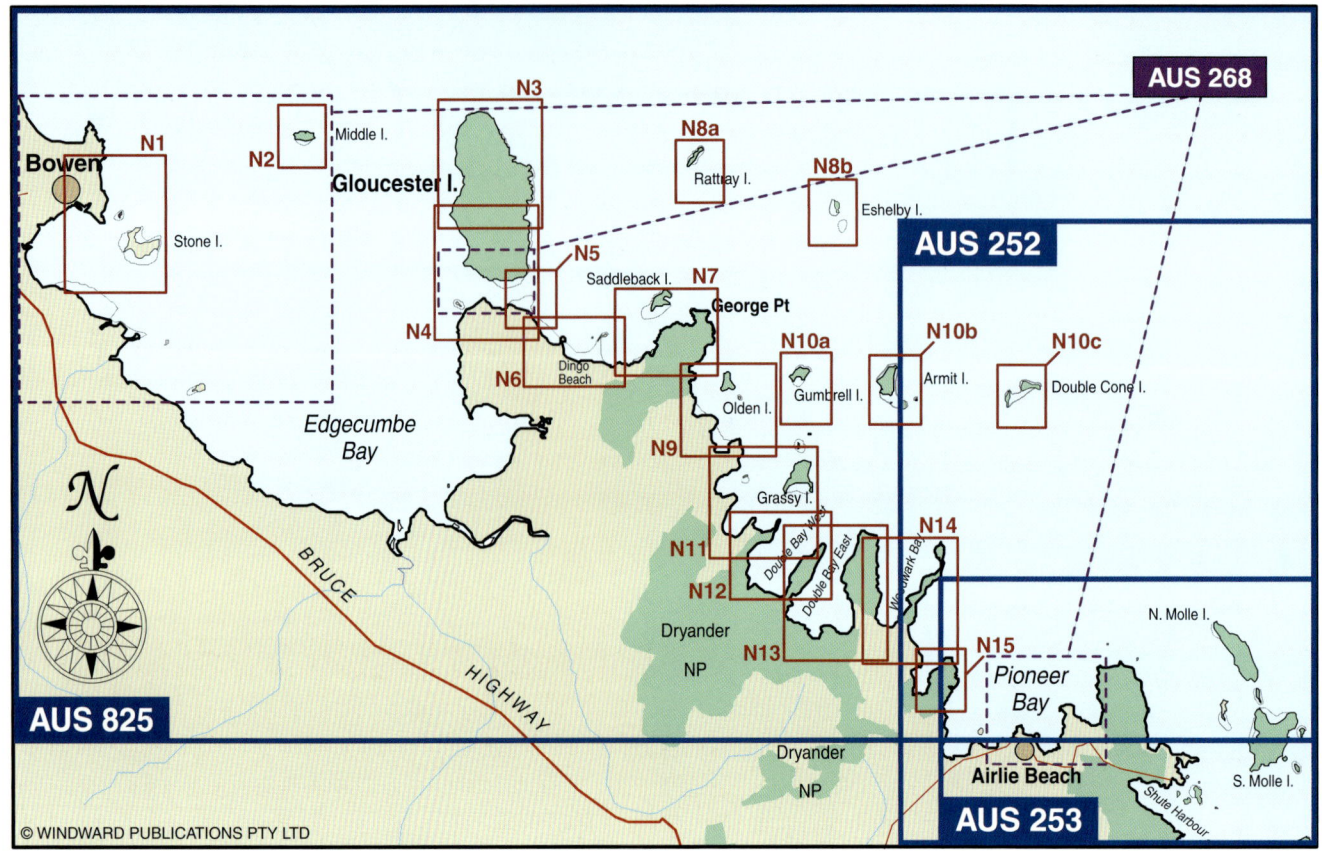

Sketch Map Index

Anchorage Description Index

Bowen

Bowen is a seaport town situated 1165 kilometres by rail north of Brisbane, exactly midway between Mackay and Townsville. It is the closest official port to the Whitsunday Group, a 40-nautical-mile sail from Airlie Beach.

Bowen's 'front door' on the world is the harbour and a pleasant esplanade of shady Moreton Bay figs, she-oaks and coconut palms which overlook it. Behind is a backdrop of attractive coastal hills. Unspoilt beach areas line the northern side of Cape Edgecumbe, which is the promontory on which Bowen is situated.

Edgecumbe Bay yawns for some 19 kilometres to the south and east, and the lofty Gloucester Island can be seen on the distant eastern horizon. Along the mainland coast to Gloucester Passage, this whole expanse of bay is lined with beaches and creeks which are excellent fishing and picnic grounds. They are popular haunts for hundreds of small boats at weekends and during holidays.

Bowen has an atmosphere of an unhurried and unspoilt northern Queensland town.

Bowen services

Air Sea Rescue
Call sign VMR487, 0800 to 1700 hours 2182 kHz, 2112 kHz, 2524 kHz, 27 MHz and VHF channels 16, 21. Tel. (07) 4786 1061.

Fuel
Diesel and ULP – Arabon Seafoods Pty Ltd at the end of the boat harbour (07) 4786 6706
Bowen Fisherman's Seafood Co. pontoon, by arrangement.

Mooring enquiries
Queensland Transport, Bowen Boat Harbour. Tel. (07) 4786 1966.
Bowen Marina Pty Ltd. Casual & long-term berths (07) 4786 6706

Slipway
Bowen Slipway (Boat Harbour). Facilities include water sprayer and sandblasting. Tel. (07) 4786 1760.

Water
Public pontoon adjacent to the yacht club

Yacht club
The North Queensland Cruising Yacht Club welcomes visiting yachtsmen. Tel. (07) 4786 3490.

BOWEN BOAT HARBOUR

The entrance to the harbour is marked by three pairs of port and starboard beacons on either side of a dredged channel with 1.4 metres depth (on a '0' tide). The harbour has two arms, the main south-western arm and a north-eastern arm.The south-western arm has a variable depth (1.4–2.5 metres), 107 pile moorings in the middle most of which are the pile type. On the south-western side of this arm is a public pontoon jetty (1-hour time limit) where water may be obtained. There is also a launching ramp, parking lot and an amenities block and a small marina belonging to the North Queensland Cruising Yacht Club.

On the north-eastern side is: a private jetty operated by Bowen Marina Pty Ltd. (casual and long-term moorings available; a slipway with chandlery; the office of Queensland Transport, which manages the harbour

and where arrangements can be made for berthing (VHF channel 16 or telephone (07) 4786 1966 (emergency telephone 0409 493 175)). At the town end of the harbour is a fish receivable and fuel depot operated by Arabon Seafoods Pty Ltd. Fish, prawns, ice, fuel and bait are sold to the public seven days a week. Casual moorings available by arrangement (07) 4786 6706.

The north-east arm is generally 2.0–4.0 metres deep. The power lines over the entrance are 21.3 metres above HAT.

The North Queensland Cruising Yacht Club is usually open after 1600 hours. This friendly club welcomes visiting yachties, offering honorary membership for those staying only a short time. Those wishing to use the bar and shower facilities for longer periods should seek temporary membership.

BOWEN BOAT HARBOUR

NOT FOR NAVIGATION: USE CHART AUS 268

SEE CAUTION ON USE OF SKETCH MAPS ON PAGES 121, 123

(1) Bowen Marina Pty Ltd; (2) Bowen Fisherman's Seafood Company; (3) Queensland Transport; (4) Air Sea Rescue; (5) Arabon Seafoods Pty Ltd

BOWEN

NOT FOR NAVIGATION: USE CHART AUS 268

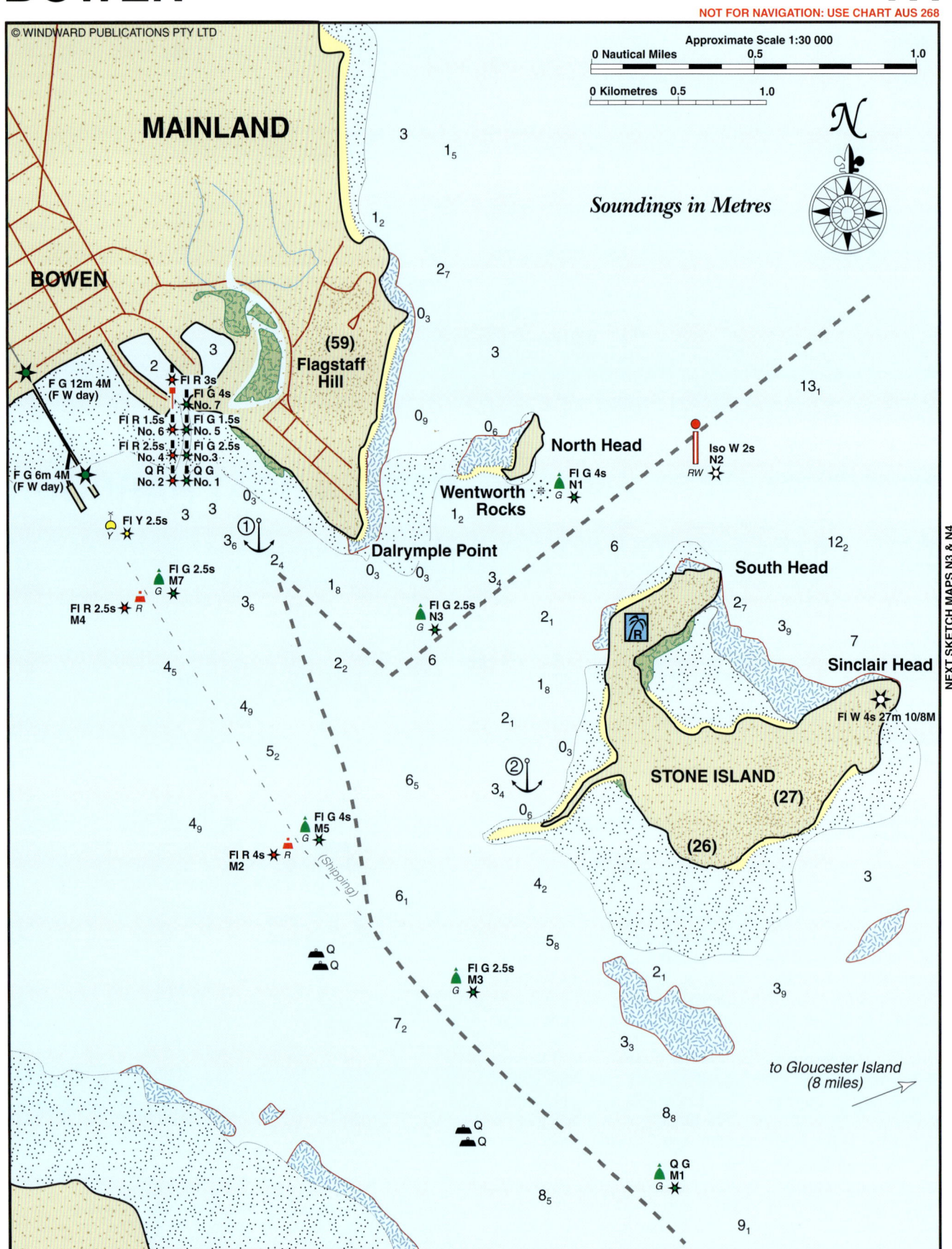

© WINDWARD PUBLICATIONS PTY LTD

Approximate Scale 1:30 000

0 Nautical Miles   0.5   1.0

0 Kilometres   0.5   1.0

Soundings in Metres

MAINLAND

BOWEN

F G 12m 4M
(F W day)

F G 6m 4M
(F W day)

Fl R 3s
Fl G 4s
No. 7
Fl R 1.5s   Fl G 1.5s
No. 6   No. 5
Fl R 2.5s   Fl G 2.5s
No. 4   No.3
Q R   Q G
No. 2   No. 1

Fl Y 2.5s
Y

Fl G 2.5s
M7
G

Fl R 2.5s
M4   R

Fl G 2.5s
N3
G

Fl G 4s
M5
G

Fl R 4s   R
M2

(Shipping)

Q
Q

Fl G 2.5s
M3
G

Q
Q

Q G
M1
G

(59)
**Flagstaff
Hill**

Dalrymple Point

North Head

**Wentworth
Rocks**

Fl G 4s
N1
G

Iso W 2s
N2
RW

South Head

R

Sinclair Head

Fl W 4s 27m 10/8M

STONE ISLAND

(27)

(26)

*to Gloucester Island
(8 miles)*

NEXT SKETCH MAPS N3 & N4

3   1₅   1₂   2₇   0₃   3   13₁
0₉   0₆   0₆   3   12₂
1₂   6   2₇   3₉   7
0₃   0₃   3₄   2₁
1₈   6   1₈   2₁
2₂   0₃
3   3   3₆   2₄
3₆
4₅   4₉   5₂   6₅   0₆   3₄   3
6₁   4₂
3   5₈   2₁
7₂   3₉
3₃
8₈
8₅   9₁

BOWEN BOAT HARBOUR (N1)

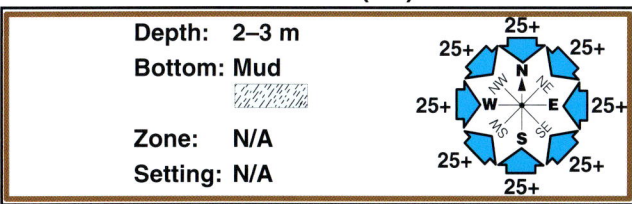

Depth:	2–3 m
Bottom:	Mud
Zone:	N/A
Setting:	N/A

Most yachts will approach Bowen from Gloucester Passage, and the easiest approach is to simply lay a course to the north of Stone Island, a more interesting sail than coming in via the main shipping channel south of Stone Island.

The entrance to the harbour is marked by port and starboard beacons (three pairs) on either side of the dredged channel. Watch the state of the tide before attempting to enter; the channel has a depth of about 1.4 metres at low water.

Berthing is arranged with Queensland Transport, whose office is on the north-eastern side of the main arm (VHF channel 16, telephone (07) 4786 1966) and is open from 0800 to 1430 hours Monday to Thursday and 0800 to 1200 hours Friday. There is also a telephone number for use only in emergencies: 0409 493 175.

The North Queensland Cruising Yacht Club has a small marina in front of the clubhouse. Enquire at the club regarding availability of berths.

DALRYMPLE POINT (N1)

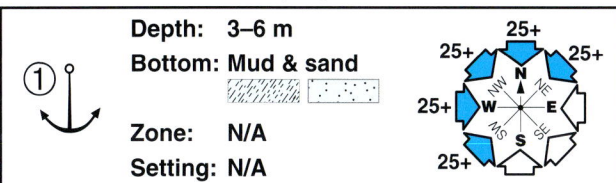

①	Depth:	3–6 m
	Bottom:	Mud & sand
	Zone:	N/A
	Setting:	N/A

Approach as shown. This anchorage can be swelly.

STONE ISLAND (N1)

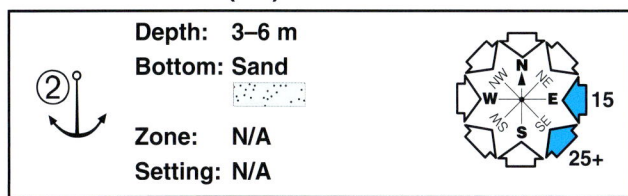

②	Depth:	3–6 m
	Bottom:	Sand
	Zone:	N/A
	Setting:	N/A

A very good anchorage. It can be swelly, especially as the wind moves more easterly.

Anchor over sand or mud and avoid coral to prevent further damage to the reefs.

MIDDLE ISLAND N2

NOT FOR NAVIGATION: USE CHARTS AUS 268/AUS 825

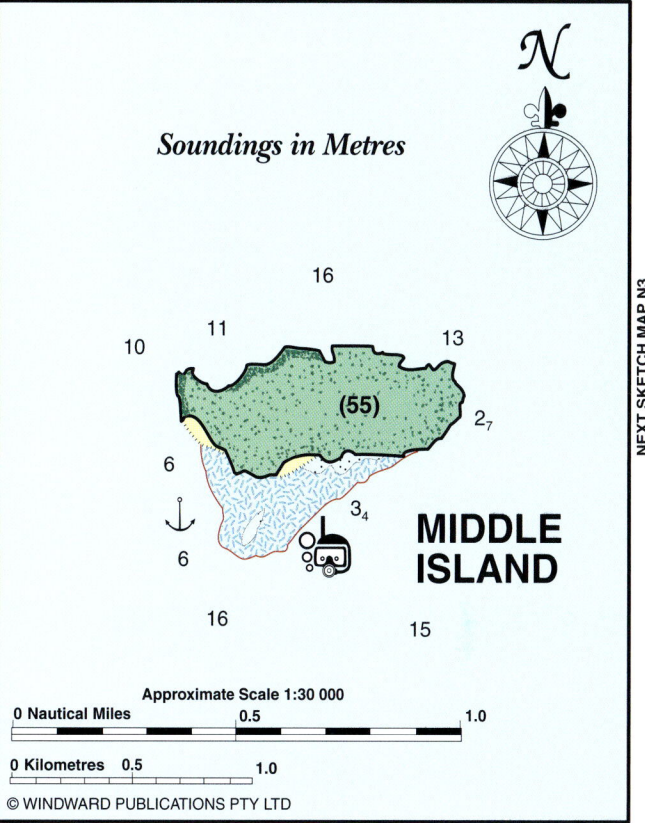

Soundings in Metres

NEXT SKETCH MAP N3

Approximate Scale 1:30 000

0 Nautical Miles   0.5   1.0

0 Kilometres   0.5   1.0

© WINDWARD PUBLICATIONS PTY LTD

SEE CAUTION ON USE OF SKETCH MAPS ON PAGES 121, 123

MIDDLE ISLAND (N2)

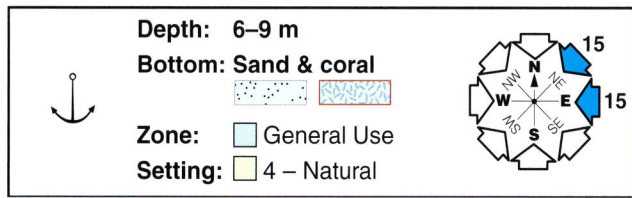

Depth:	6–9 m
Bottom:	Sand & coral
Zone:	General Use
Setting:	4 – Natural

In calm conditions, Middle Island can offer pleasant daytime anchorage. Years ago it boasted some of the most spectacular coral in the district, but cyclone damage has somewhat diminished its lustre. It is still a good snorkelling and diving spot. The reef on the south-south-east side is best. Good fishing.

Try to avoid disturbing seabirds (you can tell when they're upset by their agitated behaviour – circling, squawking, divebombing). Observe access restrictions and speed limits around significant bird sites, which are marked with red broken circles on the sketch maps.
(See also pages 114–115.)

GLOUCESTER NORTH

N3

NOT FOR NAVIGATION: USE CHART AUS 825

© WINDWARD PUBLICATIONS PTY LTD

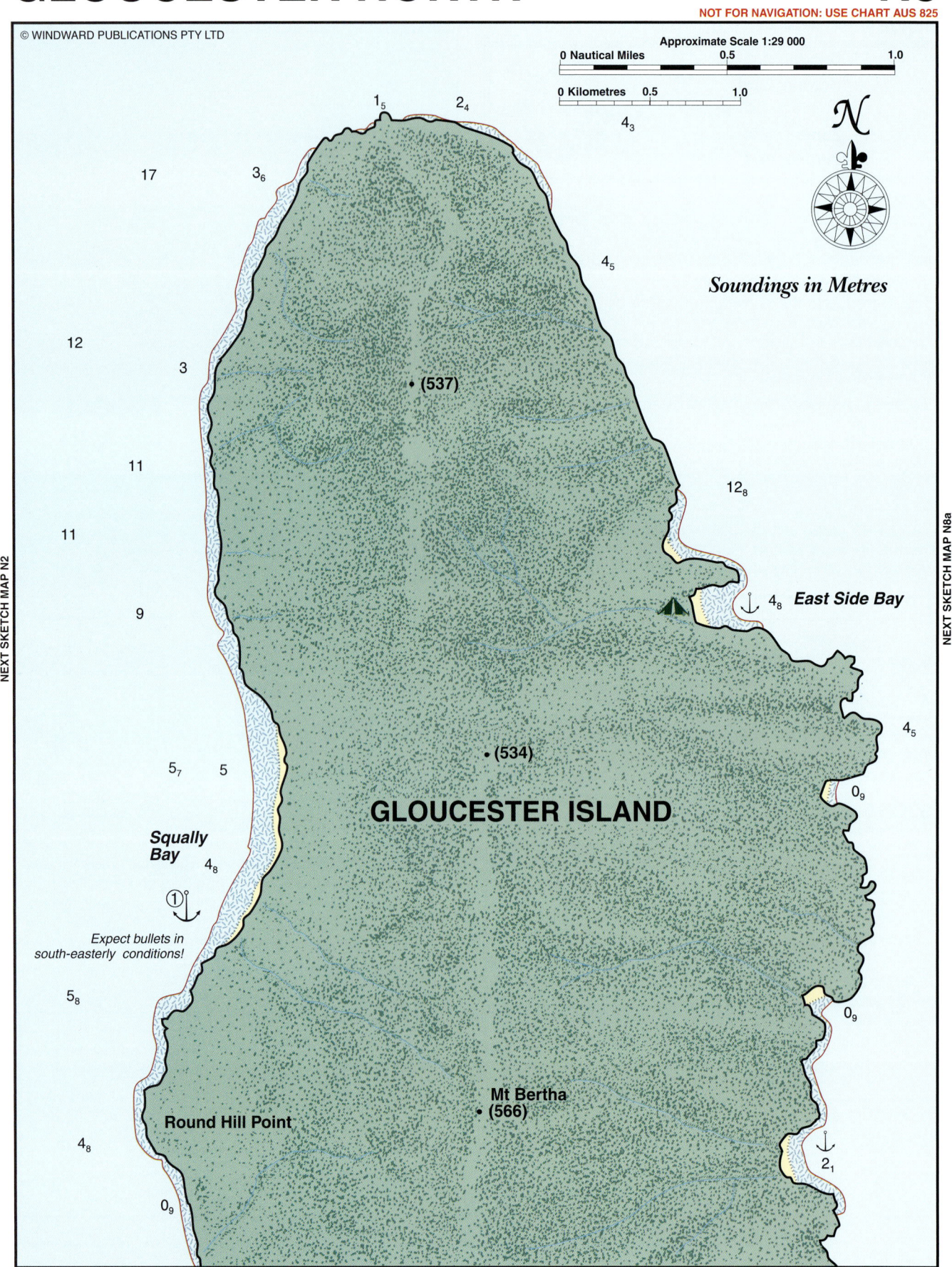

Approximate Scale 1:29 000

0 Nautical Miles   0.5   1.0

0 Kilometres   0.5   1.0

4_3

Soundings in Metres

1_5 2_4

17   3_6

4_5

12

3

• (537)

12_8

11

11

9

East Side Bay 4_8

5_7 5

• (534)

4_5

GLOUCESTER ISLAND

0_9

Squally Bay

4_8

①

Expect bullets in south-easterly conditions!

5_8

0_9

Mt Bertha
• (566)

Round Hill Point

4_8

2_1

0_9

NEXT SKETCH MAP N2

NEXT SKETCH MAP N8a

SQUALLY BAY (N3)

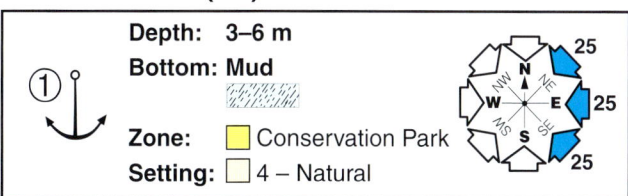

Depth:	3–6 m
Bottom:	Mud
Zone:	☐ Conservation Park
Setting:	☐ 4 – Natural

Anchorage is good virtually anywhere along the west side of Gloucester Island; there are no real dangers, nor is there much tidal run.

Squally Bay, popular with trawlers, lies in between the 566-metre-high Mt Bertha and another 534-metre hill to the north. These hills funnel and accelerate the wind very efficiently, hence the name of the bay, which it lives up to in fresh conditions. This may not be an exactly quiescent spot; but it does offer a long, lonely expanse of anchorage. The holding is good.

EAST SIDE BAY (Gloucester Island) (N3)

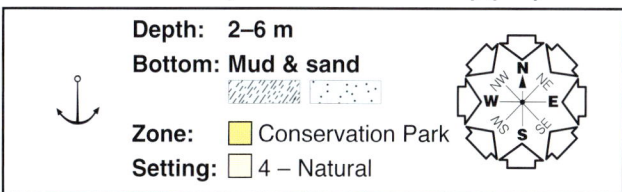

Depth:	2–6 m
Bottom:	Mud & sand
Zone:	☐ Conservation Park
Setting:	☐ 4 – Natural

On the eastern side of Gloucester Island are two very nice bays for daytime anchorage in calm conditions. Both have deserted, sandy beaches. East Side Bay has a lagoon which abounds with crabs and fish.

GLOUCESTER PASSAGE (N4)

Gloucester Passage marks the favoured route to Bowen from the Whitsundays and takes you in between a vast and lofty wind generator, Gloucester Island, and the mainland. The passage has ample water at all tides for vessels drawing up to 1.8 metres; deeper draught vessels should go through on the flood tide. The tidal stream flows easterly on the flood and westerly on the ebb. It may be as swift as 2–3 knots.

The passage is marked with a mixture of IALA lateral marks (laid towards Bowen) and IALA cardinal marks (best water east, west, and so forth). Gloucester Shoal is marked by an IALA east cardinal mark (best water east) at the east end and an IALA west cardinal mark at its west end. Don't attempt to go between the cardinal marks, and give them a healthy berth as this passage has strong currents and constantly shifting sands.

The final marker is a starboard lateral mark; give this a generous berth as there is some shoaling to the south of it.

Entrance from the east

Entry from the east requires avoidance of a dangerous reef extending north-east from the mainland; keep well to the north. From Saddleback Island, for example, to clear the reef, head directly for the south-east corner of Gloucester Island before entering the passage.

When approaching from the south – Jonah Bay or Dingo Beach – head far enough to the north-east to clear the protruding reef, and line up the north side of Saddleback Island with the south-east corner of Gloucester Island (to keep you north of the reef area) before entering.

Proceeding from the east, you will pass two port lateral marks. There is a shoal in the middle of the passage marked by east and west cardinal marks, and it is possible to pass either north or south of it. Shifting sands make it difficult to get unanimous agreement upon which is the best way to go. The general feeling of locals (including those at the North Queensland Cruising Yacht Club) is that the southern route is the easier and preferred route. After passing port beacon No. 4, turn south-west and travel parallel with the shore towards Monte's (anchorage No. 2). Then hold the port marks on the reef areas (east and north of Shag Islet) to port and the west cardinal mark on Gloucester Shoal to starboard. Turn to the south-west around Shag Island. The final marker is a starboard lateral mark on the edge of the foul ground at the western end of the passage.

The route north of the shoal is as shown on map N4, turning south-west after the west cardinal mark and proceeding between Passage Islet and the starboard beacon which marks the foul ground at the end of the passage.

Entrance from the west

Head directly for Passage Islet, leaving the 'green' marker to port and giving it a generous berth. Directions are then just the reverse of coming from the east.

Beware the shallow area westwards of the bay, although it can be crossed by shoal-draught vessels at the top of the tide.

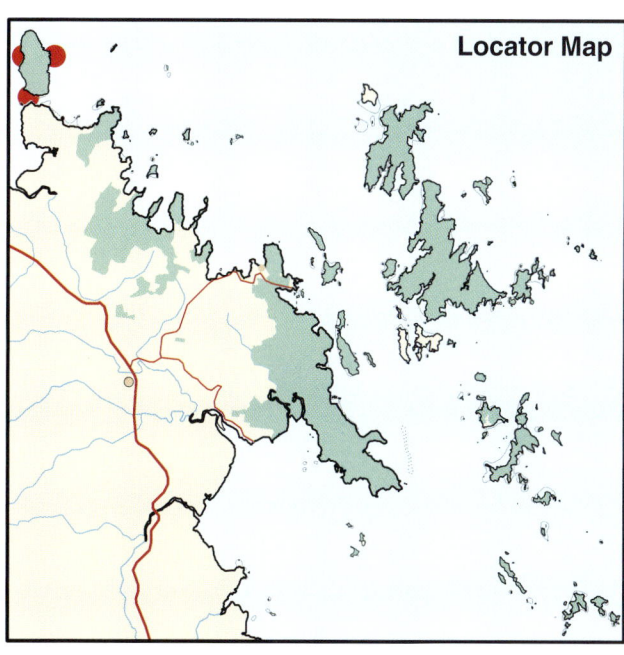

Locator Map

GLOUCESTER PASSAGE WEST

N4

NOT FOR NAVIGATION: USE CHARTS AUS 268/AUS 825

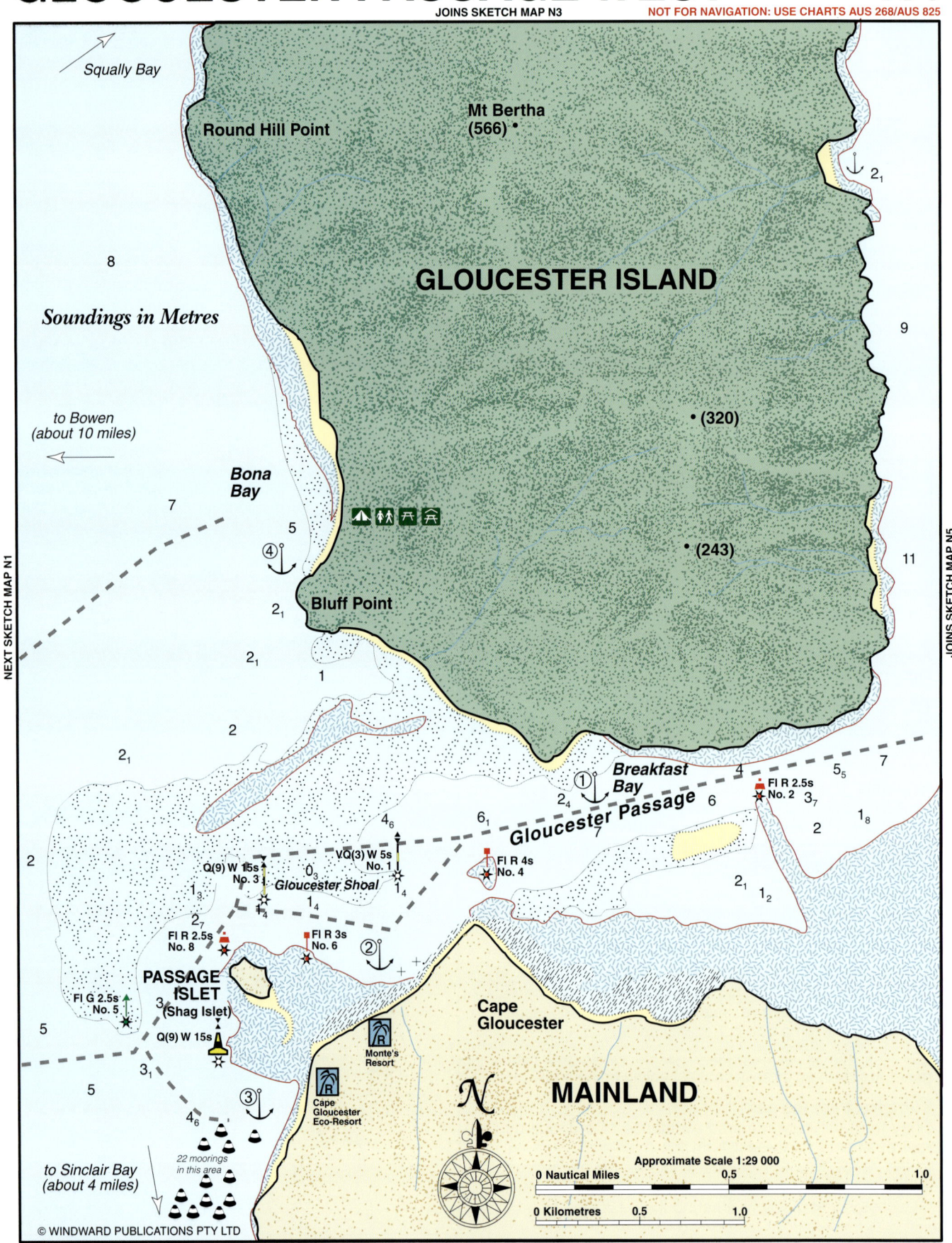

Squally Bay

Round Hill Point

Mt Bertha
(566) •

8

GLOUCESTER ISLAND

Soundings in Metres

9

to Bowen
(about 10 miles)

• **(320)**

Bona
Bay

5

④

• **(243)**

11

2_1

Bluff Point

2_1

1

2

Breakfast
Bay

4

5_5 7

2_1

①

2_4 **Gloucester Passage** 6

Fl R 2.5s
No. 2 3_7

6_1

1_8

4_6

6_2

7

2

VQ(3) W 5s
No. 1

2

2_1

Q(9) W 15s
No. 3

0_3

Gloucester Shoal

1_4

Fl R 4s
No. 4

2

2_1 1_2

1_3

1_4

1_4

2_7

Fl R 2.5s
No. 8

Fl R 3s
No. 6

②

PASSAGE
ISLET

Fl G 2.5s
No. 5

3

(Shag Islet)

Cape
Gloucester

5

Q(9) W 15s

5

3_1

③

Monte's
Resort

MAINLAND

5

4_6

Cape
Gloucester
Eco-Resort

N

to Sinclair Bay
(about 4 miles)

22 moorings
in this area

© WINDWARD PUBLICATIONS PTY LTD

Approximate Scale 1:29 000

0 Nautical Miles   0.5   1.0

0 Kilometres   0.5   1.0

SEE CAUTION ON USE OF SKETCH MAPS ON PAGES 121, 123

NEXT SKETCH MAP N1

JOINS SKETCH MAP N5

BREAKFAST BAY (N4)

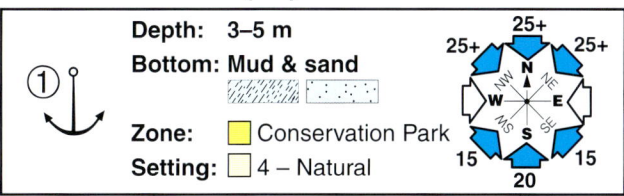

Anchor within 30 metres of the beach to keep out of tide.

Breakfast Bay is a popular little bay with an extensive beach leading west to Bona Bay. It has several creeks with freshwater ponds in the wet.

BONA BAY (N4)

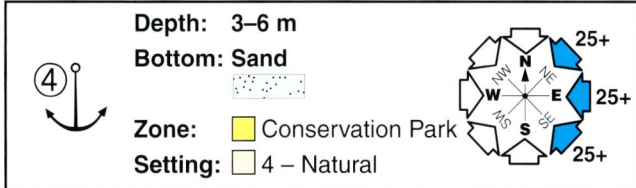

If coming from Gloucester Passage, give the foul ground at the west of the passage a sufficient berth. Although this may be crossed by shoal-draught craft at the top of the tide, it is not the recommended approach, especially without good local knowledge.

Anchorage at Bona Bay can be close to the beach, but leave enough swinging room in case the wind changes to the south-west at night.

During heavy south-east weather this is also a favourite shelter for trawlers.

Bona Bay is popular with Bowen weekenders and particularly at holiday time. It has a lovely beach.

There are death adders about; if you are moving around at night, always carry a torch so that you can see where you are going.

GLOUCESTER PASSAGE E.   N5

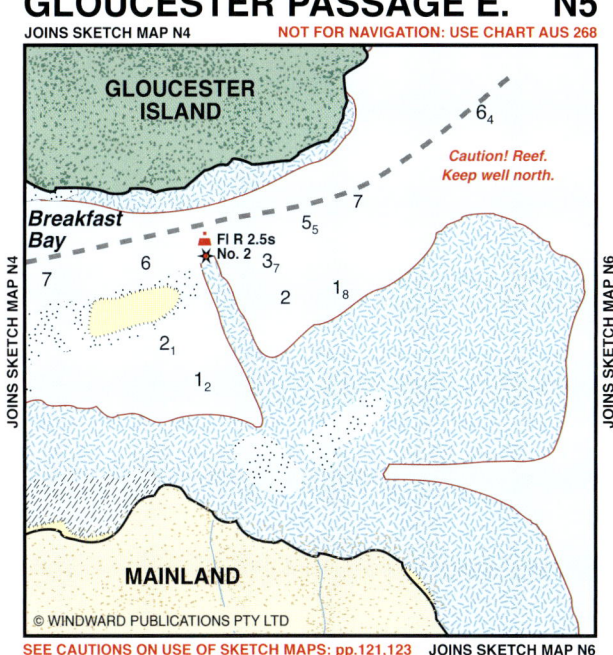

Monte's Reef Resort

MONTE'S REEF RESORT (N4)

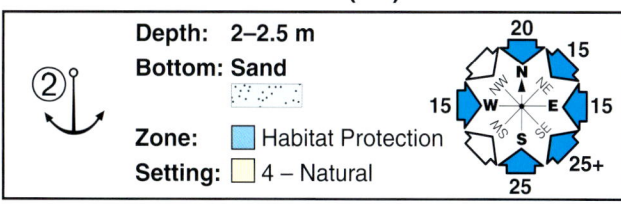

Watch out for reef area to the west. This is good anchorage in most weathers except from the north-west and south-west. Watch the depth, as there has been some silting Keep an eye out for isolated bommies.

Visiting the resort

Monte's Reef Resort is a low-key hideaway right on the water in picturesque Gloucester Passage. Food and drink is available at a small public bar and bistro. Limited supplies – milk, bread, ice, bait – may be purchased. Visitor's showers and laundry are also available at a small charge.

The resort itself caters for about 50 people in 8 separate self-contained bungalows set in the gardens along the water's edge. Visitors arriving by sea are welcome. Telephone (07) 4945 7177.

CAPE GLOUCESTER ECO RESORT (N4)

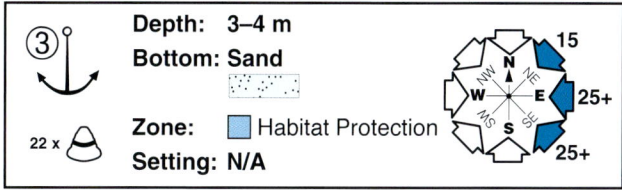

Do not attempt passage between Passage Islet, so-called 'Shag Islet' (because there are a lot of cormorants (shags) on it), and the mainland. The anchorage is reached from the western side of the island. Keep west of the western cardinal buoy, and watch out for isolated bommies just off the beach. Anchor behind the island close to the beach in front of the resort. The resort has installed 22 moorings.

Visiting Cape Gloucester Eco Resort

The resort is located on an isolated stretch of coastline with lovely sand beaches. It has 6 self-contained cabins and 4 units, a 25-metre saltwater pool, the Oar bar/bistro (which serves breakfast, lunch and dinne)r, a toilet/shower block and coin laundry. Visitors arriving by sea are warmly welcomed by management. Contact the resort on VHF channel 16/81 or telephone (07) 4945 7242.

(See photos next page)

DINGO BEACH

Gloucester Passage
(beware reef!)

Soundings in Metres

5   7   *to Saddleback Island*
(1.2 miles)

7

Shoal Bay

7   **BLACK**   Q(9) W 15s
CURRANT
ISLAND 5   Exposed   **MANTA RAY**
① ⚓   rocks   **ISLAND**

5   5

5 5 5   5

② ⚓

Nellie Bay

Approximate Scale 1:29 000

0 Nautical Miles   0.5   1.0   Swimming
enclosure   Ramp
0 Kilometres   0.5   1.0   **Dingo Beach**

© WINDWARD PUBLICATIONS PTY LTD

JOINS SKETCH MAP N5

JOINS SKETCH MAP N7

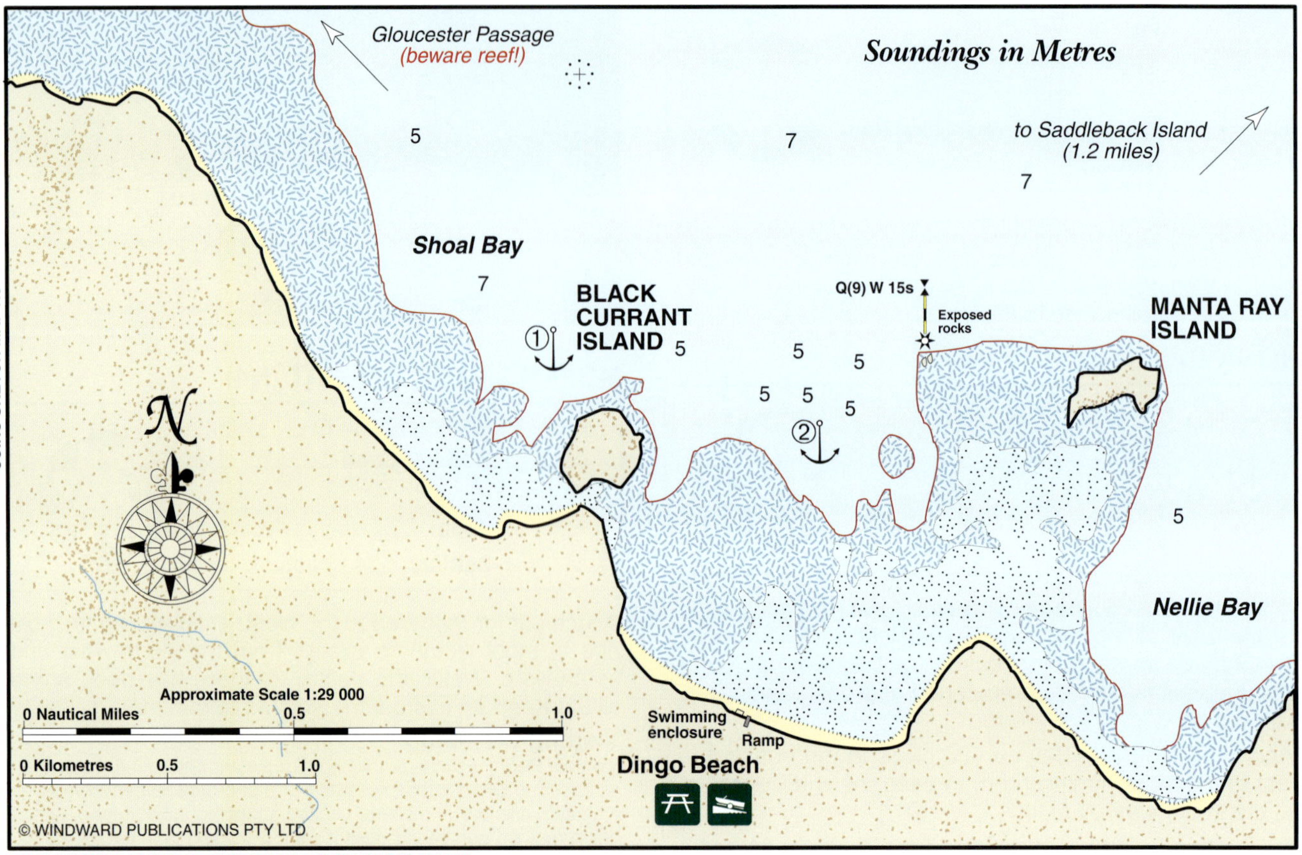

SEE CAUTIONS ON USE OF SKETCH MAPS ON PAGES 121,123

Cape Gloucester Eco Resort saltwater pool

The Oar bar/bistro at Gloucester Eco Resort

Further anchorages and beaches may be found for several miles to the south of the Eco Resort, all of which offer good shelter in south-east to east winds that often blow during the night (i.e. anchor far enough out). Sinclair Bay also has a small settlement, coconut plantation and excellent beach, but anchor well off, as it is shallow.

DINGO BEACH (N6)

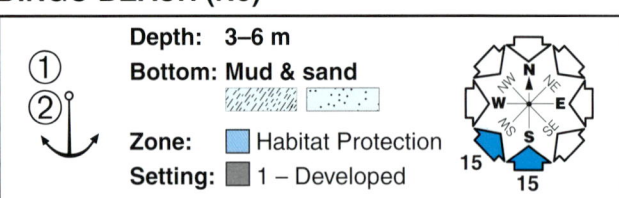

①	**Depth:** 3–6 m	
②	**Bottom:** Mud & sand	
	Zone: ■ Habitat Protection	
	Setting: ■ 1 – Developed	15 15

The waters off Dingo Beach are shallow, and there are extensive reef areas, particularly north-west of Nellie Bay. It is not suitable for keel boats. Use care, particularly if your draught is more than 0.7 metre.

This area is probably best known for its fishing. Much of the reef exposes at low tide. Dingo Beach is accessible by road, and it is a very busy spot during holiday periods.

Dingo Beach was so named because of (guess?) the preponderance of dingoes that used to frequent the area.

GEORGE POINT

N7

NOT FOR NAVIGATION: USE CHART AUS 825

Approximate Scale 1:29 000

0 Nautical Miles   0.5   1.0

0 Kilometres   0.5   1.0

Soundings in Metres

N

24

• (80)

14   20   24

• (143)

SADDLEBACK
ISLAND

1₈   7   4₆

⊕ Wreck *Jay Bee*

5

George Point
(96)•

George
Bay   2₇

8   ②   3₄

③   2₇

to Gloucester Passage
(about 3.5 miles)

④   6

7   2₇

Little
Jonah
Bay   7   to
Olden Island
(0.5 miles)

Dingo Beach   ⑤   • (265)

6   10

Jonah Bay

5   ⑥

5   5

MAINLAND

⚓

© WINDWARD PUBLICATIONS PTY LTD

JOINS SKETCH MAP N6

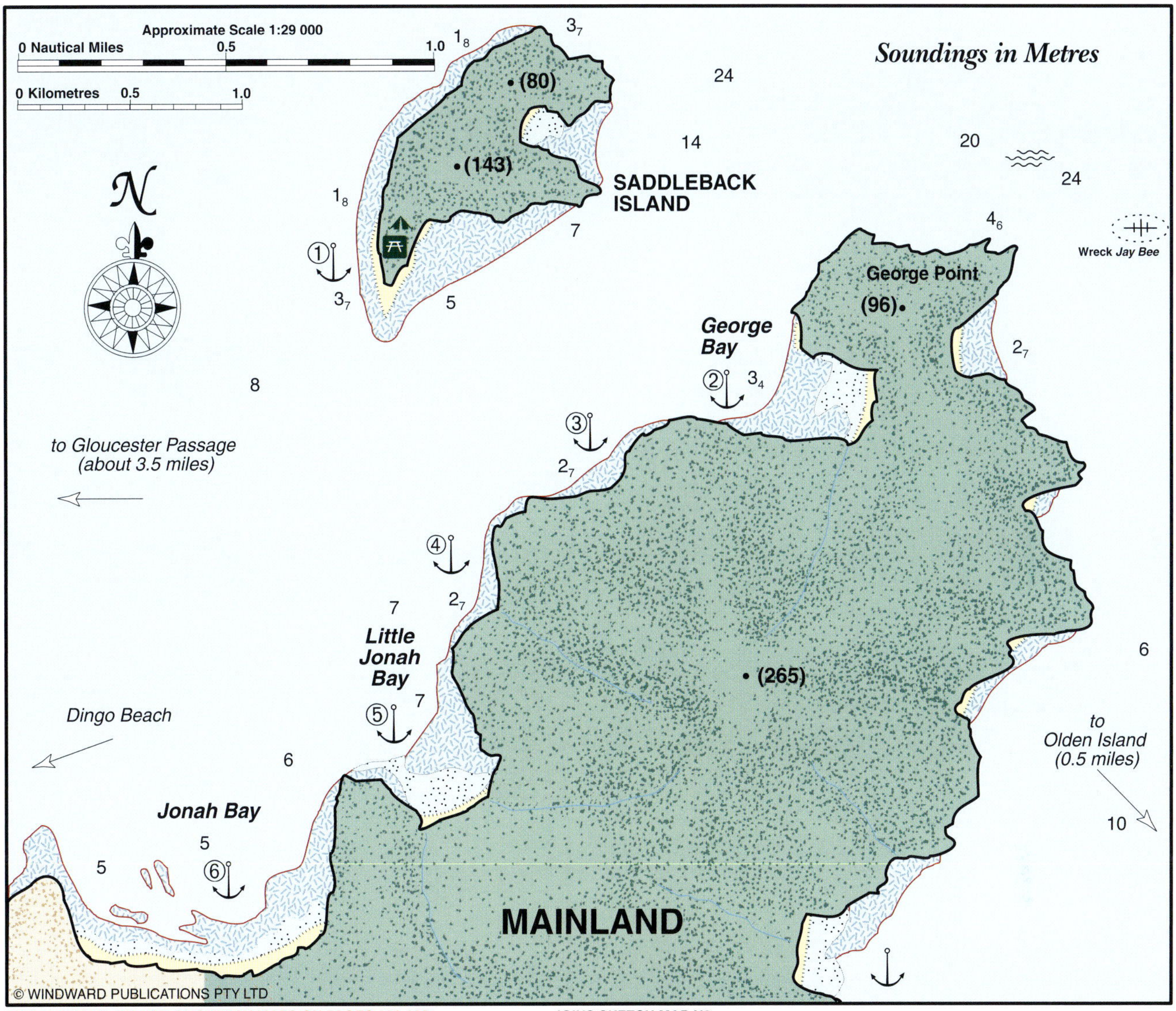

NEXT SKETCH MAP N10a

SEE CAUTIONS ON USE OF SKETCH MAPS ON PAGES 121,123   JOINS SKETCH MAP N9

SADDLEBACK ISLAND (N7)

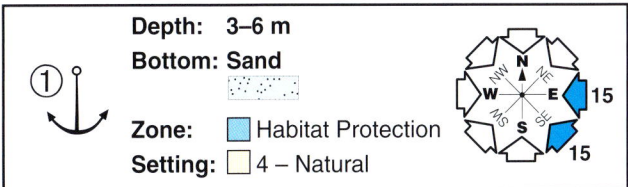

① Depth: **3–6 m**
Bottom: **Sand**
Zone: ⬜ Habitat Protection
Setting: ⬜ 4 – Natural

15
15

When approaching from George Point, keep well off the point, where there are frequently overfalls. From Gloucester Passage head straight for the northern side of Saddleback to avoid reefs and shoals south-east of the passage.

Saddleback is not a brilliant anchorage, although the holding is fine. On the southern tip of the island are the remains of a hut.

Anchorage is also possible on the south-east to east side of the island in north to north-west winds.

Keep an eye out for death adders, which have often been seen in the vicinity of the picnic table on Saddleback. These snakes conceal themselves very effectively amongst leaf litter. Have a torch in hand when moving about after dark.

GEORGE BAY (N7)

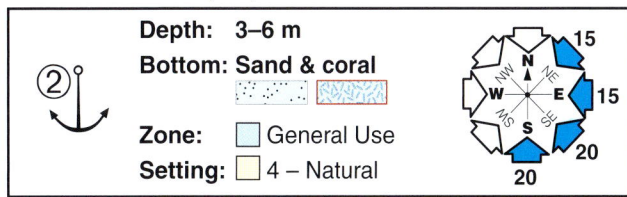

② Depth: **3–6 m**
Bottom: **Sand & coral**
Zone: ⬜ General Use
Setting: ⬜ 4 – Natural

15
15
20
20

The whole area from George Point to Gloucester Passage is subject to quite a large, long swell. Anchorage is possible along much of the whole expanse as far as Dingo Beach, in suitable weather. The deeper bays are less subject to swell; all may be gusty in fresh conditions.

As with many mainland areas, the water around these anchorages is often murky and unsuitable for snorkelling. However, in weather ranging from light to medium, good beach barbecue areas ashore are a plus. George Bay can be subject to occasional bullets in fresh south-easterly conditions; it starts to get swelly after winds reach 20 knots from the south-east.

SOUTH-WEST OF GEORGE BAY (N7)

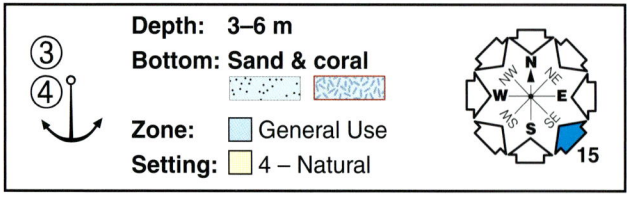

These anchorages are not as protected as George Bay to the north or Little Jonah and Jonah Bay to the south, but in moderate conditions they are quite habitable. Can be swelly.

LITTLE JONAH BAY (N7)

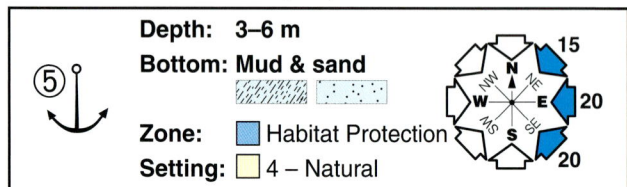

Excellent holding.

JONAH BAY (N7)

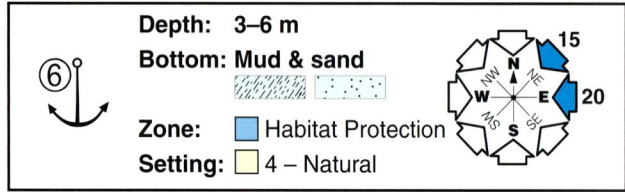

Excellent holding.

RATTRAY ISLAND (N8a)

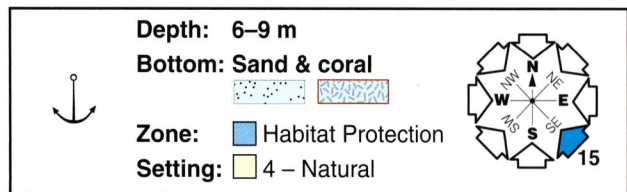

Rattray Island is a pile of rocks 111 metres high with wind-sheared vegetation; it is isolated and surrounded by currents. The island was named after Alexander Rattray, RN, ship's surgeon aboard the survey ship *Salamander*, which conducted surveys of the Whitsundays in the 1860s.

RATTRAY ISLAND   N8a

NOT FOR NAVIGATION: USE CHART AUS 825

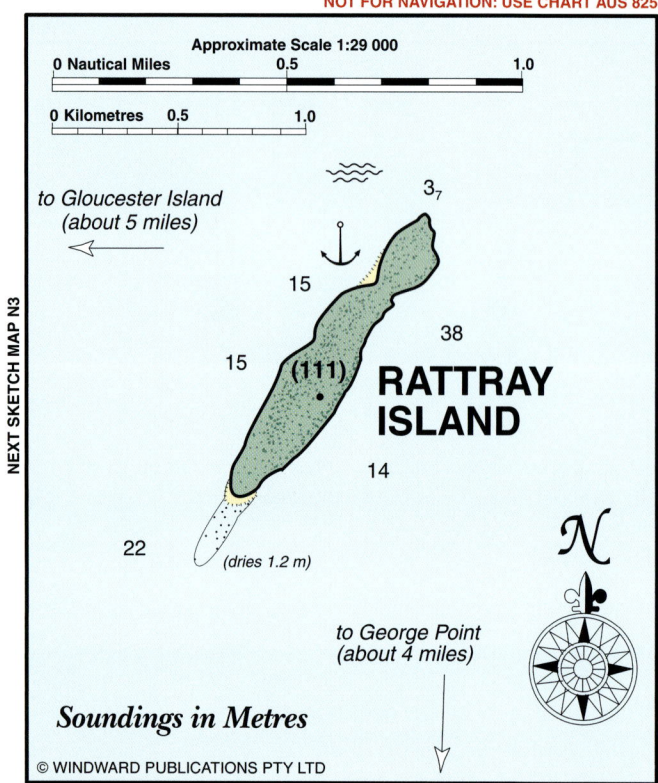

Soundings in Metres

© WINDWARD PUBLICATIONS PTY LTD

SEE CAUTIONS ON USE OF SKETCH MAPS: PAGES 121,123   NEXT SKETCH MAP N7

ESHELBY ISLAND   N8b

NOT FOR NAVIGATION: USE CHART AUS 825

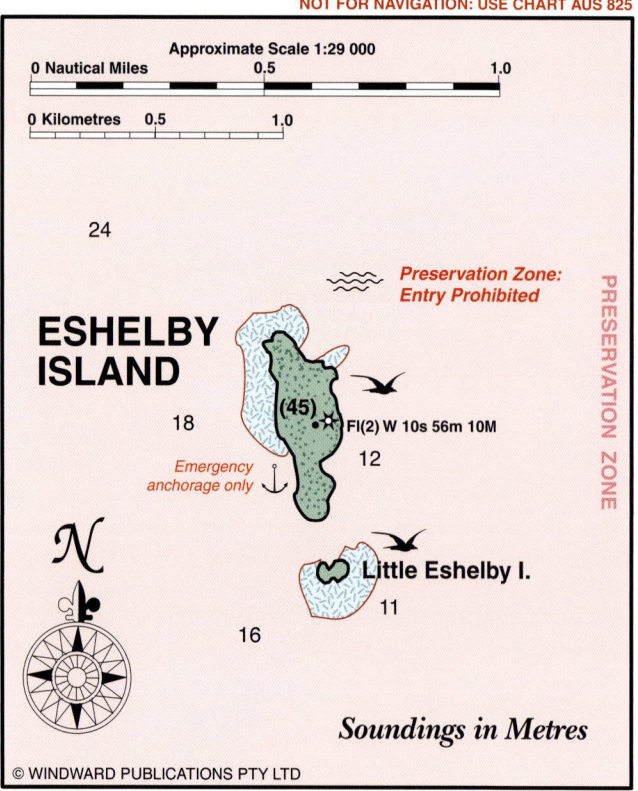

Soundings in Metres

© WINDWARD PUBLICATIONS PTY LTD

NEXT SKETCH MAPS N10a, N10b

OLDEN ISLAND N9

NOT FOR NAVIGATION: USE CHART AUS 825   JOINS SKETCH MAP N7

JOINS SKETCH MAP N7

Excellent beach

11   9   0 9   14

② ⚓

OLDEN
ISLAND

9

Excellent beach

9   ① ⚓   (85)
·

9   8

9

Olden Rock

**Significant Bird Site
Restricted Access**
*Do not approach within 200 metres
from 1 October through 31 December.*

*A 6-knot speed limit applies
within 200 metres from
1 October through 31 March,*

③ ⚓

Excellent beach

MAINLAND

N

7
to Earlando Bay (about 1 mile)

④ ⚓

3 7

Soundings in Metres

© WINDWARD PUBLICATIONS PTY LTD

SEE CAUTIONS ON USE OF SKETCH MAPS ON PAGES 121,123 JOINS SKETCH MAP N11

JULY 1995 APPROXIMATE SCALE 1:40 000

Olden Island

Earlando Bay

Aerial photograph reproduced with permission of the Department of Environment and Resource Management

---

ESHELBY ISLAND (N8b)

⚓	**Depth: 3–9 m** **Bottom: Sand & coral**

Zone: ▨ Preservation
Setting: ■ 5 – Protected

20
20

Eshelby Island is in a Preservation Zone because it is a significant seabird nesting site. Entry within the pink area is prohibited (except in cases of emergency). The anchor shown in map N8b is, therefore, of academic interest only. This special status is given to Eshelby because it is an important bridled tern (*Sterna anaethetus*) rookery, one of the few such areas left in Australia, and this threatened species needs to be protected from disturbance by man.

Albert Eshelby was a sub-lieutenant on the survey ship *Salamander*.

MAINLAND ANCHORAGES (N9)

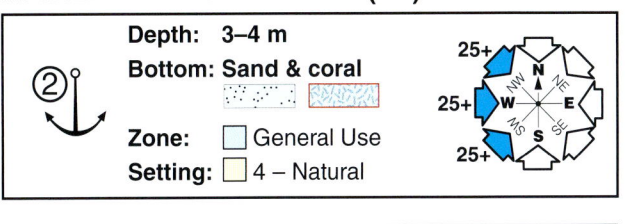

② ⚓   **Depth: 3–4 m**
Bottom: Sand & coral
Zone: ☐ General Use
Setting: ☐ 4 – Natural

25+
25+
25+

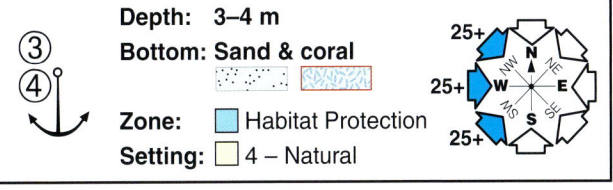

③
④ ⚓   **Depth: 3–4 m**
Bottom: Sand & coral
Zone: ☐ Habitat Protection
Setting: ☐ 4 – Natural

25+
25+
25+

Opposite Olden Island on the eastern side of George Point there are a number of beautiful, deserted mainland beaches which offer good shelter in south-west to north-west winds. Anchor about 100 metres off the beaches to avoid scattered coral heads.

Olden Island next page

OLDEN ISLAND (N9)

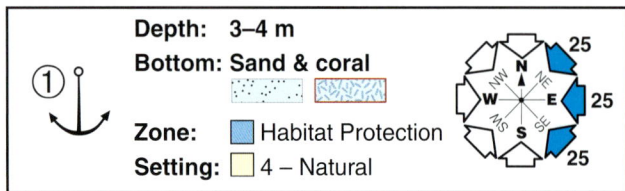

	Depth:	3–4 m
	Bottom:	Sand & coral
	Zone:	Habitat Protection
	Setting:	4 – Natural

Watch out for shallow area south of the beach if approaching from that direction. Anchor at the south-west end of the beach (perhaps a little further north if staying overnight).

The anchorage can be swelly in 25-knot winds but the holding is very good. Olden has a pleasant sand beach. It is a deserted, peaceful anchorage, ideal for a lunch stop and used by some overnight.

Olden Rock is a significant seabird site. To protect the birds from disturbance, approach within 200 metres is prohibited from 1 October through 31 December, and a 6-knot speed limit applies within 200 metres from 1 October through 31 March. (*See photo of Olden Island on page 139.*)

GUMBRELL ISLAND (N10a)

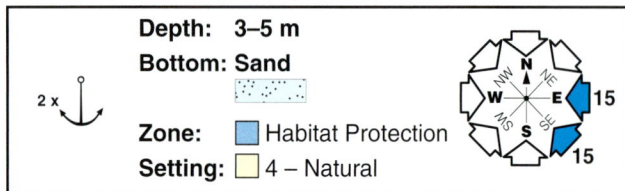

	Depth:	3–5 m
	Bottom:	Sand
	Zone:	Habitat Protection
	Setting:	4 – Natural

Pleasant daytime stopping-off spots. The northern anchorage gives better protection in south-east conditions.

A lonely, deserted island with some nice beaches.

ARMIT ISLAND (N10b)

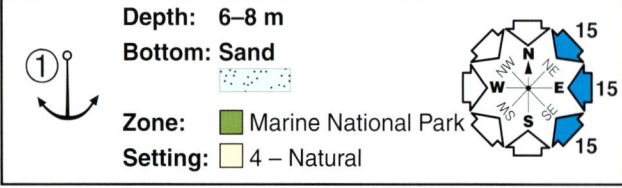

	Depth:	6–8 m
	Bottom:	Sand
	Zone:	Marine National Park
	Setting:	4 – Natural

Avoid the reef areas which join Armit and the small islets to the south-east.

Anchor close in as the bottom slopes steeply off. Good holding, although the anchorage is not particularly comfortable in fresh conditions.

Armit and Little Armit islands are significant bird sites. To reduce disturbance to nesting birds, a 6-knot speed limit applies within 200 metres of both sites from 1 October through 31 March. This anchorage is a no-fishing zone.

Armit was named after Robert E. Armit, RN, a sub-lieutenant on the survey ship *Salamander*.

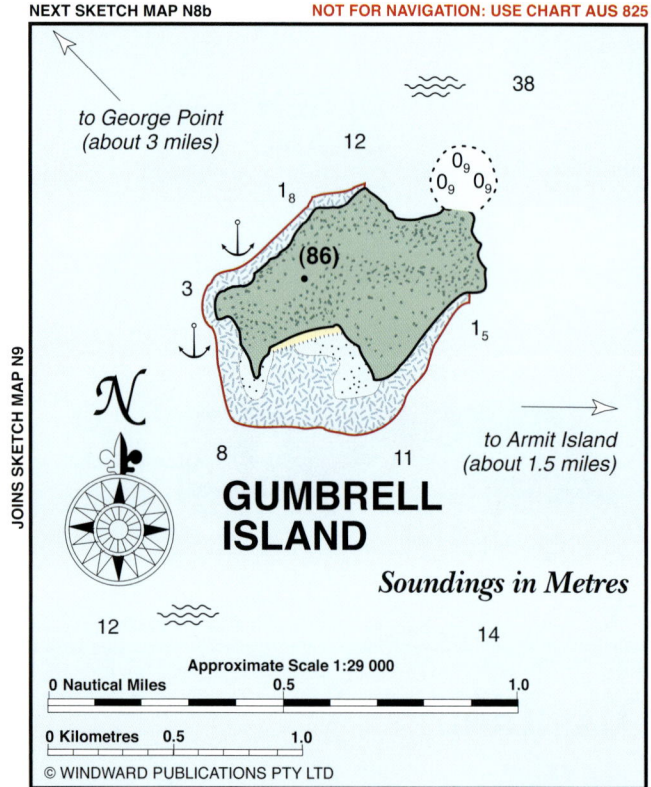

GUMBRELL I. N10a

NEXT SKETCH MAP N8b   NOT FOR NAVIGATION: USE CHART AUS 825

JOINS SKETCH MAP N9

to George Point (about 3 miles)

to Armit Island (about 1.5 miles)

GUMBRELL ISLAND

Soundings in Metres

NEXT SKETCH MAP N10b

Approximate Scale 1:29 000

0 Nautical Miles   0.5   1.0

0 Kilometres   0.5   1.0

© WINDWARD PUBLICATIONS PTY LTD

SEE CAUTIONS ON USE OF SKETCH MAPS pp.121,123   NEXT SKETCH MAP N11

ARMIT ISLAND N10b

NEXT SKETCH MAP N8b   NOT FOR NAVIGATION: USE CHART AUS 825

NEXT SKETCH MAP N10a

Soundings in Metres

ARMIT ISLAND

NEXT SKETCH MAP N10c

Significant Bird Site
6-knot speed limit applies within 200 metres from 1 October through 31 March

Significant Bird Site
6-knot speed limit applies within 200 metres from 1 October through 31 March

LITTLE ARMIT I.

to Airlie Beach (about 8 miles)

© WINDWARD PUBLICATIONS PTY LTD

SEE CAUTIONS ON USE OF SKETCH MAPS pp.121,123   NEXT SKETCH MAP N14

JULY 1995 APPROXIMATE SCALE 1:40 000

Aerial photograph reproduced with permission of the Department of Environment and Resource Management

Armit Island

Little Armit Island

DOUBLE CONE I.   N10c

NOT FOR NAVIGATION: USE CHART AUS 252

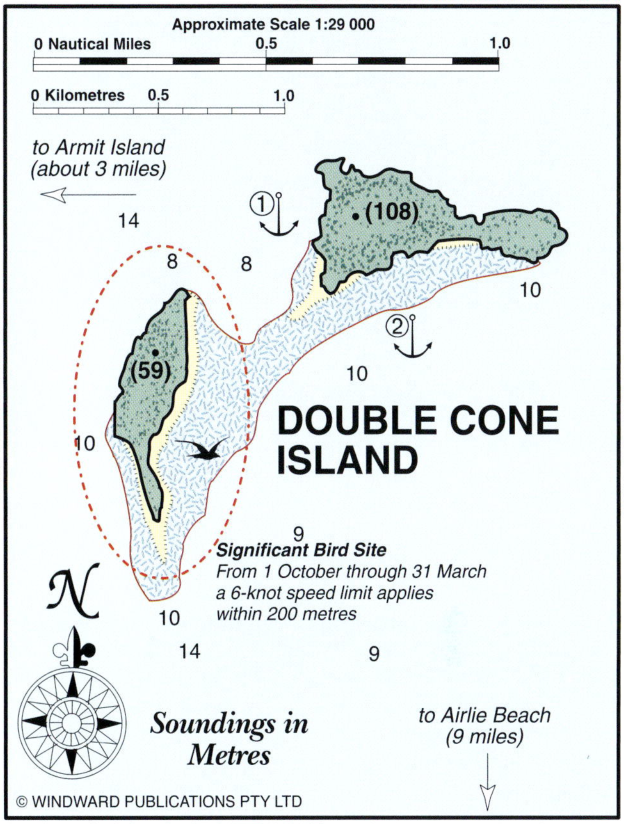

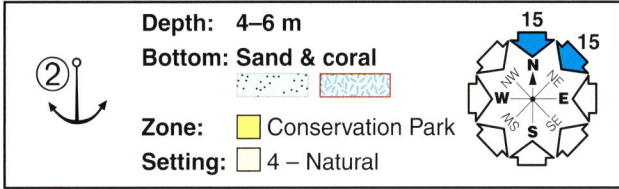

Approximate Scale 1:29 000

to Armit Island
(about 3 miles)

DOUBLE CONE
ISLAND

Significant Bird Site
From 1 October through 31 March
a 6-knot speed limit applies
within 200 metres

Soundings in
Metres

to Airlie Beach
(9 miles)

© WINDWARD PUBLICATIONS PTY LTD

NEXT SKETCH MAP N10b

NEXT SKETCH MAPS C11, C12, C13

SEE CAUTIONS ON USE OF SKETCH MAPS: pp.121,123   NEXT SKETCH MAP C1

DOUBLE CONE ISLAND (N10c)

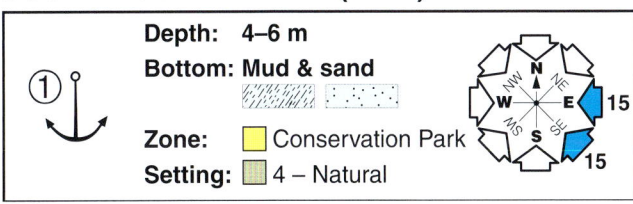

① Depth: 4–6 m
Bottom: Mud & sand
Zone: ☐ Conservation Park
Setting: ☐ 4 – Natural

Approaching from the south, keep well off the south-west tip where the reef runs off for several hundred metres.

Double Cone Island is seen for miles from the south-east, sitting up prominently on the horizon. It is an interesting daytime stopoff spot (in suitably light weather) that offers excellent beach exploration and good fishing. Some time ago a trawler was wrecked on the south-western end of the eastern 'cone', and some remains may still be visible on the beach.

An ironic aspect of its name is that it is indeed an island of double cones – in addition to its three conic hills, there are reportedly significant numbers of the venomous cone shell, *Conus geographus*, in residence (these, needless to say, are best left to their 'poisonous' selves).

Double Cone Island is an important nesting site for the Torresian imperial pigeon (*Ducula spilorrhoa*) of which there are about 2500 pairs. Other bird species nesting there are the beach stone-curlew (*Esacus neglectus*), the white-bellied sea eagle (*Haliaeetus leucogaster*) and the osprey (*Pandion haliaetus*). To allow these species to nest in some peace, a 6-knot speed limit applies within 200 metres of the western island from 1 October through 31 March.

DOUBLE CONE ISLAND (N10c)

② Depth: 4–6 m
Bottom: Sand & coral
Zone: ☐ Conservation Park
Setting: ☐ 4 – Natural

This is the preferred anchorage in northerly conditions.

Try to avoid disturbing seabirds (you can tell when they're upset by their agitated behaviour – circling, squawking, divebombing). Observe access restrictions and speed limits around significant bird sites, which are marked with red broken circles on the sketch maps.
(See also pages 114–115.)

GRASSY ISLAND (N11)

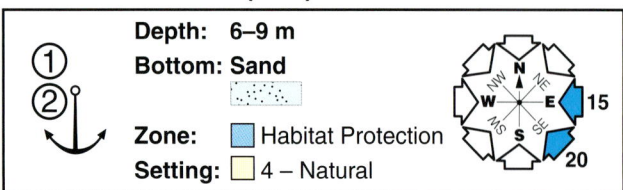

Coming from the south, watch out for the sand spit which extends for some distance off the south-western tip of the island. Coming from the north, keep west of Edwin Rock and pass outside of Little Grassy Island (immediately north of Grassy Island).

This anchorage has good holding and is suitable for overnight stops; it may be swelly as the wind easts. The tidal flow past this side of Grassy Island tends to keep you pointing either straight north or south, which is useful because of the depth and it also makes any swell less annoying. Beware of occasional bommies where the southern of these two anchors is shown.

In 1929 Boyd Lee and his family took over the island lease and built a large grass house and a variety of outbuildings and accommodation for trippers from the mainland, who were transported to the island from Cannonvale on the Lee's boat Reliance. Boyd Lee was nicknamed 'Alligator' by the locals for his escapades with saltwater crocodiles.

Edwin Rock, to the north-east of Little Grassy Island, is a significant seabird nesting site. To protect nesting birds from disturbance, approach within 200 meters is prohibited from 1 October through 31 December, and a 6-knot speed limit applies within 200 metres year-round.

GRASSY ISLAND (N11)

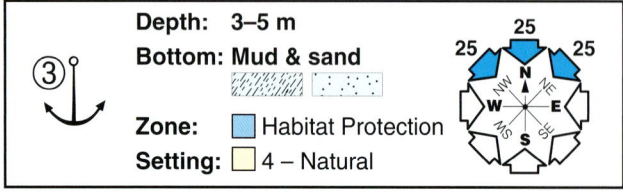

The south side of Grassy Island gives protection from northerly winds. Pleasant exploring. There is a 6-knot speed limit within 200 metres of the beach from 1 October through 31 March.

EARLANDO BAY (N11)

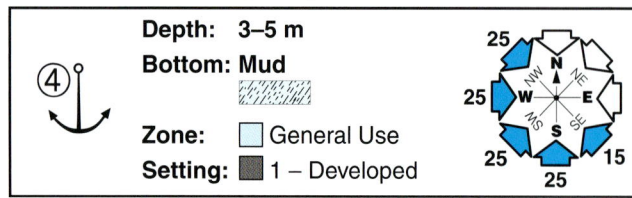

Stay south of Low Islet and the reef which extends south-west from it.

MAINLAND (N11)

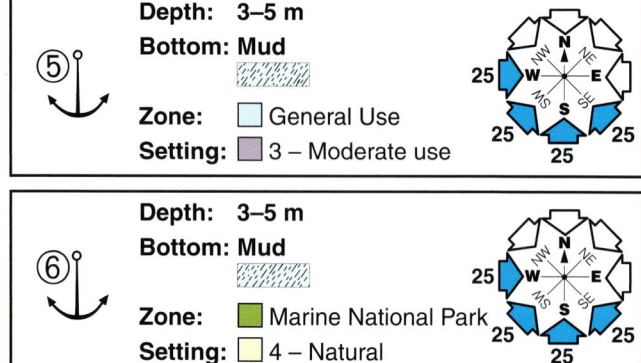

These anchorages are not frequently occupied and offer privacy and solitude.

Jetty and launching ramp, Earlando

David Colfelt

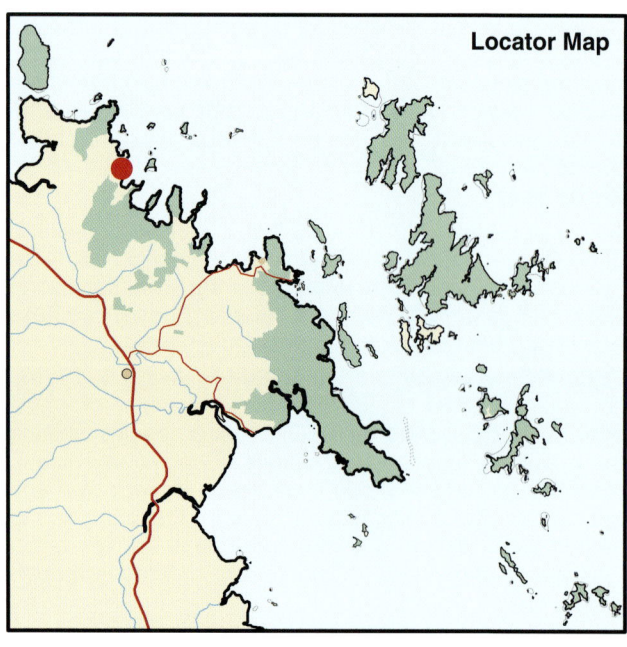

GRASSY ISLAND

N11

NOT FOR NAVIGATION: USE CHART AUS 825

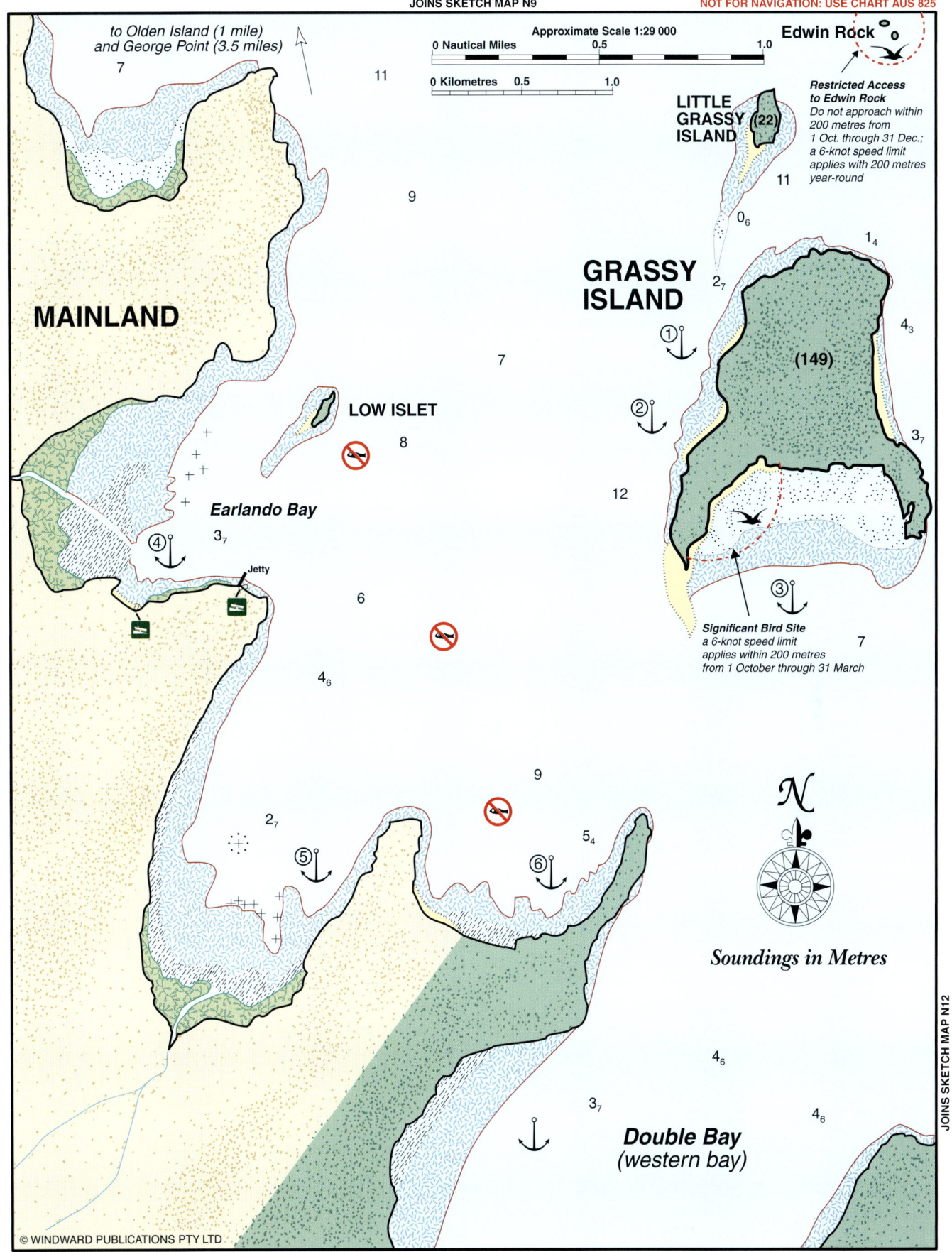

to Olden Island (1 mile)
and George Point (3.5 miles)

Approximate Scale 1:29 000

0 Nautical Miles   0.5   1.0

0 Kilometres   0.5   1.0

Edwin Rock

**Restricted Access
to Edwin Rock**
*Do not approach within
200 metres from
1 Oct. through 31 Dec.;
a 6-knot speed limit
applies with 200 metres
year-round*

**LITTLE
GRASSY
ISLAND** (22)

**GRASSY
ISLAND**

MAINLAND

(149)

LOW ISLET

Earlando Bay

Jetty

Significant Bird Site
*a 6-knot speed limit
applies within 200 metres
from 1 October through 31 March*

Soundings in Metres

Double Bay
(western bay)

© WINDWARD PUBLICATIONS PTY LTD

SEE CAUTIONS ON USE OF SKETCH MAPS ON PAGES 121,123

See pages 112–115 for information about marine park zones and settings

DOUBLE BAY (western) N12

JOINS SKETCH MAP N11

NOT FOR NAVIGATION: USE CHART AUS 825

JOINS SKETCH MAP N11

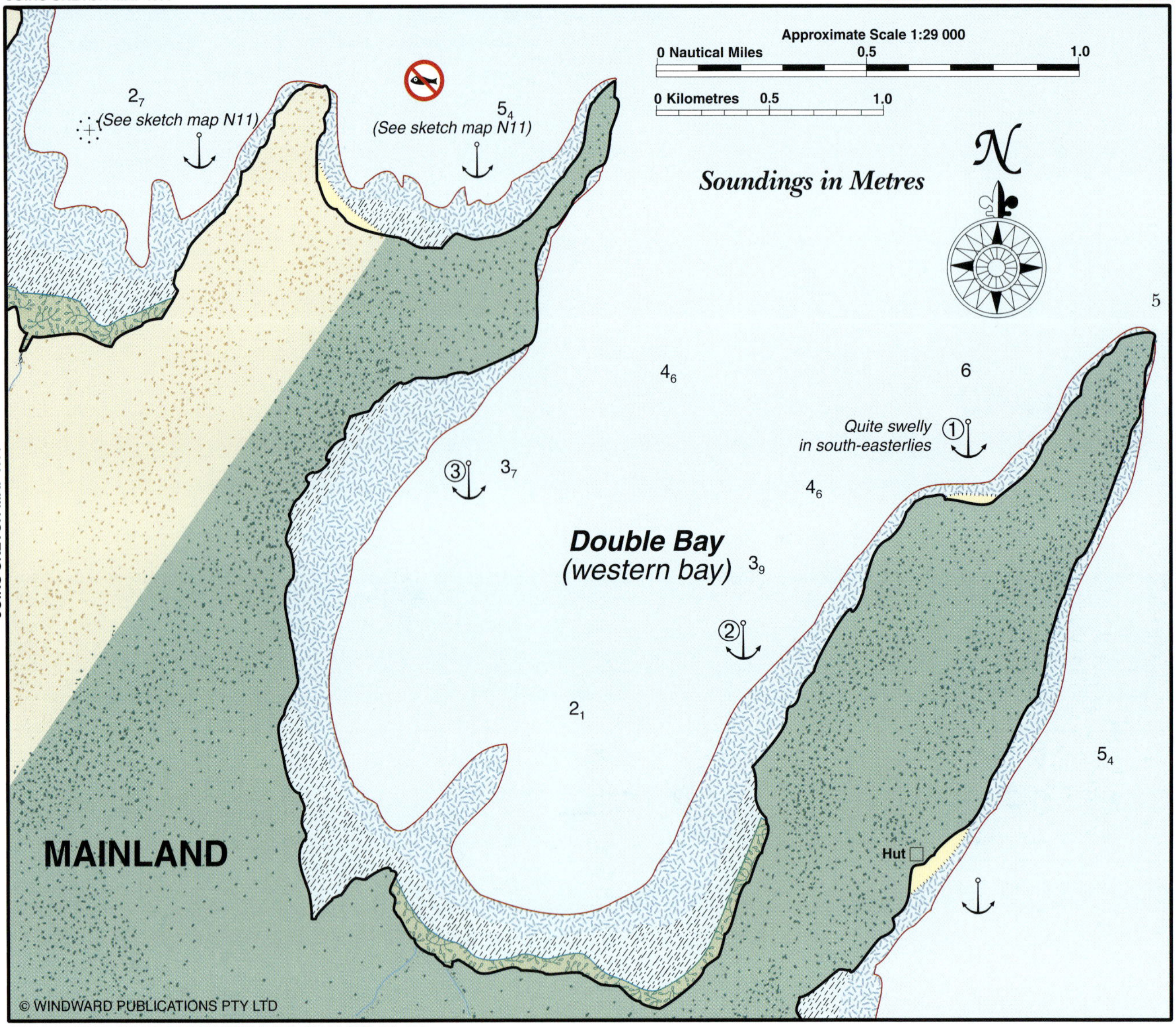

Approximate Scale 1:29 000
0 Nautical Miles 0.5 1.0
0 Kilometres 0.5 1.0
Soundings in Metres
N
2_7
(See sketch map N11)
5_4
(See sketch map N11)
5
4_6
6
Quite swelly in south-easterlies
①
③
3_7
4_6
Double Bay
(western bay)
3_9
②
2_1
5_4
Hut
MAINLAND
© WINDWARD PUBLICATIONS PTY LTD

JOINS SKETCH MAP N13

SEE CAUTIONS ON USE OF SKETCH MAPS ON PAGES 121,123

DOUBLE BAY (Western Bay) (N12)

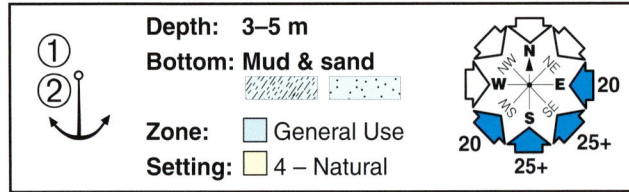

① ②

Depth: 3–5 m

Bottom: Mud & sand

Zone: General Use

Setting: 4 – Natural

N
NE
E
SE
S
SW
W
NW
20
20
25+
25+

There are several good anchorages in the western embayment of Double Bay, quiet and secure even in fresh south-east winds. As with many of these northern mainland bays, there is a rich food supply for fish and the fishing can be good.

Anchorage No. 1 may be swelly, especially as the wind gets into the east. Double Bay (eastern bay) is less swelly. Anchorage No. 2 may be marginally less swelly than No. 1 and gives slightly better protection from the south-west.

DOUBLE BAY (Western Bay) (N12)

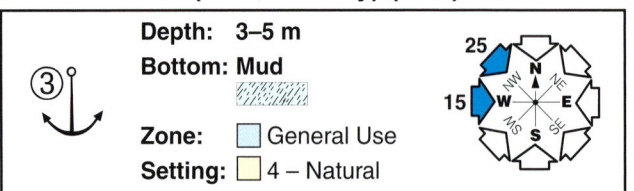

③

Depth: 3–5 m

Bottom: Mud

Zone: General Use

Setting: 4 – Natural

25
15
N
NE
E
SE
S
SW
W
NW

Anchorage No. 3 offers some protection from the north-west and west; it is also tenable in moderate south-east to east winds, but it may be swelly.

ULY 1995 APPROXIMATE SCALE 1:40 000

Grassy Island

Double Bay West

Double Bay East

Woodwark Bay

DOUBLE BAY (eastern)

JOINS SKETCH MAP N11

N13

NOT FOR NAVIGATION: USE CHART AUS 825

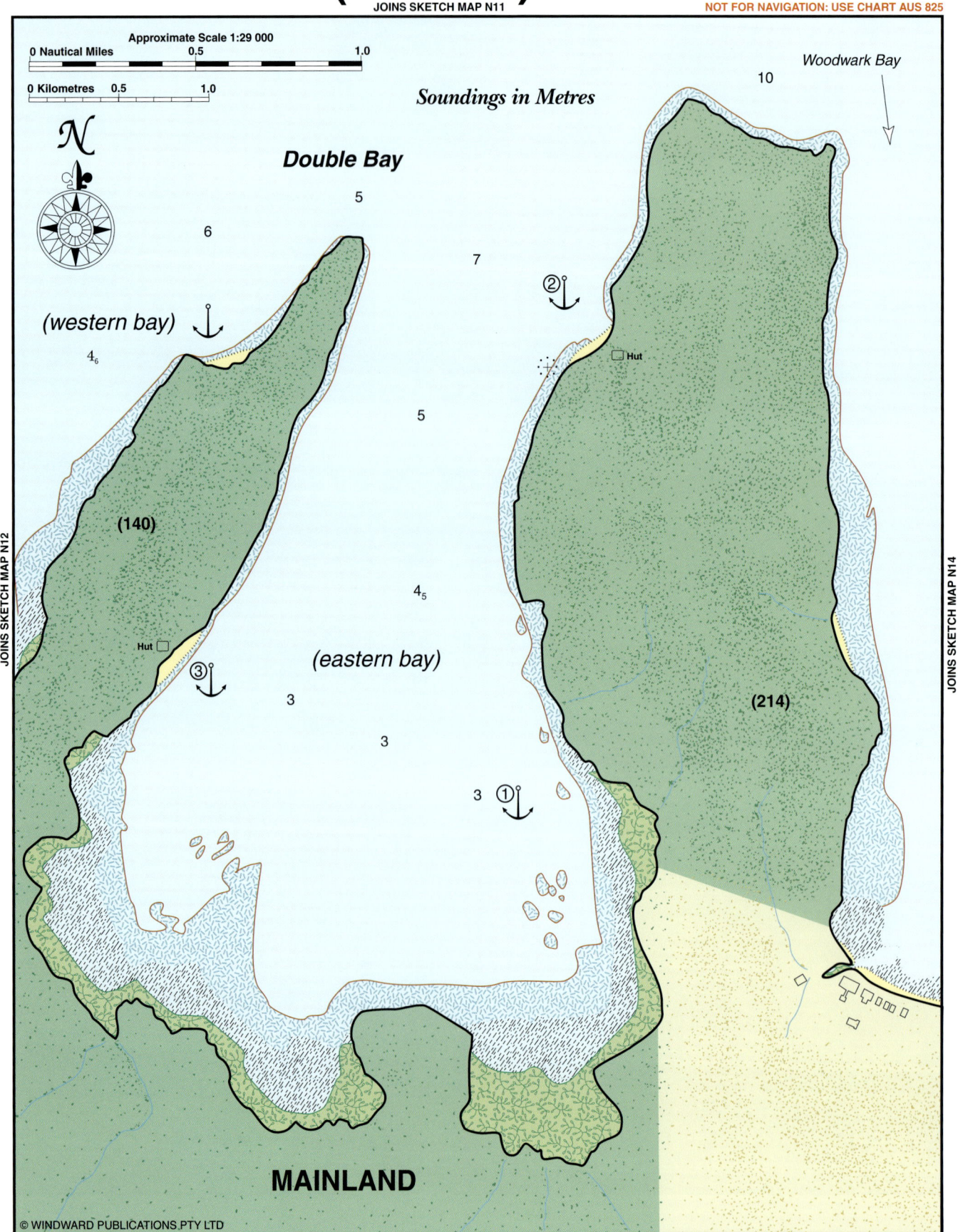

Approximate Scale 1:29 000

0 Nautical Miles   0.5   1.0

0 Kilometres   0.5   1.0

Woodwark Bay

10

Soundings in Metres

Double Bay

5

6

7

②

(western bay) ⚓

4₆

Hut

5

5

(140)

4₅

(eastern bay)

Hut

③ ⚓

3

3

(214)

3 ①

3

JOINS SKETCH MAP N12

JOINS SKETCH MAP N14

MAINLAND

© WINDWARD PUBLICATIONS PTY LTD

See pages 112–115 for information about marine park zones and settings

DOUBLE BAY (Eastern Bay) (N13)

① | Depth: 3–5 m
Bottom: Mud
Zone: ☐ General Use
Setting: ☐ 5 – Protected

Watch out for scattered bommies. Double Bay has several good anchorages, quiet and secure even in fresh south-east winds. There is a rich food supply for fish provided by the mangrove communities, and the fishing can be good. A delightful anchorage offering peace and solitude.

Double Bay east has a 'protected' setting, having significant mangrove communities.

DOUBLE BAY (Eastern Bay) (N13)

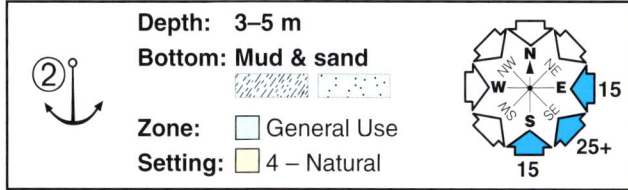

② | Depth: 3–5 m
Bottom: Mud & sand
Zone: ☐ General Use
Setting: ☐ 4 – Natural

Watch out for the reef area which extends some distance north-west of Datum Rock. Anchor off the pleasant little expanse of sand.

DOUBLE BAY (eastern bay) (N13)

③ | Depth: 3–5 m
Bottom: Mud
Zone: ☐ General Use
Setting: ☐ 4 – Natural

There are probably better choices for overnight anchorages than this one, but there is a little beach and hut on the shore which makes a pleasant picnic spot for lunch.

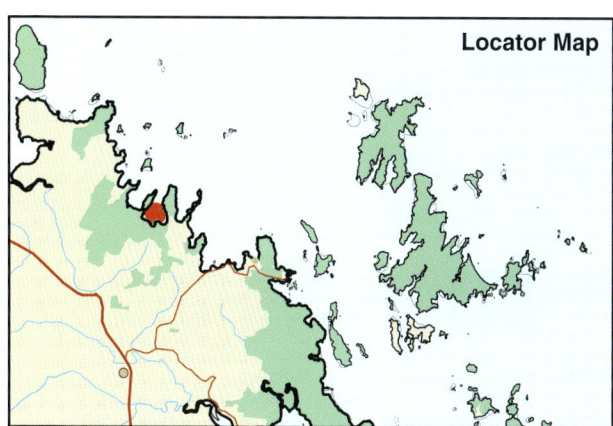

Locator Map

Woodwark Bay inlet

David Colfelt

WOODWARK BAY

N14

NEXT SKETCH MAP N10b

NOT FOR NAVIGATION: USE CHART AUS 825

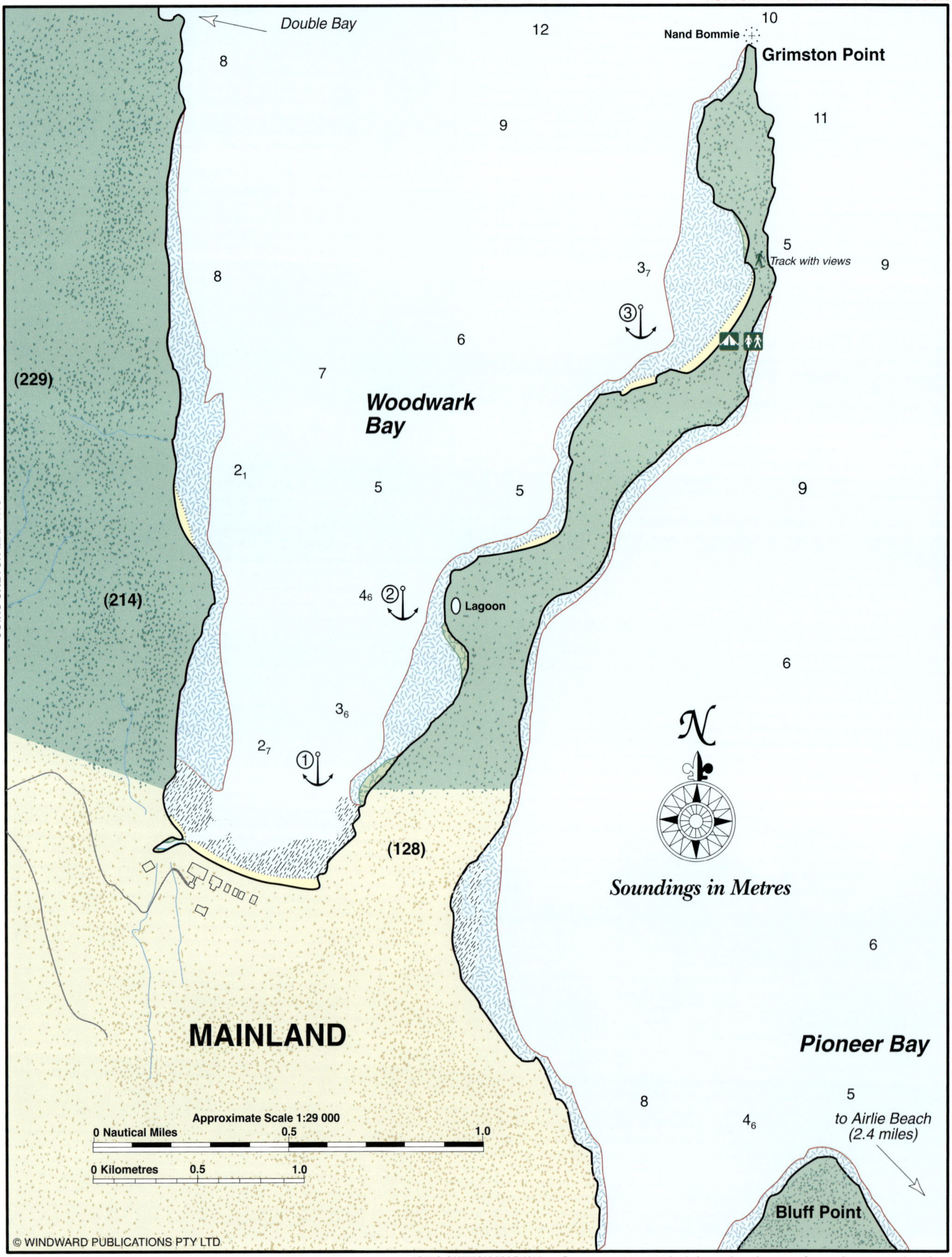
Double Bay
12
10
Nand Bommie
Grimston Point
8
9
11
5
Track with views
9
3₇
8
③
6
7
(229)
Woodwark Bay
2₁
5
5
9
JOINS SKETCH MAP N13
NEXT SKETCH MAP C1
4₆
②
Lagoon
(214)
6
3₆
2₇
①
N
(128)
Soundings in Metres
6
MAINLAND
Pioneer Bay
8
5
4₆
to Airlie Beach
(2.4 miles)
Approximate Scale 1:29 000
0 Nautical Miles
0.5
1.0
0 Kilometres
0.5
1.0
Bluff Point

© WINDWARD PUBLICATIONS PTY LTD

SEE CAUTIONS ON USE OF SKETCH MAPS ON PAGES 121,123

JOINS SKETCH MAP N15

See pages 112–115 for information about marine park zones and settings

WOODWARK BAY (N14)

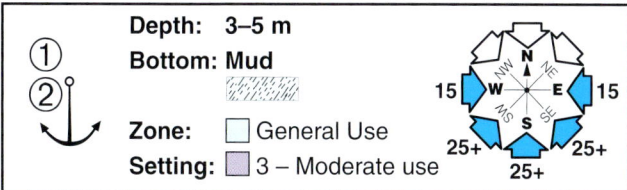

① ②

Depth: 3–5 m
Bottom: Mud

Zone: ☐ General Use
Setting: ☐ 3 – Moderate use

Woodwark Bay is large and lonely with a vast area for exploring, with some mangroves and good fishing. There is a nice beach at the head of the bay.

Grimston Point, the headland at the eastern side of Woodwark Bay, has strong currents flowing around it, as do many headlands in this area. A vessel called *Nand* struck a bommie when rounding it several years ago. Give it a good berth.

JULY 1995 APPROXIMATE SCALE 1:40 000

Aerial photograph reproduced with permission of the Department of Environment and Resource Management

WOODWARK BAY (N14)

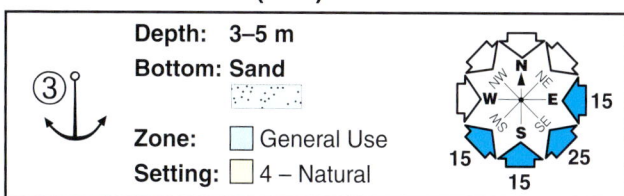

③

Depth: 3–5 m
Bottom: Sand

Zone: ☐ General Use
Setting: ☐ 4 – Natural

This anchorage can be swelly. It has a lovely little sand beach – with a spot in the corner for a picnic.

BLUFF POINT   N15

JOINS SKETCH MAP N14   NOT FOR NAVIGATION: USE CHART AUS 825

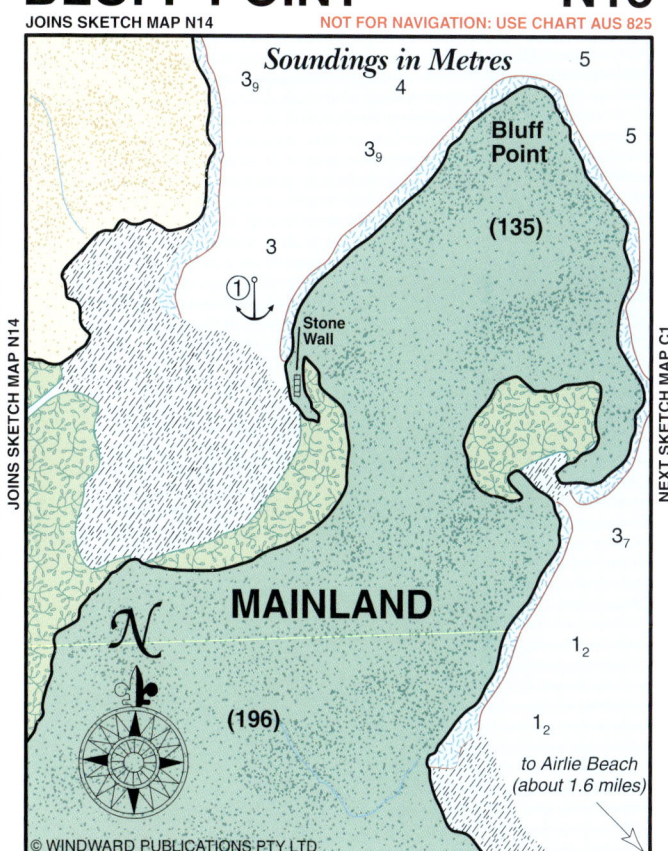

SEE CAUTIONS ON USE OF SKETCH MAPS ON PAGES 121,123

BLUFF POINT (N15)

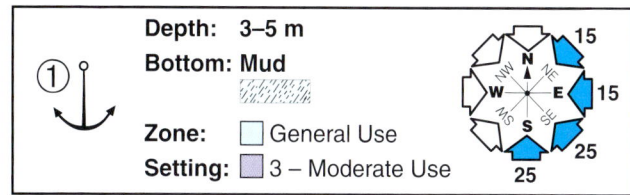

①

Depth: 3–5 m
Bottom: Mud

Zone: ☐ General Use
Setting: ☐ 3 – Moderate Use

This anchorage may be swelly as the wind easts. It is another mangrove-filled mainland bay in which you might catch a fish. A rarely visited anchorage, and perhaps not as good as Woodwark Bay or Double Bay, it is closer to Abell Point and is sometimes used as a first-night anchorage by bareboat charterers. Anchor just off the rocks north of the first mangrove trees (in a depth of about 3 metres at low tide).

THE CENTRAL GROUP

C1–33

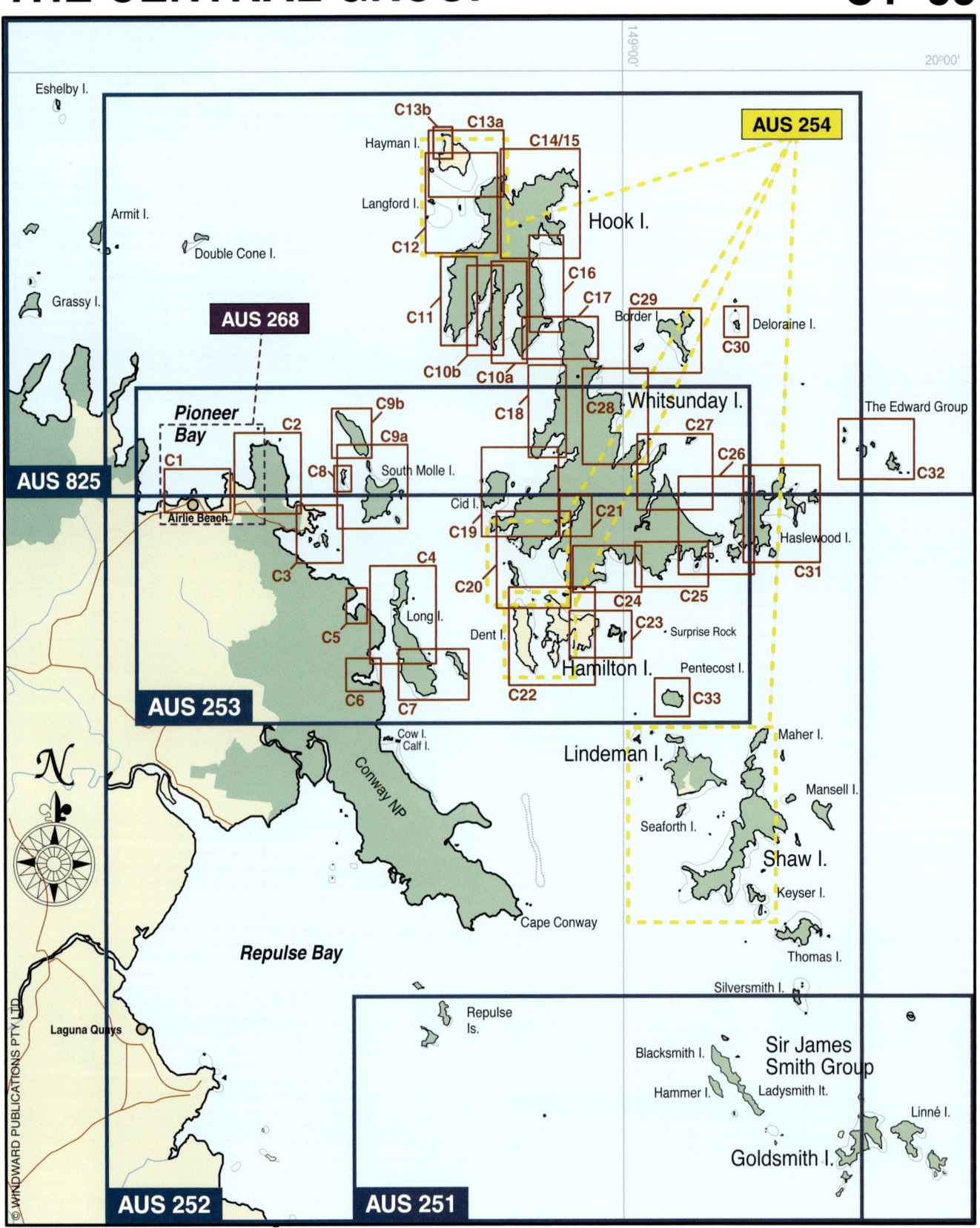

Sketch Map Index

Anchorage Description Index

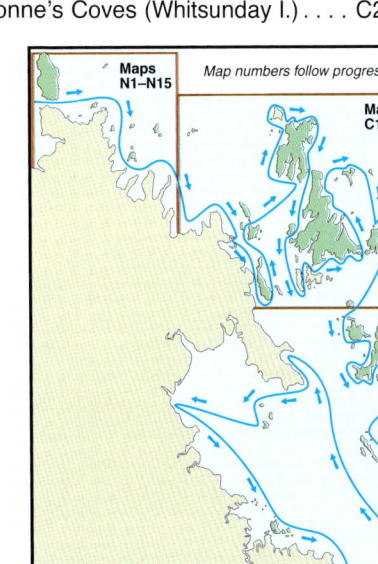

Maps N1–N15

Map numbers follow progression of arrows.

Maps C1–C33

Maps S1–S20

The Airlie Beach seascape

THE WHITSUNDAY MAINLAND

Airlie Beach and Cannonvale to its west are the principal coastal mainland centres for the Whitsundays, providing manpower, services and supplies for the island resorts and for the bareboat charter industry. These villages comprise a tourist destination in their own right, with resorts, luxurious condominiums, motels, holiday flats, backpackers' hostels, camping and caravan parks, a variety of shops and services, and restaurants. Night-time entertainment is available at several establishments. Shute Harbour (about 8 km to the east) is a major embarkation point for the islands.

The Airlie Beach skyline

AIRLIE BEACH

Airlie Beach looks northwards over Airlie Bay and Pioneer Bay onto a spectacular seascape, a brilliant blue expanse of sparkling ocean. These waters are shielded from the prevailing south-east winds by the Conway Range, and Airlie Bay is a refuge for itinerant vessels in need of rest and provisions, particularly in the trade winds season when it is well protected from sou'-easterlies. When the winds pipe in from the north, it's not a very good anchorage at all; Abel Point Marina is the best choice for good all-weather anchorage in the area.

The town of Airlie Beach is not a large town, and all shops and services are within easy walking distance along the main street, Shute Harbour Road.

Just behind the waterfront is a big man-made lagoon that affords safe, year-round aquatic recreation with a huge swimming area, wading pools, picnic facilities, children's playground equipment, walkways and lots of grassy verges for sunbaking and taking in the scenery.

The Airlie Beach lagoon

Airlie's beach

Meridien Abel Point Marina

Boating facilities

Meridien Abel Point Marina

Abell Point is the site of the largest marina complex in the Whitsundays. It is owned and operated by Meridien Marinas Abel Point Pty Ltd. Meridien is also the developer of the new Port of Airlie under construction in Muddy Bay. Abell Point is named after the Abell family that originally settled there; sometime since, the second 'l' in their name was dropped by clerical mishap, resulting in road signs, maps, charts and the name of the marina showing 'Abel' instead of 'Abell'.

The marina was the first in the area (1989); extensions to the original marina have been completed progressively over the years with final stages now complete; there is a total of 500 berths for vessels 11–60 metres in length. It is a modern facility with 24-hour CCTV, security and swipe access, private, gated berthing, wireless internet network access and secure car parking. Berths have single- and three-phase power available (34, 64, and 125 amps). Fuels, including diesel (80, 160 and 400 litres per minute flow rate), unleaded, outboard fuel and LPG are available. There is a sewage pumpout facility. Situated in the northern section of the marina complex are a number of bareboat charter companies, marine service providers (sailmaker, diesel mechanic, refrigeration, engineering, electronic and electrical services, chandlery), dive shop and bottle shop.

Office hours are Monday to Friday 0800 to 1700. Contact both offices on VHF16/09 (telephone 07 4946 2400, FAX 07 4946 2444). The marina website (*www.abelpointmarina.com.au*) gives extensive information on berthing, navigation, maps and links to other useful sites. Reservations are essential and can be made by email at reservations@abelpointmarina.com.au.

Hawkes Boatyard

Hawkes Boatyard is situated next to Abel Point Marina. All-tide lifts are possible with a 50-tonne Travelift for vessels up to 30 metres long drawing up to 5 metres. Work areas are clean, with industrial-strength trestles and planks for hire. Paint screens and ladders are provided. Marine services include high-pressure water blasting, antifouling, airless paint spraying, polishing topsides, chandlery, shipwright, and electricians. Three-phase 415V and single-phase 240V power outlets are available at all cradle positions. The yard welcomes DIY and provides toilet and shower facilities for live-aboards.
Tel. (07) 4946 6700. Email: hby@hawkesboatyard.net.au
www.hawkesboatyard.com

Edge's Boatyard (Campbell's Creek)

Campbell's Creek empties through mangroves into the head (southern end) of Muddy Bay. The creek is navigable at high tide for some distance (via a narrow channel with buoys on either side). Edge's Boatyard sits on a 2-acre site reclaimed from the mangroves about 500 metres in from the entrance. There is a shallow spot right at the the first set of markers which at times dries to 1m; the bottom is soft mud. Access to the boatyard requires a depth equal to the draft of the vessel plus 1.1m (e.g a vessel with 1.4m draft requires 2.5m of tide. Edge's boatyard can lift vessels up to 40 tonnes and up to 21m in length with the Travelift, and there are 25 hardstand sites with power and water. There is an onsite shipwright, painter and chandlery. All other services are available through private contractors in the area. Dry storage is also available. There are laundry facilities and an amenities block.
Web: *www.edgesboatyard.com*
Email: enquiries@edgesboatyard.com
Tel. (07) 4948 2607. Mob. 0413 548 323.

Launching ramps

A public launching ramp and dinghy pontoon is located immediately west of Abel Point Marina, with adjacent parking facilities for trailers. Ramps and parking are also available adjacent to Whitsunday Air Sea Rescue west of Abel Point Marina and at the Whitsunday Sailing Club (members only).

Fuel

Abel Point Marina VHF 16/09. Tel. (07) 4946 6695, 4946 2400.

Marine search and rescue

Volunteer Marine Rescue Whitsunday VMR442

Altman Avenue, Cannonvale. Tel. (07) 4946 7207.

VMR is an accredited service linked to the State Emergency Service via the Queensland Water Police and is dedicated to respond to emergencies. If called upon, VMR may also assist vessels that are not in an emergency situation but require assistance due to breakdown, etc. Calls to VMR442 will be answered on HF 2524 kHz, VHF channels 16, 22, 81, 82.

Whitsunday Sailing Club

The Whitsunday Sailing Club has an enviable position on Airlie Beach's south-eastern promontory. From any of the tables on the veranda there is a million dollar view, and this friendly club welcomes visitors and is more than happy for visiting yachtsmen to bring their dinghies into its protected lagoon and use their pontoon for loading and unloading (don't leave the dinghy tied to the pontoon). The water in the main channel is 1.5 m deep (on a '0' tide). A concrete launching ramp is for members only. The club has a washing machine and drier downstairs, and water is available at the top of the boat ramp. With its licensed bar and meals service, this is a very popular spot.
Tel. (07) 4946 6138. Web: *www.whitsundaysailingclub.com.au*

The Whitsunday Sailing Club has a protected dinghy harbour and is the easiest place to land for those coming ashore at Airlie Beach. Visitors are welcome to use its facilities, including the bar and restaurant. Sitting on the verandah, one is treated to a spectacular view northwards. The launching ramp is for use of members only.

NEARBY ANCHORAGES

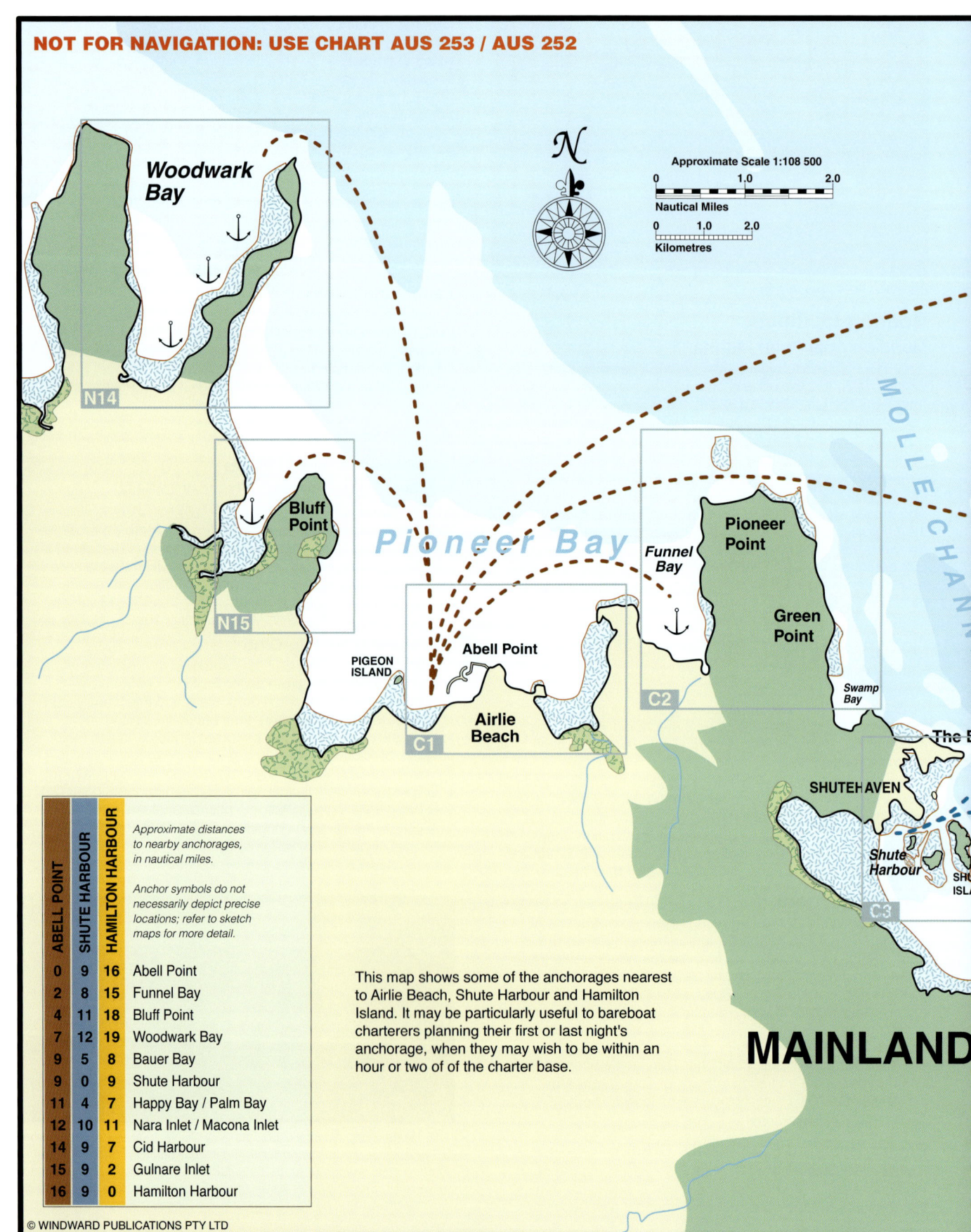

NOT FOR NAVIGATION: USE CHART AUS 253 / AUS 252

Woodwark Bay

N14

Bluff Point

N15

PIGEON ISLAND

Pioneer Bay

Abell Point

Airlie Beach

C1

Funnel Bay

Pioneer Point

Green Point

C2

Swamp Bay

The

SHUTE HAVEN

Shute Harbour

SHU ISLA

C3

MAINLAND

N

Approximate Scale 1:108 500

0   1,0   2,0
Nautical Miles

0   1,0   2,0
Kilometres

Approximate distances to nearby anchorages, in nautical miles.

Anchor symbols do not necessarily depict precise locations; refer to sketch maps for more detail.

ABELL POINT	SHUTE HARBOUR	HAMILTON HARBOUR	
0	9	16	Abell Point
2	8	15	Funnel Bay
4	11	18	Bluff Point
7	12	19	Woodwark Bay
9	5	8	Bauer Bay
9	0	9	Shute Harbour
11	4	7	Happy Bay / Palm Bay
12	10	11	Nara Inlet / Macona Inlet
14	9	7	Cid Harbour
15	9	2	Gulnare Inlet
16	9	0	Hamilton Harbour

This map shows some of the anchorages nearest to Airlie Beach, Shute Harbour and Hamilton Island. It may be particularly useful to bareboat charterers planning their first or last night's anchorage, when they may wish to be within an hour or two of of the charter base.

© WINDWARD PUBLICATIONS PTY LTD

SEE CAUTIONS ON USE OF SKETCH MAPS ON PAGES 121,123

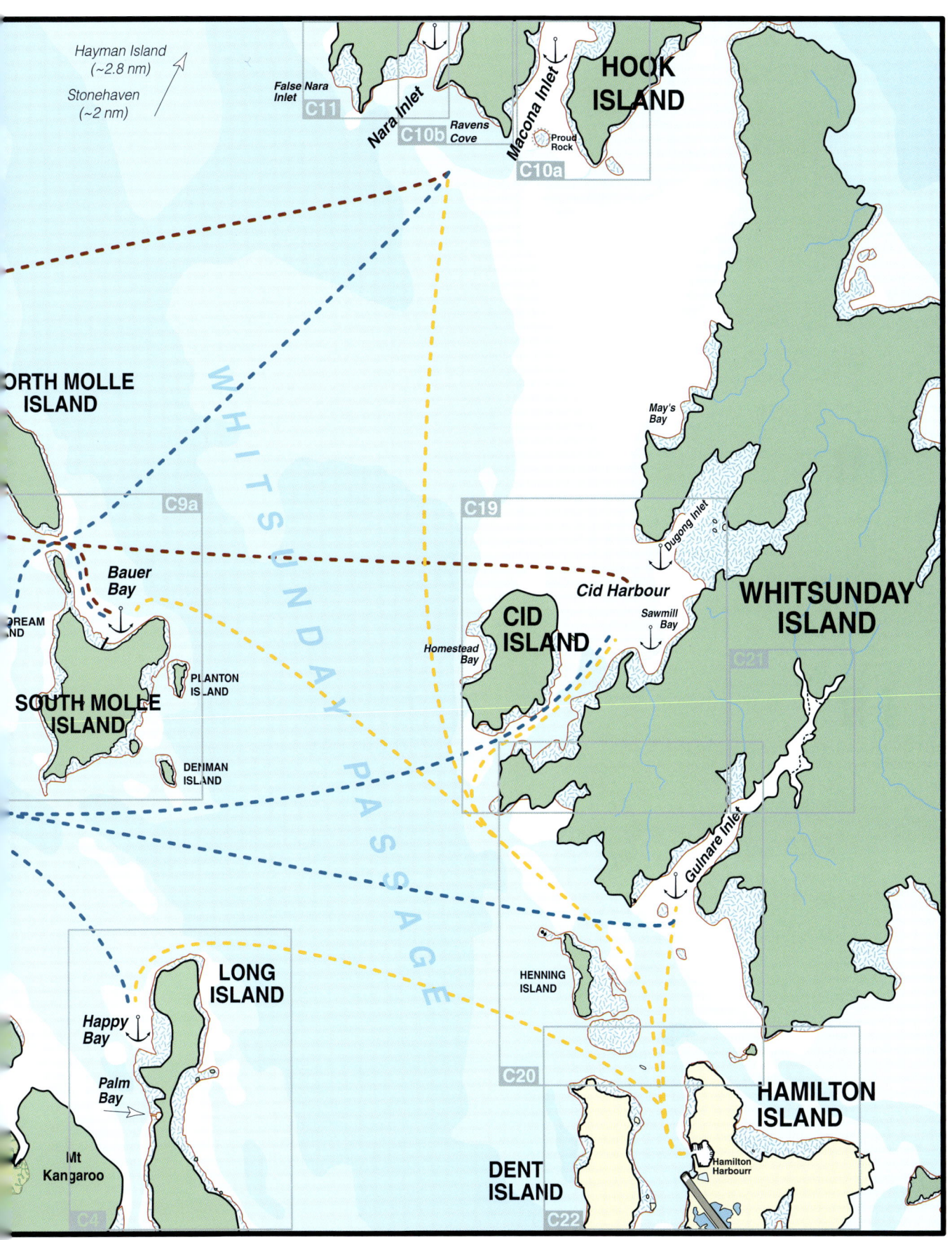

Hayman Island
(~2.8 nm)

Stonehaven
(~2 nm)

False Nara
Inlet

C11

Nara Inlet

C10b

Ravens
Cove

Macona Inlet

C10a

Proud
Rock

HOOK
ISLAND

ORTH MOLLE
ISLAND

May's
Bay

C9a

Dugong Inlet

Cid Harbour

WHITSUNDAY
ISLAND

C19

Bauer
Bay

CID
ISLAND

Sawmill
Bay

REAM
ND

Homestead
Bay

C21

PLANTON
ISLAND

SOUTH MOLLE
ISLAND

DENMAN
ISLAND

Gulnare Inlet

WHITSUNDAY PASSAGE

LONG
ISLAND

HENNING
ISLAND

Happy
Bay

C20

Palm
Bay

HAMILTON
ISLAND

Mt
Kangaroo

Hamilton
Harbourr

DENT
ISLAND

C4

C22

AIRLIE BEACH

C1

NEXT SKETCH MAP N10c

NOT FOR NAVIGATION: USE CHART AUS 268

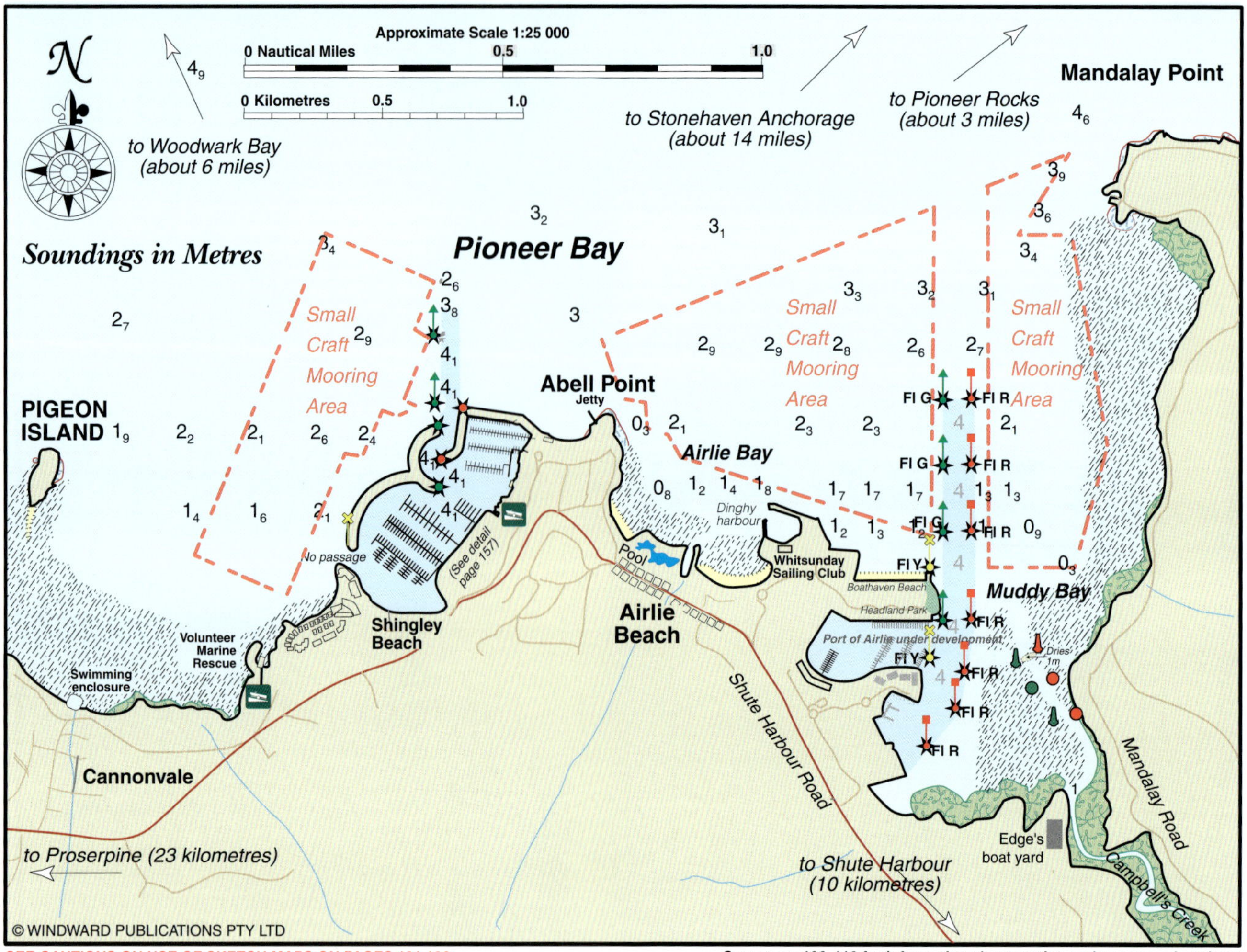

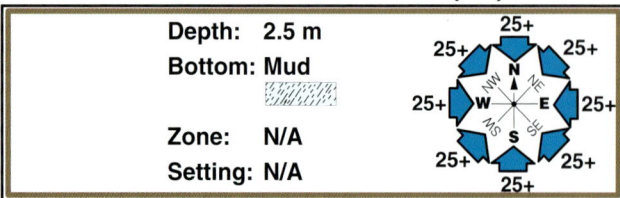

Approximate Scale 1:25 000
0 Nautical Miles 0.5 1.0
0 Kilometres 0.5 1.0
N
to Woodwark Bay (about 6 miles)
to Stonehaven Anchorage (about 14 miles)
to Pioneer Rocks (about 3 miles)
Mandalay Point
Soundings in Metres
Pioneer Bay
Small Craft Mooring Area
Small Craft Mooring Area
Small Craft Mooring Area
PIGEON ISLAND
Abell Point
Jetty
Airlie Bay
Dinghy harbour
Whitsunday Sailing Club
Boathaven Beach
Headland Park
Port of Airlie under development
Muddy Bay
Dries 1m
Fl G
Fl R
Fl Y
No passage
(See detail page 157)
Pool
Shingley Beach
Airlie Beach
Volunteer Marine Rescue
Swimming enclosure
Cannonvale
Shute Harbour Road
Mandalay Road
Campbell's Creek
Edge's boat yard
to Proserpine (23 kilometres)
to Shute Harbour (10 kilometres)
NEXT SKETCH MAP N15
JOINS SKETCH MAP C2
© WINDWARD PUBLICATIONS PTY LTD

SEE CAUTIONS ON USE OF SKETCH MAPS ON PAGES 121,123

See pages 108–113 for information about marine park zones and settings

MERIDIEN ABEL POINT MARINA (C1)

Depth: 2.5 m
Bottom: Mud
Zone: N/A
Setting: N/A

25+
25+
25+
25+
25+
25+
25+
25+
N
NE
E
SE
S
SW
W
NW

The channel and main entrance to the marinas is about 4.1 metres deep; this depth is maintained into both marinas, shoaling to 3.5m in the southern section and 2.5 in the northern section (see larger sketch map of the marina opposite). There is only one entrance to the marina (on the north); the western gap is a wash gate that allows water to circulate but it is not an entrance (there are yellow buoys and a floating yellow boom barring the passage) The marnina operates on VHF channel 16/09. Fuel (outboard, diesel, unleaded, LPG) and water are available. The southern section has a sewage pumpout facility. At the northern section a full range of marine services is available.

PIONEER BAY (C1)

Depth: 1–4 m
Bottom: Mud & coral
Zone: N/A
Setting: N/A

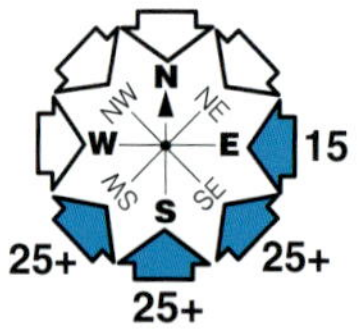

N
NE
E
SE
S
SW
W
NW
15
25+
25+
25+

Pioneer Bay (including Airlie Bay and Muddy Bay) is a broad, shallow body of water protected from southerly winds but very exposed to the north. It is the traditional refuge of itinerant cruising yachts sheltering froms seasonal SE trade winds and affording access to the amenities of the resort town of Airlie Beach.

The anchorage may be swelly as the wind easts.

The coral/rock/sand/mud off Airlie Beach dries extensively. The best dinghy access in the area is at the Whitsunday Sailing Club's dinghy harbour which is protected by a seawall. Visitors are welcome to use the dinghy harbour and club facilities. Don't leave your dinghy tied up to the pontoon (pull it up on the shore).

Muddy Bay dries extensively; it is the site the new Port of Airlie marina and condominium development.

ABEL POINT MARINA

NOT FOR NAVIGATION

[Sketch map with depth soundings and navigation markers: FI G, FI R markers, 4₁ channel markings, Northern Marina Office, Slipway, Jetty, Gov't Pontoon - No Public Access, Public Access Pontoon (tenders), Fuel Jetties, Southern Marina Office, No passage]

© WINDWARD PUBLICATIONS PTY LTD

SEE CAUTIONS ON USE OF SKETCH MAPS ON PAGES 121,123

Above: Commercial tenants at the northern section of Abel Point Marina include: kiosk-snack bar, booking office, boutique, a number of bareboat charter offices, sailmaker, marine refrigeration specialist, marine and electrical services, chandlery, dive shop, bottle shop, dive school, marina office, laundry, toilets and showers.

Much of the bay from Mandalay Point to west of the Abel Point Marina is a designated Small Craft Mooring Area, which means that yachts may anchor within the area only if they do not interfere with any yacht on a permanent mooring. Care needs to be exercised to avoid hooking a mooring with the anchor and to maintain adequate swinging room at all times. Never leave a yacht on anchor unattended in these areas. Should contact result in damage to either vessel, a 'marine incident' is created which could result in legal penalty.

Port of Airlie

The channel into the marina (*see sketch map C1 opposite*) is 40 metres wide with a design depth of 4m LAT; the declared depth (at time of printing – September 2011) is 1.8m due to siltation, and mariners should check Notices to Mariners http://www.msq.qld.gov.au/Notices-to-Mariners/Ntm-whitsundays.aspx) and/or contact the marina before entering for the latest declared depth.

Meridien Marinas Port of Airlie project has involved the reclamation of 15 hectares of Muddy Bay and the construction of a significant marina that will ultimately berth 289 yachts ranging from 10–50 metres and will provide full fuel service, sewage pump-out facilities, a Travelift capable of handling vessels up to 110 tonnes and a hardstand area. Marina berths associated with the Boathouse Apartment complex have

recently been completed. Construction is underway for a new ferry terminal just south of the man-made harbour, and super-yacht marina berths are under construction along the northern seawall within the harbour.

Ferry and cruise services

Fantasea Adventure Cruising will, upon completion of the ferry terminal, move the bulk of its operations to Port of Airlie from Shute Harbour. Fantasea offers regular inter-island ferry service to Hamilton Island marina and airport as well as cruises to to the outer Barrier Reef (Reefworld, at Hardy Reef), cruises to Whitehaven Beach, Hamilton Island and the Dent Island Golf Course. The first and last Hamilton Island commuter trips each day will continue to operate from Shute Harbour.

Other Port of Airlie infrastructure

Construction around the marina includes the Boathouse Apartments, which consist of 56 privately-owned, luxury units operated by Outrigger Resorts and Hotels. A dining and fashion precinct facing directly onto the marina is open to the public.

Additional construction planned includes two international hotels, 365 waterfront apartments, 15 absolute waterfront home sites and 39 marina-front home sites. A 240-metre white sand beach (Boathaven Beach) with boardwalk is now open to the public. However, at the time of going to press the Port of Airlie is under administration, and the extent and timing of future construction is uncertain.

Port of Airlie Boathouse Apartments and marina berths (July 2011)

MERIDIEN MARINAS

Port of Airlie (July 2011)

MERIDIEN MARINAS

FUNNEL BAY

Funnel Bay has one of the traditional 'cyclone anchorages' of the Whitsundays. Although there is '0 water' (at low tide) over the bar in front of the creek, just inside the entrance is a depth of 2.4 metres in a large pool. There are lots of mangroves.

If you are unfortunate enough to experience the thrill of a cyclone in this area and are unable to get into Abel Point Marina, you can tie to the mangroves along the bank at the head of the bay (don't anchor 'mid-stream'; there will be heaps of water and piles of logs and debris racing down the valley). Keep your lines high, and tie so that your bow faces the onslaught. (See also 'Riding out a cyclone' in 'Boating in the Whitsundays'.)

Approaching Funnel Bay from the south and east, Almora Islet may be mistaken for Pioneer Rocks, with unfortunate results, as there is no passage between Almora Islet and the mainland. Pioneer Rocks has a beacon and light.

Just to the north-west of where map C2 ends is a designated cruise ship anchorage, so don't be surprised if you see a rather large 'yacht' anchored there from time to time.

FUNNEL BAY (C2)

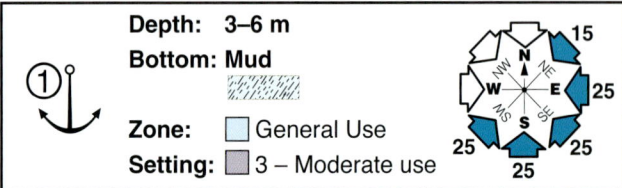

Depth:	3–6 m
Bottom:	Mud
Zone:	☐ General Use
Setting:	☐ 3 – Moderate use

Funnel Bay is at the northern end of a valley with high hills on both sides, hence its name. The area from the mouth of the bay seawards can be very squally, so be prepared for bullets in south-east conditions when sailing across to Airlie Beach or when approaching the bay itself.

Like so many of these northern mainland anchorages, the fishing can be very good.

FUNNEL BAY (C2)

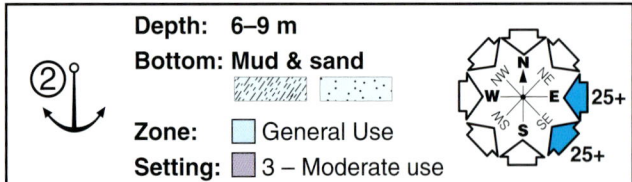

Depth:	6–9 m
Bottom:	Mud & sand
Zone:	☐ General Use
Setting:	☐ 3 – Moderate use

An anchorage with good holding and suitable for overnight stops, although being close to the point, it can be a bit rolly.

PIONEER POINT (C2)

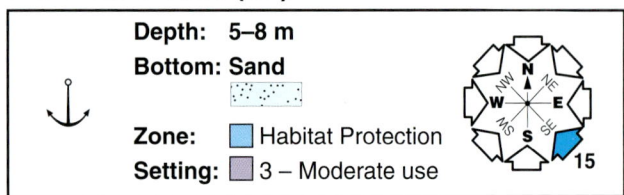

Depth:	5–8 m
Bottom:	Sand
Zone:	☐ Habitat Protection
Setting:	☐ 3 – Moderate use

This anchorage is just off Pioneer Point is suitable in light conditions.

Schooner off Funnel Bay

David Colfelt

Feeding sea gulls turns them into pests. Thereafter, they badger humans for food, and they can also become a positive threat to other seabirds.

To preserve the beauty of the beaches and avoid damage to native vegetation, don't light a fire on any national park island.

Don't fish in a green zone (Marine National Park Zone), and observe the fishing restrictions within a yellow zone (Conservation Park Zone). Be mindful of size and bag limits and seasonal closures when these apply (see pages 88–93).

FUNNEL BAY

C2

NOT FOR NAVIGATION: USE CHART AUS 253

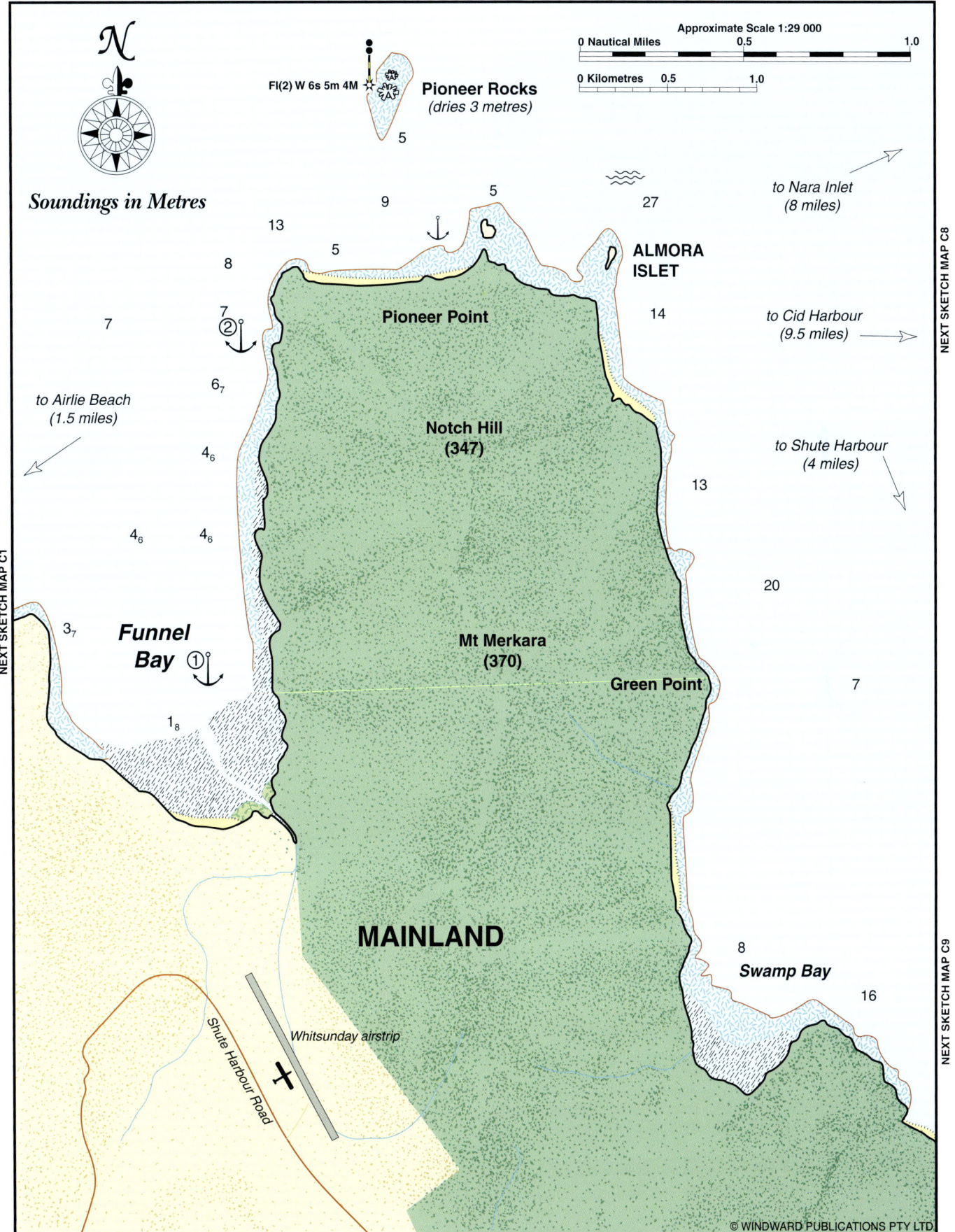

N

Soundings in Metres

Fl(2) W 6s 5m 4M

Pioneer Rocks
(dries 3 metres)

5

Approximate Scale 1:29 000

0 Nautical Miles 0.5 1.0

0 Kilometres 0.5 1.0

9

5

5

13

27

to Nara Inlet
(8 miles)

5

8

7

ALMORA ISLET

Pioneer Point

14

to Cid Harbour
(9.5 miles)

7

2

6 7

to Airlie Beach
(1.5 miles)

Notch Hill
(347)

to Shute Harbour
(4 miles)

4 6

13

4 6

4 6

20

3 7

Funnel Bay 1

Mt Merkara
(370)

Green Point

7

1 8

MAINLAND

8

Swamp Bay

16

Whitsunday airstrip

Shute Harbour Road

© WINDWARD PUBLICATIONS PTY LTD

David Collett

SHUTE HARBOUR

Shute Harbour is historically the focal point of communications between the mainland and the Whitsunday islands. Protected in all weathers, it is surrounded by the lofty hills of Conway Range. It is the best mainland natural harbour for some miles along this stretch of the south-central coast of Queensland. Here the dreams of enchanted holidays among 'South Pacific islands' begin; at 0800 hours each day the island cruise boats assemble, their hulls gleaming in the morning sun. Famous retired yachts of Australian ocean racing take passengers out to enjoy a tropical lunch at Langford Island or Whitehaven Beach, some diving or snorkelling, sailboarding, and then an exhilarating sail up the Whitsunday Passage to finish off a perfect day.

Shute Harbour has two council jetties, the larger (southern) being known as the Lloyd Roberts Jetty, which is dedicated to tourist boats. Both were designed for use by relatively large commercial craft rather than yachts. Yachts visiting the Whitsunday mainland are not encouraged to use either of the jetties and are much better catered for at Abel Point Marina (sketch map C1).

The jetty master may be contacted, if necessary, by phone (07 4946 0557) or on VHF channel 16.

Bus and taxi services

Buses run regularly between the harbour and Airlie Bach and Proserpine. Taxis are available from Airlie Beach by free phone.

Ferry services

Fantasea Adventure Cruising operates a fleet of catamaran ferries providing regular shuttle service throughout the day to and from Hamilton Island marina and airport and from Hamilton to Lindeman as required. When the new ferry terminal at Port of Airlie is complete, most services will operate from that facility with the exception of the first and last commuter services to Hamilton Island each day.

Cruise Whitsundays operates ferry services from Shute Harbour to South Molle Island, Daydream Island, Long Island and Hamilton airport.

Other charter boats and services

A number of day-cruise boats operate from Shute Harbour. There is a barge service for island campers and kayakers, and a kayaking company uses Shute Harbour as its base.

Air services

Whitsunday airstrip, a few kilometres down the road from Shute Harbour, is the base for several companies operating helicopters, amphibians and fixed-wing aircraft. These provide a wide range of services: helicopters and sea planes can pick up passengers at appropriate locations throughout the islands; fixed wing aircraft operate air taxi services to airports in the area.

Parking

Paid parking is available in the jetty area and also on the hill above; a, wooden staircase (with 96 steps) leads down to the sea-level parking lot. A 500-car lock-up garage (operated by private enterprise) is next to the service station.

Launching ramp

Shute Harbour has a concrete ramp for launching trailer yachts and a pontoon for temporary tie-up. Parking for trailers is available in designated space between the service station and the harbourside parking area.

Shops and services

Fantasea at Shute on the Lloyd Roberts Jetty sells souvenirs, T-shirts, postcards, film, books, sunscreen creams, maps, cruise tickets, and the like. Immediately adjacent is a café/sandwich/take-away shop where you can also get breakfast before departing for the islands.

Small Craft Mooring Area

Much of Shute Harbour is a designated Small Craft Mooring Area, which means that yachts may anchor within the area only if they do not interfere with any yacht on a permanent mooring. Care needs to be exrcised to avoid hooking a mooring with the anchor and to maintain adequate swinging room at all times. Never leave a yacht on anchor unattended in these areas. Should contact result in damage to either vessel, a 'marine incident' is created which could result in legal penalty.

Negotiating Shute Harbour

Shute Harbour may be entered from two directions, the preferred one being from the north-east, passing on either side of Low Rock. Low Rock is actually a pile of rocks and coral north-east of Shute Island. Thanks to several bareboat charterers having in the past unintentionally careened their yachts there, Low Rock is marked on all four sides by cardinal marks. Give it a decent berth, and watch the tidal run, which can be particularly strong coming around The Beak. There are leading lights on the jetties ('white' by day – they actually appear slightly yellowish – blue at night) to guide you into the harbour. The channel into the harbour is thereafter deep and well buoyed. \

Don't go too close to any of the beacons from Low Rock on into the harbour, as reefs sometimes extend a distance beyond the marks.

Entry to Shute Harbour from the south is possible via a channel marked by a series of port and starboard beacons. Bareboat charter operators do not permit use of this entrance.

Except during the first hour of the flood in the vicinity of the main jetty, the tidal stream always flows from south to north through Shute Harbour.

Fuel is available at Shute Harbour in an emergency but yachts are better served by Abel Point Marina or Hamilton Island marina.

(Continued on page 162)

SHUTE HARBOUR

NOT FOR NAVIGATION: USE CHART AUS 253

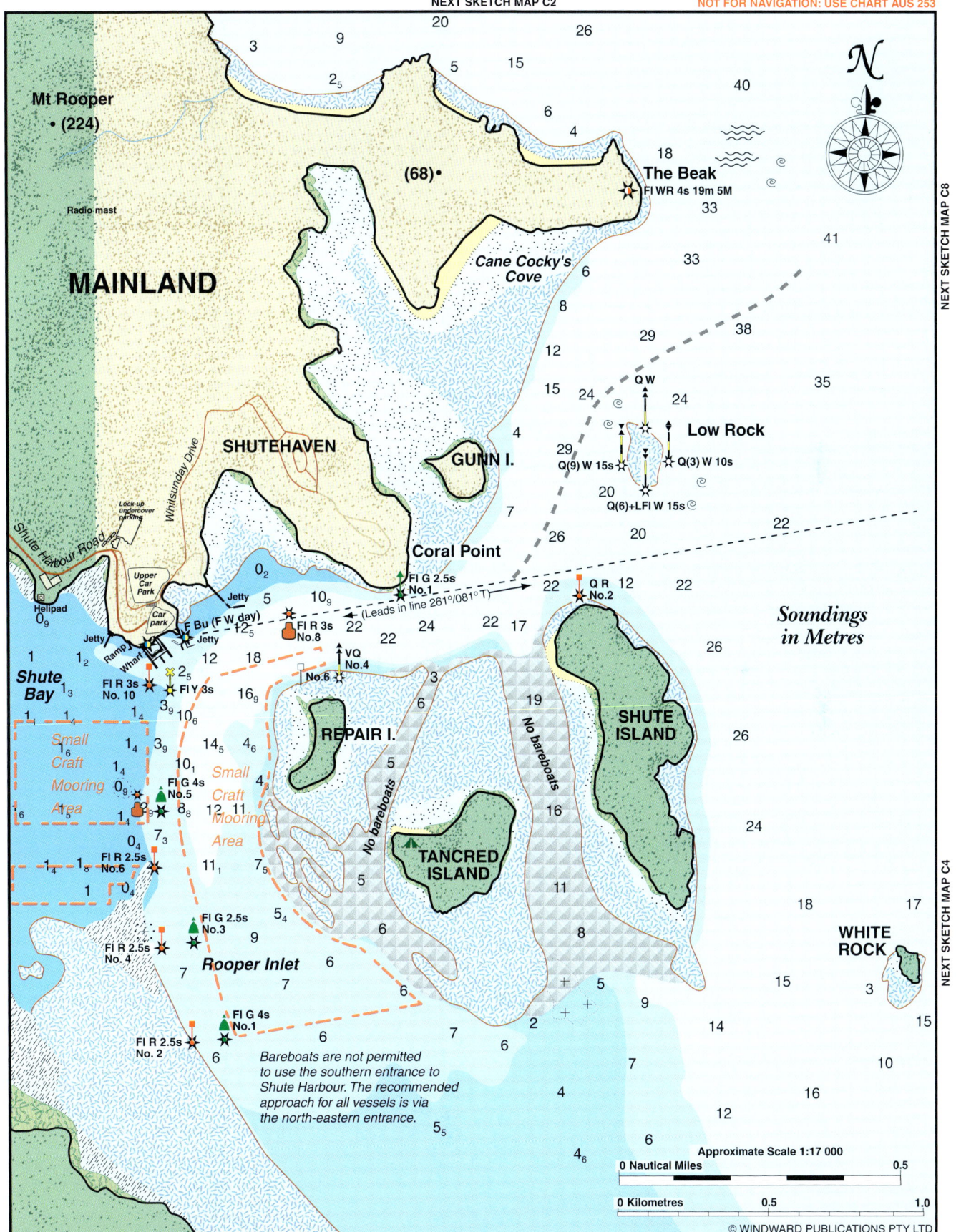

MAINLAND

Mt Rooper
• (224)

Radio mast

(68)•

SHUTEHAVEN

Whitsunday Drive

Lock-up
undercover
parking

Upper Car
Park

Car park

Helipad

Jetty

Ramp

Wharf

F Bu (F W day)

Jetty

Jetty

Fl R 3s
No. 10

Fl Y 3s

**Shute
Bay**

**Small
Craft
Mooring
Area**

Fl G 4s
No.5

Fl R 2.5s
No.6

Fl R 2.5s
No. 4

Fl G 2.5s
No.3

Rooper Inlet

Fl G 4s
No.1

Fl R 2.5s
No. 2

Fl R 3s
No.8

VQ
No.4

No.6

Fl G 2.5s
No.1

(Leads in line 261°/081° T)

**Small
Craft
Mooring
Area**

REPAIR I.

GUNN I.

Coral Point

**Cane Cocky's
Cove**

The Beak
Fl WR 4s 19m 5M

Low Rock
Q W
Q(9) W 15s
Q(3) W 10s
Q(6)+LFl W 15s

Q R
No.2

No bareboats

No bareboats

**TANCRED
ISLAND**

**SHUTE
ISLAND**

*Soundings
in Metres*

**WHITE
ROCK**

Bareboats are not permitted
to use the southern entrance to
Shute Harbour. The recommended
approach for all vessels is via
the north-eastern entrance.

Approximate Scale 1:17 000

0 Nautical Miles   0.5

0 Kilometres   0.5   1.0

© WINDWARD PUBLICATIONS PTY LTD

SEE CAUTIONS ON USE OF SKETCH MAPS ON PAGES 121,123

NEXT SKETCH MAP C8

NEXT SKETCH MAP C4

(Continued from page 160)

Water is not always readily available on the islands: from time to time when rainfall is low, water is of major concern to the resorts, and supplies have to be brought by barge from the mainland. It can be a precious and not inexpensive commodity, and the resorts are not always willing to part with it.

Shute Bay, a shallow, muddy estuary which dries extensively at low tide, is territory favoured by the toadfish, a species that is usually small and has parrot-beak-like teeth; it patrols the shallows, picking off molluscs and crabs. Many years ago there were a number of bizarre attacks by a giant toadfish in the Shute Harbour area, the victims being unsuspecting children and local fishermen, and the odd toe was lost. Never wade in muddy coastal areas without shoes on your feet. (For more lurid details

HAPPY BAY (C4)

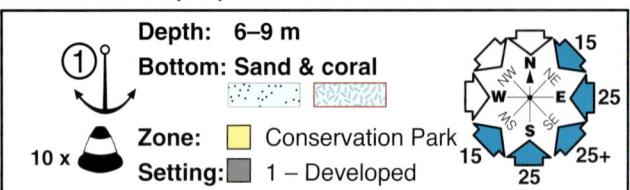

Historically, Happy Bay has been a popular first-night anchorage for bareboat charterers, who often haven't time to get to another overnight anchorage after their briefing in Shute Harbour but who want to get on their way rather than spending the first night at Shute. It is the site of the Long Island Resort, and moorings are available for hire from the resort (see 'Visiting the resort').

The reef at the southern end of the anchorage is deceptive; it extends beyond a line between Base Point at the north of the bay and Humpy Point at the south. If you do anchor on the south-west side, keep a healthy distance away from the reef to avoid several isolated bommies.

The stream that flows through 'The Narrows', between Spit Point and Fire Point, may reach 4–5 knots in spring tides. Approaching Happy Bay from the south, take special note of the prevailing wind and tide conditions. In fresh south-easterlies and a flooding tide, strong eddies and overfalls occur at the southern end of Long Island Sound, and patches of similar conditions will be present elsewhere in the Sound. These disturbances can generally be avoided by steering for adjacent quieter waters, but conditions at the southern entrance may be unavoidable. Whether travelling north or south, it may be preferable to bypass the Sound and travel outside Long and Pine islands (see sketch map C7), avoiding the passage between the two which will also be disturbed.

The jetty at Happy Bay.

Visiting the resort at Happy Bay

Radio ahead on VHF channel 16/09 and speak to the water sports manager to book one of ten moorings that are available. Payment of the fee entitles you to use of showers and all resort facilities, including tennis courts, swimming pools, and nightly entertainment. The jetty is for resort use only; permission may be given to pick up or discharge passengers, but check with the water sports manager before going alongside. Long Island is a national park with good graded walking tracks.

PALM BAY (C4)

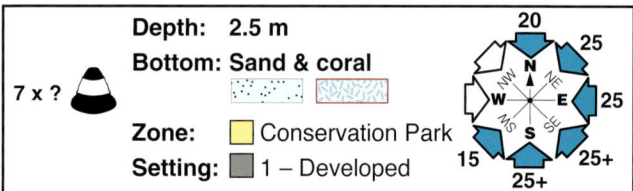

Palm Bay has a dredged channel and lagoon, offering another good overnight anchorage near Shute Harbour (although not a free one). Depending on the tide, there's room in the lagoon for five vessels with draught up to 2.5 metres, and there are two moorings outside the lagoon as well. This is part of a private lease. ***Do not enter the harbour without local advice/assistance***. There is a bar at the entrance, and at a '0' tide at Shute Harbour there is a depth of only 1.5 metres in the channel; therefore, the tide must be a minimum 0.7 metres at Shute Harbour before boats can be admitted. The entrance is marked by port and starboard markers and there are lighted leads on the shore. Once in the harbour, yachts pick up a mooring and tie to a stern line ashore.

Visiting Palm Bay

The lagoon provides a snug anchorage and can afford a peaceful night. Visiting yachts should contact the caretaker on 0429 873 938. A fee is payable for use of a mooring in the lagoon or one of two outside the reef, and this entitles you to use the swimming pool, toilets, showers and barbecue area. No food or drink is available.

The individual cabins, burés, bungalows and suites at the top of the beach are individually owned. Some owners let their units for a per-night fee plus a cleaning fee at the end of the stay. Arrangements may be made by contacting *nqpc@mackay.net.au*.

LONG ISLAND NORTH

C4

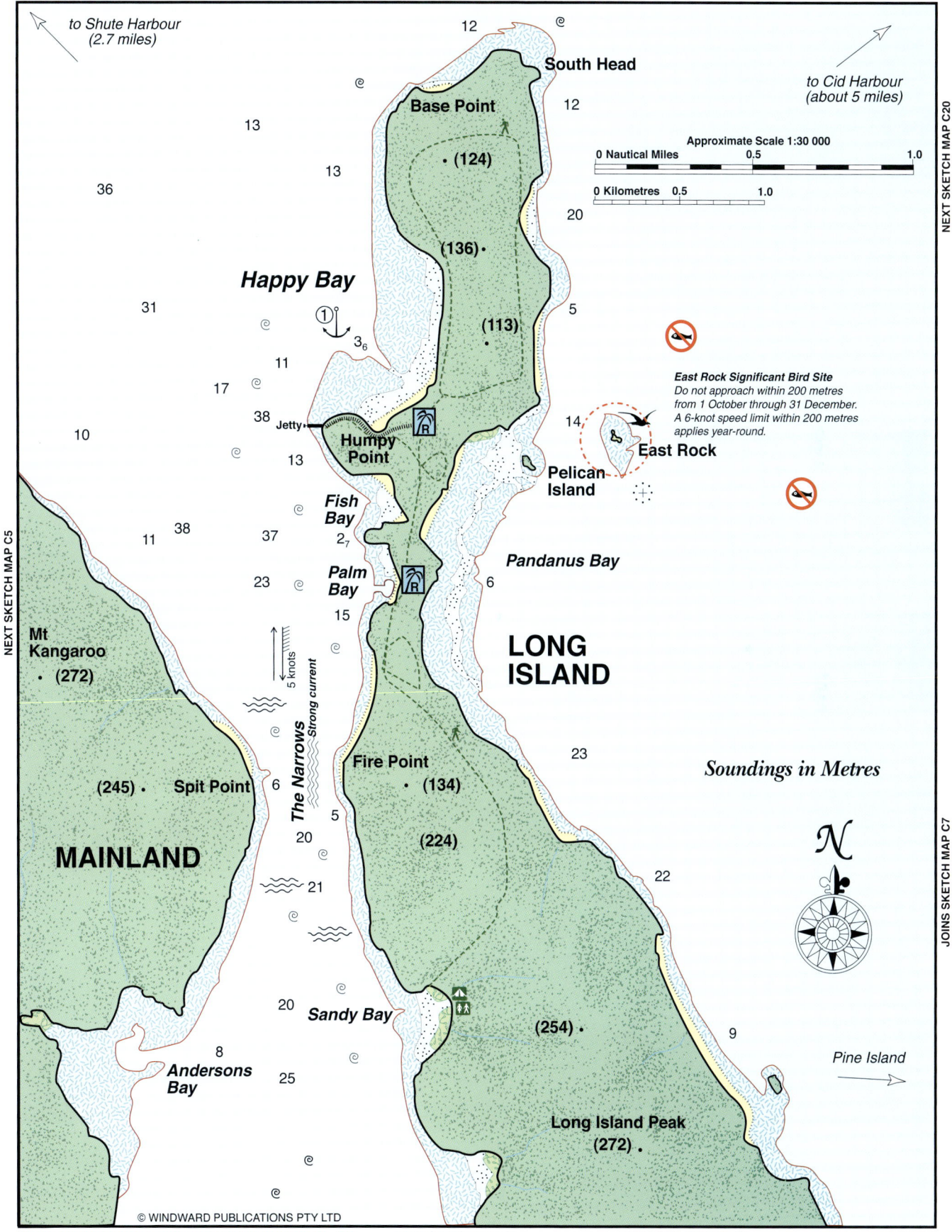

to Shute Harbour
(2.7 miles)

to Cid Harbour
(about 5 miles)

South Head

Base Point

12

12

13

36

13

(124)

20

(136)

Happy Bay

31

5

(113)

NEXT SKETCH MAP C20

Approximate Scale 1:30 000

| 0 Nautical Miles | 0.5 | 1.0 |

| 0 Kilometres | 0.5 | 1.0 |

11

3 6

17

38 Jetty

14

Humpy Point

13

East Rock

10

Pelican Island

East Rock Significant Bird Site
Do not approach within 200 metres
from 1 October through 31 December.
A 6-knot speed limit within 200 metres
applies year-round.

Fish Bay

11   38   37   2 7

Pandanus Bay

23

Palm Bay

6

15

NEXT SKETCH MAP C5

LONG ISLAND

Mt Kangaroo

(272)

5 knots
Strong current

(245) • Spit Point   6

Fire Point

23   **Soundings in Metres**

5

(134)

MAINLAND

20

(224)

21

22

N

JOINS SKETCH MAP C7

20

Sandy Bay

(254) •

9

8

Pine Island

Andersons Bay   25

Long Island Peak

(272) •

© WINDWARD PUBLICATIONS PTY LTD

JULY 1995   APPROXIMATE SCALE 1:40 000

Happy
Bay

Trammel
Bay

Palm
Bay

LONG
ISLAND

Sandy
Bay

Andersons
Bay

Woodcutter
Bay

Paradise
Bay

Pine
Island

Aerial photograph reproduced with permission of the Department of Resources Queensland

TRAMMEL BAY   C5
NEXT SKETCH MAP C3   NOT FOR NAVIGATION: USE CHART AUS 253

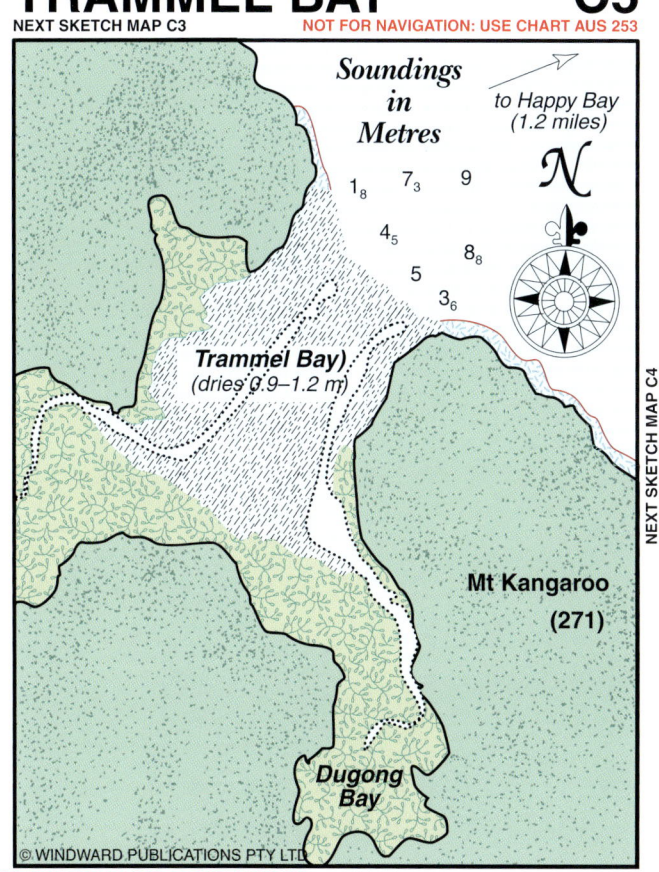

Soundings in Metres

to Happy Bay
(1.2 miles)

N

1_8 7_3 9

4_5

8_8

5

3_6

Trammel Bay)
(dries 0.9–1.2 m)

Mt Kangaroo

(271)

Dugong Bay

© WINDWARD PUBLICATIONS PTY LTD

NEXT SKETCH MAP C4

SEE CAUTION ON USE OF SKETCH MAPS pps. 121, 123   NEXT SKETCH MAPS   C4 & C6

WOODCUTTER BAY   C6
NEXT SKETCH MAP C4   NOT FOR NAVIGATION: USE CHART AUS 253

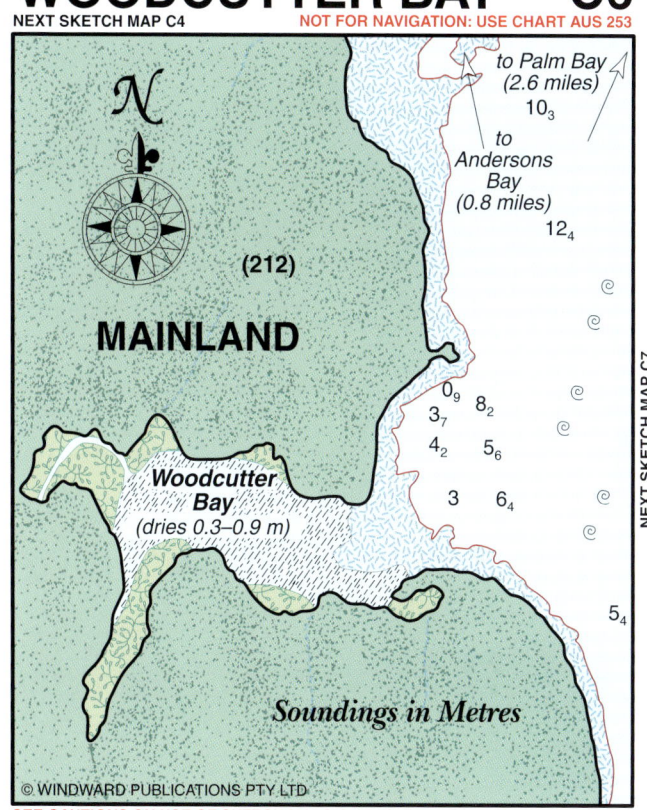

N

to Palm Bay
(2.6 miles)

10_3

to
Andersons
Bay
(0.8 miles)

12_4

(212)

MAINLAND

0_9 8_2

3_7

4_2 5_6

3   6_4

Woodcutter Bay
(dries 0.3–0.9 m)

5_4

Soundings in Metres

© WINDWARD PUBLICATIONS PTY LTD

NEXT SKETCH MAP C7

SEE CAUTIONS ON USE OF SKETCH MAPS ON PAGES 121, 123

TRAMMEL BAY (C5)

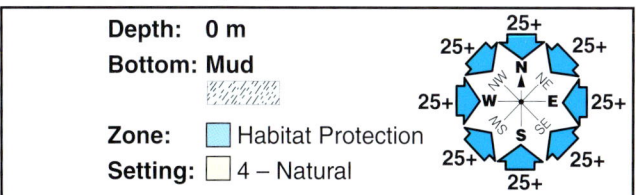

Depth: 0 m

Bottom: Mud

Zone: ☐ Habitat Protection

Setting: ☐ 4 – Natural

25+   25+   25+
25+   N NE   25+
25+   W E   25+
25+   S   25+
25+

Trammel Bay is a shallow mangrove creek accessible at neap high tides to yachts with draught of up to 2.1 metres. In the past, stakes have been put in by private individuals to mark the channel(s), and there have been private moorings (which may no longer be there). Care is obviously required in picking a suitable spot so as not to block access to moorings.

WOODCUTTER BAY (C6)

Woodcutter Bay is another 'anchorage' that is only sought in an emergency (cyclone). It offers a number of spots among the mangroves where a yacht can be tied to weather a tropical storm.

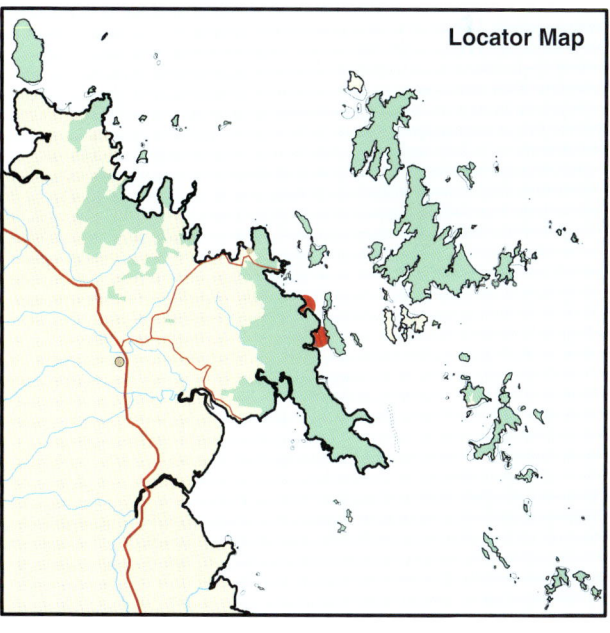

Locator Map

LONG ISLAND SOUTH / PINE ISLAND C7

JOINS SKETCH MAP C4

NOT FOR NAVIGATION: USE CHART AUS 253

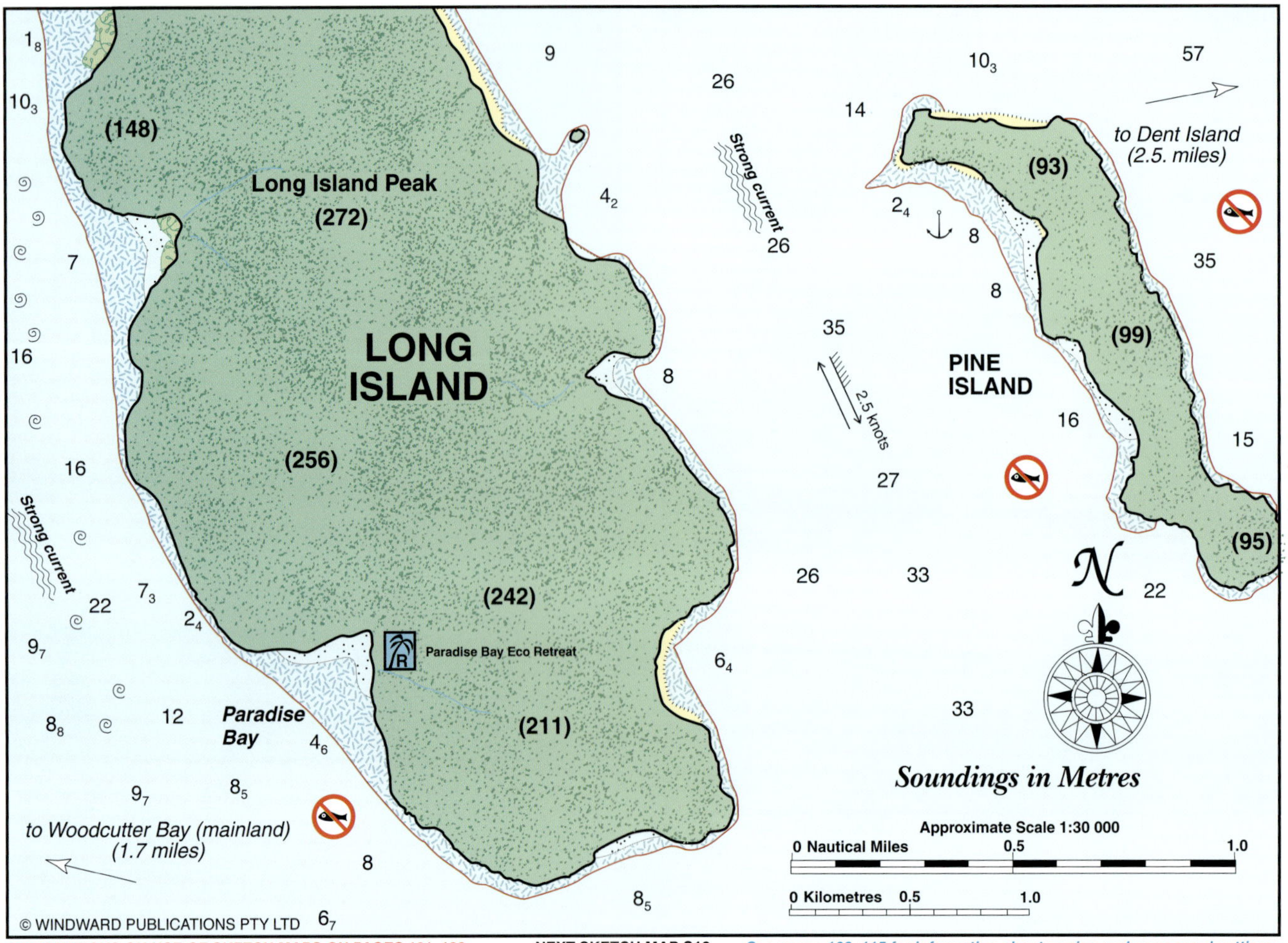

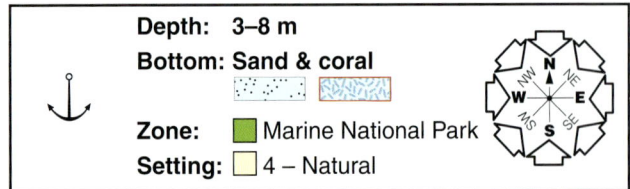

NEXT SKETCH MAP C6

NEXT SKETCH MAP C22

(148)

Long Island Peak
(272)

LONG ISLAND

(256)

(242)

Paradise Bay Eco Retreat

Paradise Bay

(211)

to Woodcutter Bay (mainland)
(1.7 miles)

© WINDWARD PUBLICATIONS PTY LTD

Strong current 26

Strong current

2.5 knots

PINE ISLAND

to Dent Island
(2.5. miles)

(93)

(99)

(95)

N

Soundings in Metres

Approximate Scale 1:30 000

0 Nautical Miles   0.5   1.0

0 Kilometres   0.5   1.0

SEE CAUTIONS ON USE OF SKETCH MAPS ON PAGES 121, 123   NEXT SKETCH MAP S19   *See pages 108–115 for information about marine park zones and settings*

PINE ISLAND (C7)

Depth:	3–8 m
Bottom:	Sand & coral
Zone:	Marine National Park
Setting:	4 – Natural

Pine Island offers limited protection and is adjacent to a channel with swift currents. It is suitable for a temporary anchorage in light conditions. There used to be a wreck on the reef at the north-western end of the anchorage.

UNSAFE PASSAGE (C9a)

Unsafe Passage is the passage between North Molle Island and Mid Molle Island (see sketch map C9a). It was given its foreboding name by a surveyor who had the navigation of ships in mind; it is perfectly safe for yachts provided you exercise due caution. Watch the run of the tide carefully and stay on track using the leads on the north-east end of Daydream Island (they line up at about 232ºM). Hold them in line one above the other until you are through and then for a safe distance beyond (hint: if leads are not lined up, steer towards the lower lead to bring them into line) The leads show fixed white lights by day and blue lights at night.

Do not mistake Unsafe Passage for The Causeway which at high tide appears to separate Mid Molle Island from South Molle Island. As its name suggests, The Causeway actually connects the two islands.

If proceeding from Unsafe Passage to Shute Harbour, watch out, as you head south, for the reef that extends for some considerable distance south from Daydream Island. Especially if the tide is ebbing (setting northwards), keep a close watch on your track to avoid being carried northwards onto the reef by the tidal stream.

Unsafe Passage (safe for small vessels, if negotiated with due care). Watch the run of the currents, and keep the leading lights on Daydream Island in line.

JULY 1995 APPROXIMATE SCALE 1:40 000

NORTH MOLLE ISLAND

'Unsafe Passage'

DAYDREAM ISLAND

MID MOLLE ISLAND

The Causeway

BAUER BAY

PLANTON ISLAND

SOUTH MOLLE ISLAND

DENMAN ISLAND

Aerial photograph reproduced with permission of the Department of Resources Queensland

DAYDREAM ISLAND   C8

NEXT SKETCH MAP C9b   NOT FOR NAVIGATION: USE CHART AUS 253

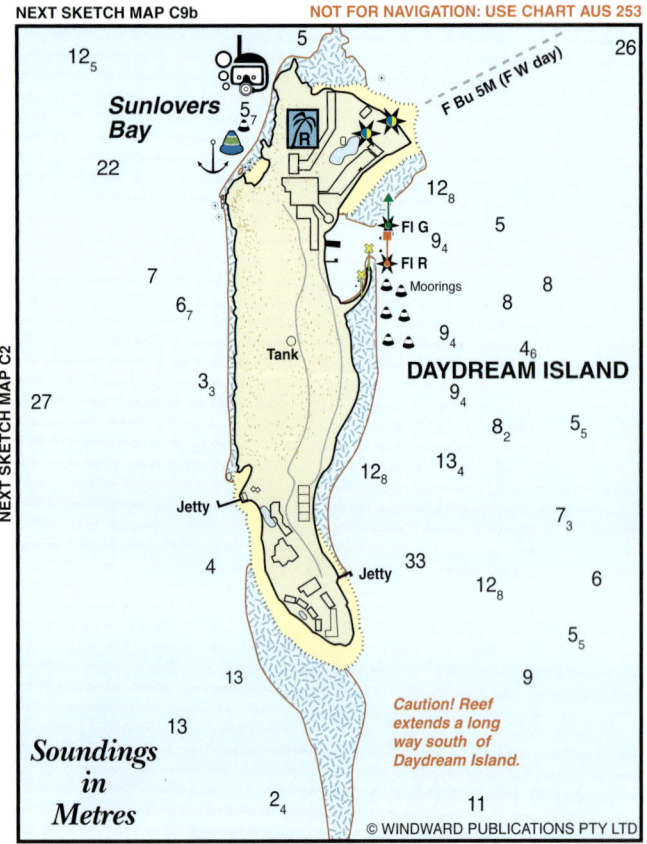

NEXT SKETCH MAP C2

Sunlovers Bay

Tank

Jetty

Jetty

Soundings in Metres

Caution! Reef extends a long way south of Daydream Island.

© WINDWARD PUBLICATIONS PTY LTD

NEXT SKETCH MAP C9a

SEE CAUTIONS ON USE OF SKETCH MAPS: PAGES 121,123   NEXT SKETCH MAP C4

SUNLOVERS BAY

NOT FOR NAVIGATION

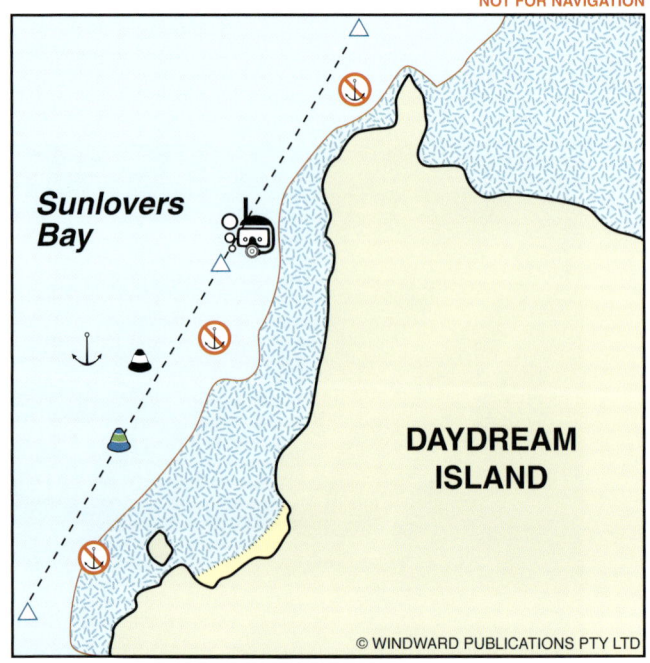

Sunlovers Bay

DAYDREAM ISLAND

© WINDWARD PUBLICATIONS PTY LTD

DAYDREAM ISLAND

Daydream Island is not a particularly good anchorage for yachts. The island is immediately adjacent to the Molle Channel and is subject to swift currents on both sides. As the tide changes, the direction of the current does too, and yachts tend to ride up over their anchors which may break lose from the bottom. If you do anchor around Daydream, always leave someone aboard on anchor watch. Moorings are available outside the harbour on the north-eastern side of the island (see 'Visiting the resort' below). If picking up the mooring nearest the harbour entrance, approach it from seawards to avoid any possibility of conflict with the adjacent reef. The jetty on the western side of the island is for commercial traffic only.

Visiting the resort

Daydream Island has a small, man-made harbour, and there are six swing moorings outside for use by visitors (two for vessels 80+ tonnes and four for vessels <40 tonnes). Yachts are welcome, and visitors who have paid the mooring fee get a free run of the island – the showers and change rooms in the departure lounge and all other resort facilities, including non-motorised water sports (catamarans and paddle skis). Other facilities, such as the bars, restaurants, The Living Reef and the Rejuvenation Spa are also available. Radio ahead on VHF channel 17 to book a mooring.
Telephone (07) 4948 8478.

SUNLOVERS BAY (C8)

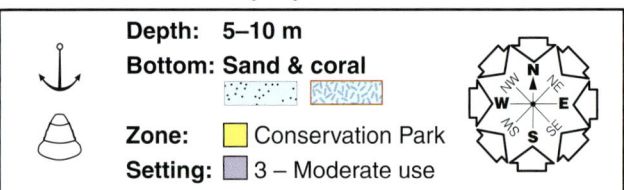

	Depth:	5–10 m
	Bottom:	Sand & coral
	Zone:	Conservation Park
	Setting:	3 – Moderate use

Sunlovers Bay has a beautiful sand beach, and the bay has obvious appeal for Daydream Island resort guests as well as visitors by sea. Reef protection buoys have been installed to protect what was some rather nice coral, and the snorkelling is still pretty good if the water hasn't been stirred up by fresh winds or spring tides. There is one public mooring for monohull yachts up to 20 metres in length (18 metres for catamarans); there is also a private commercial mooring which you will be asked to relinquish if you are tied there when the owner arrives. If anchoring, keep offshore of an imaginary straight line between the reef protection buoys; watch the state of the tide.

BAUER BAY (C9a)

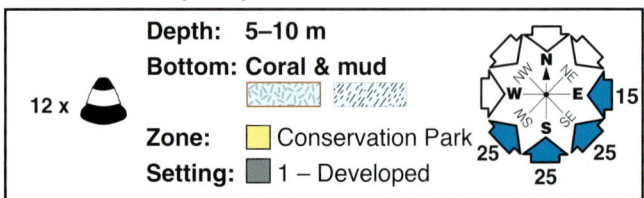

	Depth:	5–10 m
12 x	**Bottom:**	Coral & mud
	Zone:	Conservation Park
	Setting:	1 – Developed

From Deedes Point southwards right around to the western side of the island, South Molle is surrounded by tidal rips and overfalls, some of which extend some distance offshore and which can give the appearance of reefs.

Bauer Bay is not one of the most quiescent anchorages among the islands. In fresh southerly conditions it is
(Continued on page 170)

THE MOLLE GROUP

JOINS SKETCH MAP C9b

C9a

NOT FOR NAVIGATION: USE CHART AUS 253

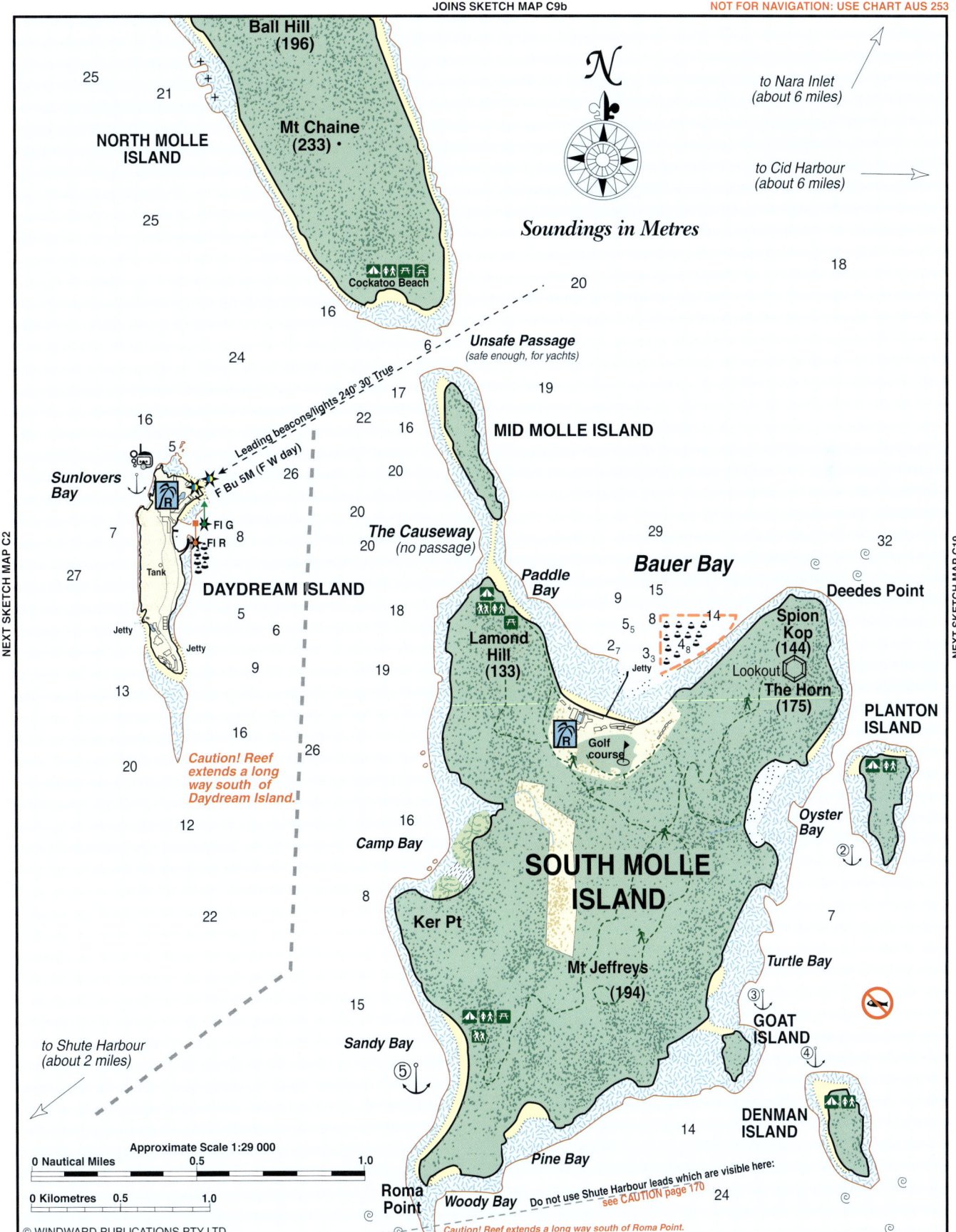

N

Soundings in Metres

to Nara Inlet
(about 6 miles)

to Cid Harbour
(about 6 miles)

Ball Hill
(196)

NORTH MOLLE
ISLAND

Mt Chaine
(233) •

25
21
25
25
16
18
20

Cockatoo Beach

24
6

Unsafe Passage
(safe enough, for yachts)

17
19

22
16

16

MID MOLLE ISLAND

Leading beacons/lights 240° 30 True

F Bu 5M (F W day)

*Sunlovers
Bay*

5
26
20
20

FI G
FI R

Tank

DAYDREAM ISLAND

The Causeway
(no passage)

*Paddle
Bay*

29

Bauer Bay

32

Deedes Point

15
9
5₅ 8
2₇ 4₈ 14
3₃

Jetty

Spion
Kop
(144)

Lookout

Lamond
Hill
(133)

The Horn
(175)

PLANTON
ISLAND

Jetty
Jetty

5
6
9
13

18
19
16

R

Golf
course

Oyster
Bay

②

7

16
20

*Caution! Reef
extends a long
way south of
Daydream Island.*

26

12

22

16

Camp Bay

8

Ker Pt

**SOUTH MOLLE
ISLAND**

Mt Jeffreys
(194)

Turtle Bay

③

GOAT
ISLAND

④

15

Sandy Bay

⑤

to Shute Harbour
(about 2 miles)

DENMAN
ISLAND

14

Pine Bay

Roma
Point

Woody Bay

Do not use Shute Harbour leads which are visible here:
see CAUTION page 170

24

Caution! Reef extends a long way south of Roma Point.

Approximate Scale 1:29 000

0 Nautical Miles   0.5   1.0

0 Kilometres   0.5   1.0

© WINDWARD PUBLICATIONS PTY LTD

SEE CAUTIONS ON USE OF SKETCH MAPS ON PAGES 121,123

NEXT SKETCH MAP C4

NEXT SKETCH MAP C2

NEXT SKETCH MAP C19

(Continued from page 168)

subject to bullets that funnel around the lofty Spion Kop, The Horn and Lamond Hill. It also tends to be swelly as the wind easts, and the anchorage may then become rolly. It is a safe anchorage.

The resort has 12 moorings in the area shown, four for large yachts (> 18.3m), which are usually occupied by the island's boats, and 8 for yachts up to 15m. The area is a declared Small Craft Mooring Area (see note about anchoring in such areas on page 160). Using one of the resort's moorings will afford more comfort than anchoring elsewhere in the bay and when going ashore for a walk or to visit the resort will give much more peace of mind.

South Molle is mostly a national park (the green areas on C9a), and its walking tracks allow spectacular views of the area surrounding the Whitsunday Passage and Molle Channel. To use the national park you do not need to pay a fee to the resort (unless using one of their moorings or if you intend using any of the resort facilities. The tracks to Mt Jeffreys and Spion Kop begin just at the back of the golf course (follow the signs from the beach along the paved road). The tracks traverse a variety of vegetation from vine forest to grasslands. Observation decks have been constructed by QPWS on Spion Kop, affording panoramic views back over Bauer Bay to the west and out towards Whitsunday Island to the east.

Visiting the resort

To arrange use of a mooring, the office can be contacted on VHF channel 16/74. Having paid the fee you are entitled to use of all facilities including the nine-hole golf course (greens fees apply), tennis courts, swimming pool, paddle boats, showers and laundry.
Telephone (07) 4946 9433.

PLANTON ISLAND (C9a)

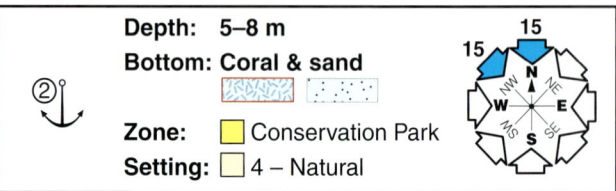

It is not advisable (nor permissible for bareboats) to use the narrow passage between Planton and South Molle islands. It is very narrow and subject to strong currents; a reef extends east for some distance off South Molle.

In suitably light conditions Planton offers a pleasant, infrequently visited anchorage. It is not a suitable overnight anchorage, and you should keep an eye on your anchor, especially if the tide is due to turn while you are ashore.

CAUTION

If proceeding around the southern end of South Molle Island bound for Shute Harbour, remember that a reef extends a long way south of the southern tip of South Molle Island (Roma Point). Give Roma Point a wide berth. The leads of Shute Harbour are visible and line up on a course that will take you right over the Roma Point reef; do not use these leads until you are much nearer to Shute Harbour

GOAT ISLAND (C9a)

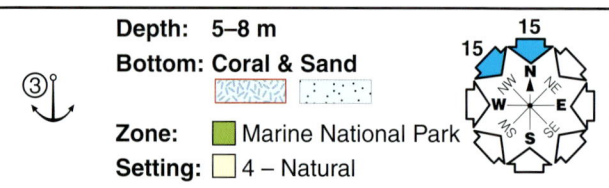

North of Goat Island is a pleasant daytime anchorage (in suitably light northerly conditions) opposite a pretty sand beach on South Molle. Watch out for the edge of the fringing reef. Anchor as close as you prudently can to minimise effects of tide flowing swiftly between Goat and Denman islands.

DENMAN ISLAND (C9a)

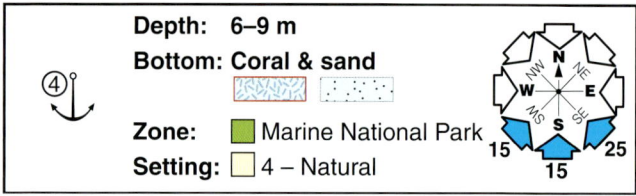

Denman Island is a pleasant daytime stopoff spot that is rarely visited. Watch out for strong currents between Denman and Goat islands. This anchorage offers surprisingly good protection from the south-east, but the sweet spot is small; it is not a good overnight anchorage.

Overfalls may occur as much as 0.5 miles east of Denman Island.

SANDY BAY (C9a)

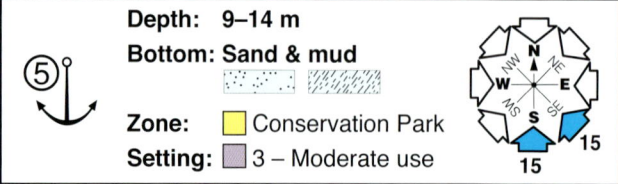

If approaching from the south or west, give Roma Point a good berth as reef and rocks extend south for some considerable distance from this point. Overfalls may at times be seen west of this point.

The anchorage is well protected with good holding, but tidal effects make it less than ideal. During the ebb a back-eddy runs south from Ker Point. Anchor as close in as practicable to minimise tide effects while keeping a safe distance from the fringing reef to allow for swing. This is a delightful, isolated expanse of sand beach.

NORTH MOLLE I. C9b

NOT FOR NAVIGATION: USE CHART AUS 253

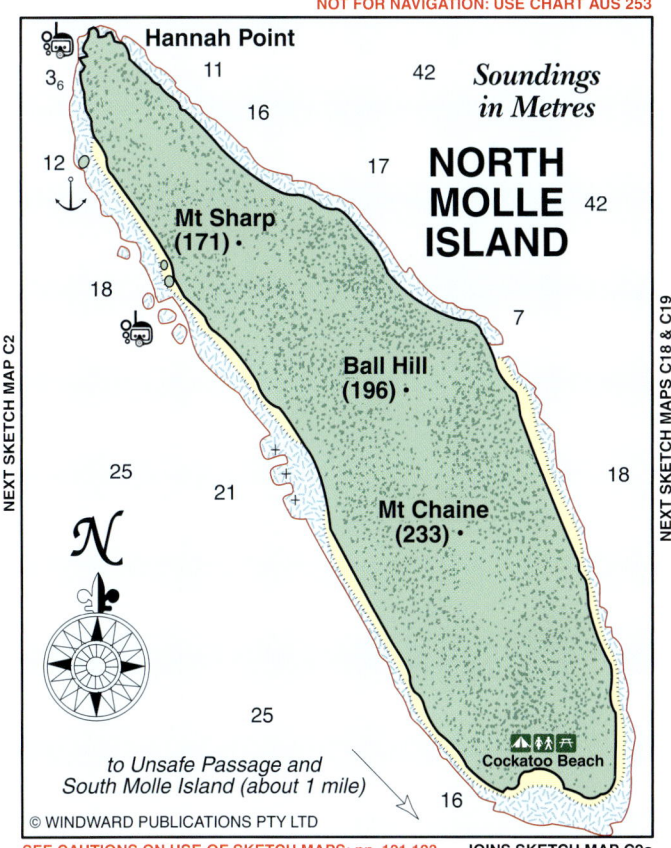

Hannah Point

3₆ 11 42 *Soundings in Metres*

16

NORTH MOLLE ISLAND

12 17 42

Mt Sharp (171) ·

18 7

Ball Hill (196) ·

25 18

21

Mt Chaine (233) ·

25

to Unsafe Passage and South Molle Island (about 1 mile)

16

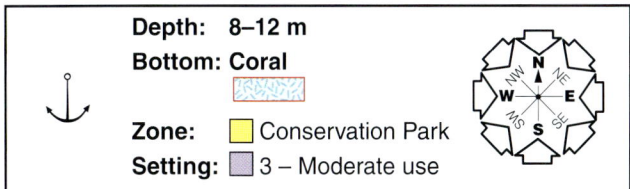

Cockatoo Beach

© WINDWARD PUBLICATIONS PTY LTD

NEXT SKETCH MAP C2

NEXT SKETCH MAPS C18 & C19

SEE CAUTIONS ON USE OF SKETCH MAPS: pp. 121,123   **JOINS SKETCH MAP C9a**

HANNAH POINT (C9b)

Depth:	8–12 m
Bottom: Coral	
Zone: ▢ Conservation Park	
Setting: ▢ 3 – Moderate use	

This anchorage on the north-west side of North Molle Island is a light-weather daytime stop and is a difficult anchorage because it drops off suddenly and is subject to tidal currents. You really need light wind and a neap tide to get the best of it.

There is a very nice sand beach; at its south end is a big rock and some interesting bommies for snorkelling. Hannah Point also offers some diving, but watch out for current, particularly as you approach the Point. Should you feel yourself getting into current, fin back straight away and don't let yourself be carried on around the point. Visibility for snorkelling and diving will not be especially good except in neap tides and when the wind is fairly light.

The Causeway separates South Molle and Mid Molle islands and is completely covered at high tide. Don't be fooled into taking a 'short cut' to Bauer Bay at high tide.

Bauer Bay, South Molle Island

Feeding native wildlife has an adverse affect on the health of individual animals and natural populations. Unnatural populations can cause animals to become competitive and aggresive. Enjoy the company of native animals, but let nature take its own course.

To preserve the beauty of the beaches and avoid damage to native vegetation, don't light a fire on any national park island.

Note. Sketch maps C10a (Macona Inlet) and C10b (Nara Inlet) are intentionally out of sequence so that these two locations lie on these pages as they appear on the chart, i.e. with Nara Inlet to the west of Macona Inlet. The description of anchorages in Nara Inlet are continued on page 174.

NARA INLET (C10b)

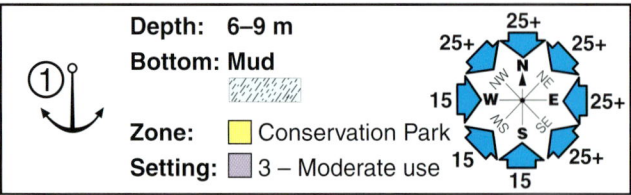

There may be disturbed water at the entrance to Nara Inlet and for some distance out in contrary wind/tide conditions. Keep to the starboard side on entering to avoid the reef area that extends over much of the entrance. Bareboats may not attempt the narrow channel at the extreme left, and no one is particularly well advised to. Once past this reef area the water is good all the way down to the end.

Anchorage No. 1 may get some chop or swell in south-south-east winds of 25+ knots as there is a clear (virtually unbroken) fetch straight in from the Whitsunday Passage and down to the end of this long narrow fjord. Refuge Bay may be smoother (as will anchorage No. 3 for smaller yachts and trailer sailers). It is possible to anchor quite close to the end of the inlet. The holding is excellent. Just before the end (on the starboard side) a waterfall runs after rain.

The Ngaro Cultural Sight is reached from a small beach on the eastern side just in from the anchorage No.1 symbol. The track ascends 170 m, initially steeply up the banks of the inlet, to a rock shelter containing Ngaro art motifs. The site includes a boardwalk, viewing area and interpretive displays.

REFUGE BAY (C10b)

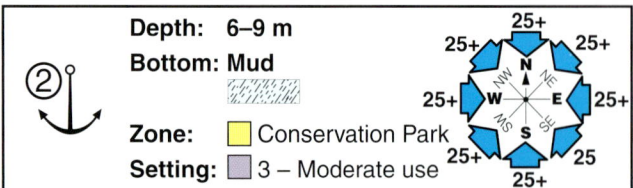

Watch out for the deceptive reef extending from the point on the northern side the end of which is marked. In the past this reef has been the undoing of more than one yacht. There are also several large bommies towards the top end of this anchorage; keep a sharp lookout!

Refuge Bay is less susceptible to swell than is anchorage No. 3 in heavy south to south-east winds; it may be blustery in winds of 25 knots and more.

This bay was formerly called 'Shark Bay', possibly because both Nara and Macona inlets are reputed to be spawning grounds for hammerheads. Nara Inlet probably isn't the best place for swimming.

NARA INLET   C10b

NEXT SKETCH MAPS C13 & C14/15   NOT FOR NAVIGATION: USE CHART AUS 252

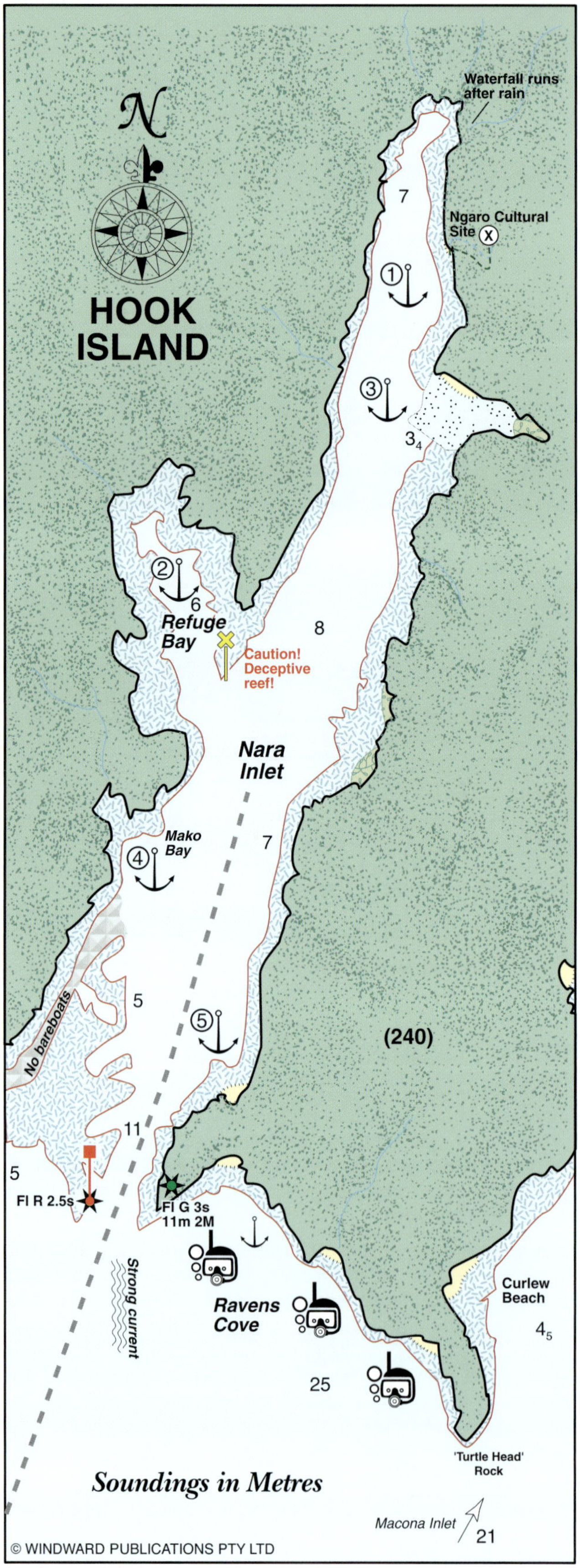

HOOK ISLAND

Waterfall runs after rain

Ngaro Cultural Site (X)

7

Refuge Bay

6

Caution! Deceptive reef!

8

Nara Inlet

Mako Bay

7

5

(240)

No bareboats

5

11

Strong current

FI R 2.5s

FI G 3s 11m 2M

Ravens Cove

25

Curlew Beach

4₅

'Turtle Head' Rock

Soundings in Metres

Macona Inlet   21

NEXT SKETCH MAP C11

NEXT SKETCH MAP C10a

© WINDWARD PUBLICATIONS PTY LTD

SEE CAUTIONS ON USE OF SKETCH MAPS: pp. 121,123   NEXT SKETCH MAP C19

MACONA C10a

NEXT SKETCH MAP C14/15 NOT FOR NAVIGATION: USE CHART AUS 252

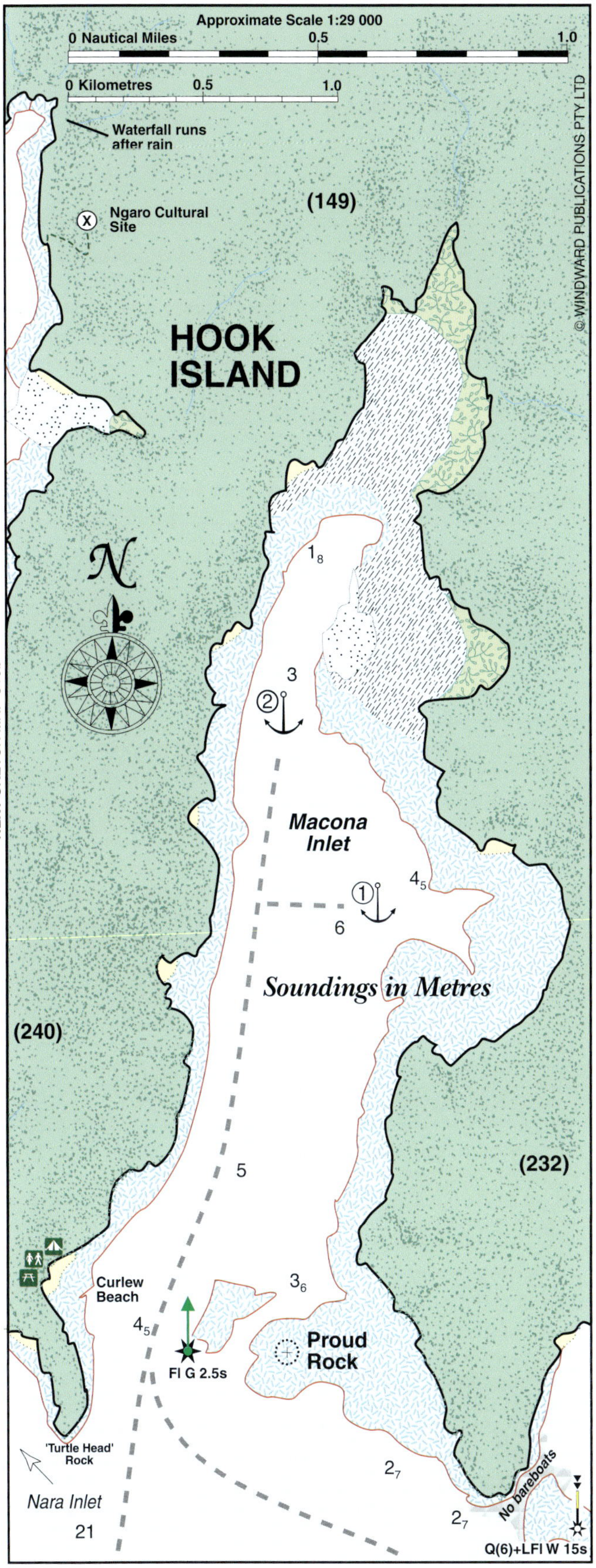

Approximate Scale 1:29 000

0 Nautical Miles   0.5   1.0

0 Kilometres   0.5   1.0

© WINDWARD PUBLICATIONS PTY LTD

Waterfall runs after rain

(X) Ngaro Cultural Site

(149)

HOOK ISLAND

N

1₈

3

②

Macona Inlet

4₅

①

6

Soundings in Metres

(240)

5

(232)

Curlew Beach

4₅

3₆

Proud Rock

Fl G 2.5s

'Turtle Head' Rock

Nara Inlet

21

2₇

2₇

No Bareboats

Q(6)+LFl W 15s

NEXT SKETCH MAPS C14/C15, C16, C17

NEXT SKETCH MAP C10b

SEE CAUTIONS ON USE OF SKETCH MAPS: pp 121,123   **NEXT SKETCH MAP C19**

MACONA INLET (C10a)

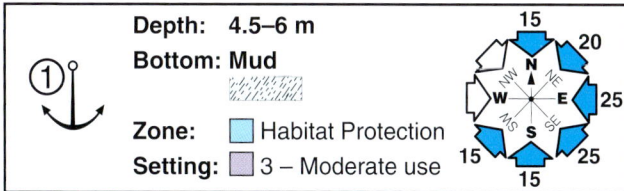

① Depth: **4.5–6 m**
Bottom: **Mud**

Zone: ☐ Habitat Protection
Setting: ☐ 3 – Moderate use

Entering Macona Inlet, keep to the port side to avoid Proud Rock. A back transit may be used to check your progress; hold Hill Rock (which is immediately west of Cid Island) to the east (left) of Pine Island.

If you are coming from Hook Passage, stay outside the south cardinal mark that marks the reef off the southern extremity of Hook Island, and don't head straight for the buoy marking the reefs in the entrance to Macona or you may cut the corner too closely (the reef area around Proud Rock).

Macona Inlet is vast, and there are numbers of sand beaches to explore. Anchorage No. 1 is preferable to anchorage No. 2 in fresh south-east conditions.

MACONA INLET (C10a)

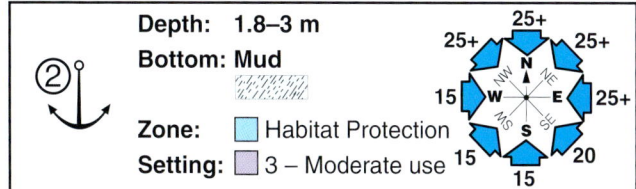

② Depth: **1.8–3 m**
Bottom: **Mud**

Zone: ☐ Habitat Protection
Setting: ☐ 3 – Moderate use

Anchor allowing sufficient swinging room.

JULY 1995 APPROXIMATE SCALE 1:40 000

Aerial photograph reproduced with permission of the Department of Resources Queensland

HOOK ISLAND

Macona Inlet

NARA INLET (C10b)

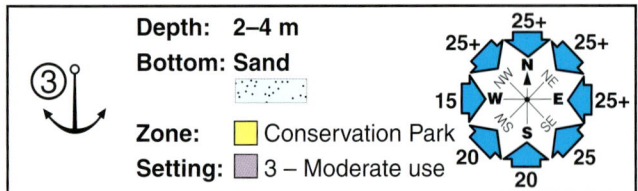

Smaller yachts and trailer sailers will be able to make use of this delightful cove with its lovely sand beach. It provides protection from chop and swell in fresh southerly conditions. Trailer sailers can anchor right over the sand beach; larger yachts should split the difference between the fringing coral reefs. There is very limited swinging room. It is shallow, and if your boat is threatening to swing the wrong way, a stern anchor may solve the problem.

MAKO BAY (C10b)

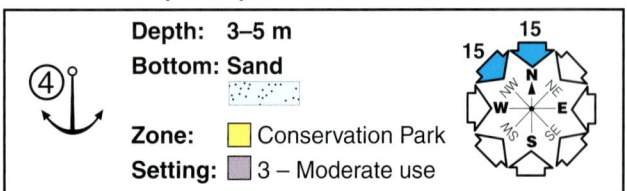

Mako Bay has a pleasant beach for a barbecue in northerly weather (when it is well protected). Anchor

outside the reef, over sand.

NARA INLET (C10b)

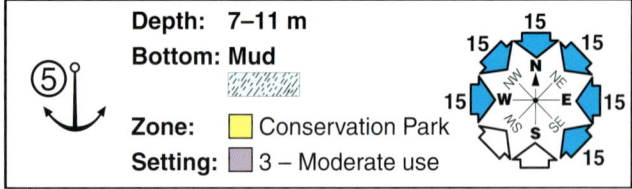

There are more-protected anchorages than this in Nara Inlet, but this one is tenable in suitably light conditions if you wish to remain close to the entrance. From this anchorage it's a short ride in the dingy to Ravens Cove (between Nara and Macona) where you can go snorkelling or perhaps drop a fishing line.

RAVENS COVE (C10b)

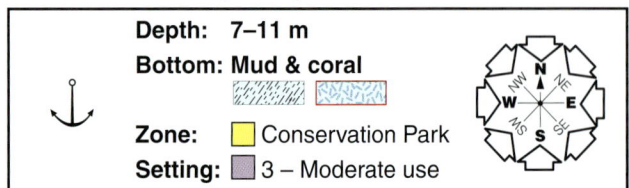

In suitably light weather the fringing reef in the bay on the point that separates Nara and Macona inlets offers good snorkelling and exploring. Ideally, the conditions should be light easterlies and neap tides, at or near the bottom of the tide.

FALSE NARA (C11)

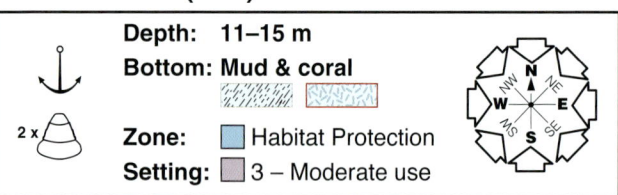

False Nara gets its name because it masquerades as Nara Inlet. You won't get far if you try to go in here. There is frequently disturbed water off this corner of Hook Island.

False Nara is not an easy anchorage because it is fairly deep. Reef protection markers have been installed; no anchoring inshore of a straight line between the buoys. The buoys may not be used as a mooring, even for tying up a dinghy. At neap tides, and when the wind is quiet (so that the water isn't too stirred up), False Nara is good for a dive or snorkel.

CAVES COVE (C11)

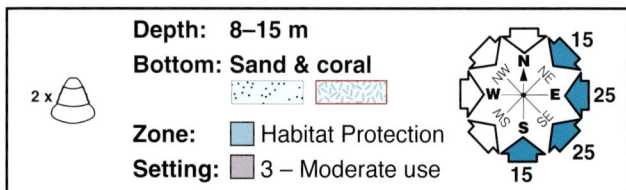

This shallow cove just south of Stonehaven has one public mooring and sometimes one or more private moorings, so it may provide an alternative shelter to Stonehaven if the latter is crowded. It is slightly closer to the mainland, too, which may confer some advantage on a first or last night out.

APPROACHING STONEHAVEN

The Stonehaven area requires particular vigilance because of the extensive fringing reefs of Langford, Black and Hayman islands. There are many potential hazards; exercise extreme care in this area.

Approaching from Butterfly Bay, beware the extensive reef off Hayman Island; at high tide, when this reef is covered, you may be deceived; stay closer to Hook Island (about two-thirds of the total distance between Groper Point and Stanley Point).

Approaching from Hayman keep a lookout for the beacon that marks the considerable bulge on Hayman's reef south-south-west of Groper Point. Keep well south until you are past this and can see the next beacon on the southern tip of the reef and the special mark on the northern tip of Black Island's reef.

Sealark Patch (south-east of Black Island) is a shallow patch of shifting sand which is not a hazard to navigation.

Stonehaven is a majestic bay surrounded by some lofty hills; it is very blustery in fresh south-east conditions, and in the anchorage there may be 'bullets' – sharp gusts of much greater force than the average wind. Because the anchorage is relatively deep, put down plenty of anchor line, and if there are other yachts anchored nearby, allow enough swinging room. Where the maximum depth at high tide is 12 metres, a yacht may have as much as 60 metres

FALSE NARA C11

JULY 1995 APPROXIMATE SCALE 1:40 000

Stonehaven Anchorage

Nara Inlet

False

Aerial photograph reproduced with permission of the Department of Resources Queensland

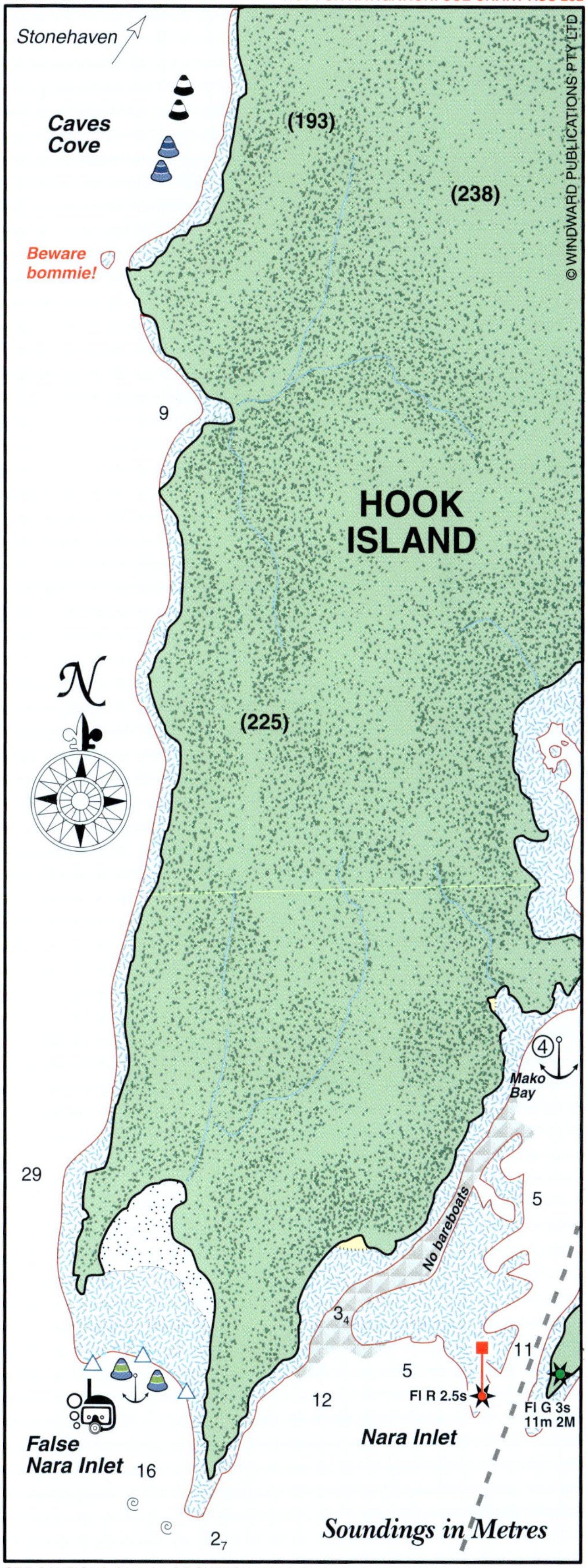

Stonehaven

Caves Cove

Beware bommie!

9

N

HOOK ISLAND

(193)

(238)

(225)

© WINDWARD PUBLICATIONS PTY LTD

JOINS SKETCH MAP C10b

Mako Bay

④

5

29

No bareboats

3₄

5

11

12

Fl R 2.5s

Fl G 3s 11m 2M

False Nara Inlet

16

Nara Inlet

2₇

Soundings in Metres

of scope out, and its maximum swinging radius may be almost 60 metres. Anchor at least five boat lengths away. The bottom is sand and coral, with isolated bommies; rig a rope snubber on the chain to reduce any noise from the anchor chain scraping over the bottom. (See pages 71–72 for more discussion of snubbers and swinging room.)

STONEHAVEN ANCHORAGE (C12)

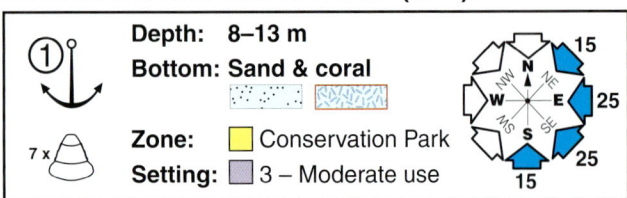

To help preserve the fringing reefs in anchorages No. 1 and No. 2, reef protection buoys have been installed, from the inlet south of Cockatoo Point right down to Ian Point. Anchoring inshore of an imaginary straight line between these buoys is prohibited. There are six 18/20 metre moorings which will make life easier than anchoring; don't lengthen the pennants for any reason as there are bommies not far to the east – these may provide some good snorkelling.

STONEHAVEN ANCHORAGE (C12)

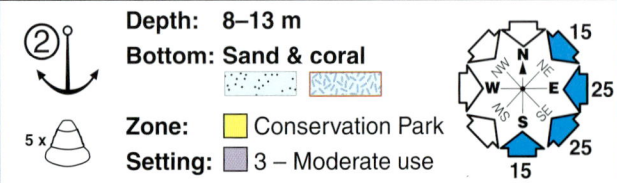

Watch out for scattered bommies. A 'finger' of reef projects into the anchorage, and the two southernmost moorings are almost surrounded by coral reef; approach these with great care, from the north-west, and keep a lookout posted on the bow; make your exit the same way. Under no circumstance lengthen the mooring pennants.

The patch of reef with the break in the middle is good for snorkelling if the wind hasn't been too strong and the tides not too great. The anchorage has a nice sand beach for exploring.

STONEHAVEN ANCHORAGE (C12)

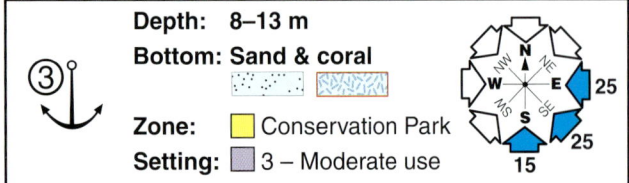

This anchorage possibly provides slightly more protection in gusty south to south-east weather, but it is not as 'cosy'. Again, watch out for scattered bommies off the fringing reef.

LANGFORD ISLAND (C12)

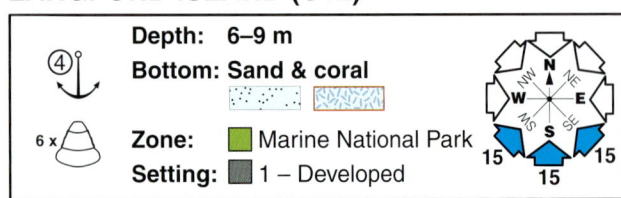

If approaching from the west, keep well outside Bird Island. Reef protection buoys have been installed along Langford's eastern reef; anchor outside (offshore) of an imaginary straight line between these buoys. This location is notorious for snagging anchors; use one of the public moorings if at all possible.

The reef here offers a good dive all along the north-east side, but particularly at the northern end. Langford, with its coral sand beach, has vegetation that gives it the feeling both of a continental island and a true coral quay. The long sand spit is interesting to explore. A nice island.

LANGFORD ISLAND (C12)

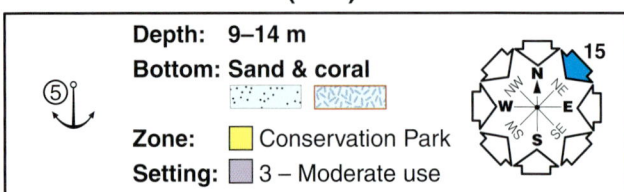

Watch out for scattered bommies lying along the reef margin. Anchorage No. 4 is preferable, and the snorkelling is better there, too.

BIRD ISLAND (C12)

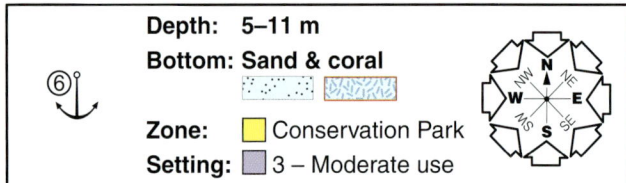

Watch out for strong currents that sweep southwards by this side of Bird Island.

As its name suggests, Bird Island is a significant bird nesting site. To protect nesting birds from disturbance, there is a 6-knot year-round speed limit within 200 metres of the island. This anchorage is of greatest interest to divers because there is an excellent drift dive

BLACK ISLAND (C12)

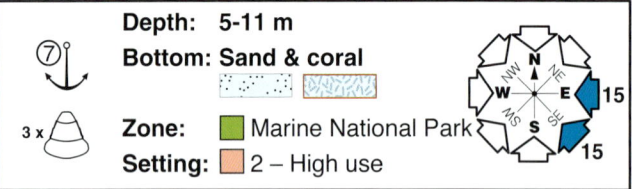

It may be possible to dive/snorkel on the western side of Black Island (known as Bali Hai to Hayman Islanders) when conditions are not as suitable at Langford Island. Black Island has picnic tables and a pit toilet. Beware the reef at the southern end of the island, which sticks out beyond the special mark planted on the reef.

Note: Great caution is needed making your way around this area. Give everything a wide berth: do not take a straight course from one beacon or buoy to the next, as the reefs often bulge out beyond the direct line.

HOOK ISLAND NORTH-WEST   C12

NOT FOR NAVIGATION: USE CHART AUS 254

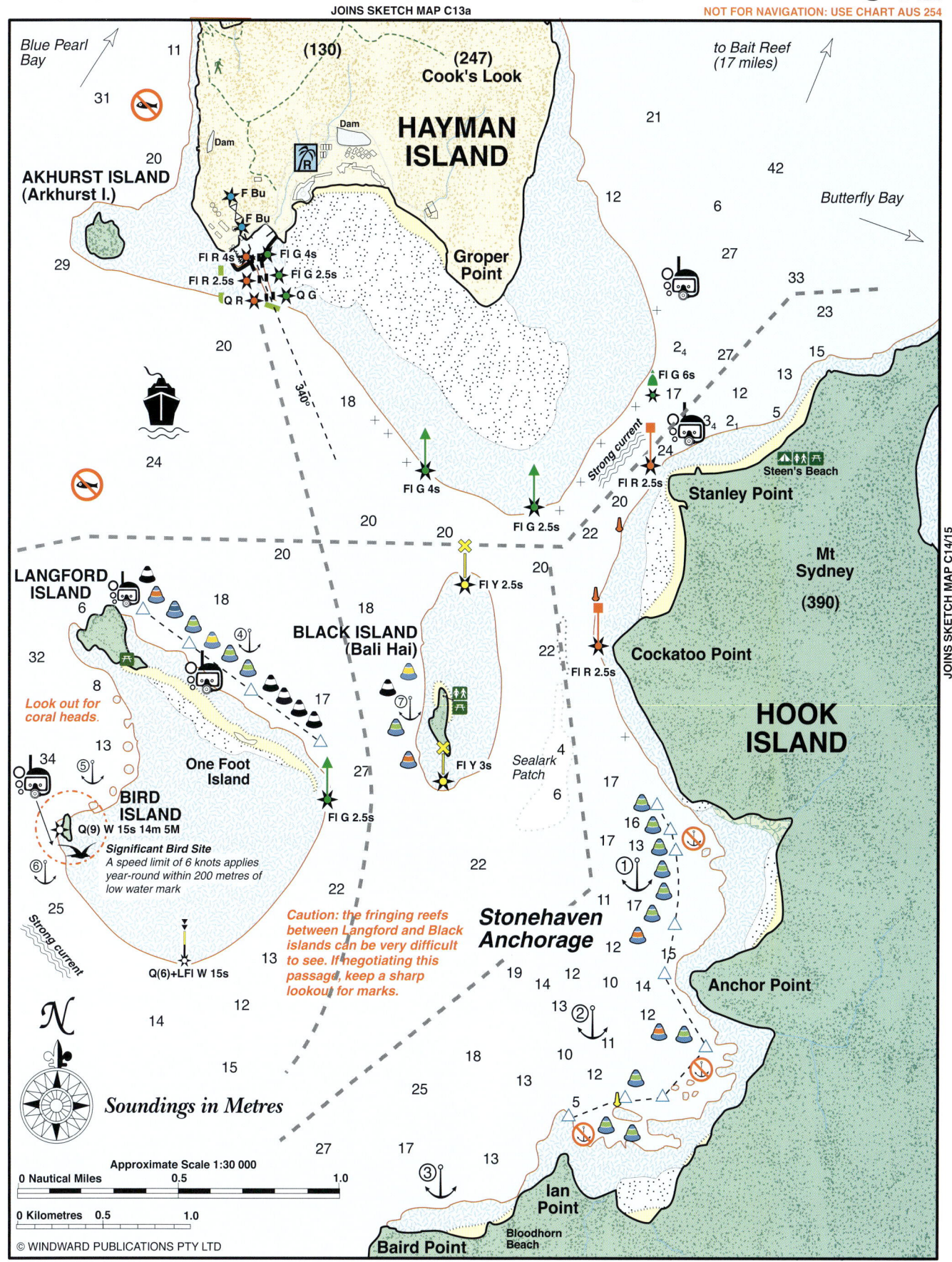

Blue Pearl Bay

(130)

(247)
Cook's Look

to Bait Reef
(17 miles)

HAYMAN ISLAND

Dam
Dam

AKHURST ISLAND
(Arkhurst I.)

F Bu
F Bu

Fl R 4s   Fl G 4s
Fl R 2.5s   Fl G 2.5s
Q R   Q G

Groper
Point

Butterfly Bay

Fl G 6s

Fl G 4s

Steen's Beach
Stanley Point

Strong current

Fl G 2.5s

Fl R 2.5s

Mt
Sydney
(390)

LANGFORD
ISLAND

Fl Y 2.5s

BLACK ISLAND
(Bali Hai)

Fl R 2.5s

Cockatoo Point

HOOK ISLAND

Look out for coral heads.

One Foot
Island

BIRD
ISLAND

Q(9) W 15s 14m 5M

Significant Bird Site
A speed limit of 6 knots applies
year-round within 200 metres of
low water mark

Fl Y 3s

Sealark
Patch

Fl G 2.5s

Stonehaven Anchorage

Anchor Point

Strong current

Q(6)+LFl W 15s

Caution: the fringing reefs between Langford and Black islands can be very difficult to see. If negotiating this passage, keep a sharp lookout for marks.

N

Soundings in Metres

Ian
Point

Bloodhorn
Beach

Approximate Scale 1:30 000

0 Nautical Miles   0.5   1.0

0 Kilometres   0.5   1.0

© WINDWARD PUBLICATIONS PTY LTD

Baird Point

JOINS SKETCH MAP C14/15

JULY 1995 APPROXIMATE SCALE 1:40 000

Aerial photograph reproduced with permission of the Department of Resources Queensland

HAYMAN ISLAND (C13a)

Hayman Island has one of Australia's most talked about resorts with a man-made boat harbour on the southern side where, in days gone by, there was a rather poor anchorage. Before entering the harbour yachts must obtain permission from the marina office (VHF channel 16/10 – see 'Visiting the resort' below).

The harbour entrance is marked by six beacons (Nos 1 to 6) lit at night. On the hill behind and in line with the entrance are two triangular leads (fixed blue lights at night) that line up 339°45'T (about 331°M).

The floating marina berths have power and water. The marina office is on the breakwater at the top of the marina. The island's functional facilities (e.g. power generation plant, desalination plant, sewage treatment plant) are located in the area beyond the marina office.

HAYMAN ISLAND

C13a

NOT FOR NAVIGATION: USE CHARTS AUS 254/AUS 252

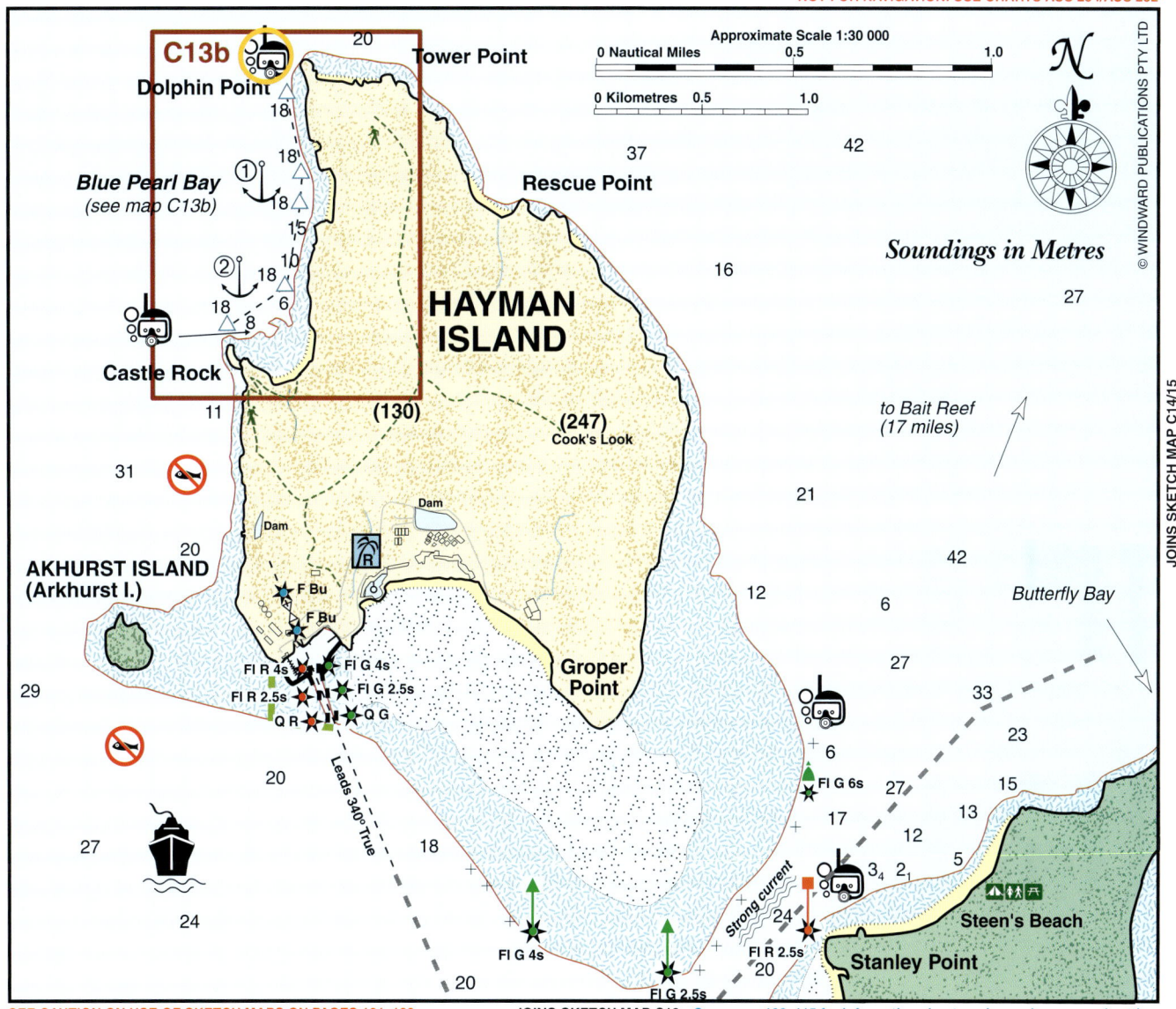

SEE CAUTION ON USE OF SKETCH MAPS ON PAGES 121, 123

JOINS SKETCH MAP C12 *See pages 108–115 for information about marine park zones and settings*

The waterway south from Hayman across to Hook Island is strewn with navigation hazards and is haunted by the spirits of defrocked mariners. A number of lights and beacons have been installed on the worst trouble spots; use extreme care in this area.

You will notice that Akhurst Island is 'Arkhurst' on the charts, a stuff-up in the Admiralty hydrographic office. John Akhurst was a crew member on HMS *Salamander*, which surveyed the Whitsundays in the 1860s. On the Admiralty chart of 1866 this island is shown as Akhurst. Somehow, from 1916 onwards, the charts show 'Arkhurst' Island. It was undoubtedly named Akhurst by *Salamander*'s captain, Commander Nares (*source*: historian, Ray Blackwood).

Visiting the resort

It is essential to make prior arrangements because space is limited (at some busy times no visitors are allowed). Day visitors are permitted to stay on the island between 1000 and 1500 hours. Overnight visitors must book into the resort; no one is allowed to stay on board a yacht in the marina overnight. An overnight marina fee applies.

Hayman has beautiful gardens and is stunningly presented. There several restaurants offering a variety of cuisine. A night ashore here can be a memorable experience (more about the resort is found on pages 34–35)

Tel. (07) 4940 1234; Marine Operations (07) 4940 1882

BLUE PEARL BAY   C13b

NOT FOR NAVIGATION: USE CHARTS AUS 252/AUS 254

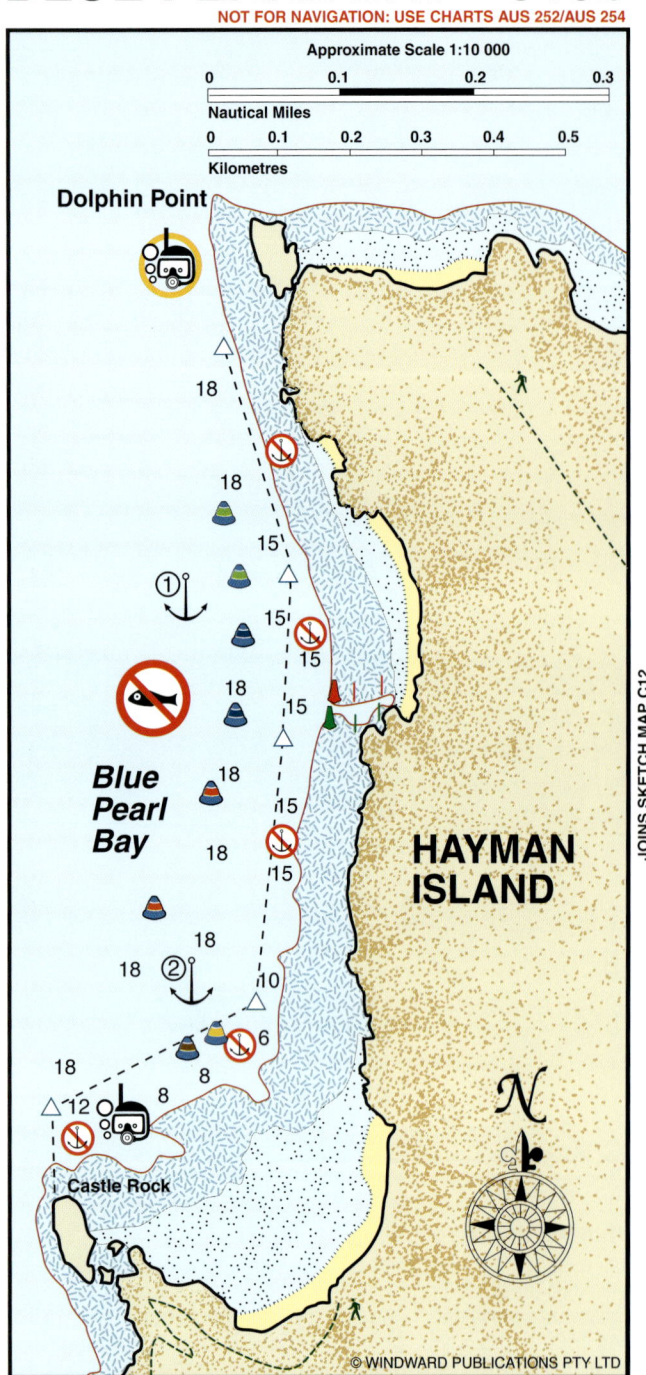

SEE CAUTIONS ON USE OF SKETCH MAPS ON PAGES 121, 123

Anchor over sand or mud and avoid coral to prevent further damage to the reefs.

BLUE PEARL BAY (C13a & C13b)

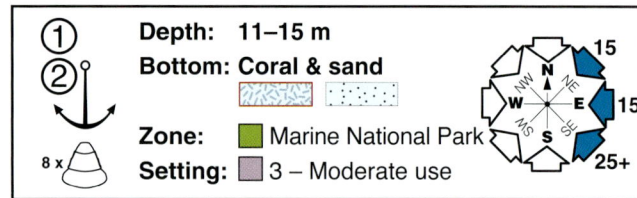

① ②
Depth: **11–15 m**
Bottom: **Coral & sand**

8 x

Zone: Marine National Park
Setting: 3 – Moderate use

Do not attempt to go between Akhurst Island and Hayman Island when sailing around to Blue Pearl Bay.

Blue Pearl is a lovely expanse of bay with beautiful beaches, and it is a very popular diving and snorkelling spot. Reef protection buoys are in place; do not anchor inshore of an imaginary straight line between these marker buoys; they are not to be used as a mooring for any size vessel. A speed limit of 3 knots applies inshore of the markers; keep a good lookout for people in the water.

Outside the no-anchoring buoys the water is 11–15 metres deep, and it drops off rather steeply, making this a difficult anchorage with potential swinging room problems. Put out plenty of scope (60 metres of chain), and leave sufficient swinging room between yachts. Blue Pearl Bay is not the most quiescent of overnight anchorages, there often being plenty of action due to swell refracting around the points and reverberating off the sheer rock faces of Hayman Island.

The best dive sites are off Castle Rock and Dolphin Point (the latter is one of the best dives in the islands). A number of large bommies lie between Castle Rock and the middle of the bay. Be mindful of the state of the tide; the currents off Castle Rock can be very swift.

A dinghy channel has been marked with port and starboard buoys and poles. The channel is to facilitate access to the beach, and dinghies are not permitted to remain in the landing area. Divers and snorkellers should not linger in this channel for obvious reasons.

NORTHERN HOOK ISLAND

The north coast of Hook Island has beautiful fringing coral reefs that offer good diving and snorkelling. These have attracted lots of attention in recent years, and there has been a considerable amount of anchor damage. To prevent further degeneration, a local volunteer group, the Organisation of Underwater Coral Heroes (OUCH), conducted underwater surveys of much of this area, and park rangers installed reef protection buoys in a number of bays.

All of the area along the north coast of Hook Island, between Alcyonaria Point (the western entrance of Butterfly Bay) and Pinnacle Point (the north-eastern tip of Hook Island) is a Marine National Park Zone (a look-but-don't-take zone – fishing and shell collecting (even empty shells) are prohibited).

Take special care to anchor over sand (light-coloured bottom) and try to keep the anchor and chain away from coral (dark patches). This will not only help preserve the coral but will save any headaches should the anchor or chain become fouled. It is an offence to damage coral in the marine park.

APPROACHES TO NORTHERN HOOK ISLAND AND BUTTERFLY BAY

If coming from the west, i.e. from Hayman Island and Stonehaven, use caution negotiating the passage between Hook and Hayman. The reef extends a long way off Hayman, and you should be much closer to Hook Island than to Hayman when negotiating this passage. If the tide is high, it's easy to be deceived.

If approaching from the east side of Hook Island, be prepared for strong currents and overfalls around Pinnacle Pt.

Butterfly Bay is tucked in behind the precipitous north-east face of Mt Sydney and is, like Stonehaven Anchorage, subject to bullets in fresh south to south-easterlies; these whistle down and strike anchored yachts like a punch. You may experience sharp gusts off Alcyonaria Point when you approach, so it's a good idea to have the motor going and to get sails down before the yacht is where manoeuvring is restricted.

A shallow patch (2.1 metres at '0' tide) is in the entrance to Butterfly Bay; this is not usually a problem for yachts, but if yours draws 2.1 metres keep an eye out if the tide is low.

If in an area where anchoring is permitted, set your anchor well; make sure you have allowed enough swinging room to avoid fringing reefs and other yachts.

Anchor chain dragging across the bottom may keep you awake; rig a rope snubber (see 'Anchor noise', page 72). There are live coral heads on the bottom, so anchor in a sandy spot and keep the chain away from dark patches.

In light north-easterlies on an anchor you may roll uncomfortably at night. Rigging a stern anchor may ease the rolling and make for a more restful night. Buoy a stern anchor so others can see that one is set.

Butterfly Bay is shaped somewhat like a butterfly with one underdeveloped wing. Coincidentally, colonies of butterflies may be found at times in the moist shade of trees along the creek beds. There are several very good dive/snorkel spots, particularly along the bay side of Alcyonaria Point, the latter named by local divers because of the abundance of that coral form there. (See 'Diving and Snorkelling in the Whitsundays' for more information on diving in this bay.)

BUTTERFLY BAY (C14/15)

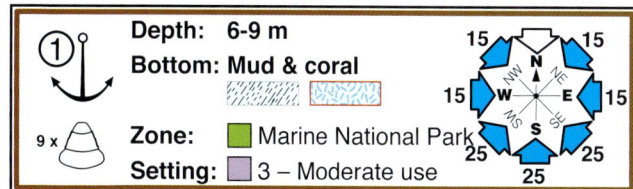

The western bay gives the best protection, particularly from swell in north-easterlies. The bottom is strewn with coral, which has suffered damage over the years, and reef protection buoys have now been installed. There are 9 public moorings inshore of these, and anchoring inside the boundary delineated by the triangular buoys is not permitted. Pick your way along the left side of the reef, which is steep-to, and have a lookout posted at all times.

NOT FOR NAVIGATION: USE CHART AUS 252

BUTTERFLY BAY

Butterfly Bay

Save your shirt and spare the corals

Butterfly Bay is often subject to sharp gusts of wind that accelerate off the surrounding hills. It is especially important, therefore, to secure items of clothing, towels, snorkels, fins, etc. that may be left on deck or hung out to dry. The annual clean-up of Butterfly Bay conducted by OUCH (Order of Underwater Coral Heroes) finds hundreds of shirts, towels, bathing suits etc. on the bottom – blown overboard from yachts. These items can smother corals if they happen to settle in the wrong place. Any item of clothing left out to dry needs to be securely **knotted** to the rails (never mind the clothes pegs) to prevent its being blown overboard.

© WINDWARD PUBLICATIONS PTY LTD

SEE CAUTION ON USE OF SKETCH MAPS ON PAGES 121, 123

HOOK ISLAND NORTH & EAST   C14/15

NOT FOR NAVIGATION: USE CHART AUS 252

The Woodpile 19 Seabiscuit Bommie

Manta Ray Bay 10 Pinnacle Bay

24

16

36

5

Luncheon Bay

24

Alcyonaria Point

16

7 6

5

5

Butterfly Bay

7 3

Maureen's
Cove

11

13

2 1

1 2

13

8

13

Raleigh Beach

Strong current

Pinnacle Point

Fl(4) W 20s 21m 10M

Pinnacle Peak
• (160)

18

JOINS SKETCH MAP C12

(233)

15 4

25

**Mackerel Bay
North**

25

*Caution:
Double Rock
(0.3 mile)*

(148)

18

(377)

16 **Mackerel
Bay** 37

Mackerel Bay
South

18 46

HOOK ISLAND

5

Crayfish Beach

42

33

*to Border Island
(about 5 miles)*

Hook Peak
• (459)

NEXT SKETCH MAP C29

18

(232)

6

(262)

0 9

17

Saba Bay

6

9

14

*to Hook Passage
and underwater observatory
(about 2.8 miles)*

Approximate Scale 1:30 000

0 Nautical Miles 0.5 1.0

0 Kilometres 0.5 1.0

Soundings in Metres

© WINDWARD PUBLICATIONS PTY LTD

SEE CAUTION ON USE OF SKETCH MAPS ON PAGES 121, 123 JOINS SKETCH MAP C16 *See pages 109–113 for information about marine park zones and settings*

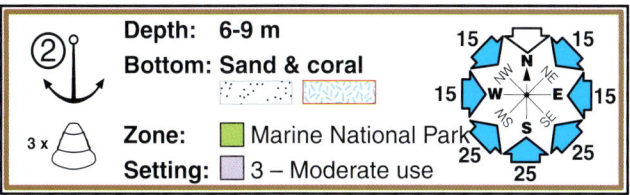

JULY 1995 APPROXIMATE SCALE 1:13 000

Butterfly Bay

Aerial photograph reproduced with permission of the Department of Environment and Resource Management

MAUREEN'S COVE

NOT FOR NAVIGATION

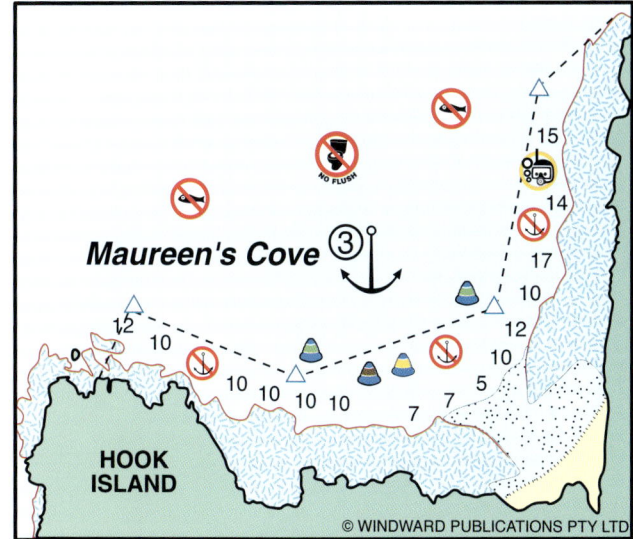

Maureen's Cove ③

HOOK ISLAND

© WINDWARD PUBLICATIONS PTY LTD

See pages 110–113 for information about marine park zones and settings

MAUREEN'S COVE (C14/15)

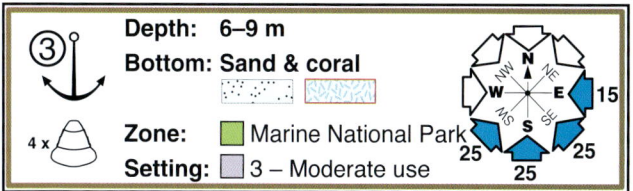

③	Depth:	6–9 m
	Bottom:	Sand & coral
4 x	Zone:	▮ Marine National Park
	Setting:	▯ 3 – Moderate use

Maureen's Cove has some good snorkel/dive spots. Reef protection buoys have been installed here; do not anchor inshore of a straight line between the buoys. A mooring is the best option, if you have a choice. This anchorage has a steep shingle beach; footwear is advisable.

LUNCHEON BAY

NOT FOR NAVIGATION

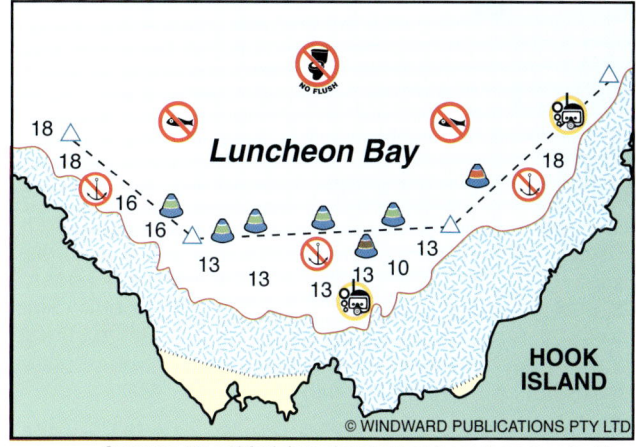

Luncheon Bay

HOOK ISLAND

© WINDWARD PUBLICATIONS PTY LTD

See pages 110–113 for information about marine park zones and settings

LUNCHEON BAY (C14/15)

Don't anchor inshore of an imaginary straight line between the reef protection buoys. Luncheon Bay is not good for anchoring, being fairly deep and subject to swift currents. Moorings for various size yachts have been installed to facilitate reef appreciation. The bay has some excellent dive and snorkelling sites and is a very pleasant spot to stop for lunch – hence its name. Occasionally you will see wild goats on the rocks above the bay. Nil discharge zone.

BUTTERFLY BAY (C14/15)

②	Depth:	6-9 m
	Bottom:	Sand & coral
3 x	Zone:	▮ Marine National Park
	Setting:	▯ 3 – Moderate use

Anchorage No. 2 is less restricted and may be less crowded for those who prefer a bit of relative isolation. However, it is subject to quite strong 'bullets'. Reef protection markers have been installed; do not anchor inshore of an imaginary straight line between the buoys. The reef and sand beach here (in the top of the 'underdeveloped wing') make for fascinating exploring. Watch out for stingrays when walking in shallow water on the sand flats (shuffle your feet). The point which separates this anchorage from No.1 has nice flat elevated rocks for sunbaking.

JULY 1995 APPROXIMATE SCALE 1:40 000

Aerial photograph reproduced with permission of the Department of Environment and Resource Management

Manta Ray Bay

Pinnacle Bay

Luncheon Bay

Steen's Beach

Maureen's Cove

Butterfly Bay

HOOK ISLAND

Mackerel Bay North

Mackerel Bay

Mackerel Bay South

Saba Bay

MANTA RAY BAY (C14/15)

Approaching Manta Ray Bay from the east, watch out for Seabiscuit Bommie which lies immediately north-north-west of the Pinnacles and which is a potential hazard at spring low tides. Give the point a good berth. The north-eastern tip of Hook Island may be subject to strong currents, overfalls and very choppy seas in fresh south-east winds with a flooding tide.

Manta Ray Bay offers some of the best underwater scenery in the Whitsundays and is a favourite spot for diving and snorkelling. Anchoring in the bay is prohibited. There are a number of public moorings. Do not secure a yacht to the brown (dinghy) moorings; they are not designed for such duty. Not a good overnight spot. Nil discharge zone and Marine National Park Zone.

MANTA RAY BAY

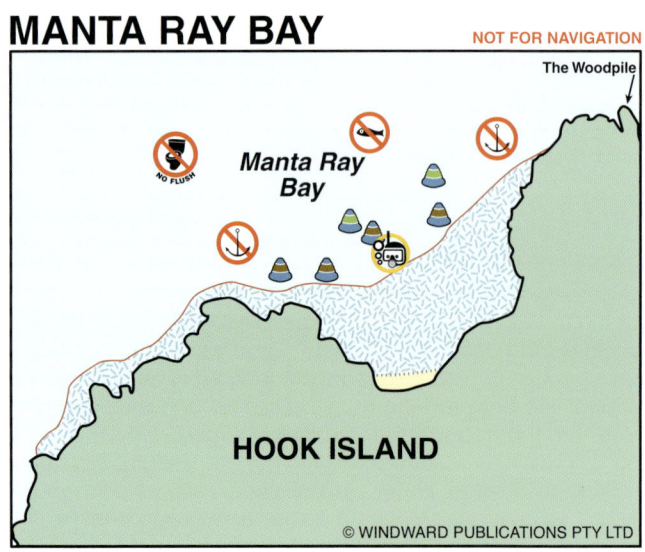

NOT FOR NAVIGATION

The Woodpile

NO FLUSH

Manta Ray Bay

HOOK ISLAND

© WINDWARD PUBLICATIONS PTY LTD

PINNACLE BAY

NOT FOR NAVIGATION

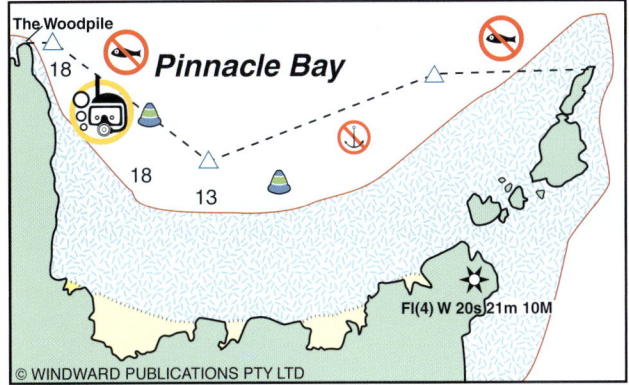

The Woodpile
18
Pinnacle Bay
18
13
Fl(4) W 20s 21m 10M
© WINDWARD PUBLICATIONS PTY LTD

PINNACLE BAY (C14/15)

The Pinnacles are some rather striking rocks on the north-eastern corner of Hook Island. The bay formed between them and 'The Woodpile' (a volcanic dyke on the most northern tip of the island that looks like a stack of logs) offers some excellent diving. Reef protection buoys have been installed in this bay; do not anchor inshore of an imaginary straight line between the buoys This is not a good bay for anchoring, anyway; it is deep, and the bottom shelves steeply. There are two moorings the use of which is infinitely preferable to anchoring. Not good as an overnight anchorage, being subject to swells and currents that make for an uncomfortable night.

MACKEREL BAY (C14/15)

④ ⑤

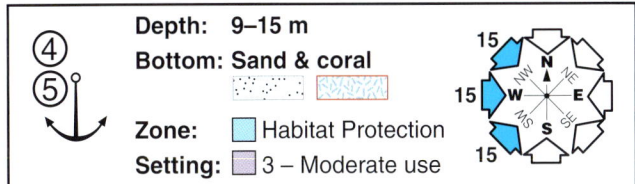

Depth: 9–15 m
Bottom: Sand & coral
Zone: Habitat Protection
Setting: 3 – Moderate use

15
15
15
N
NE
E
SE
S
SW
W
NW

If proceeding to Mackerel Bay (see sketch map C14/15) from northern Hook Island, consider carefully the state of wind and tide, as the area around Pinnacle Point can be *very* rough in wind-against-tide conditions. Mackerel Bay has two infrequently explored anchorages; both are exposed in sou'-easterlies, even No. 5, which suffers from refracted swells. The reef offers some interesting exploring with the dinghy or in the water with snorkelling gear. Good fishing.

SABA BAY (C16)

⑥

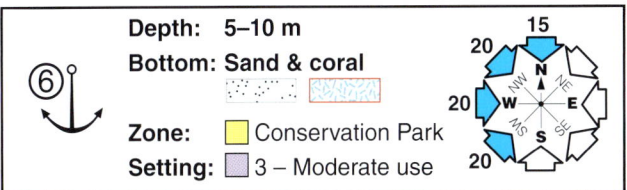

Depth: 5–10 m
Bottom: Sand & coral
Zone: Conservation Park
Setting: 3 – Moderate use

15
20
20
20
N
NE
E
SE
S
SW
W
NW

Exercise extreme caution in negotiating the reef. Saba Bay is exposed to the south and east and is suitable as an overnight anchorage only after the trade winds season is over. It has some excellent fringing reefs for snorkelling and diving. Anchor with extreme care to avoid the anchor or chain coming in contact with coral.

HOOK SOUTH-EAST C16

JOINS SKETCH MAP C14/15

NOT FOR NAVIGATION: USE CHART AUS 252

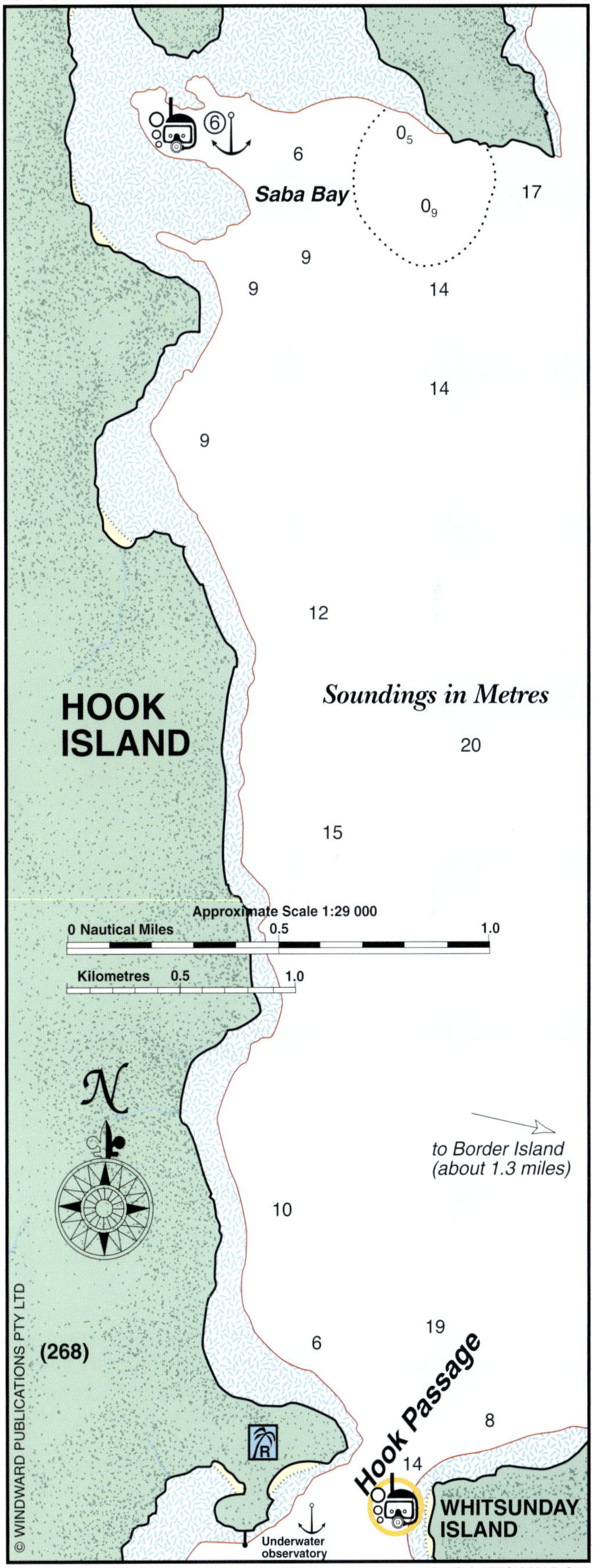

⑥
Saba Bay
6
17
9
9
14
14
9
12
HOOK ISLAND
Soundings in Metres
20
15
Approximate Scale 1:29 000
0 Nautical Miles
0.5
1.0
Kilometres
0.5
1.0
to Border Island (about 1.3 miles)
10
(268)
6
19
Hook Passage
8
14
WHITSUNDAY ISLAND
Underwater observatory
JOINS SKETCH MAP C10a
JOINS SKETCH MAP C29
© WINDWARD PUBLICATIONS PTY LTD

SEE CAUTIONS ON USE OF SKETCH MAPS ON PGS 121, 123

JOINS SKETCH MAP C17

HOOK PASSAGE

C17

NOT FOR NAVIGATON: USE CHART AUS 252

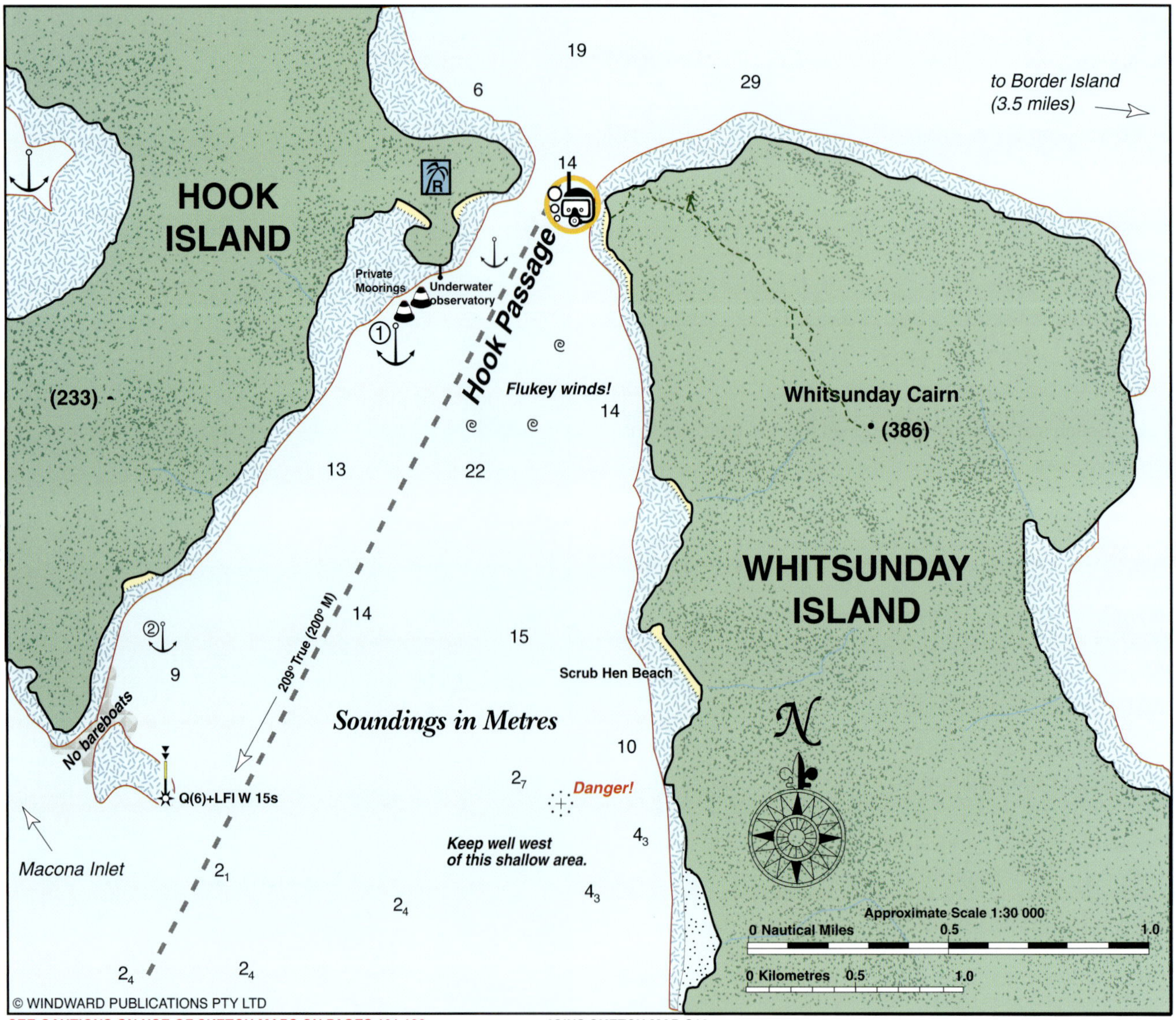

Map:

JOINS SKETCH MAP C10a

19

6

29

to Border Island
(3.5 miles)

HOOK ISLAND

14

Private Moorings

Underwater observatory

Hook Passage

①

(233)

Flukey winds!

14

Whitsunday Cairn

• (386)

13

22

209°True (200° M)

14

15

WHITSUNDAY ISLAND

9

②

Scrub Hen Beach

Soundings in Metres

10

No bareboats

Q(6)+LFl W 15s

2₇

Danger!

4₃

Keep well west of this shallow area.

4₃

Macona Inlet

2₁

2₄

4₃

N

2₄

Approximate Scale 1:30 000

0 Nautical Miles   0.5   1.0

2₄

2₄

0 Kilometres   0.5   1.0

© WINDWARD PUBLICATIONS PTY LTD

NEXT SKETCH MAP C29

SEE CAUTIONS ON USE OF SKETCH MAPS ON PAGES 121,123

JOINS SKETCH MAP C18

HOOK PASSAGE (C17)

Hook Passage is a relatively narrow obstruction to the tidal stream and is therefore subject to strong currents and eddies. The high land on either side guarantees fickle winds which veer 180°. Be prepared.

When heading north through the passage in flood tides and when the wind is fresh from the south-east, be prepared for overfalls on the other side.

If you are proceeding south from the passage, note that there is a large shallow area with some dangerous bommies on the north-western side of Whitsunday Island. So, when heading south, keep to starboard (west of centre) between Hook and Whitsunday islands (steer about 200°M) until one nautical mile south of the south cardinal mark on the reef off Hook Island's south-eastern corner.

HOOK RESORT/OBSERVATORY (C17)

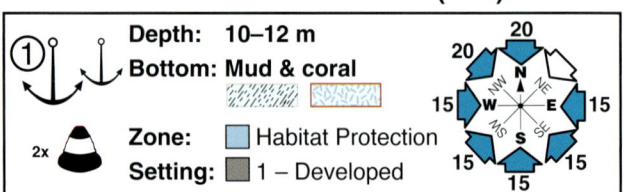

①	**Depth:**	10–12 m
	Bottom:	Mud & coral
2x	**Zone:**	☐ Habitat Protection
	Setting:	☐ 1 – Developed

The Hook Island Wilderness Resort and underwater observatory is located on the western side at the northern end of Hook Passage. Anchorage No.1 is not a good place to anchor, there being all manner of hazards on the bottom, and many an anchor has been lost there. There are two moorings available for visitors. (See 'Visiting the resort' on the next page for contact information.)

Temporary anchorage is available off the beach in front of the resort, but this is a current-swept channel and the boat shouldn't be left unattended.

The observatory dates back to days before motorised catamarans made it possible to take day trips to the Barrier Reef. Visibility underwater is not always all that good in Hook Passage, particularly with winds from the northern sector or at times of spring tides with strong south-east winds, which cause fine sediments to rise. But it provides an opportunity to view fish at very close quarters, and to observe some corals, without getting wet. For legal reasons there are signs inside the observatory warning that the building contains asbestos and that visitors may possibly come in contact with asbestos dust.

Visiting the resort

Contact the office on VHF channel 16/74 or telephone (07) 4946 9380. The resort style is informal, affordable and welcoming. Inexpensive meals are served in the café, and the bar/lounge, which has a large TV (drop in and don't miss your favourite sporting event), is open most of the day. Milk, ice and bread may be obtained from the small shop. Snorkelling has always been a feature here, and this can be done right from the beach. Beach staff also conduct snorkel tours to coral gardens across the passage on the northern end of Whitsunday Island. (See page 43 for more about the resort.)

HOOK PASSAGE (C17)

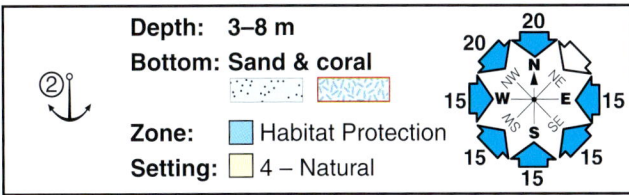

Depth:	3–8 m
Bottom:	Sand & coral
Zone:	☐ Habitat Protection
Setting:	☐ 4 – Natural

This is a pleasant daytime stopoff with a lovely little beach. Hook Passage is subject to strong currents, and this is therefore not really suitable as an overnight anchorage; changing tidal currents may cause the yacht to ride up on its anchor, which may dislodge it.

MAY'S BAY (C18)

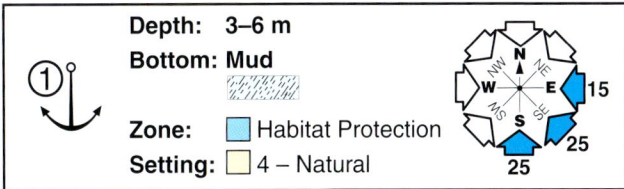

Depth:	3–6 m
Bottom:	Mud
Zone:	☐ Habitat Protection
Setting:	☐ 4 – Natural

If coming from Hook Passage, watch out for two bommies off the north-western shore of Whitsunday Island which are hazards to navigation at low tide. Proceeding southwards, stay to the right of centre in the passage and don't turn for May's Bay until you are at least one nautical mile beyond the south cardinal mark on the reef on the south-east tip of Hook Island.

The anchorage can be swelly as the wind easts. The water is deeper towards the western end of the beach. Watch out for isolated bommies and one in particular about 3 metres in diameter that lies about 300 metres north-west of the rocks on the beach (GPS 20° 13.527'S, 148° 56.612'E). At an average low tide the bommie has 0.5 metre water over it; the surrounding depth is 3.0 metres.

Historical note: 'May' was the wife of Lindsay Heiser; together they built the Hook underwater observatory which opened in 1969. Before their observatory accommodation was finished, they lived on their boat, retreating to this lovely, sheltered anchorage when SE winds made the observatory anchorage uncomfortable. The sandy beach here, called Bernie's Beach, was named after Bernie Katchor, a charter yacht pioneer of the early '70s.

WHITSUNDAY I. NW C18

JOINS SKETCH MAP C17 — NOT FOR NAVIGATION: USE CHART AUS 253/AUS 252

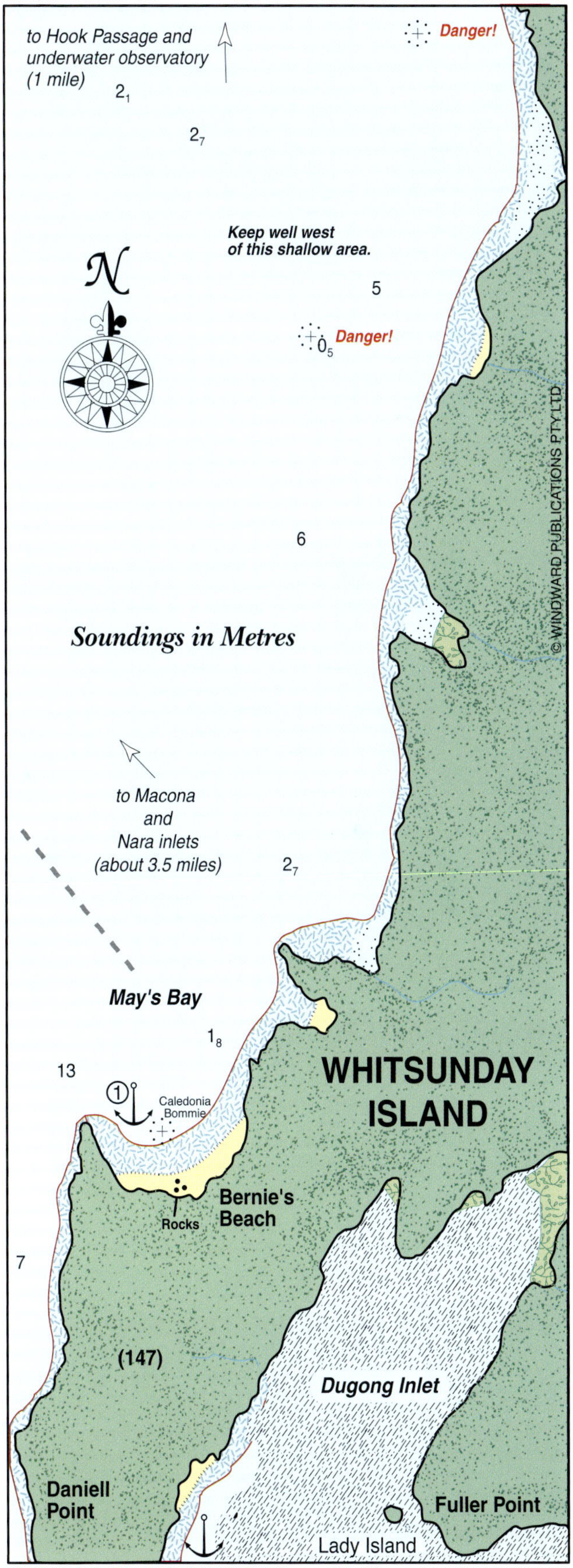

to Hook Passage and underwater observatory (1 mile)

Danger!

Keep well west of this shallow area.

Danger!

N

Soundings in Metres

to Macona and Nara inlets (about 3.5 miles)

May's Bay

Caledonia Bommie

Bernie's Beach

Rocks

WHITSUNDAY ISLAND

(147)

Daniell Point

Dugong Inlet

Fuller Point

Lady Island

© WINDWARD PUBLICATIONS PTY LTD

JOINS SKETCH MAP C28

JULY 1995 APPROXIMATE SCALE 1:40 000

Aerial photograph reproduced with permission of the Department of Environment and Resource Management

Dugong and Sawmill beaches are popular with trailer sailers.

A 1-kilometre track follows the 20-metre contour from Sawmill to Dugong Beach. And a new track to Whitsunday Peak is accessed from Sawmill Beach picnic area (see page 103 for details).

Ross Islet, also called Orchid Rock, is sometimes a nesting place for sea eagles. Keep well away in nesting season (August to September) because, if disturbed, these raptors can take fright and abandon their eggs, leaving them exposed to the elements. As the island's other name suggests, it is one of many rocky places in the Whitsundays where wild orchids (*Dendrobium discolor*) grow. (Orchids are protected in Queensland.)

SAWMILL BEACH (C19)

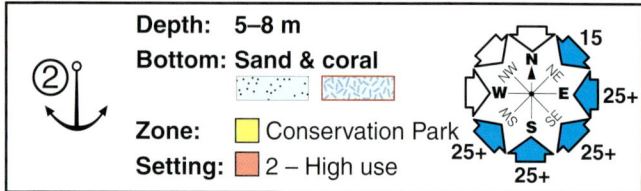

Approach cautiously and be aware of the state of the tide as the beach slope is fairly gradual. Give Hughes Point a wide berth, as there are off-lying bommies.

This is the best of Cid's beaches and picnic tables are available. A great spot for a picnic. All rubbish created ashore must be taken away with you. Access to the new track to Whitsunday Peak from the southern end.

DUGONG INLET (C19)

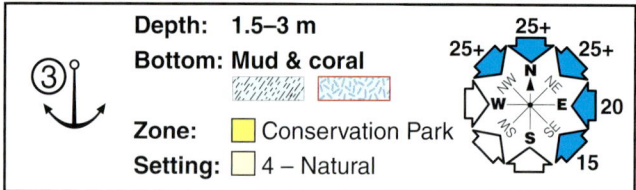

Approach is from Cid Harbour. Stay about 150 metres off the port shore and keep a lookout.

This is a shallow anchorage but one in which the bottom is very soft mud, so not much damage can be done if you do find yourself settling in at low tide. If there are a number of boats already in this anchorage, it is possible to anchor outside the indicated area (off Daniell Point). If the wind changes you should be able to make your way across to one of the south-east anchorages without difficulty.

HOMESTEAD BAY (C19)

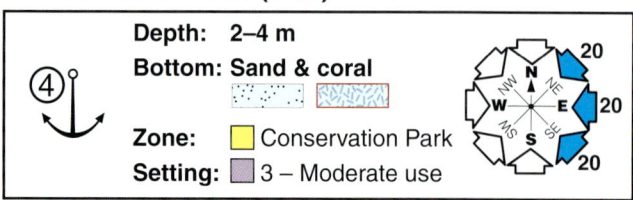

Homestead Bay is a pretty bay and makes a good picnic spot. Anchor off the southern end of the beach. There are excellent views of the passage from Cid Island.

SAWMILL BAY (C19)

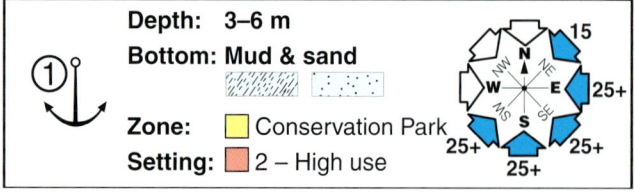

Watch out for strong currents and gusts of wind when entering from the south between Cid Island and Loriard Point. Give Reef Point a good berth. Give Hughes Point a wide berth, too, as there are isolated bommies within 25 metres of the shore.

Cid Harbour is a very large harbour and one of the all-weather anchorages of the Whitsundays. Occasionally used as an anchorage by the Australian and allied navies during World War II, it was not a marshalling point for the US Fleet prior to the Battle of the Coral Sea. There are several sand beaches. There is a campsite at Dugong Beach, with toilets, and tank water may be available. Both

CID HARBOUR

C19

NOT FOR NAVIGATION: USE CHART AUS 253

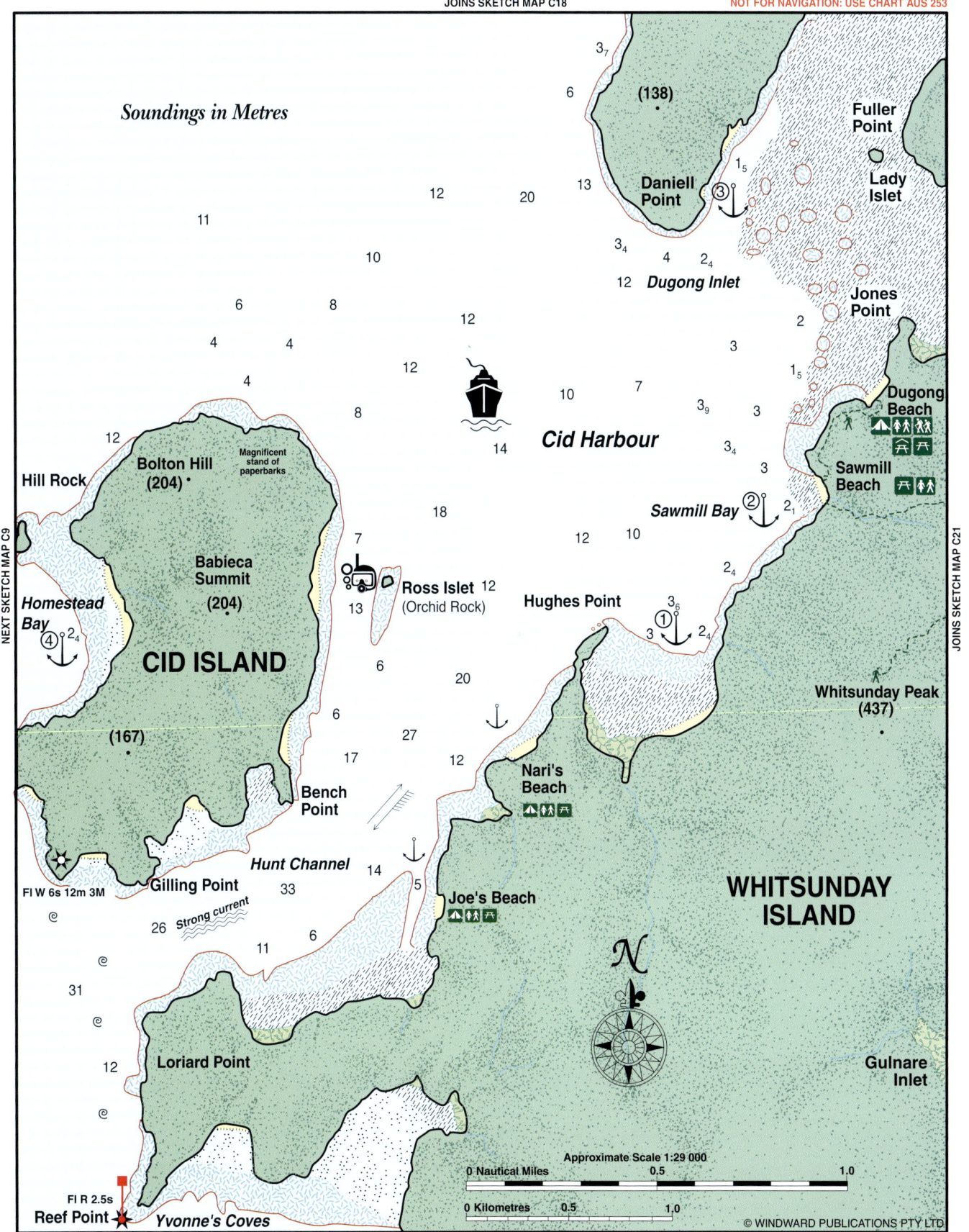

Soundings in Metres

3_7

6

(138)

Fuller
Point

13

**Daniell
Point**

③

1_5

Lady
Islet

11

12

20

3_4

4

2_4

10

12

Dugong Inlet

Jones
Point

6

8

2

12

3

7

Cid Harbour

1_5

4

4

10

3_9

3

Dugong
Beach

12

4

12

8

14

3_4

3

12

Bolton Hill
(204)

Magnificent
stand of
paperbarks

Sawmill
Beach

Hill Rock

7

3

18

Sawmill Bay ②

2_1

**Babieca
Summit
(204)**

Ross Islet
(Orchid Rock)

12

13

Hughes Point

12

10

CID ISLAND

6

2_4

*Homestead
Bay*
④ 2_4

3_6

① ⚓

2_4

3

(167)

6

**Whitsunday Peak
(437)**

17

27

20

12

**Bench
Point**

⚓

Hunt Channel

14

**Nari's
Beach**

⚓ FI W 6s 12m 3M

Gilling Point

33

5

26

Strong current

6

Joe's Beach

**WHITSUNDAY
ISLAND**

11

31

N

12

Loriard Point

**Gulnare
Inlet**

Approximate Scale 1:29 000

0 Nautical Miles   0.5   1.0

FI R 2.5s

0 Kilometres   0.5   1.0

Reef Point ⚓ *Yvonne's Coves*

© WINDWARD PUBLICATIONS PTY LTD

NARI'S BEACH (C19)

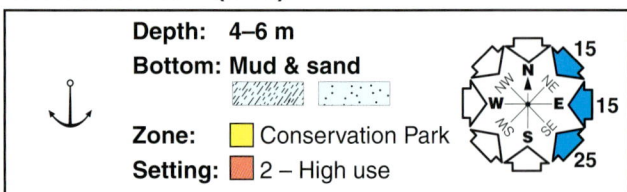

Depth: 4–6 m
Bottom: Mud & sand
Zone: ☐ Conservation Park
Setting: ☐ 2 – High use

JOE'S BEACH (C19)

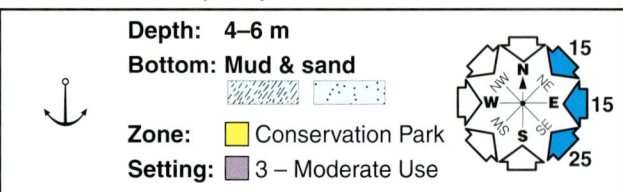

Depth: 4–6 m
Bottom: Mud & sand
Zone: ☐ Conservation Park
Setting: ☐ 3 – Moderate Use

Nari's and Joe's are nice sand beaches that are good for a lunchtime stopoff. Because anchorage is either in, or very near, the narrow channel between Cid and Whitsunday islands, these locations are subject to tidal influences and are not really satisfactory overnight anchorages. You should also keep an eye on your anchor. There are scrubfowl (*Megapodius reinwardt*) mounds behind some of these beaches. Don't climb on the mounds (both for the fowl's and your own sake – there are sometimes mites and snakes in them).

A channel in the coral by Joe's Beach can be an interesting place to paddle around, but the visibility may not always be particularly good in this current-prone channel. Never attempt to swim across Hunt Channel to Cid Island; the currents are very swift, and occasionally very large motorised catamarans and other cruisers come through the channel at speed and may not see you in the water.

YVONNE'S COVES (C20)

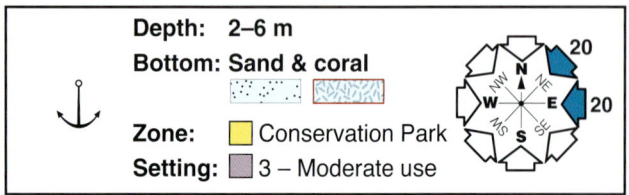

Depth: 2–6 m
Bottom: Sand & coral
Zone: ☐ Conservation Park
Setting: ☐ 3 – Moderate use

Yvonne's Coves offer fascinating reef exploring in suitably light weather. Anchor off the edge of the reef, allowing enough swinging room. There is much interesting reef life, including armies of soldier crabs.

HENNING ISLAND (C20)

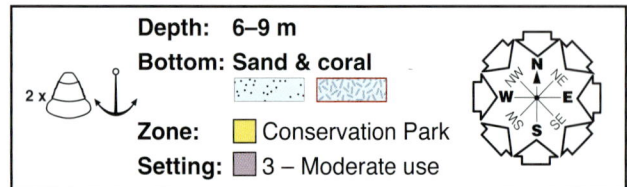

Depth: 6–9 m
Bottom: Sand & coral
Zone: ☐ Conservation Park
Setting: ☐ 3 – Moderate use

Henning Island has two daytime anchorages, one off the north-east side, where there is a very pleasant sand beach, and one off a little sand beach in the middle of the western side. At times of neap tides and light southerly winds, the visibility may be good enough to enjoy the coral on the reef that extends west from the northern tip.

A relatively shallow spot (about 7 metres) exists (where the yellow buoy is moored) ESE of the north-east beach, and here the water becomes quite disturbed in some tidal conditions.

GULNARE INLET (C20)

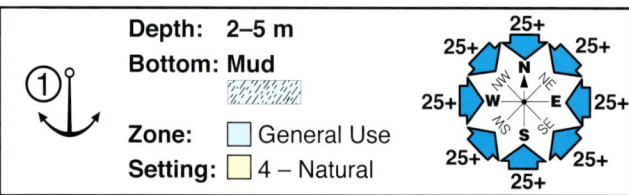

Depth: 2–5 m
Bottom: Mud
Zone: ☐ General Use
Setting: ☐ 4 – Natural

Gulnare Inlet is a well-protected anchorage; there are a few very shallow spots on the way in, and then it gets a little deeper where the anchor is shown on the map. Be aware of the state of the tide; it's probably best to enter on a rising tide.

Approaching from Fitzalan Passage, beware of the submerged reef area shown. Don't turn into the inlet until you are on the back bearing that aligns Dent and Pine islands (see below). Coming from Dent or Hamilton islands, stay east of Plum Pudding Island. Approaching from the north, keep well south until picking up the Dent Island/Pine Island bearing (see below). Don't mistake the rocks that lie off the northern entrance with the submerged patch of reef just to their east.

A back bearing, using Dent and Pine islands as leads, is a useful guide to the entrance: the south-east tip of Pine Island is held in line with the extremity of the rocks on the north-west tip of Dent Island. The outer rock on Dent Island submerges at high tide, so make a small allowance for this if the tide is high. This back bearing, which is approximately 202°M, avoids the patch of reef just inside the entrance on the port side. The reciprocal (the course on which you will be heading) is 022°M. There is a shallow spot abeam of the reef patch. Once past the reef stay about mid-channel. Go in till the water starts to get deeper again, and anchor at the mouth of an embayment on the port side where anchorage is shown.

Gulnare has room for quite a number of boats, being shallow and calm and therefore not requiring a lot of anchor chain to be put down (swinging circles are therefore small). There are endless opportunities for exploring in the dinghy. It is possible at high tide to go for miles up the estuary through mangroves. Watch the tide, though; it's a long way up (and back). About half a mile from the anchorage on the right there is a mangrove creek that turns back to the south. Around the turn of the 20th century Martin Cunningham built a tramway to move timber from the surrounding hills along the flat and into the inlet, from where it was towed back to the sawmill at Cid Harbour.

A cruise ship anchorage has been established where shown on sketch map C20. Keep well clear of any ship in this area, as it will have its hands full just manoeuvring in this current-swept area.

GULNARE INLET

C20

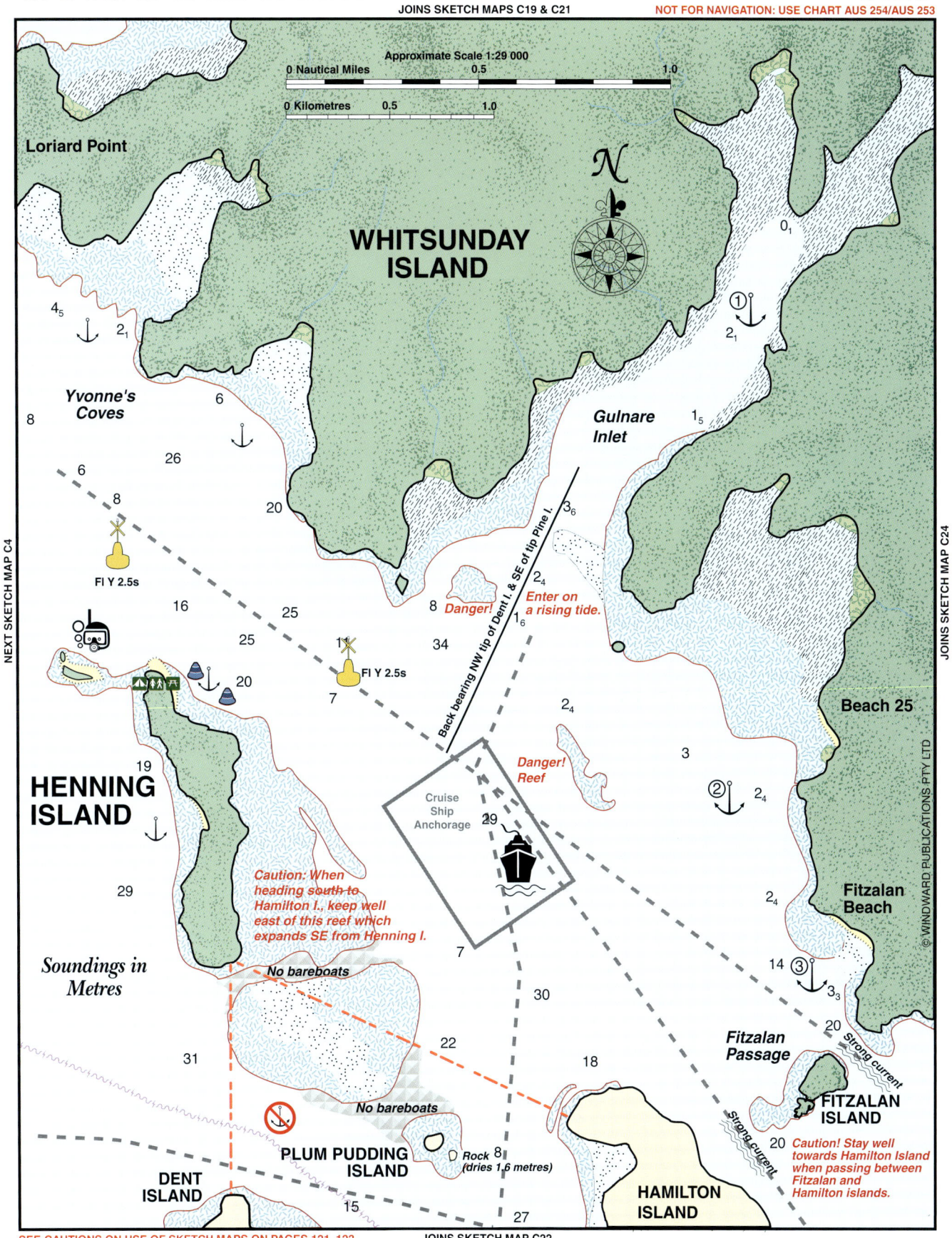

Approximate Scale 1:29 000

0 Nautical Miles   0.5   1.0

0 Kilometres   0.5   1.0

Loriard Point

WHITSUNDAY ISLAND

N

0_1

4_5

2_1

Yvonne's Coves

6

8

1_5

6

Gulnare Inlet

8

26

20

NEXT SKETCH MAP C4

JOINS SKETCH MAP C24

3_6

Fl Y 2.5s

8

2_4

Enter on a rising tide.

Danger!

1_6

16

25

25

25

34

Fl Y 2.5s

7

20

2_4

Back bearing NW tip of Dent I. & SE of tip Pine I.

Beach 25

19

HENNING ISLAND

3

②

2_4

Danger! Reef

Cruise Ship Anchorage

29

Fitzalan Beach

29

2_4

Caution: When heading south to Hamilton I., keep well east of this reef which expands SE from Henning I.

14 ③

3_3

Soundings in Metres

No bareboats

7

20

Strong current

Fitzalan Passage

FITZALAN ISLAND

31

22

18

30

No bareboats

20

Caution! Stay well towards Hamilton Island when passing between Fitzalan and Hamilton islands.

Strong current

15

Rock 8 (dries 1.6 metres)

DENT ISLAND

PLUM PUDDING ISLAND

27

HAMILTON ISLAND

© WINDWARD PUBLICATIONS PTY LTD

JULY 1995 APPROXIMATE SCALE 1:14 000

Cid Harbour

Nari's Beach

Joe's Beach

Yvonne's Coves

Gulnare Inlet

Henning Island

Beach 25

Fitzalan Beach

Aerial photograph reproduced with permission of the Department of Environment and Resource Management

BEACH 25 and FITZALAN BEACH (C20)

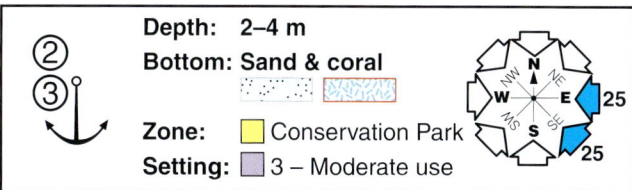

② ③ ⚓	**Depth:** 2–4 m	
	Bottom: Sand & coral	
	Zone: ☐ Conservation Park	
	Setting: ☐ 3 – Moderate use	

Just north of Fitzalan Passage are a couple of anchorages that may be useful in the event of being blown out of a south-exposed anchorage at night, such as one of those along the south side of Whitsunday Island. Anchorage No. 2 is preferable in fresh conditions and it is more removed from the tidal stream which courses through Fitzalan Passage at a rate of knots. Watch out for scattered bommies.

Both anchorages have nearby pleasant sand beaches, but take insect repellent ashore with you, as Whitsunday Island has many resident sandflies.

Beach 25 (incorrectly called Beach 23 by some locals) is the name of the beach east of anchorage No. 2, which, according to historian Ray Blackwood, was used by a fisherman, Harold Hurst, during the 1950s and early '60s to dry his nets. The '25' was the licence number of his fish trap located near the rocky point south of the beach.

UPPER GULNARE C21

NEXT SKETCH MAP C18   **NOT FOR NAVIGATION: USE CHART AUS 253**

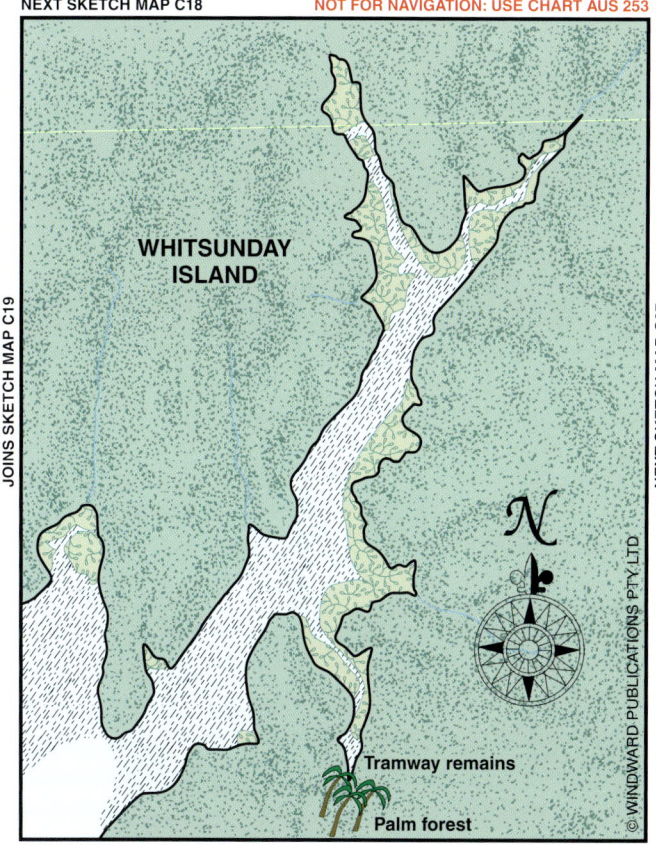

JOINS SKETCH MAP C19

WHITSUNDAY ISLAND

NEXT SKETCH MAP C27

N

Tramway remains

Palm forest

© WINDWARD PUBLICATIONS PTY LTD

SEE CAUTION ON USE OF SKETCH MAPS pps. 121, 123   **JOINS SKETCH MAP C20**

View of Fitzalan Island and Passage from Hamilton Island. Note the reef patch extending west-south-west from Fitzalan island. At high tide this disappears, so be careful, and keep well towards Hamilton Island if using this side of the Passage

David Colfelt

UPPER GULNARE INLET (C21)

Just beyond the creek that courses south-west to the palm forest is another broader mangrove creek that has been used by some local skippers as a cyclone anchorage. You will obviously need to enter on a high tide. (The smallest high tide you are ever likely to strike here would be 1.9 metres at normal atmospheric pressure.)

APPROACHING HAMILTON ISLAND

Approaching Hamilton Island from the north (coming down the east side of Henning Island or from Gulnare Inlet), watch out for the extensive reef areas south of Henning Island. Do not attempt passage north of Plum Pudding Island as you may run afoul of extensive reef there. Don't be tempted by the presence of other boats that may apparently be moored in this 'passage'; always pass south and east of Plum Pudding Island. If approaching from the Whitsunday Passage, favour the northern side of Dent Island to avoid the extensive reef area south of Henning Island and keep a sharp lookout for the reef surrounding Plum Pudding Island.

FITZALAN PASSAGE (C20/22)

Fitzalan Passage is actually two passages, on either side of Fitzalan Island, between Whitsunday Island and Hamilton Island. It is possible to use either.

Fitzalan restricts the flow of the tidal stream, and there can be 4+ knots of current during spring tides, and up to 3 knots in neap tides. Always use your motor, and watch to be sure that you aren't being set off course.

If using the southern passage (between Fitzalan and Hamilton islands), keep closer to Hamilton Island to avoid a reef that extends west-south-west from Fitzalan Island towards Hamilton Island, the position of which can be quite deceptive.

In wind-against-tide conditions, particularly south-east winds against a south-east-moving flood tide stream, the passage may become quite turbulent and lumpy. When travelling south-east through the passage towards the east you may encounter a dramatic change to quite turbulent conditions within a distance of a few hundred metres.

HAMILTON HARBOUR (C22)

Depth:	1.6–4.5 m
Bottom:	Mud
Zone:	Conservation Park
Setting:	1 – Developed

Hamilton Harbour is marked by port and starboard beacons that show lights at night. The lighthouse (port side breakwater as you enter) is for decoration. Depths in the harbour vary between 2 and 4.5 metres; check with the harbourmaster for specific details.

Caution about flight path

Hamilton's jet airport poses a potential hazard for both yachts and aircraft. There have been occasions when commercial passenger jet planes have had to abort landings at the last minute due to a yacht's mast restricting the approach path. A small dinghy was once overturned by the jet blast from a departing plane. Yachts are advised to avoid, if possible, the area of the flight path, which can be at any time of day or night. Stay east of the flight path when approaching the harbour, if possible. If you unavoidably find yourself on the flight path when a plane is arriving, be sure to keep the minimum distance away from the runway (depending upon the height of your mast shown on sketch map C22).

Hamilton harbour has 230 marina berths and has a full-service shipyard with fuel, water, supplies, chandlery, shipwright, Travelift, refrigeration, electrical and engineering services. There are many restaurants, a bakery, a fish-and-chip shop, Trader Pete's store, several boutiques, a supermarket, bottle shop, chemist, pub, showers, toilets, and lots of amusements.

No anchoring in Dent Passage

Due to the presence of high-voltage undersea cables connecting Hamilton with the mainland and power cables and water and sewer pipes between Hamilton Island and and Dent Island, anchoring is prohibited anywhere in the area bounded by:

> ... the southern tip of Henning Island down to the northern tip of Dent Island, then following Dent's east coast to a point just south of Cowrie Island, then east across to Hamilton Island, then north following the west coast of Hamilton Island to its north-western extremity and then back up to the southern end of Henning Island.

Moorings in Dent Passage

In Dent Passage north of the golf course jetty there are 10 private moorings with orange floats and black tops, which belong to Hamilton Island. They are suitable for for vessels up to 30 metres or 150 tonnes and are available to rent.

HAMILTON HARBOUR

NOT FOR NAVIGATION

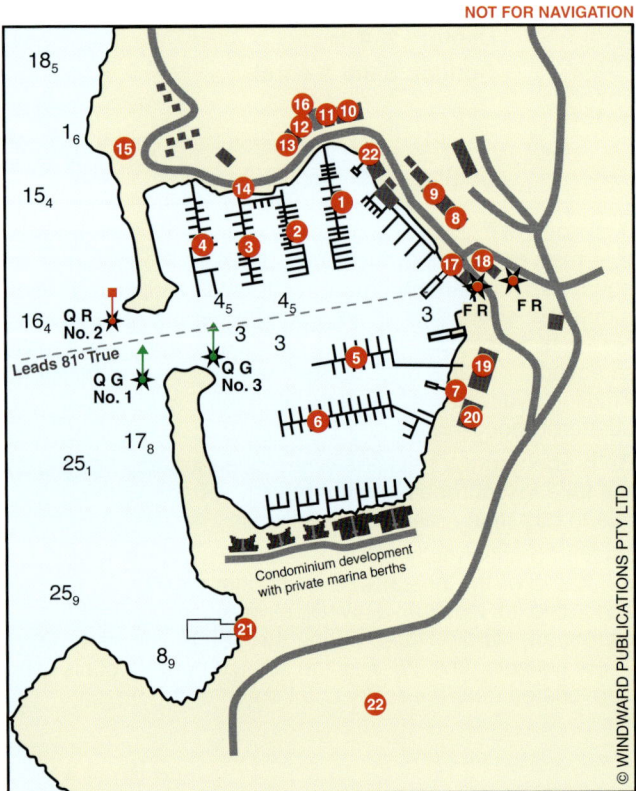

© WINDWARD PUBLICATIONS PTY LTD

SEE CAUTION ON USE OF SKETCH MAPS ON PAGES 121, 123

1. B-Arm marina berths	9. General Store, PO	17. Passenger jetty
2. C-Arm marina berths	10. Coin Laundry	18. Trader Pete's store
3. D-Arm marina berths	11. Pharmacy	19. Shower/toilet block
4. E-Arm marina berths	12. Bakery	20. Marina Office, chandlery
5. F-Arm marina berths	13. Bottle shop	21. Airport pontoon
6. G-Arm marina berths	14. Sunsail	22. Airport terminal
7. Fuel jetty	15. Yacht club	
8. NAB Bank	16. Shower/toilet block	

Visiting Hamilton in a yacht

Hamilton welcomes visitors by sea; marina berths and moorings are available. Radio ahead (several days, during busy times) to the harbourmaster on VHF 16/68 and make arrangements for a berth; call again on arrival and you will be directed to a berth or mooring. The overnight fee entitles you to 'the keys to the island'. For more about the resort, see pages 38–41. Telephone (marina office) (07) 4946 8353.

Anthony Colfelt

HAMILTON ISLAND

C22

NOT FOR NAVIGATION: USE CHART AUS 254/AUS 253

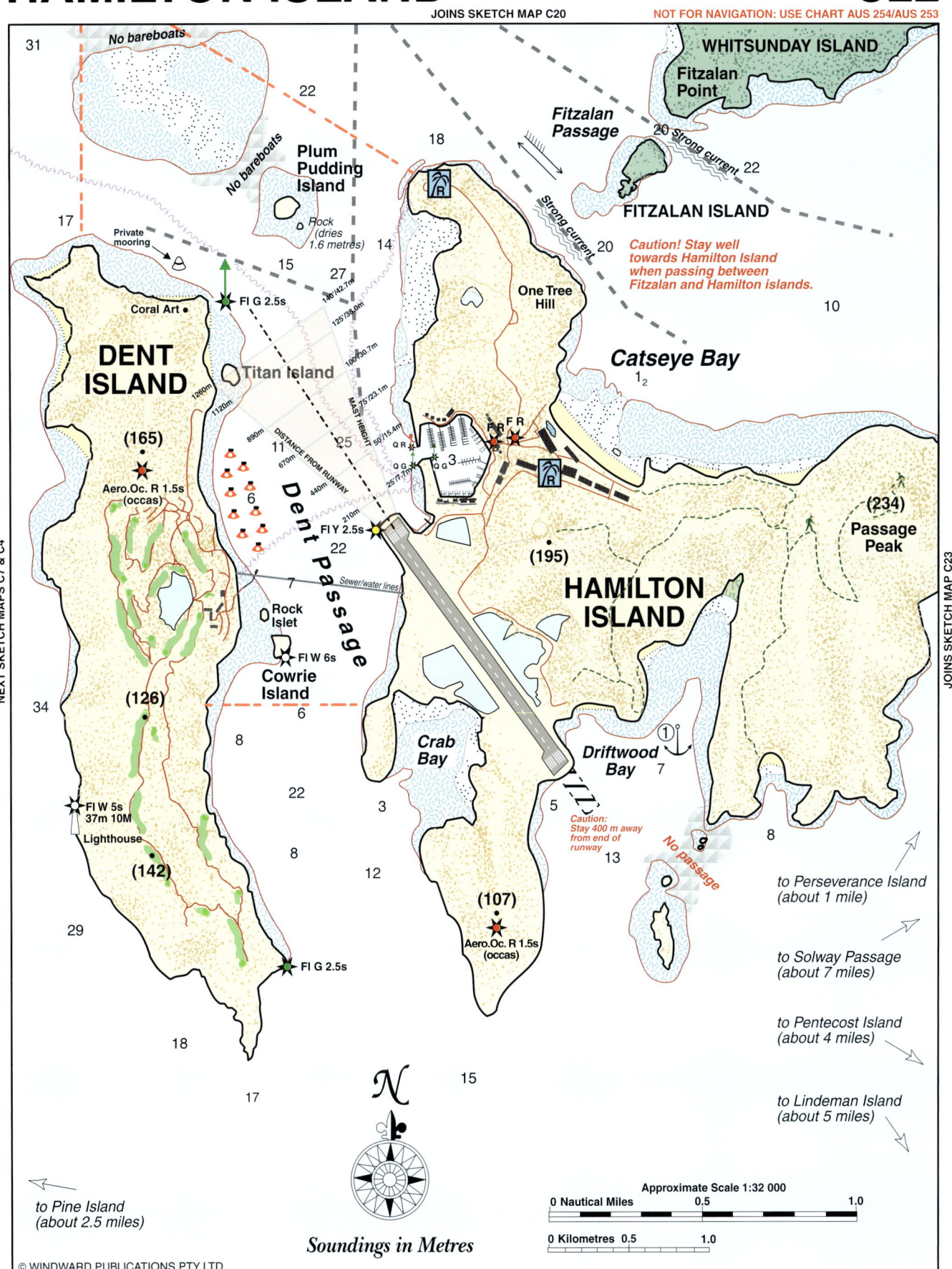

31

No bareboats

22

No bareboats

Plum Pudding Island

18

Rock (dries 1.6 metres)

14

15

27

17

Private mooring

Coral Art •

Fl G 2.5s

WHITSUNDAY ISLAND

Fitzalan Point

Fitzalan Passage

20 Strong current 22

Strong current 20

FITZALAN ISLAND

Caution! Stay well towards Hamilton Island when passing between Fitzalan and Hamilton islands.

10

One Tree Hill

Catseye Bay

1 2

DENT ISLAND

Titan Island

(165)

Aero.Oc. R 1.5s (occas)

1260m
1120m
890m
670m
440m
210m

DISTANCE FROM RUNWAY

MAST HEIGHT

140/42.7m
125/38.0m
100/30.7m
75/23.1m
50/15.4m
25/7.7m

11

25

6

Fl Y 2.5s

22

7

Sewer/water lines

Rock Islet

Fl W 6s

Cowrie Island

6

Q R
Q G
Q G

F R F R
F R
3

R

R

(195)

HAMILTON ISLAND

(234)
Passage Peak

NEXT SKETCH MAPS C7 & C4

34

(126)

8

22

8

Crab Bay

3

12

Fl W 5s 37m 10M
Lighthouse

(142)

(107)
Aero.Oc. R 1.5s (occas)

Driftwood Bay

1

7

5

Caution: Stay 400 m away from end of runway

13

No passage

8

JOINS SKETCH MAP C23

to Perseverance Island (about 1 mile)

to Solway Passage (about 7 miles)

to Pentecost Island (about 4 miles)

to Lindeman Island (about 5 miles)

29

Fl G 2.5s

18

17

15

N

to Pine Island (about 2.5 miles)

Soundings in Metres

Approximate Scale 1:32 000

0 Nautical Miles   0.5   1.0

0 Kilometres   0.5   1.0

© WINDWARD PUBLICATIONS PTY LTD

SEE CAUTION ON USE OF SKETCH MAPS ON PAGES 121, 123

NEXT SKETCH MAP C33

HAMILTON ISLAND EAST

NEXT SKETCH MAP C4

C23

NOT FOR NAVIGATION: USE CHART AUS 253

20

to Fitzalan Passage
(about 1.3 miles)

to Solway Passage
(about 4.5 miles)

(234)
Passage
Peak

PERSEVERANCE ISLAND

Surprise Rock
(about 1.3 miles)

020° 21.30'
149° 01.60'
Q(2) W 6s

10

17

3

HAMILTON
ISLAND

8

18

8

8

12

YOUNG ISLAND
(DUNGURRA ISLAND)

Soundings in Metres

JOINS SKETCH MAP C22

①

7

No passage

8

10

Approximate Scale 1:26 000

0 Nautical Miles   0.5   1.0

0 Kilometres   0.5   1.0

© WINDWARD PUBLICATIONS PTY LTD

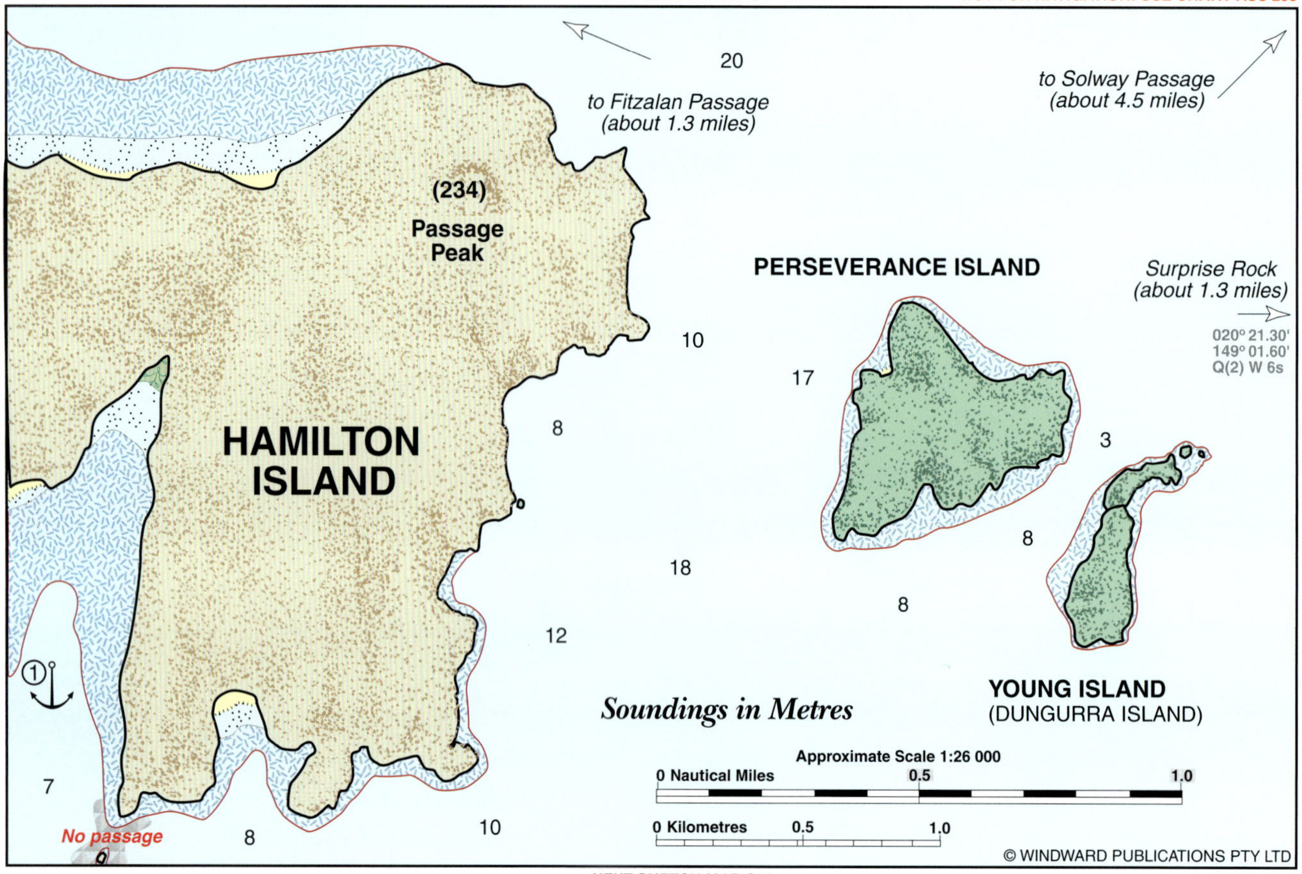

SEE CAUTION ON USE OF SKETCH MAPS ON PAGES 121, 123

NEXT SKETCH MAP C33

DRIFTWOOD BAY (C22)

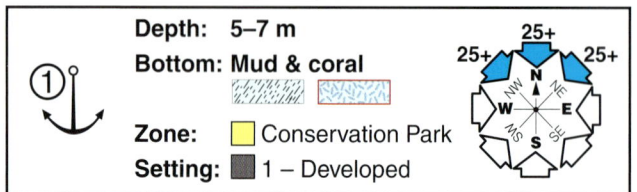

Air traffic at Hamilton airport has rendered this anchorage less peaceful. Post a lookout when going into the anchorage to avoid the reef and bommies. There are some walking tracks around the bay.

TURTLE BAY (C24)

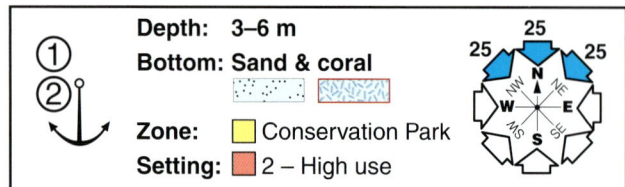

Turtle Bay consists of a beautiful series of bays just east of Fitzalan Passage. There are a number of good lunchtime spots in suitable weather during the April to August/September trade winds season, when it is advisable not to stay overnight to avoid being caught on a lee shore by a middle-of-the-night southerly change (which happens not infrequently during these months).

Anchorage No.1 gives the most protection. The water is shallower on the west side of the anchorage.

There is some good snorkelling on the reef just north of the anchorage No. 2 symbol. Visibility will be best in neap tides and if the wind has been in the northern sectors for a day.

TORRES HERALD BAY (C24)

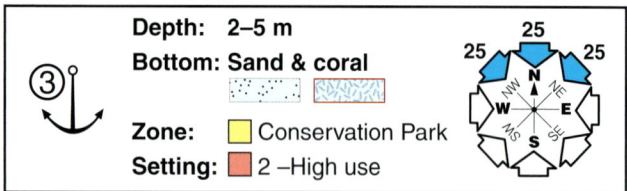

This used to be a favourite lunchtime spot of the charter vessel *Torres Herald*.

CRAYFISH BAY (C24)

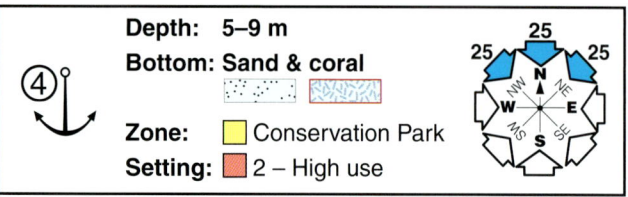

Watch out for bommies. Leave adequate swinging room.

TURTLE BAY

C24

NOT FOR NAVIGATION: USE CHART AUS 253

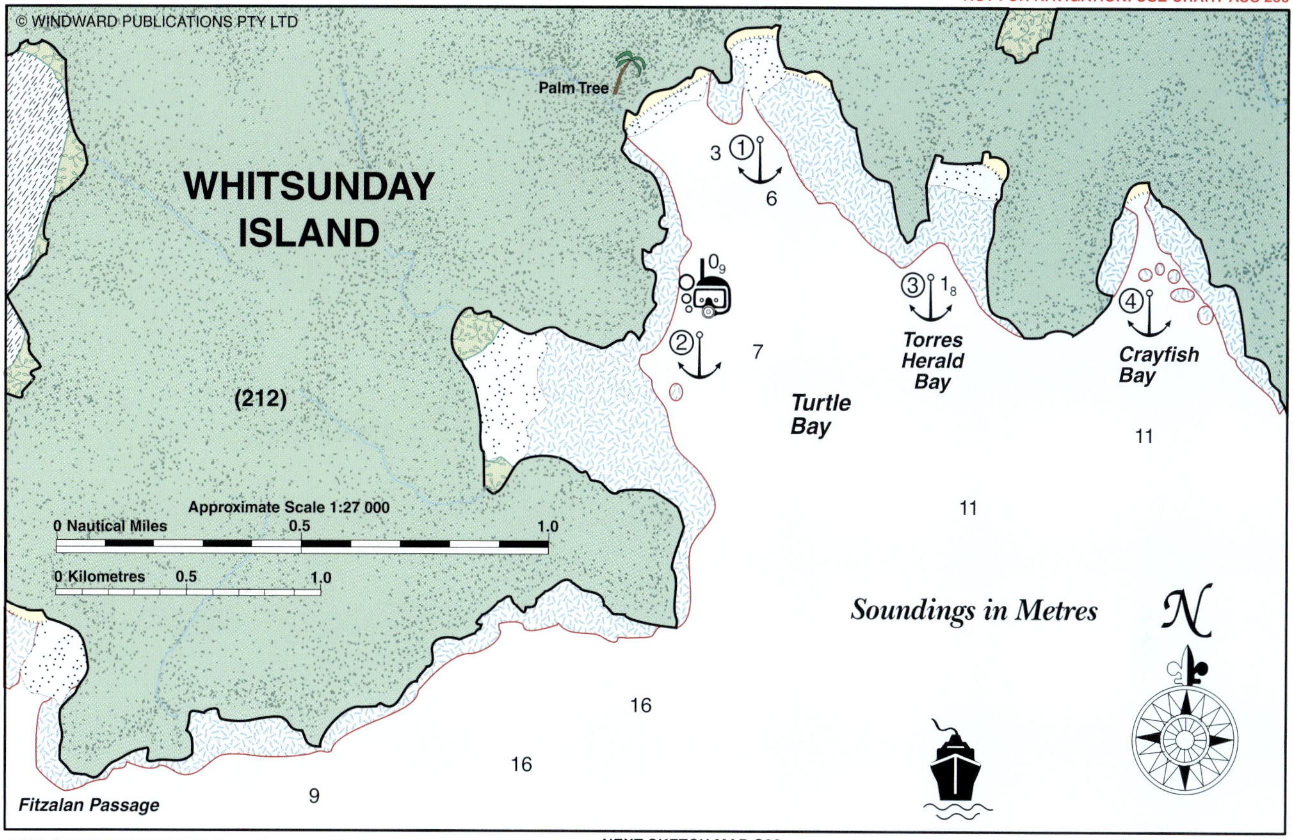

© WINDWARD PUBLICATIONS PTY LTD

Palm Tree

WHITSUNDAY ISLAND

3 ①
6

②
7

0₉

Turtle Bay

③ 1₈

Torres Herald Bay

④

Crayfish Bay

11

11

JOINS SKETCH MAP C20 & C22

JOINS SKETCH MAP C25

(212)

Approximate Scale 1:27 000

0 Nautical Miles 0.5 1.0

0 Kilometres 0.5 1.0

Soundings in Metres

N

16

16

9

Fitzalan Passage

SEE CAUTION ON USE OF SKETCH MAPS ON PAGES 121, 123

NEXT SKETCH MAP C23

JULY 1995 APPROXIMATE SCALE 1:40 000

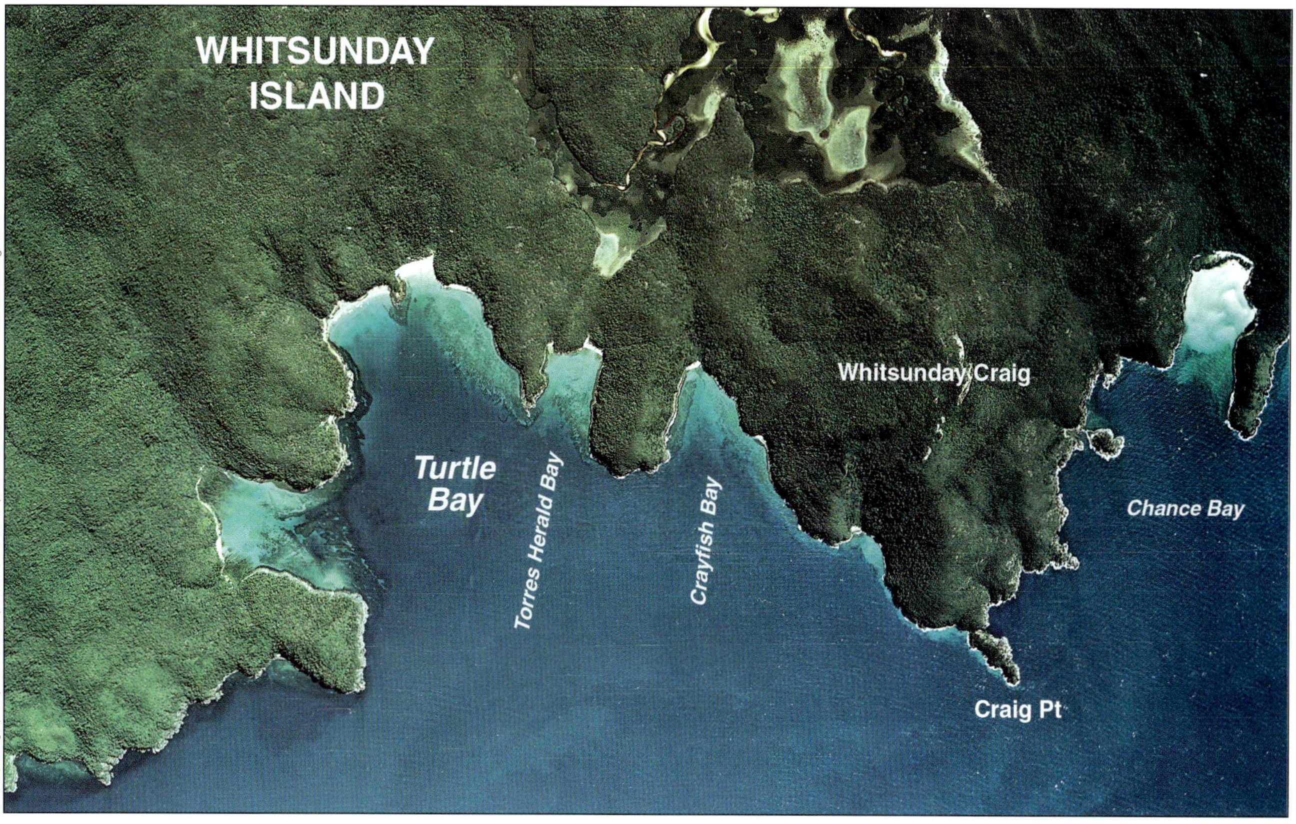

Aerial photograph reproduced with permission of the Department of Environment and Resource Management

WHITSUNDAY ISLAND

Whitsunday Craig

Turtle Bay

Torres Herald Bay

Crayfish Bay

Chance Bay

Craig Pt

CHANCE BAY

C25

NOT FOR NAVIGATION: USE CHART AUS 253

Whitehaven Beach

JOINS SKETCH MAP C24

Whitsunday Craig
(349)

WHITSUNDY ISLAND

WHITSUNDAY ISLAND

① Theo's Point

②

JOINS SKETCH MAP C26

④

Crayfish Bay

11

9

Chance Bay

15

MOON ISLAND

18

Craig Point

20

to Solway Passage
(about 1 mile)

Surprise Rock
(about 2 miles)
020° 21.30'
149° 01.60'
Q(2) W 6s

4₆

This area becomes
very rough in
heavy south-east conditions

Soundings in Metres

© WINDWARD PUBLICATIONS PTY LTD

SEE CAUTION ON USE OF SKETCH MAPS ON PAGES 121, 123

NEXT SKETCH MAP C33

JULY 1995 APPROXIMATE SCALE 1:40 000

Aerial photograph reproduced with permission of the Department of Environment and Resource Management

Whitehaven

Martin Islet

WHITSUNDAY ISLAND

Solway Passage

Chance Bay

CHANCE BAY (C25)

① ② ⚓	**Depth:** 5–10 m **Bottom:** Sand **Zone:** ☐ Conservation Park **Setting:** ☐ 2 – High use	compass rose

Keep a lookout posted. When picking your way into anchorage No. 2, set your transom on Theo's Point and head directly for the centre of the right-hand sandy beach. That should keep you clear of the reefs.

Chance Bay is a 'double' bay with two beautiful sand beaches. There is good snorkelling around the reef areas and around the little islet to the west of anchorage No.1. Anchorage No. 2 may provide some protection in moderate south-east to east winds. As with other south-exposed anchorages along these islands, this one is risky for overnight use during the trade winds season (April to August/September) when strong southerlies may come roaring in during the night.

A track which is part of the Ngaro Sea Trail leads from Chance Bay to Whitehaven Beach. It passes through some of the Whitsundays' finest forest and woodland and joins the Solway Circuit to Whitehaven.

SOLWAY PASSAGE (C26)

Solway Passage is another of the Whitsundays' restricted passages through which spring tides race at about 5 knots. When a fresh south-east trade wind is bucking a south-flooding tide, Solway Passage can become 'spectacular' with curling waves, overfalls whirlpools that spin a yacht around 90°. Some argue that it is not really dangerous; without debating the point, the average skipper in the average-sized yacht may, in these conditions, get a bit of a fright. Solway Passage should be avoided in strong wind-against-tide conditions, particularly by smaller craft, including trailer sailers. If possible it should be negotiated when the tide is slack or when wind and tide are together, i.e. in southerly winds when the tide is ebbing and in northerly winds when the tide is flooding.

Frith Rock is in the middle at the southern end of the passage and is always exposed, with good water either side.

The passage between Teague Island and Haslewood Island is extremely narrow with an underwater reef extending out from Haslewood Island; it is also subject to tidal currents. Bareboats are not permitted to use this passage, and only the adventurous would use it in preference to going around Teague Island.

Note: *A tidal anomaly has been reported near Haslewood Island south of Martin Islet; during ebb tide, which normally flows north, the stream runs south from Martin Islet for some half mile before recurving to join the north-moving main stream.*

Looking along the south-east side of Whitsunday Island towards Solway Passage, Teague and Haslewood islands.

David Colfelt

WHITEHAVEN BAY

C26

NOT FOR NAVIGATION: USE CHART AUS 253/AUS 252

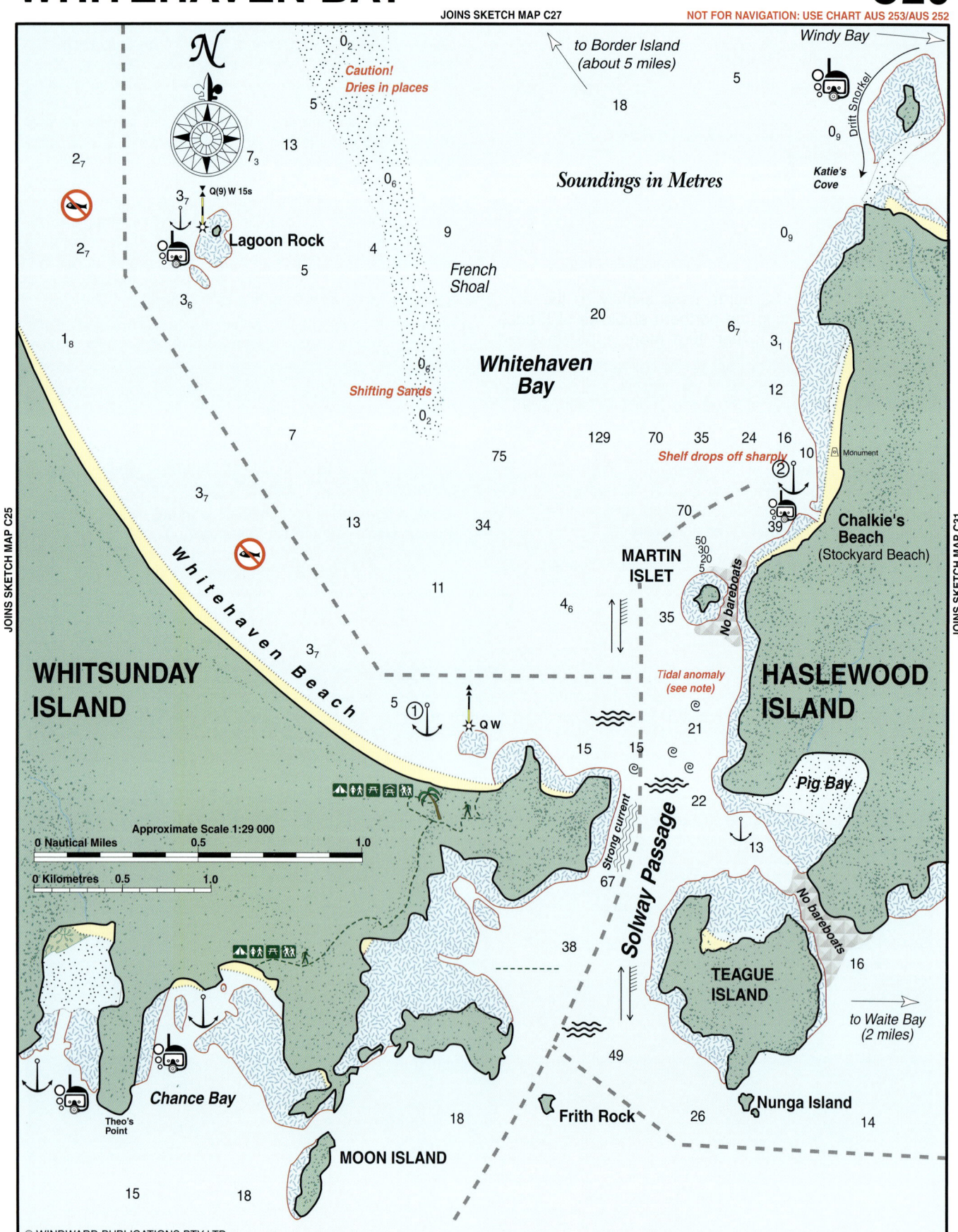

Caution!
Dries in places

to Border Island
(about 5 miles)

Windy Bay

Drift Snorkel

Katie's
Cove

Soundings in Metres

Q(9) W 15s

Lagoon Rock

French
Shoal

*Whitehaven
Bay*

Shifting Sands

Monument

Shelf drops off sharply

Chalkie's
Beach
(Stockyard Beach)

MARTIN
ISLET

No bareboats

Tidal anomaly
(see note)

**WHITSUNDAY
ISLAND**

Whitehaven Beach

**HASLEWOOD
ISLAND**

Pig Bay

Strong current

Solway Passage

No bareboats

Approximate Scale 1:29 000

0 Nautical Miles   0.5   1.0

0 Kilometres   0.5   1.0

**TEAGUE
ISLAND**

to Waite Bay
(2 miles)

Chance Bay

Theo's
Point

Nunga Island

Frith Rock

MOON ISLAND

© WINDWARD PUBLICATIONS PTY LTD

WHITEHAVEN BEACH (C26)

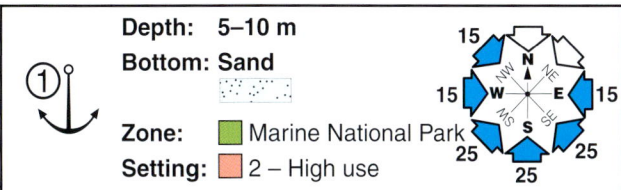

Depth:	5–10 m	
Bottom:	Sand	
Zone:	☐ Marine National Park	
Setting:	☐ 2 – High use	

If coming from Solway Passage, watch out for the reef area, which is always covered, at the south-east end of Whitehaven Beach. It is marked with a north cardinal mark. Proceed north until you are well clear of the passage before turning to port and heading for the beach.

Approaching from the north, pass slightly to the west of Esk Island, avoiding the northern shallows of French Shoal (see map C27); then turn more south to avoid shifting sands at the mouth of Hill Inlet and head just west of Lagoon Rock. Follow your way down, closing gradually with the beach.

Alternatively, you can come straight down, leaving Esk Island and French Shoal to starboard until you are almost abeam of Martin Islet, then turn towards the anchorage. The former track avoids guesswork as to the exact whereabouts of French Shoal and the coral patches at the southern end of Whitehaven.

Note: The anchor is shown slightly west of north of the lone palm tree on the beach. If you're directly opposite the palm tree you may find yourself too close to the reef patch. Keep the palm tree to your south-east.

If you never anchor in less than 5.5 metres or in more than 9 metres of water, you will never have to worry whether the tide is coming or going.

Whitehaven can be very rolly and, therefore, an uncomfortable anchorage at night. A stern anchor buried in the beach at high tide level can be used to pull your stern around to keep your bow towards the swell. This is a busy spot, and a buoy on the line will let others know not to pass between you and the beach.

Whitehaven is an incredible expanse of pure white sand, a magnificent beach and one that is popular with all and sundry, from itinerant yachts to motorised catamarans complete with rock bands. It is also popular with sandflies and mosquitoes; take plenty of insect repellent with you.

There is a walking track from the southern end of the beach to Chance Bay (see page 103 for details).

CHALKIE'S (STOCKYARD) BEACH (C26)

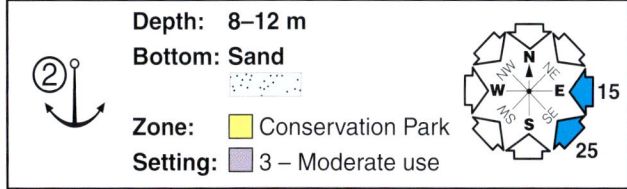

Depth:	8–12 m	
Bottom:	Sand	
Zone:	☐ Conservation Park	
Setting:	☐ 3 – Moderate use	

Stay outside Martin Islet if coming from the south; approach from the southern end of the anchorage closing gradually to pick up the fringing reef. Anchor north of the gap in the reef; further south is deep water.

This anchorage has a lovely beach. If Whitehaven is overcrowded, this is a good alternative provided there are not too many yachts already there. It is a somewhat difficult anchorage because it shoals off very steeply and is swept by currents, so it may be necessary to put down quite a lot of chain (be sure to allow for a rising tide), which may create swinging circle clashes with other yachts behaving differently in the current. In neap tides and light southerly winds, snorkelling at the northern end of the beach is good.

Don't feed the gulls, which are becoming a nuisance both to other birds and to humans having picnics on this beach. A monument on the beach is in memory of Captain Kris Finato, a well-known local diving instructor who trajically drowned here in 2003.

PIG BAY (C26)

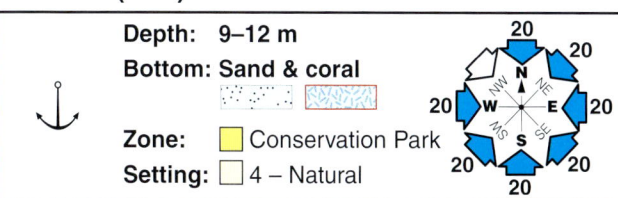

Depth:	9–12 m	
Bottom:	Sand & coral	
Zone:	☐ Conservation Park	
Setting:	☐ 4 – Natural	

Temporary anchorage is possible opposite this pretty bay just north of Teague Island. Needless to say, watch the run of the tide. It gets its name from wild pigs that used to inhabit the island and which were often sighted here.

HILL INLET (entrance) (C27)

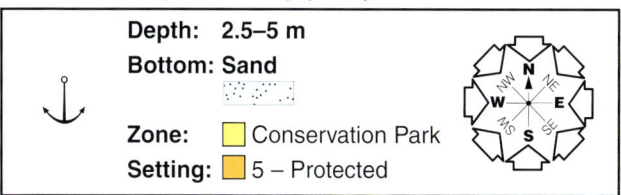

Depth:	2.5–5 m	
Bottom:	Sand	
Zone:	☐ Conservation Park	
Setting:	☐ 5 – Protected	

Hill Inlet is a large estuary, with mangroves and shifting sands. It is not really accessible to keel boats (although at high tide you could pick your way up one of the shifting channels for some little distance). It offers trailer sailers magnificent exploring and many spots for allowing the yacht to dry out at low tide. Because it is tidebound, go in near the top of the tide and be prepared to wait for the next tide to get out, if you're not staying overnight.

The anchorage shown just south of the entrance is a light-weather temporary stop-off only and may provide an opportunity to explore the inlet in the dinghy, or to go ashore and loll around on the northern end of Whitehaven Beach, away from the crowd that may be madding away at the southern end.

Hill Inlet is of tremendous significance to the local ecology, being a major source of food for hungry and growing young fishes. Human visitors to Hill Inlet are also an important source of food – for the local mosquitoes and sandflies, of which there are plenty. Take insect repellent ashore with you.

The inlet is also an important resting place for migratory wading birds that come from as far as arctic climes to fossick on these sandy foreshores. The inlet is classified as 'protected', and restrictions on access may from time to time be imposed according to the dictates of good environmental management.

HILL INLET

C27

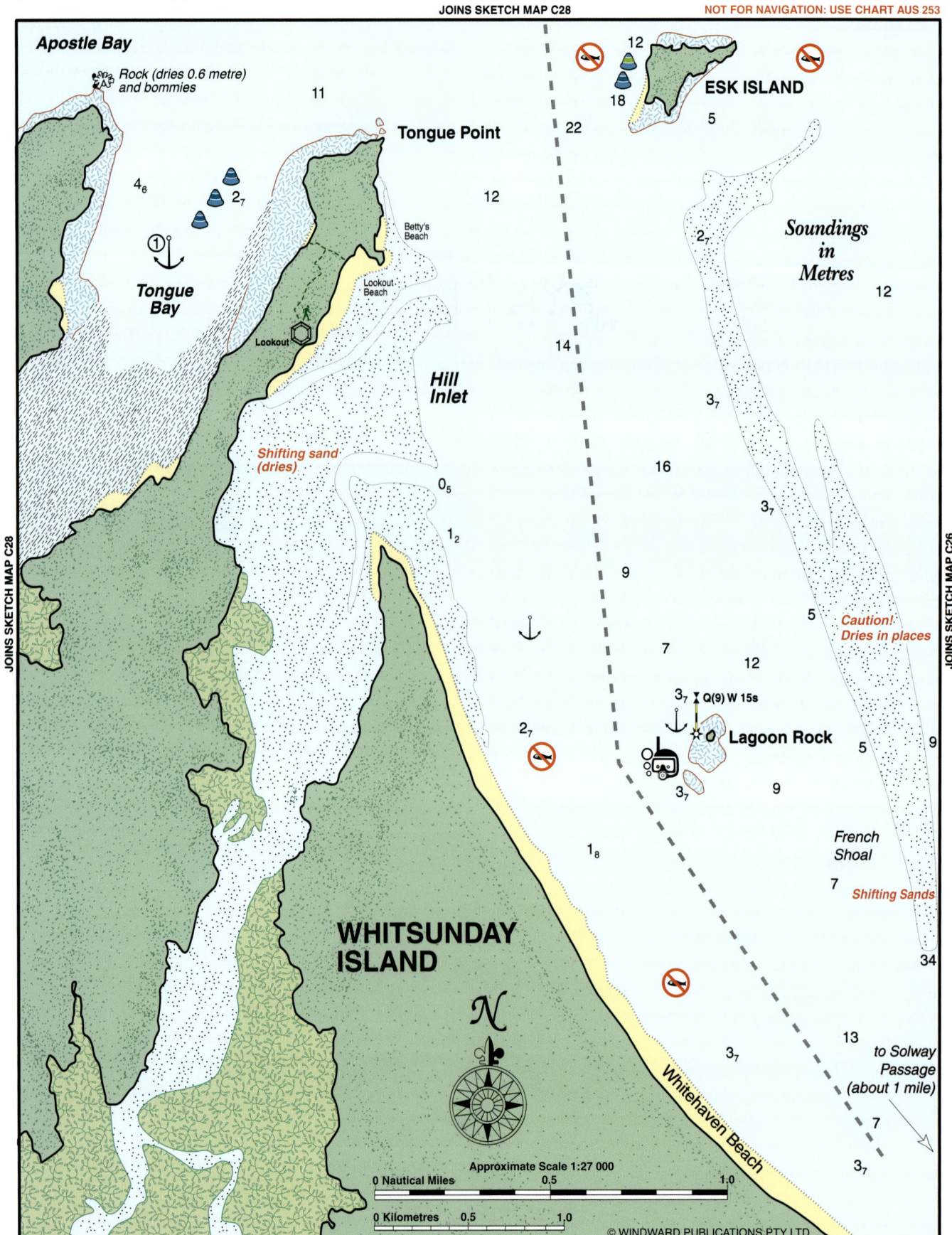

NOT FOR NAVIGATION: USE CHART AUS 253

Apostle Bay

Rock (dries 0.6 metre) and bommies

11

Tongue Point

4_6

2_7

① Tongue Bay

Betty's Beach

Lookout Beach

Lookout

Hill Inlet

Shifting sand (dries)

0_5

1_2

2_7

1_8

WHITSUNDAY ISLAND

12

22

ESK ISLAND

18

5

Soundings in Metres

12

2_7

3_7

14

16

3_7

9

5

Caution! Dries in places

7

12

3_7

Q(9) W 15s

Lagoon Rock

3_7

9

5

9

French Shoal

7

Shifting Sands

34

13

to Solway Passage (about 1 mile)

3_7

7

3_7

N

Whitehaven Beach

Approximate Scale 1:27 000

0 Nautical Miles   0.5   1.0

0 Kilometres   0.5   1.0

© WINDWARD PUBLICATIONS PTY LTD

SEE CAUTION ON USE OF SKETCH MAPS ON PAGES 121, 123

JOINS SKETCH MAP C28

JOINS SKETCH MAP C26

LAGOON ROCK (C27)

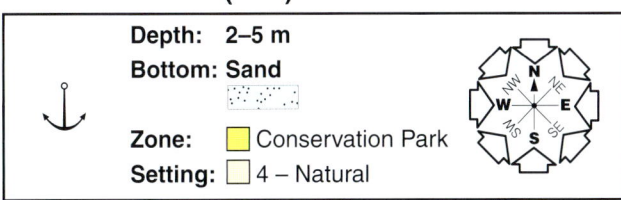

Depth:	2–5 m
Bottom:	Sand
Zone:	☐ Conservation Park
Setting:	☐ 4 – Natural

Lagoon Rock, in suitably light south-east to east weather and at neap tides, may provide some interesting exploring from the water. Anchor on the lee side as shown.

TONGUE BAY (C27)

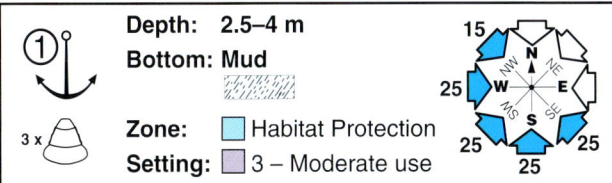

Depth:	2.5–4 m
Bottom:	Mud
Zone:	☐ Habitat Protection
Setting:	☐ 3 – Moderate use

Tongue Bay is quite a large anchorage that offers a secure haven for keel boaters who want to explore Hill Inlet having fled the crowds or the swell at Whitehaven. It is fairly shallow and the holding good.

A track leads from the little beach across Tongue Point to a silica sand beach on the other side, where the amazing spectacle of Hill Inlet and Whitehaven beach unfolds. Halfway across the neck another track branches at right angles to the south-west and heads up the neck and crosses to a platform lookout that allows magnificent views straight into the inlet and across to the long sweep of Whitehaven Beach. It is well worth the minor effort required to get there once you effect a landing; be sure to take a camera. The beach on the Tongue Bay anchorage side is accessible only at high or near-high tide, and while it is possible to get ashore at other times, this involves a certain amount of heroics and isn't advisable for those who aren't both sure-footed and semi-masochistic. Alternatively, if the weather is favourably light, you can go, in a dinghy, around Tongue Point where there is all-tide access to Betty's Beach on the other side.

ESK ISLAND (C27)

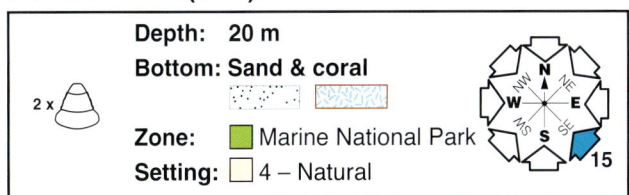

Depth:	20 m
Bottom:	Sand & coral
Zone:	☐ Marine National Park
Setting:	☐ 4 – Natural

Esk is a small island, its shores eroded by waves into small cliffs and coves, with a deep saddle in the middle and forested by hoop pines. It was named by a naval surveyor Cmdr Bedwell, RN remembering the turbulent history of Scotland (there is an 'Esk' in Cumberland, England and in Scotland). One mooring has been installed just off the coral shingle spit on its western side. If the weather is right, it's only a short dinghy ride from here across to Hill Inlet. A lonely, deserted isle with some nice bays to explore on the northern and southern sides.

The lookout on Tongue Point surveys Hill Inlet and the sweeping silica sands of Whitehaven Beach.

Secluded cove on the northern side of Esk Island

WHITSUNDAY NORTH-EAST C28

NEXT SKETCH MAPS C17 & C29

NOT FOR NAVIGATION: USE CHART AUS 253/AUS 252

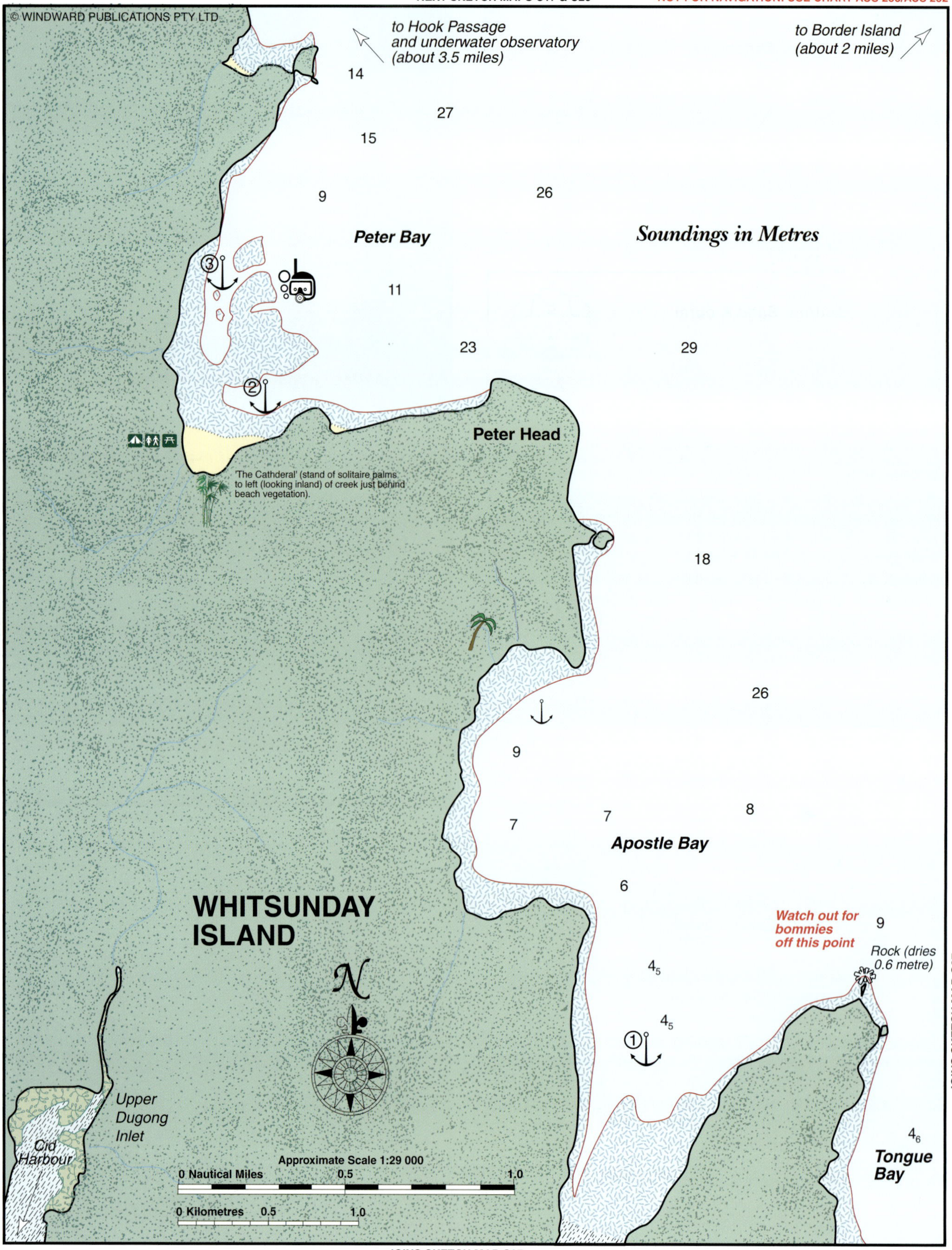

© WINDWARD PUBLICATIONS PTY LTD
to Hook Passage
and underwater observatory
(about 3.5 miles)
to Border Island
(about 2 miles)
14
27
15
9
26
Peter Bay
Soundings in Metres
3
11
23
29
2
Peter Head
'The Cathderal' (stand of solitaire palms to left (looking inland) of creek just behind beach vegetation).
18
26
9
7
7
8
Apostle Bay
6
WHITSUNDAY ISLAND
N
Watch out for bommies off this point
9
Rock (dries 0.6 metre)
4₅
4₅
1
Upper Dugong Inlet
Cid Harbour
Approximate Scale 1:29 000
0 Nautical Miles 0.5 1.0
0 Kilometres 0.5 1.0
4₆
Tongue Bay
JOINS SKETCH MAP C18
JOINS SKETCH MAP C27

SEE CAUTION ON USE OF SKETCH MAPS ON PAGES 121, 123

JOINS SKETCH MAP C27

APOSTLE BAY (C28)

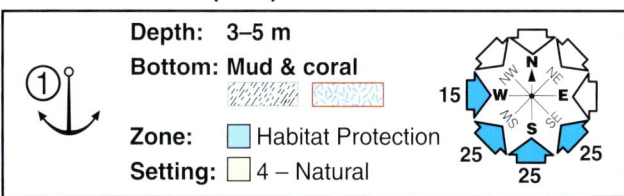

①	**Depth:** 3–5 m
	Bottom: Mud & coral
	Zone: ☐ Habitat Protection
	Setting: ☐ 4 – Natural

Apostle Bay is another quite large anchorage that may not be crowded. It may be a bit swelly as the wind easts. Be on the lookout for scattered bommies as you pick your way into the anchorage.

PETER BAY (C28)

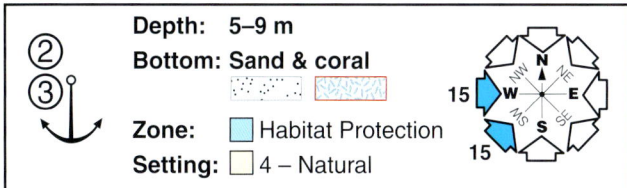

② ③	**Depth:** 5–9 m
	Bottom: Sand & coral
	Zone: ☐ Habitat Protection
	Setting: ☐ 4 – Natural

Peter Bay is swelly in south-east conditions and, from a distance off, it normally looks foreboding. There are a couple of places to tuck in snugly if the weather is favourable, using great care to avoid the fringing reef (particularly in Anchorage No. 3). Good fishing and snorkelling or diving. Behind the beach vegetation on the eastern side of the creek outlet (left looking inland from sea) there is a stand of palm trees that has been likened, somewhat imaginatively, to 'standing in a cathedral'.

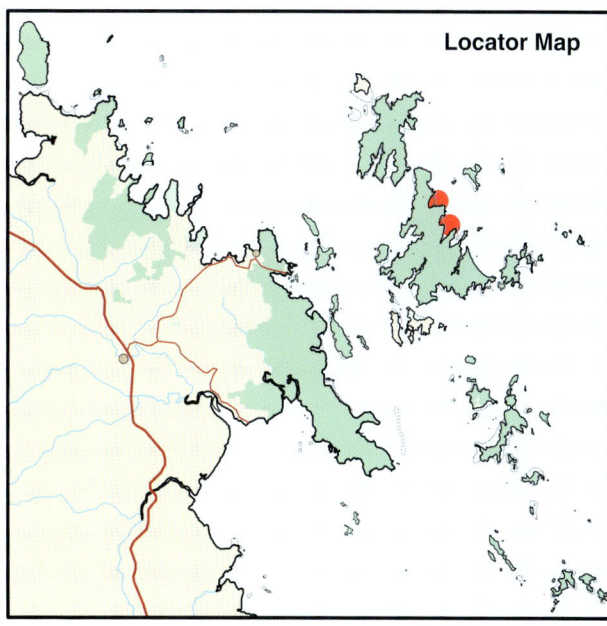

Locator Map

JULY 1995 APPROXIMATE SCALE 1:40 000

Aerial photograph reproduced with permission of the Department of Environment and Resource Management

Peter Bay

Apostle Bay

Tongue Bay

Tongue Pt

Esk Island

BORDER ISLAND

C29

NOT FOR NAVIGATION: USE CHART AUS 252

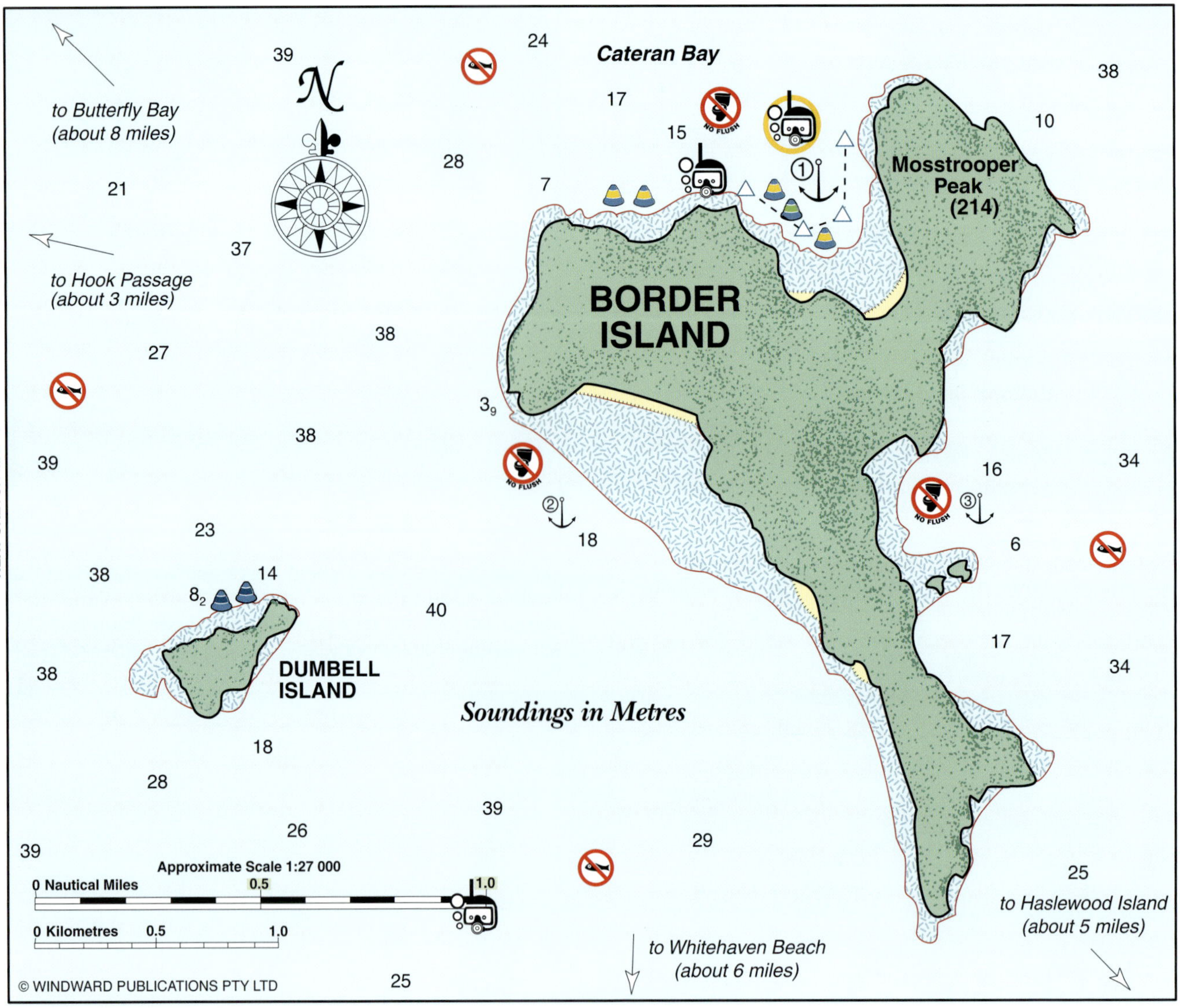

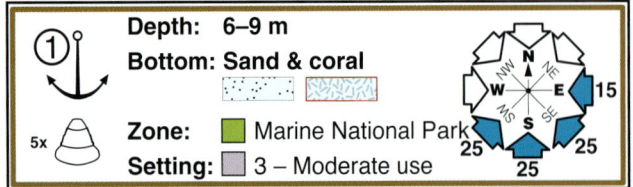

*to Butterfly Bay
(about 8 miles)*

*to Hook Passage
(about 3 miles)*

Cateran Bay

**BORDER
ISLAND**

**Mosstrooper
Peak
(214)**

**DUMBELL
ISLAND**

Soundings in Metres

NEXT SKETCH MAP C17

NEXT SKETCH MAP C30

Approximate Scale 1:27 000

0 Nautical Miles   0.5

0 Kilometres   0.5   1.0

© WINDWARD PUBLICATIONS PTY LTD

*to Whitehaven Beach
(about 6 miles)*

*to Haslewood Island
(about 5 miles)*

SEE CAUTION ON USE OF SKETCH MAPS ON PAGES 121, 123

NEXT SKETCH MAP C28

CATERAN BAY (C29)

① ⚓	**Depth:** 6–9 m
	Bottom: Sand & coral
5x	**Zone:** 🟩 Marine National Park
	Setting: ⬜ 3 – Moderate use

Border Island is one of the 'outlying' islands that will reward your efforts for going there. Reef protection buoys have been installed to prevent further damage to the island's excellent fringing reef. Do not anchor inshore of an imaginary straight line between the reef protection buoys. Public moorings have been installed in the bay and just west of the bay.

Cateran Bay is subject to bullets when the wind is over 20 knots. It is swelly when the wind easts. If the wind is light, you will also roll around on your anchor as the tide changes. A stern anchor, if the anchorage is not crowded, may help. Your anchor chain will make a dreadful noise scraping over the bottom, so rig a rope 'snubber'. There are occasional bommies on the bottom. Anchor over sand (light-coloured bottom); avoid dark patches.

Border can be a delightful anchorage if the wind isn't too brisk. The bay has very good coral. Snorkelling/diving is best in neap tides and light southerly winds (northerly winds cause the rising of fine sediments that are deposited on the 'lee side' of the islands, and visibility is poor). In spring tides some colourful coral exposes at the bottom of the reef, just off the sand beach. The beaches are accessible in the dinghy at high tide.

If you go ashore at low tide, don your footwear and be careful where you tread to avoid stepping on live corals or a stonefish.

All around Border Island is Marine National Park Zone; fishing and shell collecting (even empty shells) are prohibited. It is also a nil-discharge zone.

CATERAN BAY

NOT FOR NAVIGATION: USE CHART AUS 252

Cateran Bay

BORDER ISLAND

© WINDWARD PUBLICATIONS PTY LTD

SEE CAUTION ON USE OF SKETCH MAPS ON PAGES 121, 123

BORDER ISLAND (C29)

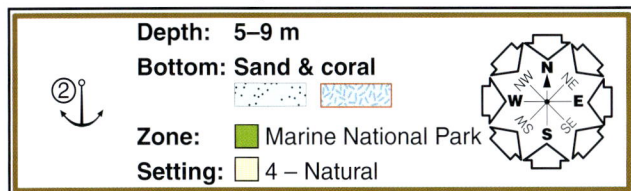

	Depth:	5–9 m
	Bottom:	Sand & coral
	Zone:	▉ Marine National Park
	Setting:	☐ 4 – Natural

This is a daytime stopoff in light easterly or north-easterly weather. Watch the flow of the current, and keep an eye on your anchor.

BORDER ISLAND (C29)

	Depth:	6–9 m
	Bottom:	Sand & coral
	Zone:	▉ Marine National Park
	Setting:	☐ 3 – Moderate use

Another pleasant lunchtime anchorage in north-westerly winds.

DUMBELL ISLAND (C29)

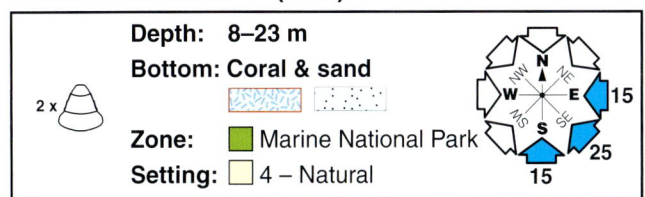

	Depth:	8–23 m
	Bottom:	Coral & sand
	Zone:	▉ Marine National Park
	Setting:	☐ 4 – Natural

A small, remote island covered in hoop pines and grass trees similar to the adjacent Whitsunday Island vegetation. There is some good coral on the southern side. Two moorings have been installed to facilitate coral appreciation; it's very deep for anchoring here.

DELORAINE ISLAND (C30)

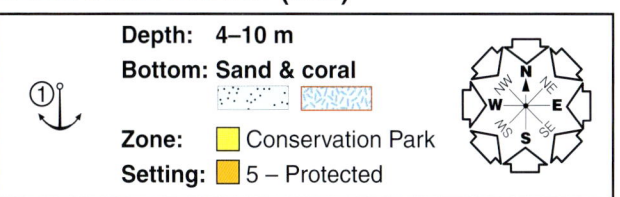

	Depth:	4–10 m
	Bottom:	Sand & coral
	Zone:	☐ Conservation Park
	Setting:	☐ 5 – Protected

Deloraine Island stands aloof, east of Border Island; it shimmers in the sunlight, its dazzling beach punctuating vibrant blue water around it, lonely and beckoning. It is a difficult place to anchor, even in the most favourable conditions, because of steeply sloping terrain and coral reef. Its outlying, exposed position has contributed to its relatively pristine condition, and it has been given a 'protected' setting in order to preserve its unique conservation values. As such, some restrictions on access may be necessary from time to time.

Anchoring should be attempted only in ideal conditions – light easterlies/north-easterlies.

Anchorage No. 1 is a magnificent but steep coral dropoff, and an anchor dropped on this face may be difficult to retrieve (quite apart from the damage the cable will do to the coral). A better plan, if tide, weather and draught permit, is to ease in over the reef flat and hang off a short anchor in one of the sandy patches that can be found there. Best to leave someone aboard if you make a shore visit, as the tide races through here.

DELORAINE ISLAND C30

NOT FOR NAVIGATION: USE CHART AUS 252

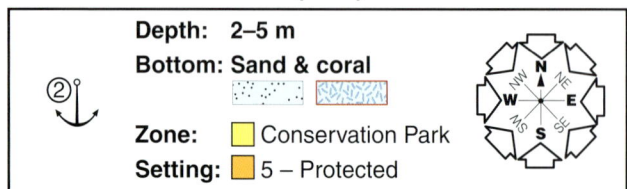

Jester Rock

47

6

Minstrel Rocks
(dries 2.7 metres)

*Soundings
in
Metres*

②

③ 4

①

22

**DELORAINE
ISLAND**

*to Border Island
(about 1.5 miles)*

22

8

Approximate Scale 1:27 000

| 0 Nautical Miles | 0.5 | 1.0 |
| 0 Kilometres | 0.5 | 1.0 |

© WINDWARD PUBLICATIONS PTY LTD

NEXT SKETCH MAP C29

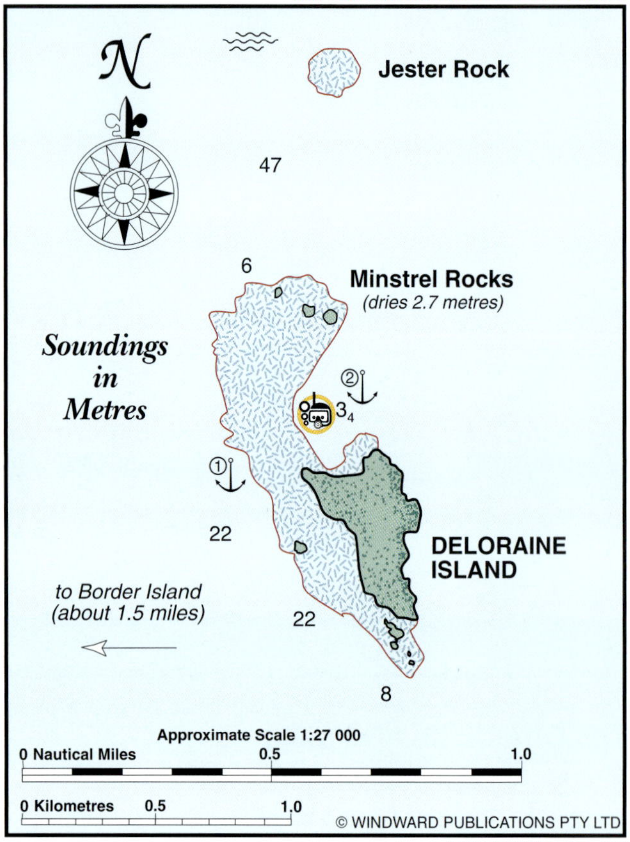

SEE CAUTION ON USE OF SKETCH MAPS pps. 121, 123   NEXT SKETCH MAP C31

DELORAINE ISLAND (C30)

② ⚓

Depth: 2–5 m
Bottom: Sand & coral

Zone: ☐ Conservation Park
Setting: ☐ 5 – Protected

Anchorage No. 2 obviously requires very light conditions and excellent visibility. This anchorage is suitable only for small, shallow-draught boats (dinghies and runabouts). Watch the current.

It's a good beach for exploring.

Feeding native wildlife has an adverse affect on the health of individual animals and natural populations. Unnatural populations can cause animals to become competitive and aggresive. Enjoy the company of native animals, but let nature take its own course.

Approach to Waite Bay (White Bay)

'White Bay' is another of those Whitsunday placenames in the process of correction. although haste is not evident. The original survey chart of this area shows Waite Bay, and as has happened in some other cases, this later somehow became 'White'. Waite is undoubtedly correct.

CAUTION

The area between Haslewood Island and Nicolson Island is hazardous. One vessel, *Pegasus*, was sunk there in 1982, and several others have done themselves serious damage while heading through the passage between Nicolson and Haslewood islands. The culprit is an elusive bommie that has variously been reported over the years as being anywhere between the southern tip of Haslewood Island and Nicolson Island itself. It has moved around the chart like an ephemeral spirit, but investigations by harbourmasters and experienced local mariners have failed to find it. There *is* a bommie (which is marked on map C31 as 'Pegasus Rock') which is deceptive and which is probably the one that has done the defrocking and which has been reported elsewhere to spare red faces. It becomes a problem at spring low tide. **Keep well over to the Nicolson Island side if you use the passage between Nicolson and Haslewood islands.** If proceeding to Waite Bay from the south of Whitsunday Island or from Solway Passage, after coming around Teague Island don't head straight for the passage or you will probably run right onto Pegasus Rock. Keep well to starboard and favour the western side of Nicolson Island (or go right outside (east) of Nicolson Island).

If proceeding from Waite Bay to Solway Passage or to the south of Whitsunday Island en route to Fitzalan Passage, the same applies; favour the western side of Nicolson Island and keep well south of Teague before turning west.

WAITE BAY (WHITE BAY) (C31)

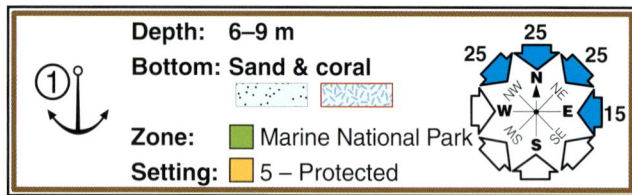

① ⚓

Depth: 6–9 m
Bottom: Sand & coral

Zone: ☐ Marine National Park
Setting: ☐ 5 – Protected

25   25   25   15

Waite Bay is formed by Lupton and Haslewood islands which are joined by a massive fringing reef. This reef is recognised to be a significant 'feeder' reef of the area, i.e. it produces larval coral recruits for many other reefs in the area. It is a significant marine wildlife habitat. As such, it has been given a 'protected' setting in order to provide the appropriate degree of ecological management; restrictions to access may be necessary from time to time.

All of the area around this bay and Lupton Island is a Marine National Park Zone; fishing and shell collecting (even empty shells) are prohibited.

Anchorage No. 1 will provide better protection in north to north-east winds, which funnel through the opening between Lupton and Haslewood islands.

(Continued on page 211)

HASLEWOOD ISLAND

C31

NOT FOR NAVIGATION: USE CHART AUS 252

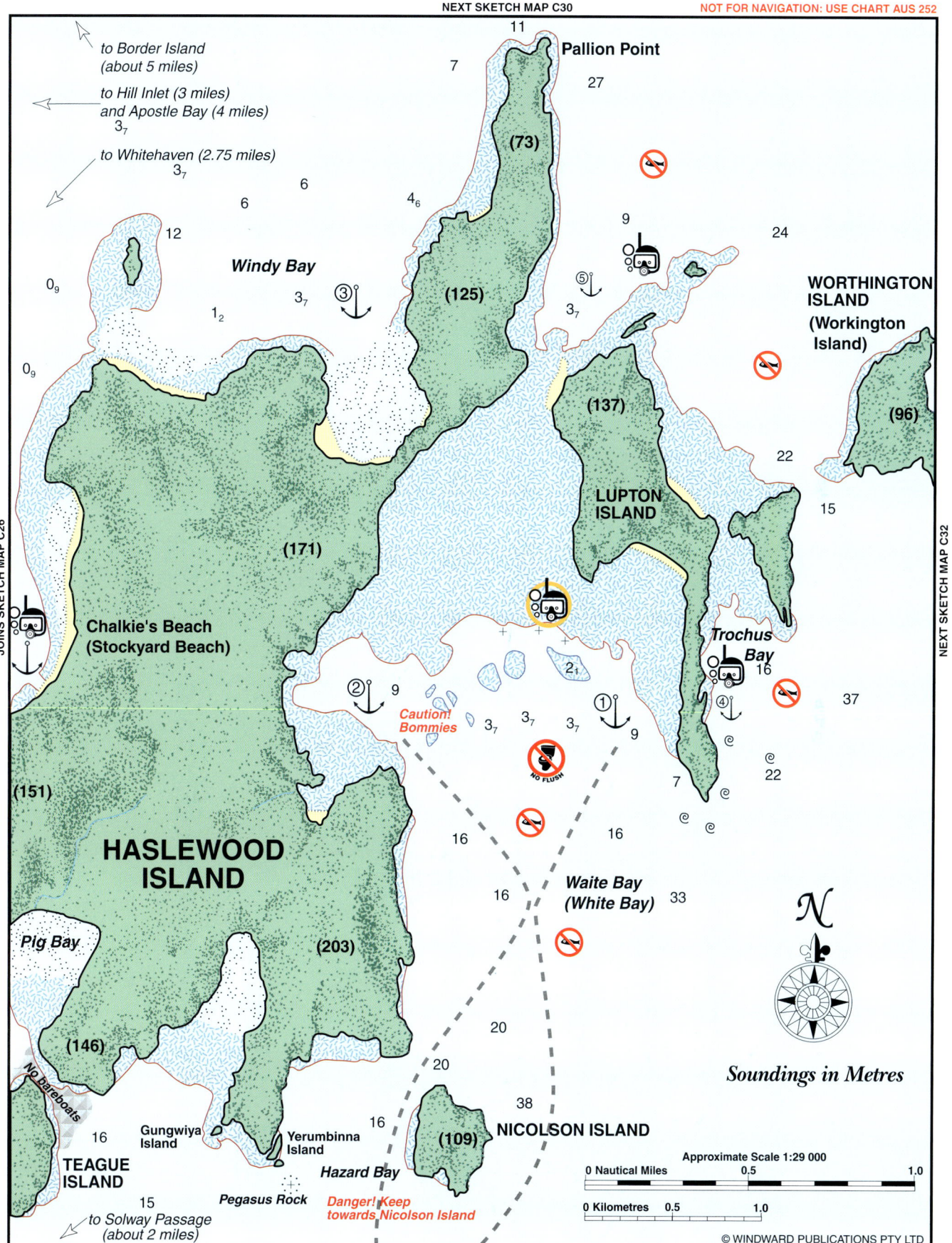

to Border Island
(about 5 miles)

to Hill Inlet (3 miles)
and Apostle Bay (4 miles)
3_7

to Whitehaven (2.75 miles)
3_7

Pallion Point

11
7
27

(73)

9
24

12
6
4_6

Windy Bay

(125)

3_7

WORTHINGTON
ISLAND
(Workington
Island)

0_9

6
3_7
③

0_9
1_2

0_9

5

(137)
22

(96)

JOINS SKETCH MAP C26

LUPTON
ISLAND

15

NEXT SKETCH MAP C32

(171)

Chalkie's Beach
(Stockyard Beach)

*Trochus
Bay*

16

② 9

*Caution!
Bommies*

2_1

① 9

37

22

(151)

3_7
3_7
3_7
④

NO FLUSH

7

16
16

**HASLEWOOD
ISLAND**

16

*Waite Bay
(White Bay)*
33

N

Pig Bay

(203)

16

20

Soundings in Metres

(146)

No Bareboats

20

Gungwiya
Island

Yerumbinna
Island

16

(109) **NICOLSON ISLAND**

38

Approximate Scale 1:29 000

0 Nautical Miles   0.5   1.0

16

Hazard Bay

**TEAGUE
ISLAND**

15

Pegasus Rock

*Danger! Keep
towards Nicolson Island*

0 Kilometres   0.5   1.0

© WINDWARD PUBLICATIONS PTY LTD

to Solway Passage
(about 2 miles)

JULY 1995 APPROXIMATE SCALE 1:40 000

Aerial photograph reproduced with permission of the Department of Environment and Resource Management

(Continued from page 208)

There is a beautiful sand beach on Lupton Island, and walking on the island is relatively easy, with excellent views back over Waite Bay and Trochus Bay to the east.

The reef, which dries extensively, provides potentially endless hours of reef exploration and, in suitable weather, snorkelling at the edge. As the tide comes up over the reef an abundance of sea life, including turtles and small sharks, returns to feed on the reef.

The best landing spot is the sand beach on Lupton Island; it is almost impossible to land a dinghy elsewhere without damaging the coral. Watch the state of the tide or you may find yourself stranded until the tide comes back in.

Be careful where you tread, avoiding stepping on live coral. Step between clumps or in places that appear like concrete, which will help to preserve the coral as well as yourself.

WAITE BAY (WHITE BAY) (C31)

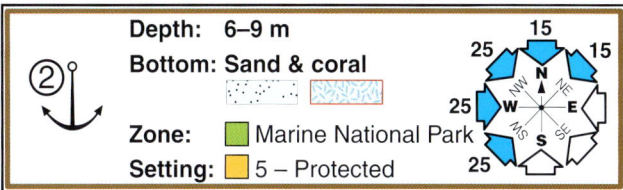

Go slowly and keep a lookout for scattered bommies in and around the area marked (and even in the approach channel marked), especially at times of spring low tides, when these bommies may constitute a hazard.

LUPTON ISLAND (east side) (C31)

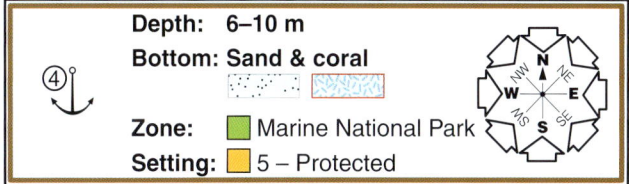

On the east side of Lupton Island, in ideal conditions, and preferably at times of neap tides, you can find temporary anchorage which will allow you to explore this isolated spot. Be careful where you drop anchor to avoid damaging coral. The area south of Lupton Island is marked by eddies and disturbed water.

LUPTON ISLAND (north side) (C31)

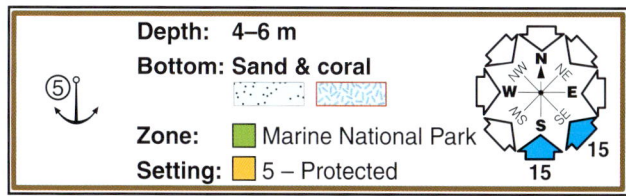

Be careful if using the passage between Worthington Island and Lupton Island, particularly at times of contrary wind and tide, when it may best be avoided. Watch out for the reef which runs for some considerable distance north-east of Lupton. For safety don't go south-west of a line from Pallion Point to the northern end of Worthington Island unless you can see your way clearly into the anchorage.

Anchorage No. 5 is a daytime stopover, not a night-time anchorage. Good snorkelling, but watch the current.

Worthington Island (Workington on the chart) is another case where at some time the name got changed through an error in the British hydrographic office. The original charts show 'Worthington' (*source*: Ray Blackwood).

WINDY BAY (C31)

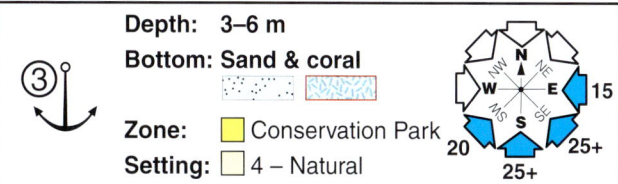

Approach cautiously, as you cannot get very deep into the bay. Windy Bay is lovely but usually not particularly quiescent. It tends to be very rolly, and it can be gusty in fresh south-east conditions.

A small sand beach north-east of the anchor symbol can serve as a platform for launching yourself onto a snorkel around the fringing reef.

Waite Bay, Haslewood Island, looking south-west

David Colfelt

Don't fish in a green zone (Marine National Park Zone), and observe the fishing restrictions within a yellow zone (Conservation Park Zone). Be mindful of size and bag limits and seasonal closures when these apply (see pages 88–93).

Feeding sea gulls turns them into pests. Thereafter, they badger humans for food, and they can also become a positive threat to other seabirds.

EDWARD GROUP

C32

NOT FOR NAVIGATION: USE CHART AUS 252/AUS 825

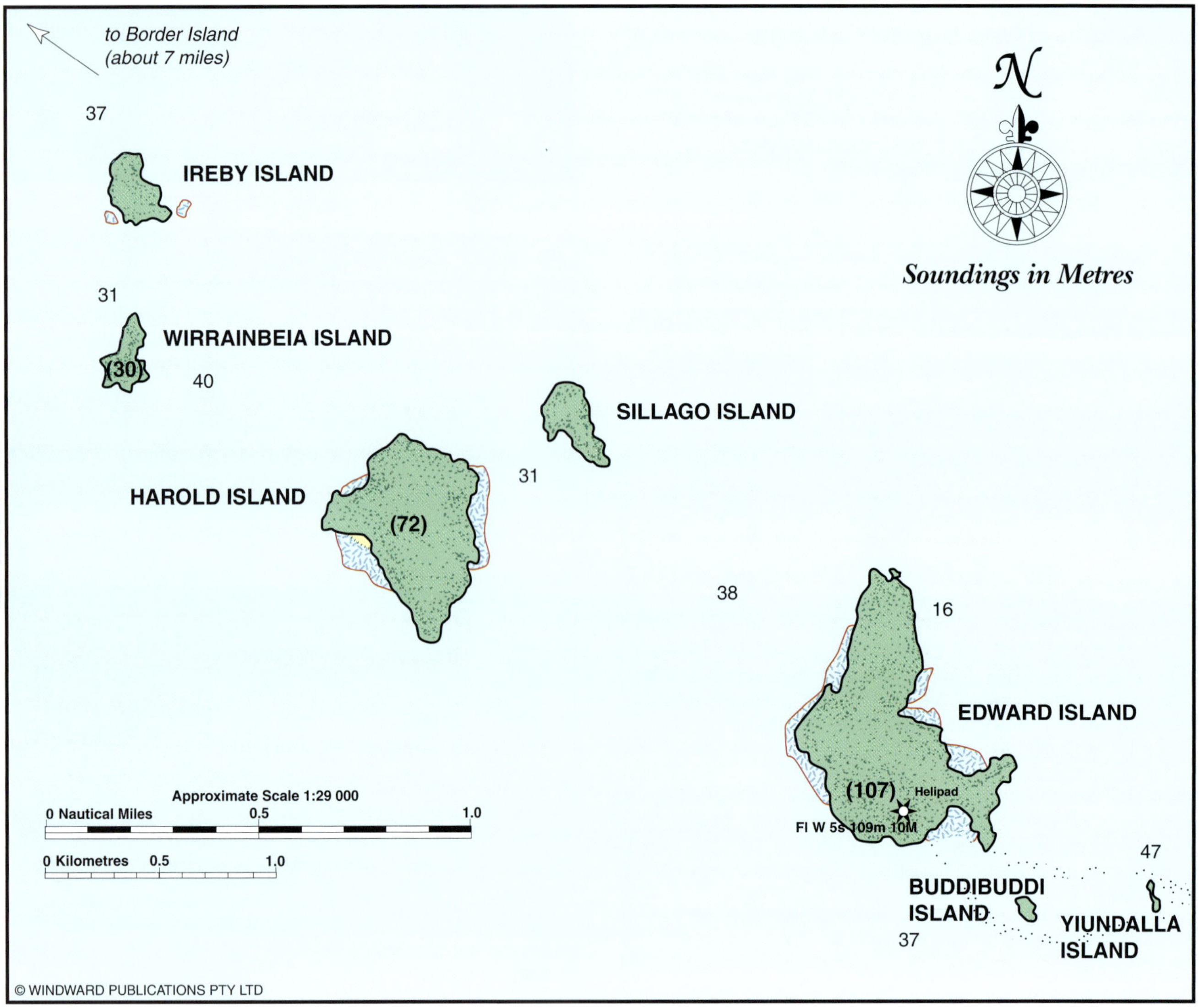

to Border Island
(about 7 miles)

37

IREBY ISLAND

31

WIRRAINBEIA ISLAND

(30)   40

SILLAGO ISLAND

HAROLD ISLAND

(72)   31

38

16

EDWARD ISLAND

(107)   Helipad

Fl W 5s 109m 10M

47

BUDDIBUDDI ISLAND

37

YIUNDALLA ISLAND

𝒩

Soundings in Metres

NEXT SKETCH MAP C31

Approximate Scale 1:29 000

| 0 Nautical Miles | 0.5 | 1.0 |

| 0 Kilometres | 0.5 | 1.0 |

© WINDWARD PUBLICATIONS PTY LTD

SEE CAUTION ON USE OF SKETCH MAPS ON PAGES 121, 123

THE EDWARD GROUP (C32)

The Edward Group lies east-north-east of Haslewood Island. These islands are not of particular interest as anchorages, but since the advent of the Hamilton Island Race Week they have seen more yachts, being a mark of one of the courses. Note the shaded line around Buddibuddi Island and Yiundalla Island, which indicates that passage between these islands is not advisable (although it may be possible at high tide, on a wing and a prayer, as one very keen yacht proved some years ago).

These islands are outside the bareboat charter limits.

Edward Island is the easternmost of the northern Whitsundays, a cliffy island with steep gullies. It has some good coral in very clear water (for the intrepid diver).

Within the Whitsunday whale protection zone (see pages 112–113) don't approach a whale closer than 300 metres. Outside the zone, stay further away than 100 metres.

PENTECOST ISLAND (C33)

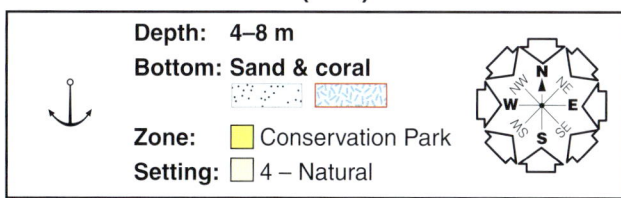

Depth:	4–8 m
Bottom:	**Sand & coral**
Zone:	☐ Conservation Park
Setting:	☐ 4 – Natural

If approaching from Haslewood or from the east side of Hamilton Island, watch out for Surprise Rock, which lies on a line between the peak of Pentecost Island and Craig Point on Whitsunday Island. Surprise Rock was given an isolated danger mark some time ago, which helps to make it visible at high tide; due to its exposed position, the mark is not infrequently carried away, so don't depend on it being there. Like many such marks on very exposed rocks in the Whitsundays, from time to time mother nature removes them, so don't rely on there being one; keep a sharp watch on your position.

A 4.9-metre rock which resembles a surfaced submarine lies one mile west-south-west of Pentecost.

As you get further south in the Whitsundays, the tidal range increases considerably. At Lindeman Island, which is the next island south from Pentecost, the tidal ranges are almost half again as big as they are at Shute Harbour. Irregular tidal eddies may be experienced throughout this area and, in fact, from Long Island to Lindeman Island.

Temporary anchorage is possible on the south side of Pentecost opposite a small sand beach. A nice lunch spot.

Pentecost was so named by Lieutenant James Cook on his voyage of discovery, which brought him through the Whitsunday Passage on Whit Sunday, 1770. It was the only island he named. Pentecost comes from the Greek word 'fifty', the association being with the religious festival celebrated on the fiftieth day after Easter, that is, Whit Sunday. Geologically, the island is a dyke of porphyry. Viewed from the west, some see, in the northern protuberance of the island, the likeness of a Red Indian head.

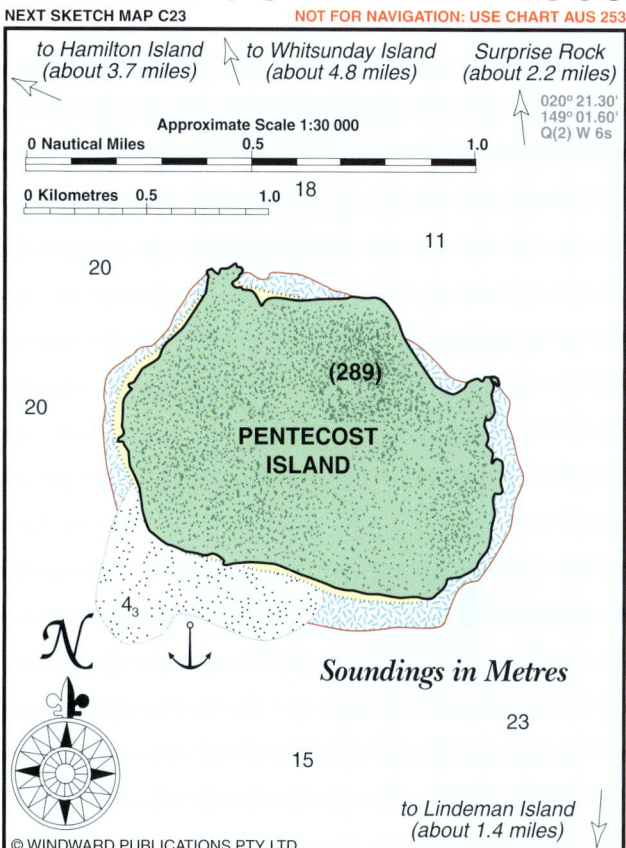

PENTECOST I.   C33

NEXT SKETCH MAP C23   NOT FOR NAVIGATION: USE CHART AUS 253

to Hamilton Island (about 3.7 miles)   *to Whitsunday Island* (about 4.8 miles)   *Surprise Rock* (about 2.2 miles)

020° 21.30'
149° 01.60'
Q(2) W 6s

Approximate Scale 1:30 000
0 Nautical Miles   0.5   1.0
0 Kilometres   0.5   1.0

18
20   11
20

(289)

PENTECOST ISLAND

4₃

Soundings in Metres

23

15

to Lindeman Island (about 1.4 miles)

© WINDWARD PUBLICATIONS PTY LTD

SEE CAUTION ON USE OF SKETCH MAPS pps. 121, 123   NEXT SKETCH MAP S1

Pentecost Island, the only island of the Whitsundays that was actually named by James Cook in 1770, viewed here from approximately east

THE SOUTHERN GROUP

S1–S21

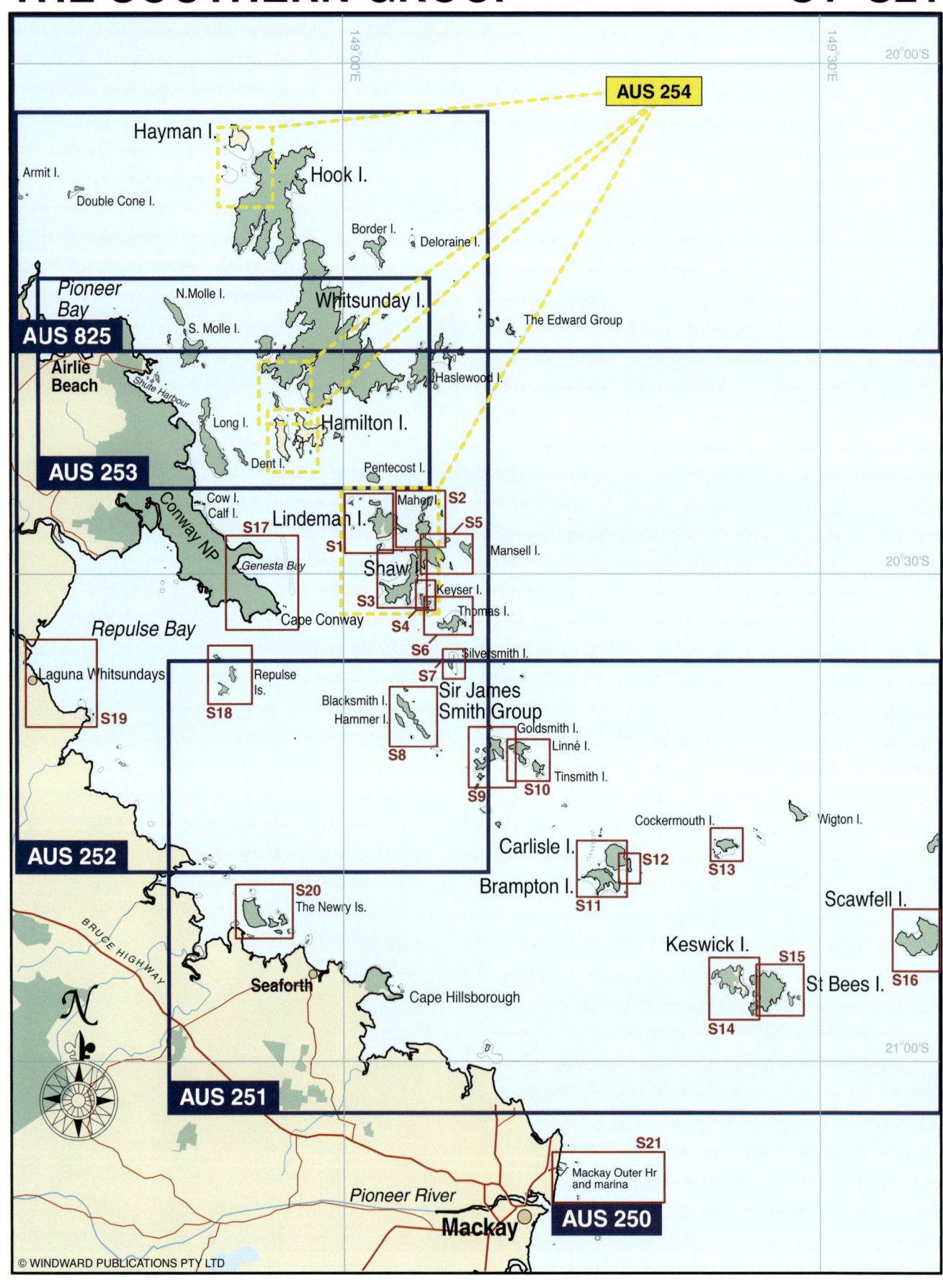

AUS 254

Hayman I.

Armit I.

Double Cone I.

Hook I.

Border I.

Deloraine I.

Pioneer Bay

N. Molle I.

S. Molle I.

Whitsunday I.

The Edward Group

AUS 825

Airlie Beach

Shute Harbour

Haslewood I.

Long I.

Hamilton I.

AUS 253

Dent I.

Pentecost I.

Conway NP

Cow I.

Calf I.

Maher I.

S2

Lindeman I.

S17

S5

Genesta Bay

S1

Mansell I.

Shaw I.

Repulse Bay

Keyser I.

S3

Thomas I.

Cape Conway

S4

Laguna Whitsundays

S6

Silversmith I.

S19

Repulse Is.

S7

S18

Blacksmith I.

Hammer I.

Sir James Smith Group

Goldsmith I.

Linné I.

S8

Tinsmith I.

S9

S10

Cockermouth I.

Wigton I.

Carlisle I.

S12

S13

Brampton I.

S11

Scawfell I.

AUS 252

S20

The Newry Is.

Keswick I.

S15

St Bees I.

S16

S14

BRUCE HIGHWAY

Seaforth

Cape Hillsborough

21°00'S

AUS 251

N

S21

Mackay Outer Hr and marina

Pioneer River

Mackay

AUS 250

20°00'S

149°00'E

149°30'E

20°30'S

© WINDWARD PUBLICATIONS PTY LTD

Sketch Map Index

Anchorage Description Index

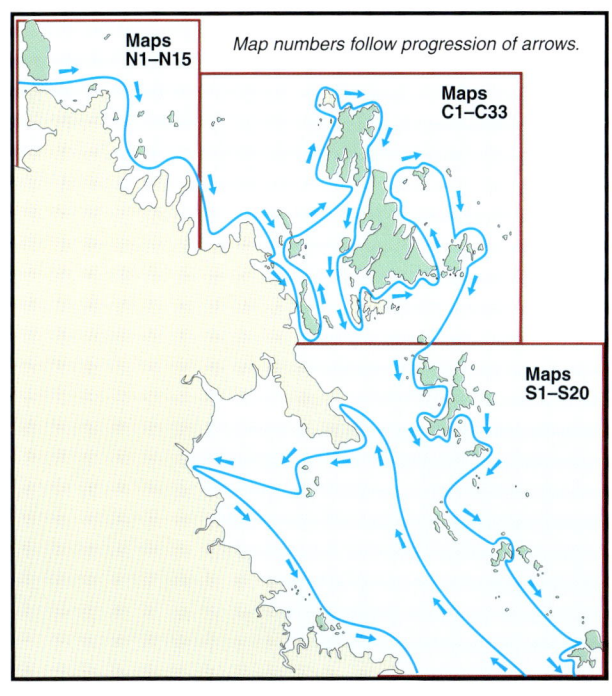

Maps N1–N15

Map numbers follow progression of arrows.

Maps C1–C33

Maps S1–S20

LINDEMAN ISLAND (S1)

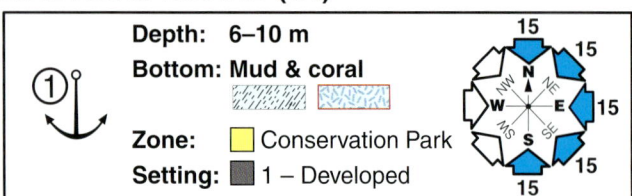

Depth:	6–10 m
Bottom:	Mud & coral
Zone:	☐ Conservation Park
Setting:	■ 1 – Developed

Tidal currents may reach 2 knots in the passage between Seaforth and Lindeman islands. If anchoring, stay outside the reef as shown and tuck in close to get out of the stream. Don't go into the dredged channel. The resort has moorings for use by visiting yachts (see 'Visiting the resort' below); a mooring is preferable to anchoring as there is quite a lot of current off the reef.

Most of the island is national park. The jetty is public and may be used for unloading/loading passengers or to tie up the dinghy (but don't leave it where boats tie up to load and unload). There is a large rise and fall of tide in this part of the Whitsundays, so tie the dinghy carefully.

The island has some marvellous graded walking tracks through vine forests and valleys filled with butterflies. The bird life is abundant. Excellent views are available from the high ground, such as from the summit of Mount Oldfield, where a sweeping panorama is available – northwards to Hamilton and Whitsunday islands, westwards to the Conway Peninsula and mainland, and southwards over Shaw Island.

Cape Lachlan and Thora Point get their names from Lachlan and Thora Nicolson, who owned and managed the resort for many years. Lachlan was one of the sons of Angus Nicolson, who moved to the island in 1923 with his wife, Elizabeth; they started the resort in the late 1920s.

Lindeman is one of the well-known Club Med establishments (see page 49 for more).

Visiting the resort
Radio reception on VHF channel 16 or the water sports manager on channel 60. Day visitors (for lunch and other activities) are permitted at the resort between 1100 and 1800 hours; night visitors (dinner, show, disco) may stay at the resort between 1800 and 0200 the following morning; overnight visitors (3 meals, activities) may stay for a complete 24-hour period (e.g. from 1100 to 1100 the following day). There is a fee for use of the mooring and a per capita charge for meals. Visitors may use all facilities, including the full-length nine-hole golf course, tennis courts, a basketball court, and an archery range. Telephone 07 4946 9333

SEAFORTH ISLAND (S1)

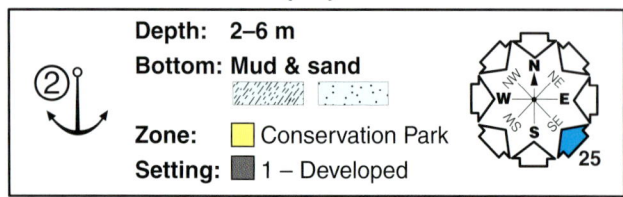

Depth:	2–6 m
Bottom:	Mud & sand
Zone:	☐ Conservation Park
Setting:	■ 1 – Developed

It is possible to tuck in on the northern side of Seaforth Island and get shelter from south-east winds.

Seaforth is a lovely little island with a picnic area and a short track through the bush to a beach across the north-east arm of the island. Queensland rock orchids abound on interesting rock formations. The island is sometimes referred to as 'Royal Seaforth', the result of a royal visit in 1954 by Queen Elizabeth and the Duke of Edinburgh, who spent an hour or so enjoying a bit of sand between their toes. Seaforth was declared a national park in 1962.

BOAT PORT (S1)

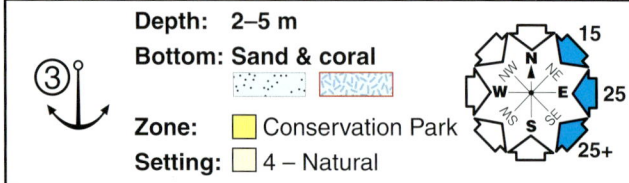

Depth:	2–5 m
Bottom:	Sand & coral
Zone:	☐ Conservation Park
Setting:	☐ 4 – Natural

There are frequently eddies around Thumb Point, and because the reef between Lindeman Island and Little Lindeman Island becomes covered at high tide, this anchorage is sometimes inclined to be rolly.

The water is frequently murky and visibility is limited. Use caution. There are several nice beaches.

LITTLE LINDEMAN ISLAND (S1)

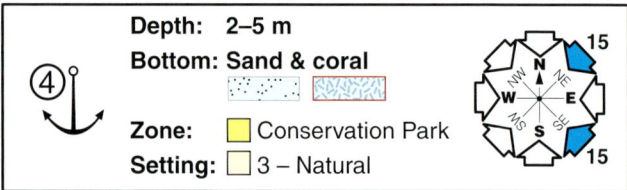

Depth:	2–5 m
Bottom:	Sand & coral
Zone:	☐ Conservation Park
Setting:	☐ 3 – Natural

At high tide don't be tempted to go between Little Lindeman and Lindeman islands.

The water is frequently murky with low visibility. Use caution. This anchorage may be rolly.

GAP BEACH (S1)

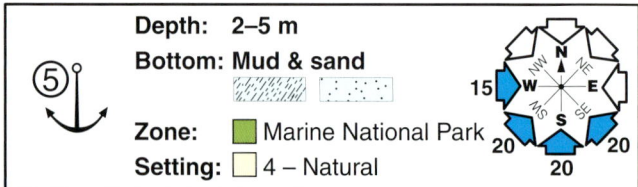

Depth:	2–5 m
Bottom:	Mud & sand
Zone:	■ Marine National Park
Setting:	☐ 4 – Natural

Gap Beach lies between two high pieces of land; it can be gusty when the wind gets above 20 knots, and it tends to be swelly. It offers beautiful views northwards towards Pentecost and the main islands of the Whitsunday Group.

Looking south from Seaforth Island's eastern beach

LINDEMAN ISLAND

S1

NOT FOR NAVIGATION: SEE CHART AUS 254

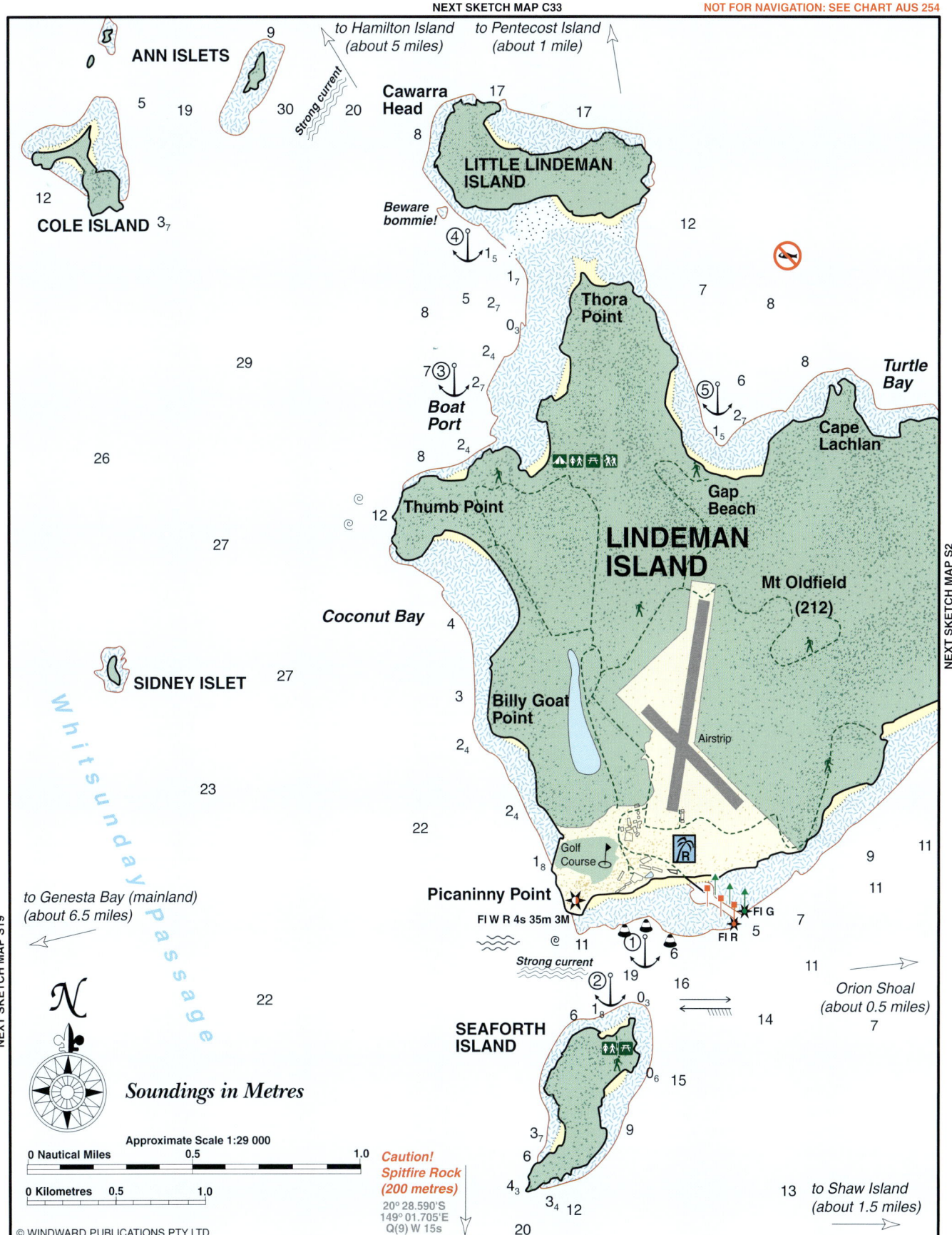

NEXT SKETCH MAP C33

to Hamilton Island
(about 5 miles)

to Pentecost Island
(about 1 mile)

ANN ISLETS

9

5   19   30   *Strong current*   20

Cawarra
Head   17   17

8

**LITTLE LINDEMAN
ISLAND**

12   7   8

**Turtle
Bay**

*Beware
bommie!*

④   1₅

1₇

5   2₇

0₃

8

**Thora
Point**

12

COLE ISLAND 3₇

2₄

7③   2₇

⑤   6   8

2₇

**Cape
Lachlan**

1₅

29

**Boat
Port**

8   2₄

8

26

Thumb Point

♣♣♣♣   ♣♣

**Gap
Beach**

12

27

**LINDEMAN
ISLAND**

**Mt Oldfield
(212)**

SIDNEY ISLET   27

Coconut Bay   4

3

**Billy Goat
Point**

Airstrip

23

2₄

22

2₄

11

Golf
Course   9

11

Picaninny Point   1₈

Fl W R 4s 35m 3M

11

①   6

②   19

16

Fl G

Fl R   5

11   7

Strong current

14

**SEAFORTH
ISLAND**

6   1₈   0₃

0₆   15

*Orion Shoal
(about 0.5 miles)*

7

to Genesta Bay (mainland)
(about 6.5 miles)

22

9

3₇

6

Whitsunday Passage

N

Soundings in Metres

3₄   12

13   *to Shaw Island
(about 1.5 miles)*

20

Approximate Scale 1:29 000

0 Nautical Miles   0.5   1.0

0 Kilometres   0.5   1.0

*Caution!
Spitfire Rock
(200 metres)*

20° 28.590'S
149° 01.705'E
Q(9) W 15s

4₃

© WINDWARD PUBLICATIONS PTY LTD

SEE CAUTIONS ON USE OF SKETCH MAPS ON PAGES 121,123

NEXT SKETCH MAP S19

NEXT SKETCH MAP S2

JULY 1995 APPROXIMATE SCALE 1:40 000

Aerial photograph reproduced with permission of the Department of Resources Queensland

Boat Port

Gap Bay

LINDEMAN ISLAND

Plantation Bay

Neck Bay

Seaforth Island

Yellow Rock

SHAW ISLAND

Brush Islet

PLANTATION BAY (S2)

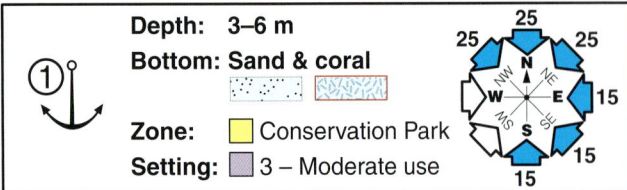

① **Depth:** 3–6 m
Bottom: Sand & coral
Zone: ☐ Conservation Park
Setting: ☐ 3 – Moderate use

Stay north of Orion Shoal if coming from the resort side of the island. Anchorage is available on either side of the reef.

This is a lovely anchorage with a delightful beach, affording excellent swimming in the right tide conditions. A track leads inland, from about the centre of the beach to what used to be the 'adventure camp' for children of resort guests.

NECK BAY (S2)

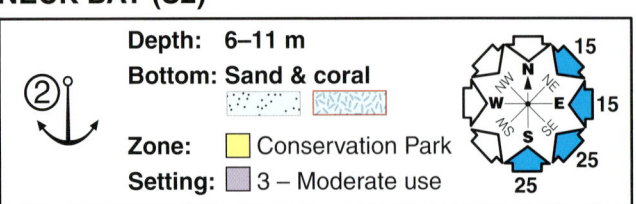

② **Depth:** 6–11 m
Bottom: Sand & coral
Zone: ☐ Conservation Park
Setting: ☐ 3 – Moderate use

The channel between Dalwood Point and Shaw Island has a very swift tidal stream (3–4 knots), which floods south and ebbs north. At times of spring tides be aware of the tide and prevailing wind conditions. Overfalls may be present in contrary wind–tide conditions.

The tide races close by Neck Bay, so stay as close in as you practicably can to keep out of it; otherwise you will be swaying and spinning on your anchor all night.

The reef is very extensive; don't go further in than a line between the vertically fluted/faulted rocks at the

(Continued on page 221)

SHAW ISLAND NORTH

S2

NOT FOR NAVIGATION: USE CHART AUS 254 / AUS 252

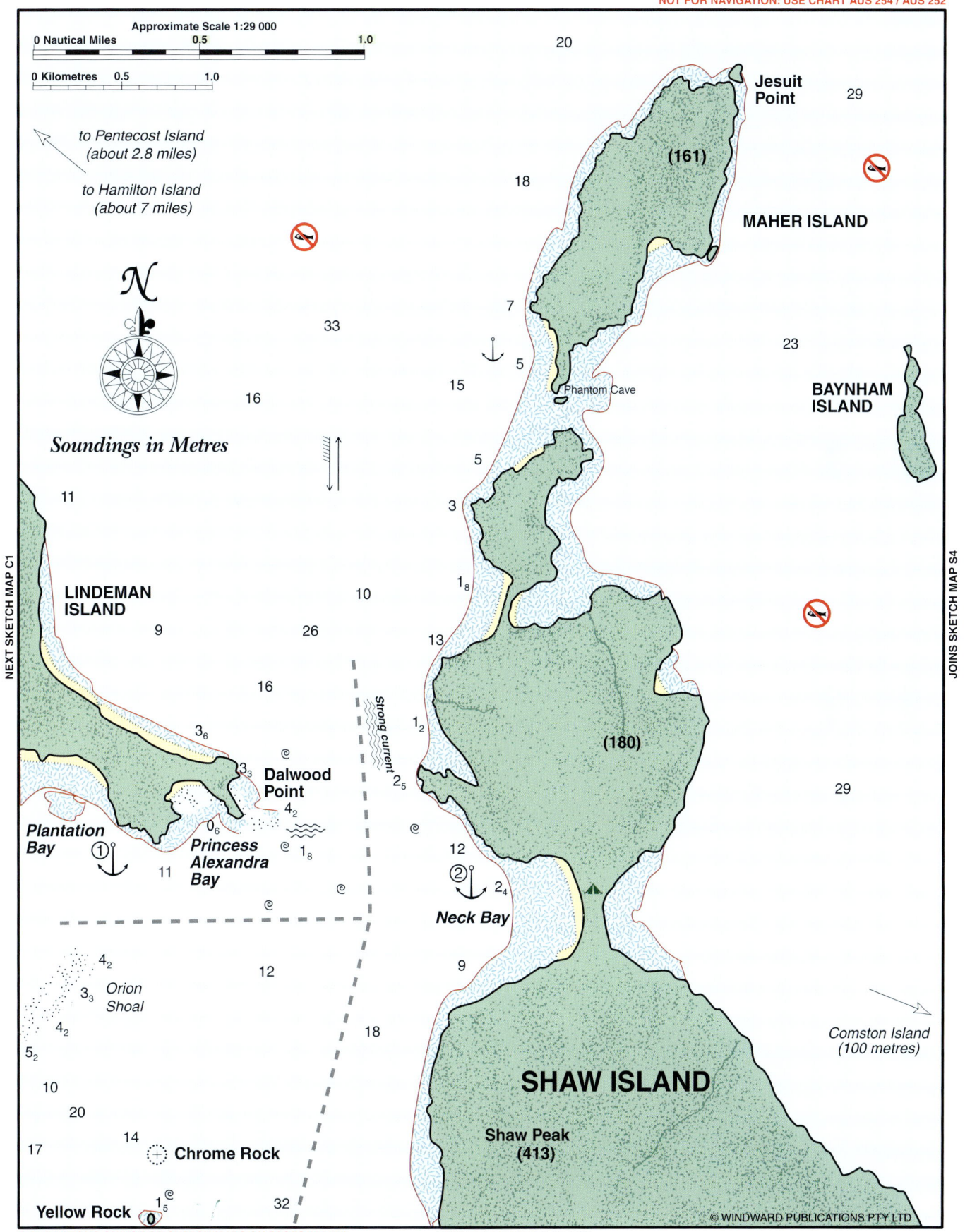

Approximate Scale 1:29 000

0 Nautical Miles 0.5 1.0

0 Kilometres 0.5 1.0

to Pentecost Island
(about 2.8 miles)

to Hamilton Island
(about 7 miles)

N

Soundings in Metres

20

Jesuit
Point

29

(161)

18

MAHER ISLAND

7

5

15

Phantom Cave

23

**BAYNHAM
ISLAND**

33

16

5

3

5

11

1₈

**LINDEMAN
ISLAND**

10

13

9

26

16

1₂

(180)

29

3₆

3₃ **Dalwood
Point**

4₂

*Plantation
Bay*

①

0₆ *Princess
Alexandra
Bay*

1₈

12

②

2₄

9

Neck Bay

12

4₂

*Orion
Shoal*

3₃

4₂

18

5₂

10

SHAW ISLAND

20

14

Chrome Rock

17

Shaw Peak
(413)

Yellow Rock

1₅

0

32

Comston Island
(100 metres)

Strong current 2₅

NEXT SKETCH MAP C1

JOINS SKETCH MAP S4

© WINDWARD PUBLICATIONS PTY LTD

SHAW ISLAND SOUTH

S3

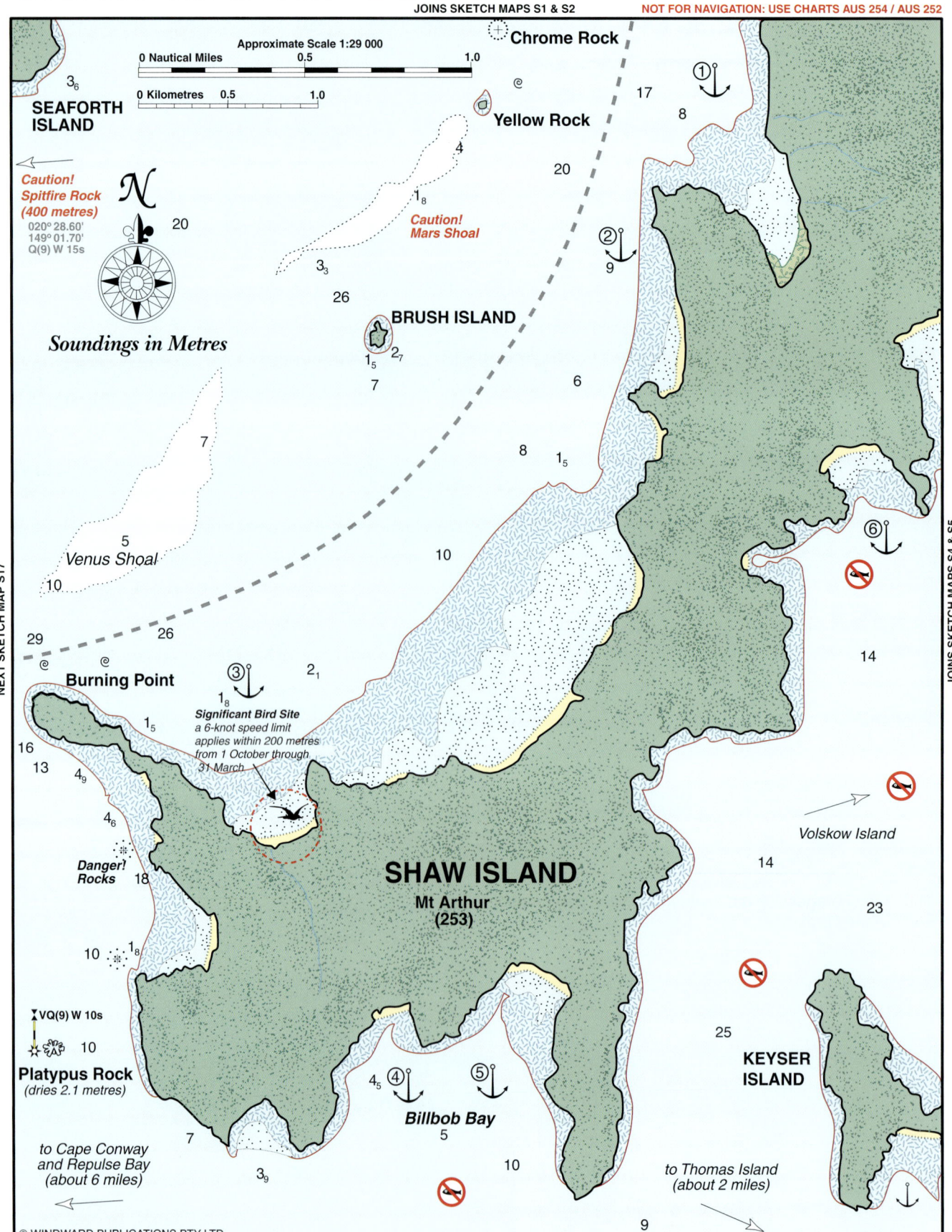

Chrome Rock

Approximate Scale 1:29 000

0 Nautical Miles   0.5   1.0

0 Kilometres   0.5   1.0

3₆

SEAFORTH ISLAND

17

①

8

Yellow Rock

20

4

Caution! Spitfire Rock (400 metres)
020° 28.60'
149° 01.70'
Q(9) W 15s

N

20

1₈

Caution! Mars Shoal

②
9

3₃

26

Soundings in Metres

BRUSH ISLAND

6

1₅ 2₇

7

7

1₅

8

6

10

7

Venus Shoal

5

10

10

29   26

②
9

⑥

🚫

14

Burning Point

③

2₁

1₅

1₈

*Significant Bird Site
a 6-knot speed limit
applies within 200 metres
from 1 October through
31 March*

16

13   4₉

4₆

Danger! Rocks   18

🚫

🚫

Volskow Island

14

SHAW ISLAND

**Mt Arthur
(253)**

14

23

10   1₈

VQ(9) W 10s

10

🚫

Platypus Rock
(dries 2.1 metres)

7

4₅ ④

⑤

25

KEYSER ISLAND

Billbob Bay

5

*to Cape Conway
and Repulse Bay
(about 6 miles)*

3₉

10

🚫

*to Thomas Island
(about 2 miles)*

9

© WINDWARD PUBLICATIONS PTY LTD

NEXT SKETCH MAP S17

JOINS SKETCH MAPS S4 & S5

(Continued from page 218)

north end (on the left as you look into the Bay) and the 'shoulder' of the island as you look to the south. The water is usually milky due to the strong tidal currents, and isolated bommies off the reef are difficult to see.

Remember, the tides here are almost 50 per cent bigger than they are at Shute Harbour; take this into account when calculating your scope and swing.

In blustery south-east conditions you may experience bullets. It may get a bit swelly as the wind easts. Neck Bay has a beautiful sand beach. You can walk over the neck to a beach on the east side. If you go ashore for a barbecue, watch the tide. Leave the dinghy anchored well out on the reef if the tide is falling, otherwise you may have to spend the night on the beach.

MAHER ISLAND (S2)

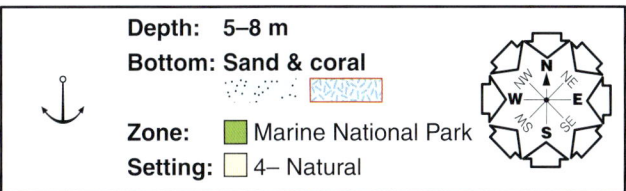

Opposite this anchorage is a nice beach and a 'hole through the island' for exploring. This is a pleasant daytime stopoff in suitably light weather, not a night anchorage.

SHAW ISLAND WEST (S3)

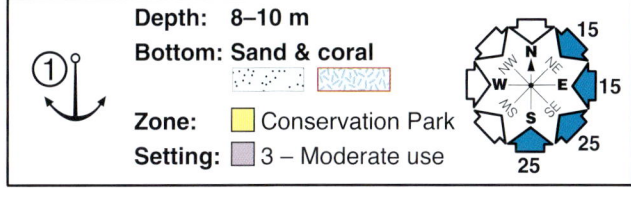

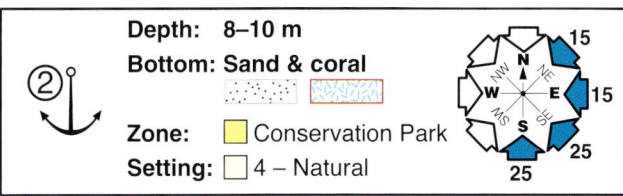

These anchorages are not as snug as Neck Bay immediately to the north.

Yachts at anchor, Burning Point

BURNING POINT (S3)

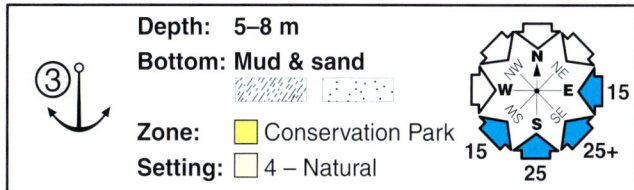

Note that the bottom is shoal for quite some distance off this little bay. Approach with care. Excellent anchorage.

This beach is a significant bird site – a nesting beach for the increasingly threatened beach stone curlew (*Esacus neglectus*). A 6-knot speed limit applies within 200 metres of the beach from 1 October through 31 March.

BILLBOB BAY (S3)

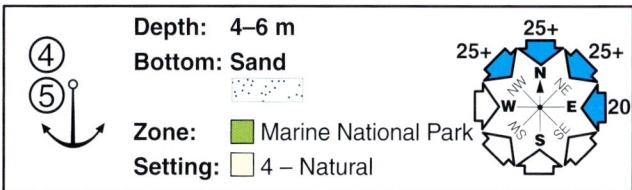

The tide sweeps around Burning Point at a rate of knots; in fresh winds from the south there may be overfalls and eddies.

Approaching anchorages 4 and 5 from Burning Point, watch out for Platypus Rock, which has been marked as a result of one or two wrecks that have occurred there.

Look out for bommies off the reef, particularly on the eastern side. These are beautiful little beaches – a nice, lonely anchorage.

As with all southerly exposed anchorages in the Whitsundays, you are potentially on a lee shore. These are not recommended for overnight during the trade winds season, from April to August/September.

The name of the bay comes from a combination of the first names of Bill Walker and Bob Gomersall, who assisted with the surveying of anchorages in the first incarnation of this book.

SHAW ISLAND SOUTH-EAST (S3)

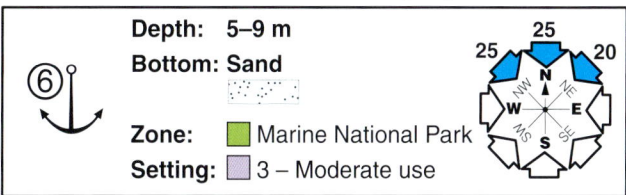

Watch the reef on the north-east side, and leave enough room to swing. There is another small beach in the opposite cove.

 In an anchorage, keep a respectable distance from other yachts (the demeanour of their crew will tell you whether you're too close).

KEYSER ISLAND   S4

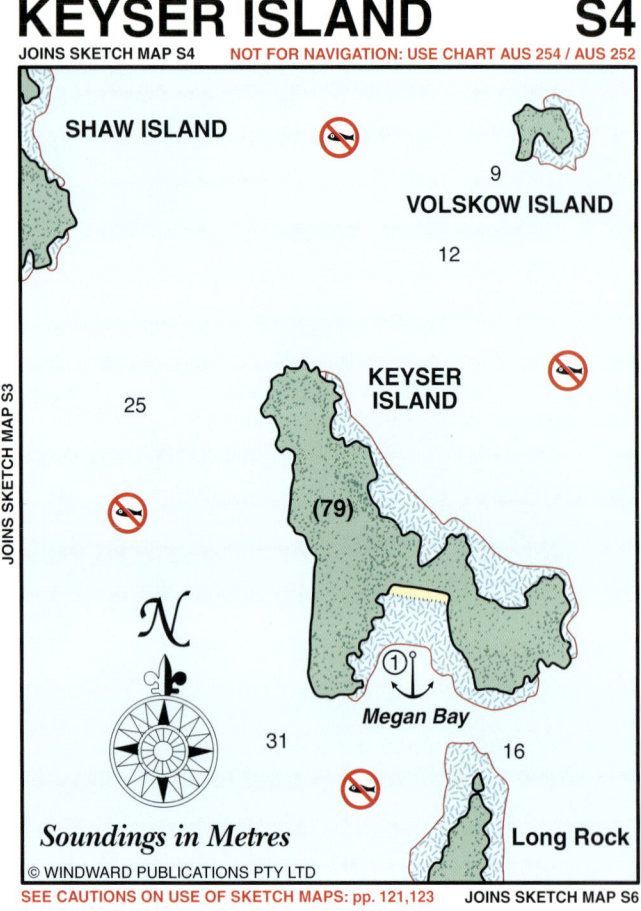

Aerial photograph reproduced with permission of the Department of Resources Queensland

MEGAN BAY (KEYSER I.) (S4)

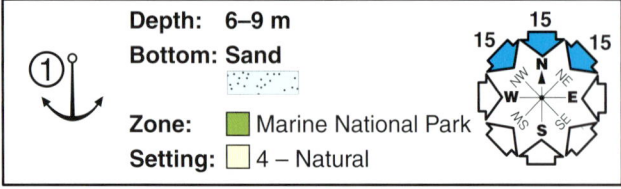

	Depth:	6–9 m
⚓①	Bottom:	Sand
	Zone:	🟩 Marine National Park
	Setting:	⬜ 4 – Natural

In moderate winds from the northern quarter this can be a delightful, isolated anchorage.

Humpback sounding off Burning Point

David Collett

ROBERTA BAY (S5)

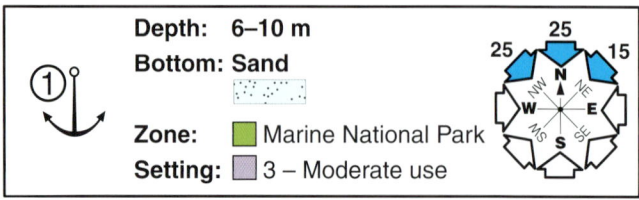

	Depth:	6–10 m
⚓①	Bottom:	Sand
	Zone:	🟩 Marine National Park
	Setting:	🟪 3 – Moderate use

This is a quiet anchorage in northerly winds and it has a pleasant beach.

SHAW ISLAND EAST

S5

JOINS SKETCH MAP S2

NOT FOR NAVIGATION: USE CHART AUS 252

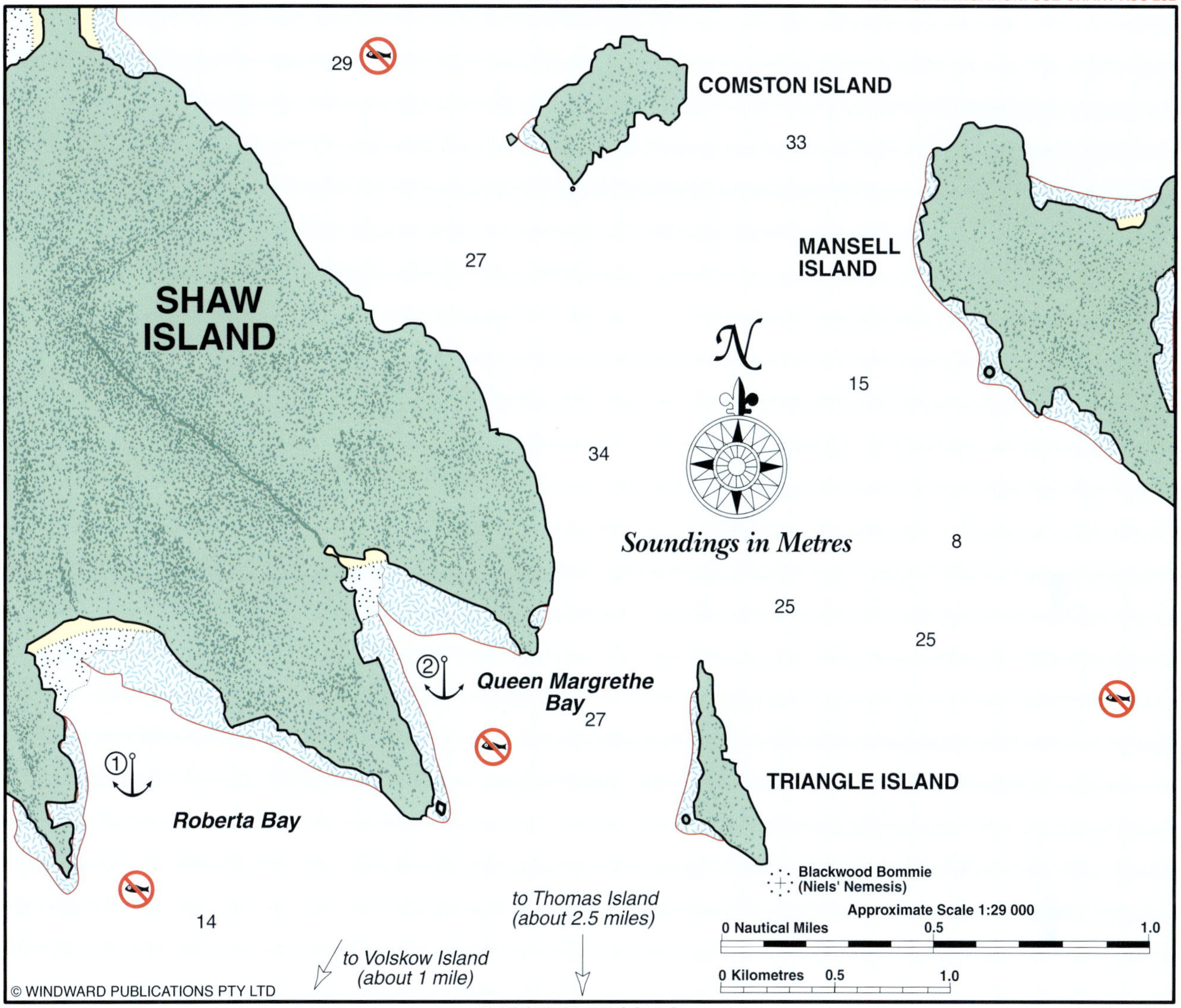

JOINS SKETCH MAPS S2 &S3

29

COMSTON ISLAND

33

MANSELL ISLAND

27

15

N

34

Soundings in Metres

8

25

25

SHAW ISLAND

② Queen Margrethe Bay

27

① Roberta Bay

TRIANGLE ISLAND

14

Blackwood Bommie
(Niels' Nemesis)

to Thomas Island
(about 2.5 miles)

Approximate Scale 1:29 000

0 Nautical Miles   0.5   1.0

0 Kilometres   0.5   1.0

to Volskow Island
(about 1 mile)

© WINDWARD PUBLICATIONS PTY LTD

SEE CAUTIONS ON USE OF SKETCH MAPS ON PAGES 121,123

NEXT SKETCH MAPS S4 & S5

QUEEN MARGRETHE BAY (S5)

②

Depth:	6–10 m
Bottom:	Sand
Zone:	Marine National Park
Setting:	4 – Natural

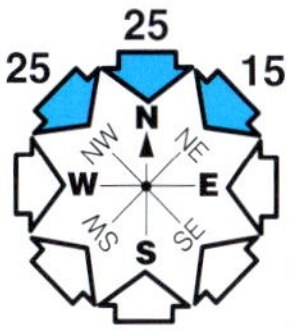

25
25   15
25

Queen Margrethe Bay has a nice beach, too. It will be less comfortable than Roberta Bay as the wind hauls more north-east.

Neither this nor Roberta Bay are recommended as overnight anchorages during the trade winds season (April to August/September).

Try to leave the park as you found it, minimising your impact, and respect the rights of other users. Activities that conflict with others (such as fishing where people are swimming, or 'buzzing' around a peaceful anchorage on a jet ski) should be avoided.

THOMAS ISLAND

S6

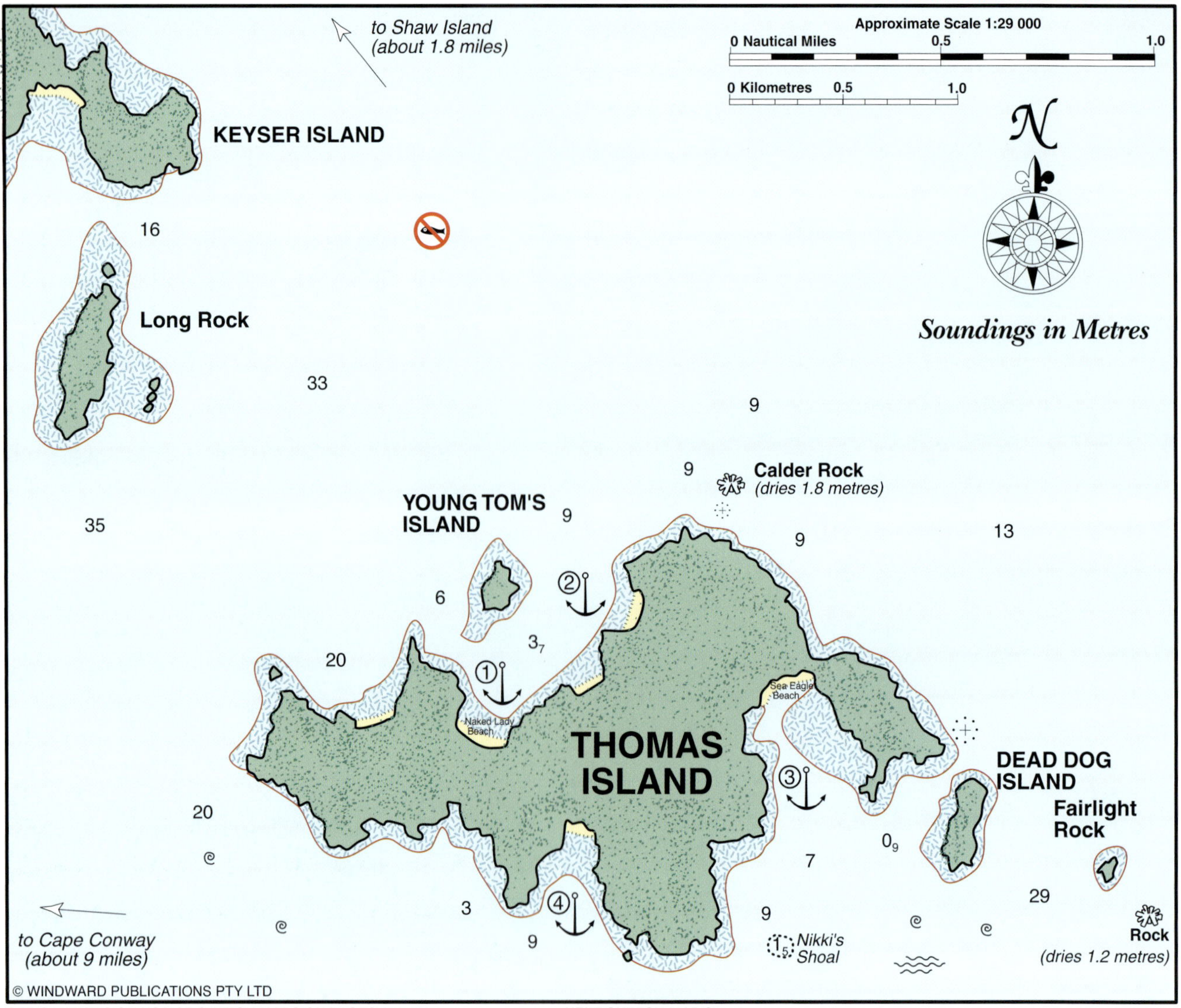

JOINS SKETCH MAP S5

NOT FOR NAVIGATION: SEE CHART AUS 252

KEYSER ISLAND

to Shaw Island
(about 1.8 miles)

16

Long Rock

Approximate Scale 1:29 000

0 Nautical Miles   0.5   1.0

0 Kilometres   0.5   1.0

N

Soundings in Metres

33

35

9

Calder Rock
(dries 1.8 metres)

9

9

13

YOUNG TOM'S
ISLAND

9

6

3 7

①

②

20

Naked Lady
Beach

Sea Eagle
Beach

THOMAS
ISLAND

DEAD DOG
ISLAND

Fairlight
Rock

20

③

0 9

29

7

3

④

9

9

Nikki's
Shoal

Rock
(dries 1.2 metres)

to Cape Conway
(about 9 miles)

© WINDWARD PUBLICATIONS PTY LTD

SEE CAUTIONS ON USE OF SKETCH MAPS ON PAGES 121,123   NEXT SKETCH MAP S7

THOMAS ISLAND (S6)

①
②

Depth: 3–5 m
Bottom: Sand

Zone: ▪ Habitat Protection
Setting: ▪ 4 – Natural

THOMAS ISLAND (S6)

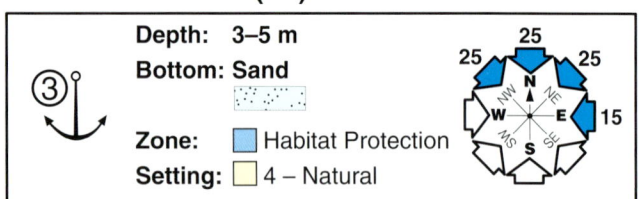

③

Depth: 3–5 m
Bottom: Sand

Zone: ▪ Habitat Protection
Setting: ▪ 4 – Natural

You can enter these anchorages on either side of Young Tom's Island; watch out for the fringing reef which makes off for some distance from its south-west side.

This anchorage can be quite 'swelly' (i.e. uncomfortable), particularly in fresh south-east winds with a flooding tide. There are several sand beaches throughout the anchorage.

Thomas Island, being somewhat remote from the centre of the Whitsundays, is likely to afford more solitude than some of the central island anchorages.

There can be overfalls south of Dead Dog Island; watch the run of the tide if you are coming between Dead Dog Island and Fairlight Rock.

This is a lovely anchorage with a beautiful sand beach that is readily accessible at all tides through the break in the reef. It has a truly 'South Pacific' atmosphere. During the trade winds season it is not suitable for overnight use as southerlies sometimes spring up in the night.

Watch out for Nikki's Shoal, a bommie with 1.5m water over it at low tide and reportedly at position 20°33.248'S, 149°07.154'E.

The south-east anchorage at Thomas Island

THOMAS ISLAND (S6)

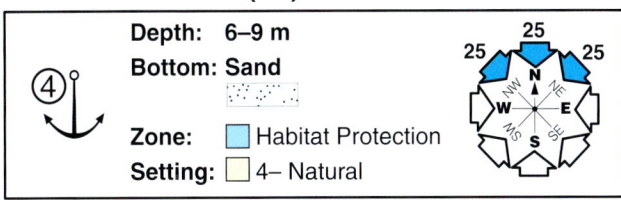

Depth:	6–9 m
Bottom:	Sand
Zone:	☐ Habitat Protection
Setting:	☐ 4– Natural

④

This anchorage also has a nice sand beach, although access to it is not as easy as anchorage No. 3 because there is no break in the reef.

SILVERSMITH ISLAND (S7)

Silversmith Island doesn't offer any anchorage. There may be overfalls to the north of Kennard Rocks.

BLACKSMITH / LADYSMITH ISLAND (S8)

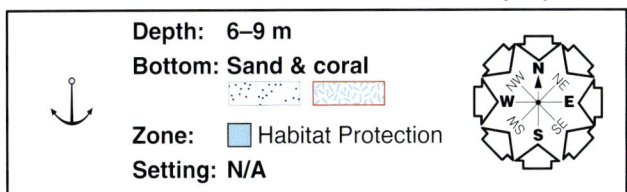

Depth:	6–9 m
Bottom:	Sand & coral
Zone:	☐ Habitat Protection
Setting:	N/A

The Anchor Islands no doubt afforded the surveyors who named them a few pleasurable minutes of name twizzling, but they do not afford the sailor very much more. They are remote and not particularly welcoming. In light conditions temporary anchorage may be had next to the sand beach at the south-west end of Blacksmith. The tide may be swift in the deep channel between Hammer Island and Blacksmith Island.

Ladysmith has prominent white cliffs on its north-eastern side. There is a shallow (4.3-metre) patch north-west of Bellows Islet which you can expect to be lively in fresh conditions with contrary wind and tide.

SILVERSMITH ISLAND S7

NEXT SKETCH MAP S6 NOT FOR NAVIGATION: USE CHART AUS 252

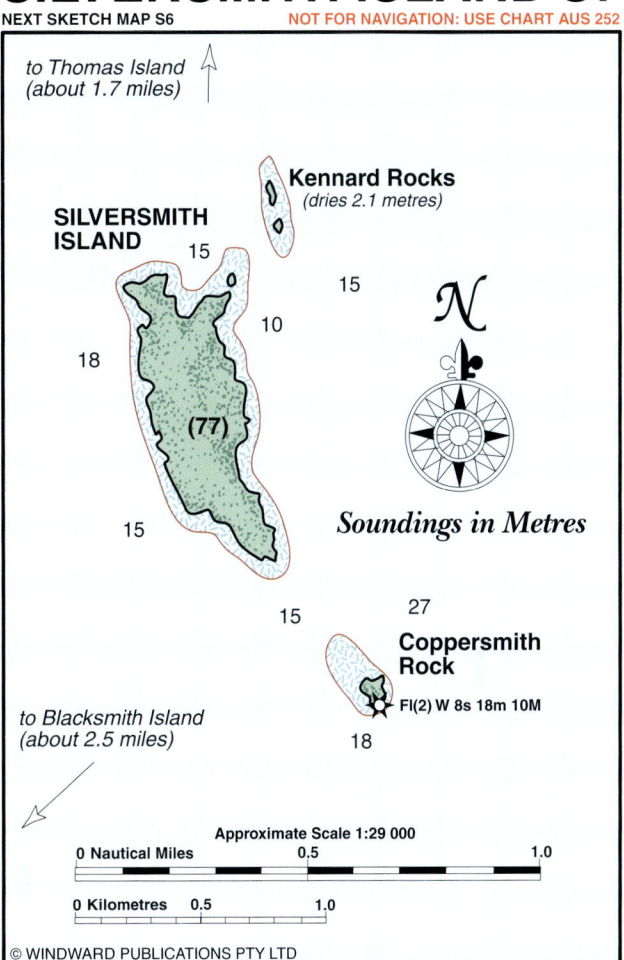

to Thomas Island (about 1.7 miles)

SILVERSMITH ISLAND

Kennard Rocks (dries 2.1 metres)

15

15

15

18

10

(77)

N

Soundings in Metres

15

15

27

Coppersmith Rock

Fl(2) W 8s 18m 10M

18

to Blacksmith Island (about 2.5 miles)

Approximate Scale 1:29 000

0 Nautical Miles   0.5   1.0

0 Kilometres   0.5   1.0

© WINDWARD PUBLICATIONS PTY LTD

SEE CAUTION ON USE OF SKETCH MAPS: pp.121,123   NEXT SKETCH MAPS S8, S9

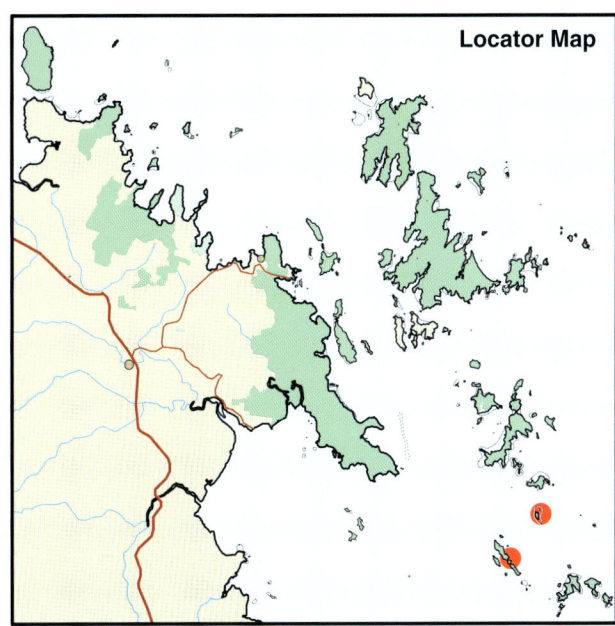

Locator Map

ANCHOR ISLANDS

NEXT SKETCH MAP S7

NOT FOR NAVIGATION: USE CHART AUS 252 / AUS 251

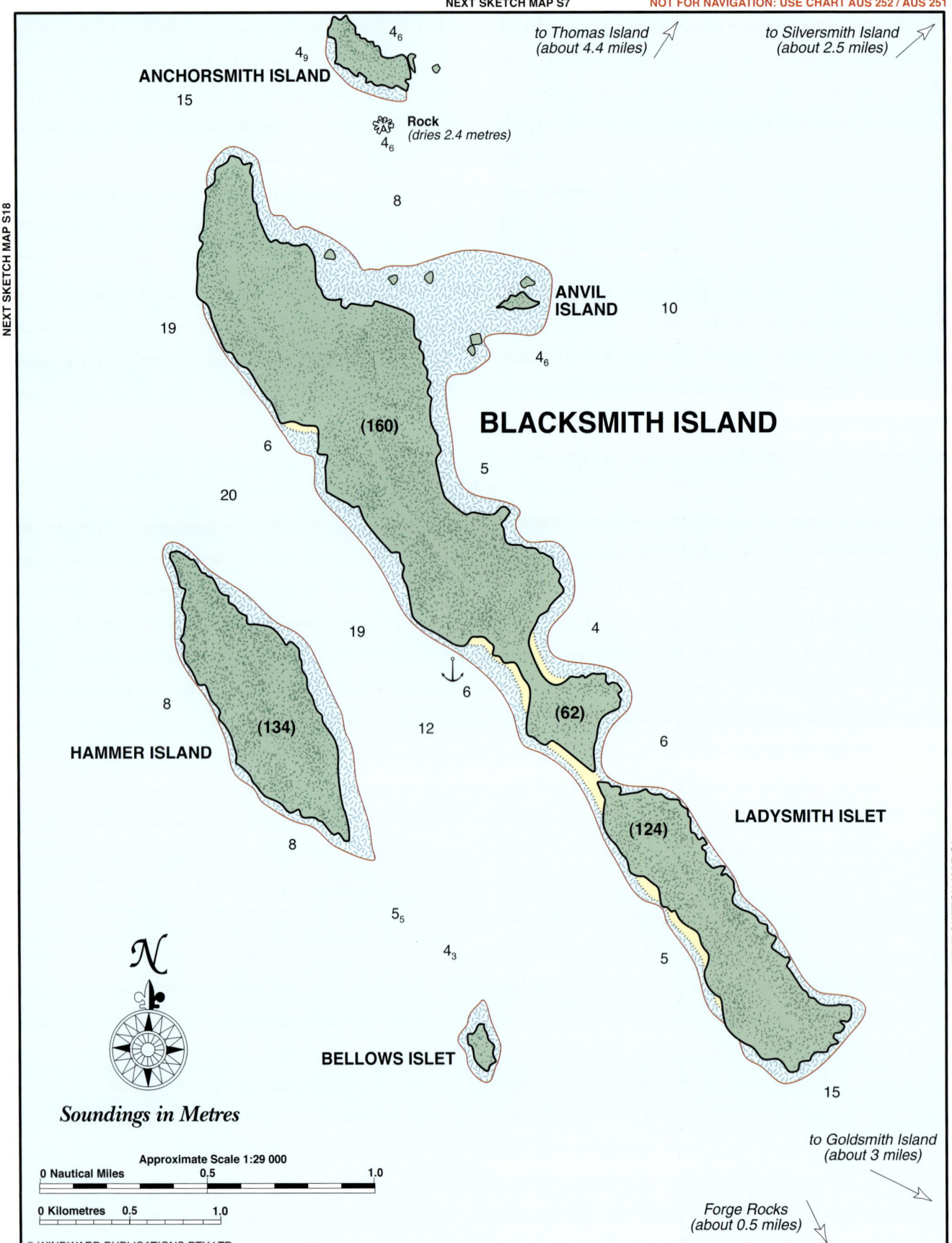

NEXT SKETCH MAP S18

4$_6$

4$_9$

ANCHORSMITH ISLAND

15

to Thomas Island
(about 4.4 miles)

to Silversmith Island
(about 2.5 miles)

Rock
(dries 2.4 metres)
4$_6$

8

19

**ANVIL
ISLAND**

10

4$_6$

(160)

BLACKSMITH ISLAND

6

5

20

19

4

(62)

6

8

(134)

12

6

HAMMER ISLAND

8

(124)

LADYSMITH ISLET

NEXT SKETCH MAP S9

5$_5$

4$_3$

5

N

BELLOWS ISLET

15

Soundings in Metres

to Goldsmith Island
(about 3 miles)

Approximate Scale 1:29 000

| 0 Nautical Miles | 0.5 | 1.0 |

| 0 Kilometres | 0.5 | 1.0 |

Forge Rocks
(about 0.5 miles)

© WINDWARD PUBLICATIONS PTY LTD

SEE CAUTIONS ON USE OF SKETCH MAPS ON PAGES 121, 123

JULY 1995 APPROXIMATE SCALE 1:40 000

Roylen Bay

Farrier Island

Minne Hall Bay

GOLDSMITH ISLAND

Southern Bay

LINNE ISLAND

Tinsmith Island

Ingot Islets

Aerial photograph reproduced with permission of the Department of Resources Queensland

GOLDSMITH ISLAND (S9)

Goldsmith is a long way south of Shute Harbour and therefore enjoys relative solitude. Approaching Goldsmith from the north, you may encounter overfalls between Locksmith Island and the northern end of the island, particularly in fresh wind-against-tide conditions. Watch out for scattered bommies off the north-west corner of the island; give it a decent berth. Approaching from south, do not attempt passage between Goldsmith and the Ingot Islets nor between the Ingot Islets themselves. Watch out for Io Reef west of the southern end of the island; it has a west cardinal mark.

About one mile south of the Ingots is Specie Shoal, which has only 4 metres of water in one spot. This whole area will be quite alive in fresh south-east conditions, particularly if the tide is making.

You can pass on either side of Farrier Island. There are often strong currents between Farrier and Goldsmith.

The mooring off Farrier Island is private.

ROYLEN BAY (S9)

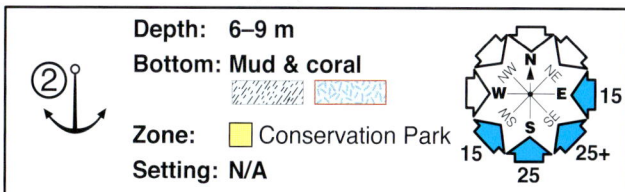

Depth:	2.5–4 m
Bottom:	Sand & coral
Zone:	☐ Conservation Park
Setting:	N/A

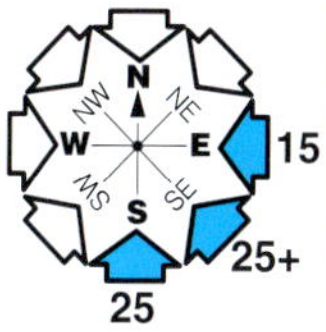

① ⚓

Watch out for scattered bommies along the edge of the reef. There is a national park campsite and toilet in the bush beyond this excellent beach.

MINNE HALL BAY (S9)

② ⚓

Depth:	6–9 m
Bottom:	Mud & coral
Zone:	☐ Conservation Park
Setting:	N/A

A snug anchorage with room for about three yachts. Wear your Polaroids to pick up the reef edge, and tuck into the gap in the reef to get out of current sweeping through the passage between Farrier and Goldsmith.

GOLDSMITH ISLAND

NEXT SKETCH MAP S7

NOT FOR NAVIGATION: USE CHART AUS 251

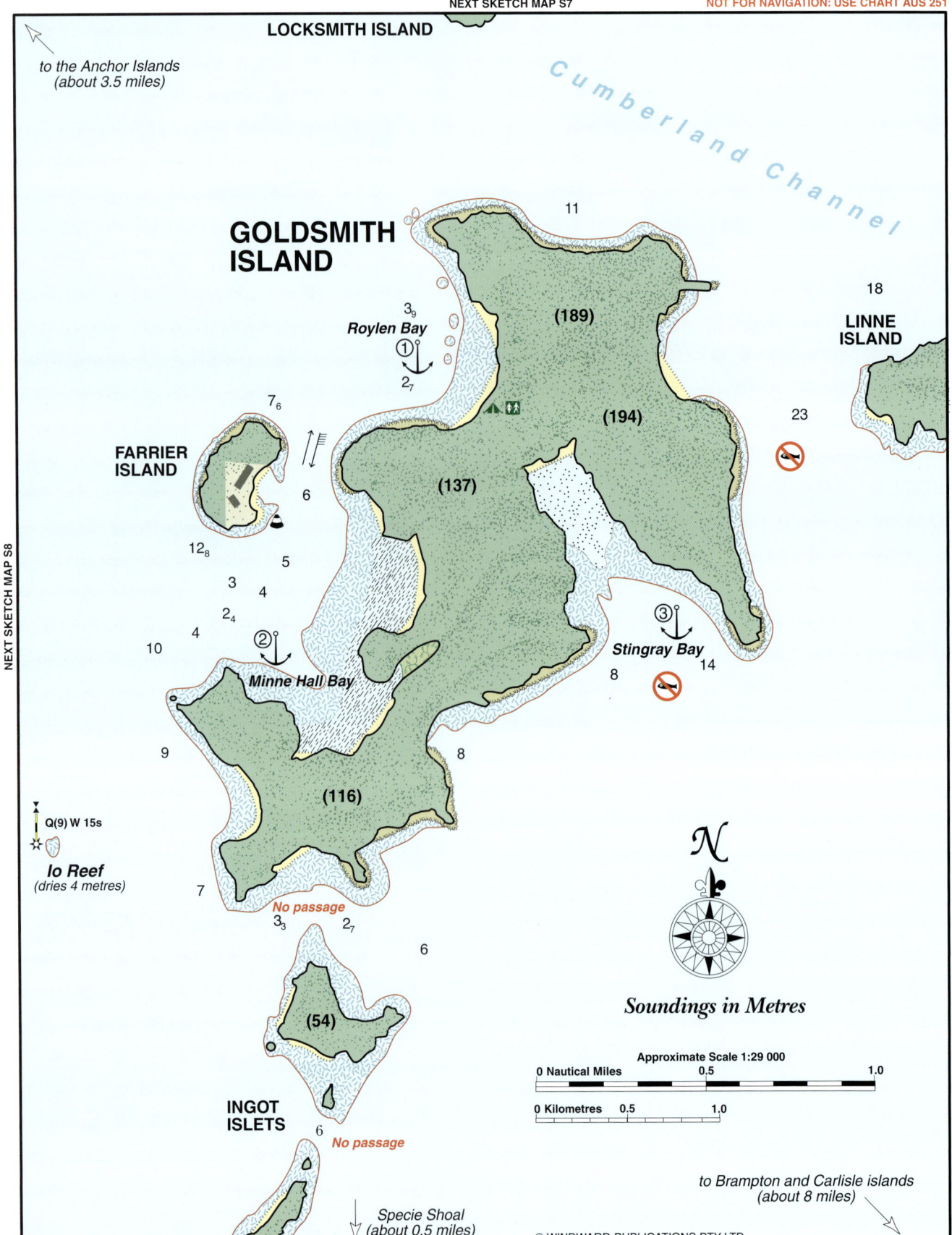

LOCKSMITH ISLAND

*to the Anchor Islands
(about 3.5 miles)*

C u m b e r l a n d   C h a n n e l

11

**GOLDSMITH
ISLAND**

(189)

18

**LINNE
ISLAND**

3₉

Roylen Bay

①

2₇

(194)

23

7₆

(137)

**FARRIER
ISLAND**

6

12₈

5

3

4

2₄

10

4

②

Minne Hall Bay

③

Stingray Bay

14

8

9

8

(116)

Q(9) W 15s

Io Reef
(dries 4 metres)

7

No passage

3₃

2₇

6

N

Soundings in Metres

(54)

**INGOT
ISLETS**

6

No passage

Approximate Scale 1:29 000

0 Nautical Miles   0,5   1,0

0 Kilometres   0,5   1,0

*to Brampton and Carlisle islands
(about 8 miles)*

*Specie Shoal
(about 0.5 miles)*

© WINDWARD PUBLICATIONS PTY LTD

SEE CAUTIONS ON USE OF SKETCH MAPS ON PAGES 121,123

NEXT SKETCH MAP S8

JONS SKETCH MAP S10

LINNE ISLAND

S10

NOT FOR NAVIGATION: USE CHART AUS 251

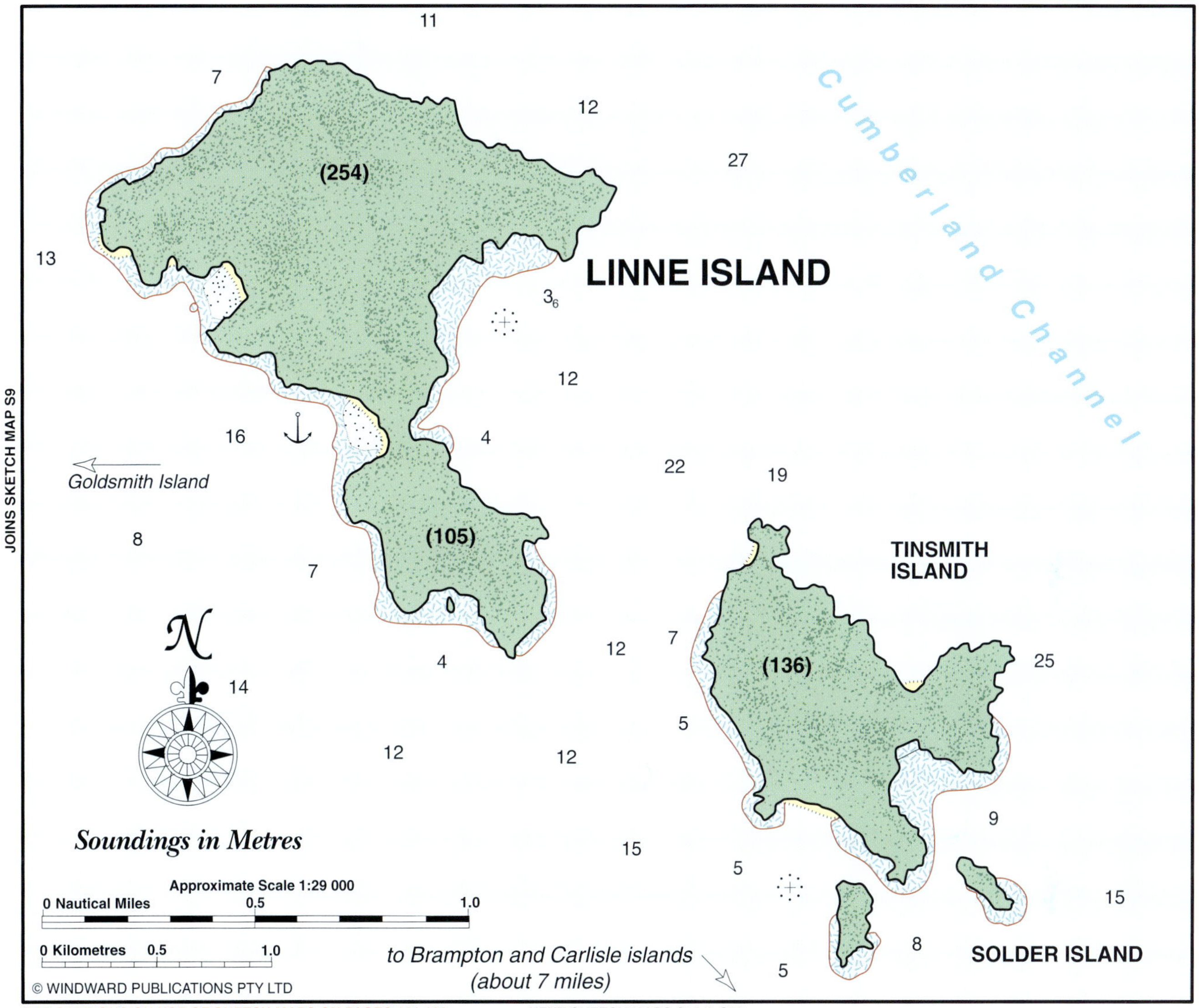

JOINS SKETCH MAP S9

11

7

12

27

(254)

13

LINNE ISLAND

Cumberland Channel

3 6

⚓

16

12

← *Goldsmith Island*

4

22

19

TINSMITH ISLAND

8

(105)

12

7

(136)

25

7

N

4

5

14

12

12

12

9

Soundings in Metres

15

5

5

Approximate Scale 1:29 000

0 Nautical Miles   0.5   1.0

0 Kilometres   0.5   1.0

8

SOLDER ISLAND

15

© WINDWARD PUBLICATIONS PTY LTD

to Brampton and Carlisle islands (about 7 miles)

5

SEE CAUTIONS ON USE OF SKETCH MAPS ON PAGES 121,123

NEXT SKETCH MAPS S11 & S12

STINGRAY BAY (S9)

Depth: 5–9 m
Bottom: Sand & coral
Zone: 🟩 Marine National Park
Setting: N/A

LINNE ISLAND (S10)

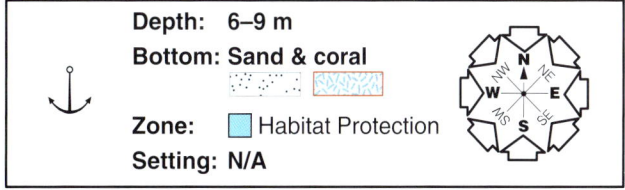

Depth: 6–9 m
Bottom: Sand & coral
Zone: 🟦 Habitat Protection
Setting: N/A

The reef extends a long way out from the sand beach; approach with care. The lonely southern anchorage looks south to the lofty peaks of Carlisle and Brampton islands. Because of its distance from Shute Harbour, it is less visited, and because it is exposed to the south, it not a good choice for anchoring overnight from April to August/September when southerly winds may arrive in the middle of the night and put you on a lee shore. But at other times it is a good anchorage, alive with reef life that seldom sees a human. Sand extends out from the beach for some distance. Small blacktip reef sharks may be seen foraging in reef pools as the tide recedes.

Linné Island is infrequently visited. The anchorage gives some protection in south-east conditions but is not an ideal overnight anchorage.

This island was the second of the Cumberland Islands to have a European man set foot on it, according to recorded history – Lieutenant John Murray, in 1802 (the first was Calder Island). Murray and his crew on the *Lady Nelson* were assisting Matthew Flinders in his coastal explorations, and they made several landings on the beaches on the western side of the island, noting evidence of visits by Aboriginal people and retrieving a wrecked canoe (*source*: historian, Ray Blackwood).

(Continued on page 231)

BRAMPTON & CARLISLE ISLANDS   S11

NOT FOR NAVIGATION: USE CHART AUS 251

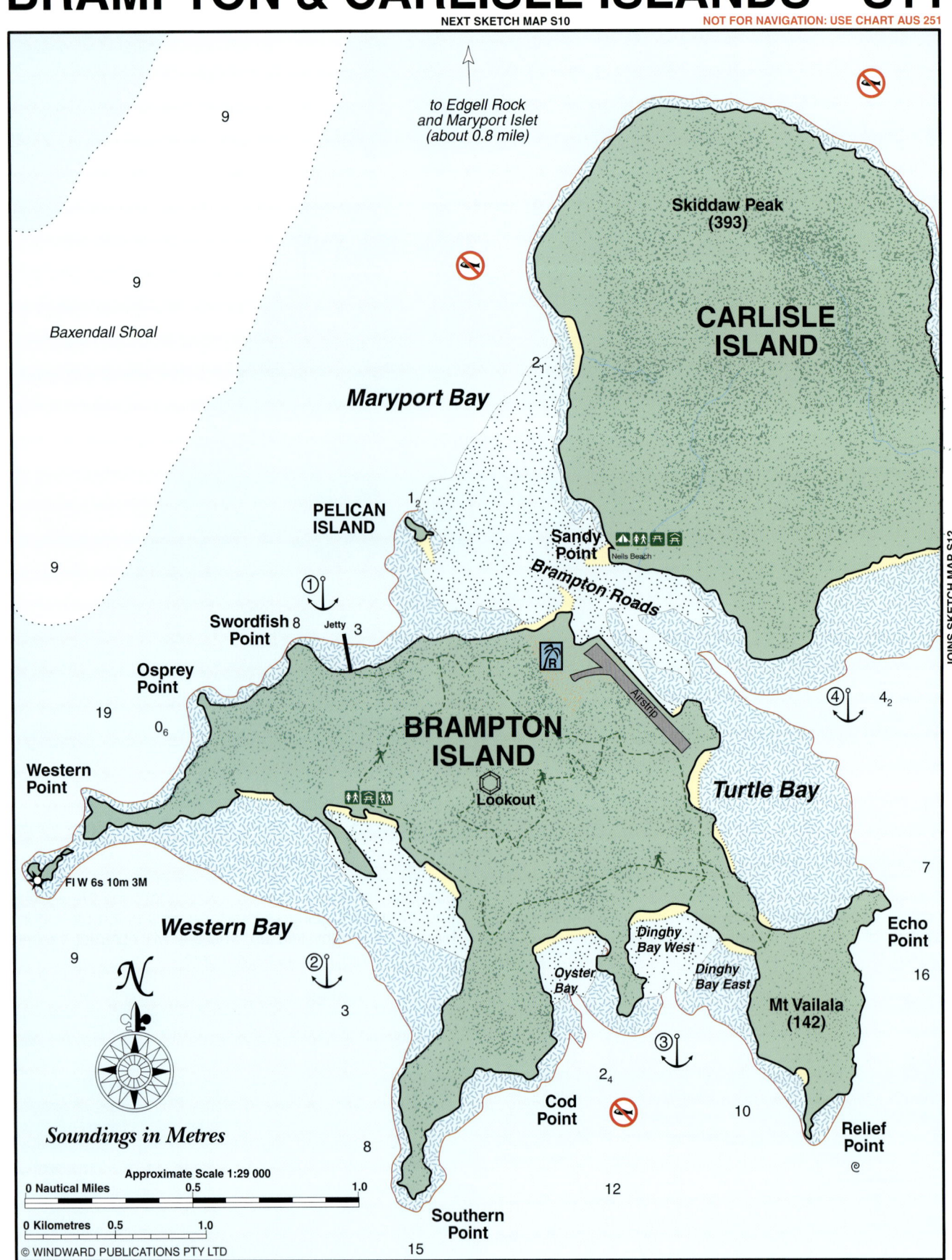

9

to Edgell Rock
and Maryport Islet
(about 0.8 mile)

Skiddaw Peak
(393)

**CARLISLE
ISLAND**

9

Baxendall Shoal

2₁

9

Maryport Bay

**PELICAN
ISLAND**

1₂

**Sandy
Point**

Neils Beach

① ⚓

Swordfish 8
Point   Jetty 3

**Osprey
Point**

④ ⚓ 4₂

19

0₆

**BRAMPTON
ISLAND**

Airstrip

**Western
Point**

Lookout

Turtle Bay

Fl W 6s 10m 3M

Western Bay

② ⚓

N

3

*Dinghy
Bay West*

*Dinghy
Bay East*

**Echo
Point**

*Oyster
Bay*

**Mt Vailala
(142)**

16

③ ⚓

9

2₄

Soundings in Metres

**Cod
Point**

10

**Relief
Point**

8

12

Approximate Scale 1:29 000

0 Nautical Miles   0.5   1.0

0 Kilometres   0.5   1.0

**Southern
Point**

15

© WINDWARD PUBLICATIONS PTY LTD

JOINS SKETCH MAP S12

Brampton Roads

JULY 1995 APPROXIMATE SCALE 1:40 000

Aerial photograph reproduced with permission of the Department of Resources Queensland

CARLISLE ISLAND

BRAMPTON ISLAND

Linné is named after the famous Swedish botanist and naturalist, Carl Von Linné, who is better known by the Latin version of his name, Linnaeus. Linnaeus formulated the system of botanical classification using Latin names for genus and species (binomial nomenclature) which is now universally used for naming all living species, plant or animal.

graded walking tracks with excellent views. The jetty is a public facility, and it leads to a road that joins the walking track system. If going ashore for a walk in the park, don't leave your dinghy tied up where it will obstruct vessels delivering or picking up passengers.

Visiting the resort
The resort is closed at the time of going to press.

BRAMPTON ISLAND (S11)

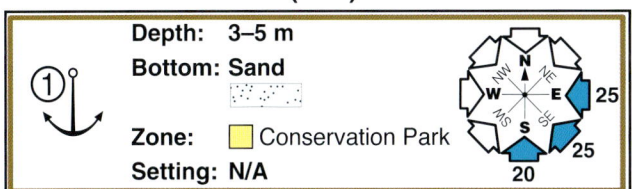

Depth:	3–5 m
Bottom:	Sand
Zone:	☐ Conservation Park
Setting:	N/A

Stay a healthy distance off southern and western points as in adverse wind/tide conditions there will be overfalls.

Brampton is a national park and has a good system of

WESTERN BAY (S11)

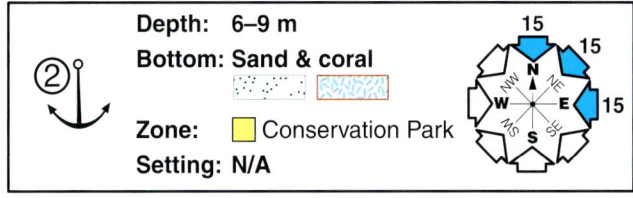

Depth:	6–9 m
Bottom:	Sand & coral
Zone:	☐ Conservation Park
Setting:	N/A

.Approach with care and anchor off the extensive reef.

DINGHY BAY (S11)

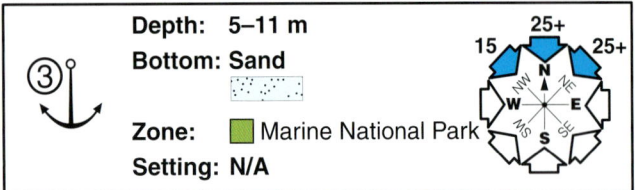

This anchorage offers good protection in north-east to north winds.

CARLISLE SOUTH (S11)

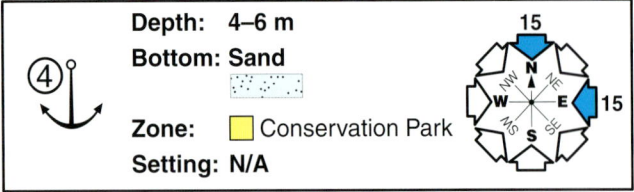

You can travel Brampton Roads in the dinghy if the tide is high. Watch for swift current through the passage. This anchorage is not as protected as anchorage No.3.

CARLISLE EAST   S12

NOT FOR NAVIGATION: USE CHART AUS 251

JOINS SKETCH MAP S11

NEXT SKETCH MAP S13

CARLISLE ISLAND

Lake

(118)

7

4

11

18

16

8

24

Devereux Rock

(dries 4.6 metres)

27

BRAMPTON ISLAND

© WINDWARD PUBLICATIONS PTY LTD

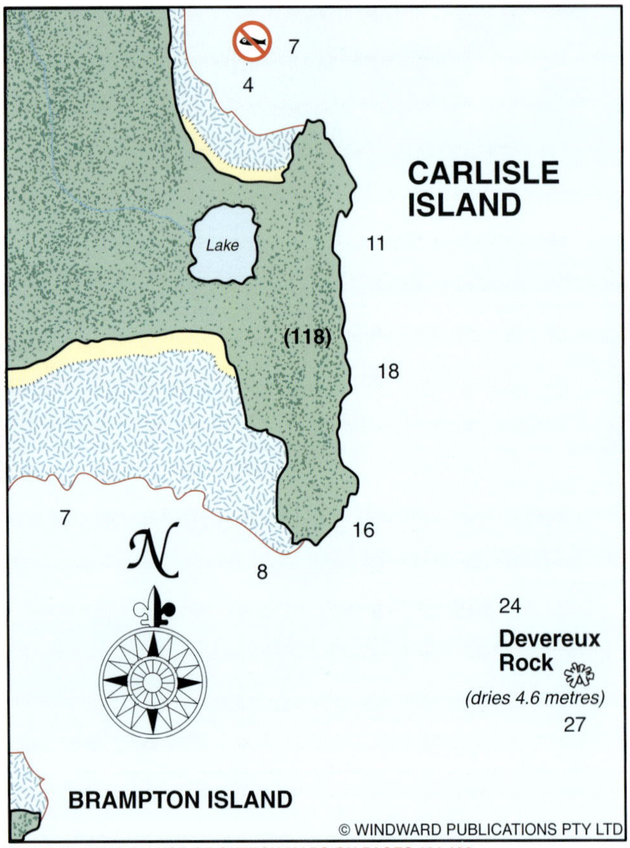

SEE CAUTIONS ON USE OF SKETCH MAPS ON PAGES 121,123

COCKERMOUTH I.   S13

NOT FOR NAVIGATION: USE CHART AUS 251

Approximate Scale 1:29 000

0 Nautical Miles   0.5   1.0

0 Kilometres   0.5   1.0

NEXT SKETCH MAP S12

22

9

(204)
COCKERMOUTH ISLAND

9

16

5

15

Soundings in Metres

© WINDWARD PUBLICATIONS PTY LTD

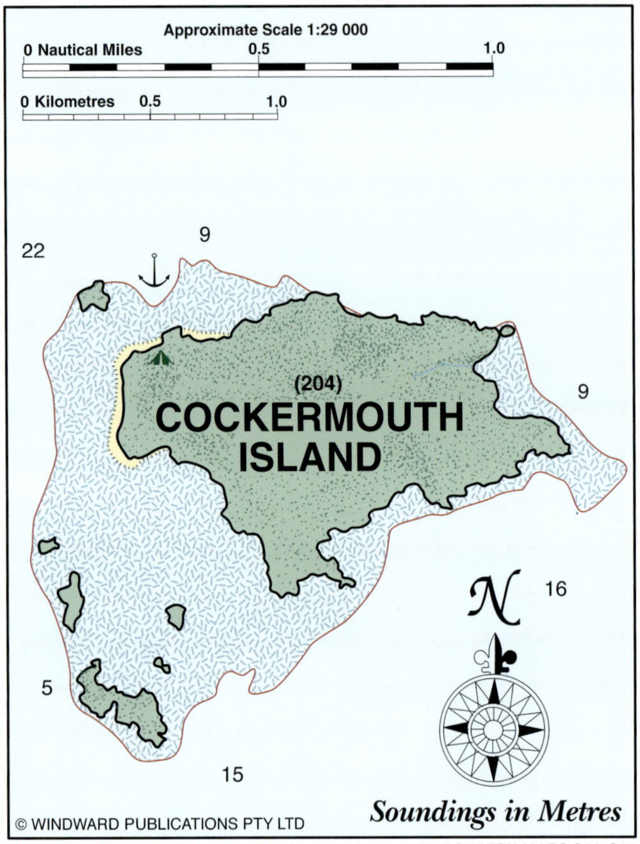

SEE CAUTION ON USE OF SKETCH MAPS: pp.121, 123   NEXT SKETCH MAPS S14, S15

COCKERMOUTH ISLAND (S13)

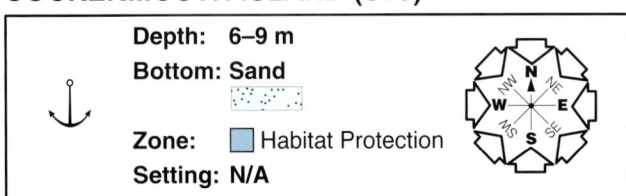

Cockermouth has a national parks campsite on its beautiful sand beach at the western end. It is a lovely island with some casuarinas and coconut palms; it is also lonely, especially as there is really no comfortable anchorage for yachts and it is thus unlikely to be visited except by adventurers. If you are one, be careful of the reef on the north side, which makes off for some distance.

It is shallow enough to anchor, but it will be swelly in all conditions.

KESWICK ISLAND *(see sketch map S14 next page)*

In 1996, 117 hectares of this national park island was zoned for special tourism facilities development, and the 99-year lease is now owned by Keswick Developments Pty Ltd, which is moving forward with a number of infrastructure projects. The construction of a 27-room worker and contractor accommodation complex near the airport and a barge ramp with mooring pylons will facilitate development that ultimately may include up to 1000 eco-conscious dwellings (all must have their own water collection/ storage and electricity generating capability). There are currently 22 lots with houses on them. A 120-metre aluminium jetty will follow shortly, and there are six swing moorings (which are serviced annually) available for use by visitors. The island has a small guest house (for those who feel like a night ashore), and there is a small store where basic provisions may be obtained. Contact with the island is on VHF channel 21 or telephone (07) 4965 8002. The developer ultimately plans to construct a marina in Horseshoe Bay (see sketch map S14, page 234).

KESWICK ISLAND – CONNIE BAY (S14)

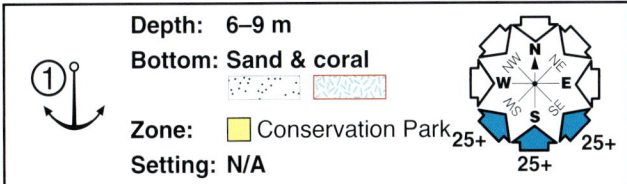

KESWICK ISLAND – HORSESHOE BAY (S14)

Keswick and St Bees islands are the southernmost of the Whitsundays to offer anchorage, and the tides here are just about as great as those at Mackay. Strong streams are encountered in Egremont Pass (3–4 knots) and around Singapore Rock, on the western side of the island, where overfalls occur. Real estate development is currently taking place on Keswick; some parts of the island are national park.

Keswick has a couple of anchorages that give shelter from southerly winds. Anchorage No. 1 can be swelly. In anchorage No. 2, tuck in as close as practicable to get out of strong tidal streams. Watch out for the fringing reef.

KESWICK ISLAND (S14)

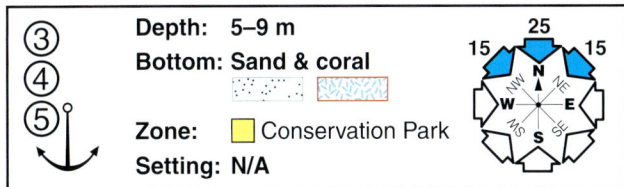

Keswick Island offers several spots on the southern side to get out of northerly weather. These anchorages, however, have a tendency to be swelly. Reef protection buoys have been installed in the bay between Keswick and Kingwell Points (see anchorage No. 3); no anchoring inshore of an imaginary line between the markers.

ST BEES ISLAND (S14)

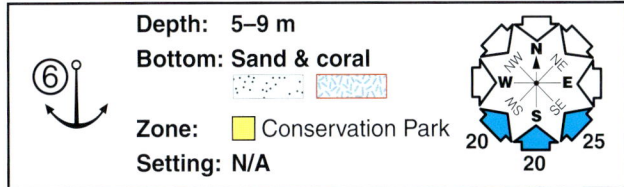

The northern bays of St Bees are not very deep and offer little protection from swell. Reef protection buoys have been installed in this anchorage to protect a nice coral reef; no anchoring inshore of an imaginary line between the buoys.

HOMESTEAD BAY (ST BEES ISLAND) (S14)

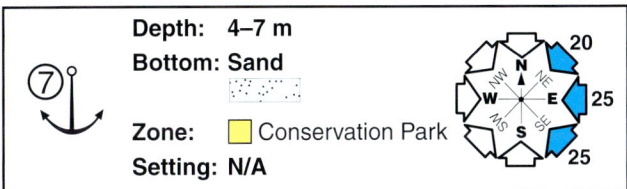

Anchorage No. 7 is at the northern end of Homestead Bay; professional fishermen report having stayed in this anchorage comfortably in 30+ knots from the south-east.

Homestead Bay is where the pioneering Busuttin family, one of the early island families, built their homestead in 1907. They began taking tourists to the island in 1926, and members of this family later established the resort on Brampton Island. The island is now a national park, with several dwellings on a small private lease in Homestead Bay.

ST BEES ISLAND SOUTH (S15)

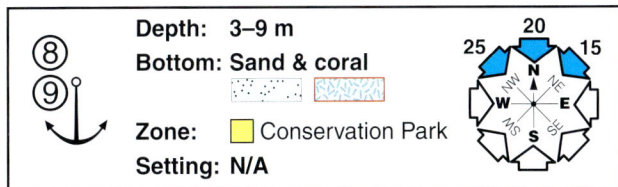

There are several places to seek shelter from northerly weather on the south side of St Bees. These anchorages tend to be swelly.

KESWICK ISLAND

S14

NOT FOR NAVIGATION: USE CHART AUS 251

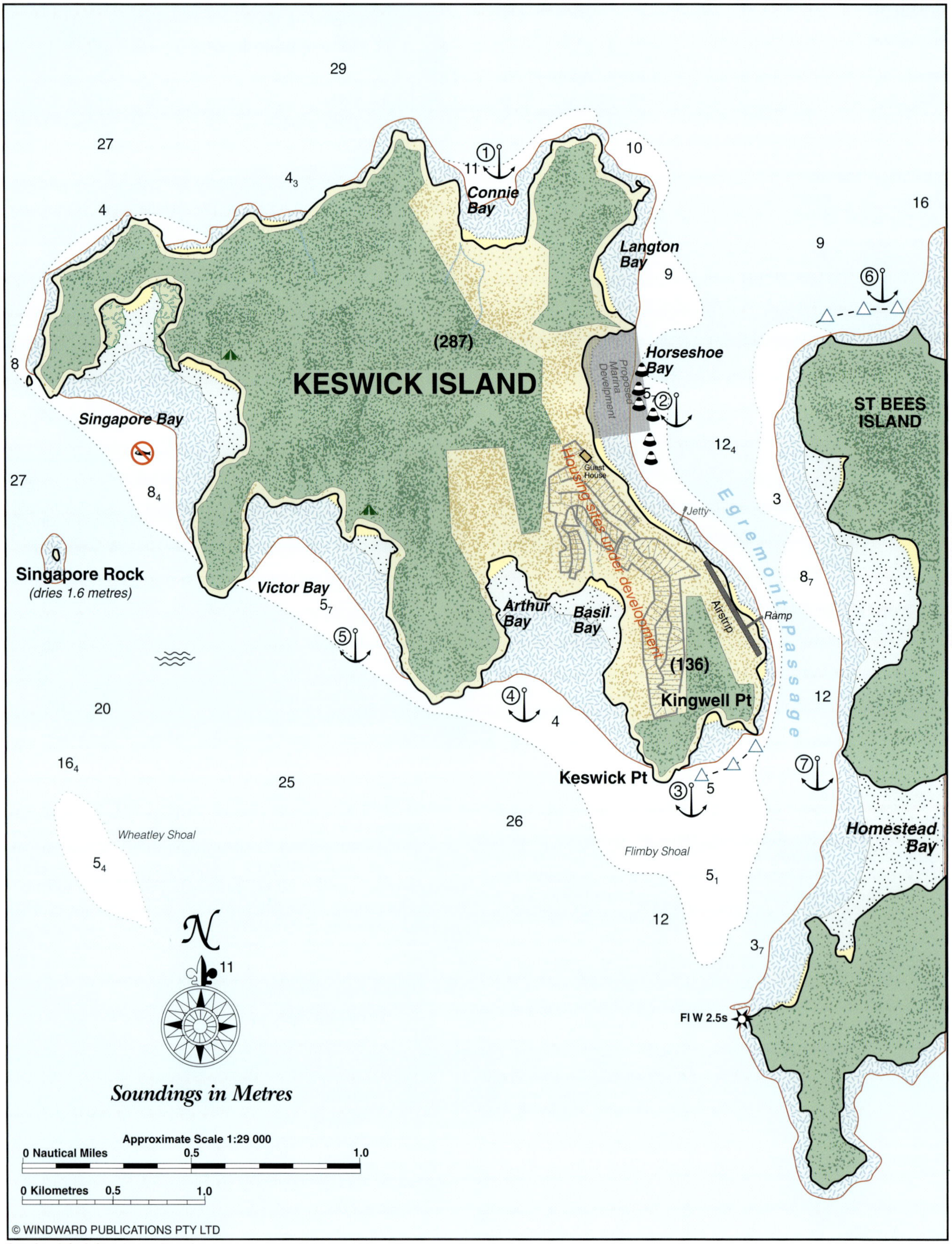

29

27

4₃

10

11 ①

16

Connie Bay

4

Langton Bay

9

9

⑥

8

(287)

KESWICK ISLAND

Horseshoe Bay

ST BEES ISLAND

0

5

②

Singapore Bay

12₄

27

8₄

Guest House

3

Housing sites under development

Jetty

Singapore Rock

(dries 1.6 metres)

0

Victor Bay

5₇

Arthur Bay

Basil Bay

8₇

Airstrip

Ramp

⑤

12

(136)

Kingwell Pt

20

④

4

16₄

25

Keswick Pt

③ 5

⑦

26

Wheatley Shoal

Homestead Bay

5₄

Flimby Shoal

5₁

12

3₇

N

11

Fl W 2.5s

Soundings in Metres

| 0 Nautical Miles | 0.5 | 1.0 |

Approximate Scale 1:29 000

| 0 Kilometres | 0.5 | 1.0 |

© WINDWARD PUBLICATIONS PTY LTD

JOINS SKETCH MAP S15

SEE CAUTIONS ON USE OF SKETCH MAPS ON PAGES 121,123

ST BEES ISLAND

S15

NOT FOR NAVIGATION: USE CHART AUS 251

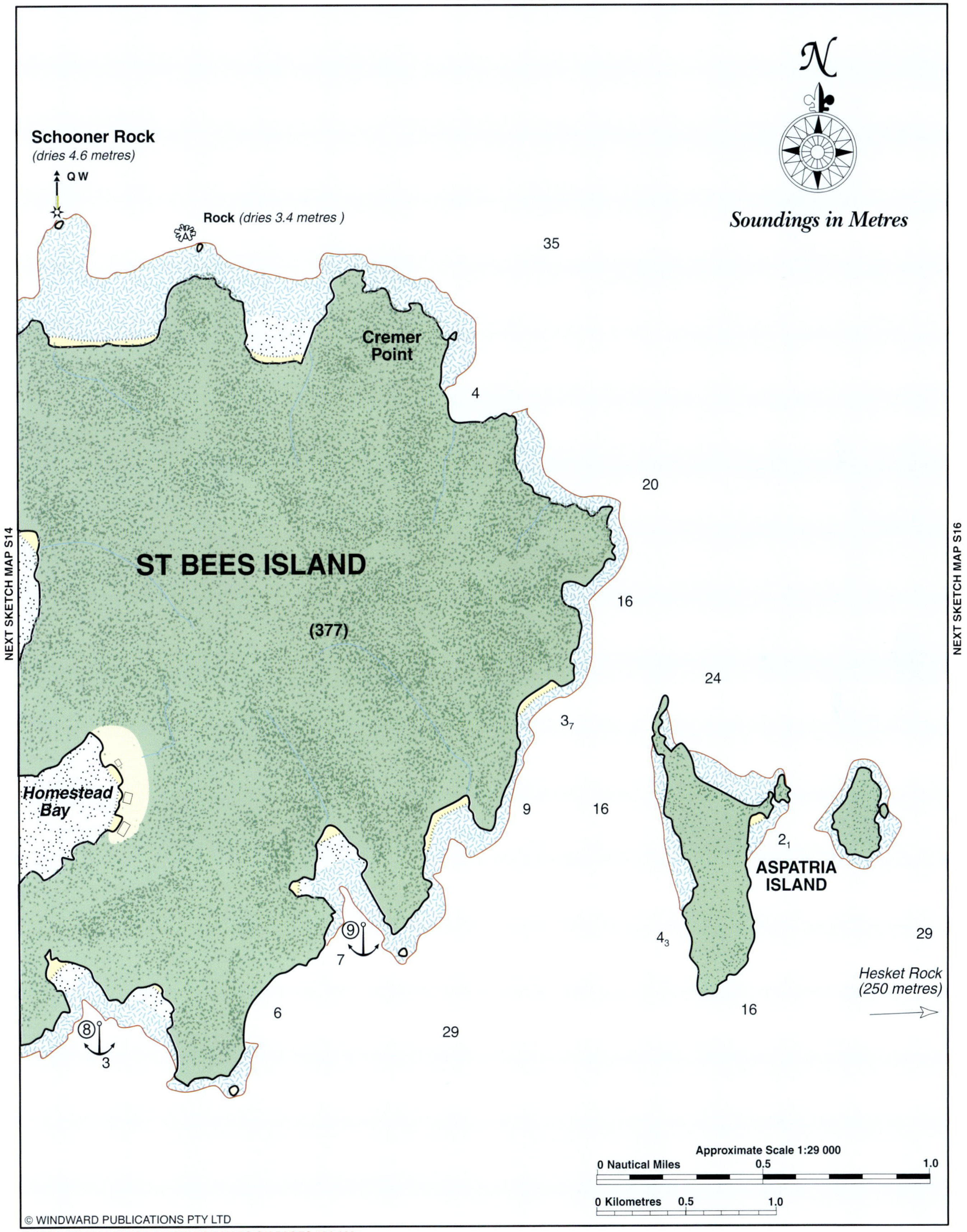

N

Soundings in Metres

Schooner Rock
(dries 4.6 metres)
Q W

Rock *(dries 3.4 metres)*

35

**Cremer
Point**

4

20

16

ST BEES ISLAND

(377)

24

*Homestead
Bay*

3$_7$

9   16

2$_1$

**ASPATRIA
ISLAND**

9

7

4$_3$

29

8

6

29

16

*Hesket Rock
(250 metres)*

3

Approximate Scale 1:29 000

0 Nautical Miles   0.5   1.0

0 Kilometres   0.5   1.0

© WINDWARD PUBLICATIONS PTY LTD

JULY 1995 APPROXIMATE SCALE 1:40 000

Aerial photograph reproduced with permission of the Department of Resources Queensland

KESWICK ISLAND

ST BEES ISLAND

REFUGE BAY (SCAWFELL ISLAND) (S16)

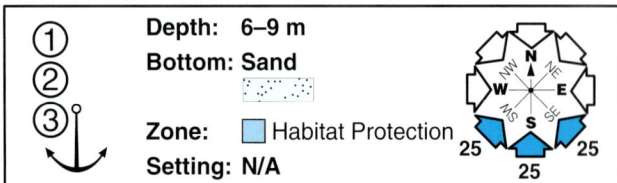

① ② ③	**Depth:** 6–9 m
	Bottom: Sand
	Zone: ☐ Habitat Protection
	Setting: N/A

25 25 25

Scawfell is a recognised convenient stopover between the Percy Islands and the Whitsundays. It is a popular anchorage with professional trawlers, and it is often possible to approach at night using their lights to guide you. Be alert, however, for vessels oblivious to the requirement to show an anchor light.

In strong south-east weather swell reaches around the points of Refuge Bay, and it may be necessary to move around to find the best situation to deal with bullets, swell and tide. Normally, anchorage close to the rock walls near anchorage No. 1 and anchorage No. 3 will be best in strong south-east weather. Anchorage No. 1 is best in strong southerlies and is also good in south-westerlies. There may be current in anchorage No. 3.

SCAWFELL SOUTH (S16)

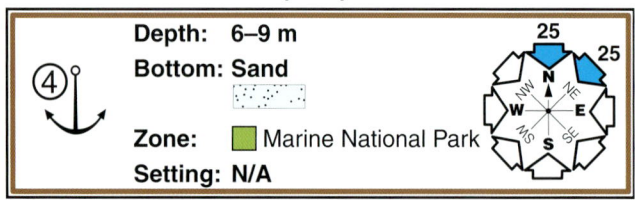

④	**Depth:** 6–9 m
	Bottom: Sand
	Zone: ☐ Marine National Park
	Setting: N/A

25 25

This anchorage is not ideal but does afford short-term protection from north to north-east winds provided there is no swell rolling in from the south-east.

Note: Sketch maps S17–S21, incorporated with later editions of this book, begin at Genesta Bay (S17) on the mainland north of Cape Conway and proceed to the Repulse Islands (S18) and then to Laguna Whitsundays Marina (S19) on the mainland opposite the Repulse Islands. From there S20 incorporates the Newry Group. Information on Mackay, at the far south of the area covered, is presented at the end of this section (sketch map S21).

SCAWFELL ISLAND

S16

NOT FOR NAVIGATION: USE CHART AUS 251

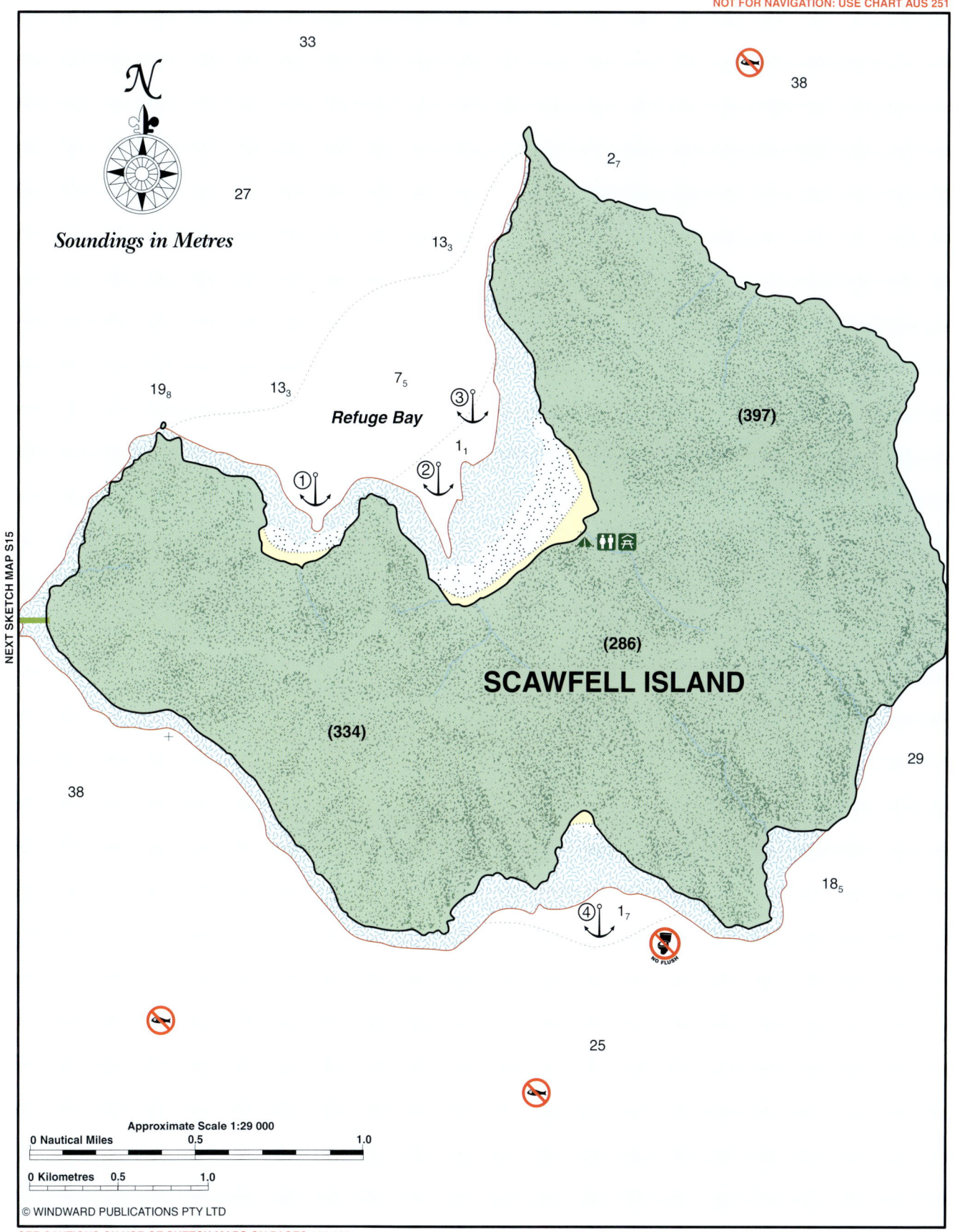

Soundings in Metres

Refuge Bay

SCAWFELL ISLAND

(397)

(286)

(334)

NEXT SKETCH MAP S15

Approximate Scale 1:29 000

0 Nautical Miles   0.5   1.0

0 Kilometres   0.5   1.0

© WINDWARD PUBLICATIONS PTY LTD

SEE CAUTIONS ON USE OF SKETCH MAPS ON PAGES 121,123

GENESTA BAY

S17

13

Puritan Bay

29

*to Lindeman Island
(about 5 miles*

Approximate Scale 1:42 000

0 Nautical Miles   0.5   1.0

5_2

1_5

*Caution!
Shoal*

6_8

0 Kilometres   1.0

0_3

2_7

2_4

N

9_4

27

Scattered coconut palms

2_7

Round Head

2_5

①

L O N G   S H O A L

5_9

13

29

Genesta Bay

3

7_1

1_8

2_8

Soundings in Metres

7_7

1_8

19_2

6_4

22

0_3

MAINLAND

14

22

6_4

Caution! Shoal

18

'Tom's
Islet'

4_9

3

Ripple Rocks

7_3

7_9

7_3

7_9

Urilla Rock
(dries 1.2 metres)

18

7_6

22

Cape Conway

7_6

8_8

Cape Rock
(dries 2.7 metres)

24

18

Repulse Bay

*Caution! Conway Shoal
(about 1 mile)*

*to the Repulse islands
(about 4.5 miles)*

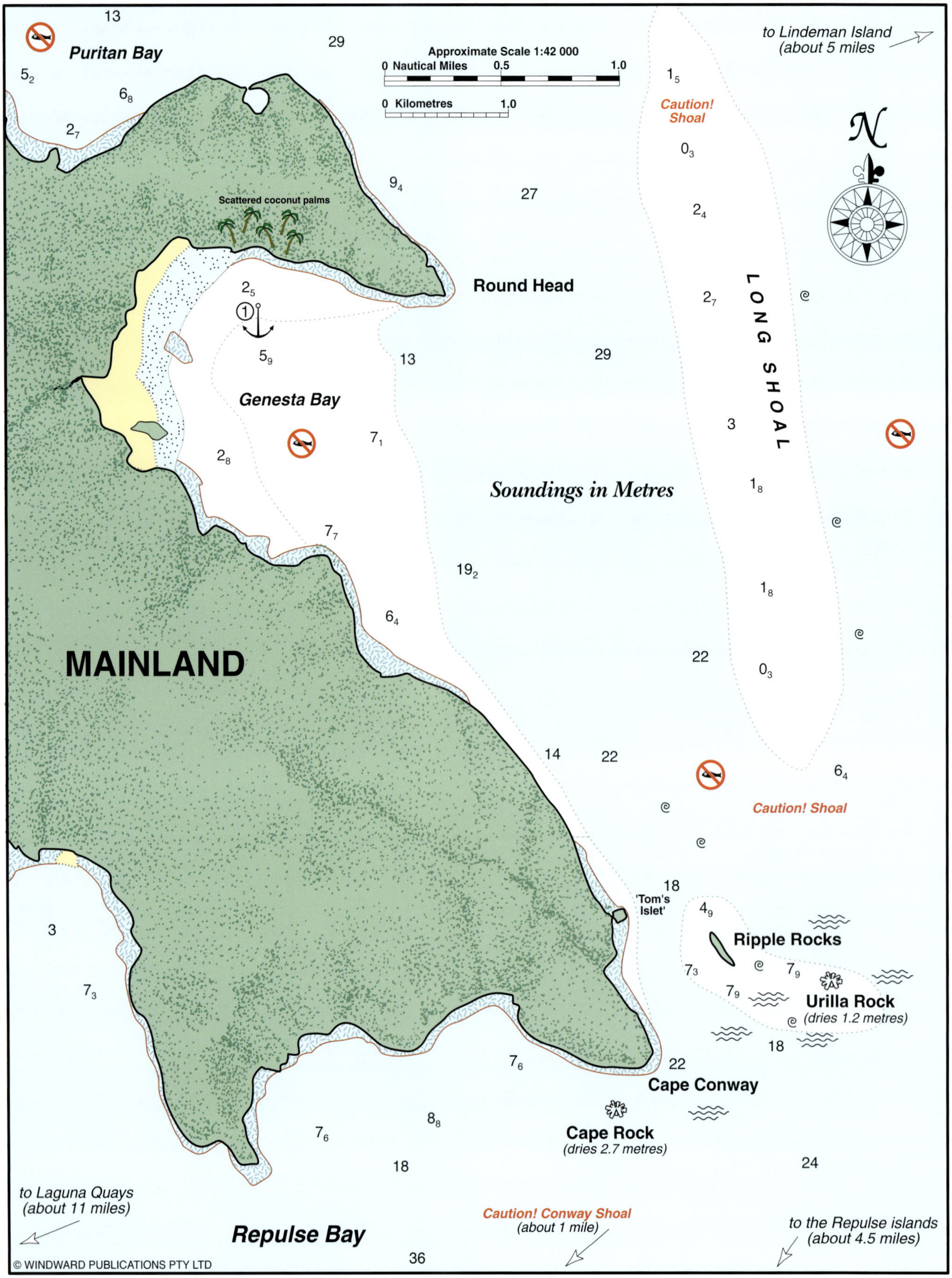

© WINDWARD PUBLICATIONS PTY LTD

36

NEXT SKETCH MAP S1

GENESTA BAY (S17)

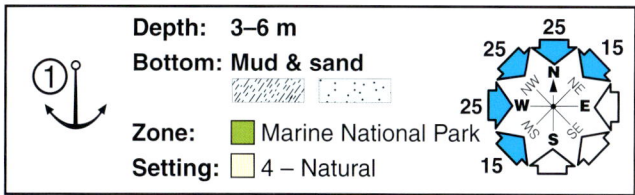

Depth: 3–6 m
Bottom: Mud & sand
Zone: ▇ Marine National Park
Setting: ☐ 4 – Natural

Watch out for Long Shoal opposite the entrance.

The water in this Bay is relatively shallow; anchor well out. The Bay has lovely beaches, and there is a deep creek that can be explored by dinghy when the tide is up.

Genesta was named by Lieutenant G.E. Richards, who conducted a survey of the area in 1885. It was a reference to the British America's Cup challenger, *Genesta*, which was sailing to New York at the time for the third America's Cup series against *Puritan*.

Round Head and Puritan Bay to the north are also associated by name. 'Roundheads' were adherents of the Parliamentary party in the Civil War of 17th century England, so-called because they wore their hair close cut (very much shorter than was the style at the time). A number of Roundheads were Puritans.

Notes on Repulse Bay

Repulse Bay is a wide expanse of quite shallow water between Cape Conway (at its north-east) and Midge Island (at its south-west). The Bay was named by James Cook, in 1770, because he was 'repulsed' by it, that is he was unable to find a passage north where he had thought there was one. This gives some clue to the size of the Bay and the expanse of low-lying land at the head of it (west of the Conway Range) where the O'Connell and Proserpine rivers make their final tortuous journey to the sea. These rivers have a combined catchment of some 12,000 square kilometres, and each year they discharge millions upon millions of cubic metres of sediment-laden water into the sea, which has contributed to the shallowness of the Bay. The combination of the south-east trade winds and the big tidal range in this area keeps the sediments stirred up so that the water is seldom clear. You cannot depend on a bow lookout to see submerged hazards.

Negotiating Cape Conway (sketch map S17)

Coming around Cape Conway, beware of the following half-tide hazards in the vicinity of the Cape: Long Shoal, which runs parallel to the eastern shore of Conway Peninsula; Urilla Rock, which is about 0.4 mile south-east of Ripple Rocks; Cape Rock, which is about 0.5 mile south-west of Cape Conway. An underwater shallow ridge runs from 'Tom's Islet' (see map S17) south-east to Ripple Rocks and Urilla Rock. ('Tom's Islet' is attached to the mainland, but it stands proud and appears to be an island at high tide.)

It is possible for small craft to go between Cape Conway and Ripple Rocks, but this route is recommended only for those with local experience; it makes for a more pleasant trip in favourable conditions (moderate winds <15 knots and, preferably, when the tide is near high). South of Ripple Rocks the water is deeper towards the mainland

and therefore may be less disturbed. For those unfamiliar with this area, and if conditions are active (caused by fresh winds and tides opposing each other, or if it's nearly low tide, particularly if there is a large tidal range), it's advisable to give the Cape and its hazards a good berth and go around to the outside (east of) Long Shoal, making a wide swing around this area. Then, watch out for Conway Shoal and stay well south of it, because it will be a very rough patch if winds and tides are jousting with each other. It is possible to go in between North Repulse and East Repulse islands, so don't turn to starboard too soon; this area is frequently like a washing machine

The Repulse Group (S18) (next page)

There are three islands: North Repulse (120 hectares), East Repulse (97 hectares) and South Repulse (40 hectares). The main human interest in them over the years was a deposit of high-grade limestone which occurs at the southern tip of East Repulse. The islands are in a fairly turbulent body of water and do not hold immense appeal for those on a time budget. South Repulse can be a good place to anchor while waiting for the right tide conditions to get into Laguna Whitsundays marina.

NORTH REPULSE ISLAND (S18)

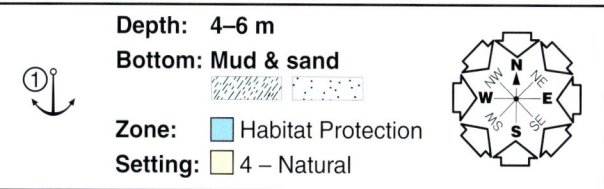

Depth: 4–6 m
Bottom: Mud & sand
Zone: ☐ Habitat Protection
Setting: ☐ 4 – Natural

This is suitable as a daytime stopoff only in light weather. North Repulse has a surprising variety of vegetation, including a lush rainforest at the northern end. The shoreline is mainly rocky and inhospitable except at this anchorage, where a pebble beach provides a landing spot in calm conditions. Torresian imperial pigeons nest here from October to March; care should be taken not to disturb them at this time.

SOUTH REPULSE ISLAND (S18)

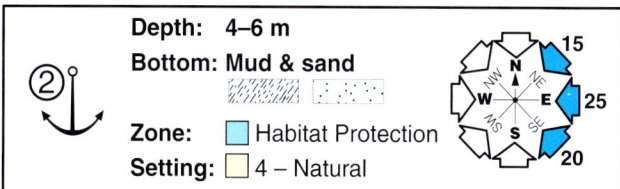

Depth: 4–6 m
Bottom: Mud & sand
Zone: ☐ Habitat Protection
Setting: ☐ 4 – Natural

The water is quite shallow in this bay; anchor well out so that you are not in danger of swinging around into shoal water. The reef has many submerged coral heads. There is a wreck in the northern part of the bay which constitutes a hazard to navigation. This anchorage becomes swelly when the wind moves into the south.

There are several pleasant beaches. The western beach is another of the Whitsunday's significant seabird nesting sites, and for this reason, to avoid disturbance to the birds, from 1 October through 31 March each year, a 6-knot speed limit applies within two hundred metres of the beach.

REPULSE Grp   S18

NEXT SKETCH MAP S17   NOT FOR NAVIGATION: USE CHART AUS 252

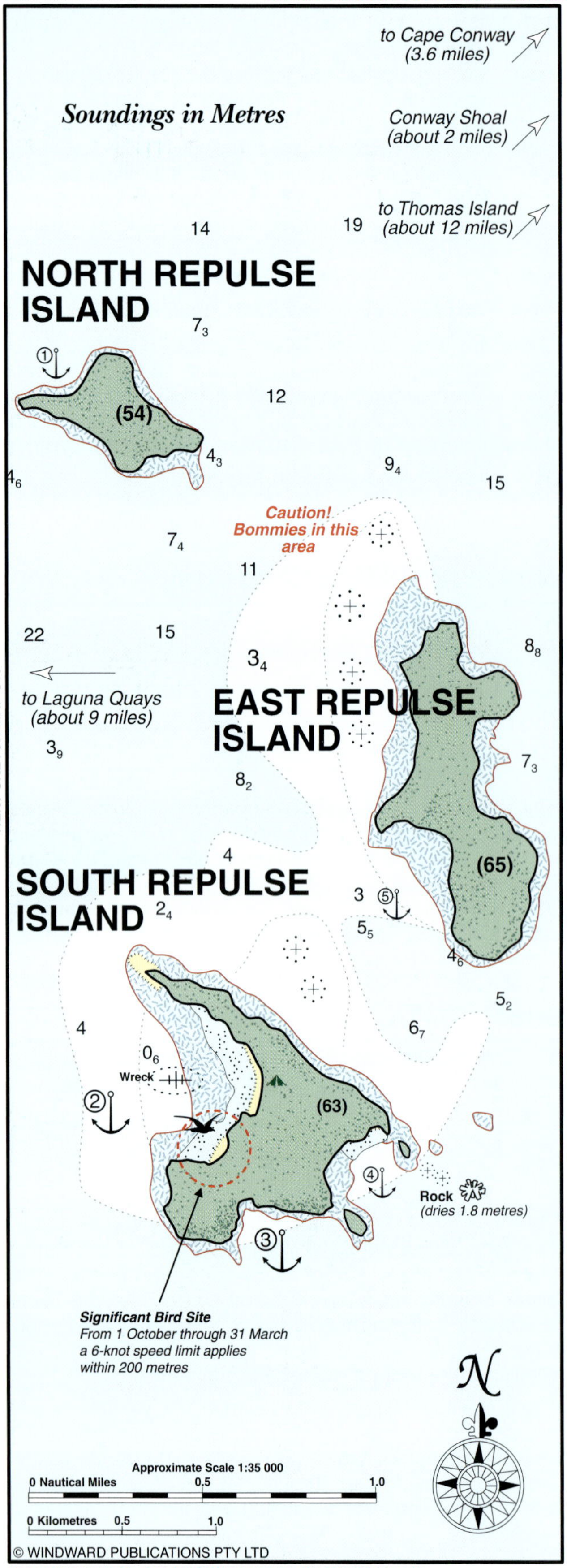

Soundings in Metres

to Cape Conway
(3.6 miles) ➚

Conway Shoal
(about 2 miles) ➚

to Thomas Island
(about 12 miles) ➚

14   19

NORTH REPULSE ISLAND

7_3

① ⚓

(54)

4_3

12

4_6 9_4

15

7_4

**Caution!
Bommies in this
area**

11

22   15

3_4

← to Laguna Quays
(about 9 miles)

3_9

EAST REPULSE ISLAND

8_2

8_8

7_3

SOUTH REPULSE ISLAND

2_4

4

(65)

3 ⑤⚓

5_5

4_6

5_2

4

0_6

Wreck

② ⚓

(63)

6_7

④⚓

Rock
(dries 1.8 metres)

③ ⚓

Significant Bird Site
*From 1 October through 31 March
a 6-knot speed limit applies
within 200 metres*

𝒩

Approximate Scale 1:35 000

0 Nautical Miles   0.5   1.0

0 Kilometres   0.5   1.0

© WINDWARD PUBLICATIONS PTY LTD

NEXT SKETCH MAP S19

NEXT SKETCH MAP S7

SEE CAUTIONS ON USE OF SKETCH MAPS ON PAGES 121,123

SOUTH REPULSE ISLAND (S18)

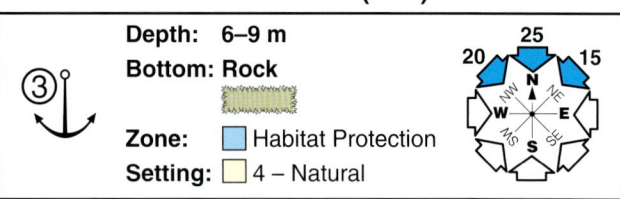

③ ⚓

Depth: 6–9 m
Bottom: Rock

Zone: ⬜ Habitat Protection
Setting: ⬜ 4 – Natural

This is not a particularly attractive bay, with a rocky foreshore, and it offers not much protection except from northerly winds. A daytime stopoff only.

SOUTH REPULSE ISLAND (S18)

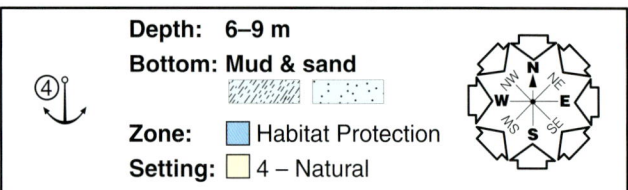

④ ⚓

Depth: 6–9 m
Bottom: Mud & sand

Zone: ⬜ Habitat Protection
Setting: ⬜ 4 – Natural

This is a more attractive anchorage than No. 3, with a pleasant beach, but there is not much protection from most winds. A daytime stopoff only.

Lieutenant Philip King and the botanist Allan Cunningham landed here in 1819 and climbed to the summit. They noted evidence of Aboriginal visitation.

EAST REPULSE ISLAND (S18)

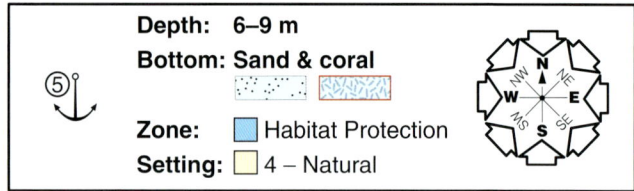

⑤ ⚓

Depth: 6–9 m
Bottom: Sand & coral

Zone: ⬜ Habitat Protection
Setting: ⬜ 4 – Natural

This anchorage is right at the side of the channel between the islands and is subject to currents and swell. The rocky beach is not particularly attractive. On the southern tip of the island are the remains of a limestone mining venture commenced during World War I.

A light-weather, daytime stopoff only.

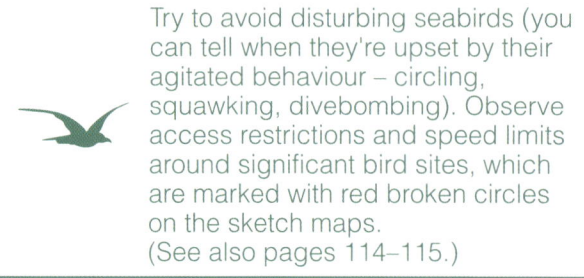

*Try to avoid disturbing seabirds (you can tell when they're upset by their agitated behaviour – circling, squawking, divebombing). Observe access restrictions and speed limits around significant bird sites, which are marked with red broken circles on the sketch maps.
(See also pages 114–115.)*

LAGUNA WHITSUNDAYS

S19

NOT FOR NAVIGATION: USE CHART AUS 252

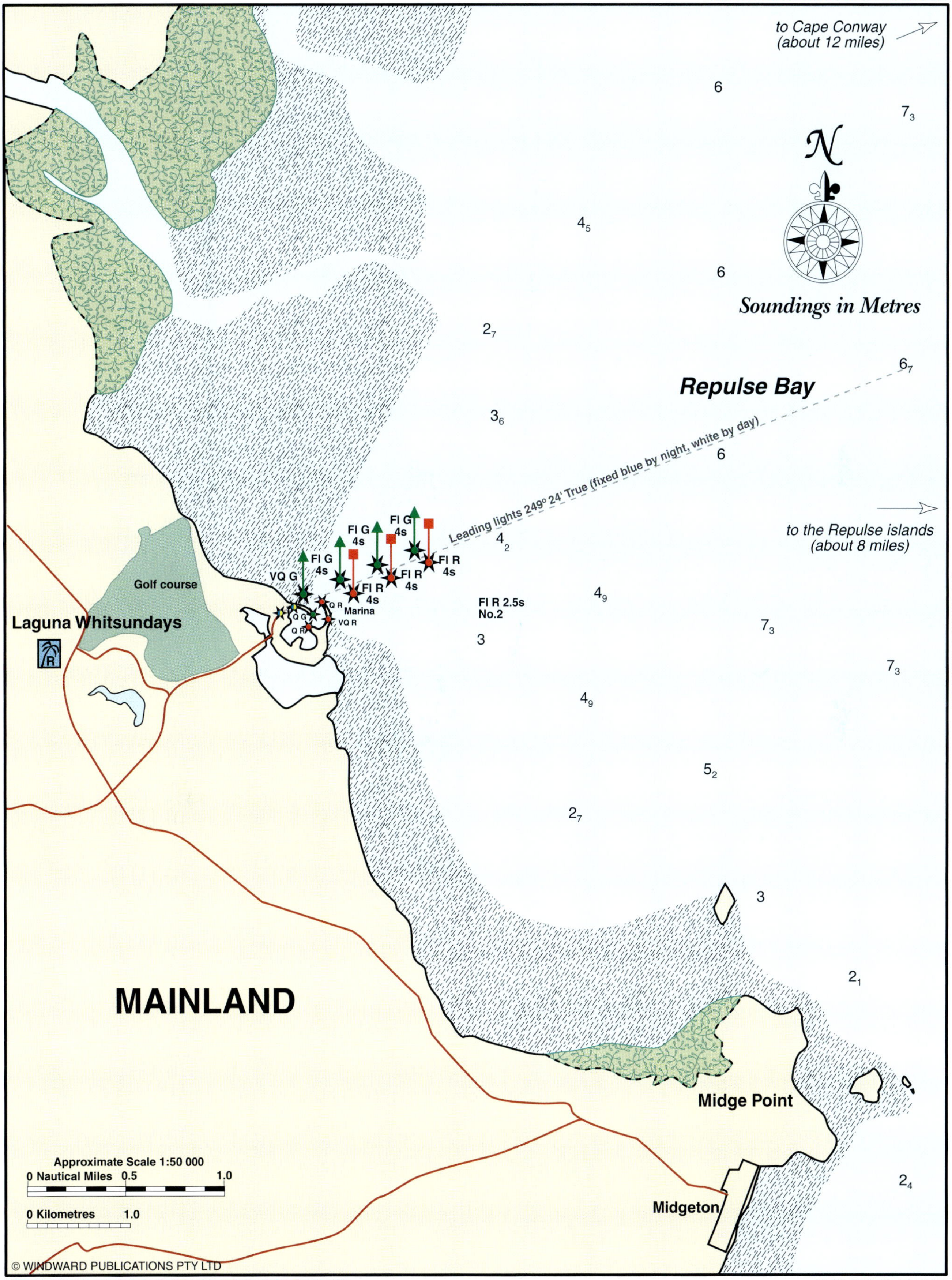

to Cape Conway
(about 12 miles)

6

7₃

N

4₅

6

Soundings in Metres

2₇

Repulse Bay

6₇

3₆

6

Leading lights 249° 24' True (fixed blue by night, white by day)

Fl G
4s

Fl G
4s

4₂

Fl G
4s

Fl G
4s

to the Repulse islands
(about 8 miles)

VQ G

Fl R
4s

Fl R
4s

Golf course

Fl R
4s

Q R

Marina

Laguna Whitsundays

Q G

VQ R

Fl R 2.5s
No.2

4₉

7₃

Q R

3

7₃

4₉

MAINLAND

5₂

2₇

3

3

2₁

Midge Point

Approximate Scale 1:50 000

0 Nautical Miles   0.5   1.0

0 Kilometres   1.0

2₄

Midgeton

NEXT SKETCH MAP S18

© WINDWARD PUBLICATIONS PTY LTD

LAGUNA MARINA

NOT FOR NAVIGATION: USE CHART AUS 252

FI G 4s
No. 5

VQ G
No. 7

?2₅

?2₅

FI R 4s
No. 6

Dries at some
low tides

F Bu
(F W day)

Leads

Q R
No. 8

Repulse Bay

Q G
No. 9

2₅

Ramp

Marina office

Car park

4

VQ R
No. 10

Q R
No. 12

4

Moorings

4

4

Watersports Area

© WINDWARD PUBLICATIONS PTY LTD

SEE CAUTIONS ON USE OF SKETCH MAPS ON PAGES 121,123

LAGUNA MARINA (S19)

Depth:	2.5–4 m
Bottom:	Mud
Zone:	N/A
Setting:	N/A

25+ (N)
25+ 25+
25+ (W) (E) 25+
25+ (S) 25+
25+

From Cape Conway the red roof tiles of the Laguna Whitsundays buildings are visible at the right-hand end of the left-hand set of hills (bearing a little south of west). After rounding the Cape, proceed well south of Conway Shoal (which has 3.6 metres of water at low tide and which can be rough) and then pass either north of North Repulse Island or in between North Repulse and East Repulse Island. In a south-easterly you can look forward to an exhilarating reach to Laguna Whitsundays! Approaching the harbour entrance, the bottom progressively rises to 3–4 metres at low tide. To avoid steering parallel to the shorter and closer seas that will occur near the marina entrance, steer a little south from the outset and then bear away towards the marina.

The mouth of the entrance channel to the man-made harbour is about two miles north of Midge Point at latitude 20° 35.94' south, longitude 148° 41.5' east, (see chart AUS 252). A river immediately north of the harbour causes siltation around the entrance and in the channel. It is imperative to call the marina office for instructions for entering the channel at least 24 hours in advance of arriving at the entrance. It may be necessary to delay your approach, perhaps for a couple of hours, and it is far better to hang about in the lee of South Repulse Island than to loiter in what may be brisk conditions around the marina entrance. White leading lights guide you into the centre of the channel to the harbour. The channel, which has three port and four starboard beacons marking the sides, was originally dredged to 2.5 metres (lowest expected tide), but silting has occurred, and this tends to be heaviest around the third set of beacons on the port side and at the entrance to the lagoon where at some tides there is no water at all. Check with the marina before approaching. Stay on the leads and execute a turn to the south-east when abeam of the marina wall. The depth in the harbour itself is 4 metres.

Contact the marina on VHF channel 21/09; they also keep a listening watch on HF 2524 kHz, from 0800 to 1700, seven days a week.

Laguna Marina
Telephone 07 4947 7844; Facsimile 07 4945 4597
Email: office@lagunamarina.com.au
Web: *www.lagunamarina.com.au*
The marina accommodates vessels up to 40 metres in length and has 110 floating berths each with water and power (single and three-phase). 10 swing moorings. Fuel and water are available. Other services and facilities include sewage pump-out, a coin-operated laundry and the friendly Mariner's Bar (named after David Marriner, the owner of the marina). There is a public launching ramp, ample car parking and dry storage for trailable boats.
Transport to Proserpine or Airlie Beach can be arranged with the marina management. Proserpine is a 20-minute drive (27 kilometres to the north); Mackay is about 100 kilometres to the south (about one hour by car).

Laguna Whitsundays golf course
As time of going to print, the golf course is not operating.

OUTER NEWRY ISLAND (S20)

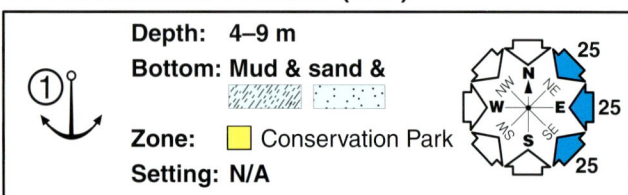

Depth:	4–9 m
Bottom:	Mud & sand &
Zone:	Conservation Park
Setting:	N/A

25 (N)
25 (W) (E) 25
25 (S)

Port Newry, as this anchorage is called, is about 25 miles north of Mackay and is a good stopover when travelling between Mackay and Laguna marina or to the Whitsundays. Trawlers often anchor here overnight, and it is popular with many small boats launched from Victor Creek immediately to the south. It gives best protection in winds from south-east to north-east. If approaching from the north, watch out for Fish Reef, which dries 2.7 metres.

THE NEWRY GROUP

NEXT SKETCH MAPS S18 & S19

S20

NEXT SKETCH MAPS S18 & S19

NOT FOR NAVIGATION: USE CHART AUS 251

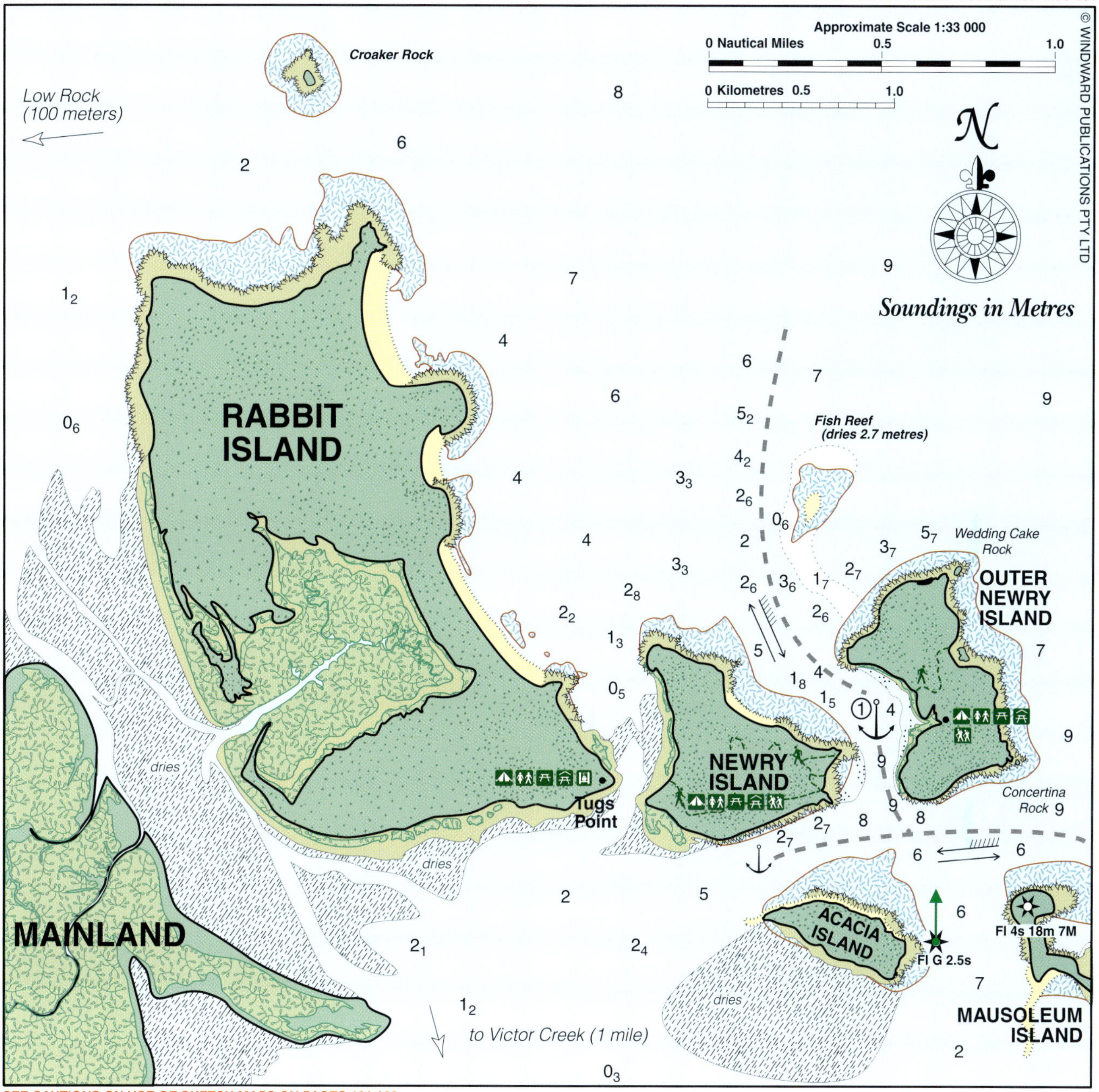

Approximate Scale 1:33 000

0 Nautical Miles   0.5   1.0

0 Kilometres 0.5   1.0

© WINDWARD PUBLICATIONS PTY LTD

N

Soundings in Metres

NEXT SKETCH MAPS S11 & S14

Croaker Rock

*Low Rock
(100 meters)*

8

6

2

7

9

1₂

RABBIT
ISLAND

4

6

7

6

5₂

*Fish Reef
(dries 2.7 metres)*

9

0₆

4

3₃

4₂

2₆

5₇ *Wedding Cake
Rock*

2

0₆

3₇

4

2₈

3₃

2₆

3₆

1₇ 2₇

OUTER
NEWRY
ISLAND

2₂

1₃

5

1₈ 4

7

dries

0₅

2₇

2₆

1₅

① ○ 4

9

9

NEWRY
ISLAND

8

9

8

*Concertina
Rock* 9

9

MAINLAND

dries

2₇

2₇

8

6 6

2

5

6

ACACIA
ISLAND

6

Fl 4s 18m 7M

2₁

2₄

dries

Fl G 2.5s

7

MAUSOLEUM
ISLAND

1₂ *to Victor Creek (1 mile)*

Tugs
Point

2

0₃

SEE CAUTIONS ON USE OF SKETCH MAPS ON PAGES 121,123

NEWRY ISLAND (S20)

Depth:	3-7 m
Bottom:	Mud & sand &
Zone:	🟩 Marine National Park
Setting:	N/A

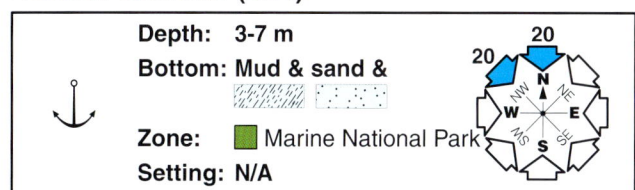

Both Newry and Outer Newry are national parks, with pleasant walking tracks and lovely views to sea and the mainland. There is a nice beach at the end of the track to the south-west corner of Newry looking over to Rabbit Island and its popular camping spot.

This anchorage offers some protection from the north and north-west but is exposed to the east and would serve as a daytime anchorage only during the trade winds season.

MACKAY HARBOUR   S21

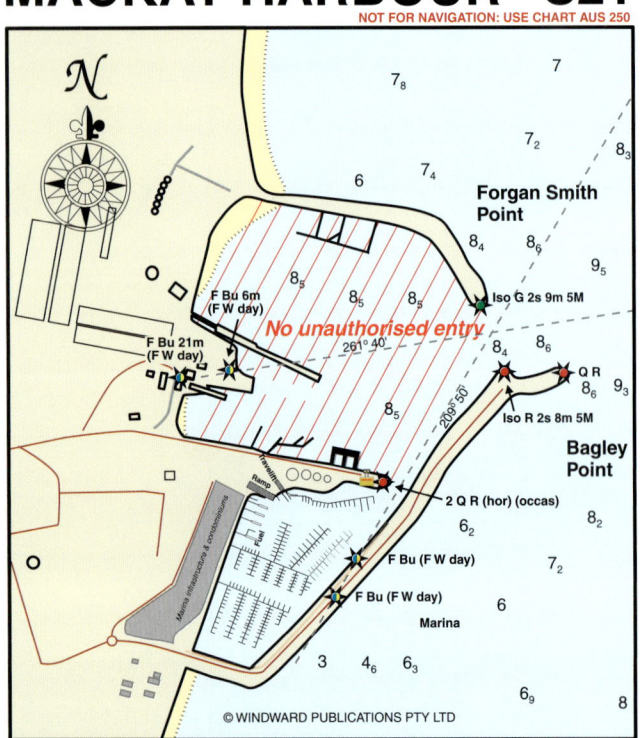

NOT FOR NAVIGATION: USE CHART AUS 250

© WINDWARD PUBLICATIONS PTY LTD

SEE CAUTIONS ON USE OF SKETCH MAPS ON PAGES 121,123

MACKAY

Mackay is a major commercial centre and the 'sugar capital' of Australia. It is smack in the middle of the Bowen Basin coal deposits, and the largest coal export terminal in the world is found at Hay Point, 45 kilometres south. The city itself is on the Pioneer River. The Mackay Outer Harbour is the southern gateway to the Whitsundays. Mackay Port Control is contactable 24/7 on VHF channel 16.

The northern section of the harbour is off limits with all berthing located at the marina in the southern section. Be alert for ship movements. There is a yellow sign with lights on the northern seawall; the lights flash when a marine movement is underway, and if you're intending to head out and you see the lights flashing, stay put until the ship movement is clear of your intended track.

The marina
The marina provides a very protected shelter, with modern facilities and services. High-rise condominium and hotel development lines the foreshore.

The marina has 479 berths, a fuel wharf with 13 pumps (unleaded and diesel), a 5-lane launching ramp with pontoon, a 65-tonne capacity Travelift (9.2 metres beam), 35 hard-stand spaces, 11 workshops including services in marine engineering/ diesel mechanics, outboard mechanics, auto electrical / refrigeration / airconditioning, and metal fabrication. There are parking spaces for over 100 cars and trailers, two toilet/shower blocks with a total of 11 male and 11 female showers and toilets, a coin-operated laundry, six restaurants, snack/takeaway/ coffee shop, bottle shop and Internet connection. It is a lock-up marina, so if you will be arriving late, arrangements need to be made to leave a keycard for you. The marina office is open from 0830–1630 hours seven days a week and may be contacted on VHF channel 16 or by phone.

The Mackay marina is an official Port of Entry for customs. Telephone 07 4955 6855.

Amber lights flash on the northern seawall of the marina when a shipping movement is in progress. If intending to head out, and the lights are flashing, stay put to allow traffic to clear.

Mackay marina – 479 berths

The promenade alongside Mackay marina. The Mackay Yacht Club is located just south of the marina foreshore development. It has a restaurant and poker machines and welcomes all visitors.

THE REEF GROUP

R1–R1b

NOT FOR NAVIGATION: USE CHART AUS 254

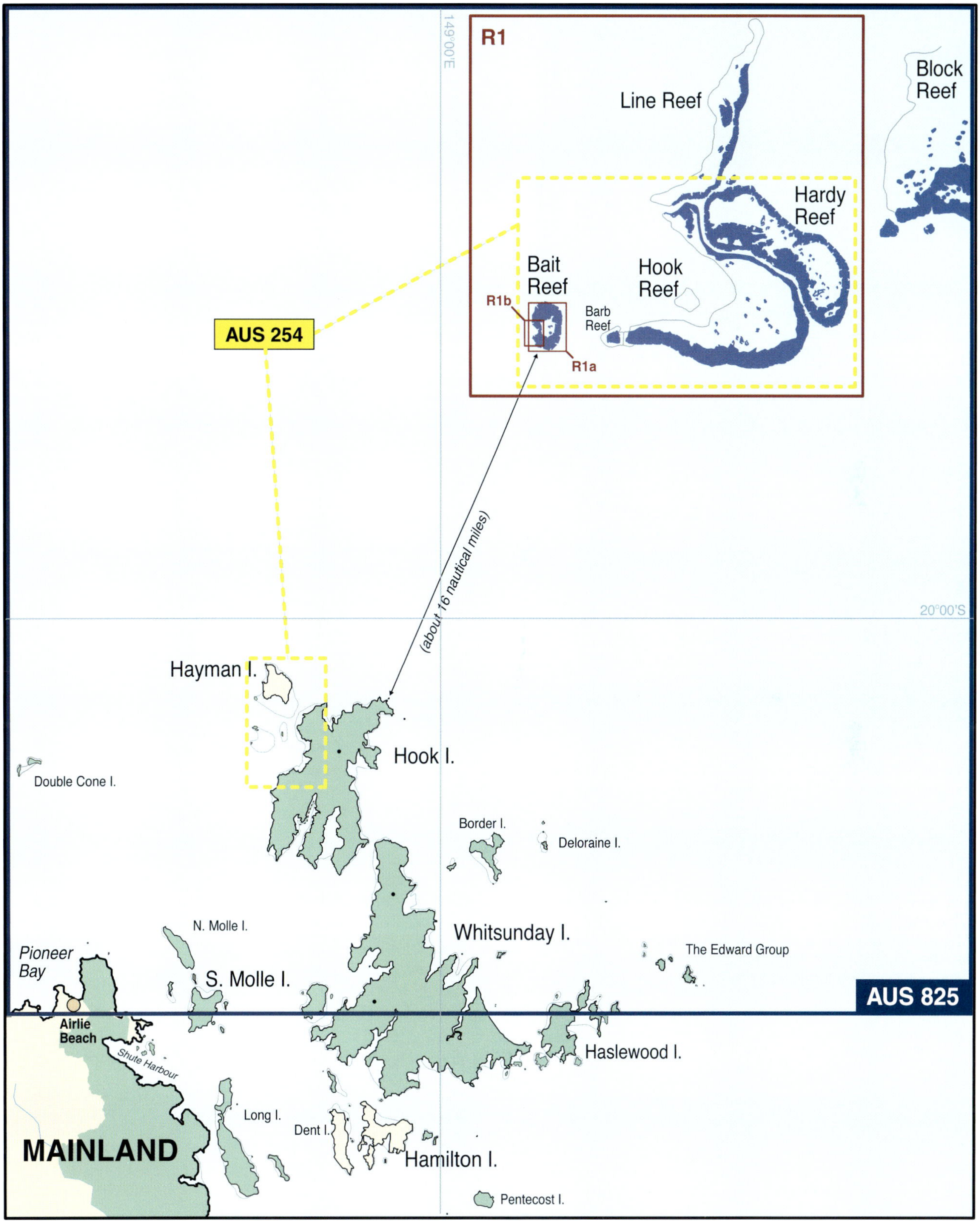

149°00'E
R1
Line Reef
Block Reef
Hardy Reef
Bait Reef
Hook Reef
R1b
Barb Reef
R1a
AUS 254
(about 16 nautical miles)
20°00'S
Hayman I.
Hook I.
Double Cone I.
Border I.
Deloraine I.
N. Molle I.
Whitsunday I.
The Edward Group
Pioneer Bay
S. Molle I.
AUS 825
Airlie Beach
Shute Harbour
Haslewood I.
Long I.
Dent I.
MAINLAND
Hamilton I.
Pentecost I.

General notes on visiting the outer reefs

Most sailors find that visiting an offshore reef is a thrilling experience. When the tide comes over the reef, you are just sitting out in the middle of the ocean. Visit these areas with the knowledge that conditions can be testing, and it's best to have as many things going for you as possible.

It is recommended that skippers not attempt their first visit to the Hook/Hardy/Bait complex if the wind is going to be blowing more than 15 knots. That advice is given by professional skippers and cruising sailors alike. It is said that the experience of being trapped in a lagoon with 30 knots of wind and the tide rising is one not soon forgotten. (Bareboat charterers are not permitted to sail themselves to the outer reefs, but there are many other ways to get there.)

Light weather and good visibility are important, especially for those going for the first time. The best time is after it has been blowing from the south-east for three to four days and the wind is starting to die off. A high pressure system, with gentle gradient, centred over Brisbane and moving very slowly, will provide good conditions – clear weather with light south-east to north-east winds and perhaps north-east sea breezes in the afternoon. If possible, go when low tide is in the middle of the day for best visibility (and for comfort at anchor during the night).

Depending upon your ultimate destination, the trip is about 17–25 miles not counting how much tide may be flowing beneath you. If you leave Stonehaven or Butterfly Bay, for example, at the start of the ebb tide, everything will be going for you. If bucking a spring flooding tide, you can add 1–2 hours to the time it would normally take to travel the distance. Nevertheless, the principal objective is to arrive at the reefs with the sun high and the tide near low.

Set a course for No.1 beacon. You will need to make some course correction to allow for set, more if going against the tide than with it. If bucking a flooding tide, steer more north than the rhumb-line course. If the tide is running with you, easterly correction will be needed.

Tidal currents are strong in the area; they flood south and ebb north. Both high and low tides are about one hour earlier than those at Mackay Outer Harbour (subtract one hour from Mackay times). The rise and fall is similar to the northern Whitsundays, about half as great as the range at Mackay. Tidal streams are seldom less than 2 knots. They may reach 8 knots in the deep channel between Hook Reef and Hardy Reef. Wind-against-tide effects should be observed carefully and certain areas should be avoided in these conditions; for example, the pass between Hook Reef and Bait Reef should not be used in south-east winds over 15–20 knots when the tide is flooding (setting south), because at such times you may encounter steep 3–4 metre waves.

Map scale

The scale of Map R1 is approximately 1:128 000 (necessarily small to get everything onto one page). Moreover, there is not very much more detailed information available from which to construct a more detailed chart. Most information exists solely in the heads of those who have acquired it by first-hand experience. Local knowledge is certainly useful, particularly in negotiating the entrance to Hardy Lagoon through the 'Waterfall'.

The distances are quite large – e.g. some 2 miles between Bait and Barb reefs, about 5 miles across the open side of Hook. It can be readily appreciated why it is desirable to go to the Reef on a clear sunny day and why you should arrive at, or near, low tide (but not earlier than 0930 hours in the winter and 0730–0800 hours in the summer, to avoid looking into the sun when it is at a flat angle). With strong tidal sets, big distances, and reefs with a low profile, you need to make the most of any available visual references.

The Hook/Hardy/Bait Reef group

Bait Reef is the nearest of the outer reefs to the Whitsunday Islands and is some 17 miles from The Narrows, between Hayman and Hook islands. Hook Reef lies in the middle of the complex, with Bait to the west, Hardy to the north-east and Line Reef to the north. Two smaller associated reefs are Sinker, immediately north of Hardy, and Barb Reef, west of the western end of Hook. A deep channel runs between Hook and Hardy reefs, with swift currents.

There are overnight anchorages at Hook Reef, at Hardy Reef in the lagoon, and on the north-west side of Line Reef. Once again, it should be stressed that these are fair weather overnight anchorages. When the tide is up, the reefs cover.

Hook and Line reefs are not only unprotected from south-west to almost north-east winds but there are strong tidal flows in and around them which can cause discomfort with contrary winds of more than 10 knots.

The outer reefs provide a taste of what the Barrier Reef is all about. The area is heavily used by tourists and divers, who fly out from the mainland in amphibians and helicopters, or travel from the mainland and islands in fast catamarans and cruisers.

Excellent diving, snorkelling, fishing and reef exploring make it worth the trip.

Approach to No. 1 beacon

If the wind freshens from the south-east and the tide is flooding, don't go between Bait and Barb reefs; conditions will be nasty there. Alter course and pass west of Bait Reef. Passage between Barb Reef and Hook Reef is possible, although locals do not recommend it to those without experience. No. 1 beacon is east of the centre of Barb Reef, and reef extends a long way to the north-west and west. Watch out.

(Continued on page 248)

HOOK/HARDY/LINE/BAIT REEFS

R1

NOT FOR NAVIGATION: USE CHART AUS 254

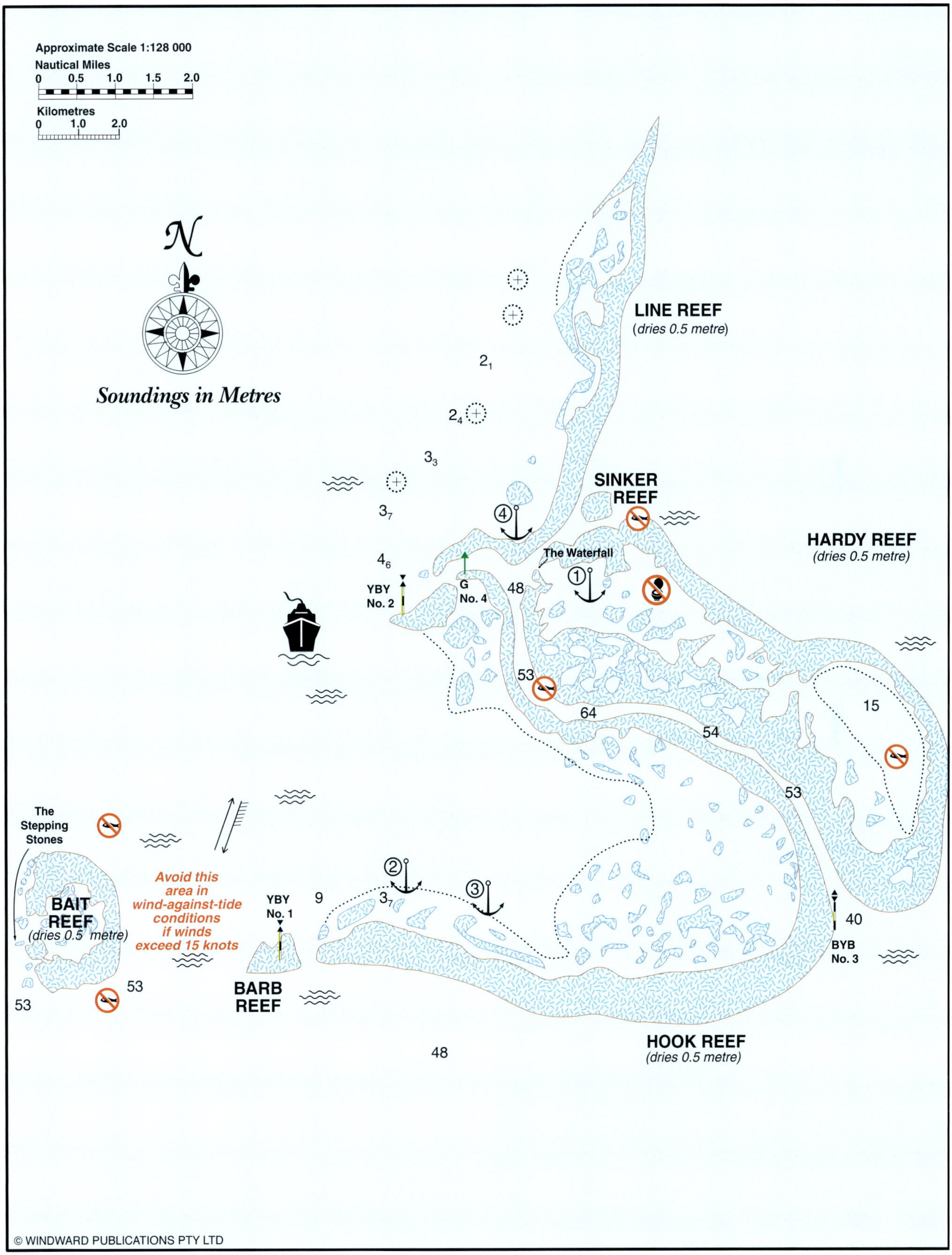

Approximate Scale 1:128 000

Nautical Miles
0   0.5   1.0   1.5   2.0

Kilometres
0   1.0   2.0

N

Soundings in Metres

LINE REEF
(dries 0.5 metre)

2_1

2_4 +

3_3

SINKER
REEF

3_7

④

HARDY REEF
(dries 0.5 metre)

4_6

The Waterfall

YBY
No. 2

G
No. 4

48

①

5_3

64

15

54

53

The
Stepping
Stones

*Avoid this
area in
wind-against-tide
conditions
if winds
exceed 15 knots*

②

③

40

BAIT
REEF
(dries 0.5 metre)

YBY
No. 1

9

3_7

BYB
No. 3

53

53

BARB
REEF

48

HOOK REEF
(dries 0.5 metre)

© WINDWARD PUBLICATIONS PTY LTD

SEE CAUTIONS ON USE OF SKETCH MAPS ON PAGES 121,123

(Continued from page 246)

No.1 beacon is usually visible as a 'black post' from some 6 to 8 miles off. Large limestone rocks and waves along the weather (south-east) side of Hook Reef are usually visible from 3 to 4 miles distance at half tide.

When approaching all of these anchorages, you should keep a lookout posted.

HARDY LAGOON (R1)

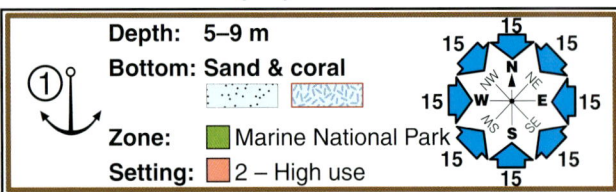

Depth:	5–9 m
Bottom:	Sand & coral
Zone:	Marine National Park
Setting:	2 – High use

Leave No. 2 and No. 4 beacons to starboard and proceed to the Waterfall, which is actually the third waterfall (gap in the reef with water moving in/out). There may be a pole (or other mark) on the left side of the entrance. Enter the lagoon immediately after the reef has just covered and is stabilised (water is no longer running out of the lagoon) or at high tide. The reef becomes stabilised about one hour after low water in neap tides or about two and a half hours after low water in spring tides. There is a depth of 2.2 metres (with '0' tide) just after stabilisation; coral is clearly visible close on both sides and the channel is unambiguous. The bommie just inside the lagoon entrance will also be sufficiently covered for vessels with 2.2 metres draught (although it may give you a momentary case of the jimjams).

Anchor as soon as you are inside and feel a comfortable distance from the reef. If you get too far in you may be frightened by amphibious aircraft that will be landing in the lagoon. The bottom is sand over coral; use plenty of chain.

The small waterfalls can be used for dinghy access at other times if you have a sufficiently powerful motor. The main waterfall in full ebb has such a volume of water pouring out that it produces a 'rooster tail'; only those with a death wish or seeking cheap thrills would attempt this one.

Hardy Reef is a Marine National Park 'Zone – 'look-but-don't-take' (see pages 106–114 for explanation of Marine Park Zones and Settings.)

'The Waterfall' entrance into Hardy Lagoon is a formidable sight when water is emptying from the reef. It becomes 'stabilised' about one hour after low water during neap tides and about two and a half hours after low water in spring tides.

BAIT REEF
R1a

NOT FOR NAVIGATION: USE CHART AUS 254

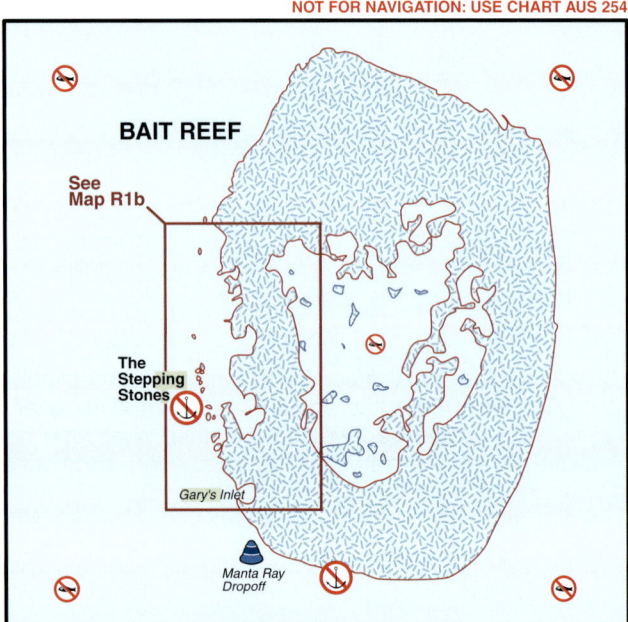

BAIT REEF

See Map R1b

The Stepping Stones

Gary's Inlet

Manta Ray Dropoff

© WINDWARD PUBLICATIONS PTY LTD

SEE CAUTIONS ON USE OF SKETCH MAPS ON PAGES 121,123

The nearest of the oceanic platform reefs of the Great Barrier system lies about 16 nautical miles north-east of Hook Island – Bait Reef, a beautiful, pristine, relatively small reef that has become a very popular scuba diving site.

The reef has a unique feature – the Stepping Stones – a series of 18 or so flat-topped coral pinnacles lined up in a row along the west to south-west side of the reef. Each pinnacle rises from a depth of 15–25 metres and stops within one metre of the surface. The pinnacles are circular in shape with absolutely vertical sides, and each is covered in coral of all varieties – huge plates on top, soft corals and gorgonian fans on the sides. Clouds of colourful tropical fish swarm around the tops of the stones. The Stepping Stones uncover only at low water springs, and they have navigable gaps between them. A cluster of four bommies guards the south side of 'the entrance', and there are deeper bommies alongside the north-west side of the reef.

There are a number of other dive sites down the western side from the Stepping Stones – Gary's Inlet, Manta Ray Dropoff (where there is a public mooring (class 'B' – 20-metre monohull or 18-metre catamaran), and the southern face. Anchoring within 100 metres of the reef edge is prohibited all along this stretch.

THE STEPPING STONES (R1b)

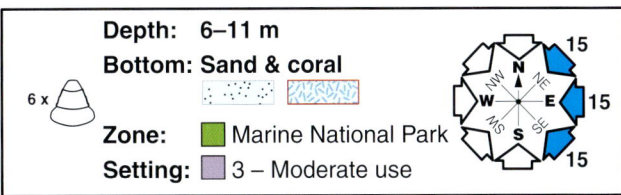

This is a temporary stopoff only for enjoyment of the reef environment, not a comfortable overnight location except in exceptionally calm circumstances. A number of public moorings for vessels up to 25 metres (22 metre catamarans) have been installed inside the Stepping Stones. Use caution going through 'The Entrance' (or between the stones if visibility is good and conditions are suitable). The Cluster of Four has about 5 metres of water over it at low tide. When bad weather or other misfortune has not befallen it, there has, in the past, been an informal mark on the southern side of the entrance just north of the Cluster of Four, and a starboard beacon with radar reflector is scheduled for installation by the Department of Transport on the first flat-topped bommie to the south of the Cluster. Thus, there is a degree of choice in negotiating the way into one of the moorings, but use care.

The Stepping Stones and bommies in the lagoon provide very good diving. One tank of air will do you for one figure of eight around a couple of bommies.

HOOK REEF (R1)

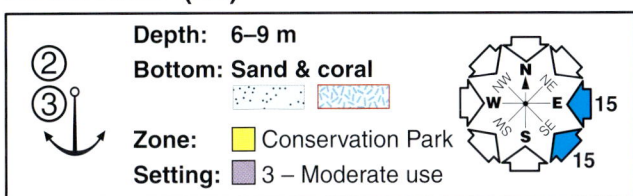

There is quite a tidal sweep right across Hook Reef and if south-east winds exceed 15 knots with a flooding tide, it is very uncomfortable. It tends to be uncomfortable in winds other than south-east or east.

You can go between Barb Reef and Hook Reef, although it is not recommended for those who are not familiar with the area. Go around Barb Reef if you are not sure.

Scuba dive boat anchored at Bait Reef

THE STEPPING STONES R1b

NOT FOR NAVIGATION: USE CHART AUS 254

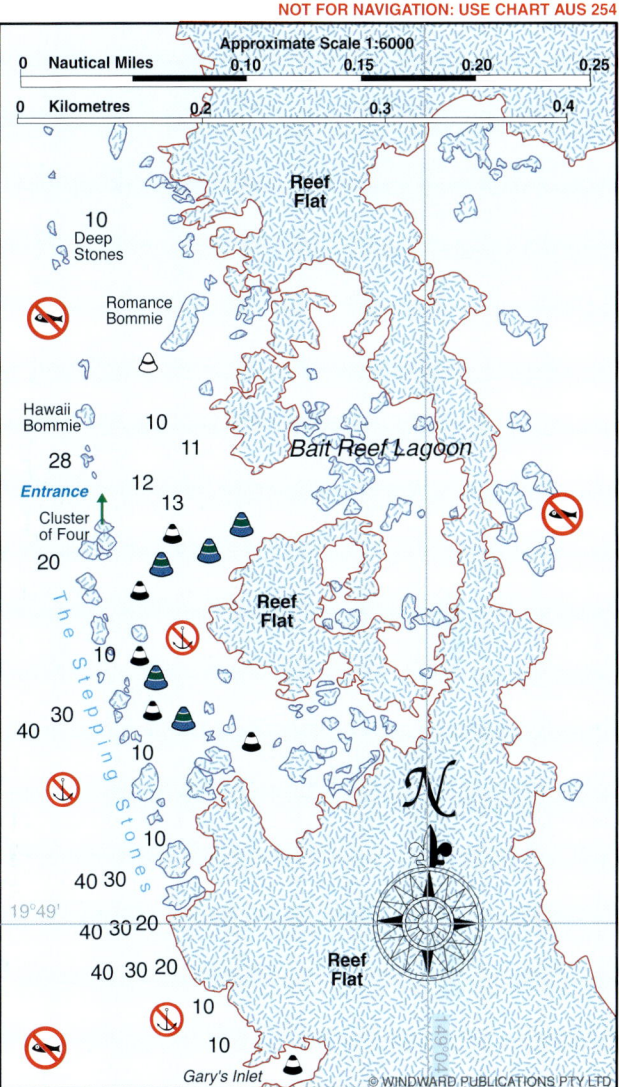

SEE CAUTIONS ON USE OF SKETCH MAPS ON PAGES 121,123

LINE REEF (R1)

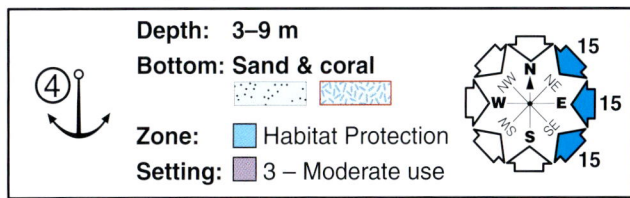

Coming from the south, after passing No.2 and No.4 beacons, there is a spot in Line Reef that has a minimum of 1.8 metres water over it which can be found by keeping No. 4 beacon in line with the gap between Hook and Hayman islands. You can go straight over the top of Line Reef until you get to a position where No.2 and No.4 beacons line up. Anchor there.

An easy way to remember the location of the anchorage is to have 'two and four in line behind Line'.

INDEX OF ANCHORAGES AND PLACENAMES

Index of Anchorages and Placenames

This index is to assist with locating and orientation but is **not to be used for navigation**. The lat.s and long.s are approximate: for islands/islets/rocks they are the approximate geographic centre of the land mass; for harbours and bays they represent the approximate entrance (at the mouth midway between enclosing headlands); for peninsulas/headlands they approximate the end of the promontory; for beaches and shoals they represent the approximate midpoint.

INDEX OF ANCHORAGES AND PLACENAMES

INDEX OF ANCHORAGES AND PLACENAMES

THE AREA COVERED

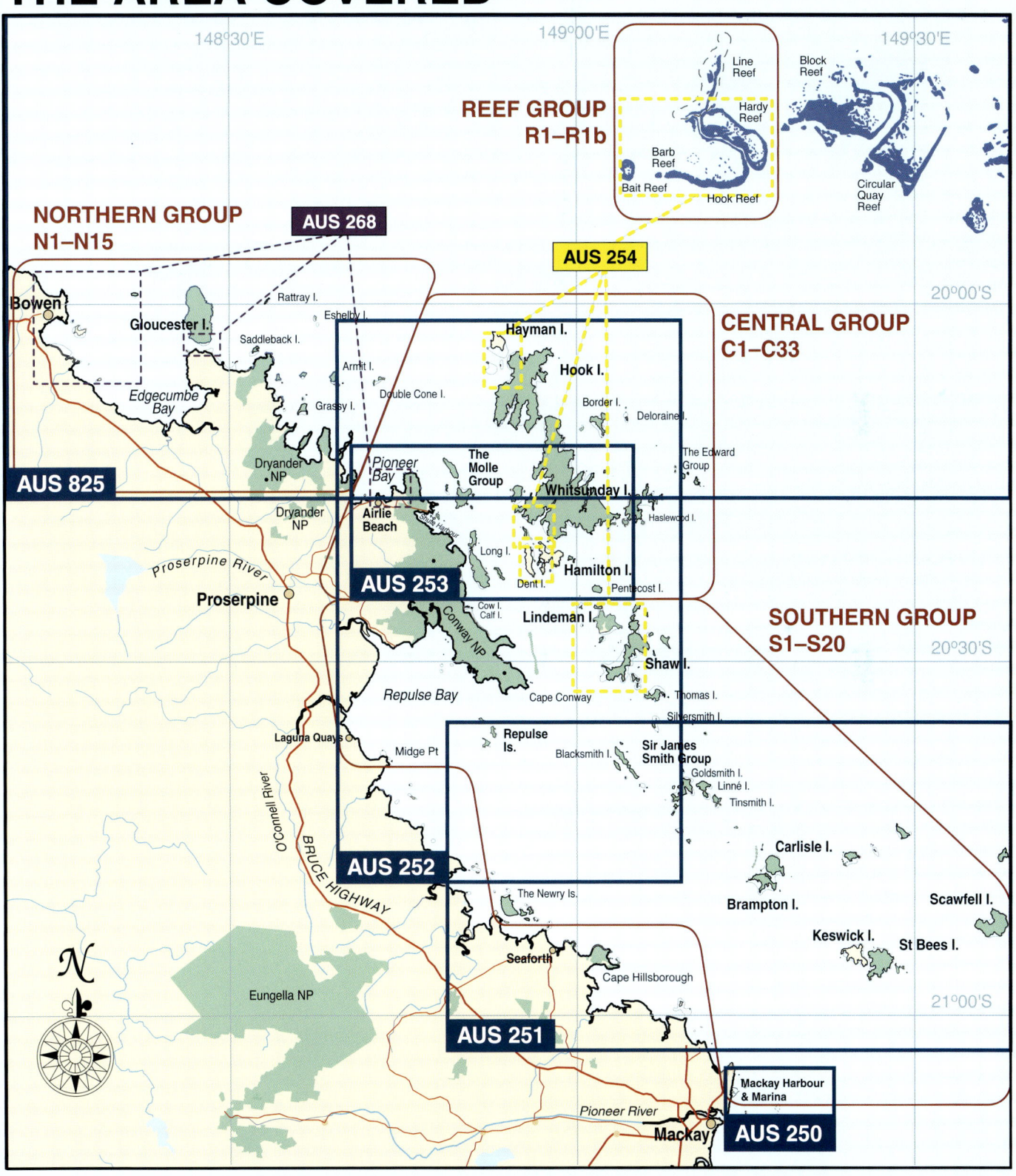

REEF GROUP
R1–R1b

Line Reef
Block Reef
Hardy Reef
Barb Reef
Bait Reef
Hook Reef
Circular Quay Reef

NORTHERN GROUP
N1–N15

AUS 268

AUS 254

CENTRAL GROUP
C1–C33

Bowen

Gloucester I.

Rattray I.

Eshelby I.

Hayman I.

Hook I.

20°00'S

Saddleback I.

Armit I.

Double Cone I.

Border I.

Deloraine I.

Edgecumbe Bay

Grassy I.

The Edward Group

AUS 825

Dryander NP

Pioneer Bay

The Molle Group

Whitsunday I.

Haslewood I.

Dryander NP

Airlie Beach

Long I.

Hamilton I.

Pentecost I.

AUS 253

Dent I.

Proserpine River

Proserpine

Cow I.
Calf I.

Lindeman I.

Shaw I.

SOUTHERN GROUP
S1–S20

20°30'S

Conway NP

Thomas I.

Repulse Bay

Cape Conway

Silversmith I.

Laguna Quays

Repulse Is.

Sir James Smith Group

O'Connell River

Midge Pt

Blacksmith I.

Goldsmith I.

Linné I.

Tinsmith I.

BRUCE HIGHWAY

Carlisle I.

Scawfell I.

AUS 252

The Newry Is.

Brampton I.

Keswick I.

St Bees I.

N

Eungella NP

Seaforth

Cape Hillsborough

21°00'S

AUS 251

Mackay Harbour & Marina

Pioneer River

Mackay

AUS 250

148°30'E

149°00'E

149°30'E

David Colfelt

Minne Hall Bay, Goldsmith Island

GENERAL INDEX

GENERAL INDEX